Athens After Empire

Athens After Empire

A HISTORY FROM ALEXANDER THE GREAT TO THE EMPEROR HADRIAN

Ian Worthington

OXFORD
UNIVERSITY PRESS

Oxford University Press is a department of the University of Oxford. It furthers the University's objective of excellence in research, scholarship, and education by publishing worldwide. Oxford is a registered trade mark of Oxford University Press in the UK and certain other countries.

Published in the United States of America by Oxford University Press
198 Madison Avenue, New York, NY 10016, United States of America.

© Oxford University Press 2021

All rights reserved. No part of this publication may be reproduced, stored in a retrieval system, or transmitted, in any form or by any means, without the prior permission in writing of Oxford University Press, or as expressly permitted by law, by license, or under terms agreed with the appropriate reproduction rights organization. Inquiries concerning reproduction outside the scope of the above should be sent to the Rights Department, Oxford University Press, at the address above.

You must not circulate this work in any other form
and you must impose this same condition on any acquirer.

Library of Congress Cataloging-in-Publication Data
Names: Worthington, Ian, author.
Title: Athens After Empire : A History From Alexander the Great to the Emperor Hadrian / Ian Worthington.
Description: New York, NY : Oxford University Press, [2021] | Includes bibliographical references and index
Identifiers: LCCN 2020018272 (print) | LCCN 2020018273 (ebook) | ISBN 9780190633981 (hardback) | ISBN 9780190634001 (epub) | ISBN 9780190634018
Subjects: LCSH: Hellenism. | Athens (Greece)—History.
Classification: LCC DF285 .W67 2021 (print) | LCC DF285 (ebook) | DDC 938/.508—dc23
LC record available at https://lccn.loc.gov/2020018272
LC ebook record available at https://lccn.loc.gov/2020018273

1 3 5 7 9 8 6 4 2
Printed by Sheridan Books, Inc., United States of America

CONTENTS

Figures vii
Preface ix
Abbreviations xi
Maps xiii

Introduction: "This Is the City of Hadrian and Not of Theseus" 1
1. Farewell to Freedom 9
2. Under the Puppet Ruler: Demetrius of Phalerum 29
3. Political and Civic Institutions 53
4. Demetrius "The Besieger" and Athens 71
5. Testing Macedonia 103
6. Independence Day 125
7. Enter Rome, Exit Macedonia 141
8. Being Free without Freedom 159
9. Social Life and Religion 181
10. Sulla's Sack of Athens 195
11. The End of "Hellenistic" Athens 223
12. Augustus and Athens 243
13. Tiberius to Hadrian 265
14. Building a New Horizon? 287
15. Hadrian's Arch 313

Timeline 337
Bibliography 349
Index 387

FIGURES

1.1 Facial reconstruction of Philip II   13
1.2 Head of Alexander the Great   15
2.1 Demetrius of Phalerum   35
2.2 Silver tetradrachm of Demetrius Poliorcetes. 289–288 BC   48
3.1 The Areopagus Hill   55
3.2 The *Bema* on the Pnyx   57
4.1 View of Acropolis from Museum Garrison   92
5.1 Portrait statue of Demosthenes, first–second century AD   109
5.2 Antigonus II Gonatas of Macedonia. Gold coin   115
6.1 Philip V of Macedonia. Coin   138
10.1 Reconstructed Stoa of Attalus   197
10.2 Sulla (Lucius Cornelius Sulla Felix)   207
10.3 Dipylon and Sacred Gates   212
11.1 Tower of the Winds   227
11.2 Bust of the Roman General Mark Antony at National Archeological Museum of Madrid   235
12.1 Roman Emperor Augustus from Prima Porto statue   244
12.2 Pedestal of Agrippa   246
12.3 Monumental Gateway to Roman Agora   251
14.1a Roman Agora (toward Gate)   289
14.1b Roman Agora (toward Tower of the Winds and Agoranomion)   290
14.2a Temple of Roma and Augustus   292
14.2b Temple of Roma and Augustus (featuring inscription)   292

14.3	Model of the Agora in the second century AD; view from the west, Odeum of Agrippa in the center 294	
14.4a	Philopappus Monument 300	
14.4b	Philopappus Monument from Acropolis 302	
14.5a	Ruins of Temple of Olympian Zeus 305	
14.5b	Temple of Olympian Zeus from Acropolis 305	
14.6a	Hadrian's Library Reconstruction 307	
14.6b	Ruins of Hadrian's Library 308	
14.6c	Ruins of Hadrian's Library (library and teaching rooms) 309	
15.1	Marble bust of the Emperor Hadrian, from the Pantanello at Hadrian's Villa, AD 117–118 315	
15.2	Hadrian's Arch 328	
15.3	Theater of Herodes Atticus 335	

PREFACE

THIS BOOK IS ABOUT A long period in Athens' history that is commonly—but mistakenly—viewed as a decline and fall after its greatness in the Classical period. Then, it was an imperial power, with a formidable fleet; a strong economy; a proud history; a flourishing intellectual, artistic, and literary life; and its people lived under a democracy that made them sovereign in the state. Athens was a city, so Pericles claimed, that everyone wanted to emulate. But in 338 that life changed forever when Philip II of Macedonia imposed hegemony over Greece. The Greeks were forced to endure Macedonian rule for almost two centuries until the new power of the Mediterranean world, Rome, secured dominion over Greece.

The common view of Athens under Macedonian and Roman dominance is of a city that was a shadow of its former self: its democracy reduced to a caricature, its economy in decline, its military prowess no more, and under its Roman masters transformed into a provincial city. But this dreary picture belies reality. As my book will show, later Athens was far from being a postscript to its Classical predecessor. It remained a vibrant and influential city, its people always resilient, even to the point of fighting their Macedonian and Roman masters, and its Classical self lived on in literature and thought. In fact, its cultural status enticed Romans to the city and to adapt aspects of Hellenism for their own cultural and political needs. Such was Athens' reputation that when the emperor Hadrian established a league of cities in the east he made Athens its center, catapulting the city to prominence in the world again.

I took longer to write this book than anticipated because of certain events, some welcome, others less so. Welcome was the big move from Missouri to Sydney in 2017—the actual move was straightforward enough, but finding our feet in a city of 5,000,000 people after living in one of 110,000 or so for nineteen years is still taking some doing. Unwelcome was that in 2018 I had a heart attack, and after getting back into the swing of things had to part ways with my gall bladder in 2019—I'm fairly sure my new colleagues at Macquarie are wondering, "What's going to happen to him this year?" I hope nothing, but to be on the safe side I thought I'd better get a move on and finish the book.

I have several people to thank for their help, patience, and friendship, who have all made the final version better.

The first is Stefan Vranka, my editor at OUP, with whom it is a pleasure to work again. He is the consummate editor, as I've said before, always patient, always diplomatic, and always giving sharp and precise comments. I thank everyone at that publisher, and also Jeremy Toynbee at Newgen UK, who helped to guide the book and me through its production.

To the anonymous referee for excellent feedback and suggestions, and generally for liking what you read: thank you.

I am much obliged to the following scholars for generously giving their time to read an earlier draft of the book, make multiple comments, and save me from glaring errors that I'd prefer to keep quiet about: Nigel Kennell, Paul McKechnie, Joseph Roisman, and Robin Waterfield.

Arthur Keaveney sent me a copy of his article on Sulla and Lucullus in advance of its publication in *Arctos*, as well as corresponded about Sulla and Athens, and I am indebted to him for all that.

I am grateful to Eric Csapo for sending me a copy of his seminar paper on Lachares and Menander that he is currently taking on tour.

My thanks also go to Arco den Heijer for sending me his chapter on St. Paul's speech to the Areopagus from his PhD thesis (Theologische Universiteit Kampen) on the depiction of Paul's performance in *Acts*.

Finally, as always, my deepest debt is to my family for tolerating what I do, at least while they have free food and wifi.

Ian Worthington
Macquarie University
February 2020

ABBREVIATIONS

BNJ	*Brill's New Jacoby*, numerous ancient writers prepared by modern scholars, editor-in-chief Ian Worthington (Leiden: 2003–)
IG	*Inscriptiones Graecae*, many volumes with different editors (Berlin: 1873–)
ISE	*Iscrizioni storiche ellenistiche*, 2 vols., editor L. Moretti (Florence: 1967–75)
SEG	*Supplementum Epigraphicum Graecum*, many volumes (Leiden: 1923–)
*SIG*³	*Sylloge Inscriptionum Graecarum*, 4 vols., editor W. Dittenberger (Leipizg: 1915–24)

MAPS

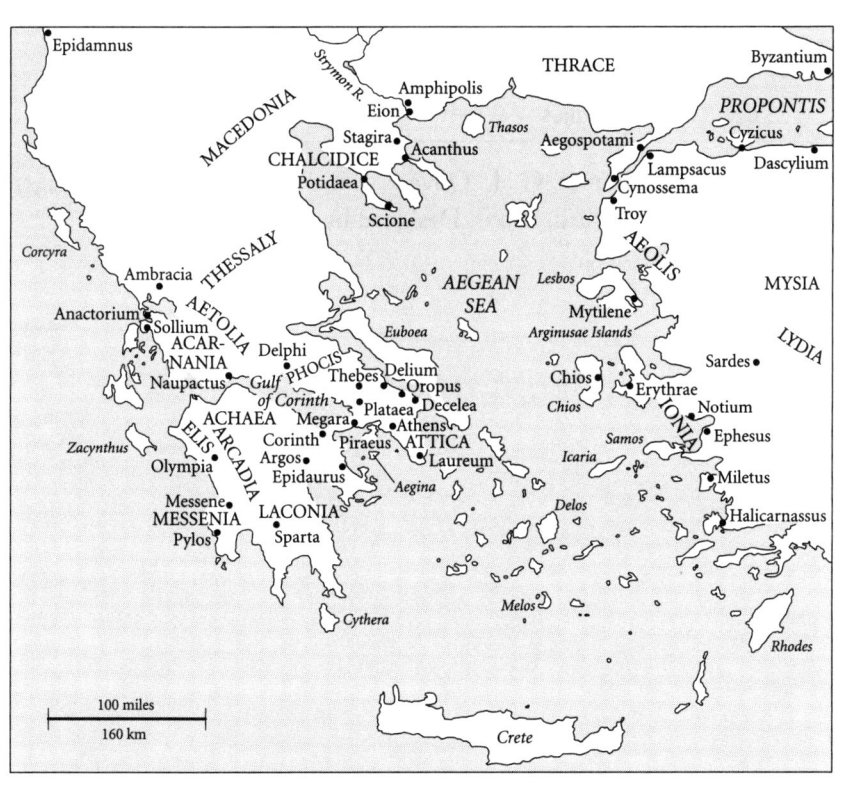

MAP 1 Greece

xiv MAPS

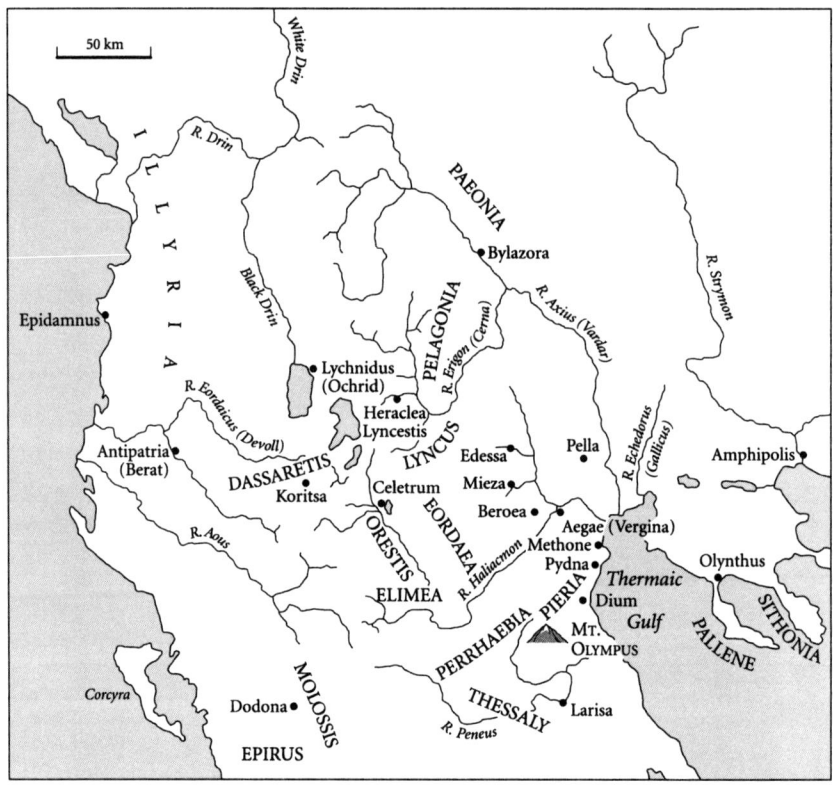

MAP 2 Macedonia. From G. J. Oliver, *War, Food, and Politics in Early Hellenistic Athens* (Oxford, 2007). Designed by Lorraine McEwan.

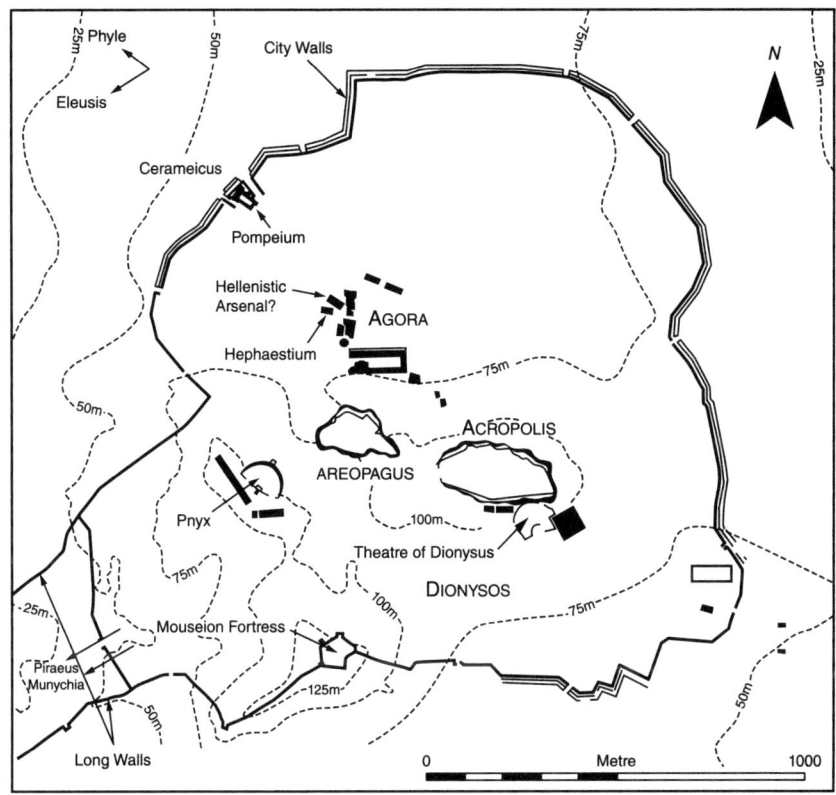

MAP 3 Ancient Athens

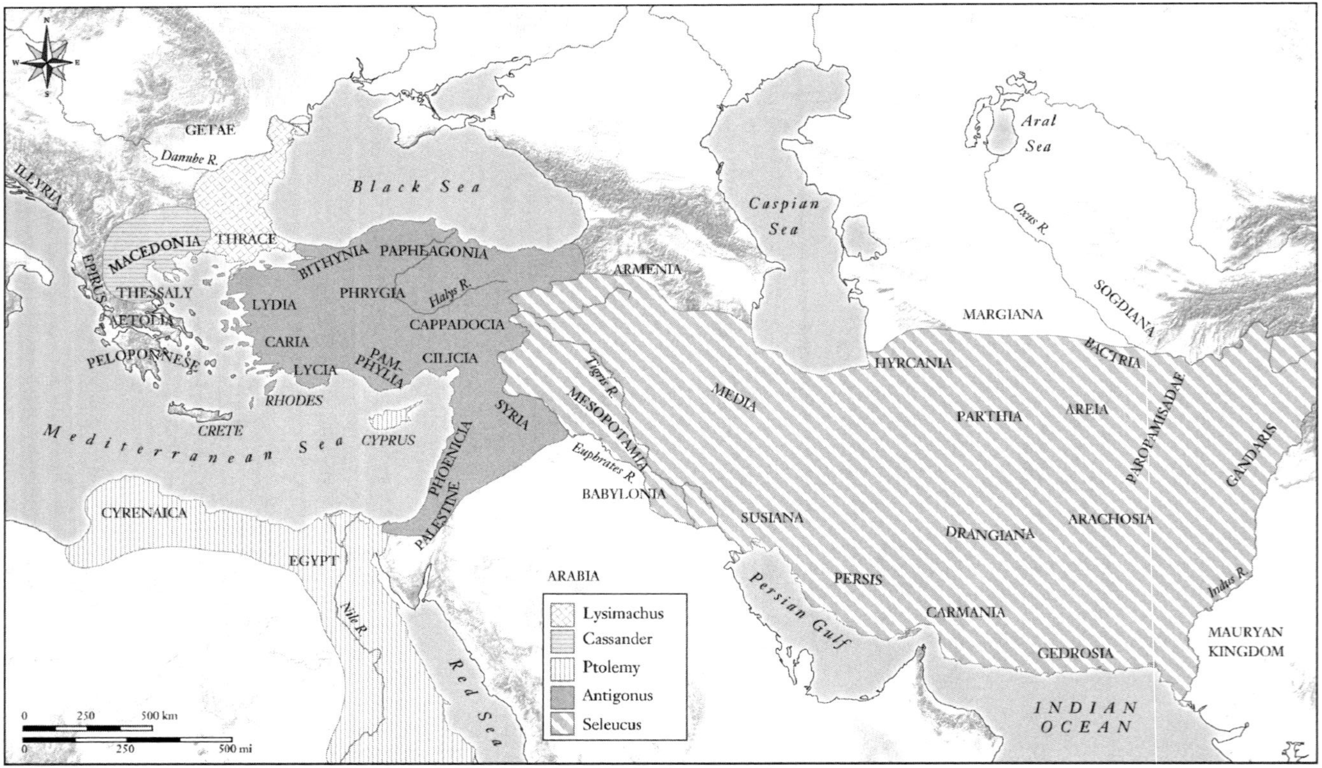

MAP 4 The Hellenistic World

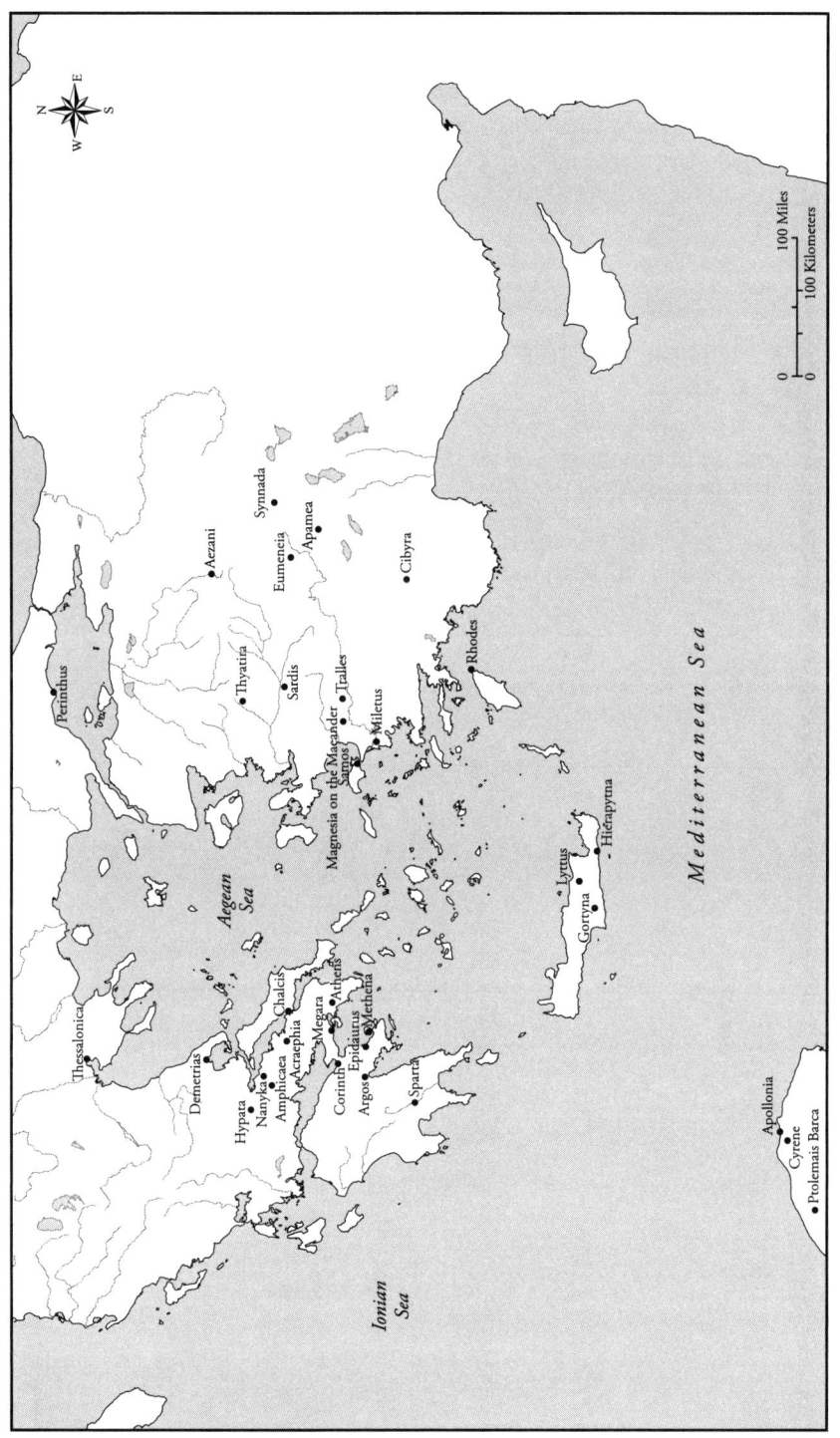

MAP 5 Hadrian's Panhellenion

Athens After Empire

Introduction

"This Is the City of Hadrian and Not of Theseus"

WHEN WE THINK OF ANCIENT Athens, the image that invariably comes to mind is of the Classical city: the Athenian military fighting the Persians for Greek freedom; monuments, like the Parthenon and Erechtheum on the Acropolis, beautifying everywhere one looked; the expansive Agora swarming with people conducting business, discussing current affairs, and generally chit-chatting; citizens taking part in their democracy; and a flourishing intellectual, artistic, and literary life, from performances of tragedies and comedies to the teaching of philosophers like Socrates, Plato, and Aristotle, to great orators like Pericles and Demosthenes declaiming in the Assembly, where domestic and foreign policy was debated and made. Life was anchored in the ideals of freedom, autonomy, and democracy, and in the fifth century at least, Athens was an imperial power second to none in the Mediterranean.

But in 338 that life forever changed, for the Athenians and for all mainland Greeks. In that year Philip II of Macedonia (r. 359–336) defeated a Greek army at Chaeronea (in Boeotia) and imposed Macedonian hegemony over Greece. Apart from some futile attempts to recapture their freedom, for well over a century the Greeks remained under that rule until the new power of the Mediterranean world, Rome, annexed Macedonia and Greece into its rapidly growing empire. Eventually Egypt was the last independent kingdom in the Mediterranean; when it fell to Rome in 30, the Romans boasted supremacy in the west and the east.

Philip II was assassinated in 336, at which time his son Alexander III ("the Great") assumed the throne. He died in Babylon in 323, having toppled the Persian Empire and marched as far east as India. The period from his death (ending the Classical period) to the battle of Actium (the defeat of Antony and Cleopatra at the hands of Agrippa) and Roman capture of Egypt is commonly called the "Hellenistic." It was the era of the great kingdoms of Seleucid Syria, Ptolemaic Egypt, Antigonid Greece, and Attalid Pergamum, among others; the age when the opening of East to West by Alexander's conquests came to fruition, with the Greeks truly realizing their world was far bigger than the Mediterranean; the time when Greek language and culture spread as far afield as India; and the rise of the new intellectual and scientific epicenter of the world centered in the Museum and Library at Alexandria. But what was Athens' place in this Hellenistic world? What was going on in the city in this period? And how different was it politically, economically, and culturally from its Classical past? These questions are what this book is all about.

It was once considered that the battle of Chaeronea in 338 spelled the end of the Greek city.[1] True, Athens as a city suffered a dramatic decline in military and naval power, and like the rest of Greece faced considerable economic distress. Under Macedonian rule it suffered a property requirement for citizenship, which saw the expulsion of thousands of its citizens. The Athenians were forced to suffer periods of autocratic rule and the imposition of Macedonian garrisons in the port of Piraeus and in the city itself, within eyesight of the great Acropolis. Once Rome had brought about the downfall of Macedonia in the earlier second century, Athens was subject to Rome's will, bowing to the likes of Sulla, Julius Caesar, Marcus Brutus, and Mark Antony (who lived there on two separate occasions), before the Roman Republic came to an end at the battle of Actium in 31 and Octavian (the future emperor Augustus) imposed stability.

During this time the Roman dominion of Greece and building activity in Athens, especially under Augustus and later (in the second part of the first century AD) under Hadrian, was steering Athens further away from what Pericles had proudly proclaimed "the school of Hellas" (the Greek word for Greece) in his funeral oration of 430.[2] The Athenians witnessed the Romans' appropriation of much of their (and Greek) culture for their own needs, and

---

[1] Gomme 1937; cf. the more realistic line of Cawkwell 1996 that the battle heralded the end of Greek autonomy.
[2] Thucydides 2.41.1.

were victim to widespread looting of artworks throughout Greece, which were taken to Rome for public and private display.³ Perhaps most grating for the Athenians, as their city became increasingly "Romanized," was watching their patron deity Athena share her home of centuries, the Acropolis, with the goddess Roma, when the imperial cult became established in the city.⁴ Arguably nowhere is the mastery of Rome more evident (literally) than the famous Arch to Hadrian that the Athenians commissioned in AD 132. On either side of it was an inscription: on the west side, "This is Athens, the ancient city of Theseus," and on the east, "This is the city of Hadrian, and not of Theseus" (on which see chapter 15).

Athens had been a great imperial power in the fifth century, and to a lesser extent in the fourth. In the Hellenistic period, it seemed only a second-rate city. But this dreary picture of decline and fall—and further fall—belies reality. It is the result of a negative image occasioned by the hostility of ancient sources, and especially the tendency to compare Hellenistic to Classical Athens in areas such as democratic participation, military power, subjection to foreign powers, and even literary life.⁵ The two cities are quite different, so much so that when comparing them the only irrefutable conclusion we can reach is that they are simply different.

True, the Athenians had been faced with adversity and quickly recovered from it in the Classical era, for example from the devastating plague that wiped out one-quarter of the city's population at the end of the first year of the Peloponnesian War, or the catastrophic defeat in Sicily in 412 that saw the annihilation of almost their entire fleet and the deaths of thousands of troops. But after Chaeronea, Athens was still a force with which to be reckoned: its people were always resilient; they still fought their Macedonian masters when they could, and later, they sided with foreign rulers against Rome, always in the hope of regaining that most cherished ideal, freedom. Many of the city's institutions were still functioning, especially religious and civic, such as the lavish festivals and the *ephebeia* (a military and intellectual training program for male youths), albeit in more restricted ways. If anything, given the city's diminished land forces and lack of its once powerful navy, the people's courageous defiance of oppression was the more remarkable.

---

[3] Appropriation: Bowersock 2002; Connolly 2007; Spawforth 2012; cf. Woolf 1994; Borg 2011.
[4] Romanization: Alcock 1997; Stefanidou-Tiveriou 2008; cf. Boatwright 2000, pp. 13–14, and also the essays in Hoff and Rotroff 1997.
[5] Very good succinct summary on why this sort of comparison is flawed and what it has meant for the "reputation" of Hellenistic Athens at Bayliss 2011, pp. 1–48; cf. Perrin-Saminadayar 2007a, pp. 7–25.

Arguably the Athenians resilience was the defining theme of their history in Hellenistic and even Roman times, when they could no longer boast a powerful land army or fleet. Thus, in 268 they idealistically joined forces with Egypt and Sparta to defy Antigonus II of Macedonia, but were totally defeated seven years later. In 229 they actually did regain independence, and with it the removal of the Macedonian garrisons, embarking thereafter on a policy of neutrality. But warfare against Philip V of Macedonia after 200 led to an appeal to Rome for help; from then on, the Athenians' future was linked to that city. In 146 Rome annexed Greece, but the opportunity to regain freedom came in the 80s when they sided with Mithridates VI of Pontus (Black Sea) against Rome. That decision would lead to their darkest hour, when in 86 the Roman general Lucius Cornelius Sulla besieged and sacked the city, with a terrible loss of life and destruction to many buildings.

But the people recovered, only to find themselves part of the downfall of the Roman Republic. Having welcomed Pompey and then Caesar, they gave refuge to Brutus after Caesar's assassination on the Ides of March in 44, and then to Mark Antony after he defeated Brutus and Cassius at the battles of Philippi in 42. Antony even lived in Athens, but his relationship with Cleopatra incurred the wrath of Octavian, and after Actium Athens had to welcome Octavian (Augustus) as ruler. Even then the people were not cowed. When Augustus visited the city in 21 he was angered that dissidents had daubed the statue of Athena on the Acropolis with blood and turned it to face westward, as though the goddess were spitting on Rome. Then a century later, under Hadrian, the city was catapulted again to prominence in the Greek world.

As one scholar succinctly said of the Hellenistic period, "Athens liked to believe that it was a centre of moderation, civilization and humanity in a sometimes irrational world."[6] And it was. As my book will show, Hellenistic Athens is far from being a postscript to its Classical predecessor; its rich and varied history continued, albeit without the same political and military emphasis, and while it has been the subject of much study in recent years, it still lives unfairly in the shadow of its more famous forerunner. Moreover, its Classical self still influenced politics, literature, and thought in the Hellenistic and Roman periods, with the pros and cons of its democracy and statesmen sparking debate.[7] It was its status as a cultural and

---

[6] Mattingly 1997, p. 120.
[7] See the collection of recent essays (of varying quality and lucidity) in Canevaro and Gray 2018 on the Hellenistic reception of democracy and political thought.

intellectual juggernaut, especially in philosophy and rhetoric, that enticed Romans to the city in increasing numbers from the second century, some to visit, others to study there—as has been well said, "Athens' ancient grandeur lived on to a great degree through the admiration of its benefactors and visitors."[8] The Hellenistic city still shines then, just not in the same way as the Classical one.

This book does not end with the commonly accepted terminal date of the Hellenistic period, but in AD 132 with Hadrian. The reason has to do with the modern construct of "Hellenistic," and what Actium and the Roman annexation of Egypt really meant for Athens—or Greece for that matter. Periodization (dividing up a historical time frame into periods and giving a name to one) is a double-edged sword: while it gives us convenient periods and labels to study, it does not necessarily follow that the beginning and end points truly reflect things starting and ending rather than merely changing as they continue.[9] Thus the dates of the Archaic (750–478), Classical (478–323), and Hellenistic (323–30) eras seem logical, but are arbitrary: why, for example, should the Persian Wars (490–478) end the Archaic rather than start the Classical (which therefore would go from 490 to 323)? The Greeks did not have those terms, and one scholar even dates Classical Athens from 322 to 230.[10]

"Periodization is also characterization."[11] In this respect, we can question the start and end dates of the "Hellenistic period."[12] That term was coined in 1836 by the German historian Johann Gustav Droysen, who saw the three centuries after Alexander's death to Roman rule in the east defined by the spread of Greek language and culture—Hellenism. But his interpretation denies other features that may equally be seen as defining, not to mention the influence of Hellenism on Roman culture and learning.[13] And that terminal date implies that history in some way ended then; it did not, but merely changed. The spread of Hellenism continued, influencing Rome,

---

[8] Stefanidou-Tiveriou 2008, p. 11.
[9] The issue of periodization has been discussed in various works: see, for example, the essays in Toohey and Golden 1997 (e.g., that of Morris, pp. 96–131); cf. Flower 2010, pp. 3–4.
[10] Dreyer 1999; cf. Dreyer 2001.
[11] Morris 1997, p. 96.
[12] See comments in Worthington 2016, pp. 5–6.
[13] Spread of Hellenism: Green 1990, pp. 312–335.

and it was Athens' cultural standing that prompted Hadrian to make it the center of a new league of Greek cities in the east called the Panhellenion.

The years 31 and 30 were demonstrably significant ones for Rome, but less so for the Greeks, even though they would suffer an economic slump after them. But in terms of domination, by 31 they had been part of the Roman Empire for over a century, and the only novelty stemming from Actium was a new master, Octavian, who was merely another in a line of Roman rulers going back to Caesar and more recently Antony. In 31 there was no new constitution foisted on the city, no reduction of any democratic functions, and no new taxes. After Actium, Octavian had traveled to Athens, where he gave the people much-needed grain. In this he was following a trend: Caesar had forgiven the Athenians for their support of Pompey, and Antony for their support of Brutus, and both had bestowed gifts on the city. It is hard to imagine, then, that the Athenians (or the Greeks) would have seen Octavian's actions, and a year later Egypt's fall to Rome, as anything special or as being the end of a period for *them*.

Indeed, previous scholars also have had different views about the period's end. All agree it began with Alexander's death, which really did herald a new era in Greek history. But W. S. Ferguson in 1911 (in a book titled *Hellenistic Athens: An Historical Essay*) and C. Mossé in 1973 (admittedly titling her book *Athens in Decline, 404–86*) both end with the Sullan sack in 86.[14] That destruction certainly was a momentous event, but it did not usher in a new age; both in 86 and 31, the new normal of Roman rule continued. Then in 1982 appeared C. Habicht's *Studien zur Geschichte Athens in hellenistischer Zeit*, and in 1995 his magisterial *Athen. Die Geschichte der Stadt in hellenistischer Zeit* (translated as *Athens from Alexander to Antony* in 1997), taking the history of the period once more to the demise of Antony and Cleopatra.[15] I have used the English translation as it contained minor updates (and will say here that my debt to Habicht's work is enormous, as most of the following pages will show).[16] Most recently, and again rightly advancing a "long" Hellenistic age, is A. Chaniotis' *Age of Conquests: The Greek World from Alexander to Hadrian* (in 2018), a broader treatment of the period (with no separate chapter on Athens itself).

---

[14] Ferguson 1911; Mossé 1973.
[15] Before the 1982 book there was his *Untersuchungen zur politischen Geschichte Athens im 3. Jahrhundert v. Chr.*, obviously focused only on the third century.
[16] Many of Habicht's articles are reprinted in Habicht 1994a.

To me, the inscription on Hadrian's Arch speaks volumes for an end date. There was of course a continuum of Roman rule long after Hadrian, but it is not just the imposition of foreign rule that drives the history of Hellenistic Athens but the changes to the physical city. Hellenistic rulers had funded buildings in Athens (the Stoa of Attalus of Pergamum in the Agora is perhaps the most famous), but they were intended to beautify the city, and earn honors for the benefactors: these men did not take over the city. But the Romans did, and their constructions, especially Hadrian's grand building program, impacted the city even more. What he had built, where, and why were his choices. Athens, then, had become as close to a provincial city as one could get, before settling into life in the later Roman Empire. The Arch is a fitting climax to a period in Athenian history that should be viewed, I would argue, as one block from Macedonian hegemony to Hadrian.

In any case, various developments and especially the quantity of publications over the past years call for a new treatment of Hellenistic Athens (since "Hellenistic" as a term has stuck, despite its limitations, I use it in this book for convenience). New insights into chronology (a complex and controversial topic) and events have been provided by the recent and much-needed epigraphical publications of the city's major state decrees and laws. So far three volumes have been published, covering the periods 352/1 to 322/1 (slightly before the focus of this book), 300/299 to 230/29, and 229/8 to 168/7.[17] New interpretations of the material remains also help to shed light on the activities and perhaps attitudes of the people, all of which add to the information provided by our increasingly scant literary sources. The picture presented of Athens in the following pages is of a vibrant city, which commanded respect in the Greek world and even in Rome. It certainly had its share of ups and downs, but the people were always buoyant despite the adversities they faced, and Greek culture, of which Athens was so integral a part, remained captivating.

My narrative is anchored in Athenian political and military history and the city's interactions with other Greeks, the various ruling powers of the Hellenistic period, and with Rome. In trying to fit half a millennium of history into one set of covers, I can give only an overview of relevant Hellenistic

---

[17] *IG* ii/iii²: Lambert 2012 (352/1 to 322/1); Osborne and Byrne 2012 (300/99 to 230/29); Bardani and Tracy 2012 (229/8 to 168/7).

history and of the city's more important institutional, social, cultural, and religious aspects. Readers eager to know more about the above should consult the works cited in the notes.

All specific dates and references to centuries are BC except where indicated.

I

Farewell to Freedom

ATHENS WAS THE LEADING *polis* of Greece in the Classical era (478–323) politically, intellectually, culturally, economically, and militarily (boasting the largest war fleet in the eastern Mediterranean). But the heyday of Athenian influence was brutally ended in 338 on the battlefield of Chaeronea in Boeotia. There, the Macedonian king Philip II (Alexander the Great's father) defeated a coalition of Greek cities led by Athens and Thebes and annexed Greece into a rapidly growing Macedonian empire. And so began a new era in Greek history, one that the Athenians, for example, could not have foreseen given the plight of Macedonia before Philip and the dominance of their city in the Greek world. It is no surprise that the Greeks hardly embraced this change, and tried to reverse it. To understand the Athenian attitude to Macedonia (and later to Rome), not to mention how Macedonia became so powerful thanks to Philip, we must begin by highlighting the last years of Greek autonomy and what cities like Athens lost.

"The School of Hellas"

In 430, Pericles delivered a solemn funeral oration (*epitaphios*) before an assembled Athenian populace eulogizing those who had died during the first year of the Peloponnesian War (431–404). Athens was unique in Greece for having this honorary speech for those who had given their lives fighting for their city's freedom, and all citizens, *metics* (resident aliens), and visitors were expected to assemble at the appointed place by the Agora to hear it. In his speech, Pericles spoke of Athens as a "role model" in the Greek world, especially for its democracy, which many other cities followed. After extolling its virtues, reputation, resources, and glorious history, he made the claim that "our city as a whole is the school of Hellas."[1]

An *epitaphios* was understandably highly rhetorical because it was intended as a tribute to the dead as well as to extol the glories of their city, its democracy, and their ancestors' exploits, but few could argue (then and now) that what Pericles said in his speech did not match Athens' position at the time. Its fifth-century empire, the Delian League, boasted allies in the triple figures all over the Mediterranean and generated substantial income. In fact, in the fifth century Athens was one of the wealthiest cities in the Mediterranean; its landscape was dotted with magnificent temples and monuments, and its citizens enjoyed splendid civic religious festivals, which included poetic, dramatic, and athletic contests. It was simply the intellectual and cultural center of the Greek world. Here, for example, Socrates, Plato, and Aristotle lived and worked, as did the great tragedians Aeschylus, Sophocles, and Euripides, along with comedic masters like Aristophanes, and master sculptors such as Pheidias and Praxiteles (Pheidias' giant statue of Athena Parthenos, the "Virgin," in the Parthenon was one of the seven wonders of the ancient world), while subjects such as oratory and rhetoric were formalized and adapted into an educational program.

The rise of Athens as an imperial power can be traced back to the end of the Persian Wars (490–479), when the city had played a key role in defeating the vast army of the Great King Xerxes.[2] Where Athens shone was not so much on the battlefield as at sea: in 480, as the Persians won their famous victory at the Pass of Thermopylae against the "300 Spartans," the Athenian general Themistocles defeated the Persian navy at Artemisium (off the northern tip of Euboea), and then at Salamis, causing Xerxes to flee back to Persia. The remnants of his army were overcome at Plataea (in Boeotia) the following year, thanks principally to the Spartan army. Because of their role in protecting Greece and their naval strength, in 478 the Athenians put together an anti-Persian confederacy, the Delian League, which attracted allies throughout the Mediterranean. The league quickly grew into an empire, and because each ally paid an annual tribute in money or ships, Athens soon became powerful and prosperous. Then in 462 an Athenian named Ephialtes introduced radical democracy, making the people sovereign in the

---

[1] Entire *epitaphios*: Thucydides 2.35–46; role model: 2.37.1; school of Hellas: 2.41.1.
[2] See, for example, Green 1996.

state (which we will discuss in chapter 3). Apart from two short periods of oligarchy (one lasting only a few months in 411, the other slightly longer-term, from 404 to 403), radical democracy remained in place until abolished by Macedonia in 322 (see below).

But the Athenians' rising influence in Greece after the Persian Wars did not sit well with the Spartans (who headed their own Peloponnesian League), and eventually led to the Peloponnesian War of 431 to 404.[3] Despite Athenian resources at the outset of hostilities and some military successes during the war, the Spartans were victorious; the Delian League was disbanded, and a pro-Spartan oligarchy, the Thirty Tyrants, installed in the city. Still, Sparta could not hold Athens down for long: the ruthless Thirty were overcome in 403, democracy was restored, and in 378 the Athenians put together a new league, the Second Athenian Confederacy, whose charter has come down to us.[4]

Although this new confederacy was never on the same scale as the Delian League, with perhaps sixty allies at its height, it may be seen as a fourth-century empire.[5] But the Athenians' exploitive practices led in 356 to an allied revolt (the Social War), which ended the following year in Athenian defeat and financial ruin. The confederacy continued to exist as a shadow of its former self, but thanks to policies of leaders such as Eubulus and Lycurgus, the Athenians rebuilt their economy, and by the middle of the fourth century were again the dominant city in Greece.

If, however, the people thought that the status quo of pre–Peloponnesian War days had been restored, they were in for a rude awakening thanks to Philip II. Since his kingdom would come to dominate Greece until the second century, let us turn to its history and rise to superpower.

Philip II and Macedonian Hegemony

Macedonia lay north of the imposing 9,461-foot Mount Olympus, Greece's tallest mountain.[6] Its original capital was Aegae (Vergina), but in 399 King

---

[3] See, for example, Kagan 2003; Hanson 2006. See too the account of the period with general comments on Athens at Harding 2015, pp. 3–46.
[4] Rhodes and Osborne 2003, no. 22 (pp. 92–105). On the confederacy: Cargill 1981.
[5] An empire: for example, Griffith 1978. Not an empire: for example, Cargill 1981; cf. Harding 2015, pp. 34–36.
[6] See Worthington 2014, pp. 14–22, for the following account, citing bibliography. On ancient Macedonia, see especially the essays in Roisman and Worthington 2010 and Lane Fox 2011a.

Archelaus established a new capital at Pella, a windswept, heavily fortified city northwest of the Thermaic Gulf on a branch of the Loudias river, with sweeping views over the plain, Lake Loudias, and the mountains behind it.[7] He did so to facilitate trade, as in antiquity Pella was coastal; today, because of the silting of the sea over the centuries, it is about 35 kilometers inland. Aegae, however, continued to be the venue for royal weddings and funerals.

The Macedonians were likely Greek-speaking, and had a rugged society akin to the Homeric or Spartan (with boys, including members of the royal family, from an early age being taught to fight, ride, and hunt wild boar, foxes, birds, and even lions). But there were clear social differences between them and the Greeks south of Olympus. For one thing, the Macedonians were polygamists—or at least their kings were—as marriages were often for political reasons, a trend continuing with the Successor kings of the Hellenistic period. Also, unlike their Greek counterparts, the Macedonians drank their wine neat (*akratos*) rather than watering it down. Thus, a Greek symposium was quite different in character from a Macedonian one, where men were drunk "while they were still being served the first course," and alcohol-fueled brash talk could lead to actual fighting.[8]

But we should not be taken in by this hard-drinking, hard-living society. Macedonian craftsmen produced artworks of stunningly beautiful quality—gold, silver, and bronze works, tomb paintings, jewelry, and especially mosaics.[9] Some kings were clearly intellectuals with cultured courts: Archelaus (r. 413–399), for example, had invited Socrates and the Athenian tragic playwrights Agathon and Euripides to move to Pella; Perdiccas III (r. 368–359) was a patron of Plato's Academy; Philip II enjoyed intellectual exchanges with the Athenian orator Isocrates and Speusippus (Plato's successor at the Academy), as well as famously hiring Aristotle to tutor his son Alexander; and Antigonus II Gonatas (r. 277–239) studied under Zeno (the founder of Stoicism) at Athens.

In 359 invading Illyrians from Macedonia's northwest killed Perdiccas III and four thousand troops in battle. At that point the Paeonians (to the north of the kingdom) mobilized to invade, and the Athenians and the king

---

[7] See Worthington 2008, pp. 225–226, citing bibliography.
[8] Ephippus, *BNJ* 126 F 1 = Athenaeus 3.120e. Ethnicity: Worthington 2008a, pp. 216–219; see in more detail Engels 2010, pp. 81–98; Hatzopoulos 2011a; Hatzopoulos 2011b. Society: Sawada 2010, pp. 392–408.
[9] Andronikos 1983; Touratsoglou 1983; Hardiman 2010; Kousser 2010; Paspalas 2011; and Palagia 2011.

FIGURE 1.1 Facial reconstruction of Philip II. Courtesy of the Whitworth Art Gallery, the University of Manchester.

of western Thrace (on Macedonia's eastern border) separately supported pretenders to the throne. Perdiccas' son and heir, Amyntas, was only a minor, but instead of appointing a regent until he came of age the people acclaimed Philip, the dead king's brother (and Amyntas' uncle), as king (Figure 1.1).

Their decision was a watershed in Macedonian history. In a remarkable reign of twenty-three years, Philip turned the kingdom into an imperial power by a dizzying and brilliant policy of deceit, diplomacy, and military force.[10] It took him only a few months to neutralize the four immediate threats to his kingdom, after which he went on to secure his borders for the first time, and then to expand in all directions. By the time he died in 336, he had doubled the size of Macedonia and its population to as many as 500,000.

---

[10] Philip's reign: Ellis 1976; Cawkwell 1978; Hammond and Griffith 1979, pp. 203–698; Hammond 1994; Worthington 2008a; Worthington 2014 (comparing and contrasting him to Alexander); see too Müller 2010, pp. 166–185. Focusing on Philip as general and tactician: Gabriel 2010.

He had also put an ambitious economic policy into place, exploiting natural resources, especially mines, like never before, to make his kingdom an economic powerhouse.

Philip also revolutionized the army, transforming it from a weak conscript one into a professional fighting force, with regular pay and a promotion pathway. New tactics such as the "shock and awe" wave of cavalry attacking the enemy before the infantry (the opposite of regular Greek warfare) and new weaponry, including the deadly sarissa, a roughly 14-foot-long cornel wood pike with a one-foot sharp pointed iron head, made Philip's army unstoppable. The army forged by Philip was the one that Alexander took with him to Asia, and which enabled his victories in epic battles and sieges; the Antigonid kings led an army modeled after that of Philip for almost 150 years until eventually the Roman legion overcame it in battle in 197 (p. 155). But thirty years after that, at the battle of Pydna in 168, the Roman general Aemilius Paullus remarked he had never been so fearful as when he faced the Macedonian phalanx in battle array (pp. 166–167).

A Macedonian king was autocratic; in his hands alone all matters of domestic and foreign policy fell, and he was also sole commander of the army, and chief priest in the state.[11] That sort of power was Philip's greatest ally, for he could move as needed and decide his own policy in contrast to the *poleis* (city-states) of Greece, with their slow-moving democracies.[12] The Antigonid rulers of Greece in the Hellenistic period were no different when it came to their speed and decisiveness.[13]

Philip's fiercest opponents were the Athenians, who by the 340s had come to follow the anti-Macedonian policy of Demosthenes, ancient Greece's foremost orator and often considered its greatest patriot (see Figure 5.1).[14] From 357 to 346 the two sides had been at war, though this had been one mostly of words while Philip expanded Macedonia's reach. The Peace of Philocrates that ended that war in 346 was soon in trouble, and thanks to Demosthenes' jingoistic rhetoric, Philip and Athens went to war again in 340.[15] When the king led an army into Greece in 338, a coalition force led by Thebes and Athens prepared to resist him at Chaeronea in Boeotia, ready to fight for the very freedom of Greece.

---

[11] King 2010, citing bibliography.
[12] Philip's speed was something even Demosthenes recognized: Demosthenes 1.12–13.
[13] On the latter, cf. Ma 2011.
[14] On Demosthenes as a politician and orator, see Worthington 2013.
[15] Harding 1985, no. 93, pp. 117–118, nos. 95–96, pp. 118–121.

FIGURE 1.2 Head of Alexander the Great. Photo: Ian Worthington. Pella Museum, Greece.

Although both sides fielded roughly equal numbers—Philip had 30,000 infantry and 2,000 cavalry and the Greeks 30,000 infantry and 3,800 cavalry—Philip crushed his enemy in battle.[16] Thousands of Greeks were slain (including 2,000 Athenians), thousands taken prisoner, and the famous 300-strong Sacred Band of Thebes was cut to pieces by Macedonian troops led by the eighteen-year-old Alexander (the king's son and heir; see Figure 1.2). Philip imposed terms on his opponents, ruthlessly installing a pro-Macedonian oligarchy and a garrison in Thebes, yet allowing the Athenians to retain their democracy and even their fleet; in fact, he tapped Alexander with returning the ashes of their dead and prisoners of war from the battle.

Then Philip moved to Corinth, a city of great strategic importance on the isthmus. There, before delegations from the Greek cities, he announced his plan to impose a Common Peace—a constitutional agreement, by which every Greek city swore a separate oath of allegiance to the other cities and to

---

[16] Worthington 2008a, pp. 147–149; Gabriel 2010, pp. 214–216.

Macedonia, promising to have the same friends and enemies and not to engage in any subversive activities.[17] These types of arrangements had collapsed before because of the distrust that the *poleis* had of each other, but Philip used that distrust as a deterrent, for if any city tried to leave his Common Peace or ally with a hostile power the others had carte blanche to attack it. Furthermore, he created a council (*synedrion*), presided over by a *hegemon* or leader, to which each city sent representatives to discuss domestic and foreign issues.[18] Macedonia would not be part of this council, making it appear that Philip was allowing the Greeks autonomy in their affairs.

The following year (337) the various representatives reconvened at Corinth, swore their oaths to each other, to Philip, and (significantly) to his descendants—and elected him *hegemon* of the council. Philip thus cannily presided over a council of which Macedonia was not a member! This administrative arrangement—given the modern name the League of Corinth—was the means by which Macedonia ruled Greece; it was anchored in the belief that the Greeks were free, but appearance was far from reality. As we shall see, future Macedonian rulers and even the Romans advocated Greek freedom, but they did so for their own ends, and turned the call to freedom into a mere slogan.[19]

Philip then declared his intention to invade the Persian Empire, ostensibly to liberate the Greek cities of Asia Minor and to punish the Persians for their invasion of Greece in the early fifth century.[20] It was not to be. The following summer (336), on the eve of leading his troops to Asia, one of his personal bodyguards (and a jilted former lover), Pausanias, assassinated Philip. Whether Pausanias acted for personal reasons or was part of a conspiracy involving Philip's fourth wife Olympias and their son Alexander is not known, though on balance the conspiracy theory has merit.[21]

The Greeks seized the opportunity of Philip's murder to revolt from the League of Corinth. However, Alexander, who had been proclaimed king on

---

[17] Harding 1985, no. 99, pp. 123–125; Ryder 1965, pp. 102–106; Perlman 1985; and Perlman 1986. See too Rhodes and Osborne 2003, no. 76, with commentary (pp. 376–379); Worthington 2008b. The league as an example of early international law: Hunt 2010, pp. 217–236.

[18] Background: Worthington 2008a, pp. 158–171, to which add Ager 1996, pp. 39–43; Dmitriev 2011, pp. 67–90.

[19] Dmitriev 2011, with a very succinct discussion on pp. 351–379; see too Gruen 1984, pp. 132–157.

[20] Worthington 2008a, pp. 166–169; Worthington 2014, pp. 103–105.

[21] Worthington 2008a, pp. 181–186; Worthington 2014, pp. 113–115.

Philip's death, ended their insurrection in a matter of weeks.[22] After restoring his father's Common Peace, he announced his intention to invade Persia for the same reasons as before: the member states of the League of Corinth had no choice but to give him this mandate. But there was campaigning to be done in Thrace and Illyria the following year before any invasion. During his operations in Illyria, Alexander was forced to put down a sudden revolt by Thebes; after a brief siege, he and his men fought their way into the city, slaughtering 6,000 Thebans and taking 30,000 prisoners, before razing the city to the ground.[23] The Athenians had toyed with the idea of supporting Thebes; fortunately, they changed their minds. Alexander's merciless punishment showed the Greeks what would happen to any city that defied Macedonian hegemony.

Alexander the Great

In the spring of 334 Alexander (aged only twenty-two) led an army of roughly 40,000 infantry and 5,000 cavalry across the Hellespont. He threw a spear, so we are told, into foreign soil before landing, a symbol to show he intended to take Persia by storm; literally "by the spear."[24] That epic campaign, one of the most celebrated of antiquity, is beyond the scope of this book.[25] Just four years after his arrival, in 330, in fierce battles and sieges, always outnumbered, but always successful, thanks to his tactical brilliance, use of psychological warfare, and at times sheer audacity, he had toppled the Persian Empire and proclaimed himself Lord of Asia.

Three years after that Alexander added Bactria and Sogdiana (Afghanistan) to his empire, and in 326 he was in what the Greeks called India (now Pakistan), where he fought arguably his greatest battle against the Indian rajah Porus at the Hydapses (Jhelum) River. But then the tide turned. An army mutiny at the Hyphasis (Beas) River a few months later forced him to start the return march westward, and in June 323 at Babylon he died.

Alexander's death had two outcomes. First, it led to a new age in Greek—indeed world—history, the Hellenistic, during which Greek language and culture spread even further in the east, and the Greeks of the Mediterranean

---

[22] Worthington 2014, pp. 126–127.
[23] Worthington 2014, pp. 131–135.
[24] Diodorus 17.17.2.
[25] See Worthington 2014, citing further bibliography; succinct survey: Gilley and Worthington 2010.

came to realize they were part of a bigger world.[26] Second, and less dazzling, it marked the end of the Macedonian Empire. Alexander had not produced an heir, a serious failing on his part as king, not least because his ambitious senior staff divided up his lands among themselves, ushering in four decades of warfare commonly referred to as the Wars of the Successors (see chapter 2). In this respect his legacy fell short of that of his father.[27]

Lycurgan Athens

While he was in Asia, Alexander had some dealings with the Athenians—such as sending three hundred panoplies to them as a dedication to Athena after his first victory against the Persian army at the Granicus River in 334.[28] But for the most part he expected Antipater, whom he had left behind as guardian (*epitropos*) of Macedonia and deputy *hegemon* of the League of Corinth, to attend to affairs in the west.[29] Under Antipater's stewardship the Greeks remained largely passive—presumably they had learned from the fate of Thebes in 335 that resistance was futile. Even Demosthenes, whose fiery speeches Philip had dubbed "soldiers because of their warlike power," was a shadow of his former self.[30] He had apparently prayed for the Persians defeating the Macedonian king, but Alexander's victories over there alerted Demosthenes, as it did the Greeks, that Macedonian rule was here to stay.[31]

The Macedonian hegemony of Greece brought a period of peace and prosperity, especially for Athens, with the city initially retaining its direct democracy.[32] But it was financially strapped. The end of the Peloponnesian War in 404 brought defeat and bankruptcy, and accompanying the end of the Social War in 355 was another round of financial ruin.[33] To the rescue

---

[26] Bosworth 2007; W. L. Adams 2007. On the Hellenistic era, see as starting points Tarn and Griffith 1952; Green 1990; the essays in Erskine 2003; Bugh 2007; and the *Cambridge Ancient History*² vols. 7–9.
[27] Worthington 2014, pp. 115–119; cf. pp. 302–309 on Alexander; see too Squillace 2015.
[28] Arrian 1.16.7; Plutarch, *Alexander* 16.8.
[29] Diodorus 17.17.3, 5. On Antipater, see Baynham 1994; Baynham 2003; Gilley and Worthington 2010, pp. 199–205.
[30] [Plutarch], *Moralia* 845d. Demosthenes in the era of Alexander: Davies 1971, pp. 113–139; Worthington 2013, pp. 275–325.
[31] Prayers: Aeschines 3.164.
[32] Worthington 1994a; Shipley 2005.
[33] Hunt 2010, pp. 259–264.

came a politician named Eubulus.[34] He instituted a series of constrictive financial and economic reforms, based on a noninterventionist foreign policy. By tightening Athenian belts, Eubulus raised state revenues from 137 talents after the end of the Social War in 355 to 400 talents.[35] He also likely created the Theoric Fund, into which was paid any and all of the city's financial surpluses. The fund (from the Greek *theoria* meaning "looking") at first provided money to the people for them to attend religious festivals and the theater, but eventually it was used for various civic projects.[36]

But Athens' growing involvement with Philip, and Demosthenes' bellicose speeches in the Assembly, undid much of Eubulus' good work and scrapped the sort of "splendid isolation" that had been a feature of his policy. Philip's benevolence to the people after Chaeronea had been a godsend, but he still insisted that they disband their naval confederacy, robbing them of income from their allies. Then in the 330s came Lycurgus, one of Athens' public treasurers and an overseer of the Theoric Fund. He rescued Athens from its financial plight and dominated civic affairs for a decade, so much so that that period is commonly referred to as Lycurgan Athens.[37]

Thanks to Lycurgus' stimuli to trade and commerce, and his increased exploitation of the city's rich silver mines at Laurium (60 kilometers south of Athens between Thoriscus and Cape Sunium), Athens' market area, the Agora, and its port at the Piraeus (about 10 kilometers from the city) thrived, and prosperity returned to the city.[38] He even launched a building program, rivaling that of Pericles a century earlier, that saw the construction

---

[34] Cawkwell 1963, pp. 48, 54–61; Hunt 2010, pp. 32, 49–50, 258; cf. Hakkarainen 1997, especially pp. 5–6.

[35] Theopompus, *BNJ* 115 F 166.

[36] Plutarch, *Pericles* 9, claims that Pericles created the fund in the 450s, but that is unlikely: Cawkwell 1963, pp. 53–58; Sealey 1993, pp. 256–258. However, Roselli 2009 argues that the Theoric Fund was not created until the middle of the fourth century, and that in the fifth century there was a system of ad hoc payments of money to the people.

[37] Mitchel 1965; Davies 1971, pp. 348–353; Mitchel 1973; Mossé 1973, pp. 80–96; Burke 1985; Bosworth 1988, pp. 204–215; Engels 1988; Engels 1992; Faraguna 1992; Habicht 1997a, pp. 22–35; Faraguna 2003, pp. 118–124; Lambert 2010; Rhodes 2010; and the reappraisal essays in Azoulay and Ismard 2011 (for example, Lambert 2011); cf. Hakkarainen 1997, pp. 5–10. Life of Lycurgus: Roisman, Worthington, and Waterfield 2015, pp. 189–211; cf. Roisman and Edwards 2019.

[38] Faraguna 1992, pp. 289–322. Further on mines: Hopper 1968; see Harding 2015, p. 87 noting the unusualness of Athens in owning its mines and its issuing of mining leases from Eubulus' time as revenue. Activity in the Agora: Thompson and Wycherley 1972, pp. 185–191; Piraeus: Garland 1987.

of the Panathenaic Stadium (not too far from the Acropolis); the theater of Dionysus (on the south slope of the Acropolis); a naval arsenal (designed by the architect Philon) at the Piraeus; and a gymnasium (the word today makes us think only of physical exercise, but in Greece gymnasia were also schools; those of philosophers like Plato and Aristotle were gymnasia).[39] In addition, Lycurgus increased the Athenian fleet to almost 400 triremes.[40]

Away from the city, he supported building projects at Eleusis (18 kilometers northwest of Athens), home of the famous Mysteries—a secret religious rite stretching back until at least the mid-seventh century that honored Demeter and Persephone and was to do with a happy afterlife.[41] Over time, the Mysteries had fallen under the mantle of the Athenians, and in the city a sanctuary to them, called the Eleusinion, was established just outside the Agora; from there, the priest would take the sacred objects to be used in the initiation to Eleusis.[42] Needless to say, the Athenians had exploited the universal appeal of the Mysteries for their own advancement in Greece, and continued to do so in Hellenistic and Roman times.[43]

Civic pride was returning to Athens. In an effort to introduce a new "theatrical heritage" with an obvious nod to the good old days of Athens at its height, Lycurgus commissioned an official edition of the fifth-century tragedies of Aeschylus, Sophocles, and Euripides, and set up bronze statues of them in the theater of Dionysus.[44] His theater program was complemented by the *ephebeia* (a type of conscription for Athenian males—called ephebes—aged eighteen to twenty), which may have come into being or at least undergone reform. In addition to military training and serving in the various fortresses in Attica, the ephebes received an education in civic duties and expectations.[45] The *ephebeia* had a very long, even if reduced,

---

[39] [Plutarch], *Moralia* 852b; Arsenal: *IG* ii² 1668.
[40] Fleet: *IG* ii² 1623–1632 (ii² 1627, line 269, shows the fleet numbered 392 vessels in 330).
[41] *IG* ii² 1672, line 11 (buildings), lines 64–65, with Faraguna 1992, pp. 355–380. On religion in the Lycurgan era: Mikalson 1998, pp. 11–45.
[42] Thompson and Wycherley 1972, pp. 150–155; Clinton 1997, pp. 161–162, and more fully Clinton 1974.
[43] See Clinton 1989a for history, and Clinton 1994 on the political use of the festival under the democracy; on the officials from Classical to Roman times, Clinton 1974.
[44] [Plutarch], *Moralia* 841f, with Roisman, Worthington, and Waterfield 2015, p. 197; Scodel 2007; on Lycurgus' vision for "theatrical heritage" see Hanink 2014, especially pp. 60–125.
[45] [Aristotle], *Athenian Constitution* 42, with Pélékidis 1962; Faraguna 1992, pp. 274–280; Steinbock 2011; especially Friend 2019; and see chapter 3.

life throughout the Hellenistic and Roman periods, as we shall see; even foreigners came to enroll in it, providing income for the city.

But no new buildings, increases in military resources, or statues of long-dead tragedians could mask the reality of Athens' declining military strength or of the new normal of Greece under Macedonian rule.[46] The war of King Agis III of Sparta proved that. Despite the terrible fate that had befallen Thebes in 335 and Antipater's tight hold, in 331 Agis called the other Greeks to arms against Macedonia.[47] The Athenians may have initially favored him, but Demosthenes, recognizing the futility of his cause, convinced them to remain neutral. His advice was right: in the spring of 330, Antipater defeated Agis at Megalopolis (in the Peloponnese), killing him and half of his men, and punishing those cities that had supported him. At the same time, the Athenians were not completely cowed; perhaps in defiance of Demosthenes' stance, Nothippus of Diomeia successfully proposed in the Assembly an honorary decree for a certain Rheboulas of Thrace (son of the king Seuthes), who had supported the Spartan king.[48] It is this defiant attitude that we will see time and again in their relations with Macedonian rulers.[49]

In 330 two trials took place in Athens that cast interesting light onto the Athenians' attitude to Macedonian rule. In the first one, Lycurgus prosecuted a man named Leocrates who had left Athens after Chaeronea, even though the people had passed a decree calling on all citizens to man the city's defenses should Philip besiege it. Lycurgus' prosecution speech survives, but the defense speech does not, though we know that Leocrates weakly claimed that he had not fled Athens but had gone abroad for trading reasons.[50] Lycurgus called for the death penalty, but perhaps surprisingly Leocrates was acquitted (but by only one vote).[51] We might imagine anyone who had deserted the city in those circumstances would have been overwhelmingly condemned, but Lycurgus' loss probably stemmed from his

---

[46] Sekunda 1992.
[47] Badian 1994; Bosworth 1988, pp. 198–204; Worthington 2013, pp. 287–289.
[48] *IG* ii³ 1, 351.
[49] The art of this period reflects anti-Macedonian bias in the honors bestowed on men who opposed Philip and Alexander: Lawton 2003.
[50] Lycurgus 1: see now Roisman and Edwards 2019. See too Mikalson 1998, pp. 11–20, on religious aspects and sentiments of the speech, and Steinbock 2011 on Lycurgus' use of the *ephebeia*.
[51] Aeschines 3.252; see further Burke 1977; J. E. Atkinson 1981; Sawada 1996; Steinbock 2011.

failure to prove that Leocrates was a traitor and especially from reminding the jurors of the ramifications of the defeat at Chaeronea.

Shortly after Leocrates' trial, Demosthenes fell victim to his political opponent (and personal enemy) Aeschines.[52] Six years earlier, in 336, a man named Ctesiphon had proposed that Demosthenes be awarded a gold crown for his various civic offices and, especially, for acting in the best interests of the city. Aeschines at the time charged Ctesiphon with making an illegal proposal, but let the case drop when Philip was killed in the same year. In 330, perhaps because of feelings of ill will to Demosthenes over the Agis affair, Aeschines revived his charge against Ctesiphon. He wanted the jury to find Demosthenes guilty, thereby establishing that his entire policy against Philip was flawed and thus that he had not acted in the city's best interests. Since Demosthenes' opposition to Philip had led to the loss of Greek freedom at Chaeronea, we might expect him to have been condemned. Instead he was overwhelmingly acquitted.

In his acclaimed defense speech (*On the Crown*), Demosthenes did not try to skirt around the prosecution's allegations but faced them head on, boldly claiming that his anti-Macedonian policy was the right one because it was the only one that could have stopped Philip—unlike that of Aeschines, who thought Philip would be Athens' friend. Although the Greeks lost at Chaeronea, Demosthenes pointed out, they had done so fighting for freedom; in that respect, they could hold their heads high and compare themselves to their ancestors who fought the Persians for the same reasons. Aeschines, like Lycurgus, had been all doom and gloom in his speech, and reminded the jury of Chaeronea in the wrong way. Demosthenes, on the other hand, turned defeat into victory, given that *eleutheria* (freedom) and *autonomia* (autonomy) were ideals the Greeks most cherished. How Alexander or Antipater reacted to these trials, given the obvious strike at Macedonia, is unknown, but no action was taken against the city.

We shall see the Athenians never lost sight of these ideals throughout the Hellenistic period, nor of their yearning for their former democracy. Among other things, they set up a statue of Demosthenes in 280/79 and even went to war against Macedonia in the 260s and Rome in the 80s, no matter how much the odds were stacked against them. Each time they were defeated and suffered, but as Demosthenes would have said, they had fought for all the right reasons.

---

[52] MacDowell 2009, pp. 382–397; Worthington 2013, pp. 294–309.

For the next six years little of public interest happened in Athens as far as we know. From about 330 there was a severe grain shortage causing prices to skyrocket; the Athenians were forced in 325/4 to establish a colony in the Adriatic to protect their precious grain convoy from pirates, and they also awarded honors to anyone giving grain to the city.[53] Then in 324/3 the city was rocked by one of its most controversial episodes, the so-called Harpalus affair, which among other things saw the public disgrace of Demosthenes.[54] In 324 Harpalus, Alexander's corrupt imperial treasurer, fled to the city with a substantial amount of money and troops to try to incite a revolt against the king. The Athenians, on Demosthenes' urging, initially denied him entry, but when he tried again (with fewer troops) he was admitted. At an Assembly, Demosthenes persuaded the people to imprison him, confiscate his money, and send an embassy to Alexander to ask what to do about him. At some point Harpalus fled; when less than half the money that he had said he had brought with him was discovered, Demosthenes and some others were accused of taking bribes to allow him to escape.

In the meantime, Alexander had issued his Exiles Decree calling for the return from the east of tens of thousands of Greek exiles (excluding murderers and the Thebans) to their native cities.[55] This measure would have caused havoc on the mainland, still reeling from the effects of the famine. For the Athenians, moreover, the decree meant that the island of Samos, which Philip II had given to them after Chaeronea, and which had on it a substantial Athenian population, would revert to its native Samian owners.[56] Thus the cities sent embassies to Alexander at Babylon to protest the decree. Against this diplomatic background, and with several thousands of exiles already back on the mainland, we can understand that Demosthenes may well have wanted to get Harpalus out of the city, thereby reducing any tension between it and the king, though that does not mean he took a bribe.

---

[53] Shortage: Demosthenes 18.89, with Tracy 1995, pp. 30–35 (rightly pointing out that Athens' dependency on imported grain made the food supply always a concern); Harding 1985, no. 121, pp. 148–150; Rhodes and Osborne 2003, no. 96, with commentary; Mossé 1973, pp. 90–96; Harding 2015, pp. 33–34, 46–51. Colony: Rhodes and Osborne 2003, no. 100, with commentary. On Athens' need to secure its food supply, see G. J. Oliver 2007a.
[54] Worthington 1992, pp. 41–77; Blackwell 1998; Worthington 2013, pp. 311–325.
[55] Worthington 2013, pp. 312–313.
[56] Errington 1975.

Despite no evidence against him, Demosthenes was put on trial in March 323. Ten prosecutors delivered speeches against him, of which only those by Hyperides and the client of a speechwriter named Dinarchus survive.[57] He was found guilty, and to escape an enormous fine of 50 talents fled into exile. With Demosthenes gone from the city, the hawkish Hyperides came to dominate political affairs. But then in late June came the news that no one expected: Alexander the Great had died in Babylon. As far as the Greeks were now concerned, his death was also the end of the Exiles Decree.[58]

The Lamian War

Most likely, it was acute alcoholic pancreatitis brought on by his excessive drinking and punishing lifestyle (exacerbated by a recent near fatal wound at Malli in India) that caused Alexander's death on June 11, 323.[59] He had married Roxane of Bactria in 327, but she was still pregnant with their child when he died, so he left no clear successor. The story goes that his generals asked him on his deathbed to whom he was leaving his empire; his reply was merely "to the best man."[60] Why Alexander said this (assuming he did) is unknown, but of course it caused chaos, as each member of his senior staff thought he was the best man. Within days of their king's passing they were all at loggerheads with each other.

The Athenian orator Demades supposedly quipped that if Alexander were dead the whole world "would smell of his corpse."[61] But once the king's death was confirmed, and with no clear immediate successor to assume the throne, the Greeks not surprisingly believed that the era of Macedonian rule was over. Beginning in Rhodes, Chios, and Ephesus, the ripple effect of insurrection quickly moved to the mainland. In Athens, Hyperides persuaded the people to give the general Leosthenes 50 talents from what was left of Harpalus' money to recruit mercenaries; with them,

---

[57] Worthington 2013, pp. 316–324.
[58] Although one city, Tegea in the Peloponnese, did take back its exiles: Harding 1985, no. 122, pp. 150–152.
[59] Depuydt 1997. Death: Worthington 2014, pp. 293–297.
[60] Diodorus 18.1.4; Arrian 7.26.3 (= Ptolemy, *BNJ* 138 F 30); Curtius 10.5.5; Justin 12.15–18. "To the best" is *to aristo* in Greek; possibly (though this is a stretch) Alexander had meant to say "*to Kratero*," in other words Craterus, who was not present at Babylon at the time, and Plutarch, *Eumenes* 6.1–2, speaks of the Macedonians wanting him to succeed Alexander. On the last words, see Antela-Bernárdez 2011.
[61] Plutarch, *Phocion* 22.3; Demades: Davies 1971, pp. 99–100.

the Athenians spearheaded a wider-scale revolt.⁶² The Greeks called it the Hellenic War, but, following the historian Diodorus, it is more commonly called the Lamian War.⁶³

The Greeks fielded an army of 30,000 men, whereas Antipater had only 13,000 Macedonian infantry and 600 cavalry, plus an additional 2,000 Thessalian cavalry.⁶⁴ Leosthenes quickly secured the pass at Thermopylae to block Antipater from marching into central Greece, forcing him to appeal urgently to two other Macedonian generals, Craterus and Leonnatus, for reinforcements. Both men were then en route back to Greece with 10,000 veterans and other troops from Alexander's army, but Athens' dominance at sea prevented them from crossing. Undaunted, Antipater tried to take Thermopylae, but the Thessalian cavalry deserted him; he retreated to nearby Lamia in Thessaly, where Leosthenes besieged him all winter.

Unfortunately for the Athenians, Leosthenes was killed in an attack on Lamia, and the following spring (322) Leonnatus successfully managed to break through the Athenian fleet and relieve Antipater.⁶⁵ In a bitter engagement, Antiphilus, who succeeded Leosthenes, killed Leonnatus, but Antipater escaped. To make matters worse, the Macedonian admiral Cleitus defeated the Greek fleet that summer, allowing Craterus to bring across his troops.⁶⁶ The victory over the Greek fleet was the turning point in the war.⁶⁷ As more Greeks deserted Antiphilus, Antipater forced him to battle at Crannon in central Thessaly in August. Antiphilus' army consisted of 25,000 infantry and 3,500 cavalry, while Antipater had 43,000 infantry and 5,000 cavalry.⁶⁸ Antipater defeated the Greeks, and followed his victory by reimposing Macedonian rule throughout Greece. He then turned to deal with the ringleader: Athens.

---

⁶² Diodorus 18.10.2, 11; Pausanias 1.25.3–4; Plutarch, *Phocion* 23.1–2; *Timoleon* 6.5. Hyperides: Davies 1971, pp. 517–520; Leosthenes: Davies 1971, pp. 342–344.
⁶³ Lamian War: Ashton 1984; Lehmann 1988; Hammond and Walbank 1988, pp. 107–117; Schmitt 1992; Tracy 1995, pp. 23–29; Habicht 1997a, pp. 36–42; Bennett and Roberts 2009, pp. 27–40; Worthington 2013, pp. 330–333; Harding 2015, pp. 55–59.
⁶⁴ Diodorus 18.12.2. Alexander's demands for reinforcements may have depleted Antipater's manpower. Diodorus 18.12.2 says that he lacked "citizen soldiers" (i.e., Macedonians): Hammond and Walbank 1988, p. 109 (cf. pp. 86–88); Bosworth 1986a and Bosworth 1986b; against this view: Billows 1995, pp. 183–212.
⁶⁵ Diodorus 18.15.1–4, with Roisman 2012, pp. 111–112.
⁶⁶ Diodorus 18.16.4–5.
⁶⁷ Bosworth 2003.
⁶⁸ Diodorus 18.17.1–8.

During the Lamian War Demosthenes had toured various cities in Greece under his own auspices urging them to join Athens. For his action he was pardoned and returned to the city in triumph; when he landed at the Piraeus, "every archon and priest was present and the entire citizen body gathered to watch his arrival and give him an enthusiastic welcome."[69] But fearing the worst after Crannon, he and Hyperides fled into exile. The Athenians hurriedly recalled the glib orator Demades (who the previous year had left the city after being fined and disfranchised for proposing Alexander be recognized a god) to treat with Antipater.[70] Also serving on this mission was Demetrius of Phalerum—the nearest coastal town to Athens and the city's port before it was eclipsed by the Piraeus, thanks to Themistocles in the 490s.[71] Demetrius was the man who in 317 would become nominal ruler of Athens (see chapter 2). But Antipater had little time for Demades and demanded nothing less than the Athenians' unconditional surrender.[72] Craterus had actually wanted to attack the city, but Antipater had dissuaded him because of his respect for Phocion, one of the period's most illustrious generals.[73]

Demochares, Demosthenes' nephew, then appeared in the Assembly, dramatically wearing a sword to rouse the people to resist Antipater.[74] Grasping reality was clearly not one of his strong suits. Another embassy, including Phocion and the metic philosopher Xenocrates (the head of the Academy), was sent to Antipater and Craterus to plead for mercy—vainly, as it turned out, though Xenocrates' speech may not have been rhetorically eloquent, as he was described as "slow and clumsy by nature."[75] Xenocrates would be the first of several philosophers used by the Athenians for diplomatic missions to Macedonian and even Roman leaders.[76]

---

[69] Plutarch, *Demosthenes* 27.6–7; [Plutarch], *Moralia* 846d.
[70] Diodorus 18.18.1–2; Plutarch, *Phocion* 26.2; Pausanias 7.10.4.
[71] Pausanias 1.1.2.
[72] Diodorus 18.18.3; Plutarch, *Demosthenes* 28.1; *Phocion* 26–29.
[73] Diodorus 18.18; Plutarch, *Phocion* 26.5–7; with Tritle 1988, pp. 129–131.
[74] [Plutarch]. *Moralia* 847c–d; with Roisman, Worthington, and Waterfield 2015, pp. 186 and 240.
[75] Description: Diogenes Laertius 4.6. Embassy: Diodorus 18.18.3–6; Plutarch, *Demosthenes* 28–30; *Phocion* 27.3, 28.1, 4, and 33; [Plutarch], *Moralia* 846e–847b, 847d, 849a–d; with Ferguson 1911, pp. 20–26; Habicht 1997a, pp. 40–49; Korhonen 1997, pp. 42–45; Baynham 2003; Green 2003; O'Sullivan 2009, pp. 26–32; Worthington 2013, pp. 334–335.
[76] Korhonen 1997, pp. 40–54. See Diogenes Laertius 4.6–15.

Antipater established a garrison on the Munychia (the steep hill, about 86 meters high, overlooking the Piraeus) to control Athens' port, imposed a heavy war indemnity on the city, insisted on the surrender of anti-Macedonians (including Demosthenes), and may have suspended the *ephebeia*, given the military preparedness of the ephebes and its importance as a civic institution.[77] But even worse, he imposed a wealth requirement of 2,000 drachmas for Athenian citizenship.[78] How many citizens were disfranchised is unknown because our ancient sources disagree. It could have been as many as 3,000 out of a total of 12,000, therefore leaving a citizenry of 9,000.[79] Our sources again disagree on the fate of those disfranchised, with Diodorus claiming they all went to Thrace and Plutarch that they all remained at home, where they eked out a miserable existence, highly resentful of their outrageous treatment.[80] Presumably a middle line, some leaving and others staying, is closer to the truth.

Athens thus became to all intents and purposes an oligarchy, in which men of property sympathetic to Macedonia dominated political life while the Piraeus garrison kept the reduced mass of the people in check.[81] If the new reality had not yet sunk in, it certainly did when the previous leaders moved the proposal—plausibly with Antipater's blessing—to execute Demosthenes

---

[77] Mitchel 1964, pp. 337–351; Tracy 2004, p. 208; *contra* Couvenhes 1998; and see p. 38, this volume. Strategic importance of Munychia and its garrison: Garland 1987, pp. 45–47, 160–161.
[78] Diodorus 18.18.4; Plutarch, *Phocion* 27.3; on the amount, cf. Baynham 2003, pp. 23–24; Bayliss 2011, pp. 68–73.
[79] The figures in the sources are problematic: Diodorus 18.18.5 claims that 9,000 citizens met the wealth requirement and that 22,000 were disfranchised, whereas Plutarch, *Phocion* 28.7, states that 12,000 were disfranchised. Diodorus' figure is thought to be too high: Green 2003, pp. 1–2. Adding the lower figures gives us 21,000, but would over half of the population really have lost its citizenship? However, the 12,000 citizens may represent the total number of citizens before Antipater's action. Thus 3,000 lost their citizenship, but the bulk of the citizens (9,000) did not; at some point Demetrius of Phalerum held a census, in which there were 21,000 citizens (presumably including at least some of the disfranchised receiving back their citizenship after the overthrow of the oligarchy in 317): see further Baynham 2003, pp. 24–26; cf. Grieb 2007, pp. 56–57; Bayliss 2011, p. 223 n. 10; cf. Harding 2015, pp. 70–73. On the census, see next chapter.
[80] Diodorus 18.18.5; Plutarch, *Phocion* 28.7; perhaps not as many went to Thrace: Baynham 2003, pp. 26–28; cf. Harding 2015, pp. 70–71.
[81] Green 1990, p. 42; Kralli 1999–2000. On Demades, see J. M. Williams 1989; on Phocion, see Bayliss 2011, pp. 129–151.

and Hyperides.[82] They were hunted down; Hyperides was captured and executed, but to avoid capture Demosthenes committed suicide.[83]

Their deaths, if we can believe Plutarch, "made the Athenians long for Philip and Alexander."[84] We can comfortably dismiss his opinion, but accept Xenocrates' comment summing up the people's feelings: Antipater's terms were reasonable for slaves but harsh for free men.[85] In fact, Antipater may have deliberately hammered home the fall of Athens by installing the garrison on the Munychia when the Mysteries were being celebrated, as though the gods themselves were abandoning the city.[86] One year later, in 321, Athenian impotence was again made clear by Alexander's Exiles Decree impacting the city after all: Perdiccas, Alexander's former second-in-command, permitted native Samians to return home.

The Athenians took care to maintain Antipater's goodwill over the next years, thanks to the careful policy of Phocion, who came to prominence after the death of Demades. Most important, they made sure that the city played no direct role in the early Wars of the Successors, which we will trace in the next chapter.[87] Some democratic organs continued to function, but on so limited a scale as to cause the Athenians to yearn for the return of their former democracy and especially their freedom.[88] In that respect, the Athenians' resilience never wavered; they were down, but over the following centuries they never considered themselves out.

---

[82] Plutarch, *Demosthenes* 28.2.
[83] Demosthenes' last days: Worthington 2013, pp. 326–337.
[84] Plutarch, *Phocion* 29.1.
[85] Antipater's terms: Diodorus 18.18.3–6; Plutarch, *Demosthenes* 28–30 and *Phocion* 29 and 33; [Plutarch], *Moralia* 846e–847b, 847d, 849a–d; cf. Pausanias 7.10.4.
[86] Plutarch, *Phocion* 28.1.
[87] J. M. Williams 1989, pp. 27–30; *contra* Green 1990, pp. 40–41.
[88] For example Grieb 2007, pp. 51–55; Bayliss 2011, pp. 63–64; and see chapter 3.

2

Under the Puppet Ruler
Demetrius of Phalerum

"ALEXANDER'S LEGACY TO THE WORLD was a mess," M. M. Austin aptly writes.¹ Shortly before Alexander died in 323, he had given his signet ring (the seal of authority) to Perdiccas, his second in command, to ensure the continued day-to-day business of running the empire.² Perdiccas quickly called a meeting of the senior staff, planning to become regent of Roxane's baby when it was born (which everyone seems to have assumed would be a boy and therefore the next king), but then the rank and file of the army forced him to recognize as king Alexander's half-brother Arrhidaeus, taking the name Philip (the name change was to emphasize a continuation of the Argead line).

At a second meeting the fate of the empire was decided; for our purposes we need mention only the key players who impact our study of Hellenistic Athens.³ Perdiccas became guardian of Philip III (Arrhidaeus) and Roxane's child. Antipater and Craterus became joint generals of Greece and Macedonia, and hence were in charge of the western part of the empire. Antigonus Monophthalmus (the "one-eyed") was reconfirmed as satrap of

---

¹ M. M. Austin 2006, p. 62.
² Curtius 10.5.4; Justin 12.15.12; Nepos, *Eumenes* 2.1.
³ Background and settlement at Babylon: Errington 1970; Bosworth 2002; Meuss 2008; Waterfield 2011, pp. 19–29; cf. Romm 2011, pp. 37–55; Anson 2014, pp. 14–28; Worthington 2016, pp. 71–83.

Greater Phrygia, Lycia, and Pamphylia, hence much of western Anatolia. Ptolemy, a royal bodyguard, received Egypt, the adjoining portion of Arabia, and Libya, and Lysimachus (another bodyguard) was given Thrace. However, it was not long before the Successors (*Diadochoi*), as these men are called, were at war with one another.[4]

The Early Wars of the Successors and Athens

When Roxane gave birth to a son, Alexander IV, a dual monarchy came into being.[5] The other Successors, however, were always suspicious of Perdiccas—suspicions well-founded, for in 322 he decided to attack Monophthalmus, forcing him to flee to Macedonia and join forces with Antipater and Craterus. Before these men went to war Perdiccas had to deal with Ptolemy, who in 321 hijacked Alexander the Great's embalmed body as it was finally en route from Babylon to Macedonia, and took it to Memphis, later burying it in Alexandria.[6] Perdiccas at once invaded Egypt (in the name of the kings), thus beginning the First War of the Successors (321–320).[7] His invasion was a disaster; after losing two thousand of his own troops in a catastrophic attempt to cross the Nile, some of his commanders murdered him one night.[8] Ptolemy then made peace and the Successors forged another settlement in 320 at Triparadeisus, in southern Syria.[9] Thus ended this first war.[10]

---

[4] Wars of the Successors: E. Will 1984a (to 301) and E. Will 1984b (301–276); Hammond and Walbank 1988, pp. 117–244; Green 1990, pp. 5–134; W. L. Adams 1997; Bosworth 2002; Braund 2003; W. L. Adams 2007; Bosworth 2007; W. L. Adams 2010; Romm 2011 (to 316); Waterfield 2011; Roisman 2012; Anson 2014; see also the papers in Hauben and Meeus 2014.

[5] Attested also by the two kings sharing the royal bodyguard of seven men (four to Philip, three to the baby Alexander): Heckel 1980.

[6] Diodorus 18.28.2–3; Arrian, *BNJ* 156 F 9, 25; Pausanias 1.6.3, with Erskine 2002, pp. 167–171; Worthington 2016, pp. 93–95.

[7] Seibert 1969, pp. 96–108; Hauben 1977.

[8] Diodorus 18.33–37; Arrian, *BNJ* 156 F 9, 28; Pausanias 1.6.3; Justin 13.8.1–2, 10, with Seibert 1969, pp. 114–128; Roisman 2012, pp. 93–107; Roisman 2014; Worthington 2016, pp. 95–99.

[9] On the Successors' choice of Triparadeisus in an attempt to reconcile differences, see Worthington 2019a.

[10] The chronology of the following decade is much disputed, and two different chronological schemes have been advanced for it, "low" and "high"; I follow the "low" one, which dates events one year later than high one, hence the Triparadeisus settlement in

The Triparadeisus settlement was largely a repeat of that at Babylon, except that Antipater was made regent of the two kings, and Seleucus, who had remained on the sidelines in 323, became satrap of Babylon.[11] Antipater's regency meant he had authority over his cogeneral Craterus, and plausibly explains why Demades, on behalf of the Athenians, traveled to Macedonia to meet him on his return to plead for the removal of the garrison from the Munychia.[12] But when Antipater came across old letters that Demades and his son Demeas had written to Perdiccas urging him to liberate the Greeks from Antipater, he had them executed.

Then in 319 came an opportunity for the Greeks to revolt: Antipater died. But it was Antipater's son Cassander who now drove events, because his father had tapped as successor not him but Polyperchon, a former infantry officer under Philip II and Alexander the Great, who was then in his midsixties, a rebuff Cassander did not take lightly.[13] As Polyperchon moved to take control of Athens, Cassander secured the Piraeus, thus denying the Athenians the means to receive supplies, and made an alliance with Ptolemy, Lysimachus, and Monophthalmus to wrest Macedonia and Greece from his rival. His actions shattered the Triparadeisus settlement, starting the Second War of the Successors (319–316), and establishing Cassander as a force with which to be reckoned over the next years.[14]

Polyperchon, in the name of the kings, at once proclaimed an amnesty for political crimes, the return of exiles, and the restoration of democracy as it had existed before the Lamian War of 323–322; in addition, the Athenians were singled out for the restoration of Samos and all their other possessions except Oropus (on the northern border of Attica with hostile Boeotia), which Philip II had given to them after Chaeronea.[15] Doubtless more taken with the chance to regain their democracy than Samos, the Athenians threw their weight behind Polyperchon. A democratic faction resolved to execute or exile anyone who had supported Antipater's oligarchy, including the

---

320 (low), not 321 (high): low chronology: Errington 1970, pp. 75–77; Billows 1990, pp. 64–80; Roisman 2012, pp. 136–144. For the higher chronology, see Bosworth 1992.
[11] Errington 1970; Billows 1990, pp. 64–71; Green 1990, pp. 12–17; Roisman 2012, pp. 136–144; Landucci Gattinoni 2014.
[12] Diodorus 18.48.1–4; Plutarch, *Demosthenes* 31.4–6; *Phocion* 30.4–6.
[13] Diodorus 18.48.4–50 (= M. M. Austin 2006, no. 31, pp. 72–74).
[14] Second War: Green 1990, pp. 18–20; W. L. Adams 2010, pp. 212–214; Waterfield 2011, pp. 75–83; cf. Braund 2003, pp. 24–30. Cassander: Landucci 2017.
[15] Diodorus 18.56, with Hammond and Walbank 1988, pp. 133–134; Dmitriev 2011, pp. 113–114 and 116–119. Philip and Oropus: Pausanias 1.34.1.

octogenarian general Phocion, a friend of the Piraeus garrison commander Nicanor.[16]

Our sources disagree on Phocion's demise.[17] Diodorus simply tells us that the Assembly decided to condemn him to show Polyperchon its support. Plutarch, however, claims that an Assembly sent Phocion and the democratic orator Hagnonides to Polyperchon to discuss his edict. Polyperchon apparently grew suspicious of Phocion; he ordered his arrest and sent him back to Athens. At that point another Assembly—packed, according to Plutarch, with jeering women, slaves, and foreigners—dragged Phocion before it. A letter supposedly from Philip III was read out denouncing Phocion and his friends as traitors, which Hagnonides seized on to propose their execution. Phocion was not allowed any defense and died by drinking hemlock—the story goes that since there was not enough to kill him, one of his friends paid the jailer 12 drachmas to make more, with Phocion saying people could not even die in Athens without having to pay.[18] The Athenians decreed he was to be buried outside of Attica; he was cremated somewhere in the Megarid area of Greece. His wife, however, who was with the body, gathered up his bones "in her bosom," and took them back to Athens to bury by their house.[19]

Plutarch's account is suspect as women, slaves, and foreigners could not attend, let alone vote, in an Assembly; his information may well come from a hostile oligarchic source.[20] On the other hand, it has been pointed out that the theatricality of his account is deliberate, as Plutarch's intention was to show how the Athenians were moved by emotion, not reason, in condemning Phocion and with him their democratic values.[21] If the Athenians acted as they did to earn Polyperchon's favor, they were soon disappointed, as there was no return to freedom and democracy. As always, when the carrot of a return to democracy was dangled in front of them, they were quick to try

---

[16] Phocion and Nicanor: Plutarch, *Phocion* 31, with Bayliss 2011, pp. 141–145; see too Tritle 1988, p. 140; Grieb 2008, pp. 58–60.

[17] Diodorus 18.65.6–67; Plutarch, *Phocion* 31.2–36; Nepos, *Phocion* 3–4; Plutarch's *Phocion* as a source: Duff 1999, pp. 133–147; Lamberton 2003; see too Bayliss 2011, pp. 129–151. Phocion subject to mob vengeance: Bayliss 2011, pp. 146–150.

[18] Plutarch, *Phocion* 36.4.

[19] Plutarch, *Phocion* 37.2–3; Nepos, *Phocion* 19.4.

[20] Mossé 1973, p. 104, notes the illegality of the meeting, but seems to accept Plutarch's account in that the Assembly showed how "the traditional ideal of the *polis* had altered in a few years."

[21] On this, see Dubreuil 2018; for Plutarch, this episode is the end of Athenian democracy.

to snatch it. Phocion's death was a sad example of their naiveté and willingness to sacrifice all and sundry.[22] As Pausanias sagely remarks, "no man who has unselfishly and completely devoted himself to politics, trusting in the loyalty of the democracy, has met with a happy death."[23] This observation could well be one of the more common threads in Athenian public life.

In the meantime, Cassander had won control of Aegina and Salamis and began his advance in Attica, where Polyperchon had been campaigning with an army of 25,000 troops, including 65 elephants (the first time that elephants were deployed in Greece).[24] Polyperchon left behind a contingent of his men to besiege the Piraeus and pushed on to the Peloponnese, but he was largely ineffective there and returned to Macedonia. Cassander was now intent on taking over guardianship of the two kings and could not allow Athens to remain free. After shoring up Nicanor's garrison in the Piraeus, he besieged the city. With their supplies shut off and their crops devastated, the Athenians sent envoys to him in the spring of 317 to negotiate a settlement.[25]

Cassander maintained the garrison in the Piraeus for obvious reasons, although not long after he appeared to grow suspicious of Nicanor and had him put to death.[26] The Athenians were to be his "friends and allies," yet he installed a governor in the city, tapping Demetrius of Phalerum (one of the envoys who had recently negotiated with him, but who seems to have been relatively obscure until this time) for that job.[27] For the next decade Demetrius, supported by a garrison, was Cassander's puppet ruler.

The Athenians had bowed to the policies of individuals before, except then they had been their own leaders; now they were forced to do the bidding of someone present in the city who had been appointed by a Macedonian. They might well worry that Demetrius' regime was going to be as bloody as that of the Spartan-backed oligarchy of the Thirty Tyrants, but Demetrius, though oppressive, would be nothing like them. Still, in an effort to appeal to Cassander, the Athenians retrieved Phocion's remains from his widow and buried them in a formal state ceremony, then erected a bronze statue

---

[22] Cf. Hammond and Walbank 1988, pp. 134–135.
[23] Pausanias 1.7.3.
[24] Hammond and Walbank 1988, p. 136.
[25] Diodorus 18.74.2–3; cf. Ferguson 1911, p. 36; Hammond and Walbank 1988, p. 137; O'Sullivan 2009, pp. 40–41.
[26] Diodorus 18.75.1.
[27] Diodorus 18.74.3 for "friends and allies." Relative obscurity in the reigns of Philip and Alexander: O'Sullivan 2009, pp. 9–24.

to him in the Agora; they executed Hagnonides, and condemned Phocion's other accusers.[28] We can always count on the Athenians to move with the times, not to mention the person.

Demetrius of Phalerum in Charge

Demetrius had been a student of Aristotle and Theophrastus and was one of the period's foremost intellectuals, having written over fifty works on diverse subjects—Homer, law, philosophy, rhetoric, and politics—and even an essay on how to interpret dreams.[29] He remained a patron of the arts and especially of philosophers, arranging for Theophrastus (Aristotle's successor as Head of the Lyceum) to own a personal garden for his school, even though as a metic Theophrastus could not legally own land.[30] Born around 360, Demetrius was now forty years old. He had had a lucky escape in 318 when the short-lived democracy of Polyperchon fell, as he was among those slated for execution. He had fled to Nicanor at the Piraeus and soon earned Cassander's trust. The irony could not have been lost on the Athenians that the man they had condemned to death one year earlier, and who had helped to negotiate the settlement in 317, was now their de facto ruler.[31] Likewise, in setting up Demetrius as his ruler, Cassander may have relished giving the Athenians "a taste of their own theoretical Platonic—or in this case Aristotelian—medicine, a real philosopher-king" (see Figure 2.1).[32]

Plutarch states that under Demetrius' regime the Athenians were subject to "nominally an oligarchy, but in reality a monarchy."[33] Demetrius was never called a king; in fact, his exact title is a mystery. Our ancient

---

[28] Plutarch, *Phocion* 38.1; [Plutarch], *Moralia* 847d. Ferguson 1911, p. 120, dates the return of Phocion's remains to 304; see too Kralli 1999–2000, p. 138.
[29] Diogenes Laertius 5.75–85 for a biography (5.80–81 for a list of his works), with O'Sullivan 2009, pp. 226–240.
[30] Diogenes Laertius 5.39, with O'Sullivan 2009, pp. 227–228, on how Theophrastus kept his land and the impact having a garden had on the future of philosophical schools.
[31] Demetrius of Phalerum's regime: Ferguson 1911, pp. 38–94; MacKendrick 1969, pp. 31–34; Davies 1971, pp. 107–110; Mossé 1973, pp. 102–108 (a "philosophical tyranny"); Green 1990, pp. 43–51; Tracy 1995, pp. 36–51; Habicht 1997a, pp. 53–66; J. M. Williams 1997; Mikalson 1998, pp. 46–74; Grieb 2008, pp. 61–68; O'Sullivan 2009 (a reappraisal—e.g., "too much of the change associated with Demetrius is based on preconceptions rather than on evidence," p. 289); Bayliss 2011, pp. 61–93; cf. Harding 2015, pp. 60–63. See too Müller's commentary on his fragments in *BNJ* 228, and cf. Gehrke 1978, pp. 142–193.
[32] Green 1990, p. 44.
[33] Plutarch, *Demetrius* 10.2.

FIGURE 2.1 Demetrius of Phalerum. Peter Horree/Alamy Stock Photo.

writers give him three: *prostates* (patron), *epistates* (overseer), and *epimeletes* (governor), whereas Pausanias makes him out to be a tyrant, which cannot be right as he allowed the democratic organs to operate.[34] Demetrius had wider-ranging powers than a mere governor, and was also elected *strategos* (general), although that office may have been more honorary than anything to do with actual military power. Likewise, his election as eponymous archon in 309/8 was presumably a sop to his power and to qualify him for the Areopagus, a body of ex-archons that had started to reassert its influence in public affairs.[35] At the end of the day the title is moot, for

---

[34] Strabo 9.1.20; cf. Diodorus 20.45.5 (second); Diodorus 18.74.3 and 20.45.2 (third); Pausanias 1.25.6 (tyrant); Plutarch, *Demetrius* 8.3 is noncommittal; cf. Habicht 1997a, p. 54. Arguments for that title: Tracy 1995, pp. 43–46; cf. Ferguson 1911, p. 47; Mossé, 1973, p. 105.

[35] Archon: *Parian Marble*, *BNJ* 239 B 24; Diodorus 20.27.1. It does not follow that he was re-elected *strategos* throughout the decade he controlled Athens: Habicht 1997a, p. 54.

Cassander had set him up to govern Athens absolutely in his name.[36] Apart from an incident in 314 when Athens almost went over to Monophthalmus' side (which we shall discuss below), it is therefore not surprising that the year of his archonship was ominously called "the year of lawlessness."[37]

Yet the city enjoyed increased prosperity under Demetrius' ten-year rule when it came to revenue and construction.[38] The Laurium silver mines in Attica were vigorously exploited, commercial activity in the Piraeus boomed, and military expenditure was negligible, given that Athens had a fleet of only twenty ships and no mercenaries to pay. Demetrius apparently came to control 1,200 talents per annum; if that represented Athens' actual annual revenue, then city life was in stark contrast to the famine and high expenditures of the past decade, although he was not worried about spending that income on himself.[39] Still, the treasury accumulated enough money to finish the Lycurgan building program elsewhere, including the portico of the temple of Demeter and Persephone at Eleusis.

The Athenians apparently voted to erect a staggering 360 statues to Demetrius, most showing him on horseback or riding a chariot, "all completed in less than 300 days because he was so revered," in an effort to endear themselves to him.[40] We must surely question the high number (and hence the cost) and apparently quick time to completion, but of special note was an honorary statue erected not in the Agora, the civic center of the city and a common area for such memorials, but on the Acropolis, the sanctuary of the patron deity Athena and "the major display case of Athenian identity and self-definition."[41] When Demetrius was expelled in 307 all his images were smashed apart from that statue, perhaps because it was a votive one to Athena and hence sacred.[42]

---

[36] Diodorus 18.74.2–3. Tracy 1995, pp. 46–47, argues that the Piraeus commander was in charge of military affairs and the troops, and Demetrius just of the city, and thus had no military power.
[37] Diogenes Laertius 5.77.
[38] Diogenes Laertius 5.75.
[39] Athenaeus 12.542b–c (revenue) from Duris.
[40] Diogenes Laertius 5.75.
[41] Von den Hoff 2003, p. 185, and see pp. 173–185 in detail. On the Agora's history and buildings, see Thompson and Wycherley 1972; Dickenson 2017 (who reevaluates the importance and continuing vitality of the Agora throughout the Hellenistic and Roman periods). On the Acropolis as the symbolic center of Athenian identity from the Archaic to Roman periods, see the comments of Krumeich and Witschel 2010a, pp. 1–53, with the essays in their volume.
[42] Von den Hoff 2003, p. 175.

One of Demetrius' first actions (possibly following Cassander's orders) was to establish a further wealth qualification for citizenship, this time of 1,000 drachmas.[43] The amount was half of what Antipater imposed at the end of the Lamian War in 322, causing us to wonder what was behind his action—after all, if some Athenians were rich enough to afford the 2,000-drachma requirement in 322, surely six years later half that amount was within their grasp. Possibly some of those earlier disfranchised had somehow rejoined the citizen body, hence Demetrius was conducting a purge; but if so, why not reset the amount at 2,000 drachmas? His measure may have not been intended to reduce the number of citizens, but was connected to his abolition of the Theoric Fund and to making entrance to the festivals free to as many citizens as possible.

Demetrius allowed some semblance of democracy, but only as he saw fit.[44] He restored the former political influence of the Areopagus, a strengthening of its power that was designed to help it enforce the various laws he enacted.[45] The Areopagus' increased influence in public affairs may have caused the Assembly to meet less regularly, as we have only two surviving Assembly decrees from this period.[46] On the other hand, it might simply be that only these two decrees have happened to survive.[47] We also have no surviving decrees of the Boule (Council) and no ephebic inscriptions (from 322 to 305). The only decree with any certain dating is to 314/13, awarding a bronze statue to a previous visitor to the city, Asander of Macedonia, and stipulating that it cannot be set up next to that of the so-called tyrannicides Harmodius and Aristogeition.[48] These two men had in 514 assassinated Hipparchus, one of the Pisistratid tyrants, which had led to the downfall of that tyranny in 510 and the introduction of democracy. They were thus revered as tyrant-slayers and their statue was the first liberation monument in the city.

---

[43] Diodorus 18.74.3; cf. Bayliss 2011, pp. 73–74, on the amount.
[44] Demetrius and democracy: O'Sullivan 2009, pp. 105–163, especially pp. 116–138 on the Assembly, Boule, and elections, and pp. 138–147 on the courts.
[45] Wallace 1989, pp. 204–205; O'Sullivan 2009, pp. 147–159.
[46] Ferguson 1911, pp. 61–62. Tracy 1995, pp. 36–41, argued that the Assembly was more active but simply reduced the number of its decrees inscribed on stone, though this seems weak (on p. 36 n. 2, he draws attention to two or three other decrees possibly from this era).
[47] Cf. the caution of Habicht 1997a, p. 63 ("very few surviving Assembly decrees").
[48] *IG* ii² 450 (of 314/13): lines 30–34 on the location of his statue; cf. *IG* ii² 453 (only the prescript, perhaps of 309).

It has been argued that Demetrius must have reinstated the *ephebeia* if Antipater (or oligarchs in the city) banned—or at the least suspended—it in 322, because of a victor list honoring a comic poet and ephebe Ameinias, which may be dated to 312/11.[49] If so, then his move took place between 317 and 312. But it has been shown that this argument is faulty and that no ephebic decrees have survived between 322 and 305.[50] That being the case, the victor list needs to be assigned to a different period, and we must accept that whatever Antipater did to the *ephebeia* was not undone until after Demetrius was displaced in 307.

Not content with allowing the Athenians to go about their business as before, Demetrius initiated a moral program encompassing all aspects of society, which has interesting affinities with the Lycurgan program of over a decade earlier. He was especially keen to impose limits on how much wealthy citizens could spend on entertainment, funerals, and religious ceremonies, and to this end he enacted laws curbing extravagance.[51] For example, he banned dinner parties and wedding feasts with more than thirty guests, limited amounts that could be spent on such gatherings, and even reduced the size of houses, which over the years had grown so enormous that, if we believe Demosthenes three decades earlier, they rivaled public buildings.[52] He decreed that all funerals had to be held before dawn, limited shrouds for the deceased, and banned large, expensive funerary monuments with elaborate reliefs; instead, only short, modest columnar headstones were allowed on graves.[53] Further, he established a group of officials known as the *gynaikonomoi*, or "supervisors of women," to make sure wealthy women dressed appropriately in public and did not parade with too many servants or ride in luxurious carriages.[54] Women in society thus seemed to be subject to the same male marginalizing attitudes as in the Classical era, except that despite the name *gynaikonomoi* men were also subject to the same rules

---

[49] Mitchel 1964, pp. 337–351; Tracy 2004, p. 208.

[50] Couvenhes 1998 (not known to Tracy 2004); cf. Chankowski 2010, p. 120 n. 283. I owe the Couvenhes reference to Nigel Kennell.

[51] O'Sullivan 2009, pp. 45–103.

[52] Demosthenes 3.29.

[53] Habicht 1997a, p. 56, on the impact this measure would have had on funerary artists, who must have been forced to leave Athens in search of work.

[54] Philochorus, *BNJ* 328 F 65 (= Athenaeus 6.245c), with the commentary of N. Jones, *ad loc.*; O'Sullivan 2009, pp. 66–72.

(we will return to women in chapter 9). All of the officials and the Areopagus worked together to enforce the new laws.[55]

Demetrius' restrictive legislation has been seen as populist because of his philosophical influences on the ideal of equality between all men. Though we cannot exclude the influence of philosophers in his work and life, we should be skeptical, as Demetrius was first and foremost a pragmatist.[56] True, over the years the rich had got richer and the poor poorer, and the wealthy certainly loved to show off, underscoring the gap between the haves and have-nots. But Antipater had imposed a wealth requirement for citizenship in 322, and Demetrius had done the same in 317, so a gap between rich and poor must necessarily have narrowed as all citizens had at least the basic wealth requirement.

Indeed, we should question whether the term "populist" applies to Demetrius' laws. He did not, for example, make any attempt to limit individual wealth and he banned liturgies—the funding of hugely expensive items of state expenditure, such as maintaining a trireme for a year, providing a chorus for a performance at a festival (*choregia*), or helping to fund Athenian competitors at the Olympic games, which the wealthiest stratum of society was expected to undertake.[57] The removal of liturgies would thus endear his rule only to the very wealthiest men (the "1 percent" of today), who saw liturgies as an enormous financial burden they were eager to have removed. Still, even though Demetrius appealed here to the superrich, they were not let off easily; in place of liturgies, *epidoseis* (so-called voluntary contributions of private money) became increasingly frequent throughout the Hellenistic era, and those who managed the festivals, games, and served on embassies were often required to foot the bill themselves.[58]

Of course, Demetrius' sumptuary legislation was not intended for himself, and he conducted his life as he wished—a clear demonstration that

---

[55] More controversial, because of the thin evidence, is that Demetrius may have made changes to the ephebic system and revised the law code: *IG* ii² 1201, lines 12–13; *Parian Marble*, *BNJ* 239 B 16; laws: O'Sullivan 2009, pp. 72–86; *ephebeia*: O'Sullivan 2009, pp. 86–89.

[56] Gehrke 1978, especially pp. 176–177 (political purposes only); J. M. Williams 1987; Mikalson 1998, pp. 60–63; O'Sullivan 2009, pp. 197–226.

[57] See the comments of O'Sullivan 2009, pp. 90–103, setting his laws in historical context (pp. 168–189 on Demetrius and liturgies). On liturgies: P. Wilson 2000. Demosthenes 20.21 claimed that there were at least sixty liturgies performed annually, but the actual figure was almost double that: Davies 1967; cf. Hakkarainen 1997, pp. 10–19; Harding 2015, pp. 89–91.

[58] See Hakkarainen 1997.

his power rested on a ruler who likewise was not bound by any moral restrictions on corruption or display. He accumulated a goodly number of honorific decrees and statues over the years, as we noted earlier. He was also said to have spent little of the city's annual income on administration and most of it on himself.[59] Among other things, he rode roughshod over his own laws, hosting lavish banquets (we do not know where his residence was in the city), dying his hair blond, wearing makeup in public ("because he wanted to have a happy appearance and be handsome to everyone he met"), and enjoying the pleasures of boys and numerous courtesans—one of whom was Lamia, the later mistress of Poliorcetes, who expelled him from Athens in 307 (see below).[60] At the same time, Demetrius' associates grew rich—his cook Moschion apparently was able to buy three houses and seduce practically anyone's wife and young boys.[61]

Away from politics, Demetrius conducted the first census in Athens' history.[62] The date is not known, nor for that matter is the reason why he held it. In it, the city's population numbered 21,000 citizens, 10,000 metics (resident aliens), and 400,000 slaves. This number of slaves is impossibly high, and probably 100,000 is closer to the mark (with perhaps 30,000 working in the Laurium mines).[63] If we can trust the other figures, then the number of citizens had grown significantly since Antipater's and Cassander's restrictions of 322 and 317. Still, the actual population of Athens in this period (including citizens, foreigners, and slaves) has been estimated at anything from 150,000 to 250,000, a reduction from the total of the fifth century.[64]

Demetrius' hold over Athens was shaken in 314 when the Athenians made a brief foray into the Wars of the Successors, nearly costing Cassander control of the city. The previous year an Athenian fleet commanded by Thymochares of Sphettus undertook a campaign against pirates, presumably with Cassander's permission, and captured the island of Cythnos in

---

[59] Athenaeus 12.542c.
[60] Diogenes Laertius 5.76.
[61] Athenaeus 12.542c–f, 13.593e–f; *contra* the laudatory remarks of Strabo 9.1.20; Cicero, *De Legibus* 3.6.14. Green 1990, p. 47, has reservations about the veracity of these stories.
[62] Stesicleides (Ctesicles?), *BNJ* 245 F 1 (= Athenaeus 6.272c), with the commentary of Hashiba, *ad loc.*; cf. Philochorus, *BNJ* 328 F 95, with the commentary of N. Jones, *ad loc*. On numbers see too: Harding 2015, pp. 70–73.
[63] Green 1990, p. 45 with n. 57, citing bibliography.
[64] Habicht 1997a, p. 58 with nn. 63–64, citing bibliography.

the Cyclades (along with a pirate named Glaucetes).[65] Thymochares' success likely led Cassander, the following year, to instruct Demetrius to deploy twenty Athenian warships under the command of a man named Aristotle against Lemnos.[66] The island, in Monophthalmus' hands, was an important stopping-off point on the sailing route from the Aegean to the Black Sea. The Athenians, along with an Egyptian fleet, besieged Lemnos, but its garrison stubbornly held out; when the enemy commander Dioscurides captured a number of Athenian vessels, the remainder turned and fled.[67]

Dioscurides followed up his victory by sailing to Delos, which he proclaimed free of Athenian control, no small blow to Athens. The Athenians were not pleased that Cassander had allowed this to happen; their discontent increased when Monophthalmus' nephew Ptolemy (not the Egyptian satrap) seized several cites on Euboea, the long island lying off Attica's eastern coastline, as well as Oropus. From either place Ptolemy (or Monophthalmus should he choose) could launch an invasion of Attica. Faced by this grave threat to their security, the increasingly isolated Athenians forced (according to Diodorus) Demetrius to allow them to dispatch an embassy to Monophthalmus with a simple objective: Since they did not think Cassander was properly protecting them, might they switch sides and join his cause?[68]

Cassander was suddenly in a vulnerable—and unusual—position, which says a lot about the influence Athens wielded as a city. If Monophthalmus decided to support Athens, then Demetrius would have been quickly bundled out of the city, and Polyperchon, who was fast winning over key towns in the Peloponnese, might exploit Cassander's weakness to rally the Greeks to him. Fortunately for Cassander, Monophthalmus decided to attack Ptolemy in Egypt, but it was Ptolemy who suddenly went on the offensive.[69] Just south of the old Philistine city of Gaza, Ptolemy engaged Poliorcetes, decisively defeated him, and sent him packing to northern

---

[65] *IG* ii³ 1, 985, lines 9–13.
[66] Diodorus 19.68.3; this mission may be connected to *IG* ii² 450; honors for Asander of Macedonia (see above) for his help in providing ships and soldiers: Tracy 1995, p. 41; O'Sullivan 2009, pp. 259–260.
[67] Diodorus 19.68.2–4. It is possible, though perhaps unlikely, that in this same campaign the Athenians attempted to recover Samos from its native owners: O'Sullivan 2009, pp. 262–263, citing sources.
[68] Diodorus 19.78.4.
[69] The chronology of the next few years is controversial: see Worthington 2016, p. 120 n. 79, citing bibliography.

Syria.⁷⁰ With Monophthalmus no longer in a position to help them, the Athenians returned to Cassander's camp.

Cultural and Intellectual Background

The uptick in finances fed into the cultural life of the city, which Demetrius enthusiastically supported. Athens remained the intellectual center of the Greek world until eclipsed by the scientific research and literary output of the famous Museum and Library at Alexandria.⁷¹ However, Athens still had a literary tradition and, even more to its benefit once Rome involved itself in Greek affairs, could rightly boast that it was the capital of philosophy.⁷² When in 155 the heads of three major philosophical schools went on an embassy to Rome (dubbed the "philosophers' embassy"), they captivated their audience, opening Roman eyes to Greek philosophy and the cultural pull of Athens, and so starting the long trend of Romans flocking to study philosophy in Athens (see chapter 10).

Beginning earlier in the 330s and 320s, there was a revival of the great fifth-century tragedies of Aeschylus, Sophocles, and Euripides, thanks to Lycurgus' canonization of their plays. It is not surprising that the "classics" would be performed in any day and age, including our own, but one reason for their revival may have been fewer tragedians at work in the fourth century. Since the Dionysia festival continued to be held throughout the Hellenistic period, which featured tragic competitions, evidently tragedies continued to be written, but roughly half of the sixty known names of Hellenistic tragedians were Athenians, and only a handful of fragments remain.⁷³ Another reason we ought not overlook, given the Athenians' attitude to the past, is that the fifth-century tragedies would call to mind the heyday of imperial power and autonomy. If so, it must have

---

⁷⁰ Worthington 2016, pp. 120–122.
⁷¹ Alexandria: Worthington 2016, pp. 133–144; Stephens 2018; cf. Green 1990, pp. 84–91 and 157–160; Hunter 2003, pp. 483–484. Hellenistic literature generally: Tarn and Griffith 1952, pp. 268–294; Gutzwiller 2007; Clauss and Cuypers 2010; see too Green 1990, pp. 65–79, 171–186, 201–215, 233–247; Hunter 2003.
⁷² Background: Habicht 1997a, pp. 98–123.
⁷³ Xanthakis-Karamanos 1980; Easterling 1993; especially Liapis and Stephanopoulos 2019; cf. Habicht 1997a, pp. 104–105. On the "afterlife" of tragedy in the later eras through to late antiquity, see the essays in Liapis and Petrides 2019; cf. Hanink 2014, pp. 159–215, 221–231.

been difficult for an Athenian audience under Macedonian rule and with a dictator actually in the city to suspend its disbelief.

Away from tragedy, the changed political circumstances helped to transform comedy. In the fifth century the genre known as Old Comedy had had a political message, anchored in scatological humor and sexual innuendo, its playwrights adopting an anything-goes attitude. Aristophanes, the greatest playwright of that genre, freely lampooned politicians, generals, and city officials; the politician Cleon, for example, was cast as a Paphlagonian slave who bewitched Demus, an old man personifying the people, in his *Knights* of 424. In Aristophanes' *Lysistrata* of 411 the titular figure unites all women of Greece in a sex strike until their husbands end the Peloponnesian War, taking over the Acropolis no less, and proclaiming that if women were running the city they would do a better job than the men.[74] Tastes and satirical slants changed in the fourth century to produce Middle Comedy, and after Alexander the Great, we have the third and final stage, New Comedy, lasting to about 260.[75] This was a popular form of drama, and there were at least fifty comic playwrights.[76]

The difference between Old and New Comedy is startling. Gone is the political plot set in the city itself, not to mention the bawdiness; instead, the action of New Comedy takes place in rural areas, its plots romantic and escapist. From the belly laughs of Aristophanes we have the gentle chuckle of Menander, Philemon, and Diphilus. Menander's only extant comedy, *The Bad-Tempered Man* (*Dyskolos*), was set in Phyle in rural Attica. In it an Athenian youth (Sostratus) falls in love with the daughter of a misanthropic farmer (Cnemon, after whom the play is titled), and has to prove his intentions are honorable to her father. He tries all manner of things to impress Cnemon, even working in the fields, all to no avail. But then Cnemon falls down a well and Sostratus rescues him, prompting the old man to allow him to marry his daughter (who has no say in all this).

It would not have been lost on the people that Menander was a close friend of Demetrius and that his *Dyskolos* won first prize at the Lenaea festival of 317—coincidentally, the same year Demetrius took over Athens. True, Menander was highly regarded as a dramatist, but he may not have

---

[74] Cf. the comments of Harding 2015, pp. 106–114.
[75] See further Ferguson 1911, pp. 73–94; Green 1990, pp. 65–68, 71–79; Habicht 1997a, pp. 99–102; Hunter 2003, pp. 481–483; Lape 2004.
[76] See the catalogue at C. Austin 1974.

been the absolute favorite as Philemon (who wrote 97 plays and had moved from his native Sicily to live and work in Athens) won more victories in the comedic competitions.[77]

This new type of comedy focused on the interactions of people in everyday life and steered well clear of anything to do with politics, a sign perhaps of the impact of changed political circumstances.[78] Obviously abuse or criticism of Macedonian rulers would not have been tolerated, though there were (infrequent) exceptions.[79] Thus, in the early days of Macedonian rule, the comic poet Archedicus had attacked Demochares for the latter's anti-Macedonian leanings.[80] And in 301 the poet Philippides famously lampooned Stratocles for his sycophancy toward the Antigonids, though the attack was a personal one and did not speak to the city's political future as Aristophanes had done (see pp. 76–77).

The rural setting also argues that the Athenians wanted to put the presence of a Demetrius, underscoring their military and political impotence, out of mind. Perhaps the people were after escapism, though it has been pointed out that the comedies were performed widely outside of Attica, hence people in different cities would not have been fussed about Athenian politics or may not have had the same penchant for bawdiness.[81] That is possible, but we would expect the same argument to apply to Aristophanes' earlier comedies or indeed any drama written in Athens and performed elsewhere.

Menander's plays may allow us a glimpse into everyday Athenian life in the early Hellenistic period, when we know so little of what people actually thought and did.[82] They also give us insights into family dynamics and the attitude toward women of the times, on which we will elaborate in chapter 9. At the same time, they sharply illustrate the reality of the changed populace of Athens: as has been said of them, missing is "the voice of the peasant," a significant change from Aristophanic plays.[83] Yet it does

---

[77] Cf. Ferguson 1911, pp. 85–86.
[78] Menander, drama, and politics: Green 1990, pp. 65–68, 71–79; Habicht 1997a, pp. 99–102; Salmenkivi 1997; Harding 2015, pp. 114–118; see especially Lape 2004; Gutzwiller 2007, pp. 50–59; Lape 2018; Konstan 2018; Heap 2019.
[79] Philipp 1973.
[80] Habicht 1993.
[81] Habicht 1997a, p. 102. But see Konstan 2018 on Athenian New Comedy's influence in other Hellenistic cities.
[82] Salmenkivi 1997; Heap 2019.
[83] Harding 2015, p. 118.

not follow that a person rich enough to remain a citizen had a "cleaner" sense of humor than a poorer man who did not meet the wealth requirement, or that everyone in the lowest social stratum was into scatological humor.

Careful to ensure that dramatic performances were properly organized after he had abolished the *choregia* liturgy, Demetrius appointed a magistrate called the *agonothetes* to oversee the festivals (and pay the choruses), theoretically with the state reimbursing expenses. But as time continued, especially in the third century, the state often ran short of funds, and so the *agonothetes* ended up paying out of his own pocket: the *agonothesia* thus became the *choregia* liturgy with a new name.[84] For his considerable private outlay the lucky person received public honors (substantial recognition) as soon as he had performed his office.

Demetrius' hands-on role in arranging the festival of the Dionysia so splendidly in the spring of 308 earned him a hymn, in which he was called *heliomorphos* or "sunlike" in his beauty.[85] He seems to have paid special attention to the Dionysia, transferring to it the rhapsodic contests (where bards recited parts of the Homeric poems for a prize) from the Panathenaea (the annual festival in honor of the patron deity Athena).[86] We will discuss festivals, an integral part of Athenian religion, in chapter 9.

Philosophy and rhetoric at Athens continued to flourish throughout the entire Hellenistic and Roman periods.[87] Rhetoric, which began to be studied more formally in Classical Athens, was seen as essential for a political or legal career, where often content was less important than delivery in persuading an audience.[88] The number of orators decreased in the Hellenistic period because of Macedonian control of Athens, but rhetoric was still studied, and the Romans were especially attracted to it.

The great philosophers of the fifth and fourth centuries, Socrates, Plato, and Aristotle, had laid the foundations of the formal study of ethics and logic and moral philosophy, with Aristotle adding music, rhetoric, biology, and zoology; they were truly the founders of Western philosophy and science. Plato had founded a school in Athens (the Academy) as had Aristotle

---

[84] See Hakkarainen 1997, especially pp. 22–23; Hanink 2014, pp. 225–231; cf. Bayliss 2011, p. 105.
[85] Duris, *BNJ* 76 F 10 = Athenaeus 12542e. Demetrius and festivals: O'Sullivan 2009, pp. 168–185; see too Mikalson 1998, pp. 54–58.
[86] Athenaeus 14.620b.
[87] Habicht 1997a, pp. 105–111; see too Perrin-Saminadayar 2007a, pp. 109–120, 535–550.
[88] See, for example, Worthington 2007.

(the Lyceum), and in our period Aristotle's former student and successor was Theophrastus of Eresus (on Lesbos). In his biography of that philosopher Diogenes Laertius lists his many works and claims that "in all he wrote 232,808 lines"—on subjects as diverse as philosophy, physics, and biology, and his two seminal works on plants, *Enquiry into Plants* and *On the Causes of Plants*, make him the father of botany.[89] By way of contrast are his *Characters*, thirty comedic vignettes of everyday Athenians highlighting flaws and bad behavior—gossips, boors, idiots, grumblers, and cowards, to name a few.[90] If they represent ordinary people of the time, we can see that society had not changed that much after all.[91]

In addition to the philosophies of Plato and Aristotle, Athens was home to other philosophical systems in the Hellenistic period and beyond. One such was Cynicism, originating earlier in the fourth century with Antisthenes, with its shunning of material possessions and focus on living a virtuous life. Two new schools were founded during the early years of Antigonid rule. First, Epicurus introduced Epicureanism, again anchored in simplicity, and rejecting the notion of divine interference in the lives of humans and the universe but attributing everything to chance.[92] Second, Zeno of Citium (in Cyprus) established Stoicism, similar to Cynicism by requiring a life of virtue, and emphasizing the value of self-control and resilience when faced with adversity.[93] Stoicism took its name from the Stoa Poikile (the "Painted" Stoa, a public portico in Athens), in which Zeno had started to teach in 301.[94] When Zeno died in 261, Antigonus II of Macedonia, who had studied under him, ordered the Athenians to honor him with a state burial (pp. 115–116).[95]

These schools were private institutions and varied in size, explaining why the more famous schools and their locations are well known, but there were

---

[89] Diogenes Laertius 5.42–50 (number of words at 5.50).
[90] Theophrastus: see Diogenes Laertius 4.36–57, and for example Green 1990, pp. 68–71; Habicht 1997a, pp. 121–123.
[91] These sketches may have been composed over a number of years rather than written in one hit, and the period 324–315 has been suggested: Habicht 1997a, pp. 122–123.
[92] Green 1990, pp. 618–630; cf. Korhonen 1997, pp. 62–66.
[93] Green 1990, pp. 631–646; cf. Korhonen 1997, pp. 66–71.
[94] Thompson and Wycherley 1972, pp. 90–94.
[95] These philosophers and Hellenistic philosophy in general: Ferguson 1911, pp. 104–107, 165–169, 173–175, 184–185, 214–216, 232–236, 257–261, 300, 333–345; Tarn and Griffith 1952, pp. 325–360; Green 1990, pp. 52–64, 95–96, 142–143, 602–646; Habicht 1994b; Korhonen 1997; cf. Mitsis 2003.

probably many philosophers who taught in private houses.[96] All in all, these places must have added an appeal and even charm to a city already full of monuments, public buildings, and areas where people collected. But education and politics mixed: the schools did not just teach philosophy, but also mathematics, music, physics, and even political theory.

Over the next centuries well-respected philosophers were used on diplomatic missions to Macedonian kings and even the Roman Senate. But the independence of schools from state oversight encouraged an involvement in public affairs not always to their credit.[97] Thus in the early Antigonid era, Sophocles of Sunium introduced a law against them (p. 75). Zeno's stance that a man still had freedom (of mind) even under a monarchy was not endearing to autocratic rulers.[98] And some centuries later, in AD 70, the emperor Vespasian introduced sanctions to curb philosophers who still commented on public affairs (pp. 282–283).

The End of the Argead Dynasty

A great deal had been going on outside Greece since Demetrius of Phalerum was installed in Athens. Cassander had seized Macedonia in 317 before attacking Polyperchon in the Peloponnese. In his absence, and with Polyperchon's support, Olympias (Alexander the Great's mother) had marched into Macedonia from her native Epirus, intending to make her grandson, Alexander IV, sole king. Olympias still had name power; when Philip III and his wife Eurydice (who unusually was trained as a soldier) led an army against her, it mutinied on them.[99] Olympias had Philip and 100 nobles (including Cassander's brother) executed; Eurydice hanged herself with her girdle to deny Olympias the pleasure of putting her to death.[100] Cassander immediately returned to Macedonia and Olympias fled to Pydna; there she was captured and put to death, with her corpse supposedly left unburied.[101]

---

[96] Camp 1989 on identifying the schools and where philosophers taught; cf. Habicht 1997a, p. 110.
[97] See, for example, Haake 2007, pp. 13–170, on Athens.
[98] See Korhonen 1997, pp. 98–99.
[99] Olympias at this time: Hammond and Walbank 1988, pp. 138–143.
[100] Diodorus 19.11.7; Justin 14.6.1–2; Eurydice: Diodorus 19.11.4–7.
[101] Diodorus 19.51.3–5; Justin 14.6.6–12; Pausanias 9.7.2 (stoning); unburied: Justin 14.6.6–12.

FIGURE 2.2 Silver tetradrachm of Demetrius Poliorcetes. 289–288 BC. Metropolitan Museum of Art. Gift of C. Ruxton Love Jr., 1967.

In 316 Cassander assumed guardianship of Alexander IV and married his aunt, Thessalonice (daughter of Philip II and his Thessalian wife Nicesipolis, and half-sister of Alexander the Great), thereby tying himself to the Argead house. He then imprisoned Alexander and Roxane in Amphipolis, organized an elaborate burial for Philip III and Eurydice at Aegae, and founded two new cities, Cassandreia (on the Pallene promontory) and the more famous Thessalonica (modern Thessaloniki), named after his wife.[102] Cassander was not, however, going to be left alone as ruler of Macedonia. Monophthalmus had been extending his territories in Asia and the Aegean, and was as ambitious as any of his former comrades in wanting a greater slice of empire, especially Greece and Macedonia. This man, tall and fat, with a loud laugh, and his son the "handsome" Demetrius Poliorcetes (who also enjoyed a good laugh), were the most charismatic of all the Successors and dominated events of the next three decades.[103] But it was Poliorcetes who would become the dictator of Athens (Figure 2.2).

Monophthalmus' son Demetrius acquired the nickname Poliorcetes, "the besieger," in 304 after his siege of Rhodes (p. 79). However, I will refer to

---

[102] W. L. Adams 2010, pp. 214–216.
[103] Monophthalmus: Plutarch, *Demetrius* 19.3. Biography: Billows 1990; Champion 2014. Poliorcetes: Plutarch, *Demetrius* 2.2–3; cf. [Plutarch], *Moralia* 458f (his son Antigonus Gonatas ugly in comparison). Laugh: Phylarchus, *BNJ* 81 FF 12 and 19, with the commentary of Landucci, *ad loc*. Biography: Manni 1951; see too E. Will 1984b, pp. 101–109.

him from now on as Poliorcetes so as not to confuse him with Demetrius of Phalerum.

The Second War of the Successors ended in 316 to Monophthalmus' benefit, and the following year he expelled Seleucus from Babylon. Ptolemy, Lysimachus, and Cassander then banded together against him, and so began the Third War of the Successors (315–311).[104] Monophthalmus supported Polyperchon in Greece and issued an edict declaring that all Greeks should be free and not subject to garrisons, purposefully to prevent Cassander and the others from garrisoning any Greek city.[105] That Cassander did not evacuate the garrison at Munychia shows what he thought of the proclamation, but this was the time when the Athenians approached Monophthalmus. Ptolemy's victory over Poliorcetes at the battle of Gaza in 312 thwarted Monophthalmus' designs on Greece and ensured that Cassander retained Athens. The battle also ended the war with a new settlement, by which Cassander, Ptolemy, and Lysimachus took over some of Monophthalmus' territory, although he remained General of Asia. Ptolemy also supported Seleucus' return to Babylon, a year marking the start of the Seleucid dynasty (311–65), the second longest of the Hellenistic era after the Ptolemaic, founded by Ptolemy (323–30).[106]

The new settlement of 311 was intended to remain in force until Alexander IV, now thirteen years old, "should reach maturity."[107] But after a dozen years of ruling their own territories and paying only lip service to the kings, the Successors had no intention of allowing him to rule in his own name.[108] In the spring of 310, or possibly early 309, Cassander ordered his execution

---

[104] Seibert 1969, pp. 138–151; E. Will 1984a, pp. 46–52; Hammond and Walbank 1988, pp. 150–162; Billows 1990, pp. 109–134; Champion 2014, pp. 69–97; Anson 2014a, pp. 129–149.
[105] Diodorus 19.62.2, with Hammond and Walbank 1988, p. 149; Dmitriev 2011, pp. 115–129.
[106] Seleucids: Bevan 1902; Bouché-Leclerq 1914; Bikerman 1938; Mehl 1986 (Seleucus I); Grainger 1999 (Seleucus I) and Grainger 2014; see too Tarn and Griffith 1952, pp. 126–163. Ptolemies: Bouché-Leclercq 1903–1907; Bevan 1927; Bowman 1986; D. J. Thompson 1994; Hölbl 2001; Huss 2001; D. J. Thompson 2003; Bingen 2007; Worthington 2016 (Ptolemy I); see too Tarn and Griffith 1952, pp. 177–209, and the essays in Van't Dack, van Dessel, and van Gucht 1983.
[107] Diodorus 19.105.1.
[108] *Contra* Hammond and Walbank 1988, pp. 161–162, that there was no doubt that they all intended Alexander to "assume the reins of government."

and that of his mother, Roxane, burying at least him at Aegae.[109] None of the others accused Cassander of regicide, but it would be four more years before they called themselves kings.[110]

But Monophthalmus was still as ambitious as ever, and Ptolemy had set his sights on Greece and Macedonia. Against this background we chart the fall of Cassander, and with it that of Demetrius of Phalerum in Athens.

The Fall of Demetrius and the Savior Kings

Ptolemy had begun a campaign against the Antigonids in 310 and in the early spring of 308 he sailed to Greece.[111] He made Corinth his base, from where he proclaimed his intention to liberate Greece from Cassander and (sounding a bit like a cracked record by now) return freedom to the cities.[112] His plan failed when few if any Greeks rallied to his cause, and he was forced to make peace with Cassander and return home, although he had added to Egypt's naval dominance in the Aegean and eastern Mediterranean.

Then Monophthalmus made his move. Early in the summer of 307 he sent Poliorcetes with 250 warships and 5,000 talents to liberate the Greek cities from Cassander, "starting with Athens."[113] Thus began the Fourth War of the Successors (307–301).[114] Poliorcetes left the bulk of his fleet at Cape Sunium, on the southern tip of the Attic peninsula, and in July or August sailed to Athens with two dozen ships. The garrison commander in the Piraeus mistook him for Ptolemy sailing to Corinth and relaxed his guard, allowing him to sail into the port and take control of it and the city.[115]

Athens thus fell to Poliorcetes, who allowed Demetrius of Phalerum to leave unharmed.[116] He made no attempt to rejoin Cassander but went first to

---

[109] Diodorus 19.105.2; see too Justin 15.2.5; Pausanias 9.7.2, with Hammond and Walbank 1988, pp. 164–167, on the reasoning and chronology.
[110] Alexander's illegitimate son Heracles and his mother, Barsine, were strangled to death on Polyperchon's orders in probably 309: Diodorus 20.28.1–2; Justin 15.2.3 (before killing Alexander IV and Roxane); Pausanias 9.7.2 (poisoned).
[111] On the campaigns and especially his ambitions, see Worthington 2016, pp. 147–154, citing bibliography.
[112] Diodorus 20.37.1–2; Polyaenus 8.58, with Dmitriev 2011, pp. 130 and 139–141.
[113] Diodorus 20.45–46.5; Plutarch, *Demetrius* 8–14.
[114] Waterfield 2011, pp. 134–154; Anson 2014, pp. 153–157; Champion 2014, pp. 109–114; Harding 2015, pp. 64–65.
[115] Plutarch, *Demetrius* 8.3–4; Polyaenus 4.7.6.
[116] Diodorus 20.45.4; Plutarch, *Demetrius* 9.2; cf. Diogenes Laertius 5.78.

Thebes and thence to Alexandria, where Ptolemy appointed him overseer of the great museum and library he was building.[117] Unfortunately, Demetrius was never able to hold his tongue. When Ptolemy was deciding his successor, Demetrius urged him to choose his eldest son, Ptolemy Ceraunus, rather than his younger one (born on Cos in the winter of 309/8).[118] But Ptolemy decided on the latter, and when he became king as Ptolemy II he remembered what Demetrius had told his father and arrested him. Demetrius died in 280, apparently by the bite of an asp while he slept one night.[119]

Before Poliorcetes disembarked from his ship in the Piraeus in 307, so Plutarch tells us, he asked the people to be quiet and spoke through a herald that he had been sent by his father and intended to free the city, expel the garrison, and "restore to the people their laws and their ancestral constitution."[120] The citizens rejoiced, Plutarch goes on, laying down their arms, applauding him, inviting him to land, and "calling him their benefactor and savior."[121] All well and good, but as events proved, the Athenians were simply swapping one Macedonian master for two new ones—one of whom, the charismatic Poliorcetes, would move into the Parthenon and turn it into a brothel.

---

[117] Diodorus 20.45.4; [Plutarch], *Moralia* 189d, with Worthington 2016, p. 140. Ptolemy had wanted to engage Theophrastus' services, but he refused: Diogenes Laertius 5.37. Alexandria: M. M. Austin 2006, no. 292, pp. 510–515 (= Strabo 17.1.6–10 abridged), and Fraser 1972 in detail.
[118] Diogenes Laertius 5.78; birth: *Parian Marble*, *BNJ* 239 B 19; Theocritus 17.58–76.
[119] Diogenes Laertius 5.78.
[120] Plutarch, *Demetrius* 8.5.
[121] Plutarch, *Demetrius* 9.1.

3

Political and Civic Institutions

IT IS NO SURPRISE THAT Athens under Macedonian and Roman rule was a very different place politically from its former democratic days. The various bodies of the civic administration continued to operate and officials still held public offices, but there were significant changes to both of these as Macedonia and especially Rome impacted all aspects of the city's civic, religious, and even architectural life.[1] Still, the Athenians did not stop hankering for a return to the autonomy, and even the democracy, they had enjoyed before Philip II. As late as the first century BC, the Athenians sided with Mithridates VI of Pontus in his war against Rome because of his promises to restore their freedom (chapter 10). To understand the Athenians' fixation with their former constitution, which underpins so much of their policies and out-and-out scheming over the next centuries, let us examine what they lost.[2]

The "Good Old Days"

From 462 Athens had been a direct or radical democracy.[3] Its constitution consisted of five major organs: the Areopagus, the Assembly (*Ecclesia*), the Boule (Council), the archons (public officials), and the law courts. Unless

---

[1] Rathmann 2010.
[2] Cf. Thompson and Wycherley 1972, pp. 25–81, on civic administration into the Roman era.
[3] M. H. Hansen 1999; Grieb 2007, pp. 27–50; Harding 2015, pp. 9–16; cf. Sinclair 1988.

disfranchised, all male citizens over the age of eighteen were eligible to take part in political life although they had to be thirty to stand for the Boule or serve as a juror, and age limits applied to some other offices (a citizen had to be in his sixtieth year to be a public arbitrator, for example). Despite their role in the *oikos* (household), and by extension the polis, women were not allowed to vote, nor could they represent themselves in court (their husbands or nearest male relatives spoke for them), hence when we refer to citizens taking part in public life we mean only males. The franchise was thus far more limited than in a modern democracy, as the political society of Athens consisted of a minority in relation to the mass of the people.

Radical democracy brought with it a new pathway to political ascendancy and introduced new men into public life. For much of the Archaic period (750–478), Athens had been an oligarchy, with aristocratic families holding the three archonships (the highest state offices) as a matter of course. These three archons were the polemarchus, in charge of military affairs; the basileus, dealing with religious matters; and the eponymous (the most important of the three), the chief civil officer. They were assisted by six thesmothetae (two per archon), originally akin to secretaries but who later took on further administrative and judicial roles. These officials served for one year, after which they joined the Areopagus, an ancient council and court taking its name from its meeting place on the steep rocky outcrop of the "Hill of Ares" by the Acropolis (Figure 3.1).[4]

A change came in 594 when the ruling families elected an Athenian named Solon to an extraordinary archonship to end civil strife due to socio-economic distress and political animosity.[5] Small farmers in Attica had become indebted to wealthy landowners; they had had their lands seized and their families sold into slavery when they defaulted on debt repayments, and the burgeoning middle stratum of society, from which hoplite infantry was drawn, was irked by having no say in political affairs despite putting their lives on the line and contributing to their polis' economic well-being.

Among other things, Solon abolished the aristocratic monopoly of power, replacing it with a wealth requirement for political office, and introduced regular meetings of the Assembly, which debated and voted on all matters

---

[4] Wallace 1989; cf. Grieb 2007, pp. 48–50. It took its name because Ares was the first to be tried there: Pausanias 1.28.5.
[5] There is a useful summary, citing sources and bibliography, of the development of democracy and of the Athenian constitution in M. H. Hansen 1999.

FIGURE 3.1 The Areopagus Hill. Photo: Ian Worthington.

of domestic and foreign policy and elected some officials, opening it up to all citizens over eighteen. He is also said to have created the Boule, initially a Council of 400 men (100 from each of the four tribes into which all Athenians were divided) to prepare the Assembly's agenda and act in an advisory capacity. Its members served for one year but re-election was possible, though not in consecutive years. We can thus credit Solon with the creation of democracy as all men, noble and non-noble, rich and poor, could now participate in Assembly meetings and so make policy, and in time those who met the wealth requirement could stand for office. Solon also abolished debt slavery and restored lands to the farmers; yet by the Roman era rich landowners had again swallowed much of the farmers' lands, practically bringing a return to the ills of Archaic Attica (p. 319).

Aristocratic men still dominated public affairs though, and the Areopagus was seen as a bastion of aristocratic power. In 508, two years after the downfall of the Pisistratid tyranny, an Athenian by the name of Cleisthenes introduced further legislation, including the creation of ten new tribes to replace the current four and tribal Assemblies, one for each tribe. Among other things, the tribal Assembly selected fifty men from its tribe to become members of the Boule in Athens, which from now on numbered 500. In doing so Cleisthenes extended the Solonian constitution and enabled citizens living in rural Attica, who could not travel to Athens to attend Assemblies there, to take a greater role in the democracy.

Cleisthenes is also credited with introducing the first professional office (to call it that) of the *strategos* (general), for which candidates were required to have military expertise. Ten *strategoi* were elected annually, and they alone of officials could be re-elected annually, given that a continuing and cohesive strategy was clearly important when the city was at war. The archon *polemarchus* continued to be an annual office, but he became more of a titular figurehead as the professional *strategoi* rose to prominence. This relationship was somewhat similar to today, where a political leader or member of a royal family is ex officio commander-in-chief, but actual military planning and execution are in the hands of the skilled professional military.

Later, in 462, came direct democracy, which changed the face of politics. In that year the Athenian Ephialtes conducted a purge of the Areopagus and transferred its political powers to the Assembly and the Boule, leaving it with only certain judicial powers (such as cases of premeditated homicide, arson, wounding, and damage to the sacred olive trees). With the increase in the Assembly's importance, non-nobles came to prominence in public life, and the key to political advancement now lay not on holding public office but on popular support in the Assembly.[6]

Assemblies were held forty times per year or four times a prytany or month—the year had twelve months in it, but for administrative purposes the Athenians divided it into ten prytanies, so each prytany lasted about six weeks. The Assembly met on the Pnyx, a large rock within easy reach of the Acropolis. Meetings began at dawn and lasted until dusk; the people brought with them their own food and a cushion for comfort, sitting in a semicircular auditorium area, and worked through a prepared agenda. In the Lycurgan period the auditorium area had been enlarged to accommodate some 13,000 attendees; of these, any citizen could speak on any agenda item, addressing his peers from a *bema* or rostrum (Figure 3.2). After the speeches and debate the people voted by a simple show of hands (*cheirotonia*); with several thousand citizens in attendance a precise count was impossible, so presiding officials estimated the votes for and against a proposal.[7] In this way, the Assembly was the "supreme democratic body in the constitution."[8]

---

[6] Worthington 2007.
[7] M. H. Hansen 1987, pp. 41–46; see too Thompson and Wycherley 1972, pp. 48–52.
[8] Aristotle, *Politics* 1299a1, with M. H. Hansen 1987; cf. Grieb 2007, pp. 42–45.

FIGURE 3.2 The *Bema* on the Pnyx. Photo: Ian Worthington.

In Athens, there were no organized political parties, no political manifestos, and no set of diehard supporters committed to one party or program. Athenian political life was dependent on interpersonal relationships and aspiring politicians usually associated with influential statesmen before becoming their own men (as was the case with Demosthenes).[9] Since the people voted for the man delivering the best speech on the day, rhetoric as a formal art developed in tandem with democracy, and with it the style of oratory in the Assembly called symbouleutic, with its emphasis on advice about the future.[10] The speakers were called *rhetores* (orators), but more pejoratively demagogues (leaders of the people).[11]

Real power, then, came to lie in the hands of a few influential speakers, for the downside was that often Assemblygoers (as they were called) were

---

[9] Cf. Worthington 2013, pp. 89–91.
[10] On which see Usher 2007.
[11] Connor 1971; M. H. Hansen 1987, pp. 50–63; cf. Worthington 2007.

swayed not so much by the content of speeches (and thus the validity of proposals) but by the speakers' rhetorical performance.[12] The first "new man" to rise to prominence in this manner was a wealthy cobbler named Cleon, so not an aristocrat but the first of the nouveaux riches to attain political power. In the 420s, when Athens was embroiled in the Peloponnesian War against Sparta, Cleon successfully challenged leaders and generals of the day on the war's progression. His new and inflammatory style of speaking appealed to the masses, for which he is commonly seen as the "prototype demagogue."[13] Other men quickly followed suit—nearly a century later Demosthenes was likewise castigating rivals and admonishing the people for their unwillingness to fight Philip. Mainly because of his social background and incendiary rhetoric, Cleon receives bad press from his contemporaries, especially Thucydides and Aristophanes, who in his comedy the *Knights* of 424 cast him as a Paphlagonian slave, contemptuous of Demus, an old man who personified the people. Cleon's name came to be associated with demagoguery; in the next chapter, we will meet the third-century politician Stratocles, who rightly or wrongly was likened to Cleon.

As the Assembly increased in importance so too did the Boule, which met in the Bouleuterium, centrally located in the Agora.[14] In 508 Cleisthenes had replaced the Solonian council of 400 with one of 500, but since five hundred was a large number of men, each tribe's fifty members served in an executive function for each of the ten prytanies into which the year was divided. Because the Boule met more regularly it came to handle the day-to-day administration of the city; a number of administrative offices were attached to it, and it could also issue its own decrees. It exercised supervisory functions over various administrative "boards" or subcommittees, dealing with such things as public works, roads, and finances, and even met foreign embassies. Elected public officials were still necessary to ensure that Athens as a city functioned smoothly and efficiently, but they had largely

---

[12] Cf. Thucydides 2.65.8–9 on Pericles' domination of political affairs: "in what was nominally a democracy power was in the hands of one man." Thucydides' comment about fifth-century democracy holds true for the fourth.

[13] Connor 1971, pp. 151–165 (wealth); Davies 1971, pp. 318–320; cf. Luraghi 2014, especially pp. 200–208.

[14] Thompson and Wycherley 1972, pp. 29–34; see too Dickenson 2017, pp. 88–95, on political buildings in this area. On the Boule, see in detail Rhodes 1972; cf. Geagan 1967, pp. 62–81 (pp. 92–103 on prytanies); Grieb 2007, pp. 45–47.

administrative duties in the city's economic, civil, and religious life, given that political power now rested on success in the Assembly.

Finally in the constitution were the law courts.[15] Athens was a litigious society; in the Classical era a panel of 6,000 citizens was annually appointed as jurors, hearing a variety of private and public cases on almost a daily basis. The Athenian judicial system seemed amateurish by our standards: for example, there was no judge in court, so the men selected to serve on a court day were literally judge and jury; professional lawyers did not exist, so prosecutors and defendants had to prepare and deliver their own cases in court; there was no time for jury deliberation as cases were heard in one day and a decision made immediately after the defense speech; and as in the Assembly, court speeches were anchored in rhetoric in order to sway the jury. Yet the Athenians took the law and their role in the judicial process seriously, as the annual oath that jurors swore to give a just and fair verdict according to the laws reveals.[16] Moreover, it was the development of law in Athens that eventually gave us fundamental rights that we take for granted today, such as trial by jury. Once past the Classical period, however, the courts continued to meet, but must have been more limited in function and meetings because of the numbers of citizens disfranchised by Antipater and then by Demetrius of Phalerum.

Radical democracy continued in existence apart from two brief interruptions of oligarchy, the first lasting a mere few months in 411, during the Peloponnesian War, and the second at the end of that war when Sparta installed the Thirty Tyrants in the city. By 403 this oligarchy had been toppled and democracy restored. Despite the specter of Sparta in Greek affairs, thanks to its victory in the Peloponnesian War, the Athenians looked forward confidently to the future. In 378/7 they formed the Second Athenian Confederacy, not as powerful or extensive as the fifth-century Delian League, but one that grew into a fourth-century empire lasting until 338. Even after the imposition of Macedonian hegemony, Athens' direct democracy continued. It is no wonder that this type of constitution, involving the whole citizenry, with the Assembly providing the path to political influence and with everyone going about their business freely, was one the Athenians did not expect to see end: when it did, they wanted it back.

---

[15] Thompson and Wycherley 1972, pp. 52–72; Boegehold 1995; Grieb 2007, pp. 47–48; Harding 2015, pp. 98–105.
[16] Demosthenes 24.149–151.

A Parody of Democracy

Antipater in 322 imposed terms that drastically altered Athens as a democracy, and Cassander's installation of Demetrius of Phalerum in the city in 317 reinforced the seeming paradox of continued democratic activity under an oligarchy. But Athenian politics did not come to a halt in 322; despite the new regime, the magistrates and other officials charged with running civic administration continued to work, and the Assembly and the Boule passed decrees—thirty-nine are known from the period 322–318, but there were probably more.[17] Likewise, ambitious men still dominated political life, even if as time progressed they needed to curry favor with Macedonian (and later Roman) masters to do so.[18] Also operating were the law courts, although we lack the abundance of information, especially court speeches, from the fourth century for what was happening in the Hellenistic period.

As noted previously, few decrees of the Assembly are known and none from the Boule. Yet even if the Assembly passed only what, say, Demetrius wanted it to do, it was still meeting rather than having been completely sidelined. The Boule itself was prone to fluctuation in numbers because of the addition of new tribes over the years (as we will see in the next chapters), each one adding fifty more members to the council. Yet declining citizen numbers may have been responsible in the third century for some men being allowed to serve three times (not the customary twice) in their lifetimes.[19] The Boule's decrees decreased in number from the third century, though perhaps not all copies of them (or Assembly decrees) were put into the Metroon—the central depository or state archives building (located close to the Bouleuterium in the Agora)—as had been the case since its creation in the early fourth century.[20]

The wealth requirements for citizenship may have meant that there was more social stability than under the radical democracy, for now the poorest people were noncitizens. But the removal of citizens who could not meet the wealth requirement meant that attendance at an Assembly must have been far less than in the period before Antipater when several thousand men went to Assemblies.[21] A significant change thanks to Demetrius was

---

[17] Poddighe 2002; G. J. Oliver 2003.
[18] Democratic activity in Hellenistic Athens: Ferguson 1911; Mossé 1973; Habicht 1997a; Dreyer 1999; Grieb 2008; Bayliss 2011, pp. 94–128; Osborne 2012, pp. 55–109.
[19] Tracy 1995, pp. 18–19; Osborne 2012, p. 63.
[20] On the Metroon, cf. Thompson and Wycherley 1972, pp. 35–38, with Sickinger 1999.
[21] Osborne 2012, p. 61, suggests in the third century a quorum of 6,000, the same number in the earlier Classical era.

the restoration of the Areopagus, charged with overseeing his laws against extravagance.[22] The aristocratic nature of this council ran counter to the influence of non-nobles, no matter how wealthy from their trading ventures, playing a role in public life. It is no surprise, as we shall see in the next chapter, that the people were euphoric when, in 307, Demetrius Poliorcetes expelled Demetrius of Phalerum, and promised them their freedom and a return to their ancestral democracy. But the Athenians' interpretation of democracy differed from that of Poliorcetes: he expected the people to follow his orders, and although a hundred Assembly decrees are known from his regime (307–301), all bestowed honors on individuals or states supporting him.

The democracy in this era has been described as "a mere caricature of the regime which had constituted the greatness of Athens," a view dismissed more recently because of the democratic leanings of its leaders.[23] Nevertheless, the city remained tightly controlled, and as time wore on there was a change in the powers of individual offices. New officials also appeared, such as the annually elected herald of the Areopagus, who among other things was in charge of the incoming board of archons.[24] Still, the eponymous archon remained influential, closely followed by the hoplite general, the herald of the Areopagus, the archon basileus, and the masters of the mint.[25] By the first century the hoplite general and the herald of the Areopagus had displaced the other officials to become the actual ruling magistrates of the city, although the eponymous archon still gave his name to the year.[26]

Equally important was the *epimeletes* (governor) of Delos, who came from the ranks of the Areopagus and rose to prominence after Athens obtained the island in 167 (pp. 170–171).[27] The office shows how important the Athenians viewed control of the island for their economy, but economic activity on the island fed into politics, as ambitious men used the wealth and prestige acquired from their trading interest on Delos to counter the aristocratic domination of the city and so change the face of political life (pp. 198–199).

The men making up Athens' political life came from usually aristocratic and certainly wealthy backgrounds as epigraphic information for the

---

[22] Wallace 1989, pp. 204–205; O'Sullivan 2009, pp. 147–159.
[23] Mossé 1973, p. 108; *contra* Bayliss 2011, pp. 51 and 94–128.
[24] Tracy 1979, pp. 213–235; Habicht 1997a, p. 288.
[25] See the discussion of Habicht 1997a, pp. 321–328; cf. Grieb 2008; on the mint, cf. Thompson and Wycherley 1972, pp. 78–89.
[26] Geagan 1979a, pp. 378 and 388.
[27] Habicht 1991a.

eponymous archons to the end of the first century attests.[28] It has even been suggested that from 103/2 to 88 Athens was a narrow oligarchy, but that was not so.[29] Some men did overstep their constitutional powers, such as a certain Medeius, whose illegal holding of the archonship over three consecutive years (91/0, 90/89, 89/8) made it look like he was aiming at tyranny. Only the hoplite general could be re-elected, and late in the first century we find prominent politicians such as Antipater of Phlya and Herodes of Marathon holding this post for several years in a row.

The revision of the citizen list in 322 and general uptick in wealth may also have impacted religious offices, especially the numerous priesthoods. In the Classical period key priesthoods were hereditary and held by members of the same group of families (*genos*). But the pool of candidates may have become more restricted, making the priesthoods the preserve of ultra-wealthy men especially in the Roman era, who came to see these positions as a means to political advancement.[30]

The type of men engaged in public life, secular and religious, explains why the socio-economic composition and age-old standing of the Areopagus made it the key organ in the Roman era. After the Sullan sack of 86 there is debate as to whether or not Sulla imposed a new constitution on Athens, one with Rome's blessing (pp. 213–214). But Sulla was not likely to have gone to this extreme measure even if the type of officials grew more pro-Roman and the Areopagus' increasing prominence can be traced to him.[31] Nevertheless, the city continued to command respect and was regularly visited for its magnificent sites and monuments.[32] But appearance was very different from reality. The days of the Classical democracy were long gone; it took the Athenians some centuries to realize that.

---

[28] Habicht 1997a, pp. 326–327.
[29] Ferguson 1911, pp. 421–437.
[30] Bowersock 1965, pp. 117–118; Walker 1997, pp. 72–73; Lambert and Blok 2009, pp. 101–102. On the increasing religious power of the elite and its exploitation for advancement, and Rome's dealings with these elite, see Grijalvo 2005; Schiller 2006; Camia 2014; cf. Geagan 1997; Baslez 2004.
[31] See especially Geagan 1967 for an in-depth discussion of public offices after Sulla and into the imperial period; cf. Geagan 1979a, pp. 373–374.
[32] See the relatively glowing description by Heracleides Creticus, written in 205, quoted on pp. 135–136.

The *Ephebeia*

Athenian males reached the age of majority at eighteen. They were then enrolled in the *ephebeia*, a form of military conscription, perhaps modeled on the Spartan system of military education, lasting for two years, and held in high regard.[33] The program is commonly ascribed to the era of Lycurgus, but there are grounds for arguing an earlier date of introduction by the law of Epicates in the 350s, in which case further reforms, such as adding intellectual study, may have taken place in Lycurgan times.[34] All expenses for the *ephebeia* (including pay for its officials and a stipend for the ephebes themselves) were covered by the state, which, like all other costs for the upkeep of the city (such as fortification walls and the military), must have been an enormous drain on the treasury.[35] In addition to their training in hoplite fighting the ephebes were taught by civilian teachers in civic duties, thus preparing them for when they could participate actively in the city's public life and to be good citizens. The *ephebeia* was thus an essential part of education, and has been described as a "training in citizenship."[36] That was one reason why ephebes attended meetings of the Assembly in the city and in the Piraeus in full armor: not to vote, but to learn how politics was conducted.[37] It was thus the expectation that eligible youths would enroll in this proud and dignified civic institution, and that their motivation to serve reflected these values; those who shirked their duties were punished.[38]

The Athenian *ephebeia* set a precedent for similar programs in towns and cities from Greece to Babylon, but that of Athens was the best known.[39] The training regimen, where ephebes served, and what else they did are described

---

[33] The most recent study is that of Friend 2019, with an excellent discussion of all aspects of the program and its place in civic life at pp. 13–184, eclipsing Reinmuth 1971.
[34] [Aristotle], *Athenian Constitution* 42; on earlier dating: Pélékidis 1962, pp. 71–79; Reinmuth 1971, pp. 123–138; Sekunda 1990, pp. 151–153; Faraguna 1992, pp. 274–280; Habicht 1997a, p. 16; Steinbock 2011, pp. 294–295; Friend 2019, pp. 34–57 (pp. 53–57 on Lycurgus); Roisman and Edwards 2019, pp. 161–162. On the Hellenistic *ephebeia*, in addition to the previous works, see Habicht 1997a, 233–237; Burckhardt 2004; Tracy 2004; Perrin-Saminadayar 2007a; Kellogg 2008; Chankowski 2010 (monumental and wide-ranging); Kennell 2015.
[35] Good comments on the high cost of state expenditure at Harding 2015, pp. 75–84.
[36] Reinmuth 1971, p. 130; cf. Kennell 2015, p. 172; Friend 2019, pp. 8–31, 136–171.
[37] Pélékidis 1962, pp. 273–274; Habicht 1997a, p. 236.
[38] Friend 2019, pp. 105–113.
[39] Kennell 2015, p. 175, and see passim on the program and training throughout the Hellenistic world.

in some detail in a late fourth-century work on the Athenian constitution, to which we can add a large number of ephebic decrees over the years, starting in 334.[40] Thus we know that ephebes spent their first year on garrison duty in the Piraeus (at Acte and Munychia, hills overlooking the port) receiving military training; in addition to learning how to use regular weaponry like swords and spears, they were taught archery and how to use a torsion catapult, developed by Philip II's engineers. At year's end the ephebes performed military drills before the people and ceremoniously received a spear and hoplite shield. Their second year was spent patrolling Attica and staying in its border fortresses (Eleusis, Panactum, Phyle, Rhamnus, and Sunium). They took an annual oath (apparently in full armor), meshing together patriotism and religion, by promising to hold fast in battle, obey their commanders, protect their city and anything sacred, and honor the ancestral shrines.[41] As well as military duties, ephebes took part in various festivals, in Athens (including escorting the image of the god Dionysus into the theater at the Dionysia), at Eleusis (honoring Demeter and Persephone), and in the annual procession to Delphi called the *Pythais*, in honor of Apollo.[42]

Several hundred ephebes were in training annually; they were under the supervision of the *kosmetes*, who had to be over the age of forty and were elected by the people. His office seems to have been annual, whereas his assistants, such as *sophronistai* or discipline officers (one from each tribe; the number was originally ten but the increase in tribes in the Antigonid era took it up to twelve), and *paidotribai* (physical fitness trainers), served without term, although the latter seem to have dropped to an annual appointment after 176.[43]

The numbers of ephebes declined considerably after the end of the fourth century. The *ephebeia* continued during the Lamian War, but at its end Antipater may have banned, or at the least suspended, it—if he did, then Demetrius of Phalerum must have reinstated it if a victor list honoring a

---

[40] [Aristotle], *Athenian Constitution* 42.2–5, with Reinmuth 1971, pp. 1–4; Kennell 2015, pp. 174–175; Friend 2019, pp. 76–87.
[41] Rhodes and Osborne 2003, no. 88, pp. 440–446; cf. Lycurgus 1.76–77 (paraphrasing parts of the oath and calling for its entirety to be read out in his case against Leocrates, but it is not included in the extant version of the speech), with Habicht 1997a, pp. 16–17; Kellogg 2008; Steinbock 2011, pp. 295–297; Roisman and Edwards 2019, pp. 161–165.
[42] Pélékidis 1962, pp. 239–247, and especially Mikalson 1998, pp. 243–255; Friend 2019, pp. 157–164.
[43] Habicht 1997a, p. 234, citing sources; officials: Friend 2019, pp. 58–69, 76–87; discipline: Friend 2019, pp. 69–76.

comic poet and ephebe Ameinias may be dated to 312/11, and we know that Poliorcetes introduced further reforms (discussed below).⁴⁴ Still, the program must have seen decreased numbers because of Antipater's wealth requirement for citizenship, which meant the ephebes would now be sons of only richer citizens.⁴⁵

Poliorcetes had gutted the numbers of ephebes by reducing the program's length to one year, making it voluntary, and no longer providing weaponry at state expense (p. 72). One obvious reason for his action was to limit any potential opposition from large numbers of trained Athenian soldiers, but given the cost of the program he may also have wanted to try to reduce expenses.⁴⁶ His measure, not to mention the Macedonian stranglehold of Athens, decreased the military capability and need of the *ephebeia* substantially; as time went on, not least because of the costs of providing personal weaponry, the aristocratic nature of the *ephebeia* turned it into more of a private association or club.⁴⁷

In 303/2 we have the last known ephebic decree until 267/6.⁴⁸ At that time, and thanks to Poliorcetes' measure, it is startling to see the drop in the annual enrollments to between twenty and forty ephebes per year (thus one or two per tribe), remaining at these levels until the mid-second century.⁴⁹ Yet they still undertook military instruction, and were called upon to fight for the city. Thus, the decree of 266/5 shows them in action during the Chremonidean War attacking the Macedonian garrison on the Museum Hill (pp. 120–121). Further, since we hear of only five ephebes in 98/7 taking part in the *Pythais*, their comrades may have been protecting other parts of Attica during a slave revolt that began around 100 (pp. 199–200).

The decline in numbers also impacted the officials responsible for their education and training: although the *kosmetes* remained in control, the

---

⁴⁴ Ban: Mitchel 1964, pp. 337–351; Tracy 2004, p. 208; Friend 2019, pp. 174–177; that the move was from "oligarchs" in the city and not from Antipater; *contra* Couvenhes 1998; cf. Chankowski 2010, p. 120 n. 283. Post–Lamian War survey: Friend 2019, pp. 172–184.
⁴⁵ See the table of serving ephebes at Perrin-Saminadayar 2007a, pp. 63–81.
⁴⁶ Perrin-Saminadayar 2007a, pp. 30–31, on a transformation over several years into the second century.
⁴⁷ Wiemer 2011; see too Ferguson 1911, pp. 127–129; Follet 1976, pp. 339–341; Habicht 1997a, p. 233; Perrin-Saminadayar 2004.
⁴⁸ Collection of fourth-century decrees: Reinmuth 1971, and the exhaustive Friend 2019, pp. 85–254. The decree of 267 is *IG* ii³ 1, 917 (= M. M. Austin 2006, no. 136, pp. 251–252, as ii² 665).
⁴⁹ Pélékidis 1962, pp. 165–172.

twelve *sophronistai* disappear. Probably numbers and the need for income explain why in the second century non-Athenians were allowed to enroll in the *ephebeia*. In 123/2 we have the first recorded foreigners, fourteen in all (with four from Rome) out of a total ephebic cohort of 107.[50] Over time foreign youths contributed to a general increase to perhaps as many as 100 to 150 by the end of the second century.[51] These foreign ephebes also had the opportunity to become citizens at the end of their training, at least until the Augustan era.[52] Nevertheless, opening up the *ephebeia* to foreigners robbed it of its predominantly Athenian military function, and in the later eras the ephebes were often reduced to putting on martial displays for visitors to the city.[53]

The ephebes' continuing role in civic and religious activity shows that in the Hellenistic and Roman periods the Athenians still took great pride in this civic program and its role in Athenian culture.[54] It has been argued that in Roman times the literary sources distorted its importance because the people wanted to elevate its standing, given the Roman appropriation of many facets of Athenian culture.[55] This may well be true, for from the time of Sulla to that of Octavian we have only five decrees honoring the ephebes and their *kosmetes*, which show that the institution was operating with restricted numbers.[56] But participation in the *ephebeia* was highly prized, as the number of aristocratic youths from major cities throughout the Greek east as well as Rome testifies.[57] The Athenians had another ephebic program on Delos, which they introduced when they acquired the island in 167, and which also admitted non-Athenians later (the first decree attesting to

---

[50] Habicht 1997a, p. 344 with n. 30; see too Burckhardt 2004, pp. 204–205; Tracy 2004, p. 209.
[51] Habicht 1997a, pp. 289–290; Habicht 1997c, p. 13.
[52] Osborne 1976.
[53] Perrin-Saminadayar 2007a, pp. 250–253.
[54] Perrin-Saminadayar 2007a, pp. 32–33. See Tracy 2004, pp. 208–209, for the view that Antigonus Gonatas possibly suspended the *ephebeia* at the end of the Chremonidean War in 261, but after returning their "freedom" in 256 the people quickly reconstituted the *ephebeia* as a sign of its importance in military and civic life.
[55] Perrin-Saminadayar 2004, pp. 90–94; ephebic catalogue and dedications: Schmalz 2009, pp. 44–55; cf. Graindor 1931, pp. 194–199 (also as artworks).
[56] *IG* ii² 1039 (79/8); 1041 (43/2 or 42/1); 1042 (40/39 or 39/8); 1043 (37/6 or 36/5); and 1040 + 1025 (depending on the dating of the archonship of Apolexis, so between 24/3 and 20/19): see further, Perrin-Saminadayar 2004.
[57] Perrin-Saminadayar 2007a, pp. 411–438.

foreigners is dated 144/3).⁵⁸ Interest in it, however, was never on a par with that in Athens.⁵⁹ The institution therefore was something to be proud of and support.

Away from military training, the ephebes had to study philosophy, and a decree dated to 123/2 lauds them for attending lectures of prominent philosophers.⁶⁰ Obviously those in Athens had an advantage over their counterparts elsewhere as they could attend the schools of the foremost philosophers of the day.⁶¹ The ephebes were instructed in the gymnasium, itself an essential component of *polis* life for the physical and intellectual environment and pursuits it provided.⁶² They shared the establishment with two other groups of students (one younger, the other older).⁶³ It became mandatory from the early first century for the graduating class of ephebes to donate one hundred books per year to the library housed in the gymnasium funded by Ptolemy III to the east of the Agora, the Ptolemaeum.⁶⁴

In other cities the supervision of the ephebes fell to the gymnasiarch—the gymnasiarchy was no different from a liturgy in reality, with the person receiving a statue.⁶⁵ The latter honor became the norm from the third century for wealthy individuals who had to foot bills from their private wealth because the state was not able to meet expenses—we mentioned the *agonothesia* as an example in the previous chapter.⁶⁶ In Athens the gymnasiarch was a very important official; he was responsible for ensuring an adequate supply of olive oil used in the gymnasium for bathing purposes at considerable expense. This perhaps caused Hadrian to set up an endowed gymnasiarchy at Athens as a means of continuing the liturgy.⁶⁷ During the archonship of Domitian (sometime between AD 84/5 and 92/3) we have the first examples of noncitizen ephebic gymnasiarchs, perhaps as a means of upward social mobility that the emperors encouraged.⁶⁸

---

⁵⁸ Habicht 1997a, p. 262.

⁵⁹ Perrin-Saminadayar 2007a, pp. 479–521.

⁶⁰ Habicht 1997a, p. 290. On philosophy as an ephebic study, see Haake 2007, pp. 46–55 (only Zenodotus the philosopher is cited in the ephebic decrees); cf. Burckhardt 2004, pp. 203–204.

⁶¹ Perrin-Saminadayar 2007a, pp. 261–266.

⁶² See the essays in Kah and Scholz 2004 as a starting point.

⁶³ See Kennell 2015, pp. 172–174.

⁶⁴ *IG* ii² 1029, 1030.

⁶⁵ Gymnasiarchy in the Roman imperial period: Geagan 1967, pp. 128–132.

⁶⁶ See Hakkarainen 1997, especially pp. 22–23.

⁶⁷ Geagan 1967, pp. 130–131.

⁶⁸ Graindor 1931, pp. 55–56 and 91; Day 1942, pp. 178–179; Baslez 1989, pp. 27 and 34.

Guilds

In the Hellenistic era various guilds of professional artists or athletes came into existence as part of a growing professionalism of athletes and actors arising from their activities in games and especially festivals. The guilds were private associations, protecting, representing, and, for want of a better word, publicizing their members—the guild of athletes, for example, was almost certainly formed before the battle of Actium in 31 and remained focused only on athletics, its members taking part in competitions in honor of various gods, and gaining recognition in Greece as a result.[69]

Of greater interest to us in this book is the Athenian guild of the festival artists, or "craftsmen (*technitai*) of Dionysus," in drama, music, dance, and literature.[70] Dionysus was the patron god since the artists performed at his festivals. The Athenian guild, which grew out of the performing arts and religion, was formed in the early third century and was soon followed by the Isthmian guild, the Nemean, and others elsewhere; it played a role in the public life of the city and may even have organized the performances of the plays at the City Dionysia.[71] Given the number of Dionysiac festivals in Greece, and the little we know about their organization, it is possible that the artists of a particular guild did not simply arrive in a place to perform but prior to their arrival finalized arrangements for their performance at the festival in question. That sort of organization (if it did happen) did not preclude artists from different guilds performing at the same musical and dramatic festivals.[72]

The religious association of the *technitai* with festivals meant that they continually travelled to perform at them. They were therefore given protection to ensure their safety and received a waiver from taking part in normal public life. Also, after 277 the Amphictyonic Council granted the members of the Athenian and Isthmian guilds exemption from paying taxes and military service, perhaps a sign of gratitude for their cities helping to protect Delphi and the Oracle of Apollo from a savage Galatian invasion in 279.[73]

---

[69] Forbes 1955.
[70] Leiwo 1997 on private associations, especially p. 117, on the Dionysiac artists; see too Day 1942, pp. 92–94; Sifakis 1965.
[71] Sifakis 1965; cf. Habicht 1997a, pp. 103–104 and 276–277.
[72] Sifakis 1965, pp. 210–213 especially.
[73] On the exemptions: Day 1942, pp. 92–93.

It is not a surprise that we find the guilds of the festival artists taking part in the *Pythais* procession to Delphi, reintroduced by the Athenians in 138 after a hiatus of two centuries. In addition to honoring Pythian Apollo with musical and dramatic performances, the procession had considerable propaganda value for Athens. The processions took place in 138, 128, 106, and 98, this infrequently probably due to their expense. The names of the participants, recorded in inscriptions, reveal an increase in numbers as time wore on: in the one of 138, there were no festival artists (but 59 members of a boys' chorus); ten years later, in 128, there were 59 festival artists and 100 in 106.[74] But we should not rule out professional standing: since artists from different guilds performed at the same festivals, those from Athens would have seized the opportunity to perform again at Delphi to promote their artistic reputation and the city's cultural standing in Greece.[75]

While the guilds were respected throughout the Greek world, that of Athens was held particularly in high regard—by the prestigious Amphictyonic Council, by Rome, and by the Athenians themselves. A case in point was in the later second century when the Athenian and Isthmian guilds were involved in a dispute (we do not know over what) and turned to Rome for arbitration.[76] The Senate's initial finding was evidently not accepted, for further disputes in 119/18 and 118/17 came before the Roman proconsul in Macedonia, Cornelius Sisenna, who split up the Isthmian guild (but made no move against the Athenian). Still, the issue was not properly resolved, and in 112 representatives for each guild appeared before the Senate—those speaking on behalf of the Athenians were actual official state envoys, a sign of the importance the city attached to its guild. On that occasion the Senate decided in favor of the Athenians, diminishing the prestige of the Isthmian guild.

The Athenian guild suffered a decline in the following century as we have only two inscriptions that show its activities at Eleusis and in the city and then nothing until the Hadrianic era.[77] We are told that in the later first century Mark Antony ordered performers to be brought across from Italy to Athens when he took up residence in the city.[78] If these were his

---

[74] Habicht 1997a, p. 276, citing sources.
[75] Sifakis 1965, pp. 208–213.
[76] Habicht 1979a, p. 278.
[77] *IG* ii² 1338 (Eleusis) of 78–76, and *IG* ii² 1340 (Acropolis); see too Geagan 1979a, p. 378.
[78] Athenaeus 4.148c.

own troupe, the Athenians might have considered it prudent, given his power over them, to "rest" their own artists, especially if they happened to be better than his. But that does not explain why Athenian artists did not make a comeback after Octavian defeated Antony at Actium in 31.

At any rate, in Athens at least guilds were not viewed as merely private associations important for theatrical and other cultural pursuits, but were recognized for the political role they played in civic life. They represented the city in the Greek world beyond mere artistic performance and even played a role in relations with Rome. Because of their religious associations, guilds also sacrificed to Rome since the Romans were usually honored as benefactors of the city—as late as Hadrian's reign (AD 117–138) we know of personal letters he sent to the Athenian guild, which sponsored a seat in the theater of Dionysus for an imperial priest, possibly of Hadrian himself.[79]

This survey of political and civic institutions has traced some of their history and workings, but most importantly has shown what the Athenians took pride in and were prepared to fight for, regardless of the odds. Those citizens who had been disfranchised were anxious for a return to the democracy of the Classical period, which would thus return them to their political role in the city, and everyone wanted the restoration of freedom and autonomy. It was not to be. Yet even with a narrower citizenry and a restricted form of democracy, institutions like the *ephebeia*, even after it had been opened to noncitizens, still contributed to Athens' greatness in the Greek world. The city, as noted in the introduction, thus continued to shine, albeit differently.

---

[79] *IG* ii² 1105, 1106, with Graindor 1934, p. 210; Geagan 1979a, pp. 394–395.

4

Demetrius "The Besieger" and Athens

HOW DIFFERENT WOULD ATHENIAN LIFE be under the Antigonids? One claim is that the city "in the years after 307 was clearly of no major importance and dependent now on this foreign potentate, now on that."[1] But that is too pessimistic a view. Athens was certainly dominated by Macedonia and needed help from foreign rulers, especially the Ptolemies and Seleucids, but "dependency" is too strong a word. As we shall see, the city could look after itself when needed and continued to play an important, albeit different, role in Greece.

Poliorcetes in Charge

At an Assembly held in July 307, the start of the new Attic year, Poliorcetes appeared to be an answer to Athenian prayers. Standing triumphantly before the people, he declared Athens free from Cassander's rule, and gave the people 150,000 bushels of grain, timber to build one hundred triremes, and allowed them to re-establish their "ancestral" democracy.[2] He also returned

---

[1] Tracy 1995, p. 22.
[2] Diodorus 20.46.1, 4 (the gifts after the people had bestowed honors on him and his father); Plutarch, *Demetrius* 10.1 (*patrios politeia*), with Ferguson 1911, pp. 96–100; Habicht 1997a, pp. 66–68; Mikalson 1998, pp. 75–104; Thonemann 2005; Grieb 2008, pp. 68–73. The present of grain reflects the Athenians' ongoing concern over their food supply: Tracy 1995, pp. 30–35, and see especially G. J. Oliver 2007a; cf. Marasco 1984a.

to them the island of Imbros, which his father had seized from Cassander.³ A committee under his auspices repealed some of Demetrius of Phalerum's laws, although those curbing excess were kept on the books. Most likely, the *ephebeia* was reintroduced (if it had not been by Demetrius of Phalerum) but was reduced from two years to one year and made voluntary, and remained that way throughout Poliorcetes' rule.⁴ These changes gutted ephebic numbers throughout the Hellenistic period.

The Athenians rushed to show their loyalty by punishing various supporters of Demetrius.⁵ These included the elderly orator Dinarchus, who had moved from his native Corinth to work in Athens some years before, and who in 323 wrote speeches for at least one of the prosecutors in the trials of those implicated in the Harpalus affair (p. 23). Menander the comic playwright was also targeted, and "nearly brought to trial for no other cause than that he was a friend of Demetrius," but Poliorcetes' cousin Telesphorus managed to protect him.⁶ Apparently on the orders of Poliorcetes, the people also revoked all decrees honoring Demetrius and tore down all the images of him—"some were sold, others thrown into the sea, and yet others, so it is said, were smashed up to make bedroom items," apart from his statue on the Acropolis, perhaps because of the sacred nature of the site.⁷ When Demetrius in Alexandria heard news of all this, he was said to have remarked that the people might well smash his statues but the reason why they had erected them in the first place could never be destroyed.⁸

On the motion of Stratocles of Diomeia, one of the period's more prominent career politicians (and one of Demosthenes' prosecutors at his trial in 323), the Athenians bestowed extravagant honors on Monophthalmus and Poliorcetes—perhaps more so on the latter, given he was actually present in the city.⁹ These included gold statues of the pair in a chariot (the vehicle of

---

³ *IG* ii² 1492, line 133; Diodorus 20.46.4, with Ferguson 1911, p. 112.
⁴ Reduction: Reinmuth 1971, no. 17, pp. 86–117, especially pp. 101–102 and 106–115; Friend 2019, pp. 179–184. The state would also benefit from the reduction in ephebes' expenses and equipment costs: Habicht 1997a, p. 137. Further on the *ephebeia*, see chapter 3.
⁵ Ferguson 1911, p. 101.
⁶ Diogenes Laertius 5.79, with Ferguson 1911, pp. 60 and 101.
⁷ Diogenes Laertius 5.77.
⁸ Diogenes Laertius 5.82.
⁹ Diodorus 20.46.1–2; Plutarch, *Demetrius* 10.2–11.1 (cf. M. M. Austin 2006, no. 42, pp. 91–93), with Ferguson 1911, pp. 108–110; Habicht 1970, pp. 44–55; Mossé 1973, pp. 108–114; Habicht 1997a, pp. 68–69; Bayliss 2011, pp. 120–124. Plutarch, *Demetrius*

the gods no less), set up next to that of the "tyrannicides" Harmodius and Aristogeiton; crowns for each of them worth (if we can believe Diodorus) 200 talents; an altar "of the saviors"; two new Athenian tribes named after them, Antigonis and Demetrias (which were placed first in the official order); annual games in their honor with a procession and a sacrifice; and weaving their images into Athena's *peplos* (robe), which was affixed to her statue in the grand annual Panathenaic procession through the city.[10]

The addition of the two new tribes meant that there were now twelve of them, and thus an increase in the Boule to 600 members. But even more overt was the change to the Monument of the Eponymous Heroes, set up in the Agora, on which details of business before the Assembly, notices of lawsuits, and the names of the new ephebes for each tribe and of those called up for military service were posted for all to see and read.[11] This monument had on top of it a row of ten bronze statues of the heroes who had given their names to the Athenian tribes. Now, statues to Monophthalmus and Poliorcetes as eponymous heroes of the two new tribes had to be added to it.[12] The image could not be more contrasting—to us, and no doubt to the Athenians. Now atop one of the key symbols of democracy, located as it was by the Bouleuterium and in front of the Metroon, were statues of two rulers who allowed only a pretense of democracy. Likewise, there was a contrast in situating their statue next to another liberation monument, the "tyrannicides" statue, for the Antigonids had saved the city not from a tyrant but merely a different Macedonian ruler.[13]

10.3 wrongly adds that the Athenians were the first to call them kings, but the Successors did not call themselves kings until 306: see below. On Stratocles see further below.

[10] Beyond the state, private individuals also set up statues, while the Acamantis tribe held its own sacrifice to them: Mikalson 1998, pp. 84–85. *Peplos*: Plutarch, *Demetrius* 12.2, tells us that a later storm symbolically ripped the *peplos*: Mikalson 1998, p. 99 (probably 302/1 Panathenaea). On the divine allusions of the chariot statue: Brogan 2003, pp. 195–196; cf. Bayliss 2011, pp. 120–124; cf. Chaniotis 2003, p. 433.

[11] T. L. Shear 1970, pp. 145–146; Monument of the Eponymous Heroes: Thompson and Wycherley 1972, pp. 38–41.

[12] T. L. Shear 1970, pp. 197–198 (during the second architectural period, pp. 171–175); see his Plate 43 for a reconstruction showing the twelve statues; on the *eponymoi*, cf. Pausanias 1.5.2–4.

[13] Brogan 2003. Shrine of the tyrannicides: Thompson and Wycherley 1972, pp. 155–160. Liberation monuments: Brogan 2003, pp. 194–198; Metroon: Thompson and Wycherley 1972, pp. 35–38.

The honors that the Athenians bestowed on the Antigonids were excessive, and Plutarch is highly critical of how the present honors "turned Poliorcetes into a foul and obnoxious man."[14] But there are precedents, and it must be remembered that they were set against a background the city had not endured since the middle to late sixth century: rule by one man.[15] There was also the danger that Cassander would try to retake the city and the Piraeus, hence the Athenians needed Antigonid support. In fact, to be on the safe side, on Demochares' motion the Athenians made repairs to the walls of the city and harbor, while Poliorcetes sent them 1,200 suits of armor from Cyprus along with grain and timber for ships.[16] The repairs were paid for by special taxes as well as contributions from citizens, metics, and foreigners.[17]

But while savior (of a city) was one thing, "savior god" was quite another. The Athenians cannot have actually believed that Antigonus and Poliorcetes were gods, especially as in official inscriptions they referred to them only as saviors.[18] Thus in 307 the Athenian honors were meant to win their favor, no different from when they had recognized Alexander the Great a god in 324, but then showed their true feelings after his death by indicting Demades, who had proposed Alexander's divine honors.[19] Nevertheless, as has been well pointed out, by recognizing the Antigonids as savior gods the Athenians embarked on a slippery ethical slope from an abhorrence of impiety to a pragmatic exploitation of it to remain on the side of Macedonia; in that they had little choice, as this was the new realpolitik.[20]

Did the Antigonids consider themselves savior gods? Poliorcetes' later actions might betray a feeling of superhuman self-importance, especially when he made the Parthenon (the monumental temple to Athena Parthenos)

---

[14] Plutarch, *Demetrius* 10.2.

[15] Habicht 1970, pp. 44–55. Mikalson 1998, pp. 79–83, discusses each one in this context.

[16] Decree: *IG* ii² 463 (= Harding 1985, no. 134, pp. 168–169); armor: Plutarch, *Demetrius* 17.1; walls: Theocharaki 2011, pp. 121–124; other things: Plutarch, *Demetrius* 10.1; cf. Ferguson 1911, pp. 112–114 ("Athens was thereby converted into a fortress of the best modern type," p. 113).

[17] Ferguson 1911, p. 113 with nn. 3–4.

[18] Ferguson 1911, p. 471, suggested that the priest of the "Savior Gods" (Antigonus and Demetrius) replaced the office of eponymous archon, but there is no evidence for this: Mossé 1973, p. 109. Demetrius seems to have relied largely on the political leaders who outdid themselves in flattery of him to help resist Cassander. Distinction on inscriptions: Mikalson 1998, p. 80; cf. pp. 82–83.

[19] K. M. T. Atkinson 1973; J. M. Williams 1989, pp. 23–24; Worthington 2013, p. 331.

[20] Mari 2003.

his home after 304 and spoke of Athena as his sister (discussed below). However, Monophthalmus was more grounded. When sycophants told him his successes would make him divine, his reply was, "My pisspot carrier knows me better."[21]

Another possible move to show loyalty to the new rulers came when Sophocles, son of Amphiclides of Sunium, introduced a law that the heads of the philosophical schools had to be approved by the Boule and Assembly, with the death penalty for any transgressors, and banned philosophers from Athens.[22] These schools believed they had freedom of speech and so were not afraid of critically involving themselves in political debate, which would not have endeared them to some rulers. But the genesis of Sophocles' aggressive action may have been Demetrius' Aristotelian leanings, since the Lyceum was one of his targets, and Theophrastus was among the philosophers who left Athens at this time.

Then the following year the people had a change of mind, perhaps because of Theophrastus' self-enforced exile, according to Diogenes Laertius.[23] Sophocles was prosecuted by a certain Philon for making an illegal proposal and was defended by Demochares of Leuconoe—Demosthenes the orator's nephew, and the man who had tried to rouse the people against Antipater after Crannon (p. 26). Demochares, "a man passably honest as politicians went," spoke in hostile terms of the treachery and immorality of philosophers, which they instilled in their followers, but his speech failed.[24] Sophocles was fined 5 talents, and any restrictions on the schools were removed, showing the Athenians held them and the whole concept of what they stood for—free speech—in high esteem, even if philosophers in New Comedy were made fun of as they had been in Old Comedy.[25] The philosophers thus returned to the city, including Theophrastus.

---

[21] [Plutarch], *Moralia* 360d–e; cf. 182c; cf. [Plutarch], *Moralia* 545b (sometimes confused with Antigonus II Gonatas, but, as Robin Waterfield commented to me, Plutarch specifies the "elder" Antigonus).

[22] Diogenes Laertius 5.38; Athenaeus 13.610e–f (cf. 11.508f), with Ferguson 1911, pp. 104–107; Habicht 1994b, pp. 236–237; Habicht 1997a, pp. 74–75; Korhonen 1997, pp. 75–85; Haake 2007, pp. 16–36.

[23] Diogenes Laertius 5.38.

[24] Fragments of his speech: Marasco 1984b, pp. 139–140 and 163–176. Quote: Tarn 1913, p. 93. Demochares: Davies 1971, pp. 141–142; Marasco 1984b; Kralli 1999–2000, pp. 153–156; Bayliss 2011, pp. 107–111 and 116–117; Canevaro 2018, pp. 73–78.

[25] Korhonen 1997, pp. 86–96.

Thus we move to the era of the Antigonid rule of Athens, lasting until 229.[26] Although Diodorus claimed that the Athenians finally restored "the constitution of their fathers," this was far from true. When Poliorcetes liberated Athens in 307, he allowed the democratic institutions, which largely remained unchanged from the fourth century, to continue to function.[27] However, he made demands of the people and expected them to follow his will, leading scholars to describe the democracy as a "caricature" and "restricted."[28] That is why we have more than one hundred Assembly decrees from the six years when he first controlled Athens (307–301), compared to only a couple from the decade of Demetrius' rule, and all sycophantic.[29] These routinely bestowed honors on individuals or states supporting Poliorcetes, but the number of Athenians proposing them was small, which could indicate he relied on only a narrow group of supporters.[30] Further, he lived in the city continuously only after 304; before then, the Athenians had to deal with his various aides or respond to his letters.[31]

Of the politicians carrying out Poliorcetes' bidding, we know of Meidias (the son of the fourth-century orator Demosthenes' wealthy opponent), Phaedrus of Sphettus, and especially Stratocles (who was responsible for over two dozen decrees).[32] What influence, if any, he had during Demetrius' regime is not known, but evidently Poliorcetes regarded him as his right-hand man. His influence certainly depended on Poliorcetes, for when the latter was absent in 305–304 and Cassander was pressuring the city, Stratocles remained on the periphery of events.[33] It is no surprise that he made enemies, such as the politically active comic writer Philippides, whose

---

[26] See Dreyer 1999, pp. 149–195, for comparative comments on Athens and the Antigonid kings to 229.

[27] See Osborne 2012, pp. 55–109; cf. Bayliss 2011, pp. 94–128, with pp. 120–124, on Demetrius the savior god and democracy.

[28] Mossé 1973, p. 108: the democracy "a mere caricature of the regime which had constituted the greatness of Athens"; cf. Dreyer 1999; *contra* Bayliss 2011, p. 51, and see pp. 49–60 on ideology in Hellenistic Athens.

[29] Habicht 1997a, pp. 71–72 with n. 15; Tracy 2000; Osborne 2012, pp. 21–22.

[30] Habicht 1997a, pp. 71–74; Kralli 1999–2000.

[31] Osborne 2012, p. 21.

[32] Stratocles: Ferguson 1911, pp. 101–103; MacKendrick 1969, pp. 35–39; Tracy 2000; Muccioli 2008; Paschidis 2008, pp. 78–106; Bayliss 2011, pp. 102, 114–116, and 152–186; Luraghi 2014; cf. Davies 1971, pp. 494–495. Meidias: Davies 1971, p. 387; Phaedrus: Davies 1971, pp. 526–527.

[33] Cf. Luraghi 2014, p. 198. Bayliss 2011, pp. 159–167, on relations between the two men ("the King and I," p. 159).

assault on Stratocles in 301 (see below) provides a rare political edge to New Comedy.[34] Plutarch was also critical of Stratocles, calling him a demagogue and a "repulsive individual," who "lived a decadent life, and was thought to match the insults and antics of Cleon in how he dealt with the people."[35] Cleon we have already met: the prototype demagogue of the 420s who opened the door to non-nobles achieving ascendancy in political affairs (p. 58).

Thanks principally to Plutarch's characterization, Stratocles has been viewed as a "radical" or "extreme" democrat. Yet there were other democrats in Athens who had showed no pro-Macedonian leanings yet were exiled, such as Demochares (see below). These democratic "labels" have recently been questioned, along with the veracity of the literary sources in making Stratocles out to be a Cleon-type.[36] Just as we should be skeptical about the view of Aristophanes and Thucydides on Cleon, given personal biases at work, so we should be about Philippides or Plutarch on Stratocles. When Philippides (whose work Plutarch presumably read) lambasted Stratocles for his baseness and venality, we should not see any agenda behind his rebukes other than it being satirical, and Plutarch's comparison of Stratocles to Cleon could likewise be unwarranted and shines no light on his character or his political sympathies.[37]

In fact, in the same year Stratocles introduced his decree honoring the Antigonids (307), he proposed a bronze statue for Lycurgus in the Agora, together with free meals (*sitesis*) in the Prytaneum (Town Hall) for Lycurgus' son Lycophron.[38] The surviving decree cites Lycurgus' building activities; his good laws; his contributions to the state; his incorruptibility; and especially his pro-democratic spirit, evidenced in his opposition to Macedonia—all of which are contrasted to the "tyrant" Demetrius of Phalerum. Stratocles' rationale for the decree shows his political alignment was anything but sycophantically Antigonid, as Lycurgus, like Demosthenes, embodied the

---

[34] Philipp 1973; cf. Habicht 1993, pp. 251–252; Hanink 2014, pp. 241–243.
[35] Plutarch, *Demetrius* 11.2. As my colleague Paul McKechnie pointed out, this sort of caricature goes back to Homer's Thersites, and so has been around a long time.
[36] See Luraghi 2014, especially pp. 200–208 on the Cleon analogy.
[37] Luraghi 2014, pp. 204–208 and 214–219.
[38] Decree 3 at [Plutarch], *Moralia* 852b and e, with Roisman, Worthington, and Waterfield 2015, pp. 275–277; Mikalson 1998, pp. 20–31 and 76–77; Bayliss 2011, pp. 105–106; Luraghi 2014, pp. 208–214. Lycurgus' statue: [Plutarch], *Moralia* 843c–e, 847d, 852e; Pausanias 1.8.2. Prytaneum: Thompson and Wycherley 1972, pp. 46–47.

anti-Macedonian spirit; he was thus sending out a "moderately conservative message."[39] This rehabilitation of Lycurgus may well indicate that the Athenians believed they were now in a new, more democratic, era, though Monophthalmus and Poliorcetes did not seem especially bothered by the honors for Lycurgus and his family.

In any case, in 306 they changed the face of the Hellenistic world when they declared themselves kings, leading the other Successors to follow suit.[40] Thus began the era of Hellenistic kingship, as the kings turned to model themselves on Alexander and base their legitimacy to rule, as he had done, on their "spear-won conquests."[41]

Declines and Falls

Not long after Poliorcetes expelled Demetrius, Monophthalmus ordered his son to capture Cyprus from Ptolemy I and win control of Rhodes and the eastern Mediterranean as a prelude to invading Egypt. Rhodes resisted Poliorcetes, but in the spring of 306, aided by an Athenian fleet of thirty triremes under the command of Medeius of Larissa, Poliorcetes decisively defeated Ptolemy's fleet in the harbor of Salamis at Cyprus.[42] The Antigonids now ruled the seas. Taking advantage of their preoccupation with Ptolemy, Cassander launched a bid to retake Athens in the summer of 306. The Athenians staved off his assault with Aetolian and Boeotian help and supplies from Poliorcetes, forcing Cassander north beyond Thermopylae.[43] Perhaps now Poliorcetes handed over the two Attic fortresses at Panactum and Phyle to the Athenians to help them protect the city.[44]

---

[39] Luraghi 2014, p. 213; *contra* Baylis 2011, p. 156 (Stratocles was motivated to endear himself to Lycurgus' son Habron, who was influential in politics).
[40] Plutarch, *Demetrius* 18 (= M. M. Austin 2006, no. 44, pp. 94–46).
[41] Mooren 1983; Walbank 1984a; Billows 1990, pp. 241–248; Hammond 1993; Hammond 2000; Bosworth 2002, pp. 246–278; Ma 2003; Chaniotis 2005, pp. 57–68; Grainger 2017; "spear won": Worthington 2016, pp. 100–101, 127–128, and 151.
[42] Diodorus 20.50–52; Plutarch, *Demetrius* 16; Justin 15.2.6–9; Pausanias 1.6.6; Polyaenus 4.7.7; Appian, *Syrian Wars* 54, with Bennett and Roberts 2009, pp. 146–153; Champion 2014, pp. 115–120.
[43] Plutarch, *Demetrius* 23.1. On the date of the alliance with Boeotia note the sage comments of Smith 1962, pp. 117–118.
[44] *IG* ii² 492, lines 8–9; Plutarch, *Demetrius* 23.1–2.

The Antigonids' invasion of Egypt turned out to be a disaster thanks to a combination of bad weather and Ptolemy's army, and they abandoned it.[45] Fortunately for them Athens had shown no signs of defecting, so in 305 Poliorcetes besieged Rhodes for its earlier defiance.[46] The siege dragged on into the following year even though various cities, including Athens, tried to resolve the standoff diplomatically.[47] Eventually Poliorcetes cut his losses; although he had failed, the enormous size and power of his siege equipment earned him the nickname Poliorcetes ("the besieger"). In gratitude for their safety, the Rhodians built a 105-foot bronze statue of their patron deity, the sun god Helios, which they stood in their harbor—this was the Colossus of Rhodes, one of the seven wonders of the ancient world.

After his string of failures, Poliorcetes returned to Greece in 304 only to find Cassander had returned with a vengeance, seizing Phyle and Panactum in Attica, together with Salamis, and besieging the city.[48] Polyperchon (Antipater's successor), who was still active in the Peloponnese, prevented any city going to Athens' aid. In desperation the Athenians turned to Poliorcetes.[49] He sailed at once with 330 ships and troops, landing in Boeotia and cannily threatening to march into Macedonia. Cassander was therefore forced to break off his siege and rush northward, where Poliorcetes defeated him and won over 6,000 of his men.

Poliorcetes moved back from Macedonia to Athens for the winter of 304–303. At the spot where he alighted from his chariot the Athenians set up a new cult to him as Demetrius *Kataibates* (Descender), an epithet referring to Zeus and in particular the spots where his lightning bolts had struck the earth.[50] They also allowed him to live in the rear chamber of the Parthenon, the great temple to Athena, but piety was far from his strong suit, and he held orgies with numerous courtesans and young men there.[51] The Athenians'

---

[45] Seibert 1969, pp. 207–224; Champion 2014, pp. 124–129; Worthington 2016, pp. 165–166.
[46] Diodorus 20.81, 100.1–4 (= M. M. Austin 2006, no. 47, pp. 98–99).
[47] Diodorus 20.98.2–3; cf. Plutarch, *Demetrius* 22.1.
[48] Plutarch, *Demetrius* 23.1; Polyaenus 4.11.1; cf. Pausanias 1.35.2 (the people of Salamis were traitors for siding with Cassander).
[49] Diodorus 20.100.5–6; Plutarch, *Demetrius* 23.1, with Habicht 1997a, pp. 74–77; see too Hauben 1974.
[50] Mikalson 1998, p. 86.
[51] Plutarch, *Demetrius* 23.2–24.1, 26.3; cf. Athenaeus 3.128a, 6.253a, with Ferguson 1911, pp. 118–119; Habicht 1997a, pp. 77–81; see Ogden 1999, pp. 173–177, on his courtesans (and wives). His activities do not suggest he garrisoned the Acropolis, as Dreyer 1999, pp. 174–180, would have it.

anger with him intensified when, so the story goes, he demanded they pay him an enormous tax of 250 talents; they scrambled to get it together, only to see him give it to his favorite courtesan Lamia for her to buy soap.[52] The veracity of the story must be suspect given the amount of money for something that cannot have cost very much, yet it gets across the very real scenario that the Athenians had to meet any of Poliorcetes' demands.

Lamia, an Athenian courtesan of great intelligence, wit, and musical ability, is one of the livelier and in many respects more powerful non-noble women in our period to have dealings with Athens (cf. chapter 9 on women). She has an interesting history with the Macedonian ruler, having previously been a mistress of Demetrius of Phalerum, and then a captive of Ptolemy, who had left her behind on Cyprus in 306 when Poliorcetes took the island.[53] Although older and "past her prime," according to Plutarch, Lamia seduced Poliorcetes and was one of his mistresses for many years, although their relationship caused friction with his closest advisers.[54] That Poliorcetes married an Athenian lady named Euthydice in this period did not endear him to the Athenians: as well as his relationship with Lamia, he had been married to Antipater's daughter Phila since 320 (as part of the Triparadeisus settlement).[55] Thus the Athenians experienced Macedonian polygamy at first hand.

The Athenians could hardly throw stones though, as their politicians had all sorts of affairs with courtesans and led scandalous lives. Stratocles, for example, took up with Phylacion, a prostitute who was nicknamed "Didrachma" because she charged anyone who wanted her only 2 drachmas (the cost of the cheapest flute girl).[56] But Poliorcetes shocked the people more because of what he got up to in the Parthenon; in the Classical period, anyone claiming familial relationship with the gods, or acting as he did in a sacred place, would have been indicted on the spot for impiety.[57] But this was no longer that time: just as when the Athenians hailed the Antigonids as savior gods, impiety had to be set aside for certain people.

---

[52] Plutarch, *Demetrius* 27.1.
[53] Plutarch, *Demetrius* 16.3; Athenaeus 3.101e, 4.128b, 13.577c–d, with Wheatley 2003.
[54] Plutarch, *Demetrius* 16.3, 27.
[55] Plutarch, *Demetrius* 14.1, with Ferguson 1911, pp. 110–111; Tarn 1913, pp. 17–18.
[56] Bayliss 2011, p. 152. On Stratocles' influence after Poliorcetes' return, see Bayliss 2011, pp. 183–185.
[57] Mikalson 1998, pp. 87–88; Mari 2003, pp. 88–90.

Poliorcetes was nonplussed by the Athenians' view of him. If anything, he was contemptuous of them and their laws—as when he became sexually involved with the young son (Cleaenetus) of a man named Cleomedon of Cydathenae, who had been fined a massive 50 talents, and overturned the father's conviction at the behest of Cleaenetus.[58] The people tried to prevent this sort of thing happening in the future by banning anyone accused or convicted of a crime from petitioning him about their case. Poliorcetes was understandably unimpressed, causing Stratocles to introduce a decree to the effect that anything Poliorcetes proposed in the future, either secular or religious, was to be accepted.[59] Demochares was openly critical of this decree, leading Stratocles to have him banished; he would not be recalled until 286/5, and during this time may have gone to Lysimachus in Thrace.[60] His son Laches later (in 271 or 270) proposed posthumous honors for his father, proclaiming he was a victim of oligarchy (presumably targeting Stratocles).[61] But if Poliorcetes was incensed with the Athenians, then Demochares' ridicule of Stratocles' decree was dangerous for the city—and provided Stratocles with a reason for ridding himself of a vocal opponent.

Poliorcetes had left the city in 303 to campaign in the Peloponnese (curiously, not making a move on Macedonia). He took Athenian troops with him as shown by a decree of the tribe Acamantis ordering a sacrifice for the safe return of its soldiers.[62] During this Peloponnesian campaign, Pausanias speaks of Macedonian troops attacking Eleusis until the Athenian Olympiodorus with a contingent of Eleusinians sent them packing.[63] The Macedonian soldiers may have been supporters of Cassander, but exactly who they were and why they undertook this offensive cannot be answered. Since their target was Eleusis, home to the famous Mysteries, they may have

---

[58] Plutarch, *Demetrius* 24.3–4.

[59] Plutarch, *Demetrius* 24.4, with Bayliss 2011, pp. 167–172.

[60] [Plutarch], *Moralia* 851f; cf. Plutarch, *Demetrius* 24.5 (clash with Stratocles); *contra* Bayliss 2011, pp. 172–176; Luraghi 2014, p. 199 n. 23, but see Roisman, Worthington, and Waterfield 2015, pp. 271–275, on the decree of Demochares. Dates: Smith 1962, and especially Dmitriev's commentary on Demochares, *BNJ* 75 T 2. To Thrace: Kralli 1999–2000, p. 154.

[61] [Plutarch], *Moralia* 851e; cf. Roisman, Worthington, and Waterfield 2015, p. 274 n. 19: the "decree resembles the last part of Decree 1 [posthumous honours for Demosthenes the orator: [Plut] *Mor*. 850f–851c] praising Demosthenes and Demochares, respectively, as exemplary democrats and patriots."

[62] Harding 1985, no. 137, pp. 171–172 (sacrifice).

[63] Pausanias 1.26.3, with Habicht 1979, pp. 102–107; Habicht 1997a, p. 75.

wanted to lull the Athenians into a fight rather than trying to besiege the city—in much the same way as in 431 when the Spartans had devastated crops hoping to lure the Athenians into a pitched battle and so win the Peloponnesian War. But the details of the present episode are so murky that Pausanias might simply have gotten his facts wrong.

In around 303 Poliorcetes announced his wish to be initiated in the Eleusinian Mysteries (on which cf. p. 20). Initiation was a long process, lasting over one year, but remembering Poliorcetes' wrath the previous year Stratocles cunningly introduced decrees renaming one of the months of the Athenian year (Munychion) twice as the various stages took place in these months. Poliorcetes thus set a record by becoming an initiate in one month.[64] It was also in this year that the people set up an expensive gold equestrian statue of him in the Agora, yet another "liberation monument" similar in intent to that of 307.[65]

But attitudes were changing toward the extravagant honors that he and his father had been paid because of a series of divine portents. At the Panathenaea of 303 Athena's *peplos* with the images of the two Antigonids on it was torn by a violent wind, hemlock was said to have grown up around their altars, and the City Dionysia was spoiled by freezing weather as—perhaps most important—were the precious grain crops of Attica.[66] The Athenians' dependency on grain for their food supply was a constant throughout their history; they were always careful to protect the grain route from the Black Sea, and their need to maintain the grain supply explains why they strove to keep the Piraeus throughout the Hellenistic era.[67] Stratocles came in for castigation. At the Lenaea of 301, Philippides made the bold claim that the gods no longer looked kindly on the city because Stratocles had made mortals divine, altered the months of the year, and turned the Parthenon into a

---

[64] Philochorus, *BNJ* 328 FF 69–70 (with N. Jones' commentary, *ad loc.*), with Ferguson 1911, p, 122; Habicht 1997a, p. 79; Mikalson 1998, pp. 89–90; Paschidis 2008, pp. 92–93; Bayliss 2011, pp. 176–179; on the renaming of the month, see Woodhead 1989, pp. 298–300.

[65] Brogan 2003, pp. 198–205, citing bibliography. Fragments of an equestrian statue were discovered in a well during excavations in the Agora, which might well be this statue, as in 200 when at war with Philip V of Macedonia, the Athenians destroyed all monuments to the Antigonids: see pp. 152–153.

[66] Plutarch, *Demetrius* 12.2–4. Grain in rural Attica: G. J. Oliver 2007a, pp. 68–73.

[67] G. J. Oliver 2007a, pp. 48–68. For all the complex issues about Athens and the grain supply (which cannot be dealt with in this book), see Oliver's exhaustive study. Grain in Classical Athens: Harding 2015, pp. 46–51.

brothel.⁶⁸ All these bad omens came together to show Stratocles guilty of *hybris*, but for now his influence remained unshaken.

Poliorcetes had left Athens (no doubt to everyone's relief) in spring 302 to travel to the Isthmian festival at Corinth. There he announced to embassies from the Greek cities his father's intention of reconstituting the League of Corinth with both of them as its hegemons.⁶⁹ Their reason had nothing to do with the original aims of the league, as crafted by Philip II in 337 (p. 16). Instead, they wanted to bring about an offensive and defensive alliance against Cassander and use the league as a springboard for invading Macedonia.⁷⁰ Cassander immediately renewed his alliance with Ptolemy, Lysimachus, and Seleucus, and decided to fight Monophthalmus in Asia rather than moving against him on Greek soil.⁷¹ He therefore distracted Poliorcetes in Greece while Lysimachus invaded Asia Minor to rendezvous with Seleucus and troops from Ptolemy. As they had anticipated, Monophthalmus immediately recalled his son, who had no choice but to make terms with Cassander.

In spring 301 the two sides met in a major battle at Ipsus, a small town in central Phrygia.⁷² Details are scarce, but we know that Lysimachus (as commander of the coalition force) led an army of 64,000 infantry, 10,500 cavalry, 400 war elephants, and 120 scythed chariots against an Antigonid one of 70,000 infantry, 10,000 cavalry, and 75 war elephants.⁷³ The Antigonid army was soundly defeated: Monophthalmus fell victim to a "cloud of javelins" raining down on him, but Poliorcetes managed to escape to Ephesus with 5,000 infantry and 4,000 cavalry.⁷⁴ Lysimachus also captured the survivors of as many as one thousand Athenian troops that Poliorcetes had taken with

---

⁶⁸ Plutarch, *Demetrius* 12.4; see further Ferguson 1911, pp. 123–124.
⁶⁹ See inscriptional evidence at Harding 1985, no. 148, pp. 172–174, and M. M. Austin 2006, no. 50, pp. 105–107, with Diodorus 20.102.1; Plutarch, *Demetrius* 25.3; see too Ager 1996, pp. 65–67. Background: Hammond and Walbank 1988, pp. 176–178; Billows 1990, pp. 228–232.
⁷⁰ Simpson 1959, p. 397; Green 1990, p. 34.
⁷¹ Billows 1990, pp. 176–185, for details.
⁷² Battle: Diodorus 21.1.2–4; Plutarch, *Demetrius* 28.3–29; Polyaenus 4.7.4, 12.1, with Billows 1990, pp. 181–184; Bennett and Roberts 2009, pp. 101–113; Champion 2014, pp. 158–161.
⁷³ According to Plutarch, *Demetrius* 28.3; Diodorus actually states 480 elephants (for Lysimachus), but this is probably his error; cf. Mehl 1986, pp. 201–202.
⁷⁴ Quote: Plutarch, *Demetrius* 29.5; cf. Diodorus 21.1.4; Pausanias 1.6.7. Poliorcetes: Diodorus 21.1.4; Plutarch, *Demetrius* 30.1.

him.⁷⁵ However, Philippides intervened on their behalf, winning their release and permission to bury the dead.⁷⁶

The battle of Ipsus ended the Fourth War of the Successors. It also marked (or seemed to mark) the end of the era dominated by Monophthalmus' imperial ambitions. The other Successors carved up much of his territory "as if it had been a huge carcass,"⁷⁷ with Cassander reconfirmed ruler of Macedonia and Greece; the Hellenic League of 302 was now abandoned. In the meantime, the Athenian Assembly voted never to accept a king within the city walls again and to pursue a policy of neutrality.⁷⁸ To remove Poliorcetes' shadow further, the people expelled his wife Deidameia (one of Pyrrhus of Epirus' sisters), escorting her as far as Megara. They sent a delegation to Poliorcetes in the Cyclades (as he was returning to Athens) with their decision; when he heard this news he was both furious and disappointed, but there was nothing he could do.⁷⁹ Against this background, Stratocles unsurprisingly fell from grace.

But Poliorcetes still had the strongest fleet in the Aegean, 5,000 troops (at Ephesus), and controlled Cyprus along with some bases in Asia Minor and Greece, including the strategic Corinth. Deprived of basing himself in Athens, he simply bided his time—and did not need to wait long. Soon after Ipsus Ptolemy and Seleucus quarreled, causing the former to strike an alliance with the increasingly powerful Lysimachus of Thrace. That made Seleucus cast around for an ally; in 298 he made a pact with, of all people, his former enemy Poliorcetes. Then suddenly in May 297 Cassander died of tuberculosis at Pella.⁸⁰ His eldest son succeeded him as Philip IV, only to succumb to tuberculosis four months later. A dual kingship followed of Antipater I and Alexander V (Cassander's other sons), with Thessalonice their mother as regent, but in 295 Antipater murdered his mother.⁸¹ Poliorcetes at

---

⁷⁵ These prisoners numbered 300, hence the estimate that Poliorcetes took 1,000 Athenians with him: Habicht 1997a, pp. 80–81.
⁷⁶ Davies 1971, pp. 549–550.
⁷⁷ Plutarch, *Demetrius* 30.1.
⁷⁸ Plutarch, *Demetrius* 30.3.
⁷⁹ Plutarch, *Demetrius* 30.2–3.
⁸⁰ Pausanias 9.7.2 ("dropsy"); Justin 15.4.24, 16.1.1. Date: Hammond and Walbank 1988, p. 208 n. 3.
⁸¹ Plutarch, *Demetrius* 36.1; *Pyrrhus* 6.2; Justin 16.1.1–9; cf. Diodorus 21.7.1; Pausanias 9.7.3. Her status as guardian or regent is controversial, but see Hammond and Walbank 1988, p. 210 n. 3, for her having this role. It is sometimes thought that the two kings divided up Macedonia into halves, but this is most unlikely: Hammond and Walbank 1988, p. 211 n. 1.

once seized his chance to become king of Macedonia—and retake Athens. But not before that city suffered a tyranny.

A Note on Chronology and the Calendar

Now that we are in the third century, the subject of this and the following two chapters in particular, some words are necessary on the vexed issue of chronology thanks to the nature of our evidence and the vagaries of the Athenian calendar. These combine to make an exact chronology, especially of archon years, hard to determine.

Not a lot of information exists on ancient Greek calendars.[82] Unlike the modern world, ancient Greek cities had their own calendars, which could differ markedly. The Athenian year was a lunar one, which ran mid-year to mid-year, and was divided into twelve months, each month having a particular name. However, while people generally lived to this calendar, and institutions like festivals were organized on it, for administrative reasons the city's political system revolved around a ten-month calendar. Each of these ten "political" months was called a prytany, hence each one lasted for roughly six weeks. That meant the Assembly, for example, did not meet four times per month (and so 48 times per year) but four times per prytany (so 40 times per year). Further, in the agricultural sector, farmers had their own seasonal calendar, which was solar (based on the twelve lunar cycles per year).

Since a lunar year has 354 days and a solar one 365, every second or third year the Athenians had to add another (intercalary) month to balance the start and finish of both types of year. That meant an intercalary year ended up having over 380 days, and when that happened the Athenians repeated a month—thus, for example, the sixth month (Poseideon) would appear twice in one year. Exactly how the Athenians worked all this out is unknown.

After 307 the Athenians added two new tribes, named after the Antigonids, taking the total of tribes to twelve, a number that stayed fairly constant throughout the following century. That meant the number of prytanies (administrative months) was increased from ten to twelve; the norm seems to have been the first six months had thirty days each, the other six months twenty-nine days, and in an intercalary year the number of days in the year was simply divided by twelve, so that all months had an equal number of days.

---

[82] Of the several modern works on the ancient calendar, see especially Meritt 1961; Mikalson 1975; Hannah 2005.

In addition to the problems posed by the differing calendars are the sources which have come down to us. Literary writers such as Diodorus, Polybius, and Plutarch do not cover the entire third century, and scattered allusions to it in other sources, such as Dionysius of Halicarnassus' brief biography of the orator Dinarchus, are not overly helpful. The amount of epigraphical material (public decrees and dedications) has increased in recent years, but it is lacunose, hard to interpret, and provides only a fraction of the many decrees and the like that must have been issued every year.[83] Indeed, not just the identities and years of the eponymous archons from the 260s to the 230s are problematic, but at times other officials, such as financial officers, are not known with certainty. Despite scholarly analysis and restorations of inscriptions, especially the stellar work of M. J. Osborne, it is still the case that many dates in the third century, especially the later part, may be off by one year.[84]

Osborne divides the third century broadly into four periods: 1) 301/1–287/6, a "period of turbulence"; 2) 286/5–263/2, the democracy of all Athenians headed by Demochares; 3) 263/2–229/8, the era of Antigonid control; and 4) 228/7–201/0, Athens free of Macedonian control.[85] The narrative in this and the following chapters follows the likely order of events and dates.[86]

The Tyranny of Lachares

Once Stratocles' political influence had declined in Athens, Phaedrus of Sphettus rose to prominence. He had a distinguished civic and military career, including being elected hoplite general in 288/7 and again in 287/6.[87]

---

[83] Excellent overview of the sources and the importance of epigraphic evidence for third-century chronology in Osborne 2012, especially pp. 111–158.

[84] Certainly, older chronologies and archon years as advanced by, for example, Graindor 1922b, Dinsmoor 1931 (still a major feat for its time), and Pritchett and Meritt 1940, are for the most part obsolete. All inscriptional evidence is gathered together in Osborne and Byrne 2012. See now Osborne 2003 and especially Osborne 2012, with Osborne 1989 and Osborne 2009. Finance officials (either individuals or possibly a board between 295 and 228): Henry 1984; Osborne 2012, pp. 92–95; cf. Geagan 1967, pp. 121–122 (into the Roman era).

[85] Osborne 2012, p. 125.

[86] On this period see Tarn 1913, pp. 311–339; Habicht 1979, pp. 113–146; Habicht 1982, pp. 159–177; Habicht 1997a, pp. 157–166; Dreyer 1999 (with caution on some redatings); Ager 2003; Osborne 2003; Scholten 2003; Rathmann 2010, pp. 69–75; Osborne 2012.

[87] Davies 1971, pp. 526–527; Osborne 2012, p. 116. On the increasingly influential position of the hoplite general, an innovation of the third century: Sarikakis 1976; cf. Geagan 1967, pp. 18–31, and Geagan 1997, pp. 21–22; G. J. Oliver 2007a, pp. 163–164.

A moderate, he saw the value of neutrality when it came to dealing with the other Greek cities and the Successors. There was clearly some value to his approach at this time, but Phaedrus was still careful to cultivate relations with any Successor willing to send the city much-needed supplies. For example, during the archonship of Euctemon (299/8) he sent an Athenian embassy under Philippides to Lysimachus, who in response gave the city 10,000 bushels of grain, enough to feed the people for the year.[88] Philippides also urged the king to meet the costs of a new mast and arm for the boat carrying Athena's *peplos* in the Panathenaic procession, since the old ones had been damaged (or even destroyed) in the winds that had ripped her *peplos* in 303. Lysimachus was quick to make this donation, perhaps to show he was different from his impious opponent Poliorcetes.[89] In return, the Athenians voted a crown for him.[90]

Despite Lysimachus' grain, by 297 a terrible shortage had the city reeling, with people apparently spending a whopping 300 drachmas for a measure of grain when the usual price was five.[91] The food crisis tested Phaedrus' leadership, but he was unable to do anything to remedy the suffering. As a result, civil strife, centered on clashes between Lachares, commander of the mercenaries in the city, and Charias, a hoplite general, broke out.[92] Lachares had been one of Poliorcetes' adherents but now declared for Cassander; in an effort to combat him Charias seized the Acropolis to defend his position in the city. Cassander saw the resulting chaos as his chance to regain the city, so out of his "deep hatred" for the people he persuaded Lachares to seize power; Charias was captured and executed on the Assembly's orders.[93]

Since Cassander died in May 297, as we noted earlier, Lachares' tyranny had to have begun while Cassander was still alive. But the chronology is controversial, and scholars are split into two camps, with some arguing the tyranny lasted from about 301 or 300 to 296/5 or (on the shorter side) from 297 to about 295.[94] The first period is based largely on a papyrus fragment

---

[88] *IG* ii³ 1, 877, lines 10–14, with Habicht 1979, p. 19; equipment: Mikalson 1998, p. 99.
[89] Mikalson 1998, pp. 98–99.
[90] Burstein 1978a.
[91] Grain prices: G. J. Oliver 2007a, pp. 241–247.
[92] *P. Oxy.* 17.2082 = Anonymous, *BNJ* 257a (= Burstein 1985, no. 5, pp. 5–6), with the commentary of Rzepka on *BNJ* 257a; see too Mossé 1973, pp. 121–123; Habicht 1997a, pp. 83–84; Hammond and Walbank 1988, pp. 204–205 and 206–207.
[93] Quote: Pausanias 1.25.7.
[94] Former: Habicht 1997a, p. 83; Osborne 2012, pp. 25–34; later: T. L. Shear 1978, pp. 52–53; Habicht 1979, pp. 1–21; Dreyer 1999, pp. 19–30.

stating that Menander wrote his comedy *The Imbrians* in the archonship of Nicocles (302/1) for the Dionysia that year (either 301 or 300), only to have it cancelled "because of Lachares, who was tyrant at that time."[95] This information means that Lachares became tyrant soon after Ipsus (301) but before the end of the archon year (mid-301). If true, the papyrus is evidence of "political interference in the theatre which is otherwise unique."[96]

There are, however, several arguments against this earlier date. For one thing, it is doubtful that a year (at most) later, in 299, a tyrant would have authorized Philippides to go to Lysimachus for grain, and even more doubtful that Lysimachus would have provided any for a city held by Cassander's man. We also have an Assembly decree passed in the archonship of Hegemachus (300/299) honoring the treasurers of Athena, who helped to provide grain for the cavalry during the famine that led to Lachares' tyranny.[97] It has been suggested that during the third century the constitution did not suffer much, even under the tyranny.[98] If so, then Lachares may have stacked the archonships and even the Boule with his own supporters and controlled Assembly meetings, yet all that does not explain Lysimachus' favorable attitude to the city. Possibly there was some connection between him and Lachares, for when the latter was eventually overthrown he may have fled to Lysimachus, but again, Lachares' dependency on Cassander would have concerned Lysimachus.

It is possible that the play could still have been written for 301 or 300 but cancelled because of the civil strife affecting the city before Lachares seized power.[99] But more important is that the archon's name in the papyrus fragment, Nicocles, may be emended to Nicias, who we know was archon in 296/5: this would allow Lachares time to seize power in 297 (possibly even late 298) before Cassander's death.[100] Accordingly, the festival at which Menander's *Imbrians* was performed was not the Dionysia of 295.

Further support for this date is that the Athenians did not cancel the entire festival, but only Menander's play, and their reasoning may be connected to

---

[95] *P. Oxy.* 10.1235, col. iii, lines 103–112, with Habicht 1979, pp. 16–21; Gronewald 1992, pp. 20–21; Luppe 1993.
[96] The phrasing of Professor Eric Csapo from a seminar paper (currently unpublished) on Lachares and Menander, which he kindly sent me.
[97] *IG* ii² 1264, with Habicht 1979a, pp. 82–83; G. J. Oliver 2007a, pp. 173–75, 234–236.
[98] Osborne 2012, pp. 55–102.
[99] The suggestion of Green 1990, p. 124.
[100] Most conveniently: Osborne 2009, p. 85 with n. 8.

the time that Poliorcetes chose to return to Athens (discussed below).[101] As we noted in chapter 2, Menander and Demetrius of Phalerum were on friendly terms; the former's victory with the *Dyskolos* was (coincidentally?) in 317, the same year that Demetrius took over Athens—on the orders of Cassander. As discussed earlier, when Poliorcetes overthrew Demetrius in 307 the Athenians were quick to condemn his supporters, including Menander, who was saved by Telesphorus (Poliorcetes' cousin). The same Cassander had encouraged Lachares more recently to take over the city, and given how the Athenians had previously treated Poliorcetes, they may well have scrambled to regain his favor by targeting Menander again, this time refusing to mount the *Imbrians*. Thus we should date Lachares' tyranny to 297–295.

Not a lot is known about the tyrant.[102] He had been "up to now a popular champion," according to Pausanias, hence Cassander might have seen him as his "man" in Athens in the same way as he had Demetrius.[103] Lachares ruled ruthlessly—"we know of no other tyrant so cruel toward men and so impious toward the gods," according to Pausanias—and he came to symbolize everything that was hated about Macedonia.[104] But when Cassander died in 297, followed soon after by Philip IV, Lachares must have realized that he had lost his main support base.

In the winter of 296/5 some of the men Lachares had used against Charias defied him and captured the Piraeus.[105] Still, Lachares maintained his rule of the city, impiously melting down the gold and silver statues in the various temples, including Athena's golden robe, to pay his mercenaries.[106] But when in the spring or early summer of 295 Poliorcetes left Asia Minor bound for Greece, more moderate Athenians, tired of the instability in the city, turned back to him. He initially failed to capture the city, so he went to campaign in the Peloponnese, where he was injured when shot in the jaw

---

[101] As argued by Csapo in his seminar paper (see n. 96).
[102] Tyranny: Ferguson 1911, pp. 132–134; Hammond and Walbank 1988, pp. 206–207 and 211–218; Green 1990, pp. 123–125; Habicht 1997a, pp. 81–87; Gabbert 1997, pp. 11–13; Dreyer 1999, pp. 17–110 (starting 295); Grieb 2008, pp. 74–77. See also the comments of Bayliss 2011, pp. 49–94, on oligarchy in Hellenistic Athens (pp. 64–65 for short comments on Lachares).
[103] Pausanias 1.25.7.
[104] Pausanias 1.25.7; cf. Plutarch, *Demetrius* 33.1.
[105] Pausanias 1.29.10.
[106] *BNJ* 257a F4; Pausanias 1.25.7 and 29.16; [Plutarch], *Moralia* 379d, with Habicht 1997a, p. 86 n. 73; Mikalson 1998, pp. 90–92.

by a catapult bolt during the siege of Messene. He returned to Attica, where he seized Rhamnus (on the east coast overlooking Euboea) and Eleusis as well as a grain ship en route to the city (hanging its crew to deter others from taking supplies to the city) before besieging Athens.[107] In the meantime Ptolemy had again appeared on the scene, still intent on expanding his influence on the mainland. He sent 150 ships to Athens, but decided the risk of battle against Poliorcetes' huge armada of 300 ships was too great, and so ordered his fleet to remain off Aegina.[108]

Poliorcetes' cruel treatment of the grain ship's crew had the desired effect, and with little to no grain getting through to the city, prices skyrocketed and the people suffered even greater famine.[109] Plutarch recounts the horror of a father and son fighting tooth and nail over a dead mouse that fell from their ceiling and the philosopher Epicurus counting out beans to give to his students to eat.[110] By spring 294, even though they had no desire to see Poliorcetes their ruler again and had even passed a decree to execute any citizen proposing to open negotiations with him, the people had had enough of the terrible conditions.[111] They rose up against Lachares, despite suffering losses in the fighting.[112] He fled to Thebes, callously throwing some of the gold he had accumulated behind him to slow down his pursuers as they scooped it up.[113] What happened to Lachares after that is not definitively known; he may have sought refuge with Lysimachus, although Pausanias claims he was murdered at Coronea (Boeotia) because of his wealth.[114]

---

[107] Initial attempt: Plutarch, *Demetrius* 33.1–2; wound: Plutarch, *Demetrius* 33.2; seizures and siege: Plutarch, *Demetrius* 33.3; Polyaenus 4.7.5.
[108] Worthington 2016, p. 177.
[109] Plutarch, *Demetrius* 33.3–4.
[110] Plutarch, *Demetrius* 34.2.
[111] Plutarch, *Demetrius* 34.1.
[112] Pausanias 1.29.10.
[113] Polyaenus 2.9.1.
[114] Pausanias 1.25.8, but Polyaenus 3.7.1–3, 6.7.2 says he was expelled from Cassandreia after trying to win over the city for Antiochus I, which would have been in 297: Hammond and Walbank 1988, p. 212 n. 4.

Encore: Athens under Poliorcetes

Athens and the Piraeus were again in Poliorcetes' grip, the people expecting no kindness from him.[115] He sent word that he wanted them to convene in the theater of Dionysus, which he proceeded to surround with armed guards before dramatically making his appearance "like the tragic actors" from one of the side entrances onto the stage (perhaps the eastern side, from which priests and other civic officials normally entered). Theatricality was always his strong suit. Yet he showed no anger over how the Athenians had earlier spurned him and expelled his wife. Instead, he immediately assured them that he bore them no ill will, gave them 100,000 bushels of grain, and allowed the public officials most acceptable to the people to take office. These included archons, secretaries, financial officials, and *strategoi*.[116] But there was no question that it was he who was master of the city, and to this end he installed a garrison on the Museum (the Hill of the Muses, directly visible across from the Acropolis).[117]

The psychological effect on the Athenians of a garrison in the very heart of their city and so close to the sacred space of the Acropolis must have been enormous. Today, it takes roughly ten minutes to walk from the Acropolis to the Museum Hill, and about a further twenty minutes to walk upward to roughly the area occupied by the garrison. Poliorcetes used the old fortification wall (built at the behest of Themistocles in the early fifth century) and the protective wall (*diateichisma*) constructed after Chaeronea in 338, when the Athenians thought Philip II would besiege the city to protect the garrison; parts of these walls still exist. The view from roughly where the

---

[115] Plutarch, *Demetrius* 34.1, 3–5, with Ferguson 1911, pp. 135 and 136–150 (July); Habicht 1979, pp. 22–33; Harding 2015, pp. 66–67; see Garland 1987, pp. 49–50, on Poliorcetes appealing to the democratic sentiments of the inhabitants of the Piraeus.

[116] Grieb 2008, pp. 77–81; Osborne 2009. But with changes; for example, there are multiple financial officials but that of treasurer of the people disappears: Henry 1984. See Osborne 1989, with comments also on the impact on chronology of the secretary cycles, first identified by Ferguson in 1898. Favoring oligarchy though, see Habicht 1979, pp. 22–26.

[117] Plutarch, *Demetrius* 34.5; Pausanias 1.25.8 with Ferguson 1911, pp. 132–138; Mossé 1973, pp. 123–124; Habicht 1979, pp. 34–44 and 103–104; Habicht 1997a, pp. 86–87; Hammond and Walbank 1988, pp. 211–212; W. L. Adams 2010, pp. 218–219; see too Dreyer 1999, pp. 111–148 on Poliorcetes and Athens. The Athenians also honored one of his agents, Herodorus, at the same time: *IG* ii^3 1, 853 (= Burstein 1985, no. 6, pp. 7–8 as ii^2 646).

FIGURE 4.1 View of Acropolis from Museum Garrison. Photo: Ian Worthington.

garrison was situated across to the Acropolis shows just how close both areas were (Figure 4.1). The Hill is also a peaceful place with relatively few tourists today; on a quiet enough day the low hum of visitors to the Acropolis can be heard. All of this means that the Athenians must have been able to see the garrison, especially at night when presumably it lit camp fires, and even hear the soldiers there. Its close proximity can only have driven home how much Poliorcetes had muzzled the city.

In what must have been genuine relief, the people, at the behest of Dromocleides the orator, offered Poliorcetes new honors and control of the Piraeus and its garrison.[118] The latter was an empty gift, as he had already taken charge of the port from Lachares and most of his fleet was anchored there. Moreover, Poliorcetes' devastation of the countryside had done more than impact the food supply: it adversely affected the mining infrastructure of eastern Attica, and as a result Athenian silver coinage went into a decline

---

[118] Dromocleides: Habicht 1979, pp. 34–44.

earlier than at the end of the Chremonidean War in 268, as is often thought (pp. 123–124).[119]

Why Poliorcetes showed this surprising clemency is unknown. Possibly a certain Herodorus of Lampsacus (or Cyzicus) had urged him to spare the city and maintain the democracy, for the following year (archonship of Nicostratus, 295/4) the Athenians made Herodorus a citizen and awarded him *sitesis* and a bronze statue in the Agora.[120] Clearly, he had done *something* to earn these things; the decree speaks of his closeness to Poliorcetes, yet that does not mean he had secured the latter's mercy. The latter was as ruthless as he was ambitious; if he were after revenge for the way he and his wife had been treated he would hardly have let himself be talked out of it. Possibly the Athenians were simply honoring an adherent of Poliorcetes in much the same way as they honored friends and associates of Lysimachus, for example. A more plausible reason for Poliorcetes' clemency is that events in Macedonia were now unfolding in a way that refocused his attention and he needed to ensure Athens' loyalty. From the time of Philip II "control of Greece had been regarded as a central tenet of Macedonian policy," and the key to holding Greece was Athens.[121] Thus tightening his control of Athens while treating the people fairly was his means to this end—which also ties in with Plutarch's claim that he "sought the favor of the Athenians more than any of the Greeks."[122]

As we mentioned earlier, in 295 Antipater I of Macedonia had mercilessly put his mother Thessalonice to death and expelled his brother and co-king Alexander V.[123] When Alexander appealed to Poliorcetes and Pyrrhus of Epirus for help, Poliorcetes broke off a Peloponnesian campaign, leaving behind his son (by Phila, daughter of Antipater) Antigonus Gonatas in Athens.[124] However, Pyrrhus, who was geographically closer to Macedonia, moved faster to expel Antipater from Pella, who fled for refuge to his father-in-law Lysimachus of Thrace (who also had designs on the Macedonian throne). Pyrrhus then restored Alexander as king, who sent a message to Poliorcetes that he was not needed after all: a fatal mistake.[125]

---

[119] Kroll 2003, especially p. 209.
[120] *IG* ii³ 1, 853, and see Habicht 1997a, pp. 88–89.
[121] Hammond and Walbank 1988, p. 280 (referring to Gonatas' rule, but relevant for all Macedonian rulers).
[122] Plutarch, *Demetrius* 42.1.
[123] On this and the following events, see Hammond and Walbank 1988, pp. 212–218.
[124] Plutarch, *Demetrius* 35–36.1; cf. *Pyrrhus* 6.2; Polyaenus 4.7.9–10; Pausanias 1.13.6. Nickname: Brown 1979.
[125] Plutarch, *Demetrius* 36.2–6; *Pyrrhus* 7.1; Justin 16.1.8–9; cf. Diodorus 21.7.1.

Poliorcetes at the time was at Dium, the Macedonian religious center in the foothills of Olympus, but he invited Alexander to dinner with him in Larissa (Thessaly), and there murdered him. The dead king's troops initially panicked, but Poliorcetes was able to assure them of his intentions to the kingdom, so much so that they declared him king (thus the army would have met in assembly).[126]

Thus, in the fall of 294, seven years after his crushing defeat at Ipsus, Poliorcetes was king of Macedonia; he would rule until 287.[127] He did not live in Athens continuously, but he certainly micro-managed affairs via his own men, such as Stratocles and Dromocleides. It is thus hardly a surprise that the Athenians called this later period an oligarchy. Another one of his agents was the Olympiodorus who had defended Athens against a shadowy Macedonian attack in 303 (discussed earlier). A decree of 293/2 speaks of him being archon for a second year, even though re-election was illegal.[128] Possibly he was trying to set himself up as tyrant, but after that second term he was certainly not archon again—Stratocles, who may have died soon after, possibly had a hand in quashing Olympiodorus' aspirations.[129] In 292/1 (archonship of Philippus), those who had been exiled for their role in the earlier oligarchy, including Dinarchus the orator, returned to the city with Poliorcetes' encouragement.[130] The recall of exiles must have been unpopular; still, the people were careful to court Poliorcetes' favor.[131]

During these years Poliorcetes campaigned vigorously. In 293 he reconquered Thessaly (founding the city and port of Demetrias, near modern Volos) and central Greece, and then with his son Gonatas invaded Boeotia, where he twice besieged Thebes (292–291).[132] There were also skirmishes with Pyrrhus and what would be a prime mover of the third to second centuries, the Aetolian League, a confederation of various cities centered in

---

[126] Plutarch, *Demetrius* 37.1–2.
[127] Demetrius as king: Hammond and Walbank 1988, pp. 219–229; Waterfield 2011, pp. 186–190 and 193–196.
[128] *IG* ii³ 1, 858, line 1, with Osborne 2009, p. 85; Osborne 2012, pp. 34–35 and 113; Gabbert 1996. The Athenians set up a statue to him on the Acropolis: von den Hoff 2003, pp. 175–178.
[129] Ferguson 1911, p. 138.
[130] Philochorus, *BNJ* 328 F 167; Dionysius of Halicarnassus, *Dinarchus* 4; [Plutarch], *Moralia* 850d, with Habicht 1979, pp. 28–30.
[131] Habicht 1979, pp. 22–33.
[132] Ferguson 1911, pp. 139–140.

Aetolia (Central Greece), and probably founded in late Classical times to check the growing expansion of Thebes.[133]

In 290 (or possibly 291) Poliorcetes went to Athens, taking with him his new wife, Lanassa of Epirus. The people greeted him with garlands and libations, while a chorus sang him an ithyphallic hymn, which began with astonishing flattery:[134]

> The greatest of the gods and those dearest to the city are present; for Demeter and Demetrios here the occasion has brought together. She, the holy mysteries of the Maiden, has come to perform and he, gracious, as a god ought to be, and handsome and laughing, is present. Something majestic has appeared, all his friends in a circle and he in their midst, his friends just like stars and he the sun. O son of the most powerful god, Poseidon, and of Aphrodite, greeting. For the other gods either are far away or they have no ears or they are not or they do not heed us, not even one, but we see you present, not wood, not stone but real; so we pray to you. First, make peace, dearest one, for you are master. Not over Thebes but over all Greece does the Sphinx hold sway, the Aitolian who, seated on the rock, even as the old Sphinx did, having seized all our bodies, carries them away, and I cannot fight. For the Aitolian used to plunder the possessions of those nearby, but now also those far away.

This time, however, sycophancy was not the only motivation; the remainder of the hymn, as we can see, shows that the people wanted his support against the Aetolian League, which since 290 had occupied Delphi. The league and the Thebans were refusing to allow the Athenians to rededicate shields from the Persian Wars in the Temple of Apollo at Delphi, and in addition the league was preventing Poliorcetes and any supporters from attending the Pythian Games, one of the four major "crown" festivals.[135]

---

[133] Grainger 1999; Scholten 2000.
[134] Garlands and libations: Demochares, *BNJ* 75 F 2 in Athenaeus 6.253b–f (= M. M. Austin 2006, no. 43, pp. 93–94); hymn: Duris, *BNJ* 76 F 13 in Athenaeus 6.253d–f (= Burstein 1985, no. 7, pp. 8–9; trans. Burstein), with Marasco 1984b, pp. 199–203; Mari 2003, pp. 89–90, and see too Ferguson 1911, pp. 143–144; Habicht 1970, pp. 214–216; Mikalson 1998, pp. 94–97.
[135] Cf. Plutarch, *Demetrius* 13.1–3 (motion of Dromocleides to seek Demetrius' help), with Habicht 1997a, pp. 93–94.

It may have adopted this stance against Poliorcetes at the behest of its ally Pyrrhus, who was none too happy that his former wife Lanassa had recently married Poliorcetes on Corcyra—perhaps more so because Corcyra was a key island on the trade route to Italy, and it was hers.[136]

Poliorcetes organized a Sacred War against the Aetolians, using, it has been argued, the Athenians' hymn as part of his war propaganda.[137] He invaded Aetolia and continued north into Epirus, intending to fight Pyrrhus, but the two of them never met. After Poliorcetes' return to Athens in most likely 290, he held his own "Pythian festival" to defy the league's action in occupying the passes around Delphi, justifying the move because Apollo had founded the Athenian race.[138] The Athenians' hymn shows that (as in 307 with both Antigonids), divinity and protection meshed together.[139]

Athens Revolts

Poliorcetes was now facing an increasingly aggressive Ptolemy, who must have pricked up his ambitious ears when news of Pyrrhus' success in Macedonia reached him. Ptolemy had restored Pyrrhus to the throne of Epirus in 297, perhaps as a means of reasserting himself into Greek affairs, and in 294 Ptolemy had retaken Cyprus and captured Poliorcetes' Aegean possessions.[140] On top of that, Pyrrhus remained a threat to his west, as did Lysimachus and Seleucus to his east. To make matters worse, Poliorcetes was also facing dissatisfaction from the Macedonians, who disliked his opulent, untraditional lifestyle, love of fancy clothes like gold-embroidered purple robes and gold-embossed shoes, and supercilious nature.[141] Nor were they pleased that he planned to use the Macedonian treasury to fund an invasion of Asia with an enormous army of 98,000 infantry, 12,000 cavalry, and 500 warships (including "superwarships" of fifteen and sixteen banks of oars) to win back his father's old empire.[142]

---

[136] Plutarch, *Pyrrhus* 10, with Ferguson 1911, p. 141.
[137] Scholten 2000, p. 20.
[138] Games: Plutarch, *Demetrius* 40.4, with Ferguson 1911, p. 144; Demetrius and Pyrrhus later reconciled: Plutarch, *Demetrius* 43.1.
[139] Chaniotis 2003, pp. 431–433; see too Habicht 1979, pp. 34–44.
[140] Worthington 2016, p. 176.
[141] Plutarch, *Demetrius* 41.4–42 (= M. M. Austin 2006, no. 52, pp. 109–110); cf. 41.4–5, 44.6.
[142] Plutarch, *Demetrius* 43.2–3.

Poliorcetes' ambition, however, brought about his downfall, as Ptolemy, Lysimachus, Seleucus, and Pyrrhus joined forces to topple him. This Fifth War of the Successors, beginning in the summer of 288, was over almost as soon as it began.[143] Ptolemy worked to win over cities loyal to Poliorcetes, while Pyrrhus invaded Macedonia from the west and Lysimachus from the east.[144] Poliorcetes marched north against them, leaving Gonatas to protect his interests in Greece. As more of his troops deserted him, Poliorcetes fled in disguise (wearing a cheap black robe), eventually to the Peloponnese, leaving behind his wife Phila, who committed suicide.[145] His flight allowed Lysimachus and Pyrrhus to divide up Macedonia between them, and probably now Lysimachus decided his son-in-law Antipater I was not going to be useful after all, so he executed him.[146]

At this point the Athenians finally revolted from Macedonian control. The timing of this short revolt hinges on a later decree (awarded in 270/69) honoring Callias of Sphettus, which provides us with "the most detailed and circumstantial account that has come to light of Athens' revolt."[147] It was originally thought that the revolt occurred in early summer of 286, but more likely it should be dated to the spring of 287.[148]

Led by Olympiodorus, the man who had been archon in two successive years (mentioned earlier), a contingent of Athenians attacked the Macedonian garrison on the Museum.[149] Pausanias, telling us these men had been inspired by the actions of their ancestors (presumably in the Persian

---

[143] Hammond and Walbank 1988, pp. 227–229.
[144] Plutarch, *Pyrrhus* 11–12; Plutarch, *Demetrius* 44; Pausanias 1.10.1–2; Justin 16.3.102; on the date, cf. Hammond and Walbank 1988, p. 229 n. 1.
[145] Plutarch, *Demetrius* 45.1; Plutarch, *Pyrrhus* 11.6.
[146] Macedonia under Pyrrhus and Lysimachus: Hammond and Walbank 1988, pp. 229–238; Lund 1994, pp. 98–100.
[147] *IG* ii³ 1, 911; T. L. Shear 1978 (= Burstein 1985, no. 55, pp. 74–76; M. M. Austin 2006, no. 55, pp. 114–116), with Osborne 1979; Habicht 1979, pp. 45–67; Habicht 1997a, pp. 95–97 and 127–129; Gauthier, 1982, pp. 221–226; Harding 2015, pp. 94–96 (though on dating see Dreyer 1996); quotation: T. L. Shear 1978, p. 14. These events are described in lines 14–32 of the decree: see Shear's commentary on them, pp. 14–22.
[148] Merker 1970, pp. 143 and 150; Grieb 2008, pp. 83–85; J. L. Shear 2010; redating: Habicht 1979, pp. 45–67; Osborne 1979; Hammond and Walbank 1988, pp. 228–233; Dreyer, 1996; Osborne 2012, pp. 36–43.
[149] *IG* ii³ 1, 918, 919 (both 266/5); Plutarch, *Demetrius* 46.1; Pausanias 1.26.1–2; revolt: T. L. Shear 1978, pp. 61–73; Habicht 1979, pp. 48–62; start of 287/6: Dreyer 1996.

Wars) and the sorry state of the city compared to its heyday, described these men as old and young; this must mean that the regular troops were with Phaedrus, the hoplite general, gathering in the harvest, as the decree honoring Callias also stipulates Athenian moves to protect vital homegrown grain.[150] We are told that the fighting was bitter, and that the first man to rush the garrison was named Leocritus, son of Protrachus, who died; in his honor, his shield with his name engraved on it was dedicated in the sanctuary of Zeus Eleutherius (Zeus of Freedom, in the northwest corner of the Agora).[151]

It appears that not all the occupying troops were willing to resist: a decree records a Macedonian soldier named Strombichus expelling his comrades, for which action he was awarded citizenship twenty years later (266/5).[152] All in all, twelve Athenians were killed in the strike and were ceremonially buried in the state cemetery in the Cerameicus district (northwest of the Acropolis), which straddled both sides of the Dipylon Gate (the main gate into the city).[153]

There was still the garrison in the Piraeus, from where the troops ravaged the countryside, and, from Corinth, Poliorcetes "in a rampage" led an army against Athens.[154] Phaedrus, worried that Poliorcetes would destroy the crops and trigger another famine, turned to Pyrrhus and Ptolemy for help.[155] Ptolemy sent much-needed grain, together with one thousand mercenaries under Callias of Sphettus (Phaedrus' brother), an Athenian exile serving in his army and who was based on Andros (the northernmost island of the Cyclades).[156] They successfully defended the grain crop, ensuring that it was safely harvested, as well as the city from Poliorcetes, although in the fighting Callias was wounded.

---

[150] Osborne 2012, p. 37 n. 7.
[151] Pausanias 1.26.2.
[152] *IG* ii³ 1, 918, lines 9–15; see too T. L. Shear 1978, p. 62. The name is a Macedonian one: Hammond and Walbank 1988, p. 230 n. 4, who say evidently he had been bribed. Citizenship decree: *IG* ii³ 1, 918, 919.
[153] Pausanias 1.29.13; cf. 1.26.2, and 1.3 on the Cerameicus. Originally the Cerameicus was the potters' and painters' quarter of the city, but by now parts of it had become a cemetery.
[154] Plutarch, *Demetrius* 46.1.
[155] Plutarch, *Demetrius* 46.1.
[156] *IG* ii³ 1, 911, lines 28–30; T. L. Shear 1978, pp. 26–27. On the establishment of this base, see T. L. Shear 1978, pp. 17–18. Rhodes may also have set a gift of grain at this time: Tracy 1995, p. 35. Callias' exile: Worthington 2019b.

Poliorcetes knew that any siege of Athens would be protracted because of the resilience of the defenders and the supplies from Ptolemy. The Athenians had sent the philosopher Crates (later the Head of the Academy) to negotiate with him, who pointed out the size of Ptolemy's fleet, and warned him that Pyrrhus' army was due any minute.[157] He was by now concerned with Lysimachus' growing influence in Asia Minor and so decided to make peace—not formally with the city but with an ambassador named Sostratus, who had been sent by Ptolemy for that very purpose.[158] This man may have been the high-ranking and wealthy Sostratus of Cnidus, who among other things financed the building of the lighthouse (one of the seven wonders of the ancient world) on the island of Pharos in Alexandria's harbor.[159] Ptolemy was likewise concerned that Lysimachus or Seleucus—or both—might move against him, hence an alliance with Poliorcetes would help maintain his naval ascendancy in the Aegean and eastern Mediterranean.[160] Thus the two men made peace with each other, and so too did the Athenians with Poliorcetes.

Callias represented Athens in the negotiations held at the Piraeus, though he may have played a junior role given that Ptolemy and Poliorcetes were the drivers of peace.[161] Afterward he returned to Egypt, but we will meet him again as an Athenian envoy to Ptolemy II (pp. 104–105). Poliorcetes thus retained control of the Piraeus, Salamis, Corinth, and Chalcis as well as the fortresses at Eleusis, Phyle, Panactum, and Sunium in Attica.[162] These terms were far from ideal for the Athenians, but Phaedrus was right to persuade the Assembly to accept them.[163] More importantly, Poliorcetes was gone—as an inscription (in the archonship of Diotimus, 285/4) puts it, "the people had rewon the city."[164] In gratitude for his assistance in helping to provide grain for the city, the Athenians honored Ptolemy's admiral Zenon in 286/5

---

[157] Plutarch, *Demetrius* 46.2, with Korhonen 1997, pp. 45–47.
[158] *IG* ii³ 1, 911, lines 32–36, with T. L. Shear 1978's commentary, pp. 22–25 and 68, and see too his discussion of the peace at pp. 74–78.
[159] Identification: T. L. Shear 1978, pp. 22–25 with n. 40. Lighthouse: Worthington 2016, pp. 144–146. Further on Callias (and the lighthouse): Meeus 2015.
[160] Habicht 1979, pp. 62–64.
[161] In the Callias decree Callias is described as an "envoy of the demos," and continuing to work for the good of the city: lines 35–39. Osborne 1979, p. 188, argues Phaedrus would also have been part of these talks.
[162] See discussion at T. L. Shear 1978, pp. 76–78.
[163] Habicht 1979, p. 56.
[164] *IG* ii³ 1, 870, line 22.

(archonship of Diocles), significantly stating that he continues "to be benevolent"—perhaps to ensure that benevolence would continue.[165] In 270/69 they finally honored Callias, setting up his decree fittingly in front of the Stoa of Zeus Eleutherius.[166] Likewise, Phaedrus was also honored with a decree (the year is not known for sure, but probably in 255/4).[167]

The relationship of Callias and Phaedrus at the time of the revolt is disputed. Phaedrus had a lengthy civic and military career, and was elected hoplite general in 288/7 and in 287/6.[168] Callias, however, was in exile and (as his decree states) had had his property confiscated.[169] That Phaedrus had initially attempted to keep Athens loyal to Poliorcetes, but Callias had been quick to help the city against him, led Shear to suggest that the two brothers were at loggerheads with each other.[170] But that does not follow. They actually worked together during the revolt, suggesting no schism, as their success in gathering in the harvest shows.[171]

Poliorcetes' invasion of Asia was a failure; he was forced to seek refuge with Seleucus, who imprisoned him, and four years later (in the summer of 283), aged fifty-four, he drank himself to death.[172] Seleucus sent his ashes to Gonatas, who buried them at Demetrias.[173] Thus ended the life of one of the early Hellenistic period's more charismatic and influential people, brought down by his personal ambition and lifestyle: we will meet someone whose declining image likewise brought him down in the late Republic and whose biography Plutarch appositely pairs with that of Poliorcetes: Mark Antony.[174]

Athens and the Piraeus were still effectively divided into two distinct entities, though at some point the Athenians tried to recapture their port.[175] They bribed

---

[165] *IG* ii³ 1, 863 (lines 12–13 for his continuing goodwill), with Habicht 1979, pp. 48–52; Osborne 1979, pp. 183–184 and 189–190; Osborne 2012, p. 48. On honors for grain gifts, see J. H. Oliver 2007a, pp. 30–37 and 204–209.

[166] Stoa of Zeus Eleutherios: Thompson and Wycherley 1972, pp. 96–103.

[167] *IG* ii³ 1, 985, with T. L. Shear 1978, pp. 65–71; Harding 2015, pp. 96–97; cf. Henry 1992; Osborne 2012, p. 38 (in 259/8). On the decree and the Athenians' looking back to the time of the revolt, see now J. L. Shear 2020.

[168] Davies 1971, pp. 526–527.

[169] Gauthier 1982, pp. 221–226, especially pp. 224–225; Worthington 2019b.

[170] T. L. Shear 1978, pp. 10–12; cf. pp. 69–71; see now J. L. Shear 2020.

[171] This again shows the importance attached to homegrown grain, rather than the harvest that year being especially significant or hazardous: Osborne 1979, pp. 185–186.

[172] Plutarch, *Demetrius* 52.1–3.

[173] Plutarch, *Demetrius* 53.1–3.

[174] A point made by Green 1990, p. 130, citing Plutarch, *Dem. Ant. Comp.* 6; see too Zanker 1988, pp. 57–65; Pelling 1996, p. 54.

[175] Pausanias 1.29.10; Polyaenus 5.17.1.

one of the Macedonian soldiers, Hierocles, to betray the garrison; he pledged his willingness, but nevertheless remained loyal, and 420 Athenians were killed in the onslaught. An epitaph of one of the dead men, Chairippus, proudly proclaims that he died "under Munychia's walls while beating back the days of slavery for his beloved country."[176] The dead were buried in the Cerameicus—Pausanias tells us that he saw their memorial when he visited the city in the mid-second century AD.[177] It has been suggested that the attack on the Piraeus took place soon after the revolt ended.[178] However, decrees throughout the entire 280s show that the port remained garrisoned, while one in 282/1 honors the previous year's archon (Euthius, 282/3) and calls for the reunification of the Piraeus and the city, hence the unsuccessful attempt probably took place in 281.[179]

For how long the people would enjoy their newly found democracy was anyone's guess. The story goes that Pyrrhus had earlier gone to Athens and sacrificed to Athena on the Acropolis, telling the Athenians that if they were wise they should never admit one of the other kings into their city.[180] But within a decade Athens would once more be under the thumb of a Macedonian king: Antigonus II Gonatas.

---

[176] *IG* ii² 5227a, lines 5–6, with Ferguson 1911, pp. 150–151.
[177] Pausanias 1.29.10.
[178] T. L. Shear 1978, pp. 82–83.
[179] Osborne 1979, pp. 192–194 with references; cf. Osborne 2012, p. 39. Dreyer 1999, pp. 257–278, argues that the Piraeus was retaken in 280; if so, it must have fallen to Macedonia again at some unknown point.
[180] Plutarch, *Pyrrhus* 12.4, with T. L. Shear 1978, pp. 74–78.

5

Testing Macedonia

THE ATHENIANS' NEW DEMOCRACY FACED immediate problems, given that the Piraeus and several border forts were in Macedonian hands, impacting food supplies from the countryside. Citizens and foreign grain merchants supplied some grain over the course of several years, but it was not enough.[1] Since the food supply was always an Athenian weakness, the people throughout this period took care to remain in the good graces of foreign rulers to help them overcome shortages.[2]

The chronology of this chapter may at times be disputed, given the problems outlined in the previous chapter of determining an exact chronology for the third century (pp. 85–86).

A New Athens?

With Poliorcetes gone from Athens, Demochares rose rapidly to political prominence. He had returned from exile in the archonship of Diocles (286/5), as we learn from the honorary decree that his son Laches brought before

---

[1] Various public decrees were passed to honor the first two groups: merchants: *IG* ii² 1, 864 (of 286/5), 1021 (of 241/0); citizens: *IG* ii³ 1, 928 (of 285–280); on awards to those giving grain to the city, see Tracy 1995, pp. 30–35.

[2] Foreign needs: G. J. Oliver 2007a, pp. 228–259 and pp. 285–290 (table of imported grain in early Hellenistic Athens); see too Marasco 1984a. O'Neil 2008, pp. 75–77; Osborne 2012, pp. 44–50 (decrees on pp. 44–47); see too Dreyer 1999. Forts and food: G. J. Oliver 2007a, pp. 138–159, citing bibliography.

the Assembly in 271.³ It spoke of his father's successes in reducing state expenditures and on two embassies to procure money from Lysimachus (30 talents of silver on the first and 100 on the second), along with a mission to Ptolemy, and winning back Eleusis.⁴ In gratitude for Lysimachus' help, the Athenians set up a statue of him in the Agora (not so much out of goodwill but because they thought he could service their needs, according to Pausanias), and, in 286, bestowed citizenship on his close friends and advisers.⁵ Their relations with Lysimachus cooled somewhat in 285 after he drove out their friend Pyrrhus from Macedonia back to Epirus to become king of all Macedonia, but they did not do anything rash to sour their association completely.⁶

The Athenians were also friendly with the Ptolemies throughout the Hellenistic period.⁷ We saw before how Ptolemy I had supplied them with grain and troops in 287, for example, and when he died in 283 his son Ptolemy II Philadelphus succeeded him as king in his own right (he had been coruler with him since 285), and ruled Egypt until 246. He continued his father's foreign policy and his connection with Athens.⁸ From the decree awarding honors to Callias (of 270/69), we learn that Callias (who had evidently returned to Athens by then) had been sent to Ptolemy II for more grain and money, financing the mission himself to reduce pressure on state expenditure; he met up with Ptolemy on Cyprus, who gave him 50 talents of silver and 20,000 bushels of grain.⁹ At Callias' request, Ptolemy also gave money for the expenses to do with the Great Panathenaea of 282,

---

³ For the circumstances of exile, see p. 81. Diocles' archonship year: Osborne 2009, p. 86; cf. Dreyer 1999, pp. 270–271.

⁴ [Plutarch], *Moralia* 851e, with Roisman, Worthington, and Waterfield 2015, pp. 271–275; T. L. Shear 1978, pp. 80–82; cf. pp. 47–50; Osborne 1979, pp. 190–192. The money from various foreign kings was probably recoined into Athenian coinage: Kroll 2003, p. 210.

⁵ Statue: Pausanias 1.9.4; *IG* ii³ 1, 866 (unknown friend) and 867 (Artemidorus); *IG* ii³ 1, 924 (Bithys of Lysimacheia), with Osborne 2012, pp. 47–48 and n. 102.

⁶ Plutarch, *Pyrrhus* 12.6–7; Pausanias 1.10.2; Justin 16.3.1–2; Polyaenus 4.12.3, with Lund 1994, pp. 105–106. Honors for those providing grain: G. J. Oliver 2007a, pp. 30–37 and 204–207.

⁷ Habicht 1992, pp. 68–90; dealing with Ptolemy III and following: Mattingly 1997, pp. 129–133.

⁸ Marquaille 2008.

⁹ T. L. Shear 1978, lines 44–55, with commentary, pp. 25–32. He was sent on the motion of Demochares: [Plutarch], *Moralia* 851e, with Roisman, Worthington, and Waterfield 2015, p. 273.

with Callias and his brother Phaedrus serving as its directors.[10] That foreign money went toward festivals is not a surprise, for their huge costs significantly stretched the state's finances.[11]

In 283 Callias was chosen to head an Athenian sacred delegation to Alexandria for the first Ptolemaea, a festival with games and a sacrifice founded by Ptolemy II to honor his newly deified father.[12] The city could offer Callias only 50 minas (5,000 drachmas) to cover his expenses, but he generously declined and paid for everything out of his own pocket—yet another indication that the state could ill afford this sort of outlay.[13] It is possible that Ptolemy's envoy Philocles personally extended the invitation to attend the Ptolemaea if a fragmentary decree and base of a statue in his honor can be connected to this period; if so, it shows Ptolemy's high opinion of Athens.[14]

We take our leave of the remarkable and patriotic Callias here, for he returned to the service of Ptolemy, and at the time of his honorary decree (270/69) was commanding troops in Ptolemy's army at Halicarnassus. However, he continued to use his influence with the king to assist embassies that Athens sent to him, as well as the city itself.[15]

Athens had been facing shortfalls for a number of years, but after 286 the new feeling of independence and, as time went on, increasing prosperity brought a more optimistic air to the city. The Athenians began minting coins for the first time in a decade, perhaps using the silver that Ptolemy and Lysimachus had given them.[16] Religious and cultural life increased, as did military activity, with the defense of Attica falling to two *strategoi*, one responsible for the inland fortresses at Eleusis, Panactum, and Phyle, and

---

[10] *IG* ii³ 1, 911, lines 64–70, with the commentary of T. L. Shear 1978, pp. 35–44 (especially see his comments on the restoration of these fragmentary lines that this was the first time after the liberation of the city in 286: pp. 35–39); cf. Habicht 1997a, p. 136; *contra* Dreyer 1996, pp. 50–56. In Phaedrus' honorary decree of 255, he was praised for how he supervised the Athenian festivals in the archonship of Nicias (282/1): *IG* ii³ 1, 985, lines 53–56.
[11] Ferguson 1911, pp. 290–298; Mikalson 1998, pp. 108–109; cf. Day 1942, pp. 37–38; on festivals, see chapter 9, this volume. Civic finances generally: G. J. Oliver 2007a, pp. 193–227.
[12] Worthington 2016, p. 204.
[13] *IG* ii³ 1, 911, lines 55–64, with the commentary of T. L. Shear 1978, pp. 33–35 (the figure of 50 minas is restored: T. L. Shear 1978, p. 34).
[14] *IG* ii² 3425, with T. L. Shear 1978, pp. 33–34.
[15] *IG* ii³ 1, 911, lines 70–83, with the commentary of T. L. Shear 1978, pp. 45–55.
[16] Mint: Thompson and Wycherley 1972, pp. 78–79.

the other for the coastal fortresses at Sunium and Rhamnus.[17] Sometime in the period September 285 to May 284, Demochares, on the Assembly's orders, recaptured Eleusis, the "first major success of the new nationalist government."[18] The Athenians later regained Rhamnus from Macedonia, but perhaps not Sunium, for during the Chremonidean War (268–261), which we will discuss, the Ptolemaic general Patroclus could not use it as a base to help Athens.

In 282/1 the cavalry corps was increased from 200 to 300.[19] Throughout Greek history only the very rich could afford their own horses, and hence serve in the cavalry, but now state loans were made available toward the cost of buying and maintaining horses. The organization of the cavalry does not seem to have altered much, for an inscription that could date to this period speaks of the *prodromoi* (the specialized advance unit or scouts) still in action.[20] On the other hand the *ephebeia*, still reeling from Poliorcetes' changes to it in 307, continued to decline in numbers.

The city was also seeing an expansion of relations and territory elsewhere. In 286 an Athenian delegation attended a meeting of the Amphictyonic Council (the body responsible for the upkeep and protection of the Oracle of Apollo) at Delphi, as well as the Pythian Games there.[21] Not long after Poliorcetes' expulsion, the Athenians made an alliance with their former opponents the Aetolian League in Central Greece.[22] They may have done so because of suspected hostility from the Boeotian League, for it would hardly have welcomed Demochares' capture of Eleusis and Poliorcetes' returning of the border town of Oropus to Athens in 291. If tensions had been building with the Boeotian League, however, they did not explode, for in the summer of 281 the city sent an official delegation comprising six infantry officers (*taxiarchoi*) to the *Basileia*, the Boeotian League's festival

---

[17] Habicht 1997a, p. 137: the innovation perhaps prompted by Demochares' recapture of Eleusis between 287 and 270.

[18] T. L. Shear 1978, p. 84. Chronology: T. L. Shear 1978, pp. 84–86 (between September 285 and May 284).

[19] Bugh 1988, pp. 186–188; cf. Habicht 1982, p. 14, and the list of cavalry commanders of 282/1 discussed in Habicht 1997b.

[20] Bugh 1998, pp. 83–90.

[21] Habicht 1979, pp. 73–75; Habicht 1997a, pp. 126–127.

[22] The belief that Athens took part in a war led by Areus of Sparta against the Aetolian League and Antigonus Gonatas of Macedonia in 280 is erroneous: Habicht 1997a, pp. 130–131 with n. 34.

in Lebadeia.²³ Finally, shortly before Seleucus' death in 281, the Athenians regained the island of Lemnos (then in his possession).²⁴

By 281 only two of the original first generation of Alexander's Successors were left: Seleucus (about seventy-five years old) and Lysimachus (about seventy-two). In the winter of 282 the former invaded Asia Minor, and these tough old men met in battle in 281 at Corupedium; Seleucus was victorious, and Lysimachus was killed.²⁵ Seleucus now added Asia Minor, Thrace, and Macedonia to his kingdom to boast an empire second only to Alexander the Great's in size. However, as he crossed to take possession of Macedonia, Ptolemy Ceraunus (the eldest son of Ptolemy I, but not his successor Ptolemy II) treacherously murdered him, and then seized all Macedonia and Thessaly apart from Demetrias.²⁶ Thus the long and bloody Wars of the Successors, which we can trace back to Alexander the Great's death, finally came to an end.

Ceraunus had not reckoned on the ambitions of Antigonus Gonatas, Poliorcetes' son, who had always regarded himself as king since his father's death in 283.²⁷ Over the next half-century, as we shall see, Greece was dragged into warfare between various Ptolemaic and Seleucid kings, with the Athenians courting these rulers to gain influence in Greece.²⁸ In doing so, they believed they "had now achieved their lasting independence."²⁹ That is why the individual politicians that dominated public affairs were all supporters of democracy, and perhaps why there was a rehabilitation of an orator and statesman often considered Greece's greatest patriot: Demosthenes. In 280 the Athenians commissioned an honorary statue of him, part of an artistic trend that we may turn to trace here.

A Statue for Demosthenes

The Hellenistic era witnessed a prodigious and innovative output of fine artworks throughout the Mediterranean and Eastern worlds, proper

---

²³ *ISE* 15, with Habicht 1997a, p. 129.
²⁴ Phylarchus, *BNJ* 81 F 29 (various benefits from Seleucus), with the commentary of Landucci, *ad loc.*
²⁵ Career of Lysimachus: M. M. Austin 2006, no. 56, pp. 117–119 (= Pausanias 1.9.5–10), with Hammond and Walbank 1988, pp. 241–243; Lund 1994, pp. 199–206.
²⁶ Memnon, *BNJ* 434 F 8.1–3, with the commentary of Keaveney and Madden, *ad loc.*; Pausanias 1.16.2, 10.19.7, with Hammond and Walbank 1988, pp. 242–244.
²⁷ Tarn 1913, p. 161; Gabbert 1997, p. 28.
²⁸ Heinen 1984.
²⁹ Ferguson 1911, p. 156.

consideration of which lies outside the scope of this book.[30] Athens was part of this movement, especially in sculpture, at times influenced by Macedonian styles, which in turn profoundly affected Roman art, especially from the time of Augustus.[31] Increasingly, mainly due to economic restraints, the quality and quantity of Athenian art declined. But what did continue uninterrupted in the city and even accelerated in the Hellenistic period was the bestowal of statues on prominent individuals. In the Roman period the Athenians took to rededicating existing statues, erasing the original name on the base and adding that of the new honoree, a measure that might have been to help save money (see chapter 14).[32]

Statues were set up to individuals for particular reasons, most often to those who performed a benefaction for the city—a foreign ruler who funded a building, for example, or who liberated the city from an oppressive regime (as Monophthalmus and Poliorcetes had done in 307). Benefactions from the state in the form of honorary decrees were also bestowed on a number of patriotic individuals—in around 292, for example, Philippides was finally awarded a statue and *sitesis* in the Prytaneum for all his efforts on behalf of the city, as were Callias of Sphettus in 270/69 and his brother Phaedrus in around 255/4.[33]

But perhaps the most remarkable award came in 280/79, when Demochares secured a posthumous statue for his uncle Demosthenes, together with *sitesis* and *proedria* (a front seat at the theater) for his eldest descendants.[34] We have Demochares' decree appended to an ancient life of Demosthenes; in it, he waxes lyrical about Demosthenes' career, donations to the city, and his constant support of "freedom and democracy."[35] The

---

[30] See for example Pollitt 1986; Stewart 2014. For a good, succinct discussion of the various stages of Hellenistic art (early, middle, and late), see for example Green 1990, pp. 92–118, 339–361, and 565–585; cf. Stewart 2007. Macedonian influence on Athenian art: Palagia 2003; Rotroff 2003; von den Hoff 2003.

[31] Cf. Torelli 1996.

[32] J. L. Shear 2007a; Keesling 2010; Krumeich 2008; Krumeich 2010b; cf. Keesling 2007.

[33] Philippides: *IG* ii³ 1, 877 (= Burstein 1985, no. 11, pp. 13–15; M. M. Austin 2006, no. 54, pp. 112–113 as ii² 657), with Davies 1971, pp. 549–550; Habicht 1982, pp. 124–127; Mikalson 1998, pp. 99–101; Luraghi 2014, pp. 214–219; Harding 2015, pp. 93–94. Decree for Callias: chapter 0000 n. 0000; for Phaedrus: chapter 0000 n. 0000.

[34] Plutarch, *Demosthenes* 30.5–6; Cicero, *Brutus* 286.

[35] [Plutarch], *Moralia* 850f–851c, with Roisman, Worthington, and Waterfield 2015, pp. 269–271; see too Bayliss 2011, pp. 108–109; Worthington 2013, pp. 339–341; Luraghi 2018, pp. 31–34.

leading sculptor Polyeuctus cast this famous statue in bronze, depicting the orator as a mature man, with his eyes gazing thoughtfully into the distance—the statue we have today is a Roman copy of the original (Figure 5.1).

As we saw in the first chapter, Demosthenes had been resolute in his opposition to Philip II, and against the odds he had crafted an alliance with Athens' most bitter enemy Thebes in 339—an alliance that forced Philip to battle at Chaeronea in 338. Less vocal in politics during Alexander's reign, Demosthenes had gone into exile after his trial in the Harpalus affair of 324/3,

FIGURE 5.1 Portrait statue of Demosthenes, first–second century AD. Photo Credit: HIP/Art. Resource, NY.

returning triumphantly during the Lamian War, but at its end in 322 he had committed suicide rather than surrender to Antipater.

Demosthenes' reputation as a patriot had suffered greatly in the intervening years thanks principally to his political disgrace in the Harpalus affair.[36] Nevertheless, his statue now has been taken to show both his rehabilitation and a new spirit among Athenians, although it is going too far to say that it "was tantamount to a declaration of war against Macedonia."[37] There may have been a feeling that the Macedonian hegemony of Greece might be teetering, with all the first-generation successors as well as Poliorcetes dead, but war was not a realistic venture at this time. But a point could certainly be made: following on from the earlier statue of Lycurgus, Athens could showcase another great patriot as the city felt it was in an era of renewed democracy.[38] Demosthenes' statue thus becomes an echo of the documentary reliefs set up in the second half of the fourth century, which by their nature proclaimed anti-Macedonian sentiment in the city.[39]

Honorary statues to foreign individuals were always placed in the Agora and not the Acropolis, home to Athena. This was deliberate, for the Athenians intended the Acropolis to be their own national monument, an attempt to show their independent spirit, not to be tainted by foreign presence.[40] Macedonian dedications or gifts to Athenian deities were fine—thus no one would have objected to Roxane's dedication of various precious objects to the age-old sanctuary of Athena Polias (the patron deity) on the Acropolis or of Antiochus IV of Syria's gold *gorgoneion* (amulet with Gorgon's head) to Athena and Zeus—just not statues.[41] That intention did not match reality, especially in Roman times, when, worse than a statue, a temple to the goddess Roma and Augustus was built on the Acropolis, a stone's throw from the Parthenon and Erechtheum (pp. 291–293).

---

[36] Cooper 2000 on how and why Demosthenes' reputation declined in the Hellenistic era as philosophers, especially the Peripatetics, coupled his alleged political dishonesty with a dishonesty in his oratory, hence his style; see also Canevaro 2018 on the later biographical tradition, and the reception of Demosthenes' politics in Hellenistic Athens; cf. Luraghi 2018, pp. 31–34.
[37] Quote: Habicht 1997a, p. 139.
[38] Bayliss 2011, pp. 94–128, on renewed democracy.
[39] See further, for example, Lawton 2003.
[40] Von den Hoff 2003; cf. Rathmann 2010, pp. 79–85. Symbolism of the Acropolis throughout the Graeco-Roman era: Krumeich and Witschel 2010a, pp. 1–53.
[41] Dedications: Themelis 2003.

The feeling (if it ever really existed) that Macedonian rule might be waning also did not match reality. Antigonus still controlled the Piraeus garrison, and he was very aware how the Athenians had treated his father. But before any confrontation occurred came an unexpected, massive invasion threat to Greece, which Antigonus used as a springboard to the Macedonian throne.

Athens and the Galatian Invasion

Beginning in 279, Galatians (a Gallic people from the area known as Galatia in present-day Turkey, who later clashed with Rome) went on several brutal marauding expeditions as far afield as Delphi and Asia Minor.[42] Ceraunus mustered a Macedonian army to do battle with a Galatian force, but its leader, Bolgius, defeated him, triumphantly impaling his head on top of a spear to dishearten his troops.[43] Macedonia was in chaos, from both the Galatian attack and a sudden fast turnaround of kings: Ceraunus' brother Meleager ruled for only two months before he was deposed; his successor, Antipater (Cassander's nephew), was king for a mere forty-five days, after which, for reasons unknown, a nobleman named Sosthenes assumed the throne, and it was he who fortunately managed to defeat Bolgius.[44]

In the meantime, another set of Galatian invaders, under a chieftain named Brennus, ravaged Paeonia. Brennus proved a greater threat than Bolgius, for he moved south through Thessaly, with his sights set on the treasuries stacked with precious items at Delphi. The Greeks could not allow Apollo's sacred site to be plundered—or more realistically, for *their* treasuries to be looted. They mobilized an army, which Pausanias tells us comprised 25,000 men from several states including Aetolia, Boeotia, Phocis, and Locris, as well as one thousand Athenian infantry (the *epilektoi* or elite soldiers), 500 cavalry, and all their seaworthy triremes, led by the aristocrat Callippus, the

---

[42] Memnon, *BNJ* 434 F 11.1–7 (= Burstein 1985, no. 16, pp. 21–22); Diodorus 22.3–4, 5, 9; Justin 24.3.10–5.11; Pausanias 1.4.1–4, 10.19.5–23, and see the commentary of Keaveney and Madden on *BNJ* 434 F 11.1–7. Invasion: Tarn 1913, pp. 139–166; Nachtergael 1977, especially pp. 126–205; Habicht 1979, pp. 87–94; Hammond and Walbank 1988, pp. 251–258; Gabbert 1997, pp. 26–27; Scholten 2000, pp. 31–37; Mitchell 2003, pp. 280–284 (pp. 280–293 on Galatians in general).
[43] Justin 24.5.6; cf. Pausanias 20.19.7.
[44] Memnon, *BNJ* 434 F 8.8; Diodorus 22.4; Justin 24.5.12–14; defeat: Justin 24.5.12; obscure elevation: Hammond and Walbank 1988, pp. 253–254.

son of the prominent later fourth-century orator Moerocles of Eleusis.⁴⁵ Antigonus and Seleucus' son Antiochus I each sent 500 mercenaries. The urgency of the mission is underscored by Athens sending 500 cavalry of its own, given that its annual cavalry corps still numbered 300; the other 200 may have been made up of a mercenary javelin-throwing unit called the Tarantines, which the Athenians incorporated into their army in the second century.⁴⁶

The Greeks established a position at the famous pass of Thermopylae, just as two centuries earlier, in 480, a Greek force had taken a stance there against Xerxes' army in the Persian invasion of Greece. But the Galatians bypassed Thermopylae, forcing the Greeks to rush after them to Delphi. There, a hard-fought battle took place; as the Greeks began to gain the upper hand, Brennus committed suicide (apparently by drinking neat wine) and the rest of his Galatian force fled northward.⁴⁷ Delphi was saved. To commemorate the victory, the Amphictyonic Council organized a new (perhaps annual) festival honoring Apollo, called the *Soteria*; the *technitai* performing at it came from all over the Greek world and hence were members of different guilds, giving the festival a Panhellenic flavor.⁴⁸ In around 250/49 the Aetolians, who had distinguished themselves in the fighting, fashioned the *Soteria* into a greater event, with its organization falling to the Isthmian guild.⁴⁹ The Aetolians thus neatly advanced their position in Greece and continued to do so over the next several years.⁵⁰

The Athenians' role in defeating the Galatians was exaggerated by Pausanias, who says that Callippus was commander-in-chief of the coalition troops and that the Athenian navy rescued straggling infantry at Thermopylae.⁵¹ However, in 250/49 Cybernis, the son of a man named Cydias who was killed in the battle, proposed an Assembly decree, which speaks of the Athenians' sending their *epilektoi* and cavalry against the Galatians but says nothing about their navy.⁵² Why Pausanias exaggerated Athens' role in

---

⁴⁵ Pausanias 1.3.5, 1.4.2, 10.20.5; see further Bayliss 2011, pp. 187–210.
⁴⁶ Bugh 1998, p. 88 n. 30, citing bibliography.
⁴⁷ Pausanias 10.21–23.
⁴⁸ Sifakis 1965, pp. 206–208.
⁴⁹ Dating (archonship of Polyeuctus): Osborne 2003, p. 73; see too Barringer 2003, pp. 252–254 (using the *Soteria* to discuss Panathenaic prize amphorae); inscriptions recording Greek states attending: Nachtergael 1977, pp. 391–495.
⁵⁰ Walbank 1984b, pp. 232–236; Scholten 2000, pp. 37–58.
⁵¹ 1.4.3–4, 10.20.5, with Habicht 1997a, pp. 132–134.
⁵² *IG* ii³ 1, 1005. Athenian navy accepted by Gabbert 1997, p. 27.

the battle (or as W. W. Tarn would more forcefully say, his story contains "some rubbish"!) is unknown.[53] Given the obvious similarities with the role of the Athenian navy in the Persian Wars, perhaps Pausanias was unduly influenced by Herodotus' account or a later pro-Athenian source. But while he was guilty of factual errors, it has been argued that there is enough in his account that is factual and especially for it to praise Callippus' role in the battle.[54] That general had a distinguished military and political career in Athens, presumably enhanced by his part in combating the Galatians.[55]

At the time of the battle Antigonus was struggling against the Spartans, who were eroding his power in the Peloponnese, and by the aspirations of Antiochus I of Syria for the Macedonian throne. In 277 Antigonus was in Thrace: since he had been embroiled in a war with Antiochus since 279, his presence in Thrace brought him closer to Asia Minor and put pressure on his enemy.[56] When a large contingent of Galatians, perhaps as many as 18,000, moved into Thrace in 277, Antigonus defeated them in battle at Lysimacheia (Thracian Chersonese), which had the ripple effect of forcing the other Galatians out of Macedonia.[57]

Antigonus was understandably hailed a hero. He immediately marched to Macedonia, where he drove out Antipater and Sosthenes (who may even have been dead by then) before retaking Thessaly. Still, it took him some years to establish himself as king because he had to deal with a major threat from Pyrrhus.[58] The latter had recently campaigned in Italy, where he had expected help from Antigonus and Antiochus; when that did not eventuate, he returned to the Greek mainland in 275, and the following year invaded Macedonia.[59] He defeated Antigonus in battle, winning over many of the king's mercenaries and citizen troops. With most of Macedonia and Thessaly now in Pyrrhus' hands, Antigonus had no option but to flee to Thessalonica.

---

[53] Tarn 1913, pp. 439–442.
[54] Bayliss 2011, pp. 192–207; cf. Luraghi 2018, pp. 34–35.
[55] Bayliss 2011, pp. 208–210.
[56] War: Tarn 1913, pp. 160–164. Green 1990, p. 134, suggests he may have wanted to usurp of some of Lysimachus' territory, but that king had been dead for four years.
[57] Diogenes Laertius 2.141–142; Justin 25.1.2–10, 2.1–7, with Tarn 1913, p. 165; Hammond and Walbank 1988, p. 256 with n. 5.
[58] On Antigonus' early years, especially against Pyrrhus, see Tarn 1913, pp. 167–222; Walbank 1984b, pp. 221–224; Hammond and Walbank 1988, pp. 259–267; Gabbert 1997, 29–32.
[59] Tarn 1913, pp. 260–261 and 264–267.

Pyrrhus, however, soon proved unpopular, especially in 272 when his Galatian mercenaries plundered the royal tombs at Aegae (Vergina) and he showed only indifference to their sacrilege.[60] Still, when he invaded the Peloponnese, since Areus I of Sparta had allied with Antigonus against him, the Athenians decided to back Pyrrhus in his struggle with Antigonus.[61] While Pyrrhus was away, Antigonus recovered Macedonia, which he followed with a campaign against Argos. Pyrrhus rushed to its assistance, but in bitter street fighting he was killed (allegedly by a tile thrown by a woman from her rooftop, hitting his head below the helmet), and his decapitated head was given to Antigonus. The Athenians' support of Pyrrhus was thus not a good move, for Antigonus now had a further reason to be displeased with them.[62]

Antigonus II Gonatas

Antigonus II was one of Macedonia's more important and successful kings (Figure 5.2). A long, stable kingship was essential if Macedonia were to recover from both the devastation that the Galatians had inflicted on it and the constitutional chaos from several short-term and weak kings. Antigonus' long reign of almost forty years, from 276 to 239, brought about that recovery, especially in the key areas of military power, natural resources, and economic stimulation.[63] And unlike his father, Antigonus remained a true Macedonian and warrior king, disavowing praise and undue flattery.[64] It is therefore not a surprise that his people actually liked him.

Antigonus was also an intellectual, having studied in Athens under Zeno, the founder of Stoicism, and many leading literary figures of the day were at his court.[65] These included the poet Aratus of Soli (who wrote Antigonus' wedding hymn to Phila, heavy on his role in defeating the Galatians), the cynic philosopher Bion of Borysthenes, and the historian Hieronymus of Cardia

---

[60] Plutarch, *Pyrrhus* 26.6, with Hammond and Walbank 1988, p. 262.
[61] Tarn 1913, pp. 269–274.
[62] Plutarch, *Pyrrhus* 32–34.4; Pausanias 1.13.8; Polyaenus 8.68; Justin 25.5.1–2.
[63] Tarn 1913; Walbank 1984b, pp. 225–229; Green 1990, pp. 138–154; Gebbart 1997; Lane Fox 2011b; Waterfield 2020; cf. Hammond and Walbank 1988, pp. 259–316; Leon 1989; W. L. Adams 2010, pp. 219–222; Waterfield 2011, pp. 197–212.
[64] Cf. the anecdote in Plutarch, *Moralia* 545b–c.
[65] Ferguson 1911, pp. 184–185; Tarn 1913, pp. 21–36; Gabbert 1997, pp. 4–6.

FIGURE 5.2 Antigonus II Gonatas of Macedonia. Gold coin. © 2019 Trustees of the British Museum.

(who wrote an account of the Wars of the Successors).[66] The cerebral nature of his court was a stark contrast to the previous decades, and a throwback to the days of Archelaus and Philip II.

Zeno's Stoic teachings had a profound influence on Antigonus; the two men remained in close contact, exchanging letters, and whenever Antigonus visited Athens he would attend Zeno's lectures, and even turn up on his doorstep with other partygoers, though Zeno would give them the slip.[67] When Zeno died in 261 (archonship of Arrheneides, 262/1), a distressed Antigonus instructed the Athenians to honor him with a burial in the Cerameicus (even though he was not a citizen), and the Athenian ambassador at his court, Thrason, sponsored the following decree:[68]

> Whereas Zeno, son of Mnaseas, of Citium was active in our city for many years as a teacher of philosophy, and not only showed himself to be a man of excellent qualities in general, but also exhorted the young men who came to him for instruction to virtuous and rational conduct, teaching them the best principles by serving as a model to them

---

[66] Teachers and youth: Tarn 1913, pp. 21–36; court: Tarn 1913, pp. 223–256; cf. Green 1990, pp. 142–143; Gabbert 1997, pp. 69–70.
[67] Diogenes Laertius 7.6–9, 13–14.
[68] Archonship: Habicht 1982, p. 13; Osborne 1989, pp. 226–227. Diogenes Laertius 7.15 (Antigonus' instruction). Decree quoted in Diogenes Laertius 7.10–12 (= Burstein 1985, no. 59, pp. 81–82); [Plutarch], *Moralia* 183d. Diogenes Laertius 7.15 (distress: "what an audience I have lost"); cf. Tracy 2003, pp. 57–58.

in his own life and actions in perfect harmony with his own doctrines, the people have decided to commend Zeno.

Zeno was buried in a public tomb in the Cerameicus, and copies of the decree were set up in the Academy and Lyceum.[69]

Antigonus may well have tried to reconcile his stoic beliefs, which taught that all mankind was equal, with the realpolitik of kingship. But this was a world where a philosopher king could trust no one and needed to act forcefully when necessary. For several years relations between him and the Athenians were amicable thanks to his intellectual ties to the city and his preoccupation with Pyrrhus. But the Athenians were fickle, and the near-slavish devotion to their new democratic regime, personified in the likes of Demochares, did not bode well.[70] They had welcomed Antigonus' overtures to them when he became king, and sacrificed to his prosperity and their own, as a decree of 249/8 indicates.[71] Later, in 274, they had dedicated paintings commemorating his victory over the Galatians in the sanctuary of Athena Nike during the Great Panathenaea. Yet in 272, the Athenians had sided with Pyrrhus on his fateful and final campaign to the Peloponnese. After Pyrrhus' death, Antigonus treated the city courteously, but that attitude could not mask the reality of his hegemony or distract the people from the garrison in the Piraeus: indeed, it was probably that garrison that affected Athenians the most.[72]

Following Philip II's example almost a century earlier, Antigonus vigorously exploited Macedonia's mines and timber resources. He built fortresses and roads in Upper Macedonia, which had the dual result of beefing up border security against the troublesome Illyrians and creating jobs. He was not so much intent on expanding his realm, as the Seleucid and Ptolemaic rulers were, but on bringing dynastic stability and economic gain to the kingdom. To this end he followed a careful and strategic foreign policy, involving himself in military conflicts only when necessary. He had his work cut out for him, as the Athenians grew increasingly belligerent, and the activities of the Aetolian and Achaean (in the Peloponnese) leagues threatened stability. To protect himself, Antigonus allied himself to the powerful

---

[69] Tarn 1913, pp. 309–310; Habicht 1994b, p. 243.
[70] Justin 24.1.2, 7; see too Dreyer 1999, pp. 167–174.
[71] *IG* ii³ 1, 1009, with Ferguson 1911, pp. 160–163.
[72] Habicht 1979, pp. 68 and 108; Garland 1987, p. 51.

Seleucid dynasty in the same year he declared himself king (276), in the process marrying Antiochus I's half-sister, Phila.[73]

Against this background, it is not surprising to see the rise of Athenian politicians who were not enamored with the city's neutral relationship with Macedonia and despised having to live with a garrison in the Piraeus. One of these was Laches, the son of Demochares, who had played a role in the movement against Poliorcetes in 287 and who some years later, in 271/0, honored his father for his patriotism.[74] Then in 270/69 Callias of Sphettus and in 255/4 his brother Phaedrus were awarded honors for fighting against Poliorcetes in 287. Significantly, Callias' decree spoke of Ptolemy the king, but did not do the same for Antigonus' father, which Shear sees as a "sign of deliberate hostility and disrespect on the part of the Athenian nationalists."[75]

And then there were the idealists, so out of touch with reality that they believed in the likelihood of returning to the ancestral constitution. One such was Chremonides, the son of Eteocles of Aethalidae, who came from a wealthy and influential family and who had also studied under Zeno.[76] His elder brother Glaucon was an Olympic winner; another brother was a *hierophantes* (chief priest in the Eleusinian Mysteries), and his sister Pheidostrate had been priestess of the oath goddess Aglaurus. Like all priests and priestesses, they were thus highly regarded in Athenian society.[77] It was Chremonides, whose decree we have that urged the Athenians to go to war, who severed the uneasy peace between Athens and Antigonus in 268.

The Chremonidean War

No one could accuse the Athenians of ignoring any opportunity, no matter how improbable, to return to their ancestral freedom and glory. Their resilience is striking, but we should not expect any less when we consider their history—during the Peloponnesian War, for example, they had suffered a devastating plague, wiping out one-quarter of the population, but within a decade had bounced back; or after losing everything in that war they had put together another empire in less than three decades. Throughout the era of Macedonian and later Roman rule, the Athenians were always

---

[73] Justin 25.1.1, with Tarn 1913, pp. 168 and 175–176; Gabbert 1997, p. 4.
[74] Laches: Davies 1971, p. 142.
[75] T. L. Shear 1978, p. 17.
[76] Ferguson 1911, p. 157; Habicht 1997a, p. 140; Bayliss 2011, pp. 109–112.
[77] See Lambert 2012; cf. Perrin-Saminadayar 2012.

going to fight for their freedom. We are reminded of Chairippus' epitaph, one of the soldiers who died in 281 attempting to retake the Piraeus, "while beating back the days of slavery for his beloved country" (p. 101). His spirit pervades Hellenistic Athens: it is seen in the message of hope and pride in Demochares' decree for Demosthenes' posthumous honors, and is even more praiseworthy, given the city's weak military condition—a stark contrast to its military power in the Classical period. Worse still, the Athenians may have been bereft of allies, for although those named in Chremonides' decree were said to be Spartan and Athenian allies, they were really allied to Sparta.[78] Not that that stopped Athens proudly declaring war.

The Chremonidean War is perhaps a misnomer, the result of giving Chremonides too much credit—and perhaps even of exaggerating Athens' role in a conflict largely involving Ptolemaic and Antigonid power.[79] We, however, are only occupied with Athens' defiance of Antigonus as a sign of its love of freedom and pride. Our two literary sources for the war (Pausanias and Justin) give us only the barest outline of its events, but fortunately we have Chremonides' decree urging war on Antigonus of 269/8 (archonship of Peithidemus); although fragmentary, it gives us additional information on the war's causes and events.[80]

The Athenians were debating whether to join with Sparta and Ptolemy II against Antigonus, for Chremonides' decree makes it clear that Ptolemy "in accordance with the policy of his ancestors and his sister" wanted to champion the cause of Greek freedom.[81] One would think that the Athenians,

---

[78] *IG* ii³ 1, 912, line 7 (previous alliance with Sparta), evocation of Persian Wars and influence of Sparta: O'Neil 2008, pp. 66–68.

[79] See, for example, Luraghi 2018, pp. 23–26, citing bibliography; see too pp. 36–41. On the war, see Ferguson 1911, pp. 176–182; Tarn 1913, pp. 295–310; Walbank 1984b, pp. 236–243; Hammond and Walbank 1988, pp. 280–289; Gabbert 1997, pp. 45–53 (outbreak in 264); see too Gabbert 1987; O'Neil 2008.

[80] *IG* ii³ 1, 912, *SIG* 434/5 (= Burstein 1985, no. 56, pp. 77–80; M. M. Austin 2006, no. 61, pp. 130–133, as ii² 687+686); Pausanias 1.7.3, 3.6.4–6; Justin 26.2, with Tarn 1913, pp. 293–297; Habicht 1979, pp. 108–112. Causes: Ferguson 1911, pp. 170–171; Hammond and Walbank 1988, pp. 276–289; Gabbert 1997, pp. 45–53; Habicht 1997a, pp. 142–149; Scholten 2003, pp. 145–148; Luraghi 2018, pp. 23–26 and 36–41. Peithidemus' archonship is commonly accepted as this year, but see Dreyer 1999, pp. 291–301, for redating it during the war to 265/4—which causes him to redate (against common opinion) the Chremonides decree to the same year: Dreyer 1999, pp. 331–341.

[81] *IG* ii³ 1, 912, lines 16–18. The plural "ancestors" will be his father Ptolemy I, who had intervened in Greek affairs several times, and perhaps also his mother; Ptolemy I and Greece: Worthington 2016, pp. 147–154 and 177.

and the Greeks too for that matter, would have learned by now not to fall for the slogan of Greek freedom again, but the carrot was too much, and the Athenians went for it: in the fall of 268 they allied to Sparta.[82] To cement the alliance they swore an oath by a number of gods, including Ares and Athena Areia, "the Athenian military deities par excellence," showing they anticipated war.[83]

Greek freedom of course was hardly at the heart of Ptolemy's thinking. He was simply exploiting that term to get what he wanted: the removal of Antigonus, who was firmly in control of Macedonia and Greece, including the strategically important "fetters" (the key strategic towns of Demetrias, Chalcis, and Corinth, by which he could control Greece), and who had been rebuilding Antigonid ascendancy over the Aegean, in the process threatening Ptolemaic naval expansion.[84] Here, Arsinoe, Ptolemy's older sister and by now his wife, makes an entrance—their union (for which he was dubbed Philadelphus or "lover of his sister"), incidentally, kick-started the Ptolemaic practice of brother–sister marriage. Now the two of them plotted to install Arsinoe's son (Ptolemy) from her previous marriage to Lysimachus on the Macedonian throne while inciting a Greek revolt against Antigonus.[85] To this end, Ptolemy allied to Areus, king of Sparta, who was always looking to expand his influence in the Peloponnese, while continuing to woo Athens with gifts of grain and appeals to traditionalists like Chremonides. With a Macedonian garrison in the Piraeus, Ptolemy knew the lure of recovering the port would prove irresistible.[86]

Arsinoe had died by July 268 (before the passage of Chremonides' decree).[87] Nonetheless, Ptolemy persevered with their plan.[88] At first sight

---

[82] Outbreak in 268: Grieb 2008, pp. 88–89; O'Neil 2008, pp. 68–71; cf. Osborne 2009, p. 89 with n. 27; Osborne 2012, pp. 49–50, 68–69 (but on pp. 127–129 dated to 265). Dreyer 1999, pp. 276, 287–288, and 301, and Gabbert 1987, pp. 230–235, still argue for 265/4.

[83] Mikalson 1998, pp. 138–139.

[84] Merker 1970; Gabbert 1997, pp. 45–46; and Marquaille 2008, pp. 47–48 especially. See Walbank 1982 on Antigonid naval policy from the time of Poliorcetes to Philip V (pp. 216–223 on Gonatas). Comments on Antigonus' fleet: Tarn 1913, pp. 340–346.

[85] On Arsinoe, see Burstein 1982; Hauben 1983; and generally Carney 2013.

[86] Habicht 1979, pp. 108–109, on exploiting the garrison's presence. Athens and need for grain: G. J. Oliver 2007a, pp. 127–131, especially.

[87] Habicht 1992, p. 72; O'Neil 2008, pp. 68–71, citing bibliography on the date of her death (p. 68 n. 11).

[88] Tarn 1913, pp. 290–293; Hauben 1983, pp. 114–119. Note the caution of Hammond and Walbank 1988, pp. 278–279.

the coalition of Athens, Sparta, and Egypt, supported by other states such as Elis, Achaea, Tegea, Mantinea, and Orchomenus, presented no small threat to Antigonus; his rapid response, however (faster probably than his opponents expected), shows that he had been expecting this situation—hardly a surprise, for Athens' contacts with the Ptolemies could scarcely have been a secret.

According to a decree of 268/7 from Rhamnus, Ptolemy's commander Patroclus and a contingent of troops sailed to Attica, intent on rendezvousing with Areus and attacking Antigonus. Patroclus set up a base on the island of Gardonisi (close to Sunium), though archaeological evidence has revealed other possible sites, including at Coroni, between Rhamnus and Sunium.[89] Patroclus' plan was for Areus and Spartan troops to confront Antigonus frontally, while he and his men would either attack him from the rear or restrict themselves to fighting at sea.[90] But thanks to Antigonus' control of Corinth, Areus was blocked three successive times from leaving the Peloponnese with his army (the summers of 267, 266, and 265); in that last year, he was defeated and killed by Antigonus close to Corinth.[91] Any hostile cities in the Peloponnese then declared for the king, who moved to besiege Athens.

With no support from Sparta, and Patroclus unable to land in the Macedonian-controlled Piraeus, the Athenians nevertheless held out against Antigonus. We do not know much about the city's fortifications at this time, but evidently they were enough to ward off the attackers.[92] In a decree of 267/6 from Eleusis, Athenian soldiers there honored Dion, the secretary of the grain treasurers, which must mean that that fortress was still in Athenian hands.[93] A decree of 266/5 (archonship of Nicias) bestows a formal vote of thanks and gold crowns on the previous year's ephebes for the way they "all held their ground, keeping good order, and obeying the laws and the *kosmetes*, and continued throughout the year to perform guard duties and all the instructions given by the general and for guarding the Museum, as ordered by the people."[94] The wording echoes the annual oath of new

---

[89] Vanderpool, McCredie, and Steinberg 1962; Vanderpool 1964; Habicht 1997a, pp. 144–145; O'Neil 2008, pp. 74–75; cf. Hammond and Walbank 1988, p. 283.
[90] Gabbert 1997, p. 47.
[91] Hammond and Walbank 1988, pp. 280–282; on Areus' campaigns, see too O'Neil 2008, pp. 78–83.
[92] Theocharaki 2011, p. 126.
[93] *IG* ii² 1272, *SIG*³ 947.
[94] *IG* ii³ 1, 917, lines 9–13 (= M. M. Austin 2006, no. 136, pp. 251–252 as ii² 665; trans. Austin). The inscription is heavily restored; it is the first ephebic inscription since 303;

ephebes, but as well as congratulating them for performing their duties, the decree suggests that they were involved in operations at the Museum. What was a major worry for the people was invading troops damaging their grain harvest, evidenced in a decree of the same year calling for the normal annual sacrifice by the eponymous archon for the welfare of Boule and the people, and unusually, of sacrifices "for the safety of the crops in the countryside."[95]

In 262 Antigonus was forced to return to his kingdom, where Pyrrhus' son and successor, Alexander II, had been continuing his father's war against him by invading Macedonia. Antigonus eventually expelled him from Macedonia, and later from Epirus itself.[96] Since the Athenians felt sufficiently safe to sow their grain crop at this time, the king may have made some sort of pact with them before he went after Alexander.[97] But once he had dealt with him he was back, crucially just as the grain crop was almost ready to be harvested, which his troops devastated. The king might have expected a cavalry attack to try to save the crops because he destroyed the grove and temple of Poseidon Hippios ("Lord of Horses"), the cavalry headquarters by the Academy.[98] Another famine gripped the city, and in the spring of 261 the Athenians had no choice but to surrender. The Chremonidean War ended in Athens' total defeat and the imposition of a Macedonian garrison in the city.[99]

The situation on the mainland at the end of the war has been likened to a cold peace, with Antigonus clearly the dominant player.[100] Stoic believer in the equality of mankind or not, at the end of the day he could not allow

---

for a collection of fourth-century decrees, see Reinmuth 1971, and especially Friend 2019. The honors bestowed on these ephebes set a trend for ephebes in future years: Perrin-Saminadayar 2007a, pp. 56–57.

[95] *IG* ii³ 1, 920, lines 8–10. The decree from Rhamnus, cited above, speaks of the general Epichares, who was in charge of the fortress of Rhamnus, protecting the farmers of the coast district as they harvested their crops. Grain in rural Attica and impact of war in the countryside on the food supply: G. J. Oliver 2007a, pp. 68–73 and 113–137.

[96] It is possible that Antigonus used his son, the future Demetrius II, in the campaign, despite his young age: Hammond and Walbank 1988, p. 285 n. 6.

[97] Polyaenus 4.6.20, with O'Neil 2008, pp. 82–83.

[98] Pausanias 1.30.4.

[99] Pausanias 3.6.6; Polyaenus 4.6.20; Apollodorus, *BNJ* 244 F 44, with the commentary of M. Williams, *ad loc.*; see too Hammond and Walbank 1988, p. 286 n. 3; O'Neil 2008, pp. 85–86; cf. Habicht 2003, pp. 53–54.

[100] Scholten 2003, p. 148.

Athens to remain independent—"it was not the time for clemency," as W. S. Ferguson so aptly states.[101]

"The Will of One Man"

Antigonus needed to safeguard himself from future revolt. Therefore, he resorted to a series of punitive measures, details for which are found in a single fragment surviving from a chronicle of world history by the second-century scholar and historian Apollodorus.[102] According to this source, Antigonus installed a garrison on the Museum, "stopped" the archons, and had everything done by "the will of one man." To these acts we can add shoring up the garrison in the Piraeus, taking control of all Attic forts, a possible check on the powers of the hoplite general, and perhaps taking possession of the islands of Lemnos and Imbros.[103] But there are problems with Apollodorus' information, for Antigonus did not install a pro-Macedonian oligarchy or abolish all public officials (according to the quotations above)— he may have directed archon elections and suspended the secretary cycles for a time, but the decree in honor of Zeno of 261 (mentioned earlier) attests to the continued workings of the Assembly.[104]

More importantly, if we follow Apollodorus on Antigonus' putting affairs in the hands of one man, presumably a governor, who was he? A passage in a later historian named Hegesander may point to the grandson and namesake of Demetrius of Phalerum.[105] This man had been summoned before the Areopagus because of his offensive lifestyle, which included building a

---

[101] Ferguson 1911, p. 182; see too Tarn 1913, p. 306; Walbank 1984b, pp. 240–241.
[102] Apollodorus, *BNJ* 244 F 44 with the commentary of M. Williams, *ad loc*.; cf. Pausanias 3.6.6, with Ferguson 1911, pp. 182–185; Tarn 1913, pp. 306–308; Pouilloux 1946; Habicht 1982, pp. 15–19; Habicht 1997a, pp. 150–172; with Habicht 2003 (modifying his views on the number of Attic forts under Macedonian control and the name of the governor; see below). On Apollodorus see the biographical essay by M. Williams in *BNJ* 244; cf. Habicht 1997a, pp. 119–121.
[103] Habicht 1982, pp. 43–63; cf. Tracy 2004, pp. 208–209, on suspending the *ephebeia*.
[104] Osborne 2012, pp. 50–51, citing bibliography; on secretaries, see pp. 74–86, 119–124; Habicht 1997a, p. 151; Habicht 1982, pp. 20–26. It may have been at this time, in tandem with these Antigonid officials, that the hoplite generalship was abandoned since no inscriptional evidence exists for this position until 229: Habicht 1982, pp. 44–47; Geagan 1997, pp. 21–22.
[105] Athenaeus 4.167e-f, with Ferguson 1911, p. 183; Habicht 1982, pp. 18–20 and 54; Tracy 1995, pp. 43–44 and 171–174; Habicht 1997a, pp. 151–154. *IG* ii³ 4, 281 appears to support the claim as this is an honorary statue set up to Demetrius the grandson at Eleusis.

viewing stand for his mistress Aristagora of Corinth for the cavalry parade (when he was cavalry commander) during the Panathenaea; since it was taller than the nearby *hermai* (quadrangular pillars with the head of a god, usually Hermes, on top and the male genitalia carved below), his gesture for her was sacrilegious. Demetrius delivered an aggressive defense speech before the Areopagus and was acquitted, impressing Antigonus.

Demetrius the grandson, however, was too young to have been governor, as his military career was only starting its upward trajectory in 256.[106] Another candidate may have been Apollodorus of Otryne, who was appointed by the king and the people to the important position of General of the Coastal Region, thereby showing the king interfering in the selection process.[107] Then again, since Antigonus had just ended the Chremonidean War, this was not the time for constitutional niceties. The existence of a governor, however, has been doubted; it makes more sense for Apollodorus' statement simply to mean it was Antigonus himself who had the final say in Athenian affairs.

Since the city did not mint silver coins for a time, it has often been supposed that Antigonus took away Athens' right to issue its own silver coinage, replacing the famous Owls (the symbol of Athena) with the Macedonian tetradrachms (4-drachma coin) or "Antigonids."[108] This action would have been a blow to nationalistic pride and the Athenian economy, yet—if Antigonus were responsible for this—it may not have been a punitive measure but to do with a shortage of silver from decreased production at the Laurium mines.[109] In any case, the Athenians had no need to mint their own coins, given the large number of Macedonian ones in circulation in the city over the next years.[110] On the other hand, it has been argued that the Athenians' silver coinage came to an end not in 262 but at least three decades earlier, and further, that the only Hellenistic kings to interfere in local currencies were the Ptolemies and Seleucids from the second century onward.[111] Still, the abandonment of the Athenian style of silver coinage under Antigonus was the result of a general decline that the city suffered

---

[106] Habicht 2003, pp. 53–54, citing bibliography; cf. Tracy 2003, pp. 56–57.
[107] *ISE* 22 (= Burstein 1985, no. 61, p. 83); note the caution of Tracy 2003, p. 56.
[108] Ferguson 1911, p. 184; Tarn 1913, p. 308; Habicht 1982, pp. 34–47; Walbank 1984b, p. 240; Hammond and Walbank 1988, pp. 286–287; Lönnqvist 1997.
[109] Day 1942, pp. 4–6; Habicht 1982, pp. 34–42; Habicht 1997a, p. 155.
[110] Lönnqvist 1997.
[111] G. J. Oliver 2001; Kroll 2003.

for much of the third century under Macedonian rule, which we may trace back to Poliorcetes' devastation of the countryside and mining interests there in 295.[112]

After the end of the war, Chremonides and his brother Glaucon fled to Ptolemy's court. Other opponents of Antigonus were executed, including Philochorus, the last of several "Atthidographers" or writers of Athenian histories from mythical times to their present day. Philochorus had been born in 340 and had seen a lot in his long life, but his apparent sympathetic view of Ptolemy II led to his death.[113] Demochares had died some time previously, so only the elderly Phaedrus of Sphettus remained in Athens, a sterling example of a politician who cannily knew that the key to a long life was to get along with everyone. He was honored for his long and generous political career in perhaps 255, though it is significant that the initiative came from him.[114]

It cannot be denied that the deaths of men such as Zeno and Philochorus decimated intellectual life in the city, causing Athens to suffer a cultural as well as a military fall.[115] The passing of another literary writer at this time also deserves mention for its symbolism with Athens' own demise. This was the New Comedy playwright Philemon, who had won more victories than his younger contemporary Menander. The story goes that Philemon, who was now almost one hundred years old, saw nine girls leaving his house the night before he died.[116] They were the Muses, said to flee from any association with death—they were leaving not only his house but also, symbolically, the city, where they had lived for the past two centuries.

---

[112] Day 1942, pp. 3–28.
[113] See the biographical essay by N. Jones in Philochorus, *BNJ* 328; cf. Habicht 1997a, pp. 116–117.
[114] *IG* ii³ 1, 985; see too Ferguson 1911, pp. 171–173.
[115] Hammond and Walbank 1988, p. 287; Habicht 1997a, p. 142.
[116] *Suda*, s.v. Philemon.

6

Independence Day

ANTIGONUS II KEPT ATHENS FIRMLY in his grasp, paring back the city's already reduced military strength with another reduction in the number of ephebes to between twenty and forty per year and the cavalry corps back down to two hundred, while the Assembly passed decrees only on routine matters, and then on his orders or those of his lackeys. Well might it appear, as at least one modern scholar once thought, that the Chremonidean War was the death knell for Athens militarily and economically.[1] Yet within several years Athens was regaining some freedom and seeing an increase in its economy, and in 229 it even regained independence. Once again, the people's resilience drives the history of their city.

Divine Honors and the End of Antigonus Gonatas

Antigonus often went to Athens, which is not surprising since he had spent a lot of time there in his youth and studied under Zeno. He may even have fathered a son with an Athenian courtesan named Demo (although the Antigonus who is spoken of in this anecdote may have been Monophthalmus).[2] When he visited the city many Athenians paid him their respects, with the notable exception of Arcesilaus, the sixth Head of the

---

[1] Gomme 1937, p. 223.
[2] Athenaeus 13.578a.

Academy, who had made it the leading school of Athens again.³ His decision to rebuff Antigonus was as philosophical as it was political: although he left no writings, he was said to have been a proponent of academic skepticism, arguing that all ideas and theories were untrue and that knowledge of anything does not exist. His views diametrically opposed stoics like Antigonus, who believed that a person could have knowledge of things.⁴ Arcesilaus also saw himself as a patriot and his school a place of liberty, so Macedonian rule was not something he tolerated.

Still, Antigonus continued to show his benevolence to the city. In 256, in response to an Athenian appeal, he withdrew the garrison from the Museum (but kept that at the Piraeus), and returned to the people all of the Attic forts except at Salamis and Sunium, and even the islands of Lemnos and Imbros.⁵ Why he did so is best explained by dating his naval victory over Ptolemy off the island of Cos to 256.⁶ The date of this battle, which robbed Ptolemy of his hegemony in the Aegean, is controversial, as it took place in the period 261 to 256. The earlier date, at the tail end of the Chremonidean War, may explain why Ptolemy gave so little support to his general Patroclus in Greece (p. 120).⁷ However, the later dating would explain the king's present magnanimity toward the Athenians.⁸

Nevertheless, Athens was still helpless. Antigonus controlled several forts, along with the fetters of Greece, and he kept a tight rein on the city's foreign policy.⁹ Although public officials were supposedly elected by lot, Antigonus appointed his own supporters to all posts, men such as Thymochares (257/6), Callimedes (252/1), Theophemus (247/6), and Eurycleides (243/2), all from the upper stratum of society.¹⁰ Eurycleides had been a state treasurer in

---

³ Diogenes Laertius 4.39 (4.28–45 for a brief life of him), with Tarn 1913, pp. 332–335; on philosophical schools in this era, see Habicht 1994b.
⁴ Ferguson 1911, p. 234.
⁵ Tarn 1913, pp. 327–328; Gabbert 1997, pp. 38–41; G. J. Oliver 2001, pp. 35–52; Habicht 2003, pp. 52–53; Grieb 2008, pp. 92–94; Osborne 2012, p. 24. Lemnos and Imbros: Tracy 2003, p. 58. See Tracy 2004, pp. 208–209, on reintroducing the *ephebeia*.
⁶ [Plutarch], *Moralia* 183c, 545b; Athenaeus 5.209e.
⁷ O'Neil 2008, pp. 84–85, 87–89. Pausanias 1.7.3 speaks of Ptolemy's assistance as minor.
⁸ Dating in favor of 256: Hammond and Walbank 1988, pp. 291–292 and 595–600. For the earlier dating, see Walbank 1982, pp. 219–223 (noting that Egypt still continued to dominate the Aegean); Reger 1985.
⁹ Ferguson 1911, pp. 191–192; Habicht 1982, pp. 20–26; Habicht 1997a, pp. 158–159; Kralli 2003, p. 63; Tracy 2003, pp. 58–60; Grieb 2008, pp. 95–97.
¹⁰ Ferguson 1911, pp. 288–289; MacKendrick 1969, pp. 39–47; Habicht 1982, pp. 179–182 (Eurycleides and Micion), and see pp. 178–197 on a selection of powerful families in

248 and was later a hoplite general. He had spent much of his own money on civic affairs, especially festivals, and along with his brother Micion sponsored a number of religious and cultural changes—his piety was apparently so great that he could not handle jokes about the Eleusinian Mysteries.[11] The two brothers came to dominate Athenian policy.[12]

The Athenians also had to support Antigonus militarily—probably not in his naval operations, but certainly on land.[13] Thus in 251 he used Athenian troops against his nephew Alexander, whom he had made governor of Corinth and Euboea, and Aratus of Sicyon.[14] Alexander had overstepped the mark when he declared himself king and, perhaps with Egyptian support, was poised to win over several Peloponnesian cities from their tyrant rulers. When Aratus of Sicyon overthrew its tyrant, the Achaean League threw its weight behind Alexander in Corinth, forcing Antigonus to go on the attack. In retaliation for the Athenians supporting the Macedonian king, Alexander's men invaded Attica; for four years they threatened the countryside until Antigonus drove them back, with Alexander dying shortly afterward.[15] At that time Antigonus retook Corinth—apparently while most of the guard were distracted at a wedding he had arranged between his son Demetrius and Nicaea, the widow of Alexander of Corinth, he simply walked up the steep hill to the citadel of Acrocorinth and demanded admission![16]

Aratus was determined to increase the role of the Achaean League in Peloponnesian and greater Greek affairs, and to this end he dictated the history of this period for the next two decades.[17] Elected general of the league, he was a formidable foe in the field, yet was the butt of many jokes about his physical stamina—how he suffered terrible bouts of incontinence before every battle, felt faint, and even asked if he had to stay for the fight, with his

---

Athenian politics into the early second century. Archonships of these men: Osborne 2009, pp. 90–91.

[11] Clinton 1974, pp. 21–22.
[12] Cf. Day 1942, pp. 14–15; MacKendrick 1969, pp. 39–43.
[13] Hammond and Walbank 1988, pp. 293–295, on Antigonus' naval operations in this period.
[14] Historical background: Tarn 1913, pp. 359–364; Hammond and Walbank 1988, pp. 296–307; Gabbert 1997, pp. 54–57 (in 252); on the date, cf. Habicht 1997a, p. 162.
[15] Tarn 1913, pp. 370–371.
[16] Plutarch, *Aratus* 17.2–5; Polyaenus 4.6.1, with Tarn 1913, pp. 372–373; Hammond and Walbank 1988, p. 305. Ferguson 1911, p. 196, calls the wedding a "fake marriage fete."
[17] On the resilient and indefatigable Aratus, see Walbank 1933. Rise of the Achaean League: Polybius 2.37.7–44 (= M. M. Austin 2006, no. 67, pp. 141–145 abridged).

name becoming a byword for good generalship and at the same time cowardice.[18] In 243 he defeated the Macedonian garrison on Acrocorinth and overran Corinth; its governor either committed suicide or fled.[19] More cities joined the league, extending it geographically to Attica and impacting the Aetolians' ambition to expand in the Peloponnese.

The following year (242) Aratus marched into Attica, presumably expecting the Athenians would seize the opportunity to throw off Macedonian rule. They did not, so he launched an attack on Salamis.[20] He likely saw that island as a base for the Egyptian fleet, for he had recently allied with Ptolemy III (who had become king on Ptolemy II's death in 246), leaving Antigonus no choice but to ally with the league's enemy the Aetolians, now with most of central Greece under their sway.[21] In the spring of 241 an Aetolian army invaded the Peloponnese, but Aratus defeated it; he tried unsuccessfully to take Athens and the Piraeus, but despite releasing Athenian captives from Salamis without ransom, and his offer of support against Antigonus, the city never joined the Achaean League.[22]

In 240/39, aged eighty, Antigonus II Gonatas died—remarkably for that period—in his sleep.[23] He had been "a Macedonian ruling Macedonians," and despite his stoic pretensions well understood the reality of the new world order of the Successor kingdoms.[24] His much-needed long reign of almost forty years (276–239) unquestionably improved his kingdom as well as stabilized Macedonian mastery of Greece. That hegemony only came under threat in those final half-dozen years.

At some point the Athenians had decided to worship him, for a decree from Rhamnus speaks of sacrifices to him at its Nemesia festival and that the Athenians conferred *isotheoi timai* (honors equal to those paid to the gods) upon him as *soter* (savior) and *euergetes* (benefactor) of the people.[25]

---

[18] Plutarch, *Aratus* 29.5–6.
[19] Tarn 1913, pp. 396–399; Hammond and Walbank 1988, pp. 309–310.
[20] Plutarch, *Aratus* 24.3, with Ferguson 1911, p. 196. An epigram survives in honor of an Athenian youth named Leon, killed in battle there, encouraging his comrades to mirror his bravery: Habicht 1982, pp. 194–197; Habicht 1989, p. 16 with n. 49.
[21] Plutarch, *Aratus* 43.9.
[22] Captives: Plutarch, *Aratus* 24.3. Attica: Plutarch, *Aratus* 33.2–4. Historical background: Hammond and Walbank 1988, pp. 311–313; Scholten 2000, pp. 123–127.
[23] Date: Hammond and Walbank 1988, p. 313 n. 6.
[24] Quote: Green 1990, p. 198. Evaluation of his kingship: Tarn 1913, pp. 394–409; Hammond and Walbank 1988, pp. 313–316; Gabbert 1997, pp. 59–72.
[25] *SEG* 41.75, with Habicht 1997a, p. 165 with bibliography in n. 58; Habicht 1996a; Mikalson 1998, pp. 160–161; Kralli 2003.

However, Rhamnus may have been exceptional because it was a fortress outside the city and after 256 was occupied by a mixed garrison of Macedonian and Athenian soldiers.[26] Yet two inscriptions record that at least by the late 250s, the Athenians were sacrificing to him and his family as benefactors in conjunction with the health and well-being of the Boule and Assembly.[27]

How these decrees describe the sacrifices is important. One speaks of sacrifices to Dionysus and the other ancestral gods "for the health and safety of the Boule, the Demos of the Athenians, their children and wives, and on behalf of King Antigonus" (lines 6–11); the other of sacrifices to various gods "for the health and safety of the Boule, the Demos of the Athenians, their children and wives, and on behalf of King Antigonos and his queen Phile and their children" (lines 9–25). Unlike the decree from Rhamnus, however, these honors are not *to* Antigonos (as a deity) but for his services to the city; further, by including his family they show "a retreat from ruler cult" as "the kings and benefactors again became men, not deities."[28] Thus the Athenians' attitude to the divinity of rulers remained the same from the days of Monophthalmus and Poliorcetes.

When the Athenians began to include Antigonus and his family in their sacrifices is unknown. The earliest decree we have dates to 249/8, but earlier decrees could have been lost, and an argument has been made to date the Athenian and Rhamnus decrees to 245.[29] In that year the four-year revolt of Alexander came to an end, during which time all of Attica (including the crops) was threatened by his troops, and the loss of Chalcis (on Euboea) was a particular danger to Rhamnus.[30] In 248/7 (archonship of Diomedon) the Athenian general Archander managed to protect Rhamnus from Alexander's raids, while the fighting in Attica was such a drain on resources that the people resorted to an extraordinary levy of between 50 and 200 drachmas per citizen to protect the countryside.[31] It is hardly a surprise, then, that when Antigonus ended the revolt and brought peace to Attica, the relieved

---

[26] Habicht 1997a, p. 167.
[27] *IG* ii³ 1, 995 (252/1 or 251/0), *SEG* 33.115 (of 246/5?), with Habicht 1982, pp. 20–24; Mikalson 1998, pp. 160–161.
[28] Mikalson 1998, p. 161.
[29] Habicht 1982, pp. 26–33; Kralli 2003, pp. 64–66.
[30] Importance of Attic crops: G. J. Oliver 2007a, pp. 68–73; see too generally pp. 113–137; see his tables listing the contributors to the *epidosis* and regional representation in it: pp. 277–284.
[31] Dating: Osborne 2003, pp. 69–70, and Osborne 2009, pp. 91–92; importance of harvest time: G. J. Oliver 2007a, pp. 132–133 and 200–204.

Athenians afforded him honors as a savior and benefactor, and an equally relieved Rhamnus added his name to its festival. By extension, the decree shows us yet again the paramount importance of the crops.

Demetrius II and Antigonus III

Antigonus' son Demetrius, now in his mid-thirties, succeeded him, ruling Macedonia from 239 to 229.[32] In 239 Demetrius II married Phthia (daughter of Alexander of Epirus), binding him closer to Epirus, and the following year they had a son, the future Philip V—naming the boy "Philip" was deliberate and would not have been lost on Macedonians.[33] The Athenians had no choice but to pledge their allegiance to Demetrius; although he may have had concerns about their loyalty, given Aratus' raids into Attica, they were not in a position to resist him, especially while Macedonian troops garrisoned the Piraeus. But more pressing for him was the fact that his strategic bond with Epirus likely prompted the Achaean League to ally with its former enemy the Aetolian League—yet another instance of that most uniform thread in Greek history, "the enemy of my enemy is my friend"—and declare war on him.[34] Breaking out in 238/7, the war lasted Demetrius' entire reign, and earned him the nickname *o Aitolikos* ("the Aetolian-fighter"), thanks to the constant opposition of the Aetolians.[35]

Demetrius received support from his father-in-law the king of Epirus, and in 236 he invaded Boeotia, which had been intriguing with the Aetolians since 245.[36] Boeotia immediately allied to him, thereby robbing the league of a powerful ally and shoring up Attica's northern border. He returned Eleusis, Panactum, and Phyle to Athens, perhaps as part of a policy of using the city to protect his interests to his south.[37] Suspecting another invasion or even a siege, the Athenian general Aristophanes of Leuconoe immediately

---

[32] Walbank 1984c, pp. 446–453; Hammond and Walbank 1988, pp. 317–336 (see p. 317 n. 1 on the poor sources for the reign); Habicht 1997a, pp. 163–166; Scholten 2003, pp. 150–153; W. L. Adams 2010, pp. 222–223. Hammond and Walbank 1988, pp. 317–318, argue that Demetrius had been coregent with his father for the last few years.

[33] Justin 28.1.2. There is some dispute about Philip's mother, but in favor of her see LeBohec 1981.

[34] Alliance and chronology: Scholten 2000, pp. 144–157.

[35] Ehrhardt 1978. Outbreak in the archonship of Lysias (238/7): Osborne 2012, pp. 53–54.

[36] Dating: *IG* ii² 1299 (c. 234), with Habicht 1982, pp. 57–59; Hammond and Walbank 1988, pp. 326–327, and pp. 326–329 on the invasion.

[37] Cf. Ferguson 1911, p. 201.

repaired the walls to these fortresses and took measures to secure the safety of the grain in the countryside.[38] Even so, the people were not able to plant crops until Eurycleides used some of his own money to this end, thus giving the city a much-needed lifeline.[39]

Sometime between 235 and 232, Demetrius' general Bithys of Lysimacheia defeated Aratus and forced him to flee to Corinth to regroup.[40] When a rumor spread that Aratus had been killed, Diogenes, commander of the Piraeus garrison, sent a letter to the Achaeans demanding that they surrender Corinth, but his demand fell flat when his letter arrived and Aratus was very much alive.[41] Aratus at once invaded Attica, plundering crops in the Thriasian Plain and inflicting damage in the grounds of the Academy, although Athenian forces under Aristophanes kept him from the city itself.[42]

In the meantime, civil strife in Epirus had brought down the ruling house and robbed Demetrius of this valuable ally. He enlisted the help of Illyrians, bitter enemies of the Macedonians for centuries, who ruthlessly put down the civil war. But their ambitious queen, Teuta, who had come to power on the death of her husband Agron in 231, raided towns along the Adriatic coast, and, among other things, invaded the western Peloponnese.[43] Teuta wanted to make Illyria a major power in Greece, but her downfall came not at the hands of a Macedonian king, but of Rome, which went to war against her in 229—we will deal with this "First Illyrian War" in the next chapter, as we chart Rome's involvement in Greece.

In 229 the Dardanians, another Illyrian tribe, raided Macedonia. Demetrius led an army against them, but he was defeated and killed in battle. Macedonia was suddenly in chaos as his son and heir, Philip, was only eight or nine years old, and the Aetolians took advantage of the situation to seize Thessaly.[44] Undaunted, the Macedonian Assembly proclaimed Philip king, but arranged a regent for him, who was also to marry his mother

---

[38] *IG* ii² 1299, lines 65–66; cf. Osborne 1989, pp. 219–220.
[39] Information in a later decree honoring Eurycleides (c. 215): *IG* ii³ 1, 1160, lines 7–9, with Osborne 2012, p. 54.
[40] Location of the battle: Hammond and Walbank 1988, pp. 331–332 (who date it to 233/2).
[41] Plutarch, *Aratus* 34.1–2; Hammond and Walbank 1988, p. 332, doubt that this happened.
[42] Ferguson 1911, pp. 202–203.
[43] Polybius 2.6.1–10, 8.4–5, with Gruen 1984, pp. 363–364; Waterfield 2014, pp. 5–10.
[44] Scholten 2000, pp. 165–170. Age of Philip: Hammond and Walbank 1988, p. 336 n. 3.

(Demetrius II's widow) Phthia.⁴⁵ And so Antigonus Doson, nephew of Antigonus Gonatas, was appointed regent (*epitropos*) and general (*strategos*) of the Macedonian military, though as Polybius says, "he was the undisputed leader of Macedonia," and later he would be king.⁴⁶ What his nickname (*doson*) meant is unknown; Plutarch explains that "he was given to promising but did not perform his engagements," but in fact he was careful to discharge his duties, and since he had agreed that Philip would succeed him, it may mean "giver."⁴⁷

Antigonus III had a short but important reign for Macedonia (229–221), forcing back the Dardanians (his biggest threat), recovering all of Thessaly, and making a settlement with the Aetolian League.⁴⁸ Less positive was the loss of Athens, which on his father's death in 229 had finally reasserted its independence.

Free Again?

Eurycleides and Micion had appealed to Diogenes, the commander of the Piraeus garrison, to hand over the port and the other forts that were in Macedonian hands.⁴⁹ He was willing to do so, encouraged also, if we can believe Plutarch, by Aratus, who at the time was confined to a bed "from a long illness" and had to be carried to Athens.⁵⁰ But there was a catch: Diogenes demanded a fee of 150 talents, ostensibly to pay his men, but some of it must have been bribe money. The sum was an enormous one, which the Athenians raised by collecting an *epidosis* (an "extraordinary gift" from rich individuals to which cities at times resorted); Aratus apparently gave 20 talents, and some Boeotian towns and perhaps even Ptolemy III made donations.⁵¹ Aratus may have intended his money to coax Athens

---

⁴⁵ Plutarch, *Paullus* 8.2–3, speaks of "the leading Macedonians," i.e., the nobility, but it is hard to imagine a decision of this nature not being made by a formal Assembly. His wife was also supposed to have been named Chryseis, but this may have been a nickname for Phthia: Hammond and Walbank 1988, p. 338 n. 1, with sources.

⁴⁶ *Epitropos* (guardian): Polybius 2.45.2; Justin 28.3.10; *epitropos* and *strategos*, then king: Plutarch, *Paullus* 8.3.

⁴⁷ That is the future participle of the Greek verb *didomi* (I give): Green 1990, p. 255. Plutarch's explanation is at *Paullus* 8.3.

⁴⁸ Walbank 1940, pp. 9–23; Walbank 1984c, pp. 453–473; Hammond and Walbank 1988, pp. 337–364; LeBohec 1993; sources: Hammond and Walbank 1988, p. 336 n. 1.

⁴⁹ Ferguson 1911, pp. 205–206; Habicht 1982, pp. 79–83; see too Habicht 2003, pp. 52–53.

⁵⁰ Plutarch, *Aratus* 34.4.

⁵¹ Plutarch, *Aratus* 34.4; Pausanias 2.8.6, with Ferguson 1911, p. 207; Migeotte 1989.

over to the Achaean League but Eurycleides and Micion were having none of that: they stayed aloof of the league, although they did keep his money.⁵²

Regardless of the controversies associated with the chronology of these decades and the uncertainty of some archon years, no one can deny that the year 229 was a watershed one for the Athenians. They had regained their independence, all forts were under their control, and the city and the harbor were finally reunited after over half a century of separation. Well might this situation have seemed like a restoration of their status quo—presumably why they started a new list of names of their eponymous archons, something they did when they believed they were at the start of a new epoch. They also began to strike their own coinage again and exploited their mines more aggressively. As a result, after a lengthy decline throughout the third century, commerce picked up as the Piraeus was again open to all Athenians, and the city prospered substantially down to the second half of the next century.⁵³ Imports increased, such as wine from the Aegean and Asia Minor; grain, hemp, and fish from the Black Sea; and luxury items including perfumes from Syria and papyrus from Egypt, while the city continued its staple exports of pottery, olive oil, figs, and Attic honey.⁵⁴

Free from Macedonia, the Athenians believed, according to Polybius, "that their liberty was now firmly secure again."⁵⁵ Their reaction to Diogenes' return of the Piraeus supports this view and speaks volumes about their attitude to Macedonian hegemony and desire to return to their former democracy. They lavished honors on him, including citizenship, a festival to him (the *Diogeneia*), a gymnasium for the ephebes named after him (the *Diogeneion*), and reserved a seat for him at the theater of Dionysus.⁵⁶ The *Diogeneia* was still going strong a century later, showing his stature as one of Athens' important saviors and benefactors.⁵⁷ By contrast, the people deliberately removed all references to any Macedonian king and his family in their public prayers, sacrifices, and state decrees—by 225 even the sacrifices to Antigonus as part of the Nemesia festival at Rhamnus had ended.⁵⁸

---

⁵² Polybius 5.106.6; cf. Plutarch, *Aratus* 41.2.
⁵³ Ferguson 1911, pp. 246–248; Piraeus: Garland 1987, pp. 58–72; prosperity: Perrin 1996.
⁵⁴ Day 1942, pp. 19–22; cf. pp. 96–104 (second century).
⁵⁵ Polybius 5.106.6.
⁵⁶ *IG* ii² 3474, with Habicht 1982, pp. 83–84.
⁵⁷ *IG* ii² 1011, line 41, 1028, line 24, 1029, line 55, 1078, with Habicht 1982, pp. 83–84.
⁵⁸ *ISE* 29, lines 16–18 of 225/4 with no reference to Antigonus.

Eurycleides and Micion were the most influential men in political life for the next three decades. They carefully guided the city down a neutral path in Greek and foreign affairs, as well as maintained a close association with Ptolemaic Egypt, for which they deserve credit.[59] They revised the laws and, celebrating the city's newfound independence, introduced religious measures, including a shrine northwest of the Agora to Demus (the personification of the Athenian people) and the *Charites* or "Graces" (the three daughters of Zeus and Eurynome, the goddesses of charm, beauty, fertility, and creativity). The *Charites* were invoked on the oath of the ephebes, presumably indicating they were charged with the welfare of young people as the best guarantee for the well-being of the state.[60] This was likely the first state cult since that to Poliorcetes, and so again indicative of a belief in a new era.[61] Although a shrine was never built, a priesthood was established— always held by one of their family members, its importance is shown by the priest having a reserved front seat in the theater of Dionysus.[62]

Nor did the brothers ignore Athens' defenses, for there was always the chance that Antigonus III or even the aged Aratus might reappear on the scene. They repaired the city's fortification wall and strengthened the Piraeus and various frontier forts, especially Rhamnus, but they paid no attention to the ruined Long Walls. Since the mid-fifth century these walls had connected Athens to the Piraeus and were an integral part of the defense system, as they offered protection for getting supplies into the city and for troops and rowers making their way to the fleet. Presumably their disregard was because of finances and of the city no longer being a naval power.

For all the desperation to reunite Athens and the Piraeus, the Athenians seemed unconcerned about the original functions of the Long Walls.[63] Still, they made sure they did not antagonize Antigonus, tasking Prytanis

---

[59] Ferguson 1911, pp. 208–221 and 252–253, especially pp. 237–257; Grieb 2008, pp. 99–107 and 110–113; Athens and Ptolemy: Habicht 1982, pp. 105–112; Neutrality: Habicht 1982, pp. 127–142.

[60] Habicht 1997a, p. 181.

[61] Mikalson 1998, p. 173, and see pp. 172–178 on the cult, with Habicht 1982, pp. 84–96; Habicht 1997a, pp. 180–182; Grieb 2008, pp. 107–110; cf. Thompson and Wycherley 1972, pp. 159–160 and 223; Grijalvo 2005, pp. 269–270. The location of the cult was deliberate and reflected the Athenians' devotion of space in the Agora to promoting their gods and religion: Dickenson 2017, pp. 97–109.

[62] Priesthood: Habicht 1982, pp. 84–96; seat: *IG* ii² 5029a and 5047.

[63] Garland 1987, p. 53. On the building of the walls to link city to port: Garland 1987, pp. 22–28; see too Theocharaki 2011, p. 126.

of Carystus, an Aristotelian philosopher whom the king held in high regard, with a mission to stress their friendship to Macedonia in 226. Prytanis was part of the trend of philosophers heading diplomatic missions that had started with Xenocrates to Antipater in 322 (p. 26). But a major reason for Prytanis' selection was his ability (like many of the others) to pay his own expenses, for which he was awarded honors (a golden wreath and public naming at the Dionysia).[64] Since Antigonus took no action against the city, we may presume he accepted its people as friends.

Our chief source for the middle to later Hellenistic era and especially Rome's intervention in the eastern Mediterranean is Polybius, who wrote when his native Greece was part of the Roman Empire.[65] Polybius does not hold back in his criticism of Eurycleides and Micion for their pacifist policy and courtship of Egypt. He claims that because of them the people passed "all manner of decrees and proclamations no matter how humiliating, and with little notice of decency thanks to the lack of judgement of their leaders."[66] But Polybius is surely too damning. It cannot be ignored that Athens (like other Greek cities) was now prospering, that the Piraeus was free, that the city was at peace, even if men who had in the past courted foreign support to throw off the Macedonian yoke—such as Chremonides—had failed miserably. The city was something of its former self again, as we can glimpse in Heracleides Creticus' description, written in 205 (as part of a wider description of central Greece), which contrasts the initial reaction of shabbiness when going to the city with its magnificent buildings and spaces and what it stood for:[67]

> The city itself is all dry and does not have a good water supply; the streets are narrow and winding, as they were built long ago. Most of the houses are cheaply built, and only a few reach a higher standard;

---

[64] *SEG* 25, 106; see too LeBohec 1993, pp. 184–189; Korhonen 1997, pp. 51–75.
[65] On Polybius' background, method, and value as a source, see, for example, Walbank 1972; Harris 1979, pp. 107–117; Gruen 1984, pp. 343–351; Green 1990, pp. 269–285; Walbank 2002; Gutzwiller 2007, pp. 144–153; G. J. Oliver 2007b; McGing 2010; Baronowski 2011; Dreyer 2011; see too Walbank 1994; Derow 1979, and the essays in Gibson and Harrison 2013.
[66] Polybius 5.106.8.
[67] M. M. Austin 2006, no. 101, pp. 198–201 (= Heracleides Creticus 1.1–2, 6–9, 11–13, 23–24, 26–30; trans. Austin). See too the comments of Mossé 1973, pp. 135–136; Habicht 1997a, pp. 170–172; Mikalson 1998, pp. 168–170. Economic changes in Athens and throughout Greece, cf. Prost 2007.

a stranger would find it hard to believe at first sight that this was the famous city of Athens, though he might soon come to believe it. There you will see the most beautiful sights on earth: a large and impressive theatre, a magnificent temple of Athena, something out of this world and worth seeing, the so-called Parthenon, which lies above the theatre; it makes a great impression on sightseers. There is the Olympieum, which though only half-completed is impressively designed, though it would have been most magnificent if completed. There are three gymnasia: the Academy, the Lyceum, and the Cynosarges; they are all planted with trees and laid out with lawns. They have festivals of all sorts, and philosophers from everywhere pull the wool over your eyes and provide recreation; there are many opportunities for leisure and spectacles without interruption.

Why, then, was Polybius so critical? The answer is likely personal. He was from Arcadia and was an active leader in the Achaean League: he may have believed that when neutral Athens turned its back on that league it failed to help prevent the massive inroads into the league's influence that Sparta would soon inflict on it (see the following section). Yet if Athens had allied with the league in 229, or even in 225 when Aratus appealed for help, there was no guarantee that Antigonus as an enemy of Aratus would not have turned on Athens. Polybius was wrong: Eurycleides and Micion rightly counseled caution, and in doing so served their city well.[68]

Philip V

The rest of the Greek mainland was nowhere near as peaceful as Athens in the last quarter of the third century. From 228 to 222 the ambitious Cleomenes III of Sparta was at war with the Achaean League, slowly but surely eroding its influence in the Peloponnese, and in the process luring Ptolemy III and the Aetolians away from Aratus to him.[69] Aratus solicited help from Athens, which, as we noted earlier, Eurycleides and Micion refused. That left Aratus with only one other place to turn: his former enemy Macedonia.[70] Antigonus

---

[68] Plutarch, *Aratus* 41.2. Polybius wrong in his censure: Ferguson 1911, p. 242.
[69] Walbank 1984c, pp. 456–459, 459, and 463–472; Hammond and Walbank 1988, pp. 342 and 345–362; Green 1990, pp. 255–261; Scholten 2003, pp. 153–156.
[70] Plutarch, *Cleomenes* 16 (= M. M. Austin 2006, no. 71, pp. 151–152), with Walbank 1984c, pp. 461–468. See too Errington 1967 on the relationship between Aratus and Philip.

was willing to offer him military support but for a price: among other things, the return of Corinth and Acrocorinth to him, and the Achaeans joining his new Hellenic League (founded in 224) to combat Cleomenes. The Achaeans thus remained under Macedonia's thumb until they sided with Rome in 198. Also, in 224 Antigonus marched into the Peloponnese, eventually defeating the Spartans at Sellasia in 222, and making Sparta join his Hellenic League.[71]

Unfortunately, Antigonus spent too much time in Greece, for in 221 the Illyrians pounced on his absence to invade Macedonia.[72] He immediately marched north and defeated them, but he was either badly wounded in the fight or perhaps broke a blood vessel "by the great shout he raised on the battlefield," according to Plutarch, and died.[73] He had been a remarkable king in many respects. The Aetolians were still a threat, but he had retaken Thessaly, defeated the Achaean League, re-established Macedonian power in Central and Southern Greece, and restored stability and morale within his kingdom. This was his legacy for the young Philip (now aged seventeen).

Philip V had a long reign, from 221 to 179, during which he and Athens were locked in bitter warfare.[74] He had been groomed by Antigonus III to succeed him, who when ill had even sent him to treat with Aratus and the Achaeans in the Peloponnese as a way of introducing him to military and public affairs.[75] Antigonus had drawn up a will appointing guardians until Philip came of age (at eighteen), but these men were soon at loggerheads with each other. Given the infighting and Philip's lack of control, the Dardanians swept into Macedonia unchecked while the Aetolians attacked the Achaeans and increased their influence in the Peloponnese. All that would change in 220 when Philip came to rule in his own right (Figure 6.1).[76]

Philip defeated the Dardanians and then turned to Greece. In 220 a conflict had broken out between the Aetolians and Achaeans, commonly known as the Social War, which would last for three years until 217.[77] Philip

---

[71] Battle: Polybius 2.65–69; Plutarch, *Cleomenes* 28; cf. *Aratus* 46.1, with Hammond and Walbank 1988, pp. 354–361.
[72] Polybius 2.70.1; Plutarch, *Cleomenes* 30.1, with Walbank 1984c, pp. 472–473.
[73] Plutarch, *Cleomenes* 30.2.
[74] Sources: Hammond and Walbank 1988, p. 367. Reign: Walbank 1940; Walbank 1984c, pp. 473–481; Hammond and Walbank 1988, pp. 368–487.
[75] Plutarch, *Aratus* 46.
[76] Philip's youth at this time much influenced Polybius in his account of the king: McGing 2013.
[77] Walbank 1940, pp. 24–67; Walbank 1984c, pp. 474–481; Hammond and Walbank 1988, pp. 371–391; Scholten 2000, pp. 200–228.

FIGURE 6.1 Philip V of Macedonia. Coin. © 2019 Trustees of the British Museum.

and his Hellenic League (which included the Achaeans and Spartans) duly declared war on the Aetolians. But when the Spartans switched sides and joined the Aetolians, all of Greece became a war zone. Battles were fought in the north and northwest in Acarnania, Aetolia, Thessaly, and Epirus; in the Peloponnese in Elis, Laconia, and Arcadia; and in 219 even at Dium, the Macedonian religious center, which the Aetolians plundered.

Philip was not prepared to let that sacrilegious act go unpunished. In the following year (218), he devastated the Aetolians' shrine at Thermum (the regular meeting place of the league). There was intense mediation by several states and eventually a peace agreement was reached at Naupactus in Aetolia in September 217, its terms re-establishing the status quo.[78] By this time Philip had heard of the Carthaginian general Hannibal's victory over the Romans at Lake Trasimene in the Second Punic War, although whether he ended hostilities with the Aetolians to turn his attention to Italy, with his borders still compromised, is unlikely.[79] He did send an envoy to Hannibal, and two years later made a treaty with him against Rome (215), which led to warfare between himself and Rome (the First Macedonian War of 214–205), which we will deal with in the following chapter.

In 220/19 and again in 218/17 an Athenian named Demaenetus of Athmonon visited Philip V and the Aetolian League to ensure that "the

---

[78] Polybius 5.100.9–105.2 (= M. M. Austin 2006, no. 73, pp. 154–156 abridged). This was the last peace agreement the Greeks ever made themselves; all future ones included Rome: Green 1990, p. 288. Mediation: Ager 1996, pp. 145–146; Scholten 2000, pp. 224–228.
[79] Cf. Gruen 1984, p. 374.

[Athenians] will continue to enjoy the friendship of both in peace, and not to engage in fighting on either side."[80] Neutrality was sensible, but the Athenians were also concerned about becoming too isolated. Antigonus' Hellenic League might well have been anti-Spartan in origins, but it could very easily switch to being anti-Athenian, leaving Athens trapped and easier prey for Philip should he decide to reassert Macedonian control over the city.

At times Athenian neutrality flouted tradition. Thus in 218, during the Social War, when some of Philip V's advisers clashed with the king over his strategy against the Aetolians, he ordered them and other critics to be executed.[81] One of them, the royal secretary Megaleas, escaped and sought refuge in Athens, but he was refused. He went to Thebes, where he committed suicide rather than be handed over to Philip.[82] It was Greek convention to accept any asylum-seeker, but clearly Megaleas' arrival at Athens placed the people in a quandary. This was not the first time they had found themselves in this position, for in 324 they had refused to accept Harpalus, a citizen seeking refuge, because of the strain it would place on their relations with Alexander the Great. However, they could not merely cast Megaleas aside without earning the contempt of the other Greeks; therefore (as with Harpalus) they made a person rather than the demos responsible: Polybius refers to "generals" turning Megaleas away, presumably Theophrastus the general of Eleusis.[83]

To counter their potentially vulnerable position the Athenians turned overseas, establishing contacts with Crete, Asia Minor (specifically Ephesus and Miletus in Ionia and Antioch in Caria), and the Seleucid court, an association lasting throughout the rest of the Hellenistic era.[84] One power Eurycleides and Micion courted in particular was Egypt.[85] In 224 or more likely 223 the Athenians founded a cult to Ptolemy III and his wife Berenice, established a festival in his honor (the Ptolemaea), erected a statue of him in the Agora, and created a new tribe named after him (Ptolemais), thereby

---

[80] *IG* ii² 1304, lines 7–8 (honors on Demaenetus of 209), with the comments of Habicht 1982, pp. 132–135.
[81] See in detail Errington 1967.
[82] Polybius 5.27.1–28.8, with Ferguson 1911, pp. 249–250.
[83] Habicht 1997a, p. 188.
[84] Habicht 1997a, p. 193, citing epigraphic sources and bibliography; Seleucids: Habicht 1989; Mattingly 1997, pp. 122–129.
[85] Habicht 1992, pp. 68–90; Mattingly 1997, pp. 129–133.

increasing the number of tribes to thirteen.[86] They also honored several of Ptolemy's courtiers, including Castor of Alexandria in 225/4 (archonship of Ergochares) and in about 215 Thraseas, an envoy who had visited Athens in 224/3, enrolling him in the Ptolemais tribe.[87] In addition, they invited other states to participate in the Ptolemaea, a move that was not necessarily diplomatic but a warning shot to Macedonia of their link to powerful Egypt.[88]

In response, Ptolemy III funded a new gymnasium in Athens, the Ptolemaeum, complete with meeting rooms and a library (which received an annual donation of books from the graduating class of ephebes).[89] It must have caused Antigonus and later Philip V to suspect Athens' policy of neutrality; but then again Ptolemy may have had his own suspicions, for while the Athenians had named a new tribe after him, they had not abolished the two Antigonid tribes (created in 307). Polybius may well have accused the Athenians of shamelessness in the way they courted Ptolemy or any foreign ruler, but reality had little room for shame—their self-serving approach characterized their relations with Hellenistic and then Roman rulers throughout their history.[90]

---

[86] Pausanias 1.5.5, with Ferguson 1911, pp. 205–212 and 237–240; Johnson 1913; Habicht 1982, pp. 103–112; Hammond and Walbank 1988, pp. 340–341; Habicht 1992, pp. 68–70; Mikalson 1998, pp. 178–179. The new tribe thus increased the Boule from 600 to 650 members.

[87] Castor: *IG* ii³ 1, 1146, with Habicht 1982, p. 102; Habicht 1992, p. 76. Thraseas: *IG* ii³ 1, 1185, with Habicht 1982, pp. 115–116, citing bibliography. See more fully Ferguson 1911, pp. 298–299.

[88] *ISE* 30: delegation to the games from Ephesus of 224–222. The Ptolemaea may well have been celebrated as late as 30 when the Romans ended Ptolemaic rule in Egypt: Habicht 1992, pp. 83–85.

[89] Ferguson 1911, p. 239. For the view that Ptolemy III not Ptolemy VI funded the gymnasium, see Habicht 1982, pp. 112–117; Mikalson 1998, p. 179.

[90] Mossé 1973, p. 133.

7

Enter Rome, Exit Macedonia

THE ATHENIANS' DIPLOMATIC RELATIONS WITH other Greek cities, Macedonia, and foreign dynasties would not be enough. A new power had begun to worm its way into Greek affairs, one that was destined to change every aspect of the landscape (rural, urban, provincial, and sacred) of Greece and the Near East over the next centuries: Rome.[1] That city had been slowly expanding in Italy and the western Mediterranean for some time.[2] Eventually the Romans turned their eyes to the eastern Mediterranean, and in 146 added Greece to their growing empire.[3] But while they had already come into contact with Greek culture thanks to the Greek cities of southern Italy and Sicily, it was their involvement in mainland Greece that really opened their eyes to Greek civilization. They became philhellenes or "lovers of Greek culture," and even more so *philathenaioi* or "lovers of Athenian culture," which they began adopting for their own ends, as our next chapters will track.

The Roman conquest of Greece splits scholars into two camps: those who see the Romans as imperialistic from the outset and those

---

[1] The standard work is still Gruen 1984; see also Errington 1971a; Kallet-Marx 1995 (from 148–162); Eckstein 2006; Eckstein 2008; Waterfield 2014; cf. Green 1990, pp. 414–432; Hoff 2013. On the changing landscape: Alcock 1993 (see her definition of the word on pp. 6–8).
[2] For example, Scullard 1989; Errington 1971a, pp. 12–34; Harris 1979, pp. 182–194; cf. Eckstein 2006, pp. 158–176.
[3] Derow 2003; Vanderspoel 2010, pp. 250–257.

who view events in Greece and Macedonia as responsible for bringing Rome into the Greek world.[4] As noted in my introduction, this book is not about Rome, hence I discuss its advance in the east only as it affects Athens and the Greek mainland and the impact of Hellenism on Rome.

Rome and Greece

Rome had some experience of Greek culture and the people before it involved itself more fully in Greece.[5] But the activities of Illyrian pirates really focused its attention on the east.[6] As Rome increased its trading network in the western Mediterranean, Italian vessels became prey to merciless Illyrian pirates, who for some time had been disrupting the trade route from southern Italy to the eastern Adriatic.[7] Enough was eventually enough, and the Romans sent an embassy of protest to the Illyrian queen Teuta, who was intent on expanding Illyrian power in Greece. She treated the Roman envoys with contempt, killing one and taking the other captive.[8] The Romans therefore declared war on Illyria in 229 (the same year as Demetrius II died and Antigonus III succeeded him). This First Illyrian War lasted only one year; it was minor as far as Roman activities in Greece went, but in many respects it opened the door to Rome's rapid and relentless advance in the entire Mediterranean.[9]

Rome sent 20,000 infantry, 2,000 cavalry, and 200 warships under the consuls for 229, Gnaeus Fulvius Centumalus and Lucius Postumius Albinus, to Illyria. Upon landing on the Illyrian coast they defeated everyone in their path, forcing Teuta to Rhizon (the Gulf of Kotor), with Albinus negotiating a peace treaty in 228. She was spared, but had to live at Rhizon, while the Illyrians had to give up all claims on towns as far north as Epidamnus and their warships could not operate south of Lissus.[10] Rome also gained control

---

[4] Former: for example, Harris 1979; Habicht 1997a (e.g., pp. 185, 194–195); latter: Gruen 1984; Eckstein 2006, for example, pp. 181–316 ("thesis of exceptional Roman belligerence"); Eckstein 2008—see his discussion of both sides on pp. 3–28.
[5] Errington 1989a, pp. 81–85; Eckstein 2008, pp. 29–30.
[6] Cf. Appian, *Illyrian Wars* 7, with Gruen 1984, pp. 359–364; Errington 1989a, pp. 85–90; Derow 2003, pp. 51–53.
[7] Polybius 2.8.2.1–2.
[8] Polybius 2.8.7–13.
[9] Gruen 1984, pp. 364–368, 438–439; Hammond and Walbank 1988, pp. 334–335; Errington 1989a, pp. 86–90; Eckstein 2008, pp. 30–41; Matyszak 2009, pp. 19–22; Waterfield 2014, pp. 21–25.
[10] Polybius 2.12.1–3.

of the ports of Epidamnus, Apollonia, and Corcyra, but did not establish any formal presence in Illyria.[11]

Albinus then reached out to the Aetolian and Achaean leagues (which had also been fighting the Illyrians); after reaching an agreement, "immediately afterwards" the Roman Senate dispatched a similar embassy to Corinth and Athens, perhaps simply as a courtesy.[12] But no embassy was sent to Macedonia, despite its enmity with Illyria and its status on the Greek mainland. The Romans might not have had much experience of dealing with Greeks, but it is hard to think they were guilty of an oversight. The only obvious reason for snubbing Antigonus III is that they did not want to send an embassy to him: Did they already have Macedonia in their crosshairs?[13]

The Athenians stayed friendly to Rome over the next few decades, although they were cautious.[14] A much later ancient writer (a twelfth-century Byzantine theologian) has it that the Athenians initiated the Roman envoys into the Eleusinian Mysteries (and that the Romans were allowed to compete in the Isthmian Games), but there is no other evidence for this and the veracity of this account is suspect.[15] Athens probably noted events to do with the island city of Pharos (not to be confused with Pharos at Alexandria), which under its ruler Demetrius went to war with Rome in 219.[16] This Second Illyrian War ended in the same year with Demetrius' defeat and flight to his ally Philip V, who was then fighting in the Social War against the Aetolian League (220–217).[17] Rome sought Demetrius' surrender but Philip refused, perhaps in retaliation for the way Rome had brushed off Macedonia at the end of the First Illyrian War in 228. It would also not have been lost on him that after defeating Demetrius the extent of Roman influence in Illyria brought it dangerously close to his border.

The Romans took no action against Philip, nor did they show any disfavor toward the Athenians, who responded positively to an appeal from Pharos for friendship and help in rebuilding. Perhaps Rome chose not to

---

[11] Alliances: Derow 1991, especially pp. 267–270, but note Eckstein 2008, pp. 45–46.
[12] Polybius 2.12.4–8 (Aetolian and Achaean leagues); Polybius 2.12.8 (Corinth and Athens).
[13] Though on this see, for example, Harris 1979, p. 138.
[14] Athens and Rome generally: Mattingly 1997, pp. 140–144.
[15] Zonaras, *Extracts of History* 8.19.
[16] On Demetrius, see Eckstein 2008, pp. 58–60.
[17] Derow 1991 (p. 262 on Athens); Habicht 1997a, p. 185. War: Errington 1971a, pp. 102–109; Errington 1989a, pp. 90–94; Eckstein 1999; Eckstein 2008, pp. 60–73; Matyszak 2009, pp. 24–27.

retaliate because the Second Punic War against Carthage had just begun (218–201), and one year later Hannibal ambushed and defeated a Roman army at Lake Trasimene.[18] His victory panicked the Romans, and it was brought to the attention of Philip V while he was watching the Nemean Games. He sent an envoy, Xenophanes, to Hannibal in either that year or 216.[19] Possibly Demetrius (the ousted ruler of Pharos) urged Philip to do so, though Philip's own ambition may have spurred him to take on Rome, and then (like every other ruler in this era), if we can believe Polybius, world conquest.[20] He had since 217 been building up an impressive fleet that could be used to attack Illyria and sail across the Adriatic.[21] For the moment he needed to make sure Macedonia was safe from any incursions, and so ended his war with the Aetolian League.

In 216, Hannibal's famous victory at Cannae (in Apulia, southeast Italy) persuaded Philip, if he needed persuading, that his future lay with the Carthaginian general. The battle was one of Rome's greatest military defeats: the consul commanders (Lucius Aemilius Paullus and Gaius Terentius Varro) and over 70,000 troops were killed in it, and several Italian allies then defected to Carthage's side. In 215, Philip made a treaty of alliance with Hannibal, "on behalf of himself, the Macedonians, and the allies."[22] Its terms included Philip taking his fleet of at least 200 ships to Italy to join with Hannibal in making war on Rome, that Philip would receive war booty and some Italian territory, that after the war ended both leaders would make war on whatever Greek enemy Philip chose, and especially "that the states on the mainland and the particular islands that lie off Macedonia should belong to Philip and be part of

---

[18] Errington 1971a, pp. 49–101; Lazenby 1978; Harris 1979, pp. 200–205; Briscoe 1989; David 2000, pp. 40–61; Hoyos 2005.
[19] Polybius 5.101.6–10; Livy 23.33.6–12, with Ferguson 1911, p. 254; Waterfield 2014, pp. 45–46.
[20] Polybius 5.101.7–10 (Demetrius). World conquest: Polybius 5.102.1, 108.4–5, against which see Gruen 1984, pp. 374–375; Derow 2003, p. 54, on Polybius' "exorbitant ascription" of these aims; cf. Waterfield 2014, pp. 38–40. All kings: see discussion in Eckstein 2006, pp. 79–117. Skepticism about Demetrius: Hammond and Walbank 1988, pp. 387–388.
[21] Philip's naval program: Walbank 1982, pp. 226–236.
[22] Preserved at Polybius 7.9 (= M. M. Austin 2006, no. 76, pp. 159–161); Livy 23.33.9–34.1, with Walbank 1940, pp. 70–72; Gruen 1984, pp. 375–376; Hammond and Walbank 1988, pp. 393–394; but see Eckstein 2008, pp. 78–84. Demetrius was also said to have persuaded Philip to make peace with the Aetolians in 217: Polybius 5.101.7–10.

his kingdom."²³ In other words, Philip intended to reassert Macedonian control over Illyria and to expand in the west.

The treaty with Hannibal has often been viewed as the cause of Rome's aggressive involvement in Greece. However, as Polybius says, having defeated the Carthaginians in the Second Punic War (in 202), the Romans "considering that they had taken the most important and necessary step toward their plan of world conquest, were now emboldened to reach out and seize the rest and to cross with an army to Greece and the continent of Asia."²⁴ In other words, it was only a matter of time before Rome turned to Greece and the east.

The First Macedonian War

Despite their dire straits, the Romans could not ignore Philip's alliance with Hannibal, which was tantamount to his declaration of war on them. In 214 they sent a fleet under Marcus Valerius Laevinus to Illyria, beginning the so-called First Macedonian War (214–205), although it is not known for certain whether the Romans formally declared war on Philip.²⁵ They had some minor successes but he was making significant gains in Illyria and threatening the Adriatic.²⁶ Therefore, most probably in 211, they turned to Philip's enemies the Aetolians, who had now regrouped after their setbacks in the war against Philip.²⁷

Eager to attack Macedonia, the Aetolians embraced an alliance with Rome, effectively breaking the terms of their treaty of 217 with Philip.²⁸ The fragments of the Greek version of the alliance with Rome (set up in Aetolia)

---

²³ Livy 23.33.9–12 (quote at 12).
²⁴ Polybius 1.3.6.
²⁵ Walbank 1940, pp. 76–105; Errington 1971a, pp. 109–118; Harris 1979, pp. 205–208; Gruen 1984, pp. 377–381; Hammond and Walbank 1988, pp. 391–410; Green 1990, pp. 297–301; Matyszak 2009, pp. 33–52; Eckstein 2008, pp. 85–116; Errington 1989a, pp. 94–106; Eckstein 2010, pp. 229–234.
²⁶ Walbank 1940, pp. 80–81.
²⁷ The date is controversial and 212 is possible: see bibliography cited at, for example, Dmitriev 2011, pp. 145–146 nn. 6–8.
²⁸ Polybius 9.39.1–3, 18.38.5–9; Livy 26.24.7–15 (= Sherk 1984, no. 2, pp. 1–2; M. M. Austin 2006, no. 77, pp. 161–163); with Walbank 1940, pp. 82–84; Errington 1971a, pp. 113–115; Gruen 1984, pp. 17–25; Hammond and Walbank 1988, pp. 400–405; Eckstein 2008, pp. 88–91 (only formally sworn to by Rome in summer 209); Waterfield 2014, pp. 49–51; treaty: Gruen 1984, pp. 25–33, 377–378, and 440–441.

are the oldest surviving of a Roman treaty, and they make it clear that Rome wanted only an ally against the king—in other words, all land operations were to fall to the Aetolians. In return they would receive all territory won in the war and the Romans all portable booty, including captured slaves. These generous terms were necessary as Rome had to stop Philip at all costs from crossing the Adriatic; but, as we shall see, Rome had no intention of honoring them.[29]

In the same year Elis, Messene, and Sparta allied with Rome against Philip and brought in the new power in Seleucid Asia Minor, Pergamum.[30] The influx of new allies spawned several battles in Greece and eventually led to the Athenians making an appearance, perhaps because the war was adversely affecting their trade. In 209 when Philip defeated an Aetolian army (which included Roman troops) at Lamia in Thessaly, the Athenians tried to broker peace. With envoys from Ptolemy IV, Rhodes, and Chios, they met Philip at Phalara, the port of Lamia, and persuaded him to adopt a thirty-day ceasefire and hold further talks at Achaea. Unfortunately, Aetolian demands wrecked the meeting and warfare resumed.[31]

Since the Athenians had stayed neutral for many years under the guidance of Eurycleides and Micion, their sudden diplomatic move may mean that both men had died or at least retired from public life.[32] Around 215 the Assembly in a justifiably laudatory decree honored Eurycleides for his lifetime of public service to the city, including his personal financial contributions, rebuilding of the defenses and sacred buildings, and moves to regrow crops on land devastated by war.[33] These honors may have been contemporaneous with his retirement, and since we do not hear of Micion, he may have also retired. With both men no longer controlling policy, the Athenians began to involve themselves more in Greek affairs.

---

[29] On the Romans' attitude to their allies and the distinction they drew between formal allies, friends, and other peoples with whom they came into contact, see Accame 1946; Gruen 1984, pp. 13–96.

[30] Heinen 1984, pp. 426–432; on Pergamum, cf. Green 1990, pp. 164–170.

[31] Habicht 1982, pp. 135–137. Attempts at mediation during the war: Eckstein 2002; Eckstein 2008, pp. 91–116; cf. Ager 1996, pp. 157–161.

[32] Ferguson 1911, p. 256 (dying within a short time of one another). Neutrality: Habicht 1982, pp. 127–142.

[33] *IG* ii³ 1, 1160 (= Burstein 1985, no. 67, pp. 90–91; M. M. Austin 2006, no. 74, pp. 156–157, as ii² 834); with MacKendrick 1969, pp. 39–43; Mossé 1973, pp. 132–137; Habicht 1982, pp. 82–89 and 118–127.

The pendulum of events in the war swung in favor of both sides over the next few years. Athens does not seem to have tried to negotiate after the collapse of the talks in 209, perhaps embarrassed at its earlier diplomatic failure.[34] When Attalus I of Pergamum was forced to return home and Rome likewise withdrew from the Greek mainland, the Aetolians had to bear the brunt of fighting themselves. Unable to get the better of Philip, they sued for peace with him in 206/5. Rome therefore had no choice but to make its own peace with Philip, bringing this First Macedonian War to an end in 205 with the Peace of Phoenice (in Epirus).[35]

Greece had little time to recover, however. Publius Cornelius Scipio Africanus' resounding defeat of Hannibal at Zama (Tunisia) in 202 brought the Second Punic War to a formal end the following year. Hatred of Philip V ran high in Rome, as did suspicions of his contacts with Egypt and Syria.[36] Earlier, in the summer of 204, Ptolemy IV had died and was succeeded by the six-year-old Ptolemy V, whose guardians, Sosibius and Agathocles, quickly made themselves the powers behind the throne. They tried to arrange a marriage between the young Ptolemy and one of Philip's daughters in case of an attack from Antiochus III ("the Great") of Syria, who had returned from a major campaign (lasting from 212 to 205) against the eastern satrapies of the Seleucid Empire.[37] However, Philip refused the Egyptian overture and in 202 made an alliance with Antiochus against Egypt.[38]

Given the anti-Macedonian sentiment in Rome, in 200 the consul Publius Sulpicius Galba, who had fought in Greece during the First Macedonian War, decided the time was ripe for revenge. Various Greek embassies to the Senate had spoken of Philip's growing influence in Greece, but news of the alliance of Philip and Antiochus persuaded the Senate to act before both of them turned against Rome.[39] After some politicking in the city, Rome

---

[34] Or possibly our sources omitted mention of further Athenian diplomacy: Ferguson 1911, p. 255.

[35] Livy 29.12.11–16 (= M. M. Austin 2006, no. 80, pp. 166–167); Justin 29.4.11, with Gruen 1984, p. 381; Hammond and Walbank 1988, pp. 408–410; Errington 1989a, pp. 104–106; Matyszak 2009, pp. 49–52; Waterfield 2014, pp. 56–57.

[36] Walbank 1940, pp. 111–118; Hammond and Walbank 1988, pp. 411–416.

[37] For example, Errington 1989b, pp. 248–250; Green 1990, pp. 193–296.

[38] Errington 1971b; Eckstein 2008, pp. 121–180, that there was no treaty. Antiochus: Grainger 2002.

[39] Eckstein 2006, pp. 257–289; cf. Eckstein 2008, pp. 230–270; imperialistic revenge: Harris 1979, pp. 207–209. Galba: Errington 1971a, pp. 141–143; Harris 1979, pp. 214–215; Gruen 1984, pp. 204–207; Errington 1989b, pp. 253–257; Waterfield 2014, pp. 62–66.

formally declared war on Philip in 200; in this Second Macedonian War (200–196), Athens found itself fighting on Rome's side.[40]

The Second Macedonian War

The Athenians probably expected Philip to be busy with offensives on various fronts, but an earlier incident unexpectedly brought them into conflict with him. In September 201, invoking an ancient law to do with the Eleusinian Mysteries, the Athenians had executed two young men from Acarnania who had gone into the temple at Eleusis, something only initiates in the Mysteries were allowed to do.[41] The youths' action may have been a genuine mistake—apparently they were following the crowd, according to Livy, though it is hard to believe they were ignorant of their location.[42] The Athenians did not give the men the benefit of the doubt, and in anger the Acarnanians, who were allies of Philip, complained bitterly to him that the Athenians had gone too far. He agreed and sent the Acarnanians Macedonian troops, who helped them raid the Attic coast while the Macedonian navy seized four Athenian warships in the Piraeus.[43] Fortunately, the commander of a Rhodian-Pergamene fleet based at Aegina saw what had happened and recaptured them for Athens.

Warfare between Athens and Philip loomed. Blame for the escalating tensions must lie with the Acarnanians, closely followed by Philip. The Athenians' action in executing the two young men was heavy handed, but it was within their legal rights; presumably they could not have anticipated that the Acarnanians would protest to Philip (rather than Athens) and that he would react by deploying troops and ships, thus bringing them to the brink of war. Philip, in turn, could have sent a letter of protest to Athens on behalf of his Acarnanian allies, asking the city to address the growing rift. Instead, he used this unforeseen opportunity to his advantage. He had

---

[40] Walbank 1940, pp. 138–185; Errington 1971a, pp. 131–155; Harris 1979, pp. 212–218; Habicht 1982, pp. 142–158; Gruen 1984, pp. 382–398; Hammond and Walbank 1988, pp. 416–446; Derow 2003, pp. 58–62; Eckstein 2008, pp. 276–282; Grieb 2008, pp. 113–118; Eckstein 2010, pp. 234–237. See too Errington 1971b; cf. Errington 1989b, pp. 261–274; Eckstein 2005; Matyszak 2009, pp. 60–98; Hoff 2013, pp. 562–563.
[41] Livy 31.14.6–8.
[42] Livy 31.14.7, with Ferguson 1911, pp. 267–268; see too Habicht 1982, pp. 143–144.
[43] Polybius 26.16.9; Livy 31.14.9–10.

recently recaptured Illyria, had seized Samos from Egypt as part of his alliance with Antiochus, and would soon be operating on the Hellespont. But he had also seen the collapse of his plans to expand in Italy when the Second Punic War ended in Carthage's defeat. Now it was time to turn to Greece, which had not been part of the Macedonian orbit since the death of Demetrius II in 229. No wonder he embraced the Acarnanian issue.

Philip's actions led the Athenians to seek allies.[44] They first turned to Egypt, but that country was being ripped apart by riots, the legacy of Ptolemy IV, during which the highly unpopular Agathocles was torn to shreds by an Alexandrian mob.[45] To make matters worse, Antiochus III and Philip were scooping up Ptolemaic possessions: Antiochus had seized Syria and Palestine, and Philip had targeted Asia Minor, taking Samos and Miletus. Egypt therefore was in no position to help Athens. That left Antiochus, a king with whom the Athenians had enjoyed diplomatic contacts for some time (and would continue to do so with his successors), but he was simply too far away.[46] Leaving their options open with Rome, they turned to Attalus I of Pergamum, also an enemy of Philip, and invited him to their city, where he was enthusiastically welcomed:[47]

> When he entered by the Dipylon Gate they placed the priestesses and priests on each side (of the street). They then opened all the temples, placed victims at all the altars and asked him to offer sacrifice. Finally they voted him honors greater than they had readily bestowed on any of their previous benefactors; for in addition to other distinctions they called a tribe after Attalus, and enrolled him among the eponymous tribal heroes.

Thus, the city began a close relationship with Pergamum that lasted for over a century.[48] Polybius has it that Attalus rushed to the city only when he discovered that the Romans had sent an embassy there to discuss relations with Philip, hence for self-serving reasons.[49] Attalus refused to appear before

---

[44] Walbank 1940, pp. 130–132; Habicht 1982, pp. 142–158; Habicht 1992, pp. 68–90.
[45] Riots: Veïsse 2004.
[46] Habicht 1989, pp. 11–26.
[47] Polybius 16.25–26 (= M. M. Austin 2006, no. 232, pp. 406–407; trans. Austin); Livy 31.14.12–15; Pausanias 1.5.5 (tribe). The Athenians continued to bestow honors on prominent Pergamenes: Mattingly 1997, pp. 134–136.
[48] Mattingly 1997, pp. 133–137; Habicht 1990; Attalids: E. V. Hansen 1971; Allen 1983.
[49] Polybius 16.25.2.

the Assembly, instead writing letters that were read out there encouraging the Athenians to join with Rhodes, Rome, and himself against Philip. The Romans may not have been seeking an actual alliance with Athens, but they must have been pleased when the city declared war on the Macedonian king in 200.[50]

Polybius, already critical of Athens' neutrality, as noted previously, is the source for Livy's critique of why the Athenians declared war at this time, believing it was for an unworthy cause and that the people "retained nothing of their former greatness except their spirit."[51] In some respects he was right. If the Athenians had punished the two violators of the Mysteries differently, the Acarnanians might not have turned to Philip as they did, triggering events that led to war. Then again, given that Philip's expansionist plans in Italy had been thwarted, and especially since he needed the Piraeus in his campaigns against Attalus and Rhodes, it would only have been a matter of time before he made his move on the city.

Cephisodorus of Xypete, who had served as military treasurer in 204/3 and treasurer of the grain fund in 203/2 (an important official tasked with ensuring a supply of grain), and who had come to the fore in public affairs, called on the Athenians to solicit the support of the Aetolians, Rhodians, Cretans, Attalus, and Ptolemy III against Philip, and to send an embassy to the Senate at Rome.[52] Polybius claims that the Romans declared war on Philip because of the king's actions against Athens, but that does not follow.[53] Nevertheless, the war was an effective entry point for them into Greek affairs, and so they sent Marcus Aemilius Lepidus to Philip at Abydus on the Hellespont ordering him not to attack Athens or any other Greeks, and to demand he compensate Attalus and Rhodes for his previous actions against them.[54] Of course the Romans had no right to make an ultimatum like this—the king had actually not broken the Peace of Phoenice, so technically was still their ally—so it is no surprise that Philip sent Lepidus

---

[50] Habicht 1982, pp. 142–150; Hammond and Walbank 1988, pp. 416–418; Eckstein 2008, pp. 206–211.

[51] Livy 31.14.6.

[52] Pausanias 1.36.5–6 (calling him "champion of the people" at sec. 5), with Ferguson 1911, p. 269; Habicht 1982, pp. 156–157. Grain officials: see the catalogue at Geagan 2011, C104, p. 48 (185–125 or later).

[53] Polybius 16.34.5. Motives: Green 1990, pp. 308–309; cf. Hammond and Walbank 1988, pp. 419–420.

[54] Polybius 16.34.2–7 (16.29.3–34 for the siege); Walbank 1940, pp. 134–135; Ager 1996, pp. 163–165.

packing, neatly laying the blame on Rome when he told Lepidus that if Rome broke the Peace, "we will defend ourselves bravely and call on the gods for help."[55]

Initially Philip did not invade Attica, but went to the Hellespont to try to block the grain route to the city. While he was there, his generals Nicanor and Philocles with 2,000 infantry and 200 cavalry invaded Attica.[56] Nicanor marched as far as the Academy, by the gates of the city, but at that point Roman envoys went to him and on behalf of the Senate requested him to cease his attack otherwise war was inevitable; Nicanor accordingly withdrew.[57] In the meantime, Philocles had been destroying small villages and even attacking Eleusis, while naval squadrons stationed in Chalcis on Euboea threatened Athenian shipping routes and the Attic coast.[58]

The Athenians, short of manpower, could only man their frontier forts—at Eleusis they cancelled religious rituals for safety's sake—and the Piraeus.[59] They were all but encircled by hostile forces, including the Boeotians (who were now firm allies of Philip), and Macedonian garrisons on Euboea and in Corinth. If they expected military help from Attalus and Rhodes, none came: the Rhodians were busy undoing Philip's recent gains at sea and Attalus had returned to Aegina, although he did send money and much-needed grain, as a later decree of 188/7 informs us.[60]

When Galba and an army of veterans from Scipio Africanus' recent north African campaign landed at Apollonia in Epirus, intent on invading Macedonia from the west, an Athenian delegation urgently petitioned him for help. Galba dispatched twenty warships and 1,000 troops under Gaius Claudius Centho to the Piraeus. In tandem with Athenian war vessels, he led a surprise night attack on the Macedonian base at Chalcis, where he burned storehouses, freed prisoners, and destroyed statues of Philip before returning to the Piraeus.[61]

---

[55] Polybius 16.34.7.
[56] Polybius 16.27.1–2; Livy 31.26.
[57] Polybius 16.27.2–3, with Ferguson 1911, p. 273.
[58] Diodorus 28.7; Livy 31.26.9–13, with Ferguson 1911, pp. 275–276; Walbank 1940, pp. 138–141; H. A. Thompson 1981, pp. 352–354; see too Mikalson 1998, pp. 190–193, on Philip's sacrilegious destructions as part of a pattern throughout Greece.
[59] Cancellations of rituals at Eleusis went on for some years: Clinton 1974, p. 24.
[60] *IG* ii³ 1, 1280, lines 3–4.
[61] Livy 31.23.

The audacity of this raid brought Philip himself on the scene. Landing at Demetrias on the Gulf of Pagasae, he hastened against Athens. The people discovered his plan in the nick of time, and with troops finally sent by Attalus held off his attack, perhaps because they had strengthened their circuit wall in anticipation of a Macedonian offensive at some stage.[62] Even so, Philip inflicted great destruction on Athenian lands, burning the Academy and even desecrating tombs and smashing the stones of temples and other monuments.[63] The scale of his wanton ruinations sets him on a par with the Persians, and it is no surprise he incurred "the absolute hatred of all mankind, which was already reviling him."[64] When Attalus and Rome deployed more troops the next day, Philip abandoned any notion of a surprise strike on the city; failing to take Eleusis, he retreated to the Peloponnese.[65]

It was probably at this time (though we cannot rule out the following summer of 199) that the Athenians went even further in their defiance of Macedonia by formally cursing Philip and all Antigonid rulers:[66]

> They immediately proposed a motion, which the people ratified, to remove and destroy all the statues and portraits of Philip and the inscriptions on them, as well as those of all his ancestors, male and female, to cancel all the holidays, ceremonies and priesthoods instituted in honour of him and of his ancestors; even the places where something had been placed or inscribed in his honour were to be put under a curse and it should be wrong in future to decide to place or dedicate anything there that religion allowed to place or dedicate in a holy spot; whenever the priests of the state offered prayers on behalf of the people of Athens, their allies, their armies and fleets, they should at the same time curse and execrate Philip, his children and his kingdom, his land and sea forces, and the entire race and name of the Macedonians.

---

[62] Theocharaki 2011, p. 126.
[63] Diodorus 28.7; Livy 31.24.18.
[64] H. A. Thompson 1981; Philip as "unhellenic" and similarity with Persian destructions: p. 354. Quote: Diodorus 28.7.
[65] Livy 31.25.2.
[66] Livy 31.44.4–5 (= M. M. Austin 2006, no. 82, pp. 169–170; trans. Austin), with Ferguson 1911, pp. 276–277; Mikalson 1998, pp. 186–188. On the Athenian curse, see especially Byrne 2010, with pp. 158–159 and 175–176 on chronology.

Thirty inscriptions with about 48 careful erasures of wording relevant to any Antigonid ruler have been identified, all in the city.[67] Two decrees that make reference to Antigonids were significantly and deliberately left intact: one for Philippides and the other for Callias of Sphettus, where both are called patriots and the kings were portrayed as enemies of Athens: "In keeping with the mood of 200 B.C., the eraser was happy to keep this much of Antigonid memory alive."[68]

Other measures included killing any Athenian speaker who spoke or moved a decree in favor of Philip with impunity; dissolving the Antigonis and Demetrias tribes (instituted in 307); and smashing all statues to Philip and his ancestors, including the expensive gold one of Antigonus and Poliorcetes set up in 307 and the equestrian one of Poliorcetes of 302. Fragments of a smashed equestrian statue, perhaps that of Poliorcetes, were discovered in a well during excavations in the Agora in 1971.[69] Also destroyed would have been the statues of Monophthalmus and Poliorcetes as eponymous founders of their tribes on the Monument of the Eponymous Heroes in the Agora, explaining why Pausanias did not see them when he visited Athens in the second century AD, but spoke only of statues of Ptolemy and Attalus.[70] Despite the Athenians' bellicose actions, Livy, who gives us this account, tellingly noted that their words were "the only weapons in which their strength lies."

The following year, 199, Philip suffered a reversal at the hands of Galba. The Athenians were quick to take advantage of his misfortune and endeavored to coax the Aetolians to their side by describing the horrors they had suffered at Philip's hands and attacking his character as sacrilegious.[71] The league held a meeting at Naupactus, attended also by envoys from Macedonia and Rome, and voted to defend Athens. The following year, the Athenians tried to drum up more support by sending an embassy to Philip's ally the Achaean League. They may have decided on this surprising action because Galba had been recalled to Rome, perhaps an indication of a wider Roman

---

[67] Byrne 2010, pp. 161–171, all confined to the Agora, the theatre of Dionysus, and the Asklepeion areas, but no public inscriptions (especially state decrees) suffered erasures on the Acropolis (on these, see Byrne 2010, pp. 167–168 with nn. 33 and 34).
[68] Byrne 2010, p. 172.
[69] T. L. Shear 1973, pp. 165–168 and Plate 36; Brogan 2003, pp. 198–203, citing additional bibliography.
[70] Pausanias 1.5.5, with T. L. Shear 1970, pp. 199–200, with Plate 44.
[71] Livy 31.30.

withdrawal. At a meeting of the Achaeans in Sicyon, the Athenian position was supported by envoys from Attalus, Rhodes, and Rome, while Philip's envoy was a man named Cleomedon. For three days pressure was put on the Achaeans to switch sides, with the envoys speaking in a fixed order: first the Roman, then those from Attalus and Rhodes, then Macedonia, and finally the Athenian. The order was clever: usually the person speaking last would be most remembered when it was time to vote. Since the Athenians had suffered the most thanks to Philip, their closing appeal was clearly intended to offset Cleomedon's preceding speech.[72] It was a close vote, but in the end the powerful Achaeans voted to join the others against Macedonia.[73]

But the war was taking its toll, and in November 198, peace negotiations were held at Nicaea (near Thermopylae), and again at an Assembly of the Boeotians in Thebes in early 197. The Achaeans spoke at both, but we do not hear anything about the Athenians doing the same.[74] This surprising silence may be because they did not attend these meetings, though that is hard to believe given their reliance on allies. Perhaps our ancient writers (Polybius and, through him, Livy) are at fault. Polybius was already hostile to the Athenians for what happened to his Arcadia when Eurycleides and Micion did not ally with the Achaeans against Sparta in 225. He also blamed them for the reason they went to war against Philip. Thus he may have downplayed their role in the peace negotiations, and since Livy used him as a major source, Livy's account would likewise have been tainted. In any case, no peace was made, but only a truce of two months.

Later that year, after a diplomatic end to the war failed, a new Roman commander, Titus Quinctius Flamininus, decided it was time to deal with Philip.[75] He expelled Macedonian influence in Epirus and then turned to Thessaly. The threat to his southern border was one that Philip could not ignore, and he immediately marched to meet with Flamininus. When their negotiations broke down the two sides did battle at Cynoscephalae

---

[72] Ferguson 1911, pp. 274–275.

[73] Polybius 16.35.1–2. Possibly now Achaea became an ally of Rome, though the date is controversial, and such an alliance might not have been made until the 180s: Gruen 1984, pp. 33–38 and 444–447; cf. Waterfield 2014, pp. 86–87: "Fear of the consequences of making enemies of the Romans was the stick."

[74] Nicaea: Polybius 18.1–10.1; Livy 32.32.9–37.5; Thebes: Livy 33.1–3, with Ferguson 1911, p. 279 (Athens sent deputations); Hammond and Walbank 1988, p. 428; Habicht 1997a, p. 202.

[75] Errington 1971a, pp. 144–151; Eckstein 1976; Gruen 1984, pp. 207–223. Diplomacy between Philip and Flamininus: Ager 1996, pp. 192–194.

(named after nearby hills resembling "dogs' heads") in June the following year (197). Flamininus fielded some 25,000 troops, including 2,500 cavalry and 20 war elephants, to Philip's 27,000 men, including 2,000 cavalry. After an initial advantage held by Philip, the Romans defeated him, killing 8,000 and capturing 5,000 of his men, whereas the Romans lost 2,000 of their number.[76]

The battle ended hostilities in the Second Macedonian War. It also ended the near-perfect run of victories that the Macedonian phalanx had enjoyed since the time of Philip II, and introduced the era of the formidable Roman legion.[77] Philip escaped the battlefield, but Flamininus overrode an Aetolian demand for his surrender, one of many spats he had with them after the battle.[78] He imposed a four-month truce to allow the Senate time to decide Philip's fate and arrangements for Greece, and for him to deal with Macedonia's ally Boeotia. With his tacit support, the pro-Macedonian Boeotarch (chief official) of the Boeotian League, Brachylles, was assassinated; in retaliation his supporters killed 500 Roman soldiers, and Flamininus invaded Boeotia, eventually agreeing to an indemnity of 30 talents and the surrender of the murderers.[79]

The Roman Proclamation of Freedom

The Senate imposed surprisingly lenient terms on Philip, and peace was sworn to in 196.[80] He was allowed to keep the throne, but from now on he had to stay in Macedonia proper (north of Mount Olympus); relinquish his fleet and the fetters of Greece; pay Rome a huge war indemnity of 1,000 talents; and surrender hostages (including his ten-year-old son Demetrius) to ensure his good behavior. As a result of his effective house arrest, Philip turned to deal with Macedonia's manpower, borders, and economic plight,

---

[76] Polybius 18.22–26, with Walbank 1940, pp. 167–172; Hammond 1988; Hammond and Walbank 1988, pp. 432–443; Matyszak 2009, pp. 88–94; Waterfield 2014, pp. 89–93.
[77] In-depth comments on the strengths and weaknesses of the phalanx and its fate against the legion at Polybius 18.28–32 (= M. M. Austin 2006, no. 83, pp. 170–172 abridged); cf. Waterfield 2014, pp. 128–134.
[78] Hammond and Walbank 1988, p. 443.
[79] Polybius 18.26, 43; Livy 33.27.5–29.12, with Ferguson 1911, p. 279; Walbank 1940, p. 178; Ager 1996, pp. 210–211.
[80] Polybius 18.44.3–7; Livy 33.30.2–11, with Walbank 1940, pp. 179–185; Gruen 1984, pp. 399–402.

and in the last years of his reign he rescued his kingdom from the years of devastation.

Then Flamininus summoned representatives from the anxious Greek cities to Corinth for an announcement at the Isthmian Games, where he issued a short and startling proclamation on behalf of the Senate:[81]

> The Senate of Rome and Titus Quinctius the proconsul [commander], after defeating King Philip and the Macedonians, leave the following peoples free, without garrison, without tribute, and in full enjoyment of their ancestral laws: the Corinthians, Phocians, Locrians, Euboeans, Achaeans of Phthiotis, Magnesians, Thessalians, and Perrhaebians.

The Greeks at first did not properly hear what he said (or perhaps did not understand what was happening) and the herald had to repeat it. Once its import had sunk in, they rose to their feet, applauding loudly, ignoring the athletes at the games, and cried out so loudly that the noise apparently disrupted the airwaves and ravens flying overhead fell into the stadium.[82] They voted all manner of honors on Flamininus, even setting up cults (hence worshipping him) in Larissa, Chalcis, Corinth, Argos, and Achaea, perhaps because of the rise of pro-Roman factions there, and an equestrian statue of him at Delphi.[83] As one scholar claims, "such expressions of gratitude may represent genuine enthusiasm—or efforts to curry favor."[84] But statues to Romans at this time were rare, so one for Flamininus was a sign of evident Greek relief; the Greeks may also have held him in high regard because of his known philhellenism and for liberating them—both reasons why Plutarch wrote so flatteringly of him in his biography.[85]

The Greek settlement of 196 has been described as "one of the most sensible and effective pieces of diplomacy in the whole course of Rome's rise to world

---

[81] Polybius 18.46.5 (= M. M. Austin 2006, no. 84, pp. 172–174; trans. Austin); Diodorus 28.9; Livy 33.32–33; Plutarch, *Flamininus* 10.3–4; Ager 1996, pp. 2113–2218. On the proclamation and Roman intentions: Errington 1971a, pp. 1533–1555; Gruen 1984, pp. 103 and 448–449; Eckstein 2008, pp. 283–305; Dmitriev 2011, pp. 153–165; Waterfield 2014, pp. 98–99.
[82] Polybius 18.46.6–15; Plutarch, *Flamininus* 10.5–6.
[83] Plutarch, *Flamininus* 10, 16–1; pro-Roman groups: Hammond and Walbank 1988, p. 446.
[84] Gruen 1984, p. 167.
[85] Bremer 2005.

power."⁸⁶ But was it? At the end of the day, the definition of "free" to Greeks was quite different from that of Romans, so Flamininus' proclamation was mere propaganda.⁸⁷ After all, it would surely not have been lost on the Greeks that Flamininus had installed garrisons in the fetters of Greece, and that as a goodwill gesture he unilaterally gave Eretria (on Euboea) to Eumenes II of Pergamum (who had recently succeeded his deceased father). As the Aetolians were supposed to have said, "what took place was a readjustment of masters and not any restoration of freedom."⁸⁸ Ironically, this proclamation marked anything but freedom, as Rome was intent on becoming the dominant power in the eastern Mediterranean, and achieved that within decades.⁸⁹ Perhaps the Greeks in their apparent euphoria were naïve to the change in masters, but all we can say with certainty is that Rome had decided not to annex Greece *yet*.

If the Senate had treated Athens high-handedly in the negotiations after Cynoscephalae, then Flamininus' treatment of the Aetolian League was worse.⁹⁰ Under the terms of its treaty of 212 with Rome (during the First Macedonian War), the league was to receive all territory won in the war while the Romans could have all portable booty. It was now time to honor those terms, but Flamininus gave the Aetolians only Phocis and the western half of Thessaly, claiming they had violated the treaty when they made an alliance with Philip in 206. Despite Aetolian protests the Senate sided with him, but it was that conduct that before long drove the Aetolians to invite Antiochus into Greece against Rome, as we shall see in the next chapter.

Athens had not been granted any material gains at the end of the war, but it still had influence in Greece, and the Piraeus was a valuable harbor used regularly by Roman and allied fleets.⁹¹ But perhaps with an eye to its future the city began to promote its culture and learning, especially in two areas that would captivate the Romans: philosophy and rhetoric. The increasing influx of visitors to the city in the shape of sailors, soldiers, visiting dignitaries, distinguished Romans, and even kings like Attalus (who visited in 199 and in 198 before dying in 197) was a boost for the local economy.⁹² But soon Romans would be going to Athens to study and simply to visit, inaugurating a new phase in relations between the two.

---

[86] Errington 1971a, p. 155.
[87] See Gruen 1984, pp. 132–157 and 448–456; Dmitriev 2011, pp. 166–199 and 228–282; Waterfield 2014, pp. 100–103.
[88] Polybius 18.45 (quote at 18.45.6).
[89] Eckstein 2008, pp. 342–381.
[90] For example, Errington 1971a, pp. 151–153 and 154–155; Waterfield 2014, p. 97.
[91] Garland 1987, p. 54.
[92] Perrin 1996.

8

Being Free without Freedom

AFTER THE BATTLE OF CYNOSCEPHALAE, Athens sent Cephisodorus of Xypete to Rome, probably so that the city could have some say in what would happen to Macedonia. He may also have petitioned the Senate to restore to Athens the islands of Delos, Lemnos, Imbros, and Scyros, which were former possessions lost to Macedonia probably at the end of the Chremonidean War in 261. That he may have done so is based on part of Polybius' account of an embassy on a similar matter to the Senate nearly thirty years later, in 168: "We do not object to them [the Athenians] for wanting Delos and Lemnos, since they have claimed these islands before."[1] When was the "before" of these claims? A plausible context is Cephisodorus' mission in 197. But even though the Athenians had fought with Rome against Philip, the Senate made no restoration (in 197), even going so far as to declare Lemnos independent.[2] Its high-handed action well illustrates that the days of Athens as a feared military power were well and truly over.

A Greek Battleground

The chances that warfare between Rome and the Aetolians would occur and that Athens would side with Rome remained high after Cynoscephalae. At a meeting on Roman-Aetolian relations organized by Flamininus at Corinth

---

[1] Polybius 30.20.3.
[2] Ferguson 1911, p. 280.

in 195, the Aetolians had criticized the Athenians for backing Roman actions in Greece, and likewise the Athenians had castigated the Aetolians for their politicking.³ In 194, Roman troops left Greece, withdrawing their control of the fetters of Greece. Unfortunately, their gesture came two years too late, for in 193 the Aetolians sent embassies to Sparta, with Philip V and Antiochus III urging them to rise against Rome. The Romans sent Flamininus to deal with the Aetolians in 192.⁴ In response, they simply told him they intended to invite Antiochus to arbitrate between them and Rome.⁵

The Athenians were in a quandary. There was every chance that Antiochus, who by now ruled an empire from Asia Minor (excluding Pergamum, Rome's ally) to Afghanistan, would use the situation that the Aetolians presented him with as a stepping-stone to involvement in Greek affairs. Antiochus was a valuable friend, but he was also a key ally of the Aetolians—and equally unsettling to Rome was that he had offered Hannibal refuge in 195.⁶ But if the Athenians sided with Rome, they would lose their standing with Antiochus. The Antiochus factor, to call it that, polarized public opinion. A group in the city, led by a politician named Apollodorus, saw in Antiochus the very real opportunity to break with Rome, and when in 192 Flamininus visited the city to persuade it not to support the Syrian king, Apollodorus and his supporters prevented him from speaking at an Assembly.⁷ He did not take any steps against Athens, but Flamininus would not have forgotten his treatment.

Antiochus had been careful not to antagonize the Romans, but their encroachment on his position and possessions led him to take the offensive, promising the Greeks their freedom if they would back him against Rome.⁸ In the fall of 192 war began when he landed a large army of 10,000 infantry

---

³ Livy 34.22.7–23.11, with Ferguson 1911, pp. 280–281.
⁴ Gruen 1984, pp. 456–462; Hammond and Walbank 1988, pp. 448–449.
⁵ Ager 1996, pp. 230–232; Eckstein 2006, pp. 301–304. The Romans were not used to how the Greeks conducted interstate relations and arbitration disputes, and the Senate had a different idea of how to reconcile issues: Gruen 1984, pp. 96–119; Kallet-Marx 1995, pp. 161–183 (after 148); Eckstein 2006, pp. 37–78. For a survey of 171 instances of arbitration from the late fourth to end of the second centuries, see Ager 1996.
⁶ Antiochus' conquests: Gruen 1984, pp. 612–619; see too M. M. Austin 2006, no. 187, pp. 337–338 (= Polybius 11.34).
⁷ Habicht 1989, pp. 10–14; Habicht 1982, pp. 194–197.
⁸ Rome's interactions with Antiochus that led to war: Walbank 1940, pp. 186–196; Gruen 1984, pp. 620–632; Errington 1989b, pp. 274–289; Eckstein 2006, pp. 292–306; Eckstein 2008, pp. 306–325; Dmitriev 2011, pp. 209–223.

and 500 cavalry at Demetrias (which the Aetolians had recently seized so as to provide him with a safe base).⁹ Apollodorus was certainly in favor of Antiochus' offer, but sanity returned when the bulk of the Athenians realized they would stand little chance against the legions that Flamininus could field against them. Leon of Aixone, another politician from a powerful family, had Apollodorus exiled, after which the Athenians opened the Piraeus to their allies.¹⁰ Nevertheless, to be on the safe side, the following year (191) Manius Acilius Glabrio, the commander of the Roman troops in Greece, sent his military tribune, Marcus Porcius Cato, to several Greek cities, including Athens, to stress Roman friendship and keep them on side.¹¹

In the spring of 191 Glabrio defeated the army of Antiochus and the Aetolians at Thermopylae, ousting Antiochus from Greece, and a Roman fleet, which had anchored in the Piraeus, inflicted damage on his vessels.¹² The Aetolians, left once more to fight on alone (as they had been in 206), appealed to Athens to act as a go-between between them and Glabrio to bring about peace.¹³ The Athenians were quick to agree, and in 190 an Athenian embassy, headed by Echedemus of Cydathenaeum, second in influence only to Leon, went to Glabrio, who was besieging Amphissa in Aetolia.¹⁴ He was open to ending the war, but despite three separate trips between Amphissa and the Aetolian authorities in Hypata to discuss each side's demands, Echedemus could only arrange a truce.¹⁵

There was always the possibility that Antiochus might return to Greece, but the Romans were not going to let that happen. In 190 they sent an army under the brothers Scipio Africanus (victor over Hannibal in the Second Punic War) and Lucius Cornelius Scipio to Asia Minor. In tandem with Eumenes of Pergamum, they defeated Antiochus at Magnesia (western Asia Minor) in 189, and the ensuing Peace of Apamea of 188 saw Antiochus,

---

⁹ Gruen 1984, pp. 632–643; Hammond and Walbank 1988, pp. 449–455; Habicht 1989, pp. 16–17; Green 1990, pp. 420–423; Grainger 2002; Eckstein 2008, pp. 325–336; Matyszak 2009, pp. 106–113.
¹⁰ Livy 35.50.4, with Ferguson 1911, p. 284. Family of Leon: Habicht 1982, pp. 194–197; cf. Grieb 2008, pp. 120–121.
¹¹ Cato spoke in Latin to the Assembly, with his speech translated by an interpreter: Plutarch, *Cato Major* 12.4–5, with Ferguson 1911, p. 283.
¹² Walbank 1940, pp. 202–204; Waterfield 2014, pp. 119–122.
¹³ Polybius 20.9–10 (= M. M. Austin 2006, no. 85, pp. 174–175 abridged).
¹⁴ Ferguson 1911, pp. 285–286; Habicht 1982, pp. 189–193.
¹⁵ Walbank 1940, pp. 209–210.

among other things, forced to pay an indemnity of a staggering 15,000 talents, stay clear of Greece and Asia Minor, and give up his war fleet and territory north and west of the Taurus Mountains.[16] He died one year later, in 187. The Peace meant that Rome had muzzled Seleucid power in the east, leaving only the Antigonid and the Ptolemaic dynasties still controlling all their territories.[17]

Greece would be next: "It is only with the defeat of Antiochus and the Peace of Apamea (188) that the nature of the Roman settlement of Greece can begin to be discerned."[18] When news of Antiochus' defeat in 189 reached the Aetolians, they asked Rhodes and Athens to negotiate peace for them with Rome.[19] An embassy from all three appeared before the Senate, where Leon's speech changed the anti-Aetolian sentiment of the senators, who saw him as someone they could count on.[20] The Senate agreed to make a treaty, thereby ending Rome's war with the Aetolian League.

What had Athens gained from siding with Rome in this war? The answer is precious little. But the Aetolian defeat opened up the opportunity of a renewed role for the Athenians in the Amphictyonic Council, which forged closer ties with Delphi for them and enabled them to mediate on a number of disputes.[21] For some time the Aetolians had controlled the Oracle of Apollo and dominated the council, controlling as many as fifteen of the twenty-four votes. The citizens of Delphi asked Glabrio to assign sole control of the shrine, Pythian Games, and the *Soteria* festival to them. Their appeal went against centuries of tradition, for the Greeks had formed amphictyonies so that no one city should control an oracular site. Glabrio refused and tasked the Thessalians (influential council members) and the Athenians with reorganizing the council's composition and organization, which they did between 186 and 184 with the Senate's approval.[22]

---

[16] Gruen 1984, pp. 640–643; Errington 1989b, pp. 288–289; Ager 1996, pp. 266–267; Eckstein 2008, pp. 333–335; Waterfield 2014, pp. 134–136.

[17] Derow 2003, p. 66. On Rome and the Seleucid decline, see Gruen 1984, pp. 644–671. See too Errington 1971a, pp. 242–256, on Rome's power after Pydna (in 167), on which battle see below. Rome's contacts with Egypt in the period down to Julius Caesar are beyond our scope, but on them see Gruen 1984, pp. 672–719. That Rome and its people always aimed at expansion in the west and east: Harris 1979, but note by contrast Kallet-Marx 1995. Later Ptolemies: H. A. Thompson 1994, pp. 310–322.

[18] Derow 1989, p. 290.

[19] Ferguson 1911, pp. 285–287; Ager 1996, pp. 258–262.

[20] Cf. Mattingly 1997, p. 123.

[21] Habicht 1997a, pp. 275–279.

[22] Habicht 1987.

One question that needs to be asked is when Athens made a formal treaty of alliance (*foedus*) with Rome. That it did is evidenced by a passage in Tacitus (admittedly writing nearly three hundred years later), which says that when Germanicus visited Athens (in AD 18), "out of respect for our treaty (*foedus*) with an allied and ancient city," he took with him only one lictor (a bodyguard carrying wooden rods and an axe to symbolize life and death), thus indicating the existence of a treaty.[23]

In 200, at the start of the Second Macedonian War, Athens did not formally ally with Rome against Philip, as we have seen. A logical time to make an alliance, therefore, might have been during or at the end of that war, because of the Roman support the city had received.[24] But Athens was pressed hard during the war and at its end was weak: Would Rome have wanted to enter into an alliance with a city in that condition?[25] We might also expect that the Athenians would have been condemned for violating any previous alliance in 192 when Apollodorus opposed Rome and favored Antiochus; that they were not castigated suggests an earlier one did not exist. Thus a more likely time for an alliance was toward the tail end, or the conclusion, of Rome's war against the Aetolians and Antiochus. Between 191 and 188, prayers accompanying sacrifices for the welfare of the state began to include the phrase "and for that of our allies," which may well include the Romans; if so, then perhaps Leon also orchestrated an official alliance with Rome.[26] That would thus give us a date of 191, after which the Senate adopted a more benevolent attitude to Athens.

When the six-month truce between the Aetolian League and Rome ended, the Aetolians refused to bow to the Senate's demand of alliance and an indemnity of 1,000 talents; instead, they attacked Philip, who received no support from the Roman troops in Greece. Philip was justifiably aggrieved, especially as he had earlier assisted the army of the Scipio brothers

---

[23] Tacitus, *Annals* 2.53.3. Malissard 2007 does not discuss the treaty but argues the passage shows Tacitus' favorable view of the Greeks. Tacitus may even refer to an informal relationship than a formal treaty as ancient writers used different terms (such as *foedus* and *amicitia*) for the same thing: cf. Burton 2011, pp. 79–84, and on informal relations between Athens and Rome, see Burton 2013. But I accept the veracity of the passage as to a formal *foedus*.

[24] For example, Accame 1946, p. 101; Hammond and Walbank 1988, p. 421; Hammond 1992, p. 345; Grieb 2008, p. 114.

[25] Indeed, Bernhardt 1971, pp. 86, 102–103 and Gruen 1984, p. 24, suggest there was no alliance before 167, while Kallet-Marx 1995, pp. 200–201, says if it happened it was sometime in the second century.

[26] Habicht 1997a, pp. 212–213, citing bibliography.

as it passed through his kingdom.[27] In gratitude for his help, Rome had cancelled the remainder of the indemnity and returned his younger son Demetrius (then about sixteen), one of the hostages demanded in 196, to him.[28] But the Romans must have been aware that some 5,000 soldiers who had been serving with Antiochus went over to Philip and that he maintained control over the Thessalian cities, which is perhaps why they did not march to his aid at that time. A resentful Philip began to plot revenge against Rome; he would not live to implement his plan, but his son Perseus would.

The Collapse of Macedonia

Rome had localized Philip to Macedonia in 196. He had done little to cause friction since then, although he had been increasing his influence in Greece, which made Rome suspicious of his aspirations.[29] It is often thought that he strove to win the support of the lower social strata in the Greek cities, but such populism was never his agenda.[30] The Romans may have hoped that his younger son Demetrius, who had been a hostage in Rome, would succeed his father and not his more militant and anti-Roman eldest son, Perseus. Flamininus may have personally liked Demetrius more, although that does not mean there was a move to secure the throne for him.[31] But Perseus seems to have seen Demetrius as a threat and convinced his father he was a traitor; despite the lack of evidence, he was executed in 180.[32]

Philip V died suddenly in 179. His long reign had certainly seen its share of ups and downs, but after 196 he had devoted considerable attention to his kingdom. Economic recovery is evidenced especially in his measures to increase agricultural production, the renewed exploitation of the mines, and new coinage. He rebuilt Macedonian manpower and crafted a foreign policy to protect his borders and extend his territory even if it did cause tension with Rome. The Macedonia he left Perseus was a strong and prosperous one, so much so that Perseus had the resources and manpower to pose a serious threat to Rome—his army comprised 43,000 troops, roughly the

---

[27] Walbank 1940, pp. 198–201; Errington 1971a, pp. 195–201; Hammond and Walbank 1988, pp. 449–450.
[28] Walbank 1940, pp. 210–211.
[29] Walbank 1940, pp. 223–257.
[30] Mendels 1977; Gruen 1981.
[31] Dell 1983; Matyszak 2009, pp. 123–124; Waterfield 2014, pp. 161–164. Though note the justified caution of Gruen 1974, pp. 234 and 245 (Roman passivity to Macedonia) and Green 1990, pp. 425–426.
[32] Walbank 1940, pp. 251–252; Dell 1983.

same number of military personnel as Alexander the Great had led into Asia in 334.³³

Because of Philip's alliance with Hannibal in 215, he could be seen as the instigator of Rome's involvement in Greece; Polybius certainly blamed him, and criticized his instability, which seemingly had him acting emotionally rather than rationally, and wrote of him as a tragic figure.³⁴ But Philip does not deserve this bad press. His ambition to extend Macedonia was no different from that of Philip II or Alexander the Great or even Poliorcetes. The last word should perhaps be from those of the times as they knew best: the Macedonians set up a dedication to him at Delos with this inscription: "the community of Macedones (honors) king Philip, son of king Demetrius, for his excellent and loyal conduct."³⁵ The Greeks also were taken enough with him to call him "the darling of the Greeks."³⁶

Perseus succeeded Philip. Ruling until 168, he would be Macedonia's last legitimate king.³⁷ No doubt hoping to prevent any Roman retaliation over the death of his brother, he successfully persuaded the Senate to renew the friendship (*amicitia*) it had had with his father.³⁸ He ruled Macedonia well (even recalling exiles), and despite opposition from Athens and the Achaean League the Greeks of the mainland and Asia Minor generally approved of him and his rule.³⁹ However, he clashed with Rome over his expansionist policies in Greece and as far afield as Thrace and Byzantium, including battling the chieftain Abrupolis (Rome's ally), who had been encroaching on his territory.

Moreover, during Philip V's last years Eumenes II of Pergamum had set his sights on Macedonia, and that goal did not change when Perseus came

---

³³ Livy 42.51 (= M. M. Austin 2006, no. 94, pp. 186–187), with Hammond and Walbank 1988, pp. 484, 515, and 541; Alexander's army: Worthington 2014, pp. 139–140.
³⁴ See Walbank 1938; cf. Walbank 1970. Against Polybius: Dreyer 2013; cf. on how Philip's youth at the time of his accession affected Polybius' view and treatment of him: McGing 2013.
³⁵ *SIG* 575, trans. Hammond and Walbank 1988, pp. 486–487. Economic recovery and coinage: Hammond and Walbank 1988, pp. 458–468; foreign policy: Hammond and Walbank 1988, pp. 468–472; general assessment of Philip's reign: Walbank 1938; Walbank 1940, pp. 258–275; Gruen 1974; Hammond and Walbank 1988, pp. 472–487.
³⁶ Nicholson 2018.
³⁷ Sources (largely hostile) on Perseus and the Third Macedonian War: Hammond and Walbank 1988, pp. 488–489 and 532–533. Reign of Perseus: Errington 1971a, pp. 202–226; Bousquet 1981; Hammond and Walbank 1988, pp. 490–558; Derow 1989, pp. 302–319; Matyszak 2009, pp. 126–156; Waterfield 2014, pp. 166–167 and 173–193.
³⁸ Gruen 1984, p. 403.
³⁹ Polybius 25.3.1–8; Livy 41.24.11–18, 42.11.6–12.10, with Gruen 1984, pp. 403–408; Hammond and Walbank 1988, pp. 494–495.

to power. He attempted to convince Rome that Perseus was preparing to invade Italy, which Perseus vehemently denied.[40] Eumenes personally went to Rome in 172, but his scare tactics did not work. En route home he decided to consult the Oracle of Apollo at Delphi. As he walked through a narrow defile, bandits, or perhaps even a small group of Macedonians, attacked him; he was struck on the head by falling rocks, and immediately accused Perseus of trying to kill him.[41] His denunciation worked, and after some diplomatic dealings with the Greeks, the Senate declared war on Perseus in 171; this Third Macedonian War would last until 168.[42]

The Athenians offered their army and navy to Rome. Sometime before they had reorganized their cavalry, phasing out the *prodromoi* in favor of another specialist unit, the Tarentines or javelin-throwing light cavalry.[43] Athens had already used them as mercenaries in 279 when fighting the Galatians. For some reason the Romans used only some Athenian troops, but they did require the people to provision their own men to the tune of 100,000 bushels of grain. As we know, Athens was always dependent on imported grain, so this demand stretched the city to its limit, especially as grain prices were sharply on the rise.[44] We can thus understand why poorer people resented Rome—generally speaking, wealthier Athenians were largely pro-Roman but poorer ones (indeed poorer Greeks) were anti-Roman, as they viewed them as supporters of the wealthy, and hence with suspicion.[45]

The events of the war do not concern us here. After several conflicts in Macedonia and Thessaly, including the defeat of a Roman army in 171 at Callinicus (Thessaly), in June 168 the newly elected consul Lucius Aemilius Paullus (the son of the Paullus who was killed fighting Hannibal in 216 at Cannae) brought Perseus to battle at Pydna (on the Macedonian coastline, near Mount Olympus). In a bloody conflict (in which Athenians fought

---

[40] Gruen 1984, pp. 550–563.
[41] Livy 42.15.4–16, 18.1; cf. Polybius 22.18.5–8. Possibly Perseus was behind the attempt, but we do not know for sure.
[42] Errington 1971a, pp. 213–226; Walbank 1977; Harris 1979, pp. 227–233; W. L. Adams 1982; Gruen 1984, pp. 408–419, 423–429, and 505–514; Hammond and Walbank 1988, pp. 505–557; Derow 1989, pp. 310–316; Green 1990, pp. 429–431; Matyszak 2009, pp. 131–155; Eckstein 2010, pp. 243–245. On the assassination story, see E. V. Hansen 1971, pp. 110–111; Hammond and Walbank 1988, p. 499.
[43] Bugh 1998, pp. 88–89, citing bibliography.
[44] Day 1942, pp. 47–48.
[45] Ferguson 1911, pp. 281–283; Day 1942, p. 29. Athens and Rome generally: Mattingly 1997, pp. 140–144.

bravely alongside him) he decisively defeated Perseus, but made the comment that "he had never seen so frightening a sight" as when he confronted the massed Macedonian phalanx bearing down on his line.[46] Perseus survived the battle and fled, but eventually surrendered. He was taken to Rome, where he was led before Paullus' chariot in his spectacular three-day triumph and witnessed the state awarding his victor the name *Macedonicus*; he was then incarcerated in the Italian town of Alba Fucens, dying there in 166.[47]

To ensure a passive Macedonia in the future, the following year (167) Rome ended the Antigonid dynasty, partitioning the kingdom into four independent republics (each one isolated from the others).[48] The people were to be free, but they were to pay Rome half the taxes they had normally paid to the Macedonian king; more significantly, their gold and silver reserves were not to be mined, nor could timber be used for a fleet, and no trade could be conducted between the four republics, thereby reducing economic activity to prevent any resurgence of power. Thus the Antigonid dynasty came to an end, as did the Macedonian state, with Rome now completely dominating the former kingdom. At the same time a good question has been posed: "How much significant change had really taken place in mainland Greece?"[49] Greece itself was still independent, and Paullus was ordered to withdraw his troops from Greece.

But a difference this time was that on the Senate's orders, in 167 Paullus invaded Epirus, which had supported Macedonia, sacking some seventy towns, destroying their fortification walls, seizing 150,000 inhabitants as slaves, and returning to Rome with immense booty and prestige.[50] That sort of conduct was the shape of things to come.

---

[46] Plutarch, *Paullus* 19.2. Battle: Hammond and Walbank 1988, pp. 547–557; Matyszak 2009, pp. 151–155; Waterfield 2014, pp. 187–190.
[47] Paullus' triumph: Plutarch, *Paullus* 32–34, with Waterfield 2014, pp. 204–206. Death of Perseus: Plutarch, *Paullus* 37.
[48] Roman settlement: Livy 45.29.3–30, 32.1–7 (= M. M. Austin 2006, no. 96, pp. 189–192), with Morgan 1969; Errington 1971a, p. 226; Harris 1979, pp. 143–146; Gruen 1982; Gruen 1984, pp. 429–436; Hammond and Walbank 1988, pp. 563–567; Waterfield 2014, pp. 190–193; Pugliese 2014.
[49] Gruen 1984, p. 517; see pp. 514–523 on Greece after Pydna, but note Errington 1971a, pp. 229–241, on the servitude of the Greeks to Roman power.
[50] Livy 45.34.1–6; Plutarch, *Paullus* 29; Appian, *Illyrian Wars* 9, with Gruen 1984, pp. 516–517; Hammond and Walbank 1988, pp. 567–569; Waterfield 2014, pp. 201–204. Good discussion of impact of Roman military intervention on civilians: Naco del Hoyo et al. 2009.

It Pays to Be Rome's Friend

After Pydna, Paullus toured Greece. At Delphi he commissioned a spectacular equestrian statue of himself atop a column, 9 meters high, in front of the temple of Apollo. To highlight his victory (if that were needed) he used column bases that Perseus had set aside for himself, adding the emphatically Latin inscription: *L. Aimilius L. f. imperator de rege Perse Macedonibusque cepet* (Lucius Aemilius, son of Lucius, Imperator, took this from King Perseus and the Macedonians).[51]

In the early fall, he and his son Scipio Aemilianus visited Athens.[52] Paullus was an intellectual and a genuine philhellene, so it is hardly surprising he wanted to visit a city steeped in history and culture.[53] In doing so, he became the first Roman we know of who went to the city for purely sightseeing purposes, thereby opening the door to an influx of Roman visitors over the following decades.[54] The Athenians welcomed him, motivated by his obvious military power, although his interest in the Piraeus, the Long Walls, and other areas of the city, as well as his sacrifice to Athena on the Acropolis, may have endeared him somewhat to the people.

When he asked for a tutor for his children and a painter to depict his triumphal procession in Rome, the Athenians offered him both in the shape of one man: Metrodorus. Paullus presumably thought he had landed a "great catch," but little is known of Metrodorus' philosophical school.[55] Still, it was Paullus' interest in Greek culture that led Plutarch to write as flattering a biography of him as he did of Flamininus as a philhellene, liberator, and man of high morality.[56] And as a mark of their regard for him, the Athenians may

---

[51] Polybius 30.10.1–2; Livy 45.27.5–7; Plutarch, *Paullus* 28.4; Sherk 1984, no. 24, p. 24; see the discussion, citing bibliography, at Hammond and Walbank 1988, pp. 613–617, M. J. Taylor 2016. Artist reconstruction: Waterfield 2014, p. 192. Rawson 1989, p. 440, is skeptical of Plutarch, *Flamininus* 12.6–7, that Flamininus composed his own dedication in Greek.

[52] Livy 45.27.11–28.1; Plutarch, *Paullus* 28.1–2.

[53] Holland 2005. Philhellenism: Gruen 1984, pp. 250–272. Romans embracing Greek artistic, literary, and other genres will feature throughout the rest of the book.

[54] Habicht 1997c, p. 9 and passim, Rödel 2010; note Rawson 1989, pp. 462–463, that for all his sightseeing Paullus was focused on strategic possibilities in Greece. See too Bowersock 1965, pp. 73–77.

[55] Rawson 1989, p. 462; Habicht 1994b, p. 245.

[56] Bremer 2005.

have presented him with a statue of Athena, which he placed in the temple of Fortuna in Rome.⁵⁷

Paullus' attitude to the Athenians was in stark contrast to how Rome treated its allies Pergamum, Rhodes, and the Achaean League for what it perceived to be too little zeal or loyalty. Eumenes II was accused of secretly intriguing with Perseus; the king personally went to defend himself in Rome, but on landing in Italy he was ordered to leave immediately. Rome chastised the Rhodians and took back Caria and Lycia, which the Romans had given to Rhodes after the war against Antiochus.⁵⁸ The most badly treated were the Achaeans, who among other things had not wanted to see the end of an independent Macedonia. The Romans seized 1,500 Achaeans, imprisoned them in Italy for fifteen years without trial, and refused any other Achaeans access to them. One of them was the historian Polybius, who was befriended by Scipio Aemilianus.

Paullus might well have treated the Athenians respectfully, and they may have enjoyed diplomatic success elsewhere, but they did not always get their own way. In 167 they sent an embassy to the Senate, petitioning that the people of Haliartus in Boeotia be allowed to return and rebuild their city.⁵⁹ The Romans had destroyed this city in 171, killing all its inhabitants apart from 2,500 troops who were sold into slavery. The Senate refused the Athenian request, at which point the ambassadors switched tack and asked for the territory of Haliartus for themselves, together with Delos and Lemnos. This time the Senate did not refuse.

Why did the Athenians' first support and then abruptly abandon the people of Haliartus? Polybius (after excusing them for asking again for Delos and Lemnos, as we noted earlier) has a long condemnation of them for their selfishness:⁶⁰

> As for the territory of Haliartus we are justified in finding fault with [the Athenians]. For not to strive by every means to restore the fallen fortunes of a city almost the most ancient in Boeotia, but on the contrary to

---

⁵⁷ Pliny, *NH* 33.135 and 34.54.
⁵⁸ Polybius 30.31 (= M. M. Austin 2006, no. 98, pp. 193–194 abridged). On the actions of the Rhodians and the decline of Rhodes' power after Pydna, cf. Gruen 1984, pp. 563–566 and 569–572; Berthold 1984, pp. 179–212; Dmitriev 2011, pp. 283–312. On Rhodes generally see Berthold 1984.
⁵⁹ Polybius 30.20, with Ferguson 1911, pp. 315–316; cf. Graindor 1927a, pp. 2–3.
⁶⁰ Polybius 30.20.3–7 (Loeb trans. modified).

erase it from the map, by depriving its unhappy inhabitants of all hope for the future, was evidently conduct unworthy of any Greek state and especially unworthy of Athens. For now, while they were making their own city the common refuge of all who wished to be citizens of it, to destroy thus the cities of others was by no means consonant with the traditions of the city.

Perhaps the Athenians were merely using the Haliartus cause as a pawn in their greater game of getting their island possessions back. If the Senate had permitted the people of Haliartus to return, then the successful embassy would have followed with its own petition about the islands. When the Senate said no, the now unsuccessful Athenians performed a *volte-face*, cobbling together Haliartian territory and their former islands as one. Polybius was right to accuse the Athenians of acting cynically, but what he did not see was how quickly the Athenians turned a diplomatic rebuff to their advantage with this self-serving request, a maneuver presumably also appealing to the Roman mindset.

Athens received Delos in 167, and in the same year Delians were forced to leave their native island to make way for Athenian cleruchs (settlers). At the same time the annual chief official of Delos, the *epimeletes* (governor), was appointed, who was always drawn from the ranks of the Areopagus in Athens.[61] But the Senate had a stipulation in giving the city this island: the Athenians could not impose any import or export tariffs on it, so they had to treat it as a free harbor. This move may have been at the behest of Italian traders, given that Delos had eclipsed Rhodes as the center of Mediterranean trade.[62] Italians came to make up the largest percentage of the island's population, and so would have expected Rome to look after their interests.[63] We also see in the Senate's ruling that Rome was starting to dictate the terms of Greek trading ventures as part of the spread of its "commercial diplomacy" in the Aegean.[64]

Delos enjoyed great prosperity, helped by its growing slave market attracting large numbers of buyers. Although Athens had been thriving, its

---

[61] Habicht 1991a; Habicht 1997a, p. 322.
[62] Rhodes' income from tariffs fell sharply by 85 per cent, from 1,000,000 drachmas to 150,000 per year: Ferguson 1911, pp. 331–333.
[63] Ferguson 1911, pp. 346–414.
[64] E. L. Will 1997.

acquisition of the island benefitted the city even more.[65] But as Polybius well remarked, in taking the island (along with Lemnos) the people had seized "the wolf by the ears."[66] Only a few years after Athens assumed control, a dispute over the Sarapeion (the temple to Serapis, a Graeco-Egyptian deity first introduced by Ptolemy I) between officials on the island and Demetrius, the head of the Sarapeion, saw him turning to Rome, which ruled in his favor.[67] The Athenian Boule had no choice but to communicate this decision to the officials, thereby showing who really controlled the island.[68]

Still, the Athenians held on resolutely to those ears for a long time—two decrees toward the tail end of the first century (in 20 or shortly after) record Athenian arbitrators to the island.[69] As well as a significant uptick in Athens' economic well-being, we will see in the next chapters a transformation of political power in Athens as rich traders involved in the island became influential in the city's public life. Rome's emerging presence on the Greek mainland led to members of influential aristocratic families in Athens, who saw their future lying with Rome, coming to the fore in public life.[70] But thanks to the money to be made on Delos the pendulum of political power in Athens swung from those of purely aristocratic blood to wealthy men of all backgrounds.[71]

In the mid-150s the Athenians again found itself involved with Oropus on its northern border with Boeotia. They were as adamant about controlling it for Attica's security as the hostile Boeotian League was of keeping it. In 164 the Athenians invaded its territory, perhaps hoping to intimidate the Oropians into surrender, but instead the latter complained to Rome. The Senate appointed the town of Sicyon—a member of the Achaean League—as arbiter, but the Athenians rebuffed any negotiating.[72] The Sicyonian

---

[65] Day 1942, pp. 50–119; Accame 1946, pp. 183–185. Prosperity of Athens before acquisition of Delos: Perrin 1996; cf. Prost 2007. Athens and Delos in detail: Ferguson 1911, pp. 347–414; Habicht 1997a, pp. 246–263; Tracy 1979; Mikalson 1998, pp. 208–241.
[66] Polybius 30.20.8–9, with Ferguson 1911, pp. 322 and 329–333; Mattingly 1997, p. 141. On Delos under Athenian control, see Ferguson 1911, pp. 347–414; Habicht 1997a, pp. 246–263. Slaves: Green 1990, pp. 528–529; cf. Ferguson 1911, pp. 316–317.
[67] Sherk 1984, no. 5, pp. 37–39.
[68] Tracy 1979, p. 214.
[69] Kallet-Marx and Stroud 1997.
[70] MacKendrick 1969, pp. 43–47.
[71] Aristocrats under Roman rule to Augustus: MacKendrick 1969, pp. 49–67.
[72] Pausanias 7.11.4–6, and on events 7.11–14, with Ferguson 1911, pp. 324–325; Ager 1996, pp. 387–388.

arbiters ordered the Athenians to pay the huge sum of 500 talents to the Oropians, but they refused, and continued to occupy Oropus. A decade passed, and then in 155 the Athenians sent a delegation to Rome to protest the amount. The Athenian representatives were not the usual diplomats, and in fact were not even Athenian: they were the heads of the three philosophical schools: Carneades of Cyrene (Academy), Critolaus of Phaselis in Lycia (Lyceum), and Diogenes from Seleuceia on the Tigris (Stoicism). Although the Senate reduced the fine to 100 talents, Athens maintained its garrison and even took hostages.[73] Oropus successfully appealed, continuing the friction with Athens, but nothing happened.[74]

This "philosophers' embassy" had another impact on the Romans, one that would shape their own culture and learning. It exposed them for the first time to these main philosophical schools, as all three men gave talks about their philosophical systems but couched in different oratorical manners. According to Polybius (who must have been in Rome to see them), using the senator Gaius Acilius as interpreter, Carneades spoke with force and speed, Critolaus with skill and smoothness, and Diogenes with modesty and sobriety.[75] The elderly censor Cato denounced the philosophers because of their sophistic trickeries, especially Carneades' ability to argue the same premise (justice as a principle of politics) differently on successive days, and told him to leave the city.[76] But the conservatism of Cato and men like him had no place in the new Roman mindset: once the Romans had experienced the "allure" of Hellenism they wanted a literary and artistic tradition akin to that of the mainland Greeks.[77]

---

[73] Polybius 32.11.4–5; with Ferguson 1911, pp. 324–328.
[74] SIG^3 675 (= M. M. Austin 2006, no. 157, pp. 284–285), a decree of Oropus of about 150 honoring Hieron of Aegeira (in Achaea) for his help in the dispute with Athens: Habicht 1997a, pp. 265–267.
[75] Polybius 33.2, with Ferguson 1911, pp. 333–345.
[76] Plutarch, *Cato Major* 22, with Rawson 1989, pp. 448–463; MacMullen 1991, p. 436; Habicht 1994b, p. 243; Korhonen 1997, pp. 40–42; David 2000, pp. 83–89; especially Powell 2013. Polybius was likewise critical (33.18.9–11) of such reaction to the potential corruption of things Greeks on Rome; cf. Waterfield 2014, pp. 232–236. Very brief life of Carneades at Diogenes Laertius 4.62–66.
[77] Plutarch, *Cato Major* 22, with Ferguson 1911, pp. 333–345; Wardman 1976; Rawson 1989, pp. 472–473 and passim; Griffin 1994 (e.g., pp. 696–700 on "Hellenization"); Habicht 1997c; Perrin-Saminadayar 2011; cf. Gruen 1984, pp. 250–272; Waterfield 2014, pp. 208–213 and 234–236.

In the first century prominent Romans and their sons went to study and live in Athens, thus bringing about the start of what has been called a "Romanization" of the city (see chapter 10). But it was not all Romans going to Athens. Some who had studied there moved to Rome, such as Philodemus of Gadara (in Syria) in the first century. An Epicurean philosopher and poet, he eventually settled in Herculaneum; his various works (on philosophy, rhetoric, and music, for example) show that intellectuals could also cross to Italy.[78]

The Athenians had played their cards well by siding with Rome in the previous three wars. They had no hostile Macedonia bearing down on them and they were prospering, with a trade network reaching to Egypt, Syria, Palestine, and as far afield as Arabia and the Persian Gulf.[79] They were not as powerful as the Achaean League or Rhodes or Pergamum, for example, but they were allies of Rome, and at least on the face of it the Romans seemed to like them. As a sign of their well-being, and a throwback to life before Macedonian rule, they most likely refounded the Greater Theseia, which had been discontinued in the fourth century; it honored Theseus, the mythical hero who had united Attica under Athens, and so made a political statement of how they saw themselves.[80] But while the Romans certainly were enamored of the city for its culture they were less charmed by its democracy; in fact, they dealt rarely with the city's institutions (other than the Areopagus) and more with individual aristocratic families, who in turn became increasingly powerful, especially through their role in priesthoods in the later Republic and imperial times.

Greece Falls to Rome

In the Peloponnese, the actions of the Achaean League led to Rome's reappearance on the Greek mainland, this time ending in the annexation of Greece in 146.[81] In 188 the league's energetic and ambitious leader, Philopoemen of Megalopolis, captured Sparta, and over the next years expanded his influence.[82] His actions contravened the Roman settlement of

---

[78] See, for example, Gigante 2002.
[79] Day 1942, pp. 84–95; see pp. 96–104 on the commodities traded.
[80] Ferguson 1911, p. 454; Bugh 1990; Mikalson 1998, pp. 252–253.
[81] Harris 1979, pp. 240–244; Gruen 1984, pp. 481–502; Derow 1989, pp. 319–323; Matyszak 2009, pp. 169–173; Dmitriev 2011, pp. 313–350; Waterfield 2014, pp. 222–225.
[82] Errington 1969.

196, protecting cities and guaranteeing independence, but for now Rome sought only a diplomatic solution, and not long after Philopoemen died, thereby preventing actual warfare.

During this period Rome had to deal again with Macedonia. By 158 the Senate had removed some of the commercial embargoes imposed on Macedonia, but in 150 a man named Andriscus claimed to be a son of Perseus and won enough support to reunite Macedonia.[83] He called himself Philip (which is why he is sometimes called Pseudo-Philip), and with the support of Thracian troops defeated a Roman army under the praetor Publius Iuventius Thalna. That victory, along with his attempt to ally with Carthage, triggered the Fourth Macedonian War (149–148).[84]

The Romans sent the general Quintus Caecilius Metellus to Greece in 148, with Pergamum supplying a war fleet. At the second battle of Pydna he defeated Andriscus, who fled to Thrace but was handed over and paraded in Metellus' triumph. Although there were two more pretenders to the Macedonian throne (in later 148 and 143), the kingdom fell under Roman control after Pydna.[85] Rome now came down hard on Macedonia, turning it and Illyria into an actual province, with its capital at Thessalonica, controlled by an annual governor from Rome.[86] It was now that the Romans began construction of the great Via Egnatia, stretching from Thessalonica to Epidamnus on the Adriatic. Macedonia's days as a superpower of the ancient world, going back to Philip II in the mid-fourth century, and even more spectacularly under Alexander the Great, were over. It remained under Rome's thumb, *Provincia Macedonia*, but enjoying some stability and prosperity until Diocletian and Constantine split it up further in the fourth century AD.[87]

South of Mount Olympus, the Achaeans' increasing resentment of Rome brought matters to their inevitable head in 146 with the outbreak of the very short Achaean War.[88] Athens supported Rome, though was not asked

---

[83] Andriscus' background and rise to power: Errington 1971a, pp. 231–233; Gruen 1984, pp. 431–432; Oikonomides 1989; Helliesen 1986; Matyszak 2009, pp. 163–168.

[84] Eckstein 2010, pp. 246–248; Waterfield 2014, pp. 218–220.

[85] Morgan 1969, pp. 430–431.

[86] Papazoglou 1979, pp. 302–325; Baronowski 1988; Kallet-Marx 1995, pp. 11–41, but Eckstein 2010, p. 248, advises caution on the use of the term "province" as the four republics continued to function even in the first century AD; *contra* Gruen 1984, pp. 481–528, that the governor was appointed much later.

[87] Sherk 1984, no. 36, p. 36; Roman Macedonia: Vanderspoel 2010.

[88] Fuks 1970; Green 1990, pp. 448–452.

to supply troops.⁸⁹ The Romans had just ended the Third Punic War with Carthage (149–146) but were quick to send troops to Greece, completely defeating the Achaeans, whose league was now dissolved. On the Senate's orders, the consul Lucius Mummius besieged Corinth, which had been the epicenter of the anti-Roman movement in the Peloponnese. When it capitulated, any male still alive after the attack was murdered, the women and children were sold as slaves, artworks were plundered, and the city was destroyed.⁹⁰ Corinth would not be rebuilt until Julius Caesar so ordered in 44. Mummius' savage reprisal at Corinth was not an isolated action, for when the Third Punic War ended in the same year Rome had destroyed Carthage.

It was obvious that a Greece left to its own devices was too troublesome, and equally apparent that the Romans had never fully grasped the interpolis dynamics and hostilities that were a common thread of Greek history.⁹¹ Thus in 146 the Senate made Greece an official province of Rome, supervised by the Roman governor of Macedonia, thereby beginning a new era in the country's history.⁹² The Athenians marked Greece's novel situation by starting a new list of eponymous archons—the last time they had done so was in 229 when they had regained their freedom from Antigonid rule (p. 133). This time there could not have been the celebrations of 229, so the symbolism of the new list was intended to curry favor with Rome.

After being a battleground going back to the Wars of the Successors, Greece now came to enjoy a peace that brought with it some prosperity. This was evident in Athens, when in 138/7 the people resumed the *Pythais* procession to Delphi, which had not been held since the fourth century.⁹³ Deliberately honoring Pythian Apollo to showcase Athens all the more at Delphi, the procession was a showy and costly affair—in the procession of 128, for example, five

---

⁸⁹ As shown by a decree passed by Athenian settlers in Myrina on Lemnos of this time referring to a military alliance between the two: Habicht 1997a, pp. 272–273.
⁹⁰ Polybius 39.2–6; Pausanias 7.16.7–17.1 (= M. M. Austin 2006, no. 100, pp. 195–196; Sherk 1984, no. 35, pp. 34–35 abridged); Dio 21.72, with Gruen 1984, pp. 520–528; Kallet-Marx 1995, pp. 84–96.
⁹¹ Gruen 1984, pp. 96–119; Eckstein 2006, pp. 37–78; *contra* Kallet-Marx 1995, pp. 42–96, on a lack of Roman interest in Greece.
⁹² Settlement: Gruen 1984, pp. 523–527; Kallet-Marx 1995, pp. 42–96; cf. Waterfield 2014, pp. 225–228; see too McGing 2003, pp. 79–84.
⁹³ Prosperity: Day 1942, pp. 94–95; cf. Habicht 1997a, pp. 276–279. On the religious nature and exploitation of the myth of Apollo, see Karila-Cohen 2005.

hundred citizens participated, including the archons, as well as the singers, musicians, and performers of the artist guild.[94]

But always Rome was center stage in Greece. In 134 the Amphictyonic Council restored the tax exemption status of the Athenian guild of artists, but did so only if "the Romans would not object."[95] And at the *Pythais* of 128 the Athenian musician Limenius composed a new hymn to Apollo.[96] It tells the story of Apollo's birth on Delos, his moves to Athens and Delphi, his battles with the Python and the dragon, and his help in expelling the Galatians in 279. What brought its audience sharply back to the present was its final ode, praising the friendship between Delphi and Athens and appealing to Apollo, Artemis, and Leto to protect Athens, Delphi, the *technitai*, and—significantly—Rome, even calling on the gods to help Rome's empire grow.

Athens in the Second-Century World

By prudently staying aloof of the principal fighting and making its allegiance to Rome known early on, Athens did not suffer anything remotely close to what the Romans had inflicted on Epirus in 167 and, more recently, Corinth. The Athenians continued relationships with other Greeks and foreign rulers as long as these were not contrary to Rome's liking, and they were also busy as negotiators in disputes that extended well beyond Attica.[97]

Thus, in 180/79 we find the Delphians turning to Athens in a territorial quarrel with a neighbor, most likely Amphissa in Locris, since that city asked Rhodes for diplomatic help at the same time and the two requests can be connected.[98] The Athenian Apollodorus resolved the dispute, implying his diplomacy won out over the Rhodian.[99] In 167/6 the Athenians dispatched five members of leading families as arbitrators in a quarrel between the people of Ambracia and Acarnania (to their south). Having suffered terribly in the recent war with Rome, in 187 the Senate declared Ambracia free, but the Acarnanians still distrusted them—until the Athenian arbitrators

---

[94] Ferguson 1911, pp. 372–373; Green 1990, pp. 527–528.
[95] Habicht 1979a, p. 277 with n. 40, for sources.
[96] The following on the hymn is based on Habicht 1997a, pp. 277–278.
[97] For a succinct account of Athens' relations with the major Greek and foreign powers in the second century, on which much of the remainder of the chapter is based, see Habicht 1997a, pp. 220–233 and 264–287.
[98] Ager 1996, pp. 314–317.
[99] Habicht 1997a, p. 228.

reconciled both sides.[100] The distance of the two in northwest Greece was a tribute to Athens' reputation.

Further afield, between 185 and 182 Athens was part of a successful thirteen-state delegation headed by Rhodes to negotiate peace between Miletus and Magnesia-on-the-Maeander (in Ionia) since the Athenians had had close contacts with Miletus for some years.[101] Decades later they were still called on for their negotiating skills, as in 111/10 when Lyttus and Olus on Crete made a treaty and sent a copy to Athens as a neutral city, and later Athenian envoys were able to secure a promise of protection for Athenian and other Greek vessels from the rampant Cretan piracy.[102]

As we have said, the Athenians' association with various Hellenistic monarchs throughout the second century was largely for self-serving reasons—military protection (when Rome could not offer it), monetary donations, and even new public buildings. Their friendship with Ptolemaic Egypt went back to when Athens had Egyptian support against the Antigonids and remained firm at least until the death of Ptolemy VI in 145 when Ptolemaic influence in the Aegean diminished.[103] In 169 they appealed on behalf of Egypt to Antiochus IV of Syria as the two kingdoms were at war; however, Antiochus won over the Athenian delegation, presumably to Ptolemy's consternation.[104] Still, they awarded honorary citizenship to Ptolemaic kings, included them in the Ptolemais tribe, venerated senior officials, and every four years sent an official delegation to Alexandria to attend the Ptolemaea.[105] Ptolemy VI even received an equestrian statue on the Acropolis no less, a clear sign of Athenian gratitude for Ptolemaic investment in the city.[106] In turn, the Ptolemies embraced Athenian citizenship, as we can see from their participation in Athenian festivals, especially the Panathenaea, in which only citizens could compete and the names of victors were inscribed on a public monument. Ptolemy V, for example, won chariot

---

[100] *IG* ii² 951, with Ager 1996, pp. 369–370; Habicht 1997a, p. 232 n. 52.
[101] Habicht 1991b; Habicht 1997a, pp. 229–230.
[102] Treaty: *IG* ii² 1135; piracy: Habicht 1997a, p. 230, citing sources.
[103] Habicht 1992, pp. 68–90; cf. Mattingly 1997, pp. 129–133.
[104] Polybius 28.19–20.
[105] For example Thraseas, an official in the courts of Ptolemy III and IV, and governor of Cilicia in the 220s, was made a citizen and enrolled in the Ptolemais tribe as a decree of about 215 attests: *IG* ii³ 1, 1185; cf. Habicht 1992, p. 76.
[106] Mattingly 1997, pp. 131–132, citing bibliography.

victories there in 182, as did Ptolemy VI in 158, and Cleopatra II in 162.[107] Such involvement also generated publicity for Athens to show that it could attract powerful kings to visit it.

Equally formidable was the Seleucid dynasty. Athens ended up siding with Rome against Antiochus III in 192, yet that did not stop the city wanting to be on friendly terms with Syria. Diplomatic ties were restored when Seleucus IV succeeded his father in 187, and they became closer when his brother Antiochus IV came to power (175–164).[108] This Antiochus had been a hostage demanded by Rome as part of the peace settlement with Antiochus III in 188. He had been released, but instead of returning to the court at Antioch he went to Athens, where he was very popular and received citizenship.[109] In fact, the Athenians were so taken with him that when his brother died and Antiochus faced a pretender threat they formally thanked Eumenes II of Pergamum and honored the brother Philetaerus for helping Antiochus secure the throne.[110] They also honored Seleucid officials, such as Arrhidaeus, commander of Antiochus' royal guard, in 173/2, and when Antiochus died in 164 the Athenians greeted the news with genuine sadness, maintaining links with his successors.[111]

The Athenians also had dealings with the independent kingdom of Pergamum (in Mysia, Asia Minor).[112] Attalus I (r. 241–197) and his son Eumenes II (r. 197–159) both visited Athens during the confrontations with Philip V and Perseus. Eumenes and his brother Attalus II (r. 159–138) took part in the Panathenaea as a means of showing off their Athenian citizenship, and their names are to be found in the chariot victory lists of 178 (with their brothers), 170, and 162.[113] In turn, the people

---

[107] Ptolemy V: *IG* ii² 2314, line 41; Ptolemy VI: *IG* ii² 2316, line 45, with Habicht and Tracy 1991, pp. 216, 218–220, and 232–233; Habicht 1992, pp. 78–79; J. L. Shear 2007b, for victories associated with the Ptolemies.

[108] Habicht 1989, pp. 18–21; Green 1990, pp. 437–440; Mattingly 1997, pp. 125–127.

[109] Zambelli 1960; Tracy 1982, pp. 61–62; *contra* Scolnic 2014, who argues that Antiochus was not in Athens during these years; but the Athenian honors to Eumenes and Philetaerus (see next note) are harder to explain if so.

[110] Eumenes II: *OGIS* 248 (= Burstein 1985, no. 38, pp. 51–52); Philetaerus: *IG* ii³ 1, 1317 (of 175/4); see too Ferguson 1911, pp. 299, 303–304; Mattingly 1997, p. 135 with n. 67.

[111] Habicht 1989, pp. 18–26.

[112] Tarn and Griffith 1952, pp. 163–170; Kosmetatou 2003.

[113] *IG* ii² 2314, lines 84–91; dating: Habicht and Tracy 1991, pp. 217–221. On the benefits of participation in the Panathenaea for all involved: J. L. Shear 2007b (list of Attalid victors on p. 136).

bestowed honors on several members of their staff, including Eumenes' doctor Menander in 190/89 (archonship of Archaeus).[114] But the Attalids had a problematic relationship with the kings of Pontus (the Black Sea area, originally territory on both banks of the Halys River and part of the Seleucid Empire, but now independent). That, in turn, caused issues for the Athenians because of their long-term dependency on grain from there and careful cultivation of Spartocid ruling power.[115] In the end grain, and money, won. In 195, despite risking Attalid disfavor, Leon headed an Athenian embassy to Pharnaces of Pontus to inform him that Athens had erected bronze statues of him and his new queen Nysa in Delos—and to remind Pharnaces that the city was still waiting for money he had promised it.[116]

Even further afield was Athens' involvement in Cappadocia, especially with Ariarathes V (r. 163–130), presumably because of his reputation as an intellectual and his interest in philosophy.[117] At some point the Athenians awarded him citizenship and also made him *agonothetes* for the Great Panathenaea and one of the two mint magistrates; there is no record of him in Athens, so most likely he simply sent money for someone else to do the work and took credit for it.[118] Not that the Athenians minded, as it was someone else's money being put to good use on their behalf.

Finally, Athens also had diplomatic and commercial contacts with the Jews. In 105 Theodotus of Sunium proposed a gold crown and bronze statue to John Hyrcanus, Prince and High Priest of Judaea (r. 134–104).[119] That Theodotus was a wealthy businessman suggests the honors were in origin to do with commerce, probably to protect Athenian trade with Palestine and Arabia.[120]

The flurry of embassies throughout the second century between Athens and foreign rulers, and between Athens and other Greek states, betrayed the reality of Roman domination. The Athenians could wheel and deal, but

---

[114] *IG* ii³ 1, 1269, with Ferguson 1911, pp. 299–300; Day 1942, pp. 38–41; Habicht 1990, pp. 564–567; Mattingly 1997, p. 136.
[115] Harding 1985, no. 82, pp. 106–107; Burstein 1978b. For Athens' relations with Pontus generally: Mattingly 1997, pp. 137–140. Source of grain: G. J. Oliver 2007a, pp. 247–255.
[116] Habicht 1997a, pp. 226–227. Pharnaces is mentioned at Polybius 27.17, a passage that may have been an obituary if the king had died in 171/0.
[117] Ferguson 1911, pp. 300–301.
[118] Habicht 1997a, p. 282; on the official, see Habicht 1997a, pp. 323–324.
[119] The decree is preserved at Josephus, *Jewish Antiquities* 14.149–155 (late first century AD).
[120] Day 1942, pp. 86–87.

only up to a point. As the discussion in this chapter reveals, at the end of the day no political treaties were agreed to or military alliances made without the input and approval of Rome. In this respect the Athenians, like the other Greeks, were free (as defined by Flamininus) but in actuality did not have freedom.

9

Social Life and Religion

EXACTLY WHAT ORDINARY ATHENIANS DID or thought about life under Macedonian and Roman rule is hard to know because of the nature of our evidence. Since no one likes to be conquered, it is no stretch of the imagination to assume that the people resented their loss of autonomy, as their various attempts to recover it in the Hellenistic era support. One crucial part of private and civic life was religion, something that we have commented on several times so far. Despite economic slumps and falling under foreign powers, the Athenians never lost faith in their gods, and they continued to honor them with festivals and the like as often and as grandly as they could, so much so that religion went hand in hand with daily life. In this chapter we will try to illuminate what social life was like in Athens, and the role of religion in the city.

Everyday Life as We Know It

Athens as a city underwent a transformation, especially in the Roman era when there was an increase in the number of monuments inspired by Roman styles and backed by Roman money (see chapter 14). There does not seem to have been a trickle-down effect as far as ordinary houses were concerned: from archaeological evidence, these remained quite small and had two stories, with the women's living quarters upstairs and the men's below.

They were set on fairly narrow streets, given that larger avenues such as the Sacred Way were major festival routes.[1]

The Athenians were used to foreign benefactions from Hellenistic rulers like the Ptolemies and Seleucids, as we have seen, and showed their appreciation in a number of ways, from simple gifts to prized Athenian citizenship.[2] But the people were not subject to the will of these rulers, as they were the Roman ones. Even though Augustus and Hadrian in particular beautified the city, as we shall see, their new buildings were overt evidence of foreign domination. What the Athenians thought of them, we do not know. But it does not follow that they suddenly changed their entire attitude toward the Athenian Agora when in the later first century Agrippa built his enormous Odeum (theater) there, whose size dominated that space (Figure 14.3). The Agora might no longer be the democratic heart of the Classical *polis*, but people still congregated in its open areas, as well as the stoas, and went about their business.[3]

How many people lived in the city? The revisions to the citizen list by Antipater in 322 and Demetrius of Phalerum in around 317 led to a smaller citizen body. But some disfranchised men and their families must have remained in and around the city to continue performing the same jobs, such as fishermen, stonemasons, potters, and furniture makers; others would have hired themselves out as laborers and the like to make ends meet. We have no idea of numbers, and our literary sources do not help us: Plutarch maintains that all the disfranchised remained home after Antipater's revision of 322, and Diodorus, less plausibly, claims that they all went to Thrace.[4] Demetrius' census tells us that there were 21,000 citizens, 10,000 metics (resident aliens), and 400,000 slaves; the first figure has been contested, and a higher one of 31,000 advanced, along with a more realistic 100,000 slaves, in which case the actual population was around 150,000 to 250,000 (p. 40). Thus, all we can safely say is that the city's population was certainly down from its fifth-century level.[5]

Away from the actual city and its nearby demes, the Piraeus was a popular living area for metics—not a surprise, as it was the hub of commercial

---

[1] Thompson and Wycherley 1972, pp. 173–184; cf. pp. 192–194 on streets.
[2] Cf. the comments of Mossé 1973, pp. 144–145.
[3] Agora and stoas: Thompson and Wycherley 1972, pp. 82–108.
[4] Diodorus 18.18.5; Plutarch, *Phocion* 28.7, with Baynham 2003, pp. 26–28; Harding 2015, pp. 70–71.
[5] Harding 2015, pp. 72–73.

activity—and Milesians in particular settled there.⁶ Once Rome took over Greece in the second century an increasing number of Romans began to visit and settle in the city on at least a short-term basis, of which the most famous was Titus Pomponius, better known by his nickname "Atticus," the correspondent of Cicero.⁷ The influx of Romans taking up residence in Athens must have added an interesting dynamic to social and even domestic life, as we shall see. Moreover, the city's prominence in the Hellenistic and especially Roman eras, and its overall prosperity when things were going well, would not have made it a cheap place in which to live—the cost of living in a big city such as Athens (or Rome) was far higher than in a smaller town, a reason why Plutarch, for example, chose to live in his hometown of Chaeronea, as its smallness suited him better and it was less expensive.⁸

Thus, those who went to Athens for work must have seen the move as a justifiably lucrative one, a testament to the city's prosperity. In rural areas life seems to have been more exploitive. Hadrian's census of all property and money held by individuals throughout Attica revealed changes in land ownership whereby wealthy landowners had taken over the lands of the smaller subsistence farmers (p. 319). Such moves were reminiscent of the plight of Attica in the Archaic period, when the suffering of poor farmers indebted to large landowners was a catalyst in civil war (p. 54). We have no idea when the loss of privately held lands began again, but Hadrian's measure may have been to redress injustices that had been ongoing for some time. Likewise, his other measures, especially his regulations for the fairer sale of olive oil in AD 126/7, may have been to remedy these social and economic grievances (pp. 319–320).

Not every leader had the same attitude to the well-being of the people. It was, for example, a shortage in grain leading to starvation that brought about Lachares' tyranny, and his focus on maintaining his own power led to his downfall (p. 89). We have seen that as the Hellenistic period progressed into the Roman there was a change in the type of men who rose to political influence. Prominent families dominated politics, but many of them had histories that stretched back only a few generations, at most into the second century, and so they were akin to new men in political life.⁹ Very few

---

⁶ Graindor 1927a, pp. 159–171; Day 1942, pp. 142–151; see too Grigoropoulos 2009.
⁷ See, for example, Habicht 1997a, pp. 293–295, and especially 342–350; and see pp. 220–221, this volume.
⁸ See Titchener 2002.
⁹ Cf. Day 1942, pp. 171–174.

could boast families with centuries of tradition. Moreover, men who held high priestly offices were favored more; Athenian elites exploited religion for their advancement as much as for the continuation of religious traditions, a neat combination of the secular and religious.[10] But they seemed less concerned with the plight of their own citizens and more with their own political advancement.

Within the citizenry there were still marked divisions: a widening gap between the haves and the have-nots, especially during the third century, though gaps had existed in the Archaic and Classical periods. The big difference was that back then there had been a wider citizen body and a correspondingly larger number of poorer people. Now, thanks to the community of disfranchised citizens, previously richer (but not superwealthy) men, who had had enough money to maintain their citizenship under Antipater and Demetrius of Phalerum, would have found themselves forming the lowest stratum of society. They may well have grown richer thanks to increased economic opportunities, especially in the second century with the boom in mining, and in particular after Athens acquired Delos in 167 and the lucrative commercial interests there, but socially they had taken a step back. It is hardly a surprise then that the Athenians, resentful of their new circumstances, seized opportunities to throw off their masters whenever they could.

One question often asked is whether the plots of New Comedy, with their gentler humor and centered more on richer workers and well-heeled urbanites, reflect a different, more elitist audience with more refined tastes than that of the earlier Old Comedy, with its emphasis on sexual innuendo and crude humor. But we should not pigeonhole the Athenians' sense of humor based on their socioeconomic backgrounds. Just because someone was rich enough to remain a citizen did not mean he did not appreciate the bawdiness of Old Comedy, nor does it follow that poorer men did not have refined tastes. We should also expect some of the disfranchised Athenians to have still wanted entertainment and therefore gone to the theater, but would they have done so if they had to sit through hours of something they did not enjoy? Perhaps, then, what we can say in terms of Menander's plays giving us a glimpse into the life and *mores* of the times is that people from all walks of life wanted escapism: the plots of these plays

---

[10] Grijalvo 2005; see too Camia 2014.

gave them that luxury by transporting them from the harsh reality of the urban setting to the fantasy of the rural.

Athens, like other Greek cities, was obviously affected by Macedonian and Roman rule, especially in its political systems and religious life. But the domestic sphere was not immune to change. Our knowledge of the household (*oikos*) is better for the Classical period, but it would seem that the same structure and family dynamics remained during the Hellenistic era. The family unit was still the husband, wife, legitimate children, and slaves; the husband was technically the master of the house, with everyone subservient to him, but the wife was in charge of running the *oikos*—a singularly important job, as the *oikos* was vital to the well-being and future of the polis.[11]

Women in particular were largely segregated in society; their public movements were closely monitored, and when they did go out in public it was mostly for religious reasons, such as attending certain festivals.[12] At home, they lived upstairs and the men downstairs, where the husband would entertain his guests or in another, separate room (*andron*).[13] Women were protected at all times—under Athenian law, for example, any man was forbidden from entering a house if only women were present in it, and until age sixty women could attend only the funerals of relatives. Any household duties that fell to women were conducted inside the house, in private. Moreover, some sort of curtain or other screen was hung behind the door of a house, so that when it was opened no one from the street could see into the inside and catch a glimpse of its female occupants.

But women's roles in the household and society began to expand, especially in the Roman era; presumably they began to do so in the Hellenistic, though that cannot be said with certainty because of the paucity of the ancient sources.[14] One reason for their emerging role may have been due to a trickle-down effect from the activities of powerful, noble women. Among these were Olympias, Alexander the Great's mother, who had intervened in the hitherto traditional male preserves of politics and warfare, and Arsinoe II, wife of Ptolemy II, who had orchestrated the Chremonidean War. As the late Hellenistic and Roman eras came about, other powerful women came to the fore, such as Cleopatra VII of Egypt;

---

[11] See Lacey 1986 for the best introduction to the family.
[12] Cf. Mossé 1973, p. 146.
[13] See in detail Walker 1983.
[14] Excellent discussion in Pomeroy 2007, for example.

Julia Balbilla, sister of the Commagenian "king" Philopappus and a close friend of Hadrian, who likely had her brother's funerary monument built in Athens; and Pompeia Plotina, Trajan's widow, who persuaded Hadrian to rescind a decree about the heads of the philosophical schools.

It is frustrating that we know so little about the lives of ordinary people in our period, though women seemed to have a generally increasing profile in economic, religious, and even intellectual life. Some were even philosophers, such as the cynic Hippachia, or successful poets, like Erina of Telos (continuing a tradition of female poets going back to Sappho of Lesbos). At the same time there was still no political equality, as women could not vote, and art and New Comedy continued with their male biases—in Menander's *Dyskolos*, for example, Cnemon's free daughter has no say in who she will marry or even whether she finds her unsolicited suitor Sostratus desirable. The young girl is rather a bland character, a contrast to courtesans in comedy, who are depicted as scheming and able to charm whomever they wished—we are reminded in real life of the famous Lamia, who ingratiated herself first with Ptolemy I and then with Poliorcetes.

In the Roman era, however, presumably because of exposure to Roman social attitudes and the relative liberty that Roman women enjoyed, there was a significant change in the freedom of Greek women and, by extension we have to think, male attitudes toward them.[15] Although we still have limited literary sources to give us insight into domestic life, we do have archaeological evidence. No complete house exists for it to be thoroughly excavated, but on the basis of what we have it seems that the central courtyard of Athenian houses was enlarged and opened out, allowing women to do work in them, and thus be seen from the street. Moreover, women seem to have socialized in public more freely, including with their husbands' friends, presumably in the *andron*, bringing about a change in previous gender distinctions.[16] Thus, women were no longer sequestered out of sight, even to someone knocking on the front door, and "the conservatism evident in some areas of public life during this period was not present in the private sphere."[17]

---

[15] See especially Nevett 2002.
[16] [Plutarch], *Moralia* 140d.
[17] Nevett 2002, p. 94.

Religion and the City

Religion in Hellenistic Athens was very much a continuum of religion in the Classical city, in close association with every aspect of public and private life. The same gods, goddesses, and heroes (such as Aphrodite, Apollo, Asclepius, Dionysus, Heracles, and Zeus) were sacrificed to and worshipped, as the number of shrines and votive monuments (inscribed on stone as opposed to other items) with their offerings proves.[18] The state managed a multiplicity of cults; their various priests and priestesses, some annually appointed and others holding the office for life, were held in the highest regard.[19] Likewise, in the political sphere all meetings were still preceded by various religious rites—before actual debate began at an Assembly, for example, a pig was sacrificed and the herald prayed to the gods for guidance. Thus there was little change as far as beliefs and rituals over time went, and the same holds true for the most lavish expression of religious fervor in city life: festivals.[20]

Previously, in the Classical era, the archons had been charged with organization of the festivals, and wealthy citizens had undertaken liturgies such as funding a chorus for the dramatic events at their own expense. But as the system of liturgies fell into disuse under Demetrius of Phalerum, a new official came into being charged with running the festival: the *agonothetes*. Since he was also expected to fund much of the activities, the office quickly became one that only the wealthy could afford to undertake, and so was akin to a liturgy, for which the *agonothetes* received public honors at the end of his office. The reward could hardly have matched the outlay, however, but public recognition was what counted. Of the festivals, that of the Eleusinian Mysteries, under Athenian control, remained the major draw card in the Greek world. The Romans were fascinated by the Mysteries, and their leaders were initiated into them as a matter of course and lavished money on Eleusis.[21] But it was thanks to Hadrian's building

---

[18] Geagan 2011, pp. 285–352. Shrines: Thompson and Wycherley 1972, pp. 117–169.
[19] The most detailed account (down to the Sullan sack of 86) is Mikalson 1998; cf. Ferguson 1911, pp. 216–232 and 290–297, for example, and Habicht 1997a, pp. 166–170, 237–242, and 323–326. See also Garland 1987, chapter 3, on religion in the Piraeus (which because of the garrisons mostly existed as an area aloof of Athens). On Athenian religion prior to the Hellenistic: Parker 1996. Generally on Hellenistic religion: Mikalson 2007.
[20] Ferguson 1911, pp. 290–297; Habicht 1997a, pp. 237–242.
[21] See Clinton 1989a.

program there that both beautified the sanctuary and brought about a renaissance of the overall site (pp. 302–303).[22]

In Athens itself the major festivals were the annual Panathenaea (honoring the city's patron deity Athena Polias), the Theseia (to Theseus), and the Dionysia (to Dionysus). The Panathenaea dated back to the Archaic period; it had been significantly enlarged by the tyrant Pisistratus in the mid-sixth century with the addition of a grandiose procession and sacrifice of 100 oxen, along with a contest to find the best rhapsode in the Greek world who could recite the Homeric poems (presumably select lines of them, given the length of the poems). From Pisistratid times the festival was celebrated more grandly every four years, when it was known as the Great Panathenaea. Its other events included horse and chariot races and athletic games (foot races, wrestling, boxing, and the infamous *pankration*—perhaps the antecedent of mixed martial arts, with its combination of boxing, wrestling, kicking, and chokeholds, and where only biting, gouging out an opponent's eyes, or kicking him in the groin were not allowed). Originally only Athenian citizens were eligible for its events, but by the Hellenistic era anyone could compete in them (though some cavalry games in the Agora remained only for citizens), attracting Greeks and foreigners from all over the Mediterranean and Near East, including foreign kings and their families.

The Theseia dated back to the second quarter of the fifth century when the supposed bones of Athens' mythical founder Theseus were found on the island of Scyros, brought back to Athens for internment, and a festival was introduced to honor him. In the Hellenistic period the Theseia seems to have been celebrated every fourth year (perhaps annually in the Classical era, when the state coffers were not quite as strained). Although similar games and age groupings to the Panathenaea were a feature of the Theseia, it was really intended for Athenian citizens; ephebes were included in its events, and members of the Boule had to be in attendance, for which each councilor received a stipend of 2 drachmas. It appears that in the 160s the festival was revamped, perhaps because of Athens receiving back Scyros (along with Lemnos, Imbros, and Delos) in 167.[23]

The Dionysia (also celebrated with additional pomp every four years) was the creation of Pisistratus to honor the god of wine and agriculture Dionysus. In doing so Pisistratus was endearing himself to his grassroots supporters,

---

[22] Clinton 1989b.
[23] Bugh 1990, pp. 20–37, for a date of 164.

principally the poorer farmers, given that Dionysus had never had a festival in his honor before. What made the festival special was the performance of tragedy. Under the Pisistratid tyranny an Ionian named Thespis "invented" the genre of tragedy (thus giving us the word "thespian"); although no one knows precisely what Thespis did (he may have simply acted out part of a Homeric poem rather than simply reciting lines), from these rudimentary beginnings spawned the great plays of master tragedians like Aeschylus, Sophocles, and Euripides, which are still performed today.

There were of course other festivals, though none as splendid as those just described. But as the Hellenistic period wore on, a change came about in the perception of religion. Classical religion was part of the democratic *polis*, but with the loss of independence and, in turn, as the city found itself needing foreign support, people's attitude to traditional religion (to call it that) altered. Foreign cults began to appear in the city, such as those to Isis and Sarapis; ambitious individuals saw priesthoods as a means to political elevation, especially in Roman times; and the move to lifetime rather than annual priesthoods gave the upper social stratum more control of religious life. New festivals came into being honoring foreign rulers, such as Ptolemy III in the early 220s. Such actions revealed a changing world and the Athenians recognizing the need to move with it.

Perhaps one of the more significant changes was the rise of ruler cult. This phenomenon was more embedded in Ptolemaic Egypt and Seleucid Syria than Antigonid Greece, though the last was not immune.[24] The Athenians had declared Monophthalmus and Poliorcetes savior gods in 307, after liberating the city from the regime of Demetrius of Phalerum, and bestowed various other honors on them, such as a cult, liberation monument, and two new tribes with their names (pp. 72–74). Thus began what has been described as a "stormy twenty-year relationship between Athens and Demetrios Poliorcetes, a relationship that brought turmoil to Athenian politics and Athenian religion."[25] Later they seem to have acknowledged Antigonus II as divine and sacrificed to him; although we are not sure of their attitude to his successors, we can certainly say that Philip V was not so revered—in fact, they cursed him and his predecessors in 200 (pp. 152–153). That being the case, we can assume that ruler cult did not have that long a life in Athens.

---

[24] See comments on ruler cult and its development in Green 1990, pp. 396–413.
[25] Mikalson 1998, p. 75.

The Athenians' bestowal of divine honors on the Antigonids did not mean they actually thought they were gods, but was in thanks for their liberation. Such a political slant is evident again in 290, when, in another over-the-top display of religious fawning, the ithyphallic hymn to Poliorcetes spoke of him as like the sun and as a god (p. 95). This came at a time when he had seized control of Athens, hence the people were striving to earn his good graces, and also needed his support against the antagonistic Achaean League. Seventy years later, in either 224 or 223, the people founded a cult to Ptolemy III and his wife Berenice, which included a new tribe named after him (Ptolemais) and a festival (the Ptolemaea) in his honor. Their action was part of their courtship of Ptolemaic Egypt for protection should they face hostilities from Philip V or the Aetolian League.

These self-serving instances capture what the people thought a god was at that time; they saw ruler cult as far from religious, but something to be exploited for secular advantages. Their formal cursing of the Antigonids in 200, followed by disbanding the tribes named after them and smashing virtually every monument to them in the city, well illustrates that the Athenians could deprive as easily as they could bestow honors on someone without fear of divine retribution.

The mixing of religion and politics was also seen in 229 when Athens reasserted its independence. The city's leaders, Eurycleides and Micion, introduced a series of religious and secular measures to commemorate the recent liberation from Macedonian domination, including the establishment of a priesthood and a shrine (never built) to Demus and the three *Charites*. Demus had long personified the Athenian people and their democracy, and connecting him to the *Charites* was a deliberate religious and ideological union of the new democracy. It has even been suggested that the new cult was a counterpart to that of the rulers the Athenians had introduced as early as the Antigonids in 307 to symbolize their independence and democracy.[26] But a change occurred in the middle of the second century when the Goddess Roma was attached to the cult and served by the same priest, an expansion that expressed "the inseparable union of the Athenian citizenry and the Roman republic."[27]

The appearance of Rome, and in particular the rule of Augustus, impacted the civic religion of Greece overall. For the Athenians, arguably the biggest

---

[26] Nilsson 1974, pp. 144–145.
[27] Habicht 1997a, pp. 181–182 (quote on p. 182).

effect was the fixture of the imperial cult in civic life. Among other things, the Athenians had to live with the goddess Roma occupying the same sacred space, the Acropolis, as Athena—the temple of Roma and Augustus was situated immediately next to the Parthenon (see Figure 14.2B). The city also became home to a large number of altars set up to various emperors, which may have been part of the imperial cult.[28] Thus, in the Roman period aspects of Greek and Roman religion were to be found side by side.[29]

This Roman presence led to the increased importance of the priests in the city's dealing with Rome. Priests and priestesses had long been respected in Athenian society, as honorary decrees to them show (and to a lesser extent on Delos when the city regained control of the island), and their services were held in the same regard as magistracies.[30] But an offshoot of this Roman influence was a secularization of sorts for some of the priesthoods, whereby those of the upper social stratum used their involvement in state cults at the higher levels and especially the imperial cult as a stepping-stone to political life, and even acted as conduits between Rome and the city.[31]

A case in point is the priesthood of Asclepius (the healing god), which every year in the Classical and Hellenistic periods rotated evenly among the tribes and so could be called a "democratic priesthood."[32] But epigraphical evidence attests that between 25 and AD 10 the priesthood became a lifetime one, with the resulting change from what used to be a public cult to one managed by a number of wealthy families, in turn introducing their own hierarchy into the cult. As Grijalvo argues, this "aristocratization" of the cult was not about whether Asclepius was popular or there was a shortage of men qualified to be his priests: instead, Athenian elites embraced the opportunity afforded by the Roman conquest to elevate their social standing in the city and in the eyes of Rome by exploiting the multiplicity of existing cults.[33]

Athenian festivals were also not immune from Roman intervention. During the Hellenistic period there had been a scaling back of the more expensive festivals like the Panathenaea, even though wealthy Athenians as

---

[28] Geagan 2011, pp. 157–170.
[29] Cf. Graindor 1931, pp. 101–129.
[30] Perrin-Saminadayar 2012 (see pp. 149–152 for names of priests); Lambert 2012 (with the other essays in Horster and Klöckner 2012).
[31] Grijalvo 2005; Camia 2014.
[32] Grijalvo 2005, p. 272; see pp. 271–275 on the following; and cf. Geagan 1991.
[33] Grijalvo 2005; cf. Mikalson 1998, p. 293.

well as foreign rulers gave money and gifts for their production.[34] In 286 the Athenians had to cancel the Great Panathenaea, but because of the interruption the one in 282 was more splendid than normal.[35] Nevertheless, the Great Panathenaea disappeared from the 240s until 170.[36] Then changes were introduced, such as awarding oil in the prize amphorae not only to athletes (as had been the norm) but also those taking part in musical contests, a change that may be attributed to Eurycleides since his name suddenly appears on these amphorae.[37] But the uniqueness of this Athenian festival disappeared in the Roman era, when emperors appropriated it for their own propaganda reasons, causing it to become a hybrid of Athenian and Roman elements (p. 275).

As the city came into more contact with foreign cultures, especially in the Near East and Egypt, we see the appearance of new gods and festivals. Two foreign gods that found their way into Athens, both from Egypt, were Isis and Sarapis.[38] In Egyptian religion, Isis was thought to assist the dead in their afterlife, but in Greece she took on various attributes of the Greek gods, including protective roles. A decree of 333/2 permitted Lycurgus to build a sanctuary to her in the Piraeus, but even though her cult was a public one it never won a large-scale following, and was always in the hands of aristocratic families and counted prominent and wealthy people among its followers.[39] Another factor counting against it, at least in the later first century, was the association of the goddess with Egypt and the Athenians' dislike of Cleopatra. Yet the Athenians did not expel Isis, and by the second century AD there were small shrines to her on the Acropolis, perhaps coupled with Sarapis, the "hybrid" god.[40]

Sarapis was the creation of Ptolemy I as part of his moves to unite his disparate people.[41] Sarapis was a combination of the Greek gods Zeus and Pluto with the Egyptian sacred bull Apis—again, we see the reassurance of

---

[34] Ferguson 1911, pp. 290–298; Habicht 1997a, pp. 237–242; Mikalson 1998, pp. 108–109; cf. Day 1942, pp. 37–38; Barringer 2003.
[35] Mikalson 1998, pp. 108–109; Habicht 1997a, p. 136.
[36] Barringer 2003.
[37] Barringer 2003.
[38] Mikalson 1998, pp. 275–277, for example. Foreign cults in general: Mikalson 1998, pp. 275–279.
[39] Lycurgus: *IG* ii² 337, and see Dow 1937 and Grijalvo 2005, pp. 277–279, citing bibliography.
[40] Walker 1979.
[41] Ptolemy and Sarapis: Worthington 2016, pp. 198–199.

life after death as Pluto was god of the underworld. The temple of Sarapis (Sarapeum) at Alexandria housed an image of Sarapis as a bearded Zeus, crowned by the *modius* (the grain measure of Egypt), with Pluto's three-headed dog Cerberus at his feet. Although both Isis and Sarapis clearly took on Greek attributes and were worshipped throughout the Greek world, they never won a large-scale following, including in Athens, as the small number of votive offerings indicates.[42] Delos was an exception, as there were cult centers on the island to Isis and Sarapis, and even to Syrian gods that were not found in Athens.

Nevertheless, there was an openness on the part of some Athenians to foreign cults, and the Athenians even allowed some freedom of religion—except of course with Christianity, which was brought to Athens by the apostle Paul when he visited in AD 51. After preaching to Jews and non-Jews in the city he was summoned before the Areopagus and delivered a sermon, among other things berating the Athenians for worshipping their pagan gods and encouraging them to worship only the one true God and to believe in the resurrection (pp. 276–277). The Areopagus did not punish him, but his departure soon after to Corinth implies that he did not want to spend too much time in Athens.

At the end of the day it was Athens' own deities that were accepted and worshipped with little question. Despite the changes in Athenian religion, the aristocratization of priesthoods, and additions such as the worship of living rulers or new foreign cults, there was still continuity: the same pantheon, the same rituals, and ultimately the same religious beliefs and attitudes were all present and accounted for in the Hellenistic and Roman eras.[43]

The Athenians' care in re-establishing relations with Delphi, home of the oracle of Apollo, maintaining control of the Eleusinian Mysteries, claiming new sanctuaries, such as that of Amphiareus at Oropus, and introducing a new cult of Demus and the *Charites*, all point to engagement with traditional deities. When the people called the Antigonids savior gods, or included them in their sacrifices, or worshipped Roman emperors, they were simply paying lip service to their masters. We are reminded of Monophthalmus' reaction when flatterers told him he would become a god: "My pisspot carrier knows me better" (p. 75). The Athenians echoed these sentiments (albeit carefully to themselves), as for the most part they followed their traditional orthodoxy.

---

[42] Geagan 2011, pp. 319–321.
[43] This is the thesis of Mikalson 1998 (whose account goes down to the Sullan sack).

10

Sulla's Sack of Athens

AS WELL AS A MUSHROOMING of Romans studying philosophy in Athens or simply visiting the city to enjoy its culture and grand monuments, there was an increase in Roman embassies from the Senate. The Athenians built a special stone rostrum in the Agora from where Roman officials and generals could address them, which survived until the Herulian sack in AD 267 (p. 335).[1] In this they were not alone, as rostra were also built in Corinth and Philippi—a sign, it has been said, not so much of helping the Romans speak to people but of Roman influence on the way an Agora was used.[2] Perhaps; although it does not follow that a platform in one part of the Athenian Agora would hardly impact all parts of it and therefore alter its purpose. Nevertheless, as the years passed "Romanizing" influences led to some sharp changes in cities, not least Athens.[3]

Foreign Investment

Greece was prospering in the later third and second centuries after a slump, and Athens was no exception.[4] An increase in exports stimulated

---

[1] Posidonius, *BNJ* 87 F 36.50 = Athenaeus 5.212f; see further Thompson and Wycherley 1972, pp. 51 and 220 n. 3; Stefanidou-Tiveriou 2008, pp. 14–15. The Athenians may also have built a private club for Roman dignitaries: Ferguson 1911, pp. 366–367 and 417–418.
[2] Dickenson 2017, pp. 159–160, and see pp. 292–299 on the later *bema*.
[3] On the issue of "Romanization," see Alcock 1997, together with the essays in Hoff and Rotroff 1997 and Vlizos 2008.
[4] Kroll 2003, especially p. 206.

economic activity in the Piraeus, and a renewed exploitation of the Laurium mines led to the first new coinage in twenty years, the "new style" silver coinage introduced in 167 (or perhaps 164), after the city acquired Delos.[5] These coins featured the helmeted head of Athena on the obverse, but while the reverse always retained the owl (Athena's symbol) the rest of the iconography changed constantly to reflect, among other things, the names of the different masters of the mint.[6] Also flourishing was the *ephebeia*, as shown by a series of decrees from 127/6 to 98/7; by the end of the second century, thanks to non-Athenians allowed to enroll in the program, there were probably as many as 100 to 150 serving ephebes per year.

Lavish new public buildings funded by foreign monarchs began to appear.[7] Eumenes II and his brother Attalus II of Pergamum, for example, both built stoas in the city.[8] For their benefactions, the Athenians set up statues of the two rulers on a monumental pedestal that was later reused to honor Agrippa (see Figure 12.2). The Stoa of Eumenes was a large, two-story one on the south slope of the Acropolis and accessible from the theater of Dionysus (parts of it are still there today and give a good impression of its size). Attalus' Stoa was also two-story, but with more rooms, including shops, meeting spaces, and viewing areas for festival crowds, and it was built in the Agora. It was restored between 1952 and 1956, and dominates views of the Agora because of its size; today it is a museum and research center of the American School of Classical Studies in Athens (Figure 10.1).

Antiochus IV of Syria was certainly a philhellene and a benefactor of the Athenians. In 174 he paid for a Roman architect, Decimus Cossutius, to continue work on the enormous temple of Olympian Zeus, close to the Acropolis.[9] Begun by the Pisistratid tyrants in the mid-sixth century, only the

---

[5] Day 1942, pp. 31–36 and 90–92; M. Thompson 1961, but dated lower by Lewis 1962, and now followed, for example, by Mattingly 1990; Habicht 1991c; Habicht 1997a, pp. 242–245. The Piraeus trade and its market: Day 1942, pp. 41–49 and 88–90; Garland 1987, pp. 58–72 and 83–95.

[6] On whom see Habicht 1991c.

[7] Day 1942, pp. 38–41.

[8] Thompson and Wycherley 1972, pp. 103–107; Dickenson 2017, pp. 170–178.

[9] *IG* ii² 4009; Livy 41.20.8; cf. Polybius 26.1.11, with Wycherley 1964; Abramson 1975; H. A. Thompson 1987, pp. 2–3; cf. Hoff 2013, pp. 564–566; see too Ferguson 1911,

FIGURE 10.1 Reconstructed Stoa of Attalus. Photo: Ian Worthington.

three steps and some column bases of the huge *temenos* (almost the size of the area of the entire Acropolis) had been built when the tyranny came to an end in 510. Cossutius swapped the original Doric columns for Corinthian ones and started on the interior, but the temple was still unfinished on Antiochus' death; it would not be completed until the early second century AD as part of the emperor Hadrian's building program (see Figures 14.5A–B).

These buildings added luster to the city; in fact, Athens received more lavish donations than any other Greek city.[10] Yet the return never seemed to match the outlays, for Athenian awards to their benefactors varied from a gold crown to a bronze commemorative tablet.[11] But for foreign rulers the value of the award was less important than where it came from. Athens remained strategically and ideologically important throughout the

---

pp. 305–306. Antiochus may also have sent a shield with the head of Medusa on it as an offering to Athena: Habicht 1989, pp. 10–21.

[10] Brogan 2003, p. 194 with nn. 2–3; cf. Hoff 2013, pp. 563–567.

[11] Day 1942, p. 41.

Hellenistic era, boasting the cultural and intellectual pedigree of centuries.[12] Alexandria, Antioch, and Pergamum had edged out Athens intellectually and artistically, with the exception of philosophy, but they were not Athens. In fact, the reason for philosophy flourishing as it did in Athens and not in other cities (especially Alexandria) was its history in the city: philosophers did not want to leave behind even the areas where greats such as Socrates, Plato, Aristotle, Theophrastus, and Zeno had walked and talked.[13]

What most benefited Athens in the latter half of the second century was its control of Delos, given the location of the island on the trade route between Italy and the new Roman province of Asia.[14] There were also lucrative jobs to be had on the island, as artworks by thirteen Athenian sculptors from nine different families show.[15] Connections to Delos also enabled upward social mobility: a family from Marathon, for example, with several males named Zenon and Pammenes, has been identified as one moving to the island probably in the 160s. From the first century to later in the reign of Augustus it became rich and prominent enough for its sons to be enrolled in the *ephebeia* and to be archons; its members also competed (successfully) in the Greater Theseia and took part in the Panathenaea and the *Pythais* to Delphi.[16] Pammenes himself became hoplite general and priest of the goddess Roma and Augustus, and it is his name in the dedication of the temple of Roma and Augustus on the Acropolis (p. 291).

Investment in Delos brought with it a different gain as wealthy families with commercial interests there displaced traditional, aristocratic landowning families of Athens when it came to wielding political influence.[17] Leading politicians from aristocratic families of the first half of the century such as Eurycleides, Micion, or Leon gave way to men such as Sarapion of Melite, Medeius of Piraeus, Theodotus of Sunium, Diodorus of Halae,

---

[12] Cf. Ferguson 1911, pp. 307–311.

[13] Ferguson 1911, pp. 307–311; see too Habicht 1994b on Classical precedents and Hellenistic philosophers.

[14] Ferguson 1911, pp. 322 and 329–333, and pp. 347–414 on Athens and Delos; Day 1942, pp. 50–84; Tracy 1979; Habicht 1997a, pp. 246–263.

[15] Habicht 1997a, pp. 290–291 with nn. 49–50. Cf. Day 1942, p. 25, on Athenian sculptors going to work in other cities.

[16] Geagan 1992.

[17] Ferguson 1911, pp. 421–427 (likening them to the *equites* in Rome); Day 1942, pp. 109–110; MacKendrick 1969, p. 55; Grieb 2008, pp. 124–126; cf. Geagan 1992; Tracy 1979, pp. 215–220; Badian 1976, pp. 106–108.

and Pyrrhus of Lamptrae, who had made their fortune on Delos—and were pro-Roman. This does not mean that only a small circle of aristocratic men with Delian connections ruled Athens for their own gain, merely that wealth from Delos enabled men from different social backgrounds to take on various public positions.[18] Moreover, members of these families would also play a role in relations between the city and Rome.[19] Thus the face of Athenian politics and by extension the city's religious and social life changed dramatically.[20]

W. S. Ferguson believed that in 103/2 a group of wealthy businessmen with close ties to Rome set up a narrow oligarchy, which was not toppled until Athens moved to support Mithridates VI of Pontus in 88.[21] That is not the case, and his view "deserves honourable burial amid the graves of its relatives among nineteenth-century interpretations."[22] A valuable inscription exists that documents the principal annual officials of Athens for the years 103/2 to 97/6; in all, 173 names were inscribed, of which 31 are connected to Delos.[23] In fact, the inscription makes clear that the *epimeletes* of the island was an important Athenian official. We can understand that some scholars would think an oligarchy was in place in Athens since according to the text some officials held more than one elected office at the same time, such as Medeius, who had been archon in 101/100, hoplite general in 99/8 (and *epimeletes* of the island in the same or following year), as well as *agonothetes*.[24] But these simultaneous office-holdings could simply indicate either the competence of these individuals or the lack of qualified men at the turn of the first century to take on these positions.

Less welcoming for the Athenians were two revolts by the slaves who worked in the Laurium mines, the first in 134, and the second some thirty years later. The first revolt was quickly put down the following year.[25] The

---

[18] Tracy 1979, pp. 229–231.
[19] Geagan 1992, Schiller 2006; on the increasing religious power of the elite and dealings with Rome, see Grijalvo 2005. Public role of priests on Delos that made them akin to public officials: Perrin-Saminadayar 2012.
[20] Tracy 1979, pp. 227–229; post Sulla: Geagan 1967, pp. 57–61.
[21] Ferguson 1911, pp. 421–437; cf. Day 1942, pp. 110–113; to an extent MacKendrick 1969, pp. 58–63; Geagan 1971, p. 103.
[22] Badian 1976, pp. 105–106 (quote on p. 106); Tracy 1979, pp. 213–235.
[23] *IG* ii² 2336, with Tracy 1979, pp. 215–231; cf. Grieb 2008, p. 132.
[24] Tracy 1979, pp. 222–225; cf. Ferguson 1911, p. 436. On Medeius, see too Badian 1976, pp. 106–107; Antela-Bernárdez 2009a.
[25] Orosius 5.9.5.

second revolt, occurring most probably in 100, was far more serious, for after killing their guards the slaves seized the Acropolis of Sunium, one of the Attic fortresses, and pillaged the surrounding countryside.[26] Some slaves even fled to join pirates, who were a menace to trading.[27] This revolt may have taken some years to put down, as in 98/7 only five ephebes took part in the *Pythais* to Delphi—this low number is best explained by their fellow ephebes being called on to protect Attica from marauding slaves (thus showing the ephebes still had a military function).[28]

But although the Romans were preoccupied from 129 with turning Asia into a province, they did not forget Greece.[29] Possibly they were behind a set of economic regulations, in which Attic weights were converted to Roman ones, presumably to make trade with Rome easier.[30] The Romans may even have backed a decree by the Amphictyonic Council that ordered "all the Greeks" (which might refer to more than its member states) to accept only Athenian silver tetradrachms at an exchange rate of 1 tetradrachm to 4 drachmas of silver, and prohibited any fees for currency exchange, with violators punished (slaves were to be whipped and free people fined 200 drachmas).[31] The Greeks had numerous coinages that made trade difficult, so this measure was an attempt at regulation, but it was a boon for Athens as its tetradrachm became the standard currency of Greece. This may well be the time when the Athenians began to mint coins with the head of the goddess Roma on them, and perhaps even to establish a cult to her in their city, since on coins she is similar in appearance to Athena, and cults of Roma

---

[26] Posidonius, *BNJ* 87 F 35 = Athenaeus 6.272e–f. Ferguson 1911, pp. 427–428, dates it to 103/2, the same year as a slave revolt on Sicily, news of which encouraged the Laurium slaves to revolt. But how did these slaves hear of the revolt in Sicily? Ferguson 1911, p. 428, suggests they did so "along mysterious channels." The date of 100 is more likely: Tracy 1979, pp. 232–235. Slaves: Day 1942, p. 105.

[27] In 102, Athens contributed warships to a fleet commanded by the proconsul Marcus Antonius in his successful campaign against piracy off the southern coast of Asia Minor following Rhodes' decline as a naval power: *IG* ii² 3218, with Ferguson 1911, p. 428; Habicht 1997a, pp. 284–285.

[28] Tracy 1979, pp. 232–235. Inscriptional evidence from 102/1 honoring the ephebes of the previous year makes no mention of any crisis in Attica at this time, which indicates the revolt broke out after the decree was passed: *IG* ii² 1028.

[29] Asia: for example, Kallet-Marx 1995, pp. 97–160.

[30] *IG* ii² 1013. One Attic mina became the equivalent of two Roman pounds (655 grams).

[31] *SIG*³ 279 (= M. M. Austin 2006, no. 125, pp. 234–235), with Day 1942, pp. 91–92; Habicht 1979a, pp. 242–245 and 275–279; see also Accame 1946, pp. 111–123.

were often connected to patron deities.[32] The cult was eventually joined to one of Octavian/Augustus after the battle of Actium.[33]

Nevertheless, after some decades of peace and prosperity, there was growing discontent in Athens between the upper and lower social strata.[34] Just because political power was no longer in the hands of rich aristocrats did not mean that the divide between rich and poor was suddenly narrowed. After the second slave revolt Athens' new leaders adopted even more of a pro-Roman stance, and they were especially keen to join the Areopagus at the end of their term of office, since it was favored by Rome.[35] It also did not help that the rich had begun to show off again as the austerity measures of Demetrius of Phalerum fell by the wayside; in the first half of the second century expensive funerary monuments began to appear, as well as endowments providing money for some public but more often than not private institutions.[36] These socio-economic divisions, as well as the city's closer ties to Rome, eventually proved too much. In 88 the people voted to support Mithridates VI of Pontus in his war against Rome, and thus steered the city to war once more, this time against Rome.

Athens, Mithridates, and Rome

The Athenians had long relied on imported grain from the Black Sea region and had maintained close relations with its monarchs.[37] In 120 Mithridates VI, at age twelve, had become coruler of Pontus with his younger brother with their mother as regent, but had left court until 112 when he was old enough to rule in his own right. He had his mother and brother put to death and married his younger sister Laodice to preserve the bloodline (later executing her for trying to kill him). A warrior king who saw himself as another Alexander, Mithridates was a philhellene, apparently spoke twenty-two languages, was immune to poison, and ruled for nearly sixty years, until

---

[32] Whittaker 2002, p. 30, citing bibliography.
[33] Whittaker 2002, p. 30, citing bibliography.
[34] Cf. Ferguson 1911, pp. 428–430.
[35] Ferguson 1911, pp. 419–420; Rawson 1985, pp. 59–66; see on this council (to 307), Wallace 1989.
[36] Day 1942, pp. 30–31. On such institutions, see Leiwo 1997; cf. Ferguson 1911, pp. 216–232.
[37] As revealed by an elaborate heroon-like monument for Mithridates, designed by the Athenian Helianax, on Delos: Hinds 1994, pp. 133–140; Kreuz 2009.

63. In the three wars that the Romans were forced to wage against him (88–84, 83–81, and 75–63), he fought against three of their distinguished generals—Sulla, Lucullus, and Pompey the Great—and when he was at last defeated the Romans celebrated with a festival.[38]

Mithridates' ambition to expand his realm inevitably led to conflict with Rome.[39] When the Greek cities along the Black Sea coast (founded as colonies by the Ionian city of Miletus) appealed for his help against Scythian and Sarmatian tribes, Mithridates was quick to position himself as a champion of their freedom—but then annexed their territories. By the early 80s, thanks to his brand of savvy diplomacy backed by military force, he had taken over much of Asia, yet he was still welcomed as a liberator from the hated Roman rule.[40] When the Romans declared war on him in 88 he turned to Greece, skillfully promoting himself as a liberator and a defender against barbarians—in other words, Rome.[41] His propaganda worked, with the Greeks even calling him, according to Diodorus, their "god and savior."[42]

From about 91 Athens had been under the sway of Medeius. He was not a popular person; among other things, he had illegally held three successive eponymous archonships in 91/0, 90/89, and 89/8 (hence four in all as he had been archon a first time in 101/0), banned assemblies, and closed gymnasia.[43] Presumably he did so with the Senate's support, for Rome was then embroiled in its own Social War at home, and needed to keep Athens under control.[44] Medeius was evidently out to establish a tyranny and it is not a surprise that in 88 he was deposed in a coup, his plea to Rome for support going unheard.

---

[38] Memnon, *BNJ* 434 F 22.1–10 with the commentary of Keaveney and Madden, *ad loc.*; Appian, *Mithridatic Wars* 112–113; Justin 37.2.4–9, and see Reinach 1980; McGing 1986; Ballesteros Pastor 1996; Matyszak 2008; Højte 2009a; Mayor 2011; cf. Green 1990, pp. 558–564; Hinds 1994; McGing 2003, pp. 84–88.
[39] Kallet-Marx 1995, pp. 250–259; Keaveney 2005, pp. 64–68.
[40] Glew 1977a, pp. 397–398. Campaign: Hinds 1994, pp. 140–147.
[41] Glew 1977a; Reinach 1980, pp. 100–205; McGing 1986, pp. 89–131; Hinds 1994, pp. 146–164; Kallet-Marx 1995, pp. 261–290; Keaveney 2005, pp. 64–90; Madsen 2009; McGing 2009. His propaganda to the Greeks: Glew 1977b; cf. Green 1990, pp. 561–562.
[42] Diodorus 37.26, with Ferguson 1911, pp. 438 and 440; Badian 1976.
[43] Ferguson 1911, p. 440; MacKendrick 1969, pp. 60–61; Badian 1976, pp. 107–108; Antela-Bernárdez 2015; Antela-Bernárdez 2019, pp. 44–45.
[44] Badian 1976, p. 108; Kallet-Marx 1995, pp. 208–209; Antela-Bernárdez 2009a; Antela-Bernárdez 2015, p. 67.

We can say that Medeius' legacy was a period of anarchy (*anarchia*) because no eponymous archon was elected for 88/7.[45] Yet other archons and officials like the herald of the Areopagus were elected, and the Assembly began to meet. Probably in the same year the latter body elected an Aristotelian philosopher by name of Athenion to go to Mithridates' court and discuss an alliance with Athens.[46] Athenion's selection as envoy is not a surprise (nor is his elevation to hoplite general when he returned), as the other magistrates for that year were all his friends.[47] When he got to Mithridates' court he sent back letters to Athens stating that the king promised he would end civil strife in the city, restore democracy, and pay the people handsomely if they joined him in his war on Rome.[48] The part about giving money to the city suggests that Athenian coffers were more empty than full, and that this was a deliberate ploy to court the Athenians.[49]

Our only source for Athenion's mission and the Athenians' reaction to it is the stoic philosopher and historian Posidonius, whose account is preserved in Athenaeus. But Posidonius speaks of Athenion in a completely disparaging manner. Thus, he claims, having ingratiated himself with Mithridates, he returned to a hero's welcome, in the process showing his venality and the gullibility of the people:[50]

---

[45] Cf. Accame 1946, p. 167; Geagan 1967, p. 17; Habicht 1976, pp. 127–135. On the term: Badian 1976, pp. 111–112. Antela-Bernárdez 2011 discusses an inscription from the Piraeus honoring a priestess of a religious association (*IG* ii² 1334) bearing the name (partly restored) of the archon Athenion (line 6). Since the latter served as envoy to Mithridates and was later elected hoplite general (see below), Antela-Bernárdez posits that he may have been elected archon in 88/7 and his name not recorded in the list of archons. This is doubtful, as Antela-Bernárdez admits, suggesting that the inscription could be wrong. Habicht 1976, p. 130, proposed that Mithridates held the archonship in this year, but as Badian shows, *anarchia* means no archon.

[46] Athenaeus 5.212a for information, stating there was a formal election, with Badian 1976, pp. 110–113 (the appointment in 89); cf. Ferguson 1911, pp. 440–441. Note that Badian 1976, p. 110 n. 23, draws attention to the opaqueness of the Greek as to the time of the election.

[47] Badian 1976, pp. 112–114 (cf. pp. 119–120), especially with his n. 30 on them.

[48] Athenaeus 5.212a (for example, he "plied the people with false hopes").

[49] Tracy 1979, p. 207.

[50] Posidonius in Athenaeus 5.212b–c, trans. Ferguson 1911, pp. 442–444; see too Accame 1946, pp. 168–170; Mossé 1973, pp. 148–149; Ballesteros Pastor 1996, pp. 121–134; Habicht 1997a, p. 300; Mikalson 1998, pp. 280–283; Grieb 2008, pp. 135–137; Antela-Bernárdez 2015; Gray 2018; Antela-Bernárdez 2019, pp. 46–49. Drama of account: Bugh 1992, pp. 108–109.

As [Athenion] entered the city almost everybody flooded out in a crush to receive him. Some, indeed, went simply as spectators in amazement at the chance which brought back to Athens in a silver-footed litter and purple wraps an imposter who had never seen so much as a streak of purple in his beggar's rags; for not even a Roman had ever paraded in such a haughty fashion in Attica. Accordingly men, women and children thronged hastily to see the sight, naturally expecting great things from Mithridates, seeing that this pauper, Athenion, who had made his living by subscription lectures, had come back from his court in grand estate, lolling along at his ease through country and town.

We will return to Posidonius' views. Athenion was greeted by sacrifices on the part of the Guild of Dionysiac performers, and the next day the people could hardly contain themselves to hear what he had to report—so much so that Athenion had to force himself through the crowd to mount the *bema* in the Agora, ironically built for Roman generals to address the masses.[51] There he gave a passionate speech, theatrically stopping at times to rub his forehead or to allow his words to sink in, praising Mithridates' power and intentions, lamenting how so many of Athens' civic and other institutions (as well as "holy places") had been shuttered, and rebuking the Senate for allowing "the state of anarchy" to continue as long as it had.[52] Excited by all they heard, the Athenians elected Athenion hoplite general and allowed him to choose his own officers.[53]

The Athenians had stayed loyal to Rome until now, but predictably they saw Mithridates as a savior come to rescue them from Rome.[54] They even put his portrait on their tetradrachm coins, portraying him as younger and looking like Alexander because he would liberate the Greeks from their oppressors the Romans.[55] Against this

---

[51] Athenaeus 5.212d–e.
[52] Athenaeus 5.212f–213d.
[53] Athenaeus 5.213e–f.
[54] Coinage proves their loyalty: Mattingly 1971, p. 86.
[55] Højte 2009b, p. 149, and see pp. 145–162 on Mithridates' statues and portraits on coins elsewhere. On the vexed chronology of the coinage, see Habicht 1976, pp. 135–142; Badian 1976, pp. 108–109 and 117–119, citing bibliography. Perhaps now a reform was introduced by Athenion's supporter Demeas supposedly to assist the lowest social stratum against Rome's revitalization of the Areopagus: Geagan 1971, pp. 101–108 (dated 84/3, so after the Sullan sack), but see J. H. Oliver 1980 (dated 87/6, so after Athenion), and especially Antela-Bernárdez 2009b, whose date of 88/7 (year of *anarchia*) I follow;

background, then, they went to war against Rome in May or June of 88.⁵⁶

But then Athenion changed dramatically, according to our ancient accounts, seizing power to become a "dictator"; ruling through fear; surrounding himself with an armed bodyguard; callously torturing and even executing opponents and fugitives from the city without trial as well as seizing their possessions and properties; imposing a curfew ("everyone must stay inside after sunset"); ordering the city gates to be closed and guarded to prevent anyone fleeing; and giving orders to hunt down and either kill or imprison anyone who had managed to escape. Further, he was forced to ration grain in quantities so small that it was like giving that amount "to cocks, not men."⁵⁷

During this time Delos unexpectedly snubbed Athens by revolting and declaring in favor of Rome, perhaps not a surprise given the island's Roman and Italian inhabitants.⁵⁸ Athenion immediately dispatched one thousand troops there under Apellicon of Teos, an Ionian Greek who had become an Athenian citizen, to seize the treasury of Apollo.⁵⁹ Apellicon, however, did not set up a well-guarded camp, and a Roman force landed stealthily one dark night and killed 600 and captured 400 of his men as they slept; its commander Orbius set up a victory monument on the beach.⁶⁰ Apellicon escaped and died in 84.

The debacle on Delos was a major setback for Athenion, but his end came when Mithridates' general Archelaus took over Delos, killed the 20,000 or so Romans and Italians living on it, and brought the temple treasury to

---

cf. Badian 1976, pp. 116–117. The inscription does not tell us exactly what the reform entailed, but instead of benefitting the poor it seems to have enhanced the influence of Athenion and his friends, given they were new men in political life, some having been metic residents of Delos who had recently acquired citizenship: Antela-Bernárdez 2009b, pp. 106–107.

⁵⁶ Antela-Bernárdez 2015; cf. Ferguson 1911, p. 444; Mossé 1973, pp. 147–151; Habicht 1976; Badian 1976; Grieb 2008, pp. 135–137. Bugh 1992, pp. 113–120, sees Athenion's regime as a neutral period before the actual outbreak of hostilities in the First Mithridatic War.

⁵⁷ Athenaeus 5.213f–214d, 214f.

⁵⁸ Ferguson 1911, pp. 359–361.

⁵⁹ Athenaeus 5.214d–e; importance of Delos: Kallet-Marx 1995, p. 210. Expedition to seize Delos: Hinds 1994, pp. 150–151.

⁶⁰ Posidonius, BNJ 87 F 36.53 = Athenaeus 5.214d–215, with Ferguson 1911, pp. 445–446; McGing 1986, pp. 118–126.

Athens.⁶¹ There he set up an Athenian citizen named Aristion, supported by 2,000 soldiers, as tyrant of the city.⁶² Athenion is never heard of again. Why Mithridates gave orders that he be removed is not known. Possibly the king had been simply using him to persuade the Athenians to side with him, and no longer trusted him, especially after the fiasco on Delos.⁶³

Athenion's sudden change of character from narcissistic envoy to bloodthirsty tyrant is startling. It is almost as if we are dealing with two different men—and almost certainly we are, because of the rise of the tyrant Aristion. Since both names are similar and the two men are active in a short time frame, Aristion and Athenion have been taken as the same person.⁶⁴ But compelling arguments have been made that they are indeed two distinct individuals, and that it was Aristion who exhibited the savagery we described here, who ordered Apellicon to Delos, and who deserves our condemnation.⁶⁵

Why then does Posidonius attribute all these ruthless and self-serving acts to Athenion? The answer now commonly accepted is that Posidonius did a hatchet job on Athenion not from any error but because of his own Stoic beliefs, which were diametrically opposed to the Epicurean Aristion. Posidonius saw Aristion as corrupt and a failure, but since he was not able to bring him into his work as it ended in 88, he therefore deliberately conflated the two men.⁶⁶ We can feel some of his contempt in his account, such as when he speaks of him as an example of the "Pythagorean doctrine of treachery," since Pythagoras was said to have aimed at becoming a tyrant.⁶⁷ Hence Athenion deserves rehabilitation.

In the meantime, Mithridates had been scoring successes against Roman troops in Asia Minor; he also organized the massacre of 80,000 Roman and Italian tax collectors, their families, and exploitive traders throughout Asia.⁶⁸

---

⁶¹ Appian, *Mithridatic Wars* 28.
⁶² Appian, *Mithridatic Wars* 28; Pausanias 1.20.5, with Ferguson 1911, pp. 446–447.
⁶³ Antela-Bernárdez 2009b, p. 108.
⁶⁴ Ferguson 1911, pp. 444–445, for example.
⁶⁵ McGing 1986, pp. 120–124; Bugh 1992; Ballesteros Pastor 2005; Antela-Bernárdez 2019, pp. 49–51; cf. Badian 1976, pp. 114–115; Hoff 1997, p. 34.
⁶⁶ His *History* ending in 88 (not 86) and Posidonius swayed by his philosophical beliefs: Desideri 1973; Kidd 1989; Bugh 1992, pp. 109–114; Bringmann 1997. On Posidonius' account being part of an ongoing debate between various writers and intellectuals about Classical Athenian civic ideal, see Gray 2018 (note pp. 168–172 on Athenion as a peripatetic and how this affected Posidonius).
⁶⁷ Athenaeus 5.2134; Pythagoras: Diogenes Laertius 8.39.
⁶⁸ On the *publicani* in the Republic: Badian 1972; Gruen 1984, pp. 299–308.

FIGURE 10.2 Sulla (Lucius Cornelius Sulla Felix). Glyptothek, Staatliche Antikensammlung, Munich, Germany. Photo Credit: © Vanni Archive / Art Resource, NY.

In 87 the Senate sent five legions to Greece as part of an offensive against the troublesome Mithridates, which were commanded by the previous year's consul, Lucius Cornelius Sulla (Figure 10.2). The latter added troops from Aetolia and Thessaly and besieged Aristion in Athens and Archelaus (Mithridates' general who had earlier seized Delos) in the Piraeus.[69] Both men were forced to act independently of each other because of the dilapidation of the Long Walls.[70] However, Sulla had no fleet and so could not sever Archelaus' line of communication to Greece or starve him into surrender.

---

[69] Siege: Plutarch, *Sulla* 12–14 (at 12.1 naming Aristion as the one who persuaded them to join Mithridates); Appian, *Mithridatic Wars* 30–41, with Ferguson 1911, pp. 415–459; Kallet-Marx 1995, pp. 198–212; Hoff 1997. On Sulla, see Seager 1994; Keaveney 2005.
[70] Hoff 1997, p. 35.

Archelaus also fought back against Sulla's attacks by setting fire to his enormous wooden siege engines, which forced Sulla to rebuild them by chopping down trees in the heavily wooded groves of the Academy and the Lyceum (where Plato and Aristotle had respectively taught), transporting them to the Piraeus on 10,000 mules, and raiding the sacred treasuries at Epidaurus and Olympia for money.[71] This sacrilegious act had become something of the norm by then.[72]

Sulla moved to Eleusis for the winter of 87/6. Fortunately for him, an informant told him when Archelaus was expecting his next batch of provisions, allowing him to intercept them. At the same time, he encircled Athens with a ditch to prevent supplies getting in—and people getting out. The scarcity of food in the city, Plutarch relates, led to grain selling for 1,000 drachmas a bushel, but the Athenians endured the conditions, eating wild flowers and "boiling down shoes and leather oil-flasks to eat."[73] Worse, according to Appian, is that when Sulla's men finally entered the city, they saw evidence of cannibalism.[74] All of this fighting and uncertainty led to many anxious people burying their coins, never to reclaim them, as the number of coin hoards shows.[75]

Eventually the Athenians could not hold out any longer and forced Aristion to send a delegation to Sulla seeking terms. The general was in no mood for long speeches; when the first envoy started off by waxing lyrical about Athens' past glory, going back as far as Theseus and the Persian Wars, Sulla interrupted him by saying he had been sent by the Senate not to learn about ancient history but to end a revolt.[76] Then some of his soldiers heard by chance elderly Athenians complaining that a part of the city wall by the Sacred Gate and the Dipylon Gate (the main entrance to the city in the Cerameicus) was in disrepair and had lax guards by it; they reported this information to Sulla, who saw his chance to overcome the city.[77] He attacked it on the night of March 1, 86. As the Romans stormed

---

[71] Plutarch, *Sulla* 12.2–3; Appian, *Mithridatic Wars* 30.
[72] Keaveney 2005, pp. 78–86, on Sulla's actions in seizing money from Greek shrines; see too Mikalson 1998, pp. 283–284.
[73] Plutarch, *Sulla* 13.3; cf. Appian, *Mithridatic Wars* 38, with Ferguson 1911, pp. 449–450; Keaveney 2005, pp. 72–75.
[74] Appian, *Mithridatic Wars* 38.
[75] Kroll 1993, p. 67; see further Habicht 1997a, pp. 309–310.
[76] Plutarch, *Sulla* 13.4.
[77] Plutarch, *Sulla* 14.1–3; [Plutarch], *Moralia* 505b; Appian, *Mithridatic Wars* 38, with Hoff 1997, p. 36; and Theocharaki 2011, pp. 128–129, on the location.

Athens, many people, too weak to resist them, committed suicide; still, furious that the people "had so suddenly joined the barbarian [Mithridates] without cause and had shown such bitter enmity toward himself," according to Appian, Sulla allowed his men to go on an orgy of murdering men, women, and children:[78]

> Sulla ... led his army into the city at midnight. The soldiers now let loose by him for plunder and slaughter, and rushed through the narrow streets with drawn swords. There was therefore no counting of the slain, but their numbers are to this day determined only by the space that was covered with blood. For without mention of those who were killed in the rest of the city, the blood that was shed in the market-place covered all the Cerameicus inside the Dipylon Gate; nay, many say that it flowed through the gate and deluged the suburb. But although those who were thus slain were so many, there were yet more who slew themselves, out of yearning pity for their native city, which they thought was going to be destroyed.

Plutarch tells us that a certain Medeius (probably not the earlier tyrant but possibly his son) and Calliphon beseeched Sulla to put a stop to the massacre and that all the senators accompanying Sulla supported their plea.[79] Sulla acquiesced, explaining that he would forgive a few for the sake of the many and the living for the sake of the dead. He ordered all the Athenians who had opposed him into the nearby Cerameicus, selected by lot one out of every ten of them (a decimation), and had that person executed.[80] As Pausanias notes, "his treatment of the Athenians was so brutal as to be unworthy of a Roman."[81]

Aristion had fled to the Acropolis, en route setting fire to the Odeum (the concert hall built in the Periclean era, next to the theater of Dionysus), so that the Romans could not use its wood for their siege engines.[82] Sulla left

---

[78] Plutarch, *Sulla* 14.3–4 (trans. Mossé 1973, p. 150), with Ferguson 1911, pp. 446–452; Day 1942, pp. 113–119; Naco del Hoyo et al. 2009, pp. 44–45. Plutarch, *Sulla* 13.1 and [Plutarch], *Moralia* 505b suggest that Sulla was motivated by Aristion's insults to him and his wife Metella; cf. Hoff 1997, p. 36.
[79] Plutarch, *Sulla* 14.5; Medeius: Badian, 1976, p. 108 n. 12.
[80] Pausanias 1.20.6.
[81] Pausanias 1.20.7.
[82] Appian, *Mithridatic Wars* 38.

his commander Gaius Scribonius Curio to besiege him while he went after Archelaus at the Piraeus. Aristion managed to defy Curio for some time before lack of water forced him to surrender—as he was led away, a sudden rainfall "that filled the Acropolis with water" was thought to show what the gods thought of him.[83] He was executed, although when is unknown.[84] His demise heralded the end of an era beginning with Medeius: the last tyrants of Athens.[85]

Archelaus was proving to be a more formidable opponent, thwarting Sulla's attempts to capture the Piraeus. But he fled when Sulla launched a successful attack on the garrison and news reached him that Athens had fallen.[86] To ensure that no enemy fleet would anchor in the Piraeus, Sulla burned down the fortifications, including its acclaimed arsenal designed by the architect Philon over two centuries earlier as part of the Lycurgan building program.[87] He then pursued Archelaus into Boeotia, defeating his army at Chaeronea.[88] His victory ended combat in Greece, given that Mithridates had unsurprisingly lost support there, and events in the First Mithridatic War switched to Asia Minor.[89] It took two more decades before Pompey the Great defeated Mithridates in 66 and Rome took over Pontus. Mithridates' threat to Rome ended in his suicide.[90]

"Its Fill of Horrors"

Athens suffered terribly when Sulla took the city in 86, although he had ordered his men not to set fire to it.[91] The damage was far worse than when

---

[83] Plutarch, *Sulla* 14.7.
[84] Appian, *Mithridatic Wars* 39 (he and other leaders executed); Pausanias 1.20.7 (after he had been expelled from the temple of Athena); *contra* Plutarch, *Sulla* 23.2 (poisoned, perhaps in 85 when Sulla was in Thessaly: Ferguson 1911, pp. 451–452; Hoff 1997, p. 37).
[85] Antela-Bernárdez 2019.
[86] Appian, *Mithridatic Wars* 40–41; cf. Plutarch, *Sulla* 14.7.
[87] Plutarch, *Sulla* 14.7; Appian, *Mithridatic Wars* 41, with Garland 1987, p. 56; Hoff 1997, p. 38 with n. 36 on buildings destroyed. Arsenal: Garland 1987, pp. 156–158; Roisman and Worthington 2015, p. 195.
[88] Appian, *Mithridatic Wars* 42–45, with Keaveney 2005, pp. 77–84; Hinds 1994, pp. 154–159.
[89] Campaign: Keaveney 2005, pp. 85–90.
[90] War: Sherwin-White 1994, pp. 233–248.
[91] Appian, *Mithridatic Wars* 38; cf. Memnon, *BNJ* 434 F 22.11 (the Senate ordered him not to). Note Keaveney 2005, pp. 74–75, that Sulla's terrible retribution should not be seen as a sign of any "perverted love of cruelty for its own sake," but from "a simple

the Persians had burned houses and looted from the Acropolis in 480, for Sulla's destruction affected the physical city and its economy.[92] Buildings in the Agora, including the Tholos, the Southwest fountain house, the so-called Heliaea (where stone catapult balls from Sulla's siegecraft were found in the excavations) and the military arsenal, as well as shops and monuments, including that of the eponymous heroes, were extensively damaged or destroyed.

Away from the Agora, buildings in the Cerameicus were wrecked as Sulla's men tore through the area heading toward the gates into the city (also ransacking the cemetery for its tombstones), as were houses south of the Acropolis and the theater of Dionysus, and the circuit wall remained damaged for some time.[93] Sulla seized much personal booty to take back to Rome with him, including columns from the unfinished temple of Olympian Zeus (reused in the Temple of Jupiter on the Capitol), the library of Apellicon of Teos (including works by Aristotle and Theophrastus), and a substantial amount of gold and silver from the treasury on the Acropolis.[94] Probably all sanctuaries were stripped of their contents, especially in the city and Piraeus, though less so in the countryside.[95] His thefts are the first, incidentally, we know of by a Roman in Athens itself—a tradition that would carry on for generations.[96]

Today the archaeological site of the Cerameicus, some twenty minutes walk from the bustling central Monastiraki area of the city, is a jewel to visit. At its far end is the wreckage of the Dipylon and Sacred Gates (Figure 10.3). In between them are the ruins of the Pompeion (where the people prepared the Panathenaic procession), with the Acropolis within eyesight from various vantage points. Standing by what used to be the large, grand Dipylon Gate into the city, it is not hard to imagine Sulla's men charging through the Cerameicus and forcing their way into the city perhaps at the very spot

---

necessity to survive," so as to appease his frustrated men and stop them turning on him; cf. Hoff 1997, p. 37.

[92] See H. A. Thompson 1987, pp. 3–4; Hoff 1997, pp. 38–43; Mango 2010, pp. 119–125; Rathmann 2010, pp. 82–84; Hoff 2013, pp. 568–569; economy: Day 1942, pp. 120–126. The damage also led to a change in memorial sites: Mango 2010.

[93] Theocharaki 2011, p. 130.

[94] Plutarch, *Sulla* 26.1; Appian, *Mithridatic Wars* 39; cf. Pausanias 10.21.6, with Day 1942, p. 126; Wycherley 1964, pp. 170–171.

[95] Mikalson 1998, p. 286.

[96] Alcock 1997, p. 306; the "specialness" of Athens on p. 4.

FIGURE 10.3 Dipylon and Sacred Gates. Photo: Ian Worthington.

where you're standing while from high on the Acropolis Athenians looked across on what was happening. That is where history comes alive.

Thus did Athens "have its fill of horrors," as Appian depressingly states.[97] Pausanias claims that thanks to its wars with Rome the city was so badly affected that it started to flourish again only under Hadrian.[98] That is not true: within a few decades several buildings were rebuilt and construction of a new market began, all funded by Roman money (see chapter 14). Nor did the Senate impose a harsh penalty on the Athenians, despite their alliance with so powerful an enemy of Rome. In fact, the Athenians (and also the mainland Greeks for that matter) were spared the massive indemnity imposed on Asia (20,000 talents), which forced the people over there to borrow to such an extent that with interest the debt ballooned to 120,000 talents in a decade.[99] Sulla also returned Lemnos, Imbros, Scyros, and Delos to Athenian control (although Delos never regained its former preeminence

---

[97] Appian, *Mithridatic Wars* 39.
[98] Pausanias 1.20.7.
[99] Kallet-Marx 1995, pp. 275 with n. 59 and 278–279.

and prosperity) and allowed the city to continue striking its new-style silver coinage.[100]

Sulla boasted that he was pleased he had not destroyed the city, which he genuinely seems to have admired.[101] But at the same time he had been tasked with defeating an enemy city, and there had to be harsh reprisals to teach the Athenians a lesson. In response the Athenians could only resort to what they did best to redeem themselves in the eyes of Rome, among other things establishing a new cycle of eponymous archons.[102] When Sulla returned to the city in 84, they set up a statue to him and may even have initiated him into the Eleusinian Mysteries.[103] The festival of the Theseia was renamed the Sylleia in his honor, as an ephebic decree of 79/8 (archon unknown) attests, although it may have been celebrated only that one time.[104] Further, the masters of the mint in 84/3, Mentor and Moschion, struck a new symbol on their silver coins, the tyrant slayers Harmodius and Aristogeiton, to evoke the downfall of Aristion—the iconography, like the new archon list, was intended to symbolize a new era.

We are told that while Sulla left Athens free and independent, men lost the right to vote in elections.[105] But according to Appian, after executing Aristion, his bodyguard, and supporters, and pardoning everyone else, Sulla "bestowed to all of them substantially the same laws that the Romans had previously laid down for them."[106] Appian's information here, in tandem

---

[100] Appian, *Mithridatic Wars* 61–62, with Ferguson 1911, pp. 452–454; Graindor 1927a, pp. 3–4; Day 1942, pp. 116–118 and 159–161; Green 1990, p. 564; on coinage, *contra* Habicht 1976, pp. 137–138.
[101] Plutarch, *Lucullus* 19.5; [Plutarch], *Moralia* 202f; cf. Appian, *Mithridatic Wars* 38. Admiration: Borg 2011, p. 215.
[102] In tandem, and to reinforce the political break from the previous regime, the first archon after Sulla (in 86/5) was not named but simply recorded by his religious title of *hierophantes* (the chief priest in the Eleusinian Mysteries): Habicht 1997a, pp. 316–317. He may have been Theophemus of Cydathenaeum, whose son or nephew was eponymous archon in 61/0 and president of the Areopagus in 56/5: Habicht 1997a, p. 325.
[103] Statue: *IG* ii² 4103 (cf. Geagan 2011, H 407, p. 223); Mysteries: Plutarch, *Sulla* 26.1, but Clinton 1989a, p. 1503, for example, suggests that Plutarch was misinformed here.
[104] *IG* ii² 1039, line 58, with Accame 1946, p. 172; Habicht 1997a, pp. 311–312 and 315–318; Habicht 1997c, p. 12. Hoff 1997, p. 42 n. 76. Cf. *IG* ii² 4, 375 for an ephebic victory in the torch race.
[105] For example, Plutarch, *Comparison Lysander-Sulla* 5.5.
[106] Appian, *Mithridatic Wars* 39, with Ferguson 1911, pp. 455–457; Day 1942, p. 126; Geagan 1967; Geagan 1979a, pp. 374–375; Kallet-Marx 1995, pp. 212–219; cf. Follet 1976, pp. 301–303; Keaveney 2005, pp. 104–105.

with subsequent changes to the Athenian constitution over the following decades, has given rise to the belief that Sulla imposed a new constitution on Athens, a clear demonstration of Rome's power.[107] But in his biography of Sulla Plutarch says nothing about any constitutional change, and in his comparison of Sulla and Lysander (the Spartan general whose life Plutarch pairs with Sulla) he contrasts Sulla with Lysander's action at the end of the Peloponnesian War in 404 of abolishing Athenian democracy and installing the ruthless Spartan-backed oligarchy of the Thirty Tyrants.[108]

The passage in Appian, quoted in the previous paragraph, is much disputed; since it comes after details of the earlier Roman conquest of Greece, it has been attractively argued that among other things, we are dealing with a corrupt tradition out to amplify the Athenians' crimes and attach a tradition to Sulla's acts that simply was not there.[109] In other words, there was no such thing as a new constitution foisted on Athens. On balance, though, it seems likely that Sulla imposed some restrictions on Athenian public life, as the Senate would not want to see the same sort of civil strife recurring that had led to Aristion's tyranny.[110]

With that in mind, Sulla likely restored the supervisory role of the Areopagus over the archons and expected archons to be pro-Roman.[111] The hoplite general and herald of the Areopagus continued as they were, but they and the return to influence of the Areopagus ought not to be considered as some Sullan attempt at oligarchic control.[112] At the same time, as C. Habicht pointed out, the small number of families holding public offices was akin to Athens being an oligarchy anyway, and in keeping with restricted voting rights the Assembly was curtailed, for we have no decrees issued by it until 49/8 (discussed below).[113]

---

[107] Ferguson 1911, pp. 455–457; Geagan 1967; Geagan 1979a, pp. 373–374; Badian 1976, pp. 115–116.
[108] See Keaveney 2018, pp. 112–116, on Plutarch's characterization of Sulla here.
[109] Kallet-Marx 1995, p. 213, and see pp. 214–218, showing that the idea of a "Sullan constitution" is a modern scholarly one.
[110] Ferguson 1911, pp. 455–457; Accame 1946, pp. 172–174; Badian 1976, pp. 115–117.
[111] Geagan 1967, p. 10. Officials: Tracy 1979, pp. 220–225; Tracy 1995, p. 18.
[112] Kallet-Marx 1995, p. 217.
[113] Habicht 1997a, pp. 327–328. The only decrees in these decades come from the Boule, mostly to do with religious affairs: Habicht 1997a, pp. 317–318, for details with bibliography. For a discussion of the organs of the constitution after Sulla and into the Roman imperial period, Geagan 1967 is essential.

The *ephebeia* continued, as shown by five decrees honoring the ephebes and their *kosmetes* from the time of Sulla to that of Octavian, roughly 79/8 to about 20.[114] Sulla does not seem to have imposed any major restrictions on the program, although after him the ephebes no longer practiced with the catapult.[115] But since Romans were enrolling in the *ephebeia*, and given the pride the Athenians had for it, we should not be surprised to find it operating even if numbers continued to be restricted.

Nevertheless, the Athenians had experienced major losses: the defection of Delos; the bloody tyranny of Aristion; the slaughter of many citizens in the city and in the Piraeus; the sale of Salamis because of poverty; the loss of their gold and silver treasury, many artworks, and the libraries of Aristotle and Theophrastus; and had to endure more oversight of their officials and hence political freedom.[116] Even the artistic life of the city was affected, as there was now a break in the types of sculpture that had been produced, indicating that sculptors may have moved from Athens to other places or even have been killed in the Sullan sack.[117] Among other things, it becomes something of the norm to rededicate existing honorary statues by erasing the original name and reinscribing a new one on the base, a practice continuing into the imperial era.[118]

It is not going too far to say that, in the aftermath of the sack, "art, philosophy, literature, rather than political achievement or imperial domination, now offered the only road to supremacy."[119] As it turned out, it was just as well that Athens had this rich cultural and intellectual history to fall back on.

---

[114] *IG* ii² 1039 (79/8); 1041 (43/2 or 42/1); 1042 (40/39 or 39/8); 1043 (37/6 or 36/5); and 1040 + 1025 (depending on the dating of the archonship of Apolexis, so between 24/3 and 20/19); on the inscriptions, see Perrin-Saminadayar 2004.
[115] As pointed out to me by Nigel Kennell.
[116] See generally on the period: Day 1942, pp. 126–128. Destructions: for example, T. L. Shear 1970, p. 201 ("the violent passage of the Roman legions is everywhere reflected"), Thompson and Wycherley 1972, p. 23. Salamis: Strabo 9.394; cf. Graindor 1927a, pp. 8–9; Day 1942, p. 127; Geagan 1979a, p. 374; *contra* Habicht 1997a, pp. 312–313; Kallet-Marx 1995, p. 219 n. 111; Habicht 1996b. Salamis was returned to Athens in the Augustan period: see pp. 260–262.
[117] Palagia 1997.
[118] J. L. Shear 2007a.
[119] Green 1990, p. 565; cf. Ferguson 1911, p. 458: "Resignation was the only policy for the Athenians; meekness their cardinal virtue."

Subject to Rome?

Life in Athens was uneventful for the next several years. Then in 68 the Roman governor in Smyrna (Asia), Publius Cornelius Dolabella, referred a homicide case that had come before him to the Areopagus.[120] A woman in his province had been accused of murdering her husband and their son because they had killed her son from a previous marriage. Dolabella knew by law he ought to convict her, but at the same time her motive put him in a dilemma. Since the Areopagus in Athens had tried cases of premeditated homicide for centuries, he called on it to decide the woman's fate, either out of respect or because he wanted to wash his hands of the case. (Another attractive suggestion is that he may have referred the case because the Areopagus was believed to be the first court to judge a domestic violence case involving a son, Orestes, who killed his mother, Clytemnestra, for murdering her husband Agamemnon.)[121] Dolabella's quandary carried over to the members of the Areopagus, who hit upon an extraordinary and smart solution: they delayed the case and ordered the defendant and prosecutors to appear before them for trial in one hundred years' time.[122]

Dolabella's referral might have given the Athenians a reason to believe that Athenian–Roman relations were returning to something like the status quo before they sided with Mithridates. But now comes a problem concerning the status of Athens as either a free city or part of a proconsul's province subject to that official's will. The issue is important not only for how the Romans viewed Athens, but also for the ability of the people to go about their daily affairs without interference by Rome.

In 58 the tribune of the plebeians, Publius Clodius Pulcher, introduced his *lex Clodia de provinciis consularibus* (the law of Clodius on the provinces of the consuls), permitting consuls to hold larger provinces than currently allowed.[123] The consuls of that year were Lucius Calpurnius Piso (Caesar's father-in-law) and Aulus Gabinius. Piso duly was assigned Macedonia, but also took over Athens and Delos; Gabinius was allocated Cilicia, along with Syria, Babylon, and Persia.[124] Clodius' law, declared C. Habicht, "turned Athens from a partner into a vassal of Rome," which was evident in Piso's

---

[120] Rawson 1985, pp. 65–66; Dolabella: Campanile 2004.
[121] By J. Roisman in his comments on my draft.
[122] Valerius Maximus 8.1, *amb.* 2; Gellius 12.7; Ammianus 29.18–19.
[123] Background: Wiseman 1994.
[124] Habicht 1997a, pp. 339–340, with sources.

overbearing attitude to the people and theft of even more artworks.[125] Yet when his term ended in 55, Athens regained its status as an independent ally of Rome.

Was Piso the de facto ruler of Athens, thereby making Athens subject to Rome, and if so, why would the city be freed from this subjection after only three years—why not simply keep Athens and Delos under the purview of the governor of Macedonia? The belief that Athens and Delos were Roman subjects for this short period is based on two passages in Cicero's works and an inscription from Delos of the dedication of a temple of Hermes.[126] All three have been vigorously disputed.[127] It now seems all but certain that the *lex Clodia* did not affect Athens and that the city maintained its independence throughout this period. For one thing, while the inscription refers to the proconsul (commander) Lucius Piso, the dating is controversial, and because of the terminology used, the Piso in question is more likely the homonymous grandfather (who was also a proconsul of Asia) of our Piso of 58. If so, the inscription is to be dated to 115 and has nothing to do with the late 50s.[128]

The Ciceronian evidence consists of two passages likewise open to interpretation. One passage merely states that Clodius' law gave Piso wider authority but says nothing of Athens.[129] The other, in a speech Cicero delivered against Piso in the Senate in 55, states: "Under that law [*lex Clodia*] which no one except you and your colleagues considers a law, all Achaea, Thessaly, and Athens—the whole of Greece—was surrendered to you."[130] The wording smacks of rhetorical exaggeration, and since Cicero launched a number of attacks on Piso, who had returned in disgrace from his province and whom he hated, he likely embellished the scope of his jurisdiction.[131] The *lex Clodia* presumably extended the operating areas of the proconsuls, but that is quite different from saying that Athens lost its sovereignty. Indeed, a sign of the

---

[125] Habicht 1997a, p. 340; artworks: Cicero, *Piso* 40.96; on Piso, see Sarikakis 1981.
[126] *Inscriptions de Délos*, ed. École Française d'Athènes (Paris: 1926–72), no. 1737; Cicero, *De domo* 23; Cicero, *Piso* 37.
[127] Eilers 2006.
[128] Eilers 2006, pp. 124–127.
[129] Cicero, *De domo* 23.
[130] Cicero, *Piso* 37.
[131] Eilers 2006, pp. 127–131 (just as Gabinius, also accused of mismanagement in his province, could hardly have received the surrender of all of Syria, Babylon, and Persia). Rhetorical exaggeration was part and parcel of a speech; we can compare Demosthenes' exaggerated claim that Philip II had destroyed every city in the Chalcidice in 348: Demosthenes 9.26, with Worthington 2013, pp. 142–143.

city's independence is that in 52 Cicero appealed to the Areopagus and not the Senate to save Epicurus' house (p. 230). Possibly adding to the belief of greater Roman control was that in 58 the consuls introduced a law in Delos waiving certain taxes imposed by Sulla to improve economic conditions on the island.[132]

In 49/8 we have the first Assembly decree of the post-Sullan period, although little of it survives.[133] That the Assembly began issuing decrees again is perhaps a sign of Rome relaxing its grip on the city.[134] An ephebic decree of 40/39 or possibly 39/8 (archonship of Nicandrus) supports this view, for usually the hoplite general and herald of the Areopagus awarded honors to ephebes.[135] However, after Mark Antony became master of Greece, these two officials put forward a decree in 37/6 or 36/5 honoring ephebes, in keeping with the usual (oligarchic) way of doing things.[136] This yo-yoing is not surprising as rapid political shifts took place during the Roman civil war when Athens was subject to Caesar, then Brutus, then Antony, and finally Octavian, as we shall see in the next chapter.

Romans in Athens

Despite the political upheavals and damage to the city, Athens was becoming more cosmopolitan because of the great esteem in which Rome held Greek culture and learning, although Athenians and Romans did not intermingle freely when in the city.[137] Over the course of the second century and well into the first, visits by Roman dignitaries increased, some en route to various commands in the east but who stopped off in Athens to attend the lectures

---

[132] *Inscriptions de Délos*, ed. École Française d'Athènes (Paris: 1926–72), no. 1511, lines 6–7.
[133] *IG* ii² 1047.
[134] Another Assembly decree of a law code possibly from this period (the date is controversial), on the motion of a certain Demeas (restored in line 6), son of Demeas, probably of the deme Azenia, appears to refer to democracy, the contrast between lots and elections, and to offices filled by lot; it seems to indicate an abandonment of Sulla's oligarchy, and hence a return to democracy: Geagan 1971, pp. 101–108 and plate 16. However, Sulla did not impose oligarchy and the decree may not be from this time: Habicht 1997a, pp. 320–321.
[135] *IG* ii² 1042; see too Rawson 1985, pp. 60–61.
[136] *IG* ii² 1043, line 55.
[137] Habicht 1997c; Rödel 2010; Perrin-Saminadayar 2011. Romans in Athens: Wardman 1976; Gruen 1984, pp. 250–272; Rawson 1989, pp. 422–476; see too Griffin 1994; Mattingly 1997; Habicht 1997a, pp. 293–295 and especially pp. 342–350.

of philosophers.¹³⁸ Thanks to the "philosophers' embassy" to the Senate in 155, interest in the systems of philosophy as well as rhetoric that were being taught in Athens had soared. Cicero visited the city twice (in 79 and 51), and together with his brother Quintus, his cousin Lucius, and friends Titus Pomponius Atticus and Marcus Pupius Piso, attended the lectures of Antiochus, Phaedrus, and Zenon of Sidon.¹³⁹ They also visited the grounds of Plato's Academy, where they saw the remains of olive trees chopped down by Sulla for his siege engines still lying on the ground, a scene that Cicero describes with a near-apologetic tone.¹⁴⁰

Educated Romans were truly appreciative of the city's philosophers, past and present, as well as their backgrounds. We can see this in Cicero's bombardment of questions about the philosophers' embassy to his friend Atticus in 45; over a century after their mission Cicero wanted to know why exactly they had gone to Rome, who the leading politicians in Athens were at the time, and any other information Atticus might have.¹⁴¹ In time Roman aristocrats and rich men sent their sons to Athens, seeing it as a finishing school of sorts, not to mention the degree of one-upmanship.¹⁴² But they also took a very real interest in education. Thus in 45 or 44 Cicero obtained Roman citizenship from Caesar for his son Marcus' teacher, Cratippus of Pergamum, but then successfully petitioned the Areopagus to allow Cratippus to continue his teaching in Athens.¹⁴³ Of course their sons and their fathers came into contact with the leading families of the city, which fostered relations between the two cities.¹⁴⁴

There was also an influx of Romans rich enough to travel who just wanted to see the city and experience its culture. Also, some Romans went to Athens for work, such as Decimus Cossutius, whom Antiochus IV appointed in 174 to work on the temple of Olympian Zeus.¹⁴⁵ Others even

---

¹³⁸ Habicht 1997c, pp. 10–11.
¹³⁹ Raubitschek 1949; Rowland 1972; cf. Rawson 1985, pp. 55–56.
¹⁴⁰ Cicero, *De finibus* 5.1–8.
¹⁴¹ Cicero, *Ad Atticum* 12.23.2. See Habicht 1994b on Hellenistic philosophy, especially in Athens, and impact on Rome.
¹⁴² Daly 1950, p. 51.
¹⁴³ Plutarch, *Cicero* 24.7.
¹⁴⁴ Rawson 1985, pp. 44–59; Cicero, *Ad Atticum* 14.16.3, 18.4, 15.16, on the interaction between Cicero's son and Herodes of Marathon, Leonides of Melite, and Epicrates of Leukonoe, who reported to Cicero on his son's conduct and studies.
¹⁴⁵ Habicht 1997c, p. 12.

took up longer-term and permanent residency in Athens.¹⁴⁶ These would include men banished from Rome or who went there before being formally exiled. In 58, for example, Cicero toyed with the idea of spending his exile in Athens; out of fear for his safety, however, he decided on Thessalonica instead.¹⁴⁷ Romans could not take part in political life, but they could own land. Also, their sons could serve as ephebes, and at the end of their service were eligible for Athenian citizenship.¹⁴⁸ In 123/2 we have the first recorded foreign ephebes, whose enlistments raised numbers substantially from the fifty since the end of the war against Perseus to 179.¹⁴⁹ Occasionally we hear of Romans who even took out Athenian citizenship, although dual citizenship was not allowed.¹⁵⁰

One famous individual who went to Athens in 86 or 85 simply out of a love of Greek culture was the twenty-four-year-old Titus Pomponius. He lived there for twenty years, spoke Greek fluently, and was nicknamed "Atticus" (Man of Attica), the name by which he is more commonly known as the friend and correspondent of Cicero, from whom he received over four hundred letters.¹⁵¹ Atticus had left Rome because of the civil war that had broken out between Sulla and another Roman general, Gaius Marius; he already had business dealings with Sicyon and Epirus, so it made economic sense for him to go to Greece.¹⁵² But equally appealing was Athens' intellectual reputation, which Atticus respected greatly, and he became a follower of the Epicurean school.¹⁵³ He quickly settled into life in the city, so much so that when Sulla, with whom he struck up a friendship, asked him to return to Rome in 84, he refused.

Atticus generously gave back to the city. He was a member of the wealthy equestrian class in Rome (which ranked below the senatorial class), and had made a fortune in real estate deals. He put that fortune and his connections to good use, twice buying large amounts of grain for the Athenians when the price soared (the first time was unknown but the second time was in

---

¹⁴⁶ Fuller details citing all sources in Habicht 1997a, pp. 342–350, from which my narrative borrows; cf. Errington 1988 (throughout the Greek world); Habicht 1997c, pp. 12–13.
¹⁴⁷ Loomis 1977.
¹⁴⁸ Perrin-Saminadayar 2007a, pp. 529–530.
¹⁴⁹ Habicht 1997c, p. 13, citing sources.
¹⁵⁰ Cf. J. H. Oliver 1981a. See Byrne 2003 for a register of Roman citizens in Athens into the Imperial era.
¹⁵¹ Perlwitz 1992; Welch 1996.
¹⁵² Perlwitz 1992, pp. 35–39.
¹⁵³ Perlwitz 1992, pp. 90–97.

50). He also dealt with venal moneylenders, usually Romans, when the city was in such dire straits it needed to borrow money, even taking out loans in his own name at more favorable rates.[154] It is hardly a surprise that the Athenians voted honors on him, which he modestly declined. He returned to Rome in 65, and died in 32 at the age of seventy-seven.

Eventually aspects of the two cultures of Greece and Rome began to merge, though while the Greeks maintained their own traditions and identity it was the Romans, especially Augustus, who came to adapt the intellectual, cultural, and artistic aspects of Hellenism into their education and intellectual life.[155] As the Roman poet Horace would aptly say, "captive Greece captured her rude conqueror and introduced her arts to the crude Latin lands," indicating that in the end the Romans might dominate but the Greeks were the cultural hegemons.[156] Not that there was every any mutual respect between Greeks and Romans, not least because of Greek fear of Roman might. In the meantime, the Athenians had to deal with ever-increasing numbers of Roman visitors, some cultivating diplomatic and social contacts with very prominent Athenians, who served as their *hospites* or guest-friends when they visited the city.[157] Against this background they found themselves involved in the fall of the Republic, to which we next turn.

---

[154] Day 1942, pp. 127 and 170.
[155] Rawson 1989; Griffin 1994; see too MacMullen 1991; Habicht 1997c; David 2000, pp. 77–89. Imperial period: Borg 2011; Dihle 2011; Hidber 2011; cf. Bowersock 1965, pp. 73–84; Spawforth 2012 (Augusta era). "Romanization": Alcock 1997.
[156] Horace, *Epistle* 2.1.156.
[157] Rawson 1985, pp. 44–59.

11

The End of "Hellenistic" Athens

GREECE HAD SEEN CORINTH DESTROYED, towns wrecked, sanctuaries despoiled, lands devastated, and artworks plundered—as Cicero wrote in a letter to Atticus in 49, "Do you suppose there is any part of Greece that will not be robbed?"[1] Athens was still suffering the effects of the Sullan sack two decades earlier; it was forced to borrow money, and yet was still unable to repair the damage caused by Sulla. On top of that the city was continually pillaged—in 80, the governor of Sicily, Gaius Verres, allegedly stole all the gold from the Parthenon that Sulla had missed.[2] There was a reason why Cicero made a point of claiming that his visit to Athens (in 51) was not a burden, unlike previous Roman visitors.[3] But Athens continued to be affected thanks to a near-constant parade of Roman rulers, each with his own demands and impact on the city.[4]

Rebuilding Athens

The days of Hellenistic kings lavishing buildings on Athens were all but gone, as were their kingdoms. The Seleucid Empire had been in decline since the end of the second century, and in 63, three years after defeating

---

[1] Cicero, *Ad Atticum* 9.9.
[2] Hoff 1989a, pp. 270–271; Hoff 2013, pp. 570–571; see too Geagan 1979a, p. 377.
[3] Cicero, *Ad Atticum* 5.10.2, 11.5.
[4] Cf. Rödel 2010, pp. 98–101.

Mithridates VI, Pompey had turned Syria into a Roman province.[5] The other great Hellenistic dynasty, the Ptolemaic, was also suffering. After the first three rulers, a series of weaker ones, combined with their exploitation of the Egyptians, had led to civil strife.[6] One king who could still benefit Athens was Ariobarzanes II of Cappadocia (r. 63–51). Educated there, he had served as an ephebe, and paid for the cost of rebuilding the Odeum, which the tyrant Aristion had burned down in 86.[7] For his *euergetism* (benefaction) the people honored him with a statue and probably inducted him into the Mysteries.[8]

Ariobarzanes had employed three architects to design the new Odeum: two Romans (the brothers Gaius and Marius Stallius) and a Greek named Menalippus.[9] Using Roman architects on Greek buildings had become something of the norm for Hellenistic monarchs—almost a century earlier (in 174), for example, Antiochus IV tasked Cossutius to work on the temple of Olympian Zeus in Athens. These rulers may have wanted some Roman influences on Greek models, or perhaps there was a dearth of skilled local craftsmen.[10] We know about Athenian artists who moved to Rome to pursue a career, such as Diogenes, who worked on Agrippa's Pantheon in Rome (dedicated in 25).[11] If he could move, then so could others; and they continued to do so, for nearly two centuries later Trajan commented to Pliny that architects were still going to Rome from Greece.[12] And Roman architects sent plaster casts of the Caryatids from the Erechtheum to Rome, where they were copied and used in the porticoes of the Forum.[13] Moreover, the round temples of Vesta in the Roman Forum and of Roma and Augustus in Athens may well trace their shape back to the Philippeum of Philip II, set up at Olympia after Chaeronea in 338.[14] Thus, the use

---

[5] Background: Green 1990, pp. 653–661; Sherwin-White 1994, pp. 248–262. Rome and the Seleucids: Gruen 1984, pp. 611–671; Kallet-Marx 1995, pp. 323–334. Impact of Roman intervention in the east on the civilian population: Naco del Hoyo et al. 2009.

[6] Background: Green 1990, pp. 647–653. Rome and Egypt: Gruen 1984, pp. 672–719; Huss 2001; D. J. Thompson 2003.

[7] *IG* ii² 3426 (honors to him by the architects he employed on the rebuilding); Vitruvius 5.9.1, with H. A. Thompson 1987, p. 4; Stefanidou-Tiveriou 2008, p. 15; Hoff 2013, pp. 566–567.

[8] *IG* ii² 3427; Mysteries: Clinton 1997, p. 164.

[9] Hoff 2013, p. 567. They were Roman residents in Athens: Habicht 1997c, p. 12.

[10] Cf. H. A. Thompson 1987, pp. 2–3.

[11] Day 1942, p. 154.

[12] Pliny, *Letter* 10.39–40.

[13] Graindor 1927a, pp. 154–155; Whittaker 2002, pp. 26 and 34.

[14] Worthington 2008a, pp. 164–166.

of Roman architects on buildings in Athens (or elsewhere in the east), while episodic, complements artists who moved from east to west.[15]

In 67 Athens prepared for the visit of Pompey (the Great), who was on his way to the east. Not able "to pass by Athens without visiting," he made a brief stop there, addressed the people, and sacrificed to the gods.[16] The Athenians appear to have bestowed divine honors on him, for Plutarch relates that on the inner and outer facades of the gate through which he left the city they inscribed these verses:[17]

> To the extent that you know yourself to be mortal, the more you are a god (interior)
>   We awaited, we worshipped, we saw, we send forth (exterior)

The Athenians were clearly expressing their gratitude for Pompey's recent victories over the pirates, who had disrupted Athenian trade in the Mediterranean, and who, some years earlier in 69, had raided Delos, inflicting damage and selling many inhabitants as slaves.[18] Numerous towns in the east had scrambled to bestow honors on Pompey after his campaigns, so it is not surprising that the Athenians followed suit.[19] But divinity was another matter, although there is no evidence that he accepted it from them.[20]

Athens still had crumbling buildings, and the people were not in a position financially to restore them.[21] They had even resorted to selling their prized citizenship and borrowing money to keep afloat, using Atticus to negotiate good interest rates.[22] Ironically, it was prominent Romans who footed the restoration bill. The list began with Pompey, who in the spring of 62 returned to the city on his way back to Italy and gave 50 talents to the people.[23] Thus the trend of foreign donations moved from Hellenistic

---

[15] See H. A. Thompson 1987.
[16] Plutarch, *Pompey* 27.3, with Hoff 2005, pp. 327–336. Pompey: Greenhalgh 1980; Sherwin-White 1994; Seager 2002.
[17] Plutarch, *Pompey* 27.3.
[18] Piracy as a threat: for example, Kallet-Marx 2005, pp. 316–317.
[19] Selection at Sherk 1984, no. 75, pp. 95–96.
[20] Hoff 1989a, p. 271; Hoff 2005, pp. 328–331.
[21] Day 1942, pp. 126–138; cf. Rotroff 1997, especially pp. 102–104, on the financial implications of the reduction in the manufacture of fine pottery. Buildings: Hoff 1997, pp. 38–44; Hoff 2005, pp. 332–333; Hoff 2013, pp. 569–570; cf. Borg 2011, pp. 215–218.
[22] Citizenship: Dio 54.7.2, with Day 1942, p. 127; Rödel 2010, pp. 98–99.
[23] Plutarch, *Pompey* 42.5.

to Roman individuals. Pompey's present may have had nothing to do with philanthropic reasons; his relations with Caesar were declining, and he probably wanted to earn the Athenians' goodwill. Whether they set up a statue to him in gratitude is unknown—if they had, they may well have destroyed it when Caesar later defeated him at Pharsalus and moved on Athens (discussed below). That they had ones of his grandfather, Sextus Pompeius, and father, Gnaeus Pompeius, on the Acropolis, does not mean anything: given the sluggishness in setting up statues to Romans, those of Pompey's relations may have been just for his visit in 62.[24]

What the people did with Pompey's 50 talents is not properly known, but it was said that he thought they had squandered it.[25] We have an inscription that refers to a *deigma* (bazaar) "of Magnus," presumably Pompey the Great (although "Magnus" is found in later inscriptions). This bazaar was probably in the Emporium or market area of the Piraeus, perhaps on a quay where goods could easily be displayed.[26] With Athens still struggling economically from the Sullan sack, it made sense to spend money to regenerate economic activity; once the Piraeus began to thrive again, other building projects in the city could be entertained.[27] On the other hand, it has recently been argued, based on a reconsideration of epitaphs in the Piraeus deme, that the settlement around the main harbor was not as affected by Sulla's attack as is often thought.[28] If so, and trade likewise was not as impacted, then perhaps not all Pompey's monetary gift was used up on work in the Piraeus; some of it may have been spent on repairing the city's circuit wall.[29]

It is even possible that part of the money was used to construct one of the more fascinating monuments in Athens, which may be dated to the mid-first century, the Tower of the Winds (Figure 11.1; see too Figure 14.1B).[30]

---

[24] Hoff 2005, p. 332; cf. Kallet-Marx 1995, p. 52.
[25] Cicero, *Ad Atticum* 6.1.25, with Hoff 1989b, p. 2; Hoff 2005, pp. 333–334.
[26] *IG* ii² 1035, line 47, with Day 1942, p. 129 (other instances of "Magnus" on inscriptions) and pp. 145–150; Garland 1987, p. 154; Hoff 1989b, p. 2 nn. 8–9 (n. 9 for references to a quay); Hoff 2005, p. 333; Borg 2011, p. 218; Hoff 2013, p. 569.
[27] Ferguson 1911, pp. 455–456; Day 1942, pp. 126 and 142–151; Garland 1987, pp. 58–72 and 83–95.
[28] Grigoropoulos 2009, especially pp. 169–172.
[29] Theocharaki 2011, p. 130.
[30] Day 1942, pp. 131–132; Noble and de Solla Price 1968; H. J. Kienast 1997a; H. J. Kienast 1997b; Webb 2017. Graindor 1927a, p. 197, suggests that Caesar was responsible for its building because of his interest in astronomy.

FIGURE 11.1 Tower of the Winds. Photo: Ian Worthington.

This 12-meter tall octagonal tower was a *horologion* (timepiece) and, arguably, the world's first meteorological station. Designed by the Macedonian astronomer Andronicus of Cyrrhus, it was built of pentelic marble near the eastern end of the Roman Agora (on which, see below) as part of the burgeoning Roman architectural presence in the city. On each of its walls was a sundial, carved for one of the eight wind deities (N, NE, E, SE, S, SW, W, and NW), and inside was a large water clock (worked by water flowing from the Acropolis). Atop it was a bronze figure of Triton with a rod in his hand; when the wind blew, the god turned into a weather vane in the wind direction.[31] The sundials and Triton were placed high enough on the structure to be visible from the Agora, so the people seemed to have intended the monument to be a clock tower.[32] Over time the tower fell into disrepair, but after two years of restoration work it was reopened (in its original location) in 2016. It is an impressive monument, and makes us wonder why Pompey

---

[31] Noble and de Solla Price 1968, p. 353.
[32] Noble and de Solla Price 1968, p. 349.

thought the Athenians had squandered his money—unless he had nothing to do with it.

A decade later, in 51, Julius Caesar and Appius Claudius Pulcher (former consul of 54, and a member of the Claudii, one of the most powerful Roman families) gave their own donations to Athens. An orator and scholar of the first rank, Pulcher was naturally attracted to the city's intellectual climate. Fascinated by the Eleusinian Mysteries (and likely initiated into them), in 51 he funded the gateway of the Lesser Propylaea in Eleusis, which was completed after his death in 48, at which time the Athenians awarded him a statue.[33] Caesar, who needs no introduction, gave 50 talents (the exact same sum as Pompey) to Herodes of Marathon (archon 60/59).[34] In a letter to Atticus, Cicero claims that Herodes "extorted" this money from Caesar, but it is hard to imagine someone like Caesar falling victim to some sort of confidence trick.[35]

No ancient writer informs us what Caesar's money was used for, but epigraphic evidence comes to the rescue: an inscription tells us that he funded the building of a Roman Agora, a project that was only finished off in the Augustan era.[36] It has been suggested that a year earlier the Athenians were planning a new agora, given the sack of Delos in 69 and its subsequent economic collapse, and approached Caesar for the money as they could not afford it themselves.[37] Caesar took advantage of the Athenians' request by deliberately gifting the same amount of money as Pompey, but wanted something grander than a bazaar, hence the other market area.[38] By extension, his gift may also have won over some of Pompey's supporters

---

[33] Clinton 1989a, pp. 1504–1506; Clinton 1997, pp. 164–165. Statue: *IG* ii² 4109; Geagan 2011, H411, pp. 224–225.

[34] Rawson 1985, pp. 47–49; cf. Graindor 1927a, p. 31. Archonship: *IG* ii² 1716.

[35] Cicero, *Ad Atticum* 6.1.25, with Rawson 1985, pp. 45–46, arguing that Caesar specified what his money was to be used for his own mercenary reasons, i.e., provincial support, in a projected clash with Pompey. Hoff 2005, p. 334, claims that Pompey could not specify what his money was used for, whereas Caesar could, and wanted something more visible to win political support in Athens, so Herodes played him off against Pompey. But Hoff does not consider the possibility that Pompey may have helped to finance the Tower of the Winds.

[36] *IG* ii³ 4, 12 (Caesar), with Rödel 2010, pp. 99–100; Borg 2011, p. 218.

[37] Hoff 1989b, pp. 2–3.

[38] Initiative from them as opposed to the Market being foisted upon them: Dickenson 2017, pp. 242–243.

to him. In gratitude, the Athenians dedicated a statue to Caesar as *Soter* (Savior) and *euergetes* (benefactor) in later 49.[39]

The Roman Agora (or Market of Caesar and Augustus, as it should properly be called) became an influential commercial area of the city, though not necessarily taking away business from the five-hundred-year-old Athenian one and surely not displacing the civic heart of the democratic city.[40] It was set into the north slope of the Acropolis, about 200 meters to the east of the old (Athenian) Agora.[41] The architecture of an enclosed large marble-paved square with shops and halls on all four sides bears no relation to anything in Athens and is a fusion of Roman and eastern elements. Caesar was clearly the driving force in its planning, as it has affinities with his Forum in Rome (begun in 51 and dedicated in 46) and perhaps with the two similar porticoed enclosures he had built at Alexandria and Antioch in 48.[42] We will return to the Roman Agora and Augustus' role in its completion in chapter 14.

One person who did not contribute anything was Cicero, who visited Athens twice (in 79 and in 51) and was even initiated into the Mysteries.[43] Neither Caesar's 50 talents, nor the following year Atticus' gift of grain, motivated him to open his purse—apparently, he thought of funding a gate at the Academy but decided that would be inappropriate.[44] But not all Roman building projects were welcomed. When the son-in-law of Sulla, Gaius Memmius, a poet banished from Rome in 52 for corruption, went

---

[39] See Geagan 2011, H251, p. 146, with Raubitschek 1954, pp. 68–69; Geagan 1984, p. 71 n. 10; see too Sherk 1984 no. 79A, p. 99.

[40] Cf. Day 1942, p. 131: "It is quite impossible to believe that the Market was built merely for the purpose of adorning the city." Location: Hoff 2013, pp. 572–573. Commercial activity in the old Agora: Thompson and Wycherley 1972, pp. 185–191. On the old Agora continuing as before, see especially Dickenson 2017, pp. 171–188 (e.g., "the grounds for thinking that the Roman Agora did take over the market function of the old square are actually rather slight," p. 171).

[41] Graindor 1927a, pp. 31–32 and 184–197; Day 1942, p. 129; T. L. Shear 1981, pp. 358–360; Kleiner 1986, pp. 9–10; H. A. Thompson 1987, pp. 4–6; see its history in Thompson and Wycherley 1972, pp. 170–173; Hoff 1988; Hoff 1989b; Stefanidou-Tiveriou 2008, pp. 15–19; Sourlas 2012; Dickenson 2017, pp. 238–252. Interruption: Hoff 1989b, pp. 3–5. Oikonomides 1979, p. 101 n. 13, believes that the Market had nothing to do with Caesar or Augustus but rich Athenians paid for it; this is unfounded.

[42] T. L. Shear 1981, p. 359 nn. 16–17, citing bibliography, though note the caution of Stefanidou-Tiveriou 2008, pp. 17–18; Borg 2011, p. 219, citing bibliography.

[43] Clinton 1989a, p. 1504.

[44] Rawson 1985, p. 46.

to the city and announced his plan to build a palace on the site where Epicurus' house stood, there was uproar from the philosopher's followers, especially when the Areopagus, presumably because of Memmius' money and influence, granted him permission. Patron, the head of the Epicurean school, turned to his Roman acquaintances Atticus and Cicero for help. Cicero believed the Areopagus would not reverse its decision—that he did not appeal to the Senate is a clear sign that if Athens had been made subject to Rome by the *lex Clodia*, it was certainly free by then.[45] Therefore he wrote to Memmius (who had just left the city for Mytilene) and managed to persuade him to abandon his grandiose project.[46] It seems ironic that Lucretius dedicated his *On the Nature of Things* (*De rerum natura*), which engages Epicurus' philosophy, to Memmius!

The Roman building projects that began at this time, continued with Augustus, and after a hiatus were resumed with gusto by Hadrian, transformed Athens into a hybrid of Greek and Roman parts, or as it has sometimes been described, a provincial city.[47] Romans were visiting and even living in the city for a variety of reasons, and everyone seems to have got along in friendly enough fashion. But then came the civil war between Pompey and Caesar, as a result of which Athens became a haven for its protagonists.[48] Against this background, we must now trace its history to the end of the Hellenistic era in 30, and with it the fall of the Roman Republic.

"The Die Is Cast"

The Roman Civil War was waged between Caesar and his supporters (the *Populares*) against the Senate (with Pompey as its military commander), and began in 49 when the Senate ordered Caesar to disband his army; instead, Caesar led his favored 13th legion across the river Rubicon (the northern boundary of Italy, though the exact location of the river is not known) on January 10 to march on Rome.[49] Supposedly, as he did so he uttered the famous phrase *iacta alea est* (the die is cast).[50] The war, ending in 45 when

---

[45] Eilers 2006, p. 130.
[46] Cicero, *Ad Atticum* 5.11.6, 19.3; *ad Familiares* 13.1.
[47] T. L. Shear 1981; cf. Kleiner 1986; Thompson and Wycherley 1972, pp. 111–116; Stefanidou-Tiveriou 2008.
[48] D. Kienast 1993, pp. 191–198.
[49] See, for example, Rawson 1994a.
[50] Suetonius, *Caesar* 32; see too Plutarch, *Pompey* 60.2.

a victorious Caesar assumed the dictatorship, was the death knell of the Roman Republic, but Greece was embroiled in it from the outset.

As Caesar approached Rome, Pompey fled to Illyria with his legions, where he had substantial support, and demanded troops and supplies from the Greek states. The Athenians, "wanting to share in the glory of the war that had become a competition for hegemony of Rome," supported him and sent him a contingent of infantry and probably three ships for his fleet in the Ionian Sea to help prevent Caesar sailing to Greece.[51] This was not the wisest move. Caesar ordered his legate Quintus Fufius Calenus to move from Illyria to the Peloponnese in 48 with fifteen cohorts of soldiers (7,500 men).[52] As he marched southward Calenus took Delphi, Thebes, and Orchomenus in Boeotia without a fight and then besieged Athens, installing troops in the Piraeus, since it was unwalled, and ravaging the countryside.[53] Athens managed to withstand his siege, "in spite of the enormous damage he inflicted on its territory," perhaps because of a frantic rebuilding of the city walls.[54]

Pompey defeated Caesar at Dyrrachium (in Albania) in July, killing one thousand of his men. But any hope that the Athenians held of him coming to their rescue was dashed when, in August 48, Caesar defeated him at Pharsalus in Central Greece. Pompey fled to Egypt, pursued by Caesar, and was murdered there by Ptolemy XIII; he sent his head to Caesar as a goodwill gesture (who was not impressed). Athens, still under siege, had surrendered to Caesar after Pharsalus, but had to wait for his terms as he decided to reinstate to the throne Ptolemy's sister-wife Cleopatra VII (whom Pompey had driven out of Egypt in 51 on their father Ptolemy XII's death).[55] It was during this short war against Ptolemy XIII (ending with his death) that parts of the great Library at Alexandria caught fire.[56] Now Cleopatra became ruler of Egypt with her young brother-husband Ptolemy XIV; she became Caesar's lover and later gave birth to his son Ptolemy Caesar (Caesarion).

---

[51] Appian, *Civil Wars* 2.70 (quote), 75 (also speaking of troops from the Spartans, other Peloponnesians, Boeotians, and Macedonians); Lucan, *Pharsalia* 3.181–183; Caesar, *Civil Wars* 3.3.1.
[52] Amela Valverde 2008.
[53] Caesar, *Civil Wars* 3.56; Dio 42.14.1. See too Oikonomides 1979, pp. 97–101; Borg 2011, p. 218.
[54] Dio 42.14.1.
[55] Background: Green 1990, pp. 664–667; Rawson 1994a, pp. 433–434.
[56] Plutarch, *Caesar* 49.6; Dio 42.38.2, with Fraser 1972, pp. 126–127, 334–335, and 476.

Caesar returned to Greece where he was met by an Athenian delegation, roughly asking it, "How often do you expect to be rescued from the ruin you bring on yourselves by the fame of your forefathers?"[57] Nevertheless, he pardoned Athens out of respect for the fame and *virtus* (virtue) of its ancestors, but likely took away some of its possessions (perhaps including Oropus).[58] The belief that he restored its democracy is unlikely.[59] In any case, the most influential body in Athens was still the aristocratic Areopagus; its members therefore would side with him to maintain power.[60] In response, the Athenians set up at least one statue to him.[61] Caesar then gave orders to rebuild Corinth, which had been razed by Mummius' army a century earlier when Rome annexed Greece in 146. The new colony of Corinth became not only the focus of new building projects, but also the center of the imperial cult.[62]

The theater of the civil war now switched to Africa and Spain, sparing Greece from further turmoil, until Caesar was triumphant and returned to Rome.[63] He took Cleopatra with him but she was unpopular with the people, with Cicero summing up the general opinion of her as arrogant and odious.[64] Her stay in Rome was dependent on Caesar, but he would soon fall victim to a group of conservatives headed by Marcus Junius Brutus and Gaius Cassius Longinus. In 44, as he made his way to the Senate on the Ides of March (the 15th), he was assassinated close to the theater of Pompey.[65] Two weeks later Cleopatra returned to Alexandria with Caesarion.

---

[57] Appian, *Civil Wars* 2.88; cf. Dio 42.14.2.

[58] Oikonomides 1979, pp. 97–101. Caesar's response has affinities with the message of Demosthenes' funeral oration (60), delivered in 338 after Chaeronea, in which he speaks of the virtue of those who died at the battle in the fight for Greek freedom (noted by J. H. Oliver 1981b, p. 412).

[59] Restored by Caesar: Graindor 1927a, p. 95; Day 1942, p. 130; *contra* Accame 1946, pp. 174–175; Raubitschek 1954, p. 66 (Brutus), but Geagan 1971, pp. 101–108, is right to fix the change to 70, when there was an anti-Sullan reaction at Rome and Athens; cf. Geagan 1979a, pp. 375–376.

[60] Rawson 1985, pp. 60 and 63–65.

[61] Geagan 2011, H249, p. 145; Raubitschek 1954, pp. 65–66; see Geagan 1984, p. 71 n. 7 and Geagan 2011, H250, pp. 145–146 for the other statue.

[62] Williams II 1987; Hoff 2014, pp. 574–577; Dickenson 2017, pp. 215–237. Spread of imperial cult: Zanker 1988, pp. 297–306.

[63] Rawson 1994a, pp. 435–467.

[64] Cicero, *Ad Atticum* 15.15.

[65] Rawson 1994a, pp. 465–467.

Rome was in shock after Caesar's assassination.[66] Mark Antony and Marcus Lepidus appeared before the Senate and arranged a compromise by which the assassins were granted amnesty and Caesar's reforms remained on the books. But the lower classes, loyal to Caesar, were far from impressed. In his will, Caesar had adopted his eighteen-year-old grandnephew Gaius Octavius, who swiftly moved from Greece (where he had been stationed with Caesar's army) to Rome and took on the name Gaius Julius Caesar Octavianus—we know him better as Octavian, the future emperor Augustus.

On November 27, in 43, the Second Triumvirate was formed, comprising Octavian, Antony, and Lepidus; tasked with restoring the state, they divided the Roman world among themselves.[67] The amnesty agreement was soon abandoned, for Antony and Octavian wanted revenge for Caesar's murder. They targeted Brutus and Cassius, who had left Rome on a hastily arranged mission to procure grain from Asia, but Cicero was not so lucky: even though he had not played a part in the assassination he had attacked Antony for his policies, and for that he was put to death.

Brutus and Cassius were not naïve enough to think that all was forgiven. They had been building up substantial support since leaving Italy, Cassius from Syria and Brutus from Greece and Macedonia. They had arrived in Greece in October 44, and even though their treacherous deed was well known, when Brutus called on the Athenians for support they threw in their lot with him—Caesar's largesse of 50 talents evidently did not win him any posthumous loyalty when the chance came to regain their liberty, not to mention the fact that Brutus was physically present in Greece.[68]

The Greeks paid all sorts of tributes to Brutus and Cassius.[69] The Athenians went so far as to place statues of them next to that of the tyrannicides (which they had done only once before, to Monophthalmus and Poliorcetes in 307), making them out to be new tyrant-slayers.[70] There is no evidence that Cassius went with Brutus to Athens—that the people set up a statue to him does not mean he actually went there, as often artworks were dedicated

---

[66] Rawson 1994b; David 2000, pp. 244–252.
[67] Pelling 1996, pp. 1–5; David 2000, pp. 252–261.
[68] Geagan 1979a, p. 377; Mango 2010, pp. 126–127.
[69] Oikonomides 1979, pp. 101–102.
[70] Brutus: *IG* 7.383 = *SEG* 17.960 (= Sherk 1984, no. 84A, p. 104); Brutus and Cassius: Plutarch, *Brutus* 24.1; Dio 47.20.4 ("thus making them out to follow their example"). Tyrannicide shrine: Thompson and Wycherley 1972, pp. 155–160.

even if the recipient did not visit.⁷¹ The warm reception Brutus received in Athens was in stark contrast to how he had been treated in Rome, and it has been suggested that his time in the city helped to restore much of his self-confidence after his hurried flight from Rome.⁷² He attended the lectures of Theomnestus at the Academy and Cratippus at the Peripatetic school, for example, as if he had nothing to fear.⁷³ But he was well aware that Antony and Octavian were mobilizing an enormous army, so he sought even wider support for his cause, attracting, among others, Macedonian troops, veterans from Pompey's army, and young Romans studying in Athens (including Cicero's son).⁷⁴

Antony and Octavian arrived in Greece in 42 intent on capturing or killing Brutus and Cassius. Athens probably did not commit troops to their cause this time. In the first of two battles at Philippi Cassius committed suicide, and in the second, a little over a week later, Brutus was defeated and also killed himself. The victors now extended their domains, marginalizing Lepidus, with Antony taking on the east and Octavian to all intents and purposes Italy and the west. Antony remained in Greece while Octavian cannily returned to Rome; in 36, Lepidus clashed with Octavian and was exiled, after which Antony and Octavian shared the world.

Antony and Cleopatra

The charismatic yet ill-fated Antony drove events of the next decade (Figure 11.2).⁷⁵ He spent the winter of 42/1 in Greece, and may have punished the Athenians by discontinuing their new-style silver coinage, introducing a new bronze coinage that proclaimed his association with Dionysus, and possibly reinstating oligarchic rule.⁷⁶ Perhaps at this time the Athenians rededicated the colossal statues of Eumenes II and Attalus II in his honor.⁷⁷ Another measure to appeal to him may have been the suspension of the Athenian guild of *technitai* of Dionysus, given that Antony had summoned

---

⁷¹ Cf. Geagan 1984; Højte 2000.
⁷² Raubitschek 1957, pp. 5 and 11.
⁷³ Plutarch, *Brutus* 24.1.
⁷⁴ Plutarch, *Brutus* 24.2, with Raubitschek 1957, pp. 5–7.
⁷⁵ Pelling 1996, pp. 9–13.
⁷⁶ Coinage: Kroll 1997; cf. Habicht 1997a, p. 365. Oligarchy: Graindor 1927a, p. 95; Geagan 1979a, p. 377; see too Rödel 2010, pp. 100–101.
⁷⁷ Plutarch, *Antony* 23.2.

FIGURE 11.2 Bust of the Roman General Mark Antony at National Archeological Museum of Madrid. Shutterstock.

performers from Italy to the city (perhaps his own troupe).[78] The Athenians may have considered it prudent to resort to this suspension, especially if their own performers happened to be better (we do not know if this was so). Their move caused the guild's influence to decline, as we might expect, yet surprisingly it remained dormant until Hadrianic times, long after Antony had ceased to have any influence in the city.[79]

Antony, who was a genuine *philathenaios*, greatly enjoyed his time in Athens (as he did on his return in the 30s), attending athletic contests and philosophers' lectures.[80] Even so, he was not prepared to favor the Athenians

---

[78] Athenaeus 4.148c.
[79] Professor Julia Kindt agrees, via personal email (for which I thank her), that the troupe was Antony's own, and wonders whether the reason for the long decline was that the new procedures had become so engrained after Actium that it was too hard to change them back. But Actium was only a few years hence; perhaps the Athenians did not at that time restore their guild because they needed to earn Octavian's favor.
[80] Plutarch, *Antony* 60.3; see too Oikonomides 1979, pp. 101–102.

above everyone else; for example, he refused their request to receive the island of Tenos (in the Cyclades), as he had just promised it to Rhodes; instead, he gave them Aegina, Keos, Ikos, Skiathos, and Peparethos.[81] In the winter of 41 he left Greece for Asia, where after some business he called Cleopatra to meet him at Tarsus (in Cilicia). Plutarch, in his *Life of Antony*, followed more famously by Shakespeare in his *Antony and Cleopatra*, have forever consigned to memory the way Cleopatra arrived in Tarsus on a magnificent barge—with sails "so perfumèd that the winds were lovesick with them," and she looking like Venus reclining under a gold canopy—and how he fell under her spell.[82] In truth this was all show, as Egypt was facing a crippling famine and distress in the rural areas.[83]

Cleopatra's sexual relationships with Caesar and Antony have given us a distorted image of her as a *femme fatale*, who seduced powerful men against their better judgment. Nothing could be further from the truth.[84] We know only of her liaisons with Caesar and Antony, hardly the mark of promiscuity, and she led both men on so as to maintain her dynasty's rule over Egypt and to ward off the spread of Roman imperialism. She may well have harbored real feelings for Antony, but at the end of the day it was country first, personal feelings second, making her one of Ptolemaic Egypt's greatest rulers.[85]

Antony spent a decadent winter with her in Alexandria before moving back to Athens in the spring of 40, where his wife Fulvia (whom he had married in 44) was waiting for him with worrying news.[86] His younger brother Lucius had fallen foul of Octavian over the latter's edict to seize land from Italian towns for thousands of Caesar's loyal veterans. Lucius championed the cause of the dispossessed, at which point Octavian besieged him in Perusia (modern Perugia); he surrendered, and was allowed to go to Spain, where he died. Antony sailed at once to Italy, where the two rulers patched things up in the Treaty of Brundisium (40): Octavian would govern the western half of the empire, and Antony the eastern.[87] To cement the

---

[81] Graindor 1927a, pp. 5–8.
[82] Plutarch, *Antony* 26.1–3; Shakespeare, *Antony and Cleopatra* 2.2.199–204.
[83] Green 1990, p. 670.
[84] Useful observations on the historical vs. legendary Cleopatra at Green 1990, pp. 662–664.
[85] There is a vast bibliography on Cleopatra: see, for example, Walker and Higgs 2001; Burstein 2004; Roller 2010.
[86] Following events: Pelling 1996, pp. 14–17.
[87] Pelling 1996, pp. 17–21.

agreement, Antony married Octavian's sister Octavia the following year—Fulvia had recently and unexpectedly died at Sicyon, and Octavia's husband Gaius Claudius Marcellus (Minor) had also died not long ago (Octavia was still pregnant with Marcellus' child when she and Antony married).

Antony remained in Italy until the late summer of 39, when he and Octavia left for Athens. There they lived virtually as private citizens, walking the streets of the city without escort, sharing meals with Greek guests, and with Antony again enjoying lectures by philosophers.[88] An inscription on an altar discovered in 1935, which we may date to 39/8, describes them both as "benevolent gods," thus showing the people had gone so far as to bestow divine honors on Octavia as well as her husband.[89] We should not be surprised they had done so for him—as early as 41, when he entered Ephesus, he was hailed as Dionysus, and that god would also associate him with the east and his conquests there.[90] The Athenians, at his behest, called him the "New Dionysus," and he held Dionysiac processions in the city, suspended a platform above the theatre where he drank all day with his friends, and (if we can believe the anecdote), as Dionysus married Athena, forcing the Athenians to pay him a vast dowry of 1 million drachmas.[91]

Divine honors to Octavia are interesting, though we need not believe that the people went so far as to proclaim her a new Athena.[92] The Athenians had not conferred the same distinction on the wives of previous rulers, even as far back as Monophthalmus and Poliorcetes. We can see that their move now had a dual purpose: to win Antony's favor as well as that of her brother Octavian. The Athenians had a history of backing the wrong Romans, and given Antony's relationship with Cleopatra, which belittled Octavia and angered Octavian, they had no wish to be on the losing side again in any showdown. They would surely have known from Roman visitors to Athens that when Caesar took Cleopatra with him to Rome in 46 he caused much

---

[88] Plutarch, *Antony* 23, with D. Kienast 1993, pp. 194–196.

[89] First published by Raubitschek 1946; see more recently Geagan 2011, H273, p. 157; cf. Robert 1948, pp. 149–150 (no. 55); Worthington 2019c.

[90] Zanker 1988, pp. 46–47; Pelling 1988, pp. 179–180. On Roman assimilations to gods in the Republic and Empire, see Poccini 1993.

[91] New Dionysus: *IG* ii² 1043, lines 22–23; Plutarch, *Antony* 60.3 (with Pelling 1988, pp. 265–266); Dio 48.39.1–2. Marriage and cost: Dio 48.39.2; Dionysiac revelry: Socrates, *BNJ* 192 F 2; see too Hoff 1989a, pp. 273–274.

[92] Octavia as Athena: Raubitschek 1946, pp. 147 and 149–150; *contra*, for example, Robert 1948, p. 150; Pelling 1996, p. 23 n. 99. The story may have originated with Octavian as part of his later propaganda war against Antony (cf. Day 1942, p. 133).

offense among conservative Romans.⁹³ Antony's relationship with Cleopatra went against Roman custom, so they had every reason to suspect that his actions would collide with Octavian's conservative beliefs and his feelings for his sister. For once, the Athenians were looking ahead.⁹⁴

Antony made a repeat visit to Italy in the spring to shore up relations with Octavian.⁹⁵ But then he embarked on a disastrous invasion of the Parthian (Arsacid) Empire, located in Iran and Iraq, where he was soundly defeated and lost one-third of his army of 100,000 close to Atropatene (modern Azerbaijan).⁹⁶ He went back to Athens the following winter, where he was elected gymnasiarch (wearing "a Greek robe and white shoes" to mark the role), and may have been awarded citizenship.⁹⁷ Possibly even the Panathenaic games were renamed the Panathenaic Antonieia in his honor, based on pottery from that festival and a restored ephebic decree referring to him as the "new Dionysus."⁹⁸

In 36 Antony sent Octavia and their daughters back to Rome, escalating the deteriorating relations between him and Octavian, who began to exploit the Romans' conservative values and create an image of Cleopatra and her relationship with Antony as part of a propaganda campaign against him. That Antony had children with Cleopatra, the twins Alexander Helios ("Sun") and Cleopatra Selene ("Moon"), born in 40, and another son, Ptolemy Philadelphus (not be confused with Ptolemy II of Egypt), born in 36, and grandly gifted Cleopatra and their children Roman territory, did not help either.⁹⁹ Cleopatra went to stay in Athens with Antony in the spring of 32 and strove to endear herself to the people with various gifts.¹⁰⁰ They had no choice but to offer her honors comparable to those of Octavia, not so much for what she gave them but to make sure they did not upset Antony. But when bad omens started to occur, such as a storm toppling the rededicated

---

⁹³ Likewise, the Athenians may have heard of Caesar's soldiers refusing to follow him and Cleopatra in Egypt: Suetonius, *Caesar* 52.1.
⁹⁴ Expansion of this argument: Worthington 2019c.
⁹⁵ Pelling 1996, pp. 24–27.
⁹⁶ Pelling 1996, pp. 28–34.
⁹⁷ Gymnasiarch: Plutarch, *Antony* 33.4. Citizenship: Plutarch, *Antony* 57.2, with Pelling 1988, *ad loc.*; Rawson 1985, p. 58.
⁹⁸ *IG* ii² 1043, lines 22–23; see too Raubitschek 1946, pp. 148–149. Pottery: Tsouklidou 2008.
⁹⁹ Analogy: Habicht 1997a, p. 363. Territory: Sherk 1984, no. 88, pp. 110–111 (Chalcis in Syria); Pelling 1996, pp. 29–30.
¹⁰⁰ Plutarch, *Antony* 57.1–2.

statue to Antony, the couple's demise seemed certain.[101] The final straw came when Antony wrote to Octavia to say he was divorcing her, causing the Senate, on Octavian's orders, to declare war—on Cleopatra, though Antony was included by association.

Once Octavian arrived in Greece most of the Greek cities, including Athens, went over to his side. Antony and Cleopatra staked everything on a final battle near Actium (at the mouth of the Ambracian Gulf) on September 2, 31, but they were famously defeated by the admiral Marcus Vipsanius Agrippa and fled back to Egypt.[102] Octavian thus acquired all of Greece in one stroke. Although Dio claims that he punished the Greeks, Plutarch's account is more credible, in which he went to Athens and "after reconciling with the Greeks he handed out the grain left over from the war to the cities, which were in a terrible state, having been stripped of money, slaves, and working animals."[103] Greece may not have suffered as much as Asia Minor in the decades of warfare, but it had still suffered.[104] Very likely Athens, despite its support of Antony, received some of the grain, especially as Octavian needed the Piraeus to anchor his fleet.[105] Also, we have a lead token given by the city to Octavian with the head of a youthful Apollo on it, a six-rayed star (representing the apotheosis of Caesar), and the inscription *Kaisar*, which therefore predates 27 when Octavian became Augustus and the Greeks started calling him *Sebastos* (the Greek version of the name Augustus).[106] Since this type of token was given to someone who had made a donation to the city, its type and historical context fit with a much-needed gift of grain after Actium.[107]

Octavian still had to deal with Antony and Cleopatra, who had lived to fight another day.[108] After a brief return to Italy to consolidate his rule with the Senate, he went to Egypt, arriving there by the middle of 30. In

---

[101] Plutarch, *Antony* 60.2; Dio 50.15.2, with Habicht 1990, p. 572; Pelling 1988, pp. 265–266.

[102] D. Kienast 1993, pp. 197–198; Pelling 1996, pp. 54–59 ("a very lame affair"); in detail: Carter 1970.

[103] Plutarch, *Antony* 68.4, with Day 1942, pp. 132–138, including the economic plight of Greece at this time.

[104] Day 1942, pp. 156–158. Levick 1996, pp. 652–653, cites Strabo that Greece reached its lowest point between the razing of Corinth and the reign of Nero.

[105] Cf. Graindor 1927a, p. 160; Geagan 1979a, p. 378.

[106] See further Hoff 1992; cf. Peppas-Delmousou 1979.

[107] Graindor 1927a, pp. 37–38 n. 2 and 118; Hoff 1992, p. 225.

[108] On the following: Pelling 1996, pp. 59–67.

the meantime Antony had requested permission to live privately in Athens (the lure of the city was still evident) if he could not live in Egypt, but Octavian refused.[109] The latter took Alexandria in August 30—the previous night, so the story goes, there was the sound of heavenly music and visions of Dionysus leading a procession from the city.[110] Antony stabbed himself to death and shortly after Cleopatra committed suicide—by the bite of an asp (or cobra) as she sat on her throne, her final act of defiance to Rome.[111] Less than one month later Octavian hunted down and executed her coruler Ptolemy XV, ending the Ptolemaic dynasty. Egypt then became a special province, the property of the emperor himself.[112]

After Actium

Thanks to the battle of Actium, the year 31 is a watershed in ancient history for several reasons. First, it is the commonly accepted terminal point by modern scholars of the Hellenistic period, which began in 323 when Alexander the Great died in Babylon—though in 31 little changed for Athens, as this book stresses (see the Introduction). Second, it led the following year to the absorption of the last independent kingdom of the eastern Mediterranean, Egypt, into the Roman Empire, and the fall of the Ptolemaic dynasty, founded by Alexander's bodyguard Ptolemy almost three centuries earlier.[113] Third, it represented the end of the five-hundred-year-old Roman Republic, for with Antony dead Octavian ruled alone: the era of the Roman Empire had begun. Four years later, in 27, he took the name Augustus and founded the first imperial dynasty, the Julio-Claudian, which ended with Nero's death in AD 68.[114]

---

[109] Plutarch, *Antony* 72.1, 73.1. Influence of Athens in the east and on Romans: Borg 2011.
[110] Plutarch, *Antony* 75.3–4.
[111] See Whitehorne 1994, pp. 186–196, for a good analysis of the various sources associated with her suicide.
[112] Commanded by an imperial prefect: Sherk 1984, no. 93, p. 114. See Spawforth 2012, pp. 233–234, on Octavian's attitude to Alexandria as the cultural capital of the Mediterranean world.
[113] On Ptolemy, see Worthington 2016.
[114] Numerous biographies of Augustus exist; more recently, see Everitt 2007; Eck 2007; Levick 2010; Galinsky 2012; and Graindor 1927a is still valuable. For a condensed consideration of Augustus' powers and accomplishments, see Crook 1996 and Gruen 1996.

What was Athens'—and Greece's—place in the Roman Empire, and what did the Romans think of both places?[115] Rome saw Greece and Greek culture as its possessions, and as we shall see, Athens experienced this firsthand. The Romans retained their love of all things Greek, taking over aspects of Hellenism, from architecture to literature to rhetoric, for their own practical and ideological needs. Still, increasing numbers of Romans in Athens, and of Greeks in Roman society, benefitted both cities.[116] But for now we leave Hellenistic Athens and turn to Roman Athens, a city that still shone radiantly in the eastern Mediterranean even as its Classical past became increasingly remote.

---

[115] There are several edited volumes containing excellent essays dealing with Greece and Hellenism in imperial times; for example Follett 2004a; Perrin-Saminadayar 2007b; Walker and Cameron 1989; Ostenfeld 2002; cf. Krumeich and Witschel 2010a (especially essays by Rathmann, Rödel, Mango); Schmitz and Wiater 2011; and see too Wardman 1976. Many individual essays are referenced in the following chapters.

[116] Habicht 1997, pp. 346–347, for comments on Greeks in Roman society.

12

Augustus and Athens

IN 27 AUGUSTUS DECIDED TO split Macedonia and Greece into two distinct areas. The former would henceforth have its capital at Beroea, with the port of Thessaloniki serving as its economic center.[1] He also based several legions in Macedonia, and recruited from there and the Danube region, as did his successors.[2] Greece was turned into the province of Achaea, consisting of Attica, Boeotia, other parts of central Greece, the Peloponnese, and the Cycladic islands, with its capital at Corinth (re-established as a colony, and now on the rise after an influx of settlers from Rome as well as Roman-backed building projects).[3] Achaea was a senatorial province (under the control of a proconsul), as opposed to an imperial province (where the emperor himself appointed governors); its governorship (based in Corinth) was a plum job, given the intellectual and cultural history of the Greek cities, especially Athens (Figure 12.1).[4]

Augustus also rekindled the former Achaean League and founded new cities, including most famously Nicopolis (city of victory), near Actium.[5] For

---

[1] Papazoglou 1979, pp. 325–328 and 351–354; see too Bowersock 1965, p. 97.
[2] Papazoglou 1979, pp. 338–351.
[3] Cf. Rizakis 2001. On the province of Achaea (especially taxation), see the survey of Alcock 1993, pp. 17–24.
[4] See Alcock 1993, pp. 224–227.
[5] Dio 51.2.3 (Nicopolis). Achaean League: Hupfloher 2007; Nicopolis: Bowersock 1965, pp. 92–95; Alcock 1993, pp. 133–137 and 141–145 (impact on the landscape and the population); Bowersock 2002, pp. 3–4; see too Spawforth 2012, pp. 33–36, on the Greek

FIGURE 12.1 Roman Emperor Augustus from Prima Porto statue. Shutterstock.

Nicopolis he joined together several surrounding communities—Ambracia, Amphilochnian Argos, and Alyzia—into one (a process called synoecism). His choice of location was deliberate, as its two harbors facilitated trade and commerce and its local economy received a boost from a festival celebrated there, the Actia (modeled on the Olympic Games), which attracted visitors from all over Greece. But there was still discontent on the mainland. At

---

aspects of the city, but that it was populated by Roman veterans, hence a deliberate hybrid of Greek and Roman elements; cf. pp. 160–162 (religious associations).

some point a man named Cassius Petraeus was burned alive in Thessaly, perhaps an indication of factional opposition, resulting in Thessaly losing its freedom, and in 2 the ambitious Eurycles of Sparta (whom the Athenians had previously honored with a statue sometime after 21) attempted to unite the cities of Achaea against Rome, forcing the emperor to banish him.[6]

Spitting Blood

Augustus went to Athens three times—in fact, our only known events of life in the city stem from his visits, though not every one of them was friendly, as we shall see.[7] As an allied free city bound to Rome by a treaty (*foedus*), Athens was in the highest hierarchy of cities in the provinces.[8] The people paid Augustus and other members of the imperial family honors throughout his reign, such as erecting statues and at least nineteen altars around the city (part of an imperial cult, at which sacrifices may have been performed).[9]

Nor was Agrippa, Augustus' right-hand man (and son-in-law), neglected. The Athenians set up a monumental statue of him in a chariot drawn by four horses just west of the Propylaea or gateway to the Acropolis in recognition of his building a huge Odeum in the Athenian Agora (see pp. 293–294).[10] The price tag was not as colossal as its size, for the Athenians reused the original pedestal on which statues of Eumenes II and Attalus II of Pergamum had stood. Possibly we can read into this that they did not feel sufficiently excited by the new building located as it was in their Agora to cast a new statue. Nowadays only the high pedestal (matching in height the Temple of Athena Nike to the south of the Propylaea) can be seen (Figure 12.2).

As time went on, relations between Athenians and the emperor cooled, as his visit of 21 shows. In that year Augustus concluded a lengthy period

---

[6] Bowersock 1965, pp. 101–111.
[7] Athens in the Augustan age: Graindor 1927a; Day 1942, pp. 134–177.
[8] Graindor 1927a, pp. 130–131.
[9] Graindor 1927a, pp. 45–53; see too Baldassari 1995a. Multiple examples of statue bases are also included in Geagan 2011; see too Hendrick 2006, chapter 9, pp. 172–207. Altars: Benjamin and Raubitschek 1959; Geagan 1984, pp. 72–75; Torelli 1995; Hendrick 2006, chapter 5; see too the examples included in Schmalz 2009, pp. 95–99; and Geagan 2011, H274–H282, pp. 157–159. Dedications to Julio-Claudian emperors and imperial family collected at Schmalz 2009, pp. 92–126 (pp. 92–99 for Augustus).
[10] *IG* ii² 4122 and 4123; Geagan 2011, H417, pp. 227–228 (= Sherk 1984, no. 98A, p. 120), with Dinsmoor 1920; Graindor 1927a, pp. 48–49; Day 1942, p. 140; Geagan 1979a, p. 380. Its base refers to him as consul for the third time (hence the date of 27).

FIGURE 12.2 Pedestal of Agrippa. Photo: Ian Worthington.

of provincial reform in the western half of his empire, especially Sicily.[11] He then decided to do the same in his eastern provinces.[12] Dio's account puts Augustus in Greece in the winter of 21–20, but given the time needed to deal with his settlement in Sicily, he may well have gone to Greece that summer or even fall. He first went to Sparta (which had supported him at Actium and which had also offered refuge in 40 to Livia and her young son Tiberius

[11] R. J. A. Wilson 1996, pp. 437–442.
[12] Bowersock 1965, pp. 42–72 and 85–100; cf. Levick 1996, pp. 647–663.

when they had fled to Greece), where he bestowed gifts of land and other favors on the city.[13] Then he moved on to Athens, perhaps arriving there after the start of the new Attic year (in the archonship of Apolexis of Oion, 21/20), as has been argued from the flurry of decrees and other diplomatic activity then.[14]

Augustus' actions in Athens were markedly different from those at Sparta, for he ended Athenian control of Aegina, Eretria, and Oropus (indicating that Caesar had not already taken away the last from Athens), banned the selling of Athenian citizenship (a practice going back to the later fourth-century Lycurgan era, when the Laurium silver mines began to dry up), and possibly also prohibited the minting of bronze coinage.[15] There were obvious repercussions for the city: the loss of Aegina and Eretria and the ban on selling citizenship must have reduced revenues, while losing Oropus again caused a worrying security issue on the border with Boeotia.[16]

Why did Augustus punish Athens as he did? According to a letter purportedly written by him on Aegina and quoted by Plutarch, "when, so it seemed, the Athenian people had committed some offense, he wrote from Aegina that he was sure they would be aware that he was angry; otherwise he would not have spent the whole winter in Aegina."[17] Thus he snubbed the city because the people had somehow offended him. What they had done meshes with when he wrote his letter. It was often assigned to 31 after Actium, but more recent arguments (commonly followed) associate it with his settlement of 21 to fit the context of the emperor's punitive measures.[18] Yet after quoting the letter Plutarch tells us that Augustus "neither said nor did anything else to the Athenians." The penalties he imposed on Athens show that he did indeed do something else, in which case we can reassign

---

[13] Suetonius, *Tiberius* 6.2; Pausanias 7.9.3–7; Dio 54.7–2, with Bowersock 1965, pp. 91–92; Rawson 1973, pp. 227 and 229. Livia: Dio 48.15.3–4. See too Spawforth 2012, pp. 86–100, on Augustus' admiration for Sparta.
[14] Chronology: Graindor 1927a, pp. 16–23, but see Schmalz 1996, especially pp. 395–397, on the decrees.
[15] Dio 54.7–2; see further Graindor 1927a, pp. 5–8; Bowersock 1964; Oikonomides 1979, pp. 102–103; Geagan 1979a, pp. 378–379; Hoff 1989a; Hoff 1989b, pp. 4–5; D. Kienast 1993, pp. 199–200; Schmalz 1996. Coinage: Kroll 1973, pp. 323–327; Hoff 1989a, p. 269.
[16] Though Schmalz 1996, pp. 384–389, argues the decision over Aegina was simply to restore the island's independence.
[17] [Plutarch], *Moralia* 207f; cf. Dio 54.7.4 (Samos).
[18] Bowersock 1964; cf. Bowersock 1965, p. 106. The year 31: Graindor 1927a, pp. 17–18; Day 1942, pp. 134–136; Schmalz 1996.

the letter to 31 after Actium.[19] The matter is worthy of more consideration, as it affords us a vivid glimpse into the fluctuating relationship between Athens and Augustus in these early years.

Dio tells us the Athenians had offended Augustus because of their dealings with Antony.[20] Yet if the letter is from 21, could Augustus really hold a grudge a decade after Actium?[21] In fact after that battle he went to Athens and gave it and the Greeks gifts of grain. But Dio also tells us that when Augustus visited Athens in 21 the statue of Athena (perhaps that of Athena Polias, the protectress of the city) on the Acropolis had been turned to face westward, and was daubed with blood to make it look as though the goddess was spitting blood on Rome.[22]

Given Greece's suffering and the widespread looting of artworks, this subversive act may have been part of a growing anti-Roman sentiment since the Sullan sack in 86.[23] The Athenians had been quick to back various Romans over the years, all of whom turned out to be failures until Octavian; as one scholar neatly sums up, "Nobody is impressed by defeat, but at least some people appear to learn something from it. Not so with the city of Athens."[24] Thus the incident involving Athena's statue shows that the Athenians were making their feelings known, in which case we can understand Augustus' displeasure.

There are sufficient reasons for returning Augustus' letter to the year 31 rather than 21 and still reconciling his displeasure with Plutarch going on to say that he did say or do anything else. Among other things, it does not follow that he spent the whole winter on Aegina and never went to Athens. It is more likely that he went to the city after Actium, giving out grain there as Plutarch tells us, but then something happened that sparked his resentment, causing him to head for Aegina and to castigate the people in a letter—after which he did not say or do anything else against the city.

---

[19] On the offense and expansion of the following arguments, see Worthington 2019d.
[20] Dio 54.7.2–4.
[21] Graindor 1927a, pp. 17–18; Hoff 1989a, p. 268.
[22] Dio 54.7.3; cf. Bowersock 1965, p. 106; Hoff 1989a, p. 269; D. Kienast 1993, p. 199 n. 5; but Schmalz 1996, pp. 385–386, contends that the statue incident may belong to the earlier triumviral period (comparing it to Dio's anecdote about the wind toppling the statues of Antony and Cleopatra on the Acropolis before Actium).
[23] Argued by Hoff 1989a, pp. 269–276; repeated in Hoff 1989b, pp. 4–5; Hoff 2013, p. 571.
[24] Oikonomides 1979, p. 97.

Plausibly, his annoyance stems not from something the Athenians did but what they did *not* do. Since he did not stay for long in the city but departed abruptly to Rome and thence Egypt, the Athenians may have dallied in expressing their gratitude for his benevolent treatment. Their behavior, if so, was a contrast to their quickness in honoring other Romans who came to their city, as we have seen, and would account for Augustus' irritation. It was now up to the Athenians to regain his goodwill, and therefore why he took no further action against them.

This scenario provides us with a context for a spate of activity that we can now date more precisely. For example, the lead token, on which Augustus is called a new Apollo, was most likely a thanks offering for his gift of grain after Actium (p. 239). All emperors tied themselves to traditional divinities, but for Augustus, Apollo was particularly important.[25] His relationship with the god stretched from Greece to Rome, preserving, for example, the local cult of Apollo at Nicopolis, and in 28 consecrating the temple of Apollo on the Palatine in Rome. And after Actium he had dedicated ships from the battle to Apollo of Actium.[26] Calling him a *new* Apollo deliberately echoed this association with Apollo while distancing the people from Antony (the new Dionysus). Further, the people may have initiated Octavian into the Eleusinian Mysteries at this time, something they had not done for Antony.[27] Finally, at Eleusis the Athenians dedicated a monument to his wife Livia and him as savior and benefactor of the people, perhaps to make their acknowledgment of the grain he gifted the city even clearer.[28] Perhaps the people deliberately continued resting their guild of Dionysiac actors in favor of the troupe that Antony had brought over as another way of pandering to Octavian, and continued to use Roman actors from then on (see p. 235).

---

[25] L. R. Taylor 1931, pp. 118–120 and 153–155; Zanker 1988, pp. 48–53; Hoff 1992, pp. 226–229; Poccini 1993; Bowersock 2002, pp. 4–5. Statues and divine associations: Geagan 1984, pp. 75–78 (citing examples of other members of the imperial family on p. 76); cf. Hendrick 2006, chapter 9, pp. 172–207; Perrin-Saminadayar 2007c, pp. 129–130.

[26] Dio 51.2.2.

[27] Dio 51.4.1; Graindor 1922a, pp. 429–434; Graindor 1927a, pp. 20–23; Bernhardt 1975; Clinton 1989a, pp. 1507–1509; D. Kienast 1993, p. 198; Spawforth 2012, pp. 167–168 (pointing out that the sanctuary at Eleusis is the only one in all Greece that Augustus visited).

[28] *IG* ii² 3238, perhaps in the Roman Agora. Its size might show it housed the imperial cult: Benjamin and Raubitschek 1959, p. 66 n. 11; Geagan 1984; Clinton 1997, pp. 163 and 165; if so, it could have been a later addition.

If the Athenians did manage to recapture Octavian's favor after Actium, they had clearly done *something* that led to his punitive measures in 21 that we outlined earlier. Here we return to Dio's account of the symbolic blood-spattering of Athena's statue that was contemporaneous with his visit in that year. With that deliberate usage of the goddess' statue we move more to the religious sphere, specifically to Augustus' cult, which had been spreading throughout the east for some time, and was probably established in Athens in 29 (discussed below).[29] If so, the timing suggests that the Athenians' scramble to win back his goodwill after Actium had been successful, and in relief, they introduced his cult on the Acropolis.[30] But he always stressed that his cult was to be connected to that of the goddess Roma.[31] That thus meant that Roma, the personification of the conquering Roman state, of Rome itself, now had a home in Athens—in the same sacred space as Athena, to boot. Thus when Augustus visited the city in 21, religion and politics mixed to produce the slight on Rome from the symbolism of Athena's blood-spitting statue. No wonder the emperor retaliated with the sorts of sanctions that he knew would hurt the city.

Yet by 19, when he again visited Athens, there was no frostiness between him and the Athenians—he even donated money toward completing the Roman Agora (which Caesar had begun thirty years earlier), including the monumental western gateway dedicated to Athena Archegetis ("the Leader," Figure 12.3; and further on the Roman Agora, see Figures 14.1A–B).

In response, the people likely initiated him a second time into the Mysteries, which they held at a different time so as to accommodate his visit.[32] It may also be at this point that on the urging of the hoplite general Antipater of Phlya the people voted to celebrate his *dies natalis* (birthday)

---

[29] Dio 51.20.7, with Benjamin and Raibitschek 1959; on the cult of Augustus in Athens see too Zanker 1988, pp. 297–306; Whittaker 2002, pp. 27–31; Lozano 2002; Kantiréa 2007; Kantiréa 2011.
[30] Cf. Hoff 1989a, p. 275 n. 45.
[31] Augustus insisting on the link to Roma: Suetonius, *Augustus* 52, with Bowersock 1965, p. 116.
[32] Graindor 1922a, pp. 429–434; Clinton 1989a, pp. 1507–1509; Hoff 1989b, p. 4 n. 21. Bernhardt 1975 argues that the Athenians altered the date of the Mysteries and specifically invited Augustus to participate in them as part of a reconciliation—but even if there had been some anti-Roman propaganda in 20 causing Augustus' displeasure, he had dealt with it then, so there was no need for any reconciliation now.

FIGURE 12.3 Monumental Gateway to Roman Agora. Photo: Ian Worthington.

on 12 Boedromion (September 25), perhaps the date of his arrival in Athens after Actium (fought on September 2).[33]

How had the Athenians won back Augustus' favor? An answer can be found in the statue of Herod the Great (ruler of Judaea from 37 to 4) they set up on the Acropolis, describing him as a benefactor.[34] What Herod actually did to win this honor is unknown, but benefactions need not refer to buildings or money, and M. Toher has persuasively argued that Herod's service for the city was a mission to Augustus to make amends.[35] Herod,

---

[33] *IG* ii² 1071: Since he is referred to as *Sebastos* on the inscription (line 5), it cannot predate 27; see too Graindor 1922a, pp. 434–440; Graindor 1927a, pp. 25–32, 101, 113, and 142; Accame 1946, pp. 178–179; Stamires in Meritt, Woodhead, and Stamires 1957, no. 98 on pp. 260–265; Benjamin and Raubitschek 1959, pp. 74–75; Geagan 1979a, p. 383; Hoff 1992, p. 230; Levick 1996, p. 655.

[34] Herod: Goodman 1996, pp. 739–742. See too Graindor 1927a, pp. 82–84; Bowersock 1965, pp. 54–57.

[35] Toher 2014. Two statue bases have been found inscribed to Herod as benefactor, though not necessarily of the same Herod: *IG* ii² 3440, of limestone, and *IG* ii² 3441 = Geagan 2011, H316, pp. 170–171 (the Herod in question) of Hymettian marble; the different

who had been a supporter of Antony, eventually became a close friend of Augustus and Agrippa.[36] He also acted as a mediator (*mesites*) in disputes between both men and various communities.[37] Herod was with Augustus in the east in 20/19, hence the Athenians may have sent an embassy to him appealing for his help, and as a philhellene he is likely to have agreed. He was successful, and in gratitude, the people erected a statue to him. Athens, then, returned to an even keel in its dealings with the emperor.

Athens in the Augustan Age

The city underwent a transformation architecturally in the Augustan era after the Sullan devastation.[38] We even speak of a "Romanization" of Athens, and certainly parts of the city, especially the Agora, were transformed into a hybrid of Greek and Roman monuments, which will be covered more fully in chapter 14.[39] At the same time, the Athenians skillfully maintained their own culture in their artwork and intellectual pursuits even as their new masters adapted it into their own.[40] Augustus and his successors exploited Hellenism for cultural and political ends, imposing Roman trends on the aspects of Hellenism that especially appealed to them (such as architecture or oratory), and in so doing constructed their own brand of classicism.[41] Not that this should be surprising—the "mutual dependence of Greeks and Romans was destined anyhow to become increasingly pronounced."[42]

Romans continued to go to Athens throughout the Augustan era, some on official business and others simply to visit or take part in the vibrant

---

materials may indicate statues to two separate Herods on two different occasions. Other types of benefactions: Toher 2014, p. 128.

[36] Toher 2014, pp. 131–132.
[37] Details in Toher 2014, p. 132.
[38] Graindor 1927a, pp. 173–245.
[39] Thompson and Wycherley 1972, pp. 204–207, and see the discussion of Dickenson 2015. New locations: Mango 2010.
[40] Bowersock 2002; cf. Woolf 1994; Connolly 2007. On Romanization see Alcock 1997, together with the essays in Hoff and Rotroff 1997 and especially on buildings and artworks; Vlizos 2008.
[41] Woolf 1994; Connolly 2007; Spawforth 2012, pp. 18–26 and 233–235 (a "Hellenism suited to Rome's usage," p. 18), and passim. Influence of Greek classicism on Roman art from Augustus onward: Torelli 1996. Augustan program of cultural renewal in Rome: Zanker 1988, pp. 101–166.
[42] Bowersock 1965, p. 140.

intellectual life, especially the study of philosophy.⁴³ So too did other foreign dignitaries, wealthy people, and even kings (from Thrace, for example, and possibly Archelaus of Cappadocia).⁴⁴ Many were honored with statues for their gifts to the city at the behest of the Areopagus, Assembly, or Boule (still composed of 600 members)—showing us that these bodies were still meeting, though surely with curtailed political powers.⁴⁵ Possibly the relocation of the marble altar to Zeus Agoraios (Zeus the divinity guiding Assemblies) from the Pnyx to the Agora is indicative of a decline in political meetings.⁴⁶ But we actually know little of politics in the city, and its formal alliance with the Romans meant that they had subsumed its foreign policy anyway.⁴⁷

Yet the various magistracies continued to be filled, such as the nine archonships, the herald of the Areopagus, the hoplite general, and the *epimeletes* (or governor) of the city, not to mention high-level priesthoods, all charged with the day-to-day running of the city.⁴⁸ At least ambitious men could still stand for office and be active, but only as long as they leaned to Rome: men such as Apolexis, whose archonship in 21/20 is the best documented of any archon in the Augustan period.⁴⁹ Politicians who also held the hoplite generalship for a number of years are also evident, such as Antipater of Phlya, who held that post no fewer than seven times and was awarded a statue.⁵⁰ The degree of importance attached to priesthoods is not surprising, as inscriptions show priests (and priestesses) had long been respected, and their services were held in the same regard as the secular magistracies.⁵¹ In fact, it has been argued that priests, in their management of state religion and coming from the same social circles as magistrates, exercised an "oligarchization" of religious power, using it as a stepping-stone into public life.⁵²

---

⁴³ Roman visitors: Graindor 1927a, pp. 55–80; see too pp. 173–245, on artistic and intellectual life in the city.
⁴⁴ Foreign kings and visitors: Graindor 1927a, pp. 81–93.
⁴⁵ Graindor 1927a, pp. 104–107.
⁴⁶ T. L. Shear 1981, p. 365, queried by Borg 2011, p. 224; Dickenson 2017, pp. 317–324, rightly noting (on p. 323) that no one explanation can account for its relocation.
⁴⁷ Graindor 1927a, pp. 100–134 (see pp. 108–109 on the Boule and Assembly).
⁴⁸ Graindor 1927a, pp. 109–125; cf. Graindor 1922b (archons), and especially see the individual chapters on all officials in Geagan 1967.
⁴⁹ Schmalz 1996, pp. 395–397.
⁵⁰ Geagan 1979b; statue: Geagan 2011, H342–H343, pp. 186–187.
⁵¹ Lambert 2012; Perrin-Saminadayar 2012.
⁵² Grijalvo 2005; see too Camia 2014.

Where Athens seemed to have greater autonomy (in keeping with its status as an allied and free city) was in judicial matters, which were supervised by the *epimeletai* of the law courts (including in particular the Areopagus).[53] Likewise, the Athenians continued to involve themselves in mediation beyond Attica. For example, they successfully resolved a land-holding dispute between the two towns of Myrina and Hephaestia on Lemnos and as a show of thanks received a monument in the agora by Lemnos' population.[54] The *ephebeia* also continued to exist, although its socio-economic composition made it more of an aristocratic club.[55] The ephebes still took part in various religious processions and were supervised by a *kosmetes*, but increasingly the gymnasiarch, the annual official who oversaw ephebes in the gymnasium and (importantly) ensured that each gymnasium had an adequate supply of oil, may also have taken on a leadership role. Only three gymnasiarchs are known from the Augustan era and only three functioning gymnasia, the Lyceum, the Ptolemaeum, and the Diogeneum.[56]

Prosperity in the city was on the rise thanks to exports including oil, marble, and lamps, and income from its possessions.[57] The Piraeus, after suffering at the hands of Sulla, had started an economic recovery in the later first century; after its rebuilding it flourished all the more, and the population of Peiraieis (the deme of Piraeus) increased from other demes and an influx of foreigners (especially Milesians).[58] Still, the need for an adequate grain supply was always in people's minds. To this end, a decree dated to the later first century tells us that a certain Xenocles, son of Theopompus of Rhamnus, who was hoplite general four times, was honored with creating a fund and twice purchased grain for the city.[59] It would thus appear that he introduced a special treasury to buy grain, and its oversight was in the hands of the hoplite general (whose military functions had decreased substantially

---

[53] Graindor 1927a, pp. 134–135.
[54] Kallet-Marx and Stroud 1997.
[55] Graindor 1927a, pp. 125–129, especially Wiemer 2011.
[56] Graindor 1927a, p. 127. Two gymnasiarchs were Leonidas and Callicratides, to which a third, Simon, may be added thanks to *IG* ii² 1965.
[57] Day 1942, pp. 153–171. Note, however, the caution of Geagan 1979a, p. 379, that the building program is not an indicator of prosperity, as much funding for it came from outside the city.
[58] Graindor 1927a, pp. 159–171; Day 1942, pp. 142–151. Population of Piraeus: Grigoropoulos 2009 (pp. 172–181 on the composition of the population).
[59] *IG* ii² 3504; Geagan 2011, H 345, p. 188; on Xenocles, see Geagan 1967, pp. 19–20; Geagan 1997, p. 22.

in favor of administrative ones), assisted by treasurers.⁶⁰ Whether Augustus had a hand in any of this is unknown, but he did get involved in the *annona* (grain distribution system) in Rome when necessary, and thus may have done so in the provinces, including Athens. In support of his intervention is a monument found in Athens and identified as a *sekoma*, a measure for dry goods such as grain; it weighed out one *medimnos* of corn that was adapted from the Roman metrological (weights and measures) system.⁶¹

The Athenians also introduced a series of religious reforms that were surely meant to appeal to Augustus. A particularly important one was the institution of a new procession to Delphi, the *Dodekais* (with its sacrifice of twelve oxen), perhaps modeled on the *Pythais*. The latter had ended in 58 because of lack of funding from economic decline and a general jaded feeling from the Roman domination.⁶² Now with Athens' economy recovering, Diodorus of Halae (archon in 26/5) created this new procession, albeit on a smaller scale than the *Pythais*.⁶³ In all, there were five *Dodekais* processions in the Augustan era, each paid for by the wealthier citizens, and each one led by the priest of Apollo Pythios, Eucles of Marathon (the man who persuaded Augustus to donate the money to complete the Roman Agora).⁶⁴ Given Augustus' relationship with Apollo, we are probably not wrong to see the *Dodekais* as another means of fawning to him. At the same time, the procession meant that an Athenian presence at Delphi was maintained, especially as Augustus revived the Amphictyonic Council.⁶⁵ More overt was the introduction of new cults, involving other important members of the imperial family, such as that of Apollo Hypoakraios, located in a cave on the north slope of the Acropolis.⁶⁶

The Eleusinian Mysteries received a makeover thanks to Themistocles of Hagnous, one of the cult's sacred torchbearers (and a descendant of the famous Themistocles, who led Athenian fleets against the Persians in the early fifth century). According to an honorary decree brought by his clan, he

---

⁶⁰ Graindor 1927a, pp. 117–119; Day 1942, pp. 163–164.
⁶¹ Peppas-Delmousou 2004, pp. 121–138.
⁶² Day 1942, p. 175. Use of Apollo myth: Karila-Cohen 2005.
⁶³ Graindor 1927a, p. 143.
⁶⁴ Graindor 1927a, pp. 139–147; Day 1942, pp. 174–175; Bowersock 1965, pp. 95–96; Hoff 1989b, p. 3.
⁶⁵ Bowersock 1965, pp. 97–98; Hoff 1992, p. 231. Athenian sacred embassies to Delphi resumed in 30/29 (archonship of Architimus): Benjamin and Raubitschek 1959, p. 74.
⁶⁶ See Nulton 2003, drawing attention to the similarity of the worship of Livia as Artemis Boulaea.

"increased the solemnity and dignity of the cult," elevating the Mysteries into a more spectacular event.[67] Themistocles' measures may have been part of a state-sponsored program, or he may have been acting out of his friendship with Augustus, especially as he likely officiated over Augustus' second initiation into the Mysteries. The point is ultimately a moot one: Augustus favored the restoration or elevation of old cults, hence the revamped Mysteries brought the city to his attention.

Another means to court Augustus was the worship of Vesta. When we hear that goddess' name we instinctively think of Vestal Virgins in Rome, but inscriptions from the Acropolis show that three Vestals were honored with statues in Augustan times.[68] When Vestals were in service they could not leave the eternal fire in the Forum unprotected, hence the Acropolis statues cannot be of Roman Vestals but Athenian ones—not a surprise given the likely crossover between Vesta and *Hestia* (the Greek goddess of the hearth).[69] For one thing, *Vesta* in Latin is the equivalent of the goddess *Hestia*; for another, there was a seat reserved for the priestess of "Hestia on the Acropolis, Livia, and Julia" (Augustus' daughter), dated between 16 and 2, next to two seats simply for the priestess of *Hestia* in the theater of Dionysus.[70] There were thus three priestesses of *Hestia*, thereby tying in with these three honorific statues. Vesta's cult was probably introduced into Athens in 12 when the emperor, then in Rome, became *pontifex maximus* (chief priest), and it may have been located in the temple of Roma and Augustus on the Acropolis (on which see Figures 14.2A–B).[71]

Aspects of these religious reforms certainly pandered to Augustus, but the city also initiated an ambitious program to restore many of the damaged sanctuaries of the gods in Attica—not only physically rebuilding them but also returning them to their original cult purposes.[72] The decree contracting this work specifies some eighty sanctuaries in the city, the countryside,

---

[67] Clinton 1974, pp. 50–53; Spawforth 2010, pp. 192–197, with additional bibliography. See Lambert 2012, pp. 89–92, on the high value the Athenians attached to Themistocles.
[68] Kajava 2001, p. 72 with n. 8.
[69] Kajava 2001; see too Graindor 1927a, pp. 53–157; Bowersock 2002, p. 8; Spawforth 2012, p. 203.
[70] *IG* ii² 5097 (with Schmalz 2009, pp. 224–225); Kajava 2001, pp. 73–77; cf. Graindor 1927a, pp. 53–54, but Livia may not have been identified with *Hestia*: Kajava 2001, p. 73 with n. 13.
[71] Kajava 2001, pp. 78–79, 80–81, and 83–85.
[72] *IG* ii² 1035, with Culley 1975; Culley 1977; cf. T. L. Shear 1981, pp. 366–367 (dating to the reign of Claudius); Borg 2011, pp. 228–231.

the Piraeus, and on Salamis. Since no emperor is named in the decree authorizing the work, and the sanctuaries in question had nothing to do with Athens but were all to do with local heroic cults, the program may have been purely for the Athenians' benefit.[73] Although the consensus date is the Augustan era, the decree mentions restorations on Salamis, presuming that the Athenians again owned the island (they likely sold it after the Sullan sack in 86).[74] Since, however, we are told that a certain Julius Nicanor restored the island to the city, who may have lived in the mid-first century AD, so after Augustus, the restoration program on Salamis at least might postdate Augustus' reign. We will meet Nicanor more fully and discuss his dates later in the chapter.

The Imperial Cult

There may have been a cult of the goddess Roma in the city since about 150, and the head of Roma began to appear on Athenian coins from about 90, but eventually a cult of the emperor was also introduced. Exactly when is unknown. In the years following Actium, altars, statues, and sacrifices to Octavian and his successors are found throughout Greece.[75] As we discussed earlier, the Athenians may well have instituted a cult to him in 30/29 as part of their measures to regain his favor. Also controversial is the focal point of the cult. One possibility is the small two-room addition behind the Stoa of Zeus Eleutherius in the Agora, especially as cults of Roma were often associated with those of Zeus in the republican era.[76] However, the Stoa's location tells against this identification, and it has been suggested that instead it housed the cult of Tiberius and Livia.[77] Likewise, the Roman Agora might have housed the cult.[78] Yet that location is removed from the center of Athens, and the Athenians could ill afford to incur the emperor's wrath again. Bearing this in mind, the only obvious location is the temple

---

[73] Borg 2011, pp. 228–231.
[74] Graindor 1927a, pp. 8–10; *contra* Habicht 1996b.
[75] Benjamin and Raibitschek 1959; Bowersock 1965, p. 116; see further Kantiréa 2011.
[76] H. A. Thompson 1966; Thompson and Wycherley 1972, pp. 102–103 (pp. 96–103 on the stoa); Whittaker 2002, p. 30; *contra* Hoff 2013, pp. 573–574.
[77] H. A. Thompson 1966 on the Tiberian date; see too Clinton 1997, pp. 168–169; Spawforth 1997, p. 186; Whittaker 2002, p. 33; also skeptical: Kajava 2001, p. 87.
[78] Benjamin and Raubitchek 1959, p. 85; T. L. Shear 1981, pp. 359–360; Hoff 1996; Whittaker 2002, pp. 33–34; Hoff 2014, p. 574.

of Roma and Augustus on the Acropolis (see Figures 14.2A–B).[79] Although it was quite small, built in perhaps 19 but certainly postdating 27, as its dedicatory inscription uses *Sebastos*, its location on the Acropolis explicitly brought to the fore the close association between Rome and the center of Athenian religious life.[80]

Augustus' family was not ignored either. We noted earlier a seat in the theater of Dionysus for the priestess of "Hestia on the Acropolis, Livia, and Julia," which must predate 2 when Julia was banished from Rome for adultery. The year 12 has been suggested, when Augustus was elected *pontifex maximus* and the cult of Vesta likely instituted in the city (see above).[81] A statue to Livia was set up just east of the Metroon in AD 14, as its base refers to her as Julia Augusta (a title she took in that year), and she may have had a shrine dedicated to her.[82]

Then in AD 2, Gaius Caesar (son of Julia and Agrippa and Augustus' grandson) went to Athens while en route to Parthia. A statue base shows us that the Athenians called him the "new Ares," a god with whom he identified himself.[83] Their action does not mean there was a cult to him—nor to Drusus Caesar (son of Tiberius), whom the Athenians also dubbed "the new Ares" during the reign of Tiberius.[84] It is often thought that contemporaneous with Gaius' visit was the relocation of the temple to Ares (the Greek equivalent of Mars) from the god's sanctuary at Acharnae to the Athenian Agora, but the temple that was moved was a different one, and so unlikely to have had anything to do with Gaius (p. 295).

The imperial cult became a launching pad for politically ambitious men into public life.[85] What the Athenians thought of it is unknown,

---

[79] Cf. Graindor 1927a, pp. 149–152; Bowersock 1965, pp. 112–121; T. L. Shear 1981, pp. 363–365; Clinton 1997, pp. 165–167; temples and altars as part of worship: Hendrick 2006, chapters 5–6.
[80] Whittaker 2002, pp. 25–30.
[81] Whittaker 2002, p. 35.
[82] Geagan 2011, H254, p. 148, with J. H. Oliver 1965a; Thompson and Wycherley 1972, p. 166; T. L. Shear 1981, pp. 363 and 364.
[83] *IG* ii² 3250; identification: Geagan 1984, p. 76 (citing examples of other imperial family members); see too Graindor 1927a, pp. 50–51; D. Kienast 1993, p. 204; Bowersock 2002, pp. 9–10; Whittaker 2002, pp. 36–37; Borg 2011, p. 226; cf. H. A. Thompson 1966, p. 183; Thompson and Wycherley 1972, p. 163; Alcock 1996, p. 121.
[84] *IG* ii² 3257, with Spawforth 1997, pp. 187–188; *contra*, for example, Kajava 2001, pp. 88–89. Drusus: Graindor 1927a, p. 50.
[85] Bowersock 1965, pp. 117–118; Walker 1997, pp. 72–73. On the increasing religious power of the elite and its exploitation for advancement, and Rome's dealings with these elite, see Grijalvo 2005; Schiller 2006; Camia 2014; cf. Geagan 1997; Baslez 2004.

but we might say their attitude was as self-serving as when they declared Monophthalmus and Poliorcetes savior gods in 307. For one thing, in Athens the cult started off slowly, and buildings associated with it were often marginalized (the temple of Roma and Augustus being an exception).[86] The Athenians did reserve a seat in the theater of Dionysus for the "priest of Augustus Caesar," reinscribing it (perhaps toward the end of his life) as "priest and high priest of Augustus Caesar."[87] Yet two statues set up to Augustus calling him *theos* (god) were not in the city, but at Delphi and on Delos.[88] Perhaps the Athenians' slowness in taking to the new imperial cult also played a role in why its center in Achaea was in the Roman colony of Corinth, not Athens.[89]

Relations between the city and Rome remained amicable after the 20s.[90] Athens remained firmly under Rome's control, well illustrated by the statue of Gaius Caesar's brother Lucius that was set atop the gate of Athena Archegetis ("Leader") at the western entrance to the Roman Agora (Figure 12.3), arguably turning it into a triumphal arch.[91] But then a year before Augustus died, Athens revolted.[92] Few details are known, and the evidence is much later, but the revolt was taken seriously enough for Augustus to send an imperial legate to the city; the man's name is not known, but he restored peace and executed the ringleaders.[93] Although the Athenians set up a statue

---

[86] See especially Spawforth 1997.
[87] *IG* ii² 5034, with Schmalz 2009, pp. 223–224; possibly there were two priests of Augustus (one of Roma and Augustus and one of Augustus Caesar, the latter serving at Eleusis): Clinton 1997, pp. 166 and 173–174; Spawforth 1997, pp. 183–185; Whittaker 2002, p. 33.
[88] Geagan 1984, p. 76, with references.
[89] Spawforth 1994; on the cult throughout Achaea: Alcock 1993, pp. 181–191.
[90] It is usually thought that Augustus' last trip to Athens was in 19: Graindor 1927a, pp. 33–36; Geagan 1984, pp. 69 and 73. But Dio 54.28.3 has been interpreted that the emperor was attending the Panathenaea in Athens when he received the news that Agrippa was ill; he left immediately for Rome, but Agrippa died before he arrived back: Hoff 1989a, p. 275; Hoff 1989b, p. 5. Thus Augustus was in Athens in 12 (on a fourth visit), the year of Agrippa's death. The view has been rebutted by Habicht 1991d on the grounds that the martial element of which Dio speaks shows that he confused the Panathenaea with the festival to Minerva in Rome and that Augustus was in Italy when Agrippa died. Augustus' third and final visit to Athens, then, was in 19.
[91] Bowersock 2002, p. 10.
[92] Sherk 1988, no. 24, pp. 39–40; Bowersock 1965, pp. 106–108, also discussing chronology.
[93] Eusebius, *Chronicle* 197.4; Orosius 6.22.2 (both much later sources), with Bowersock 1965, pp. 106–108; Geagan 1979a, p. 379; Hoff 1989a, pp. 275–276; D. Kienast 1993,

to him, it was not enough to prevent Augustus from restricting the city's coinage to bronze.[94]

What caused the revolt is unknown, but two years later, in AD 15, the provinces of Achaea and Macedonia protested to the new emperor Tiberius the costs of their taxes and maintaining their proconsuls.[95] That defiance may have arisen from the financial difficulties faced by Athens two years earlier, together with the declining health of Augustus, and so prompted a revolt. In a speech of AD 18 by Piso, the Athenians were accused of being troublemakers "for joining with Mithridates against Sulla and with Antony against the deified Augustus," which may not mean they were looking to revolt, but could indicate continued factionalism among the elite that had dogged Athenian life since the Classical period.[96]

Julius Nicanor: Man of Mystery

Various individuals acted in a liaison role between Athens and Rome, rising to prominence from their roles in the imperial cult. But one person stands head and shoulders above the rest: Gaius Julius Nicanor of Hierapolis (in Syria). Even so, we are in the dark about many of his activities in Athens, and even why he made it his adopted home.[97]

To begin with, two men of the same name are known, one from Alexandria and the other from Hieropolis. The former was most likely the son of the philosopher Areius of Alexandria, one of Augustus' teachers, making the latter man our Nicanor.[98] Enormously wealthy, he moved from Syria in the early imperial era to Athens, but eventually became a Roman citizen. His philanthropism was such that he acquired Salamis and gave it to the city, for which the people honored him with a statue and the appellations "New

---

pp. 203–204. Graindor 1927a, pp. 41–45, discusses the revolt, but describes it as a minor domestic matter.

[94] Statue: *IG* ii² 3233; Geagan 2011, H 420, pp. 228–229; Ehrenberg and Jones 1976, no. 81a, p. 74.

[95] Tacitus, *Annals* 1.76.4.

[96] Tacitus, *Annals* 2.55.1–3.

[97] See C. P. Jones 1978, pp. 222–228; Geagan 1979a, p. 282; Habicht 1996b; Bowersock 2002, pp. 11–16; Byrne 2003, pp. 312–322; C. P. Jones 2005; Follett 2004b; C. P. Jones 2011; Spawforth 2012, pp. 113–116.

[98] Graindor 1927a, pp. 8, 51, and 168; Follett 2004b, pp. 145–146.

Themistocles" (presumably linked directly to Salamis) and "New Homer."⁹⁹ The restored decree announcing the honors (with a copy set up at Eleusis) belongs to the later first century after his death.¹⁰⁰

Nicanor's dates impact the Athenian program of restoring sanctuaries in Attica and on Salamis that we mentioned earlier. Different inscriptional evidence has been interpreted to place him as hoplite general in AD 61/2 and holding for the first time the office of *agonothetes* (overseer of the festivals) of the Augustan Games in AD 41.¹⁰¹ In light of this, he could not have been active in Augustan Athens, which means that the Athenian restoration project was either much later or that the island sanctuaries were restored afterward, between AD 41 and 61.¹⁰² However, a statue base dated to AD 41, the start of Claudius' reign, names a certain Tiberius Claudius Novius (high priest of the imperial cult) as the first *agonothetes* of the Augustan Games, and arguments for a later dating of Nicanor's life have been compellingly attacked.¹⁰³ Nicanor, then, was active in the Augustan era.

But did Nicanor buy Salamis and simply give it to the Athenians? The restorations advanced in his decree have resulted in two significantly different readings. The first possible reading is that he bought back Salamis, but instead of giving it outright to Athens he and the city controlled it jointly; after his death, the island reverted to Roman control.¹⁰⁴ But the second reading, which is preferable, supposes that the decree is a contract between Athens and Nicanor, with no reversion of the island to Rome.¹⁰⁵ Building on this, it would seem that Nicanor only bought titles to parts of Salamis gained during the troubles of the Republic and turned these

---

⁹⁹ *IG* ii² 3786, 3789 (statue bases); Dio of Prusa 31.116; Stephanus of Byzantium, s.v. Hierapolis. The statue may have been that of Themistocles in the Prytaneum, which was reinscribed to him: Spawforth 2012, p. 114.

¹⁰⁰ C. P. Jones 2005, pp. 161–167.

¹⁰¹ Hoplite general: *IG* ii² 1723, lines 14–17; *agonothetes*: *IG* ii² 1069; later dating: Kapetanopoulos 1976; Kapetanopoulos 1981; Habicht 1996b, pp. 83–84; Walker 1997, p. 73; Byrne 2003, pp. 321–322; Follet 2004b.

¹⁰² T. L. Shear 1981, pp. 366–367.

¹⁰³ *IG* ii² 3270, lines 4–5; on Novius, see Geagan 1979c; Spawforth 1997, pp. 189–191. Dating arguments: Bowersock 2002, pp. 12–15; C. P. Jones 2005; Schmalz 2009, pp. 16–17, and 28; C. P. Jones 2011. On the *agonothesia* in the Roman imperial period, see Geagan 1967, pp. 132–136.

¹⁰⁴ Follett 2004b, especially pp. 155–157.

¹⁰⁵ C. P. Jones 2005, pp. 167–170.

properties over to the city, perhaps also reserving a life-interest for himself (and his descendants).[106]

Why was Nicanor bothered with Salamis in the first place? If he wanted to ingratiate himself with the Athenians, why not improve the city's roads or construct some new building? The answer is to play up to Rome for his own self-advancement. The Romans for some time had been keenly interested in the Persian Wars era, from which they drew parallels to contemporary threats from the east.[107] Augustus also held in very high regard the battle of Salamis of 480, at which Themistocles defeated the Persian fleet. He even held a mock version of the battle, complete with an artificial lake, an islet for Salamis, and prisoners and criminals acting the part of the Greeks and Persians, when he dedicated the Forum of Augustus and temple of Mars Ultor in 2.[108] Salamis became "a metaphor for Actium," as A. Spawforth puts it, with Augustus the champion of civilization against eastern barbarians.[109] Nicanor's gift of Salamis therefore both benefited the city and resonated with Augustus—but as a result it was Nicanor himself who gained the most.

At some stage after his death the Athenians erased the nicknames "New Themistocles" and "New Homer," earning the first century AD orator and philosopher Dio of Prusa's anger.[110] The former title aligned Nicanor to one of Athens' most famous generals and families, whose valor during the Persian Wars had never been forgotten; the latter may be because he fancied himself as a poet (we have no idea how good or bad he was), so the Athenians decided to pander to his poetic pretensions.[111] Why they erased both appellations is unknown, but it is plausible that Nicanor's unabashed self-aggrandizement and perhaps even his receipt of Roman citizenship, together with his popularity among the lower social stratum, earned him the suspicion of the aristocratic families and brought about his downfall.[112] Still in this vein is the attractive suggestion that descendants of the famous fifth-century Themistocles were active in Augustan Athens, and if the boastful

---

[106] C. P. Jones 2005, pp. 170–172; C. P. Jones 2011, p. 79; cf. Bowersock 2002, pp. 15–16.
[107] Spawforth 2012, pp. 103–141, especially pp. 113–116.
[108] Trend: Spawforth 2012, pp. 103–141. Generally on Augustus' allusions to the Actium victory: Zanker 1988, pp. 82–85.
[109] Spawforth 2012, p. 103.
[110] Dio of Prusa 31.116.
[111] Bowersock 2002, p. 16, while noting that the reasons for the nickname "are beyond divining," suggests that he may have written an epic about Augustus or Augustan Athens.
[112] Cf. Schmalz 2009, p. 163.

Nicanor were flaunting his association with their great ancestor they may have secured the erasure of his Themistoclean sobriquet.[113] In keeping with Nicanor's apparent fall from grace, the Athenians then erased mention of him as a new Homer.

Back to the Classics

We have commented several times about the impact of Greek culture on the Romans, and how they would assimilate aspects of Hellenism for their own culture and learning, with subjects like philosophy, architecture, and rhetoric being especially appealing. The fascination and need continued into the later imperial period—rhetoric, for example, was required for public affairs and a philosophical system such as Stoicism vital for daily life.[114] Athens in particular found itself at the center of what would become the Romans' definition of "Greekness" on literary, philosophical, and artistic grounds.[115]

Augustus and his successors were the principal exploiters of Hellenism for cultural and political ends.[116] In doing so they did not merely take over Greek practices or systems but fused them with Roman trends and beliefs to create their own brand of classicism.[117] The term "imperial hellenism" has been used to describe this new order, which brought benefits for the Greeks but did not really allow them any sort of self-differentiation.[118] The Greeks, as we have noted, strove to maintain a sense of their own identity as the Romanization of Greece grew, though they were not always successful.

At the same time, the Romans helped to promote works uniquely Greek. During the Hellenistic period the Greek language had come into contact with many different languages and new "Asianist" styles of rhetoric from the various kingdoms of the Greek east.[119] The simpler form of language known as *koine* (common) had, however, been criticized as early as Cicero, who saw it as a debasement of Classical Greek.[120] It also did not sit well with a circle

---

[113] C. P. Jones 2011, pp. 81–82. Themistocles' priestly offices in Augustan Athens: Spawforth 2012, pp. 192–196.
[114] Cf. Bowie 2000, especially pp. 900–907, on rhetoric and philosophy.
[115] Cf. for example the essays in Schmitz and Wiater 2011, especially Borg 2011.
[116] See Spawforth 2012.
[117] Spawforth 2012, pp. 18–26.
[118] Connolly 2007, especially pp. 31–37; cf. Woolf 1994.
[119] For example Wooten 1976.
[120] Cicero, *Brutus* 13.51; Cicero, *Orator* 24–27; cf. Quintilian 12.10.16–24.

of Greek writers of various genres in Augustan Rome, including the noted literary critic and historian Dionysius of Halicarnassus, who called for a return to the loftier power and style of Classical Greek.[121] Among Dionysius' circle was the scholar and rhetorician Caecilius of Calacte (in Sicily), who most likely was responsible for compiling the so-called Canon of the Ten Attic Orators. This was a collection of some speeches of selected fifth- and fourth-century orators including Demosthenes, Hyperides, and Dinarchus, perhaps reflecting the literary tastes of all the Augustan critics.[122] Especially noteworthy here is not what this group did, but that it existed and was influential in Rome, a clear sign of the entrenchment of Hellenism in Roman life. This fascination with the Greek, especially Athenian, literary past would continue from the mid-first century AD until the middle of the third century AD with a group of writers known as the Second Sophistic, as we shall see later in chapter 15.

Augustus died in AD 14. He had expanded the empire; introduced all manner of military, economic, social, and moral reforms in Rome and throughout the provinces; and was famously said to have proudly boasted that he found Rome a city of brick and left it in marble.[123] Now it was time to find out what his successors would do.

---

[121] See, for example, Dihle 2011; Hidber 2011, and on Dionysius especially see Hunter and de Jonge 2019. On the following writers and on Greek literature and its impact on the Augustan age: Bowersock 1965, pp. 122–139; see the essays in Hunter and de Jonge 2019 on Augustan literature and cultural change in the Mediterranean.
[122] Worthington 1994b.
[123] Suetonius, *Augustus* 28.3.

13

Tiberius to Hadrian

ATHENS IN THE PERIOD FROM Tiberius to Trajan "was not marked by any notable event."[1] Written almost a century ago by the French scholar P. Graindor, whose three-volume work on Roman Athens is still valuable, this comment at first sight rings true. After Augustus, the next emperor to travel to Athens was Trajan in AD 113; Nero did go to Greece but stayed away from Athens (and Sparta), as we will see. Other Romans, as well as dignitaries and rulers from the Greek east, continued to go to the city, but numbers were not as high as in the Augustan period.[2] The reason for the lengthy gap in imperial visits is unknown, but may well have been due to the peaceful relations between Greece and Rome as a result of Augustan policy.[3] At the same time, we cannot discount that emperors may no longer have held Greece in the same high regard as before.

This was also a period when the economy of Greece slumped; fewer new buildings were constructed in cities, Roman rulers continued looting Greek artworks, religious festivals were scaled back, and as always, there were taxes to pay to Rome. Yet despite this lackluster background emperors were still

---

[1] Graindor 1931, p. 1: "n'est marquée par aucun événement saillant." On this period, see Graindor 1931.
[2] For Romans: Graindor 1931, pp. 29–45, including a register of such notables; for non-Romans: Graindor 1931, pp. 47–58.
[3] Geagan 1979a, pp. 383–384; Geagan 1984; Perrin-Saminadayar 2004–2005; Perrin-Saminadayar 2007c, especially pp. 135–141; Spawforth 2012, pp. 235–241; see too Hendrick 2006, chapter 3, pp. 56–75.

involved in Greek affairs as well as in Athenian civic life, and despite the declines, Athens did not fall into an abyss.[4]

While literary writers maintained an interest in past events for obvious reasons, what was being lost over time for all Greeks was the memory of the ravages caused by the wars and invasions of the previous century; in the process there was a reshaping of attitude to Rome.[5] The Romans still exploited the cultural and intellectual aspects of Hellenism, but as the first century AD progressed, the Greeks' perceptions of Roman involvement in their land changed. Cities like Athens strove to protect their own civic identity, and while they did not morph completely into provincial ones their character underwent change.[6]

Meet the Emperors

In this chapter we will discuss three imperial dynasties and their relations with Greece and especially Athens: the Julio-Claudian, the Flavian, and the Nerva-Antonine.

First, the Julio-Claudian dynasty. After Augustus' death in AD 14, the throne passed to Tiberius. Augustus had indicated the succession in a group of statues he set up on the Acropolis of himself, Tiberius, Germanicus, and Drusus (son of Tiberius) in AD 4, when he adopted his stepson Tiberius.[7] As Tiberius' reign progressed his initial popularity plummeted.[8] Germanicus died in AD 18 and Drusus in AD 23; Tiberius' death in AD 37 brought the young Caligula to the throne, whose exploits led to his assassination in AD 41.[9] Claudius was then proclaimed emperor, and in a brighter reign ruled until his wife Agrippina likely poisoned him in AD 54.[10] Then came the dismal rule of Nero; faced by insurrection, and with the Senate declaring

---

[4] J. H. Oliver 1981b; cf. Fernández Uriel 2007, and see Hendrick 2006, chapter 3, for example.
[5] Memories of the Republic: C. P. Jones 2011.
[6] Schmalz 1994. See too Graindor 1931, pp. 160–171, on architecture in the Julio-Claudian-Flavian era.
[7] *IG* ii² 3253, 3256, with Geagan 1984, pp. 71–72; cf. Rödel 2010, pp. 109–110.
[8] On Tiberius' reign, see Levick 1999; Seager 2005; cf. Wiedemann 1996a, pp. 198–221.
[9] On Caligula see, for example, Winterling 2011; Barrett 2015; cf. Wiedemann 1996a, pp. 221–229.
[10] On Claudius see, for example, Osgood 2011; Levick 2015; cf. Wiedemann 1996a, pp. 229–241.

against him, he committed suicide in AD 68, ending the Julio-Claudian dynasty.[11]

Second, the Flavian dynasty. Nero's suicide brought chaos to Rome and the Empire. Over the following year there were no fewer than four emperors: Galba (who had engineered Nero's demise), Otho, and Vitellius, each ruling for mere months, and the fourth and final one, Vespasian, who restored order in AD 69.[12] Vespasian brought much-needed continuity to Rome by founding the Flavian dynasty.[13] On his death from acute diarrhea in AD 79, his son Titus succeeded him.[14] The latter ruled for only two years before he died in AD 81 (during his reign the Flavian amphitheater or Colosseum begun by his father in Rome was finished and Mount Vesuvius erupted). His death led to his younger brother Domitian assuming the throne until his assassination in AD 96 brought with it the end of that dynasty.[15]

Finally, there was the Nerva-Antonine dynasty. Domitian's adviser Nerva, then aged sixty-six, was proclaimed emperor the same day his master was killed. He founded the Nerva-Antonine dynasty, ending with Commodus in AD 192, although we are concerned in this book only with its first three emperors (Nerva, Trajan, and Hadrian).[16] Nerva was never able to control the army, and died of natural causes in AD 98. Since he was childless he had been forced to adopt Trajan, who succeeded him the same year. Trajan was a soldier-emperor in the mold of Augustus and expanded the Empire greatly; he died suddenly of a stroke in AD 117. His death brought his adopted son Hadrian to power (117–138), who deserves his own chapter because of his relationship with Athens (chapter 15).

---

[11] On Nero see, for example, Malitz 2005; Shotter 2008; cf. Wiedemann 1996a, pp. 241–255; Wiedemann 1996b, pp. 256–261.
[12] Sherk 1988, no. 79, pp. 117–118; in detail Wellesley 2000; Morgan 2006; cf. Wiedemann 1996b.
[13] Dynasty: Griffin 2000a. Vespasian: Levick 2016.
[14] See B. W. Jones 1984.
[15] See B. W. Jones 1992; Southern 1997.
[16] See Griffin 2000b on Nerva and Trajan. For individual biographies, see on Nerva Grainger 2003, and on Trajan Bennett 2000.

The Emperors and Greece

All of the emperors were philhellenes who had a high regard for Greece and Hellenism, or at least the brand of Hellenism that the Romans molded for their own usage.[17] During his stay on Rhodes in 6 (so before he was emperor), Tiberius surrounded himself with Greek intellectuals and poets, and kept similar company after he took the throne. Caligula patronized Greek poets; in his reign, Philip of Thessalonica compiled the works of Greek poets known as the Garland of Philip.[18] Claudius apparently toyed with the idea of moving the "Eleusinian rites" (Mysteries) to Rome (whatever that meant).[19] A letter of Pliny the Younger in Trajan's time to Valerius Maximus, a Roman administrator about to leave for Greece, warned him not to offend the Greeks and called Achaea the "true" (*vera*) Greece, where civilization (*humanitas*), literature, and even agriculture originated.[20]

Still, the emperors' love of Hellenism did not stop them from plundering artworks, such as the famous Eros of Praxiteles from Thespiae, taken by Caligula.[21] We do not know the extent of the looting in the province: a passage in Pliny claims there were at least 3,000 statues in Athens, Olympia, and Delphi in his time; presumably there were many more in Greece before the Romans began to remove them in 146.[22]

The Greeks favored some emperors more than others. One was Claudius, who returned statues seized by Caligula, and who may have brought Macedonia into the Amphictyonic League so that it could enjoy a greater role in Greek affairs as partial compensation for its loss of influence in the south when Augustus divided two provinces.[23] The Greeks were careful to set up altars and statues to all emperors (whether they visited their cities or not), since these memorials were not only honorary but also functioned as part of the imperial cult.[24] Perhaps a sign of the

---

[17] Bowersock 1965, pp. 140–141; Connolly 2007; cf. Woolf 1994; Spawforth 2012, pp. 18–26, and passim.

[18] Cameron 1980.

[19] Suetonius, *Claudius* 25.5, with Graindor 1931, pp. 11 and 102–110; Clinton 1989a, pp. 1513–1514, accepting this was a real attempt to move them that was resisted.

[20] Pliny, *Letters* 8.24.2, 4, with Spawforth 2012, pp. 239–240.

[21] Graindor 1931, p. 9.

[22] Pliny, *NH* 34.7.36. See Sherk 1988, no. 75, p. 114, for Nero's "confiscations" of statues in Greece.

[23] J. H. Oliver 1981b, p. 416; see too Sordi 2007.

[24] Geagan 1984; Højte 2000 (reigns of Trajan, Hadrian, and Antoninus Pius), also noting that it does not follow that a statue base was contemporaneous with the statue

economic times is that a number of dedications can be found on reused bases, a practice that had begun under Augustus (for further discussion, see pp. 296–297).[25]

Nero was the only Julio-Claudian emperor after Augustus to go to Greece (in AD 66/7), though not for any diplomatic reason: he "crossed over into Greece, in no way like Flamininus or Mummius or as Agrippa and Augustus, his ancestors, had done, but with the intention of driving chariots, playing the lyre, making proclamations, and acting in tragedies," according to Dio.[26] In other words, he had no interest in listening to philosophers in Athens or taking in the sights.[27] He wanted to become a *periodonikes*—a victor (even more prestigious than an Olympic one) in at least four of the six Panhellenic festivals of the Pythia (Delphi), Olympic (Olympia), Isthmia (Corinth), and Nemea, to which the Actia (Nicopolis) and Heraria (Argos) had been added in the Roman era.[28] To this end, he ordered the six festivals to be held at irregular times so he could participate in all of them in the same year and added musical contests. He took part in musical and charioteering events—unsurprisingly, he won his four victories to become a *periodonikes*, even though, according to Suetonius, he fell out of his ten-horse chariot at Olympia and though he managed to pull himself back into it, he could not finish the race.[29]

Avoiding Athens and Sparta must have been difficult for Nero.[30] He stayed at Corinth, the capital of Achaea and imperial-cult center, possibly to show he was out to visit "Imperial Achaea" (the present) and not "Old Greece" (the past).[31] According to our ancient writers, he avoided Athens

---

on it or even had one on it at all. Dedications to Julio-Claudian emperors and imperial family collected at Schmalz 2009, pp. 92–126, and see too Hendrick 2006, chapters 6 and 9 on altars and statues; Geagan 2011, pp. 157–170, for a catalogue of imperial altars.

[25] J. L. Shear 2007a; Krumeich 2008; Krumeich 2010b; Keesling 2010. See Sève 2004 for a reused dedication to Tiberius and his brother Drusus at Philippi in Macedonia.

[26] Dio 62.8.2; visit: Dio 62.8.2–10.1.

[27] On the visit: Alcock 1994; Hoët-van Cauwenberghe 2007; see too Bradley 1978.

[28] Dio 62.8.3, with Kennell 1988; Alcock 1994, pp. 98–99 and 105–107.

[29] Suetonius, *Nero* 24.2; cf. Dio 62.14.1, 62.10.1 (his four victories). Perhaps he realized that he could never match his predecessors when it came to military glory and so took part personally in the games (unlike them) to forge his own brand of imperial glory: Griffin 2007. Spawforth 2012, pp. 237–238, argues that Nero was deliberately self-distancing from Augustus' brand of Roman Hellenism, with its focus on Sparta and Athens, but this is too strained; Alcock has the best analysis of Nero's policy in Greece.

[30] Cf. J. H. Oliver 1981b, p. 417. Kennell 1988 is best on why he avoided the two cities.

[31] Alcock 1994, pp. 105–107; Spawforth 1994. On the privileging of Corinth, see too Williams II 1987.

out of fear of the Furies (goddesses who hunted down murderers) because he had had his mother, Agrippina, killed (in AD 59).³² For the same reason, Nero gave the Eleusinian Mysteries a wide berth since the "godless and wicked" were warned away at their outset; he also steered clear of Sparta because the laws of the fabled lawgiver Lycurgus would show he was a tyrant.³³ It is hard to imagine someone like Nero anxious about vengeful mythological characters or concerned that people thought he was tyrannical. He simply stayed away from these cities, as N. Kennell argues, because neither was part of the "Panhellenic circuit," hence Athens did not have a festival that would count toward his shot at becoming a *periodonikes*.

The damnation of Nero's memory (*damnatio memoriae*) by the Senate on his death has colored the literary sources' presentation of him.³⁴ But on reflection, certain actions surely endeared him to the Greeks. One was his grandiose plan of digging a canal though the isthmus of Corinth to facilitate trade and communication, something Julius Caesar and Caligula had thought about; he even broke ground for it himself, but it was abandoned on his death.³⁵ More important was his announcement of the freedom of Achaea and a remission of taxes on November 28, AD 67.³⁶ He had just participated in the Isthmian games at Corinth, so the venue and his declaration were perhaps deliberate, calling to mind Flamininus' proclamation there in 196, and even that of Philip II, who first brought Greece under outside control.³⁷ Nero's grant of freedom would not last long. In AD 70, Achaea embroiled itself in a civil war; Vespasian immediately made

---

³² Suetonius, *Nero* 34.3–4.
³³ Suetonius, *Nero* 34.4; Dio 62.14.3, with Geagan 1979a, p. 384; Geagan 1984, p. 74; Clinton 1989a, p. 1514 (doubting), but Graindor 1931, p. 16, accepts the stories.
³⁴ Hoët-van Cauwenberghe 2007. On *damnatio memoriae*: Follet 1976, p. 60.
³⁵ Dio 62.16.1; Sherk 1988, no. 72, p. 112. His aim may have been to follow and (as with his personal participation in the Panhellenic games) even eclipse his predecessors: Alcock 1994, pp. 101–103.
³⁶ Suetonius, *Nero* 24.2; Pliny, *NH* 4.6.22; Pausanias 7.17.3; Sherk 1988, no. 71, pp. 110–112, with the discussion of Pavan 1987. Chronology: Bradley 1978. To offset the loss of income for Rome, he gave to the Roman people the prosperous island of Sardinia.
³⁷ Nero's action might appear impulsive, but there is a tradition of foreign rulers proclaiming the freedom of Greece, although at this time a large part of Achaea, including its two principal cities Athens and Sparta, was already free: Alcock 1994, pp. 103–104. On Athens' status as allied free city (*civitas foederata et libera*), see Graindor 1927a, pp. 130–131; cf. Graindor 1931, pp. 97–100.

it subject to a governor and reimposed the tribute, saying "that the Greek people had forgotten how to be free."[38]

The high rates of taxation imposed on the provinces by Rome affected all Greeks. The Athenians had revolted from Rome in AD 13. That revolt may be connected to still simmering discontent in AD 15 when Achaea and Macedonia complained to Tiberius about their rates of taxation and the cost of maintaining proconsuls in the provinces. The emperor wasted no time in diplomacy. As punishment for their protests, according to Tacitus, he decided that Achaea and Macedonia would no longer have their own governors and folded them into the province of Moesia.[39] His high-handed treatment did not solve any economic issues, and shows he did not view either province with the importance that Augustus had. Achaea and Macedonia remained under the jurisdiction of Moesia's governor until Claudius restored them to senatorial control in AD 44.

Greece's economic recovery of the Augustan era was not able to sustain itself over the following decades.[40] Nero neatly summed up the decline, lamenting that his good news of declaring the freedom of Achaea did not come when the province was more prosperous. In the Flavian era, it was claimed that all of Greece could not muster even 3,000 hoplites, the same number that the Megarians had put into the field against the Persians in the last battle of the Persian Wars, Plataea in 478.[41] Perhaps because of the economic decline, Trajan based an agent to Greece in AD 107 to 108, given the widespread corruption, abuse of governors, and ineptitude of city administrators that plagued the eastern provinces.[42] Later in the second century Hadrian's measures to moderate rates of taxation and support the poor, as well as his bestowal of gifts to communities, show us that Greece, including Athens, was still suffering badly.

As time went by, Greeks became involved more in Roman affairs. For example, some had already been attached to prominent men like Sulla and Pompey, but from Augustus' time the numbers of those working for him and provincial governors increased.[43] Using Greeks in the imperial civil

---

[38] Pausanias 7.17.4; see Griffin 2000a, pp. 26–32; cf. Levick 2000, pp. 604–605.
[39] Tacitus, *Annals* 1.76.4, with Levick 1996, pp. 655–656 and 663–664; cf. Bowersock 1965, p. 108.
[40] Day 1942, pp. 176–183.
[41] [Plutarch], *Moralia* 414a; cf. Hdt. 9.21, 28 on numbers at Plataea.
[42] Levick 2000, pp. 614–620; Griffin 2000b, pp. 117–123.
[43] Bowersock 1965, pp. 30–41.

service made sense: they were educated, literate, spoke Greek, and could act as go-betweens between the areas in which they worked (or came from) and Rome. Trajan's reign saw the first senators from mainland Greece to Rome: the distinguished Tiberius Claudius Atticus Herodes of Marathon (also chief priest of the imperial cult) and Gaius Julius Eurycles Herculanus of Sparta; their elevation may have been due to the contact they had with Hadrian before he became emperor.[44] No senator is known from Corinth, the Roman colony and capital of Achaea, perhaps because unlike Athens or Sparta, no Corinthian was considered a member of a prominent enough family.

Life in Athens

We are none too sure about political life and civic institutions between the time of Augustus and Hadrian because of a lack of evidence.[45] The *ephebeia* continued to exist, with the ephebes taking part in various religious processions, holding games, and putting on drill displays, though the Athenians seem to have made the institution out to be more important than it may have been as a throwback to the days before Roman rule.[46] The ephebic lists of the Roman era permit a glimpse into the ratio of citizens to noncitizen ephebes, who seem to have been kept separate, with Milesians (a significant part of the foreign immigrants in the Augustan era) forming a special group.[47] It appears that during the archonship of Domitian (sometime between AD 84/5 and 92/3) we have the first examples of noncitizen ephebic gymnasiarchs, although these foreign officials were always in a minority.[48]

The hoplite general and herald of the Areopagus were still the top officials in Athens, even though archons continued to be appointed and the

---

[44] J. H. Oliver 1983, pp. 116–117. However, Birley 1997 argues they did not become senators until Hadrian's reign. Subsequent Hellenizing of the Senate: Bowersock 1965, pp. 141–143.
[45] On the following: Graindor 1931, pp. 59–100 (to Trajianic era); cf. Geagan 1979a, p. 388.
[46] Perrin-Saminadayar 2004; cf. Wiemer 2011; see too Follet 1976, pp. 339–341.
[47] Graindor 1922c; cf. Graindor 1927a, p. 124, and Graindor 1931, pp. 85–97, on the *ephebeia* being its own little city; cf. Day 1942, pp. 142–151; Baslez 1989. Population of Athens using lists of ephebes: Graindor 1931, pp. 136–138; cf. Thomas 2006 (ephebic list of first century AD); ephebic catalogue and dedications: Schmalz 2009, pp. 44–55. Population of Piraeus: Grigoropoulos 2009.
[48] Graindor 1931, p. 91; Baslez 1989, pp. 27 and 34–36.

eponymous archon gave his name to the year.⁴⁹ But the Boule (of 600) had evidently declined in activity—we do not know of any statues it dedicated, for example, and the prytany decrees that it alone passed fall into abeyance until the time of Hadrian. Private associations continued to pass decrees, such as one honoring a Nicias, son of Nicias, for serving as president of the *eranistai* (an association making loans).⁵⁰

Ambitious individuals still exerted influence in civic life, though it was those who had Roman citizenship or at least were favored by Rome who rose to prominence. One such was Tiberius Claudius Novius of Oion.⁵¹ From a family of modest means, he grew rich and acquired Roman citizenship; in a career stretching over twenty years, he was hoplite general eight times (the first time in AD 40/1 and the eighth in AD 60/1); herald of the Areopagus, priest of Delian Apollo, *epimeletes* of the city, and gymnasiarch; and in AD 47/8 he served as *agonothetes* of the Panathenaea. He was awarded a statue in AD 51/2 when he was also high priest of Antonia Augusta, and in AD 61 seems to have been the organizer and first high priest (*archiereus*) of the imperial cult of the *Sebastoi* (the emperors). Another person who deserves mention is Diocles, son of Themistocles, who had introduced religious reforms under Augustus. Diocles was an eponymous archon and a hoplite general under Caligula and Claudius, and in AD 41 was *epimeletes* of the Piraeus. Despite his prominence he never sought Roman citizenship, although he did make a private donation to the imperial legate Gaius Memmius Regulus.⁵²

Economically, Athens was suffering like other cities—in an oration written between AD 79 and 82 Dio of Prusa claims it was at the end of its resources, and Pausanias contends that Greece suffered ruin and devastation because of the gods.⁵³ Foreign workers (from abroad, not so much from other Greek cities) were still found in goodly numbers, and Athens

---

⁴⁹ Graindor 1931, pp. 72–85; see too Geagan 1967 for a discussion of public officials and organs of the constitution.
⁵⁰ Graindor 1931, pp. 71–72; on associations, see Leiwo 1997; Baslez 2004.
⁵¹ Graindor 1931, pp. 141–143; Geagan 1979c especially; Geagan 1997, pp. 25–26; Spawforth 1997, pp. 183–186 and 188–194; Byrne 2003, pp. 170–173; Schmalz 2009, pp. 290–292.
⁵² Schmalz 2009, pp. 251–252 and 307.
⁵³ Dio of Prusa 31.123; Pausanias 7.17.1, with Graindor 1931, pp. 55–56; Day 1942, p. 178, who notes that Dio's view may be exaggerated as Rhodes was the subject of his oration, so he had to make it better than Athens. Decline: Day 1942, pp. 177–183; Geagan 1979a, pp. 385–386.

continued to export Attic products, including honey and olive oil, as well as marble—that from Pentelicus was used in the stadium at Delphi; the temple of Demeter and Persephone at Olympia; the Capitoline temple at Rome; and in the rebuilding in Athens of the Panathenaic Stadium.[54] But against these exports was the large number of commodities the Athenians needed to import, including copper, gold, ivory, terracotta from Italy, and even (under Trajan) lamps from Corinth.

And as always, there was the perennial problem of grain importation. We noted that in the Augustan era a special treasury had been created, supervised by the hoplite general no less, to pay for grain (pp. 254–255). But when the money in it was insufficient to meet the needs of the people, riots broke out in the city.[55] Financial straits perhaps explain why the *Dodekaides* to Delphi are not recorded after Tiberius' accession until Domitian (and then on only two occasions), although the city continued to play a role in amphictyonic affairs.[56] Nor did Athens coin during the first years of the second century AD, but used coinage minted in the previous century, perhaps also due to monetary pressure from Trajan's costly wars.[57] There may also have been increasingly tough conditions for smaller farmers in Attica: a measure Hadrian introduced to record property in Attica revealed large estates owned by the wealthy, perhaps at the expense of the smaller farmers (p. 319). Certainly, the stimulus to the local economy from visitors, in particular when the Mysteries were held, was not enough to run a city.[58]

Outside politics and the economy, philosophical schools were flourishing, and local and foreign poets were at work.[59] Sculptors increased in number, producing statues and busts of officials, funerary monuments, and information reliefs such as ephebic lists.[60] Their artworks were exported throughout Greece and Asia Minor well into the second century AD.[61]

---

[54] Day 1942, pp. 203–204; Geagan 1979a, p. 384.
[55] Day 1942, p. 210.
[56] Graindor 1931, pp. 105–107; Day 1942, p. 183.
[57] Graindor 1931, pp. 19–22; Geagan 1979a, pp. 385–386; Griffin 2000b, pp. 123–128 (eastern campaigns).
[58] Graindor 1931, pp. 30–45, 47–58, 101–105 (for lists of visitors), and 131–133; Day 1942, pp. 182–183; Bowersock 1965, p. 78.
[59] Cults: Graindor 1931, pp. 107–116. Schools and poets: Graindor 1931, pp. 149–160.
[60] Graindor 1931, pp. 171–203, with his register of known sculptors on pp. 174–188, and on sculptors see too Fittschen 2008.
[61] Day 1942, pp. 203–206, citing sources.

Festivals continued to be held, of which the Mysteries were the most important.[62] Choregic dedications—albeit surviving in fragments—to victorious dithyrambic choruses at the Great Dionysia attest to the continuing popularity of that festival, and give us valuable information on the winners, chronology, and personnel involved from the fifth century BC to the imperial period.[63] The Panathenaea had seen declining numbers of foreign athletes for some time, but most likely under Claudius it expanded into an imperial festival honoring the emperor, the *Kaisareia Sebasta* (see below). At the same time, although the Romans inserted themselves into this prestigious event they still had to recognize Athenian traditions, as a large helmeted head from a Roman statue of Athena of the mid-first century AD, found in fragments in the Agora and on the Pnyx, nicely tells us.[64] Finally, the imperial cult gained traction and was firmly rooted in the city by the reign of Nero.[65]

Paul the Apostle and Other Visitors

Many prominent individuals went to Athens in the first century AD.[66] They included the biographer Plutarch; he was born and raised in Chaeronea, but always saw Athens as the center of a literary world, even though he preferred to live in his smaller (and less expensive) hometown.[67] His lives of famous Greeks and Romans are valuable sources for their times, even though he was less interested in historical veracity and more in the characters and lifestyles of his subjects.[68] Plutarch studied philosophy under Ammonius, a follower of Plato and also a three-term hoplite general, and wrote a biography of him that is lost to us.[69] He had several friends in the city, including Julius Antiochus Philopappus, whose enormous funerary monument atop

---

[62] Day 1942, p. 183; Graindor 1931, pp. 101–105; Geagan 1979a, p. 385.
[63] See, for example, Follet and Peppas-Delmousou 2001.
[64] Ajootian 2009.
[65] Kantiréa 2001. Imperial cult between Augustus and Hadrian: Geagan 1979a, pp. 386–387.
[66] Graindor 1931, pp. 29–58; Geagan 1979a, pp. 387–388.
[67] Graindor 1931, pp. 53–54; Swain 1997. Plutarch's living in Chaeronea as opposed to a bigger city: Titchener 2002.
[68] See, for example, Duff 1999; Pelling 2002; cf. Pelling 1988, pp. 10–18 and 26–36 (on Plutarch's *Antony*, but the comments on treatment of sources and method are relevant to Plutarch's works as a whole).
[69] Graindor 1931, pp. 150–152.

the Museum Hill could be clearly seen from the Acropolis (see chapter 14). Another was the stoic poet Sarapion of Melite, for whose victory as *choregos* at the Dionysia Plutarch wrote a celebratory dialogue.[70] Sarapion perhaps changed his name to reflect his association with the Egyptian deity Sarapis, whom we discussed in chapter 9.

The first century AD was also the era of the historical development of Christianity. Here, Athens' most famous visitor was the apostle Paul.[71] He had arrived in Macedonia at the end of the forties, where he was assaulted and imprisoned in Philippi and suffered further hostility at Thessalonica and Beroea.[72] He travelled to Athens, perhaps arriving in the city in AD 51, but certainly during the reign of Claudius.[73] There he was shocked and alarmed at the number of idols he saw, hardly a surprise for a city with its centuries of diverse religious traditions and, more recently, emperor cults. In fact, the portrayal of Athens in *Acts* during the era of Paul's visit gives us a vivid insight into how the city was seen by Christians—as has been well pointed out, "this city of Greek culture *par excellence*, is in the perspective of *Acts* the city of idolatry and of a reproachable longing for things that are new."[74]

After addressing the Jews in the city, he started preaching to non-Jews in the Agora, an obvious environment to reach the largest number of people going about their business. His message about the resurrection of Jesus and the danger of worshipping false divinities led to him being ordered to appear before the Council of the Areopagus on its rocky setting (see Figure 3.1). There he delivered his famous sermon (recounted in *Acts* 17:16–34) in which he condemned pagan worship, and proclaimed the need to worship the one true God, that idols of gold, silver, and stone were objects of false worship, the belief in the resurrection, and the promise of salvation.[75]

---

[70] [Plutarch], *Moralia* 628a and following. Victory monument: Geagan 2011, C187, pp. 104–107 (with H377, pp. 202–203, on its later rededication); Sarapion: C. P. Jones 1971, pp. 13–19; C. P. Jones 1978, pp. 228–231. Sarapion's victory must predate AD 116–118 when Philopappus, who is mentioned in the choregic dedication, died; possibly the victory was in AD 87/8, when Philopappus himself was an *agonothetes*: Geagan 1991; Kapetanopoulos 1994.
[71] Graindor 1931, pp. 116–129.
[72] Clarke 1996, pp. 858–859.
[73] Graindor 1931, p. 125.
[74] Den Heijer forthcoming, section 7.2.1, and see further his sections 7.2.1–7.2.3.
[75] Graindor 1931, pp. 120–124; Geagan 1967, p. 50; Barnes 1969; Clarke 1996, pp. 859–860.

Although some members of the Areopagus condemned Paul's beliefs, others seem to have been genuinely interested in them, including a certain Dionysius the Areopagite, who may have converted to Christianity. The lack of unanimity among the members of the Areopagus presumably explains why the council made no move against Paul and he could leave the hill without standing trial.[76]

Today an engraved plaque at the foot of the Areopagus contains Paul's sermon. In 1990 Pope John Paul II likened the modern "world of communications" and its impact on the youth to a "New Areopagus," where "the Christian message and the Church's authentic teaching" could be explained and defended.[77] Another example of the ancient world informing the modern.

Individual Emperors and Athens

We have so far treated the three dynasties and their backgrounds thematically, but now we should say something about the Athenians' specific dealings with individual emperors.

Tiberius

Tiberius' time on Rhodes before he became emperor had given him experience of living in the east, and it has been suggested that while he was there he may have "called in" on Athens.[78] On his accession in AD 14 the Athenian ephebes held a festival to him.[79] The people also set up several statues to him, including six before he became emperor and three that we know of after he assumed control.[80] One of these, a large bronze one in front of the Stoa of Attalus II (originally dedicated to Attalus to thank him for the Stoa), they likely erected early in his reign when he was still popular.[81] The base has on it the epithet *theos* (god), which may indicate the Athenians worshipped

---

[76] Den Heijer 0000, section 7.2.2.
[77] *Redemptoris Missio*, December 7, 1990, chapter 4, 37 (c).
[78] Geagan 1979a, p. 384; cf. Graindor 1927a, p. 50.
[79] Graindor 1931, pp. 2–5.
[80] Graindor 1927a, pp. 4–6; Graindor 1931, pp. 102 and 113–116; Geagan 1979a, p. 386; T. L. Shear 1981, p. 363. Before emperor: *IG* ii² 3254, 3243 (= Geagan 2011, H252, pp. 146–147), 3244, 3245, 3246, 3247; after: *IG* ii² 3262, 3264, with Geagan 1984, p. 70.
[81] *IG* ii² 4209 (= Geagan 2011, H253, p. 147), with Vanderpool 1959; Schmalz 2009, pp. 105–106.

him, even though, like Augustus, he always politely refused the honor if he could.[82]

Perhaps also in an effort to ingratiate themselves with Tiberius, the Athenians dedicated a statue to Augustus' wife Livia, just east of the Metroon in the Agora, since its base refers to her as "Julia Augusta," a title she took in AD 14, and even a shrine to her.[83] A cult to Tiberius and Livia may have been housed in the small two-room structure behind the Stoa of Zeus Eleutherius in the Agora; if so, then perhaps there is credence to the view that "Tiberius dominated the Agora while Augustus and Rome held sway on the Acropolis."[84] The Athenians also set up a statue of Drusus Caesar (son of Tiberius), dubbing him "the new Ares," as they had done Gaius in AD 2 (p. 258).[85]

In AD 18 Athens received the Roman general and consul Germanicus Caesar (adopted son and heir of Tiberius), en route to his command in Asia.[86] The visit is significant as Germanicus was accompanied by only one lictor, out of respect, according to Tacitus, for the "time-honored" alliance (*foedus*) between Athens and Rome, which had likely been formed after the Second Macedonian War, perhaps in 191 (p. 163).[87] His visit spawned the ephebic games called the *Germanikeia*, which continued to be held annually after his death in the same year.[88]

Caligula

Altars and statues were set up to Caligula, with one in the Agora supervised by the priest of Apollo Patroos and the imperial family.[89] Interestingly, the

---

[82] Cf. Tacitus, *Annals* 4.37; see Sherk 1988, no. 31, p. 57, for a letter declining honors in Gytheion (Laconia).

[83] Schmalz 2009, p. 107 (arguing for the restoration of Hestia instead of Artemis Boulaea as Livia's cult title); see too Graindor 1927a, pp. 153–157; J. H. Oliver 1965a; Thompson and Wycherley 1972, p. 166; T. L. Shear 1981, pp. 363 and 364.

[84] Clinton 1997, pp. 168–169 (quote on p. 168); cult of Tiberius also at Eleusis: Clinton 1997, p. 167.

[85] Graindor 1927a, p. 50.

[86] Graindor 1931, pp. 5–7; D. Kienast 1993, pp. 204–205; Perrin-Saminadayar 2007c, pp. 131–133.

[87] Tacitus, *Annals* 2.53.3.

[88] Graindor 1931, p. 6; Follet 1976, pp. 321–322; Geagan 1979a, p. 384.

[89] Schmalz 2009, pp. 110–111 (arguing it was not Neronian, as is commonly thought, as by then the city's imperial cult was no longer associated with Apollo Patroos).

Athenians had a statue to Caligula's sister Drusilla as "the new goddess Aphrodite" in the Agora, as well as one of both of them on the Acropolis.[90] Two statue bases might be connected to a cult of the emperor, although no official cult is known.[91] Caligula was generally well disposed to Athens, but the Athenians had little time for him, especially as he had seized artworks from the city. His short reign is perhaps also a reason why contacts between the city and emperor were minimal.

Claudius

The Athenians held Claudius in esteem, despite his apparent wish to move the Mysteries to Rome (or perhaps establish some Roman variation of it there). The bases for eight statues of him in Athens are preserved, with five from his first two years as emperor.[92] One of these was of him as Apollo Patroos (the divine ancestor of the Athenians), set up in the Agora probably soon after AD 41/2.[93] Several refer to him as "savior and benefactor."[94] The titles display his generosity in returning statues seized on Caligula's orders, and he may also have initiated building projects in the city and helped it with its grain supply—since under him a *curator annonae* (official in charge of the grain supply) appears at Corinth, Claudius would surely not have neglected Athens' problems with grain procurement.[95] Claudius was the most liked emperor before Hadrian, yet curiously his name is not found on any altar in the city.[96]

At some point in his reign, and in keeping with honors to the imperial family, the Athenians set up a dedicatory inscription to Livia (as *thea* or

---

[90] Schmalz 2009, pp. 111–113; Geagan 2011, H257, p. 149. A fragment of a statue to an emperor, probably Caligula, who suffered a *damnatio*: Geagan 2011, H256, pp. 148–149; cf. Follet 1976, p. 60.

[91] *IG* ii² 3266, 3277.

[92] *IG* ii² 3268, 3269, 3270 (AD 41), 3271, 3272 (AD 42), 3273, 3274, 3276 (not dateable to actual years); Geagan 1984, p. 70.

[93] *IG* ii² 3274 (= Geagan 2011, H258, pp. 149–150), with Graindor 1931, pp. 11 and 114; T. L. Shear 1981, p. 363; Schmalz 2009, pp. 119–120.

[94] *IG* ii² 5173–5179, with Geagan 2011, C214, p. 126; see too Graindor 1931, pp. 9–10; Day 1942, p. 179; Raubitschek 1966, pp. 246–247 and n. 22; Geagan 1979a, p. 384; T. L. Shear 1981, p. 367.

[95] Return of statues: Dio 60.6.8; monument: Geagan 2011, C214, p. 126; see too Geagan 1979b; Geagan 1984, p. 71; Levick 1996, p. 666; cf. Perrin-Saminadayar 2007c, p. 142.

[96] Geagan 1984, p. 73.

goddess) and rededicated to her the fifth-century BC temple of Nemesis at Rhamnus (in northeast Attica).[97] There is a belief that the dedication dates to Augustus' time, which would mean the Athenians had deified her long before the Romans did (in AD 41).[98] However, given the Athenians' pattern of honoring new emperors and members of the imperial family at the start of a reign, it is more likely that the Rhamnus dedication was in the Claudian era. The Athenians may also have been behind a cult to Claudius at Eleusis.[99]

It was probably under Claudius that the cult of Roma and Augustus at Athens was converted to the collective one of the *Sebastoi*, its focal point likely the temple of Roma and Augustus (see Figures 14.2A–B).[100] The conversion must postdate AD 45/6 as the cult of Roma and Augustus still had its own priest then.[101] The high priest of the *Sebastoi*, a lifelong position, was considered superior to the Eleusinian priesthoods, which were seen as a stepping-stone to the imperial cult.[102] The position also underscored the mixing of religion and politics, for only men who previously had held one of the three highest state offices (eponymous archon, hoplite general, or herald of the Areopagus) were eligible for it. Possibly the cult may date to the Neronian era, for Novius (whom we met earlier) seems to have been its organizer and first high priest in AD 61, for which he was honored with a statue at Eleusis.[103]

Novius himself was busy in Athens during the Claudian period. He likely oversaw the construction of a marble stairway to the Propylaea (discussed in chapter 14) and expanded the Panathenaic festival into the *Kaisareia Sebasta*; this may have been in AD 41, as in that year (as the festival's first *agonothetes*) he dedicated a statue to the

---

[97] *IG* ii² 3242, with Lozano 2004 on the date and importance of the inscription; cf. T. L. Shear 1981, pp. 367–368; Spawforth 1997, p. 194; Hendrick 2006, chapter 5, pp. 111–116; Schmalz 2009, pp. 103–105.

[98] Livia on Athenian inscriptions as "plain" Livia and the significance of *thea* in her name at Eleusis for dating: Lozano 2004, pp. 178–179.

[99] Clinton 1997, pp. 170–171 (or possibly Nero).

[100] Graindor 1931, p. 11 (with pp. 113–116 on the imperial cult); Baldassari 1995a; Spawforth 1997.

[101] *IG* ii² 3242.

[102] Camia 2014.

[103] Graindor 1931, pp. 13 and 142–143; Clinton 1997, pp. 170 and 171–172; Spawforth 1997; Kantiréa 2001, pp. 58–59.

new emperor Claudius.¹⁰⁴ Also in AD 41/2 or 42/3 he was supervisor of a public building project, possibly the restoration and rededication to Claudius of the monument of Attalus II on the Acropolis.¹⁰⁵ Finally, in AD 44/5 (archonship of Antipater of Phlya) he served as gymnasiarch, in which year the ephebic *Germanikeia* games were held.

Nero

Only five altars to Nero are known (two of which were reinscribed ones to Augustus); on two, which may be dated between AD 60 and 68, he is called the "new Apollo" (an interesting affinity with Augustus), and possibly also on two others if that restoration is correct.¹⁰⁶ In the eighth hoplite generalship of Novius, so AD 61/62 (archonship of Thrasyllus), the Areopagus, the Boule, and the people set up a dedication in Nero's honor in bronze letters on the architrave of the Parthenon no less. Originally thought to be part of the Parthenon's rededication to Nero, the inscription is more likely to be for his Armenian wars.¹⁰⁷ The emperor's avoidance of Athens when in Greece (discussed earlier) would account for no more altars to him, as would the Senate's damnation of his memory on his death, which resulted in the Athenians erasing the Parthenon dedication.¹⁰⁸

In addition to snubbing Athens on his trip to Greece, Nero's unpopularity may also stem from ordering, in AD 64, his agents to seize offerings and statues of the gods from the temples of Achaea and Asia, causing one ancient writer to claim hyperbolically that he seized most of those in Athens and Pergamum.¹⁰⁹ One of these agents was Gaius Carrinas Secundus, surely the same man referred to as eponymous archon in an Athenian dedicatory inscription, suggesting that the people resorted to this flattery so he would remove fewer artworks than originally intended.¹¹⁰ Their attempt mirrors their practice of

---

¹⁰⁴ *IG* ii² 3270, with Schmalz 2009, pp. 115–116; cf. Graindor 1931, pp. 141–143; Follet 1976, pp. 331–333; Geagan 1979c, pp. 281–282; Spawforth 1997, pp. 189–191; Ajootian 2009, p. 495.
¹⁰⁵ *IG* ii² 3272, with Schmalz 2009, pp. 117–119.
¹⁰⁶ Schmalz 2009, pp. 121–124; see too Graindor 1931, pp. 114–115; Geagan 1984, pp. 73–74 and 76; Geagan 2011, H 283, pp. 159–160; cf. Perrin-Saminadayar 2007c, pp. 138–139.
¹⁰⁷ *IG* ii² 3277 (= Sherk 1988, no. 78, p. 115), with Schmalz 2009, pp. 124–125; cf. for example Graindor 1931, pp. 12–13 (rededication of Parthenon).
¹⁰⁸ Hoët-van Cauwenberghe 2007; cf. pp. 228–234 on Athens.
¹⁰⁹ Dio of Prusa 31.148–149 (= Sherk 1988, no. 75, p. 114).
¹¹⁰ Graindor 1931, pp. 15–16; Day 1942, p. 180; Geagan 1979a, p. 384; Levick 1996, p. 665.

rededicating important earlier Greek statues to Romans in an effort to keep them in the city and protect the artistic heritage (pp. 297–298).

Vespasian and Titus

Like Tiberius, Vespasian may have stopped off in Greece on his way back to Italy as emperor after the chaos following Nero's assassination. There is no evidence he went to Athens other than an early altar to him adding his cognomen (an additional personal name) to the formula of Augustus to show a continuity of rule.[111] Vespasian and Titus were not interested in Athens, nor were the Athenians in them, as their practice of rededicating altars shows: an altar originally to Augustus and rededicated to Nero had his name erased and was reused for Vespasian, and then for Titus.[112] Whether the people actively worshipped these two emperors is unknown, but no high priest of them in the city occurs in any extant source.[113]

We noted earlier that in AD 70 Vespasian restored the province of Achaea, which Nero had freed. He also interfered in the philosophical schools of Athens. A clash had been growing between Roman administrators and philosophers who hearkened back to the likes of Aristotle and Theophrastus in the fourth century BC on the best constitution for the city and how to establish it.[114] Philosophers had been vocal in public affairs since the Classical era, and in the time of Mithridates they usually sided against those who were pro-Roman—thus the envoy who urged the Athenians to support Mithridates VI in his war against Rome was the Aristotelian philosopher Athenion, who was belittled by the stoic philosopher and historian Posidonius (pp. 203–204 and 206).

Vespasian saw the philosophical schools as crossing the line into the political arena, and decided to do something about it, perhaps before they began to criticize him.[115] He introduced a system whereby the heads of the four philosophical schools—Platonists, Aristotelians, Stoics, and Epicureans—had to be Roman citizens and to submit a testament, written in Latin, as to why they were the right men for the job. His measure reined in the schools by controlling any political activity and altered eligibility for headship in

---

[111] Geagan 1984, pp. 70 and 74–75.
[112] Augustus (*IG* ii² 3229); Vespasian (*IG* ii² 3281); Titus (*IG* ii² 3282): Geagan 1984, p. 74.
[113] Geagan 1979a, p. 387.
[114] J. H. Oliver 1981b, p. 418; on the philosophers, cf. Graindor 1931, pp. 150–157.
[115] J. H. Oliver 1981b, p. 418.

the emperor's favor—the first head under the new system was Titus Flavius Menander, who bore the emperor's *nomen*, a sign that the emperor wanted him for the headship and so sponsored him for citizenship.[116] This system remained unchanged until Hadrian in AD 121 (pp. 323–324).

Domitian

Domitian did not visit Athens, but he was the first reigning emperor to serve as eponymous archon, sometime between AD 84/5 and 92/3.[117] In taking that office he may have wanted to show he held the city in more esteem than his immediate predecessors. On an ephebic decree he is identified with Zeus Eleutherius, and a statue of him, of unknown date, stood on a reused base.[118] Domitian patronized some building projects and sent an imperial freedman named Antiochus to oversee them.[119]

Domitian is usually condemned in our literary sources (Tacitus and Suetonius especially) for his cruelty and venality. That image may not be fully historical, but an example of his ruthlessness and greed is the fate of Tiberius Claudius Hipparchus of Marathon, grandfather of the famous sophist and multimillionaire of the second-century Herodes Atticus (on whom see p. 334).[120] Hipparchus had begun a civic career perhaps under Claudius; he had been a hoplite general and eponymous archon, and by Domitian's time he was imperial high priest and priest of Apollo Pythios, and had briefly revised the Augustan-era *Dodekais* processions to Delphi, initiated by his grandfather Eucles. He was also very wealthy, with landholdings apparently valued at 100 million sesterces.[121] His wealth was eyed greedily by Domitian, who callously had Hipparchus executed for "aspiring to tyranny" and confiscated his lands for the *fiscus* (the emperor's personal treasury).[122]

---

[116] Cf. J. H. Oliver 1979; J. H. Oliver 1982, pp. 69–70.
[117] Graindor 1931, pp. 18–19; Geagan 1979a, p. 384; J. H. Oliver 1981b, p. 418; D. Kienast 1993, p. 206; Perrin-Saminadayar 2007c, pp. 142–143.
[118] *IG* ii² 3283b, with Graindor 1931, p. 115; Geagan 1984, p. 70.
[119] Geagan 1979a, p. 384; cf. J. H. Oliver 1941, pp. 243–244; J. H. Oliver 1963, p. 87.
[120] Schmalz 2009, pp. 266–268; see too Follet 2007.
[121] Day 1942, p. 242.
[122] Graindor 1931, pp. 19–22 and 24; Graindor 1934, p. 191; Day 1947, p. 231; Griffin 2000a, pp. 77–78.

In Domitian's time a man named Quintus Trebellius Rufus of Tolsa in Gallia Narbonensis (now Toulouse in southern France), who had been a high priest of the emperor in his hometown, became the first Roman knight (*eques*) to accept the Athenian citizenship. He was also archon, between AD 85/6 and 94/5, and he, his wife, and son were honored with a statue.[123]

Nerva and Trajan

We would know nothing about Nerva and Athens except for an anecdote in the Greek sophist Philostratus about Atticus, the son of the Hipparchus whose lands Domitian had confiscated after he had had him executed (discussed earlier).[124] Atticus had bought a house and claimed to have discovered treasure in it. Remembering how his father had been brutally hounded for his money, Atticus told the new emperor, Nerva, who was a very different person from his predecessor. He allowed Atticus to keep the money and even told him to enjoy his good fortune. Nerva was not the only ruler to be critical of Domitian's action against Hipparchus, for at some point before AD 126/7 Hadrian enacted a law regulating the sale of olive oil, in which Hipparchus' estates are referred to as being "plundered by the *fiscus*."[125] It is hard to imagine that Atticus was simply lucky to have bought a house that happened to have hidden riches; more plausibly, Hipparchus was able to bury a substantial amount of money in a house that he instructed his son to buy, and then to wait for a change in emperors.[126] Atticus was thus able to restore his family's fortune; he married well, nearly doubling his wealth, and his son Herodes Atticus became one of Athens' greatest benefactors.[127]

Trajan went to Athens once as emperor, probably in AD 113 en route to the east. Three statues were set up to him in the Agora between his accession and his Dacian triumph in 102 (which led to the erection of the famous Trajan's Column in Rome).[128] Another one found on the Acropolis

---

[123] Statue: Geagan 2011, H398, pp. 216–219, with Graindor 1931, p. 144; Geagan 1979a, p. 387; J. H. Oliver 1981b, p. 417; Pailler 1988, especially pp. 100–101.
[124] Philostratus, *Lives of Sophists* 548.
[125] *IG* ii² 1100, lines 4–5 and 30.
[126] Although Day 1942, pp. 242–243, gives the story credence.
[127] Graindor 1931, pp. 22–25 and 138–141; cf. Follet 2007.
[128] Sherk 1988, no. 120, pp. 161–163, with Geagan 1984, p. 71. Dacian Wars: Griffin 2000b, pp. 109–113.

has *invictus* (undefeated) on its base, suggesting it should be associated with the visit, and also the word *theos*, although we do not know if he was worshipped as a god.[129] So few statues of an emperor who actually visited the city is at first sight surprising, yet overall only a few dedications have been found to him throughout the east, despite his various travels there.[130]

Athens' influence and even reputation declined as the first century progressed. Nevertheless, its new life was still positively summed up by Aelius Aristides, who in the mid- to later first century AD wrote that the city was enjoying "the place of honor in the whole Greek world, and has so fared that one could not wish for her the old circumstances instead of the present."[131] Then under the emperor with whom we finish this book, Hadrian, the city was catapulted once more to greatness in the Greek world.

---

[129] *IG* ii² 3284; Geagan 2011, H260, p. 150, with Geagan 1984, p. 77.
[130] Of these only 51 can be dated: Højte 2000, p. 228.
[131] Aelius Aristides, *Panathenaecus* 234.

14

Building a New Horizon?

FROM THE LATTER HALF OF the first century BC, increasing Roman involvement in Athens was evident in the numbers of Romans visiting, studying, and living there (some, like Antony, happening to be rulers at the same time), and especially in terms of building activities. Roman rule affected Athens in far greater ways than Macedonian control had; literally the most obvious was in the building projects funded by Rome, to be discussed in this chapter. These have been taken together to trace the steps by which Athens over the years turned into a provincial city, seemingly defined by the inscription on Hadrian's Arch proclaiming Athens to be the city of that emperor and Theseus (p. 327). But the extent to which Roman architecture altered Athens as a city should not be exaggerated, nor should we neglect how the artistic and intellectual interchanges affected the Romans.

Still the City of Theseus

It cannot be argued that Roman architecture brought about changes to the physical presence of the city. Augustus undertook extensive building projects throughout Greece, at Olympia, Sparta, and Messene, for example, which would not be matched until Hadrian over a century later.[1] At Athens,

---

[1] Spawforth 2012, pp. 159–168, especially pp. 207–232 and 382–383; cf. Alcock 1993, p. 93; see her chapter (pp. 93–128) on the civic landscape of Roman Greece, namely the interaction of town and countryside, with emphasis on nucleation (living in more populous towns as opposed to more isolated rural ones).

Augustus' substantial patronage saw the completion of the Roman Agora, the construction of the temple to Roma and Augustus, and the restoration of several buildings, while Agrippa (Augustus' son-in-law) was responsible for an enormous Odeum (theater) in the Agora.[2] All of this construction (which incidentally provided jobs and so for that reason would have been embraced) was meant to denote a new phase in the urban planning and architecture of the city as the Athenians carried out public works (even if funded by Rome), bringing into the city a distinctive Roman stamp.[3]

Yet let us not forget that Athens was the largest city in Greece, sprawling out to its fortification walls for quite some distance, and it had monuments all over it—the vast majority stretching back to the Classical era. Although some city demes (what we might call suburbs today) were only a few minutes' walk from the Acropolis or Agora, others were farther away—to walk to the far end of Ceramicus, takes about twenty minutes today, and the Piraeus was considerably farther. We should not imagine that even with the extensive building programs of Augustus and Hadrian, the city skyline was suddenly transformed into a Roman vista. The Parthenon and the Erechtheum dwarfed their neighbor, the temple of Roma and Augustus, for example, and although the sheer size of the Odeum of Agrippa in the Athenian Agora made it impossible to miss, it still had Corinthian façades and capitals to allow some blending in of Greek styles—and likewise the mammoth temple of Olympian Zeus with its Corinthian capitals. Even the amount of construction associated with Hadrian, not least the completion of the temple of Olympian Zeus, could not have prohibited anyone from appreciating how the Classical monuments on the Acropolis dominated all views (as they do today).

It is these uniquely Athenian buildings, as well as the Greek architectural influences in Roman ones, that show us how the Greeks and not just the Athenians strove to retain their identity, but only in the literary, cultural, and artistic areas that the Romans were now commandeering and defining.[4] At the end of the day, everything was on Roman terms.

---

[2] See the summary at Geagan 1979a, pp. 379–381, with Graindor 1927a, pp. 173–245; Day 1942, pp. 139–142; Thompson and Wycherley 1972, pp. 160–168; T. L. Shear 1981, pp. 359–362; Kleiner 1986, pp. 8–10; Hoff 1989b; Mango 2010, pp. 129–138; Rödel 2010, pp. 102–110; Borg 2011, pp. 219–224; cf. Schmalz 1994. On the architects and other specialists used on the constructions, see Burden 1999.

[3] Stefanidou-Tiveriou 2008, pp. 27–28, and passim.

[4] Cf. the essays in Schmitz and Wiater 2011, especially that by Borg 2011 on this point.

FIGURE 14.1A Roman Agora (toward Gate). Photo: Ian Worthington.

Augustus and the Roman Agora

Work on the Roman Agora had progressed slowly since Caesar's time; probably by the Augustan era his money had run out, and with no new infusion of money in the interim work had stopped.[5] Then in 19, Augustus was returning to Italy after successfully retrieving the Roman legionary standards lost by Crassus at the battle of Carrhae in 53, and stopped off in Athens. The tension existing between emperor and city in 21 had been resolved by now, perhaps thanks to the diplomatic intervention of Herod (pp. 251–252), so he now pledged money to complete the Roman Agora (Figures 14.1A–B, and see too Figure 12.3 for the monumental gateway).[6]

The Roman Agora was nowhere near as extensive as the Athenian one, as its ruins demonstrate. But from the monumental gateway from the west to its end, it was impressive, with its buildings and colonnades decked out

---

[5] Day 1942, p. 141.
[6] Hoff 1988; Hoff 1989b, pp. 3–5; Hoff 1992, p. 231. Market: Graindor 1927a, pp. 184–198; Thompson and Wycherley 1972, pp. 170–173; T. L. Shear 1981, pp. 360–361; H. A. Thompson 1987, pp. 4–6; Hoff 1988; Hoff 1989b; Stefanidou-Tiveriou 2008, pp. 15–19; Rödel 2010; pp. 102–103; Sourlas 2012; see too Schmalz 1994.

FIGURE 14.1B Roman Agora (toward Tower of the Winds and Agoranomion). Photo: Ian Worthington.

in marble. The inscription on the architrave of its massive gateway (see Figure 12.3) tells us that it was dedicated to Athena Archegetis ("Founder") in the archonship of Nicias (perhaps 10/9), when the hoplite general Eucles (son of the Herodes who had been given money by Caesar in 51) had approached Augustus for financial help.[7] Eucles' success was probably also due to his being priest of Apollo Pythios, given Augustus' close association with that god. The new agora had a Greek architectural design, but there was no mistaking Roman influence. Further, the addition (perhaps later) of a statue of Lucius Caesar atop its gate effectively turned a "traditional" gate into a Roman triumphal arch.[8]

---

[7] IG ii³ 4, 12, with Schmalz 2009, pp. 79–80 (preferring 25 BC). Eucles: Graindor 1927a, p. 32; Day 1942, p. 137; Hoff 1989b, pp. 3–5. Hoff 1996, p. 192, on an earlier date in the 20s, even after Actium, but see Graindor 1927a, p. 32; Schmalz 2009, p. 80. Inauguration: Graindor 1927a, p. 32; Day 1942, pp. 130–131. Oikonomides 1979, p. 101 n. 13, believes that the Market had nothing to do with Caesar or Augustus but rich Athenians paid for it, given that there is no mention of it in the *Res Gestae* (in which Augustus recorded donations to many other cities); still, this is unfounded.

[8] Graindor 1927a, pp. 51–53 and 189; Bowersock 2002, p. 7; Borg 2011, p. 219.

The Temple of Roma and Augustus

In front of the Parthenon on the Acropolis was the temple of the goddess Roma and Augustus (Figures 14.2A–B).[9] It was a *monopteros* or circular structure, consisting of nine Ionic columns of white Pentelic marble, without walls, roughly eight meters in diameter and perhaps nine high, with a conical roof of marble. Its small size made it more of a shrine than a temple.[10] In it were statues of Augustus and perhaps other members of the imperial family, as well as the goddess Roma, and most likely it housed the imperial cult, given that temples, like altars, were part and parcel of emperor worship. Interestingly, no literary source mentions this important building, so were it not for the dedicatory inscription (Figure 14.2B), the few fragments of it on the Acropolis would be a mystery.

When the temple was dedicated is a matter of conjecture. Its inscription uses *Sebastos*, the Greek equivalent of Augustus, so it must postdate 27.[11] We can narrow the date further on two grounds. First, there is a reference in the inscription to the influential hoplite general and priest of the goddess Roma and Augustus *Soter* on the Acropolis, Pammenes of Marathon. His family had moved from Marathon to Delos some generations earlier, made its money on the island (like many families), and returned to Athens, where it played an influential role in political and religious affairs; Pammenes' hoplite generalship was in the period 27–18.[12] Second, the archon is named as Areus; since we know the names of the archons from 17 to 11, the temple must have been dedicated in the period 27–18 (to align with Pammenes) or after 11. On balance, and perhaps in tandem with the Roman Agora, a date of 19/18 may be advanced.[13]

---

[9] Graindor 1927a, pp. 30–31, 97–100, and 180–184; Geagan 1979a, pp. 382–383; T. L. Shear 1981, p. 363; Spawforth 1997, pp. 186–188; Bowersock 2002, pp. 8–9; Hoff 2013, pp. 573–574. Temple: Binder 1969 (though his location of it opposite the Erechtheum is doubtful); Baldassari 1995b; Kajava 2001, pp. 80–83; Whittaker 2002; Fecchi 2004; Stefanidou-Tiveriou 2008, pp. 21–23 (with comments on its shape); Dally 2008; Rödel 2010, pp. 106–107; Fouquet 2012.

[10] Kleiner 1986, p. 9.

[11] *IG* ii³ 4, 10: *Sebastos* was added over the word *Soter* (Savior), which the letter cutter erased.

[12] Geagan 1992, with Geagan 2011, H347, p. 189; Pammenes' background in other cults: Baslez 2004, p. 107. The reference to "on the Acropolis" shows there was another priest of Augustus in the lower city: Kajava 2001, p. 80 with n. 40.

[13] Schmalz 2009, pp. 80–82; see too Hoff 1989b, p. 60; Baldassari 1995a, p. 73; cf. Whittaker 2002, pp. 26–27 and 32; for 27: Graindor 1927a, pp. 30–31. At the same time, we should not exclude the possibility of a date after 11 BC, perhaps even as late as AD 2, with the visit of Gaius Caesar to Athens: Baldassari 1995a, pp. 80–83; Whittaker 2002, pp. 33–36; see below on the visit.

FIGURE 14.2A Temple of Roma and Augustus. Photo: Ian Worthington.

FIGURE 14.2B Temple of Roma and Augustus (featuring inscription). Photo: Ian Worthington.

The Parthenon dwarfed the temple, as the illustrations show, even though we would think there would have been room to build a larger one to Roma and Augustus. Still, location was everything. Because it was built on so sacred and symbolic an area as the Acropolis, immediately neighboring the Parthenon, the ruined temple to Athena Polias (destroyed by the Persians in 480), and the Erechtheum (dedicated to Athena and Poseidon, supposedly the burial place of the first mythical king of Athens, Erechtheus), all visitors to the Acropolis would have seen it.[14] Likewise, three centuries earlier all visitors to the sacred grove at Olympia would have seen the round Philippeum of Philip II, which he built to acknowledge his victory over the Greeks at Chaeronea and house statues of himself and members of his family. The propaganda effect of both buildings emphasized the mastery of the respective rulers over Greece (though Philip was not worshipped).

Agrippa's Odeum

In around 15 another significant addition to Athens appeared when Agrippa built an Odeum (theater)—not in the Roman Agora but in the old Athenian one.[15] It was a massive building, with a seating capacity of one thousand, and "out of scale with the setting" (Figure 14.3).[16] Although it had Greek architectural elements to it (especially a Corinthian façade and capitals), the Odeum was based on a smaller theater at Pompeii (of 80–75), again showing the impact of Roman architects at work on a monument in Greece.[17] In a show of gratitude, the Athenians erected a statue of Agrippa in a chariot drawn by four horses, sited just west of the Propylaea; today only its base remains (see Figure 12.2). How genuine that gratitude was cannot be known, but the fact that they reused an earlier statue of Eumenes II and Attalus II

---

[14] Hoff 1996, pp. 185–194. The Acropolis as the sacred center of Athens: Krumeich and Witschel 2010a, pp. 1–53.
[15] Thompson and Wycherley 1972, pp. 111–114; Geagan 1979a, p. 380; H. A. Thompson 1987, pp. 6–9; Torelli 1995, pp. 27–29; Stefanidou-Tiveriou 2008, pp. 23–24; Mango 2010, p. 136; Rödel 2010, pp. 103–104; Spawforth 2012, pp. 59–86; Dickenson 2017, pp. 258–266. Spawforth 1997, pp. 186–188, believes the building of Agrippa's Odeum prompted that of the Temple to Roma and Augustus, but the date of 15 is awkward for the connection.
[16] T. L. Shear 1981, p. 361. The building was intended for dramatic performances but also for the more Roman practice of declamation: Spawforth 2012, pp. 72–79.
[17] Kleiner 1986, p. 9; H. A. Thompson 1987, p. 7. Odeum: Thompson and Wycherley 1972, pp. 111–114; T. L. Shear 1981, p. 361; H. A. Thompson 1987, pp. 6–9; Rödel 2010, pp. 103–104. On the building and its history: H. A. Thompson 1950.

FIGURE 14.3 Model of the Agora in the second century AD; view from the west, Odeum of Agrippa in the center. Athens, Agora Museum. akg-images/jh-Lightbox_Ltd./John Hios.

might have been for economic reasons or because they had no desire to pay for a brand-new one of Agrippa.

It had been centuries since the old Agora had seen a new building; even the stoas of the Attalids were carefully positioned along its borders so as not to affect the sorts of buildings, like the Bouleuterium, which were associated with democracy and the dispensation of justice.[18] Now the Roman Odeum seemed to dominate the open space of the center of civic life, just as the Roman temple to Roma and Augustus appeared in the very citadel and spiritual center of Athens. But the Odeum's location does not mean the old Agora suddenly stopped being a place for the citizenry to go about their

---

[18] T. L. Shear 1981, pp. 360–361; see too Thompson and Wycherley 1972, pp. 103–107 with plate 8, on the Attalid stoas.

business or to gather and talk about life and current affairs (which we will discuss later). Still, the city was turning into a different place.[19]

Wandering Temples and Reused Statues

The restoration of sanctuaries that the city undertook in the Augustan era may provide the context for another, uniquely Athenian, undertaking, the "wandering" (or "itinerant") temples and shrines.[20] At some point in this period several monuments were transplanted from the countryside to the Athenian Agora. Among these was a fifth-century temple, thought to have been that of Ares from his sanctuary at Acharnae, brought to honor the visit of Gaius Casar to the city in AD 2 (p. 258). But the temple in question was originally dedicated to Athena Pallenis at Pallene.[21] Each of its marble blocks was carefully lettered to aid reconstruction in its new home, with a roof made of marble taken apparently from the temple of Poseidon at Sunium.[22]

The temple was deliberately positioned in the Agora on the east–west axis of the square with the Odeum on the north–south axis, with an altar of Ares set up where their axes crossed, an axial design that Roman architects favored, and which linked the two buildings.[23] This does not mean that the initiative came from Agrippa, for there was nothing stopping the Athenians having this configuration.[24] Three other partially transplanted temples have been found around the periphery of the Athenian Agora; one seems to have been the temple of Athena at Sunium, another a temple (perhaps) from Thoricus, and the third is unknown; materials from other rural temples were used in other building projects in the city.[25]

---

[19] Agora: Dickenson 2015; Dickenson 2017.
[20] Thompson and Wycherley 1972, pp. 160–168; Geagan 1979a, pp. 380–381; T. L. Shear 1981, pp. 361–362 and 364; Alcock 1993, pp. 191–196.
[21] Ares: H. A. Thompson 1966, p. 183; Thompson and Wycherley 1972, p. 163; Borg 2011, p. 226; cf. Alcock 1996, p. 121. Identification: Geagan 1984, p. 76 (citing examples of other members of the imperial family). But see now T. L. Shear 2016, pp. 230–262, on the identification with Athena Pallenis—I owe this reference to Nigel Kennell.
[22] McAllister 1959; Thompson and Wycherley 1972, pp. 162–165; Dinsmoor Jr. 1974; H. A. Thompson 1987, pp. 6–9; Stefanidou-Tiveriou 2008, pp. 24–27; Mango 2010, pp. 132–136; Rödel 2010, pp. 104–105.
[23] T. L. Shear 1981, p. 362; H. A. Thompson 1987, pp. 6–9.
[24] Cf. Spawforth 1997, p. 187.
[25] T. L. Shear 1981, pp. 365–366; Walker 1997, pp. 71–72.

We do not know why these temples were moved, who was responsible for their relocation, and why the phenomenon was unique to Athens. One rather doubtful explanation is that as people moved from rural areas in Attica to the city they took some buildings with them—a substantial undertaking, and with no guarantee (we presume) of restoring them in the Agora.[26] Alternatively, there may be a connection with Augustus' exploitation of Greek art in an outdoor museum of sorts—his restoration policy at Rome included exhibiting looted artworks from Greece in temples, not just for their own beauty, but to link them to his moral reforms and make the center of Rome a sacred space.[27]

The thought of the Agora becoming an outdoor "museum" has been questioned because it signifies the area lost some of its vitality.[28] Surely not: for one thing, temples continued to function as centers of cult, attracting all and sundry, and for another, more monuments would have been an incentive for people to visit and see the sights. The corollary of this is that the relocation was good for Athenians who did not have to make the trip out to the original locations.[29] Thus, Augustus' policy may have spurred the Athenians to display artworks that had not been seized by Romans in fifth-century shrines in their own equivalent of a functioning outdoor museum.

Perhaps also the Athenian practice of rededicating earlier bronze statues to prominent Romans, to which we can now turn, also plays a role in the wandering monuments.[30] Reuse of statues took place throughout the Greek world, but the practice was different in Athens and linked to its association with Rome. Such refashioning began in earnest in the first century, when the Athenians rededicated the two colossal statues of Eumenes and Attalus to Mark Antony after he became master of Greece. Reworking existing ones was cheaper than casting from scratch, yet at the same time sculptors of the period were still crafting new honorary statues—one was

---

[26] Alcock 1993, pp. 193–196.
[27] Spawforth 2012, pp. 4–11 and passim; cf. Walker 1997, p. 72; Kleiner 1986, p. 9, also drawing attention to Agrippa's Pantheon in Rome, dedicated 25, with a caryatid porch by an Athenian sculptor named Diogenes, but see Borg 2011, pp. 224–226. Cf. Dickenson 2017, p. 279, on Athens capitalizing on its cultural heritage.
[28] Dickenson 2017, pp. 279–280.
[29] As J. Roisman pointed out to me.
[30] See in detail J. L. Shear 2007a; Krumeich 2010; with Keesling 2010 on the impact of reusing dedications on the Acropolis' "sculptural legacy." The practice of reusing dedications is also found in Macedonia: Sève 2004.

a descendant of the famous fourth-century master Praxiteles, also named Praxiteles, in the first century.[31]

Thus, the practice does not look like it arose purely for money-saving reasons. Possibly a number of Athenian artists had been killed in the Sullan sack, leading to a new tradition of reusing statues.[32] Yet even if there were a decline in sculptors, we would surely expect the trend to have been reversed by now, a half-century after Sulla took Athens. Indeed, this is a practice not just found in the first century; it continues into the late first century AD in the reign of Domitian.

The circumstances leading to reusing existing statues suggests that the people wanted to turn the Romans they honored into "virtual" Athenians to garner their favor and protection. They thus honored a Roman benefactor with the equivalent of a bronze "Old Master portrait," given that the greatest artists of Classical Athens had sculpted some of the reused statues, including Kritios and Nesiotes (who had sculpted the statue of Harmodius and Aristogeiton).[33] Certainly the idea of rewarding private benefactors with an Old Master portrait cannot be disregarded, nor should we ignore the possibility that the Athenians had their own agenda in doing so. But perhaps there is another, simpler explanation, linked to the itinerant temples: that the Athenians were protecting their artistic heritage. Acutely aware that at any time the Romans could pillage artworks as they saw fit, the Athenians hit on a way to keep some of their great ones.

In support is that the reused statues were dedicated on the sacred space of the Acropolis and deliberately identified the honorees with the original Athenian dedicatee. To give one example: the name L. Cassius, a consul in either AD 11 or 30, is carved onto the base of a statue dating to the 470s or 460s, sculpted by Kritios and Nesiotes; a man named Hegelochus, who may have fought against the Persians when they invaded Greece, had originally dedicated it to Athena.[34] Hegelochus' dedication showed his nobility and his patriotism in fighting for Greek freedom against the Persians; by replacing his name with that of Cassius on its base, the Athenians likewise portrayed him as a warrior, a patriot, and significantly like Hegelochus, a local who

---

[31] Keesling 2010, pp. 309–313.
[32] Palagia 2007.
[33] J. L. Shear 2007a, pp. 242–246; the analogy of Old Master portrait on p. 245. Shrine of the tyrannicides: Thompson and Wycherley 1972, pp. 155–160.
[34] J. L. Shear 2007a, pp. 235–238 and 242–243; Krumeich 2010, pp. 338–339; on sculptors, see Keesling 2010.

had dedicated to Athena Parthenos—hence his statue should remain on the Acropolis. Their act was deliberate flattery, then, for a pragmatic reason: to keep it on the Acropolis for all to see it. We encountered something similar in Nero's reign when the Athenians flatteringly made Carrinas archon, the very man the emperor had tasked to seize more of their artworks, in an effort to limit his plundering (pp. 281–282). The temples and reused statues may therefore be a way of keeping the Athenian cultural heritage alive.

From Tiberius to Hadrian

There was still building activity under the other Julio-Claudians, focused on the Acropolis and both Agoras, albeit not as prolific as in the Augustan and Hadrianic periods.[35] For example, in Claudius' reign a marble stairway to the Propylaea of the Acropolis was built, which the emperor may have funded, given its expense.[36] Another stairway around the mid-first century AD was built from the Athenian Agora to the temple of Hephaestus, this one funded by the Athenians and hence less costly, and in the same Agora the baths in the southwest corner were rebuilt, together with a public latrine.[37] Nero's reign also saw activity. Before AD 61, an unknown private individual rebuilt the theater of Dionysus, dedicating the *skene* to Dionysus Eleutherius, Nero, the Areopagus, the Boule, and the Demos.[38] More imposing was the Agoranomion, dedicated by a certain Hermogenes, son of Hermogenes of Gargettus, next to the Tower of the Winds in the Roman Agora (see Figure 14.1B). Exactly what the building was used for is unknown, but since it was dedicated to Athena Archegetis and the *Theoi Sebastoi*, it has been suggested that it was the home of the cult of the *Sebastoi* and perhaps even the headquarters of the market police.[39]

Nothing of great consequence was built under the Flavians, but the Nerva-Antonine era saw more activity. Of note is the benefaction of a certain Demetrius of Sphettus, possibly between AD 100 and 102, who paved the entranceway to the temple of Asclepius, on the south slope of the

---

[35] Graindor 1931, pp. 160–171; T. L. Shear 1981, pp. 363–373.
[36] Geagan 2011, C215, pp. 126–127; see too Graindor 1931, pp. 11 and 160–163; Day 1942, pp. 180–181; Geagan 1979a, p. 384; T. L. Shear 1981, p. 367 with n. 52; Levick 1996, p. 665.
[37] T. L. Shear 1981, p. 367.
[38] *IG* ii² 3182 (cf. Schmalz 2009, pp. 85–88), with Graindor 1931, pp. 13 and 164–166; Day 1942, p. 181; Geagan 1979a, p. 384; Geagan 1997, p. 26.
[39] See Hoff 1994; cf. Kantiréa 2001, p. 59.

Acropolis, in marble.[40] Grander was a library (complete with books) in the Athenian Agora dedicated (perhaps in the same period) by a non-Athenian, Titus Flavius Pantaenus (a priest of the Philosophical Muses and later archon), to Athena Polias, Trajan, and the city of Athens.[41] Commonly called the "Library of Pantaenus," the structure was more than a library as it included outer stoas and a peristyle (an open-colonnade area), and was only surpassed by the later Library of Hadrian (discussed below). The term "Priest of the Philosophical Muses" is not found in any other inscription, and so is the likely title of the librarian in the Trajanic period.[42]

In about AD 100 (during Trajan's reign) colonnaded streets—wide avenues often paved in marble with arches, stoas, and other monumental architecture flanking them—made their appearance in Athens, and were soon found in every provincial city.[43] Their design probably came from Syria, going back to Antioch-on-the-Orontes under Herod the Great at the end of the first century BC.[44] In Athens, one of the most beautiful streets had to have been the paved one leading to the Roman Agora, with a marble arch at the entrance and marble gracing the walls of buildings along its way.

The Philopappus Monument

Although not strictly a Roman construction, the Philopappus monument must be discussed here because of its fusion of Roman and Greek elements (Figure 14.4A).

At the top of the Museum Hill was built an elaborate funerary memorial of Gaius Julius Antiochus Philopappus of Commagene (a small prosperous kingdom in eastern Anatolia, founded in 165 and annexed by Rome in AD 72) sometime between AD 114 and 116 (hence late in Trajan's

---

[40] *IG* ii² 3187 (cf. Schmalz 2009, p. 91), with Graindor 1931, p. 164; Day 1942, pp. 181–182; dated slightly earlier by Geagan 1979a, p. 384.

[41] Geagan 2011, C217, pp. 127–128 (= Smallwood 1966, no. 395, p. 132), with Day 1942, p. 181; Thompson and Wycherley 1972, pp. 114–116; Geagan 1979a, p. 385; T. L. Shear 1981, pp. 370–371 (especially the comments in n. 62 in light of more recent excavations); Dickenson 2017, pp. 374; cf. Clinton 1974, p. 30. Pantaenus: Follet 1976, pp. 56–57; J. H. Oliver 1979.

[42] J. H. Oliver 1979, p. 158, also drawing attention to the "Philosophical Muses" in Plato, *Republic* 545d–548c.

[43] T. L. Shear 1981, pp. 368–370; Kleiner 1986, p. 9; Mango 2010, pp. 130–132; Rödel 2010, pp. 105–106, but note Thompson and Wycherley 1972, pp. 108–109.

[44] T. L. Shear 1981, pp. 371–372 (influence of the East on their architecture).

FIGURE 14.4A Philopappus Monument. Photo: Ian Worthington.

reign).[45] Philopappus was the grandson of Antiochus IV, the last ruler of Commagene, who had been a distinguished visitor to Athens probably in Tiberius' time; after the annexation of the kingdom, Vespasian allowed the ruling family to live in Rome.[46]

Philopappus was never a king, but he was referred to as one.[47] He moved from Rome to Athens, where he became a citizen, and between AD 75 and 87 served as archon and *agonothetes* of the Dionysia.[48] He befriended Trajan, who made him a senator (the first senator from Athens, even though he was not a native Athenian), and he was elected a Roman consul in AD 109.

---

[45] Graindor 1931, pp. 51–52 and 166–169; Geagan 1979a, p. 384. Full information on Commagene, Philopappus, and the monument: Kleiner 1983 (from which the following section is drawn) and Kleiner 1986, pp. 11–27. See too Baslez 1992; Steinhart 2003; cf. Perrin-Saminadayar 2007c, pp. 133–135. On the date, its inscription gives two of Trajan's titles he used after 114 (Germanicus and Dacicus) but not the third (Parthicus), which he received after 116.

[46] Graindor 1931, p. 47. On notable visitors to Athens: Graindor 1931, pp. 29–45.

[47] Smallwood 1966, no. 207, p. 78.

[48] Perrin-Saminadayar 2007c, pp. 134–135, with sources; see too Follet and Peppas Delmousou 2001, pp. 97–98.

Philopappus was probably not himself responsible for the construction of his memorial, but instead his younger sister Julia Balbilla. She was another of the period's "power women," and a poet, becoming a friend of Hadrian and his wife Vibia Sabina, accompanying them to the Valley of the Kings in Egypt in 129, and writing of their time there in four epigrams inscribed on colossal statues of Memnon (Amenhotep III) at Thebes.[49] Her relationship with her brother was such that she would have wanted to undertake a final resting place of such magnitude.

The monument was a fusion of Philopappus' backgrounds: Commagenian prince, Roman consul, and Athenian archon, showing the "eclecticism of Roman provincial art."[50] The frieze on the low first story depicts his inauguration as consul in AD 109. In the middle of the taller upper story was a large seated portrait of him nude from the waist up, and above his head a rayed crown (worn by his ancestors to denote their divinity). To his right was a smaller figure of Antiochus IV, and to his left (now lost) Seleucus I, one of his mother's distant relatives, and founder of the Seleucid dynasty after Alexander the Great's death. These three elements fuse in the rayed crown showing his Commagenian background, the consular procession displaying his relation to Rome, and his naked torso depicting Greek heroic nudity.

Philopappus presumably chose the Museum Hill as it was next to the Acropolis so that his striking memorial would be seen by anyone close to, and on, the Acropolis (Figure 14.4B). That a tomb was set so high, making his monument stand taller than the Acropolis, went against Athenian practice, but not so for the Commagenian royalty, whose burial place was on the highest point of their kingdom (Nemrud Dagh).[51] The monument is well worth the climb to the top of the Museum Hill as it affords striking views from one side to the Piraeus and from the other across the city with the Acropolis in the forefront. It is also a reminder of the painful memories that the Museum must have had for the Athenians as you pass by the area where Poliorcetes' garrison had been based in the early third century.

In its heyday the monument must have been very impressive—as it still is, even with its rear and interior, where Philopappus would have been interred, missing (the stones were used for other buildings in the Middle

---

[49] On the fascinating Julia, see Rosenmeyer 2010.
[50] Kleiner 1986, p. 12.
[51] H. A. Thompson 1987, p. 14.

FIGURE 14.4B Philopappus Monument from Acropolis. Photo: Ian Worthington.

Ages). But not everyone was dazzled by it. Pausanias, the first to describe it, did not even name its occupant, but referred to the memorial as simply one erected "to a Syrian."[52]

City of Hadrian (and Theseus)

Hadrian undertook an ambitious construction program throughout his empire, which saw at least ninety new buildings, engineering projects (such as aqueducts), and monuments in fifty-four cities.[53] But it was Greece to which he paid special attention. As the cultural center of the Roman Empire, he set up buildings and monuments in various places, including the temple of Apollo at Megara and an aqueduct at Argos, and carried out some makeovers on monuments at Eleusis.[54] In fact, Hadrian paid such attention

---

[52] Pausanias 1.25.8.
[53] Boatwright 2000, pp. 108–143 (see her tables on pp. 109–111 and 144–171).
[54] Clinton 1997, pp. 174–175; Levick 2000, p. 621.

to the sanctuary at Eleusis and the Mysteries that Eleusis enjoyed a renaissance it had not seen since the Classical period.[55]

Athens saw a building frenzy unmatched by Augustus, and even by Pericles in the fifth century or Lycurgus in the fourth.[56] The city's slump after Augustus was so much that "it would not be an exaggeration to describe Athens as a provincial backwater by comparison with the great capitals of the eastern provinces at Antioch, Ephesus, or even at Corinth."[57] Pausanias is invaluable for his eyewitness descriptions of Hadrian's projects and comments on their purpose: the temple of Olympian Zeus; a temple of Hera and Zeus Panhellenius; a basilica; a sanctuary of all the gods or Pantheon; a building "in which books are kept"; and a gymnasium, to which we can add an aqueduct and a bridge over the Cephisus River.[58]

These buildings also provided labor for Athenians, and their sculptors regained something of their former prominence in the world.[59] But they were not intended simply to beautify the city as they were connected to the emperor's "Panhellenion"—a league of cities of the east with Athens at its center, established by Hadrian, principally to maintain Roman rule in the east while stimulating trade and other contacts. We shall consider the Panhellenion in more detail in the next chapter, which deals with Hadrian's political relations with Athens.[60]

After six hundred years from its foundation, with centuries of neglect, the great temple of Olympian Zeus was finally completed and dedicated by Hadrian during his third visit to the city in the winter of AD 131/2.[61] The temple's initial phase in the later sixth century had seen the construction of the three steps and some columns' drums, but it had been abandoned after the fall of the Pisistratid tyrants in 510. Antiochus IV of Syria undertook

---

[55] Clinton 1989a, pp. 1516–1523; Clinton 1989b; cf. Clinton 1997, pp. 174–175.
[56] Graindor 1934, pp. 214–252; Day 1942, pp. 185–187; Kokkou 1970, pp. 150–173; Follet 1976, pp. 107–135; Geagan 1979a, pp. 395–397; T. L. Shear 1981, pp. 373–377; Spawforth and Walker 1985, pp. 92–100; Boatwright 2000, pp. 144–157 and 167–171; the papers in Vlizos 2008; Spawforth 2012, pp. 246–252.
[57] T. L. Shear 1981, p. 372.
[58] Pausanias 1.18.6–9. On Pausanias here, though a tad harsh on his defects as he was hardly an archaeologist, see Thompson and Wycherley 1972, pp. 204–207.
[59] Graindor 1934, pp. 253–284; Day 1942, pp. 206–207. Sculptors: see too Fittschen 2008.
[60] Buildings connected to the Panhellenion: Spawforth and Walker 1985, pp. 92–98.
[61] Graindor 1934, pp. 218–225; Kokkou 1970, pp. 154–157; D. Kleiner 1986, p. 10; H. A. Thompson 1987, pp. 2–3; Willers 1990, pp. 26–53; D. Kienast 1993, pp. 207–208; Hoff 2013, pp. 564–566; see too Wycherley 1964; Abramson 1975; Boatwright 2000, pp. 150–153.

more work on the temple in 174, swapping the original Doric columns for Corinthian ones and beginning work on the interior, but on his death work again stopped.

When Hadrian began to put his Panhellenion together he decided to make the temple the focal point of that league, and so oversaw its completion. The dedication ceremony in 131/2 therefore marked the formal start of this league and, to help celebrate it, he introduced the Panhellenia games.[62] It is ironic that the sanctuary was never popular under the democracy because of its association with the Pisistratid tyrants, yet Hadrian, emperor of Rome and ruler of Greece, made it his center point for bringing all Greeks together.

Exactly what was left to do on the temple is unknown.[63] Livy claimed that it was already an object of wonder, suggesting that Cossutius had added substantially to it, although Sulla was said to have carried off columns from the temple to be reused in the Temple of Jupiter on the Capitol at Rome.[64] Pausanias says that Hadrian merely dedicated the temple and the statue of Zeus, so he may have added terracing, the paved walkway around the *temenos*, the gold and ivory statue to Zeus in the *cella*, and perhaps a roof.[65]

Although in ruins today, we can still visualize its vastness and grandeur from the size of its remaining columns, which absolutely dwarf visitors, and huge *temenos* (Figure 14.5A). Even from the height of the Acropolis the temple's enormity is obvious (Figure 14.5B, in which the Arch of Hadrian is visible to the left in the foreground).

Hadrian also had a personal reason for finishing the temple because of his associations with Zeus, Dionysus, and Theseus.[66] He put himself and Olympian Zeus on his coinage by the time of his second visit to Athens (AD 128/9), and he is even called son of Zeus Eleutherius on an inscription from the Acropolis; further, he took on the epithets reserved for Zeus (Olympius, Eleutherius, and Panhellenius), and was called Olympius after AD 128/9 and Panhellenius after his death.[67] He also set up a statue of himself (made of

---

[62] Spawforth and Walker 1985, p. 79; C. P. Jones 1996, p. 33.
[63] Willers 1990, pp. 34–35.
[64] Livy 41.20.8; see too Stefanidou-Tiveriou 2008, pp. 12–13.
[65] Pausanias 1.18.6, with Willers 1990, pp. 26–53; cf. Boatwright 2000, pp. 152–153.
[66] Karivieri 2002; cf. Willers 1990, pp. 58–60.
[67] Inscription: Raubitschek 1945, pp. 131–132. Epithets: Karivieri 2002, p. 42; cf. Boatwright 2000, pp. 170–171 (Hadrian Panellenius identified with Zeus Panhellenios; *contra* Benjamin 1963, p. 58).

FIGURE 14.5A Ruins of Temple of Olympian Zeus. Photo: Ian Worthington.

FIGURE 14.5B Temple of Olympian Zeus from Acropolis. Photo: Ian Worthington.

chryselephantine, hence a cult statue) as the son of Zeus Eleutherius in the temple, clearly marking his identification with Zeus as well as Athena.[68] In fact, of all the emperors, he is the one who most consistently parallels himself with a divinity at Athens.[69] Added to his portrayal of himself is that when the temple was dedicated (and the Panhellenion officially came into being), embassies from all the cities of the east were in attendance, bringing with them statues of the emperor in stone and bronze from their cities—so many that when they were set up in the temple they practically filled it.[70]

As splendid and imposing as the temple of Olympian Zeus must have been, according to Pausanias, Hadrian's so-called library was the most striking of all his buildings, as an artistic reconstruction shows, and another example of a trend in the use of cultural space (Figure 14.6A).[71] Pausanias described it as a "building with 100 columns, with walls and colonnades of Phrygian marble, and a gilded roof," and adds the detail that in the rooms "books are kept."[72] His last comment has led to the building being dubbed a library, though it was more than just a place to hold books: like the famous library at Alexandria, it was an arts precinct, grander even than the Library of Pantaenus (discussed earlier). It stood to the east of the Agora, alongside the Market of Caesar and Augustus, thus making that whole area akin to the imperial *fora* in Rome.[73]

The Library was a large walled enclosure, with just one entrance through a porch (with seven columns on either side) in the middle of the west wall. It was open to the air, with a pool down the middle surrounded by a garden with statues, and bordered on all four sides by colonnades. Along the eastern side were five rooms. The largest was intended for books, and so was the actual library; the adjoining ones may have been picture galleries, and the two

---

[68] Raubitschek 1945; Geagan 1979a, p. 399.
[69] Geagan 1984, p. 77.
[70] Pausanias 1.18.6; see too Højte 2000, pp. 230–231.
[71] Graindor 1934, pp. 230–245; Kokkou 1970, pp. 162–165; T. L. Shear 1981, pp. 374–376; H. A. Thompson 1987, p. 10; Willers 1990, pp. 14–21; Willers 1996, pp. 4–6; Boatwright 2000, pp. 153–157; Choremi-Spetsieri and Tinginagka 2008 (including its later history); Tinginagka 2008 (building techniques); Spawforth 2012, pp. 247–248 (a "tribute to the Athenian origins of Greek high culture"); Dickenson 2017, pp. 374–375; in detail Choremi-Spetsieri 1996; Tinginagka 1999.
[72] Pausanias 1.18.9.
[73] Graindor 1934, pp. 230–245; T. L. Shear 1981, pp. 375–376; H. A. Thompson 1987, p. 10; Spawforth and Walker 1985, p. 96.

FIGURE 14.6A Hadrian's Library Reconstruction. Courtesy Dimitris Tsalkanis and Chrysanthos Kanellopoulos, www.AncientAthens3d.com.

FIGURE 14.6B Ruins of Hadrian's Library. Photo: Ian Worthington.

corner ones may have been teaching rooms as one had a sloping floor (for banks of seats) and a marble-paved orchestra.[74]

The whole complex was probably modeled on the temple of Peace at Rome (begun by Vespasian in AD 70 and dedicated in AD 75), which had a library, art gallery, and garden; if so, we see another example of the use of earlier Roman architecture in buildings in Athens (and the east), and a Roman architect may even have traveled from Rome to design the Library.[75] Today the impressive ruins of the wall and seven columns from the west or entrance side of the enclosure still allow us to gauge its size, and we can also see the actual library or room where the books were kept and one of the corner teaching rooms (Figures 14.6B–C).

We do not know as much about Hadrian's other buildings in the actual city. The Pantheon, built fifty meters to the east of the Roman Agora and Library of Hadrian, was most probably the meeting place for the members of the Panhellenion rather than an actual temple, although Dio does (perhaps

[74] Willers 1990, pp. 16–17.
[75] H. A. Thompson 1987, p. 10; T. L. Shear 1981, pp. 374–375; cf. Willers 1990, p. 23.

FIGURE 14.6C Ruins of Hadrian's Library (library and teaching rooms). Photo: Ian Worthington.

mistakenly) speak of a building called the Panhellenion.[76] The temple to Hera and Zeus Panhellenius may be a shrine of the Panhellenion.[77] The basilica in the northeast corner of the Athenian Agora may have had something to do with public business, given its location outside the Roman Agora.[78] The gymnasium, one of the few secular buildings that Hadrian had constructed, lay close to his Library and had one hundred columns. It certainly outrivaled the gymnasium for the ephebes named after Diogenes in 229 or that of Ptolemy III in the later 240s.[79] Finally, the bridge over the Cephisus River, 50 meters in length, connected Athens to Eleusis, and was built probably during Hadrian's first visit to Athens.[80]

---

[76] Dio 69.16.1, with Kokkou 1970, pp. 159–161; Spawforth and Walker 1985, pp. 97–98; Willers 1990, pp. 21–25 and 60–65; Willers 1996, pp. 7–8; Boatwright 2000, pp. 169–170.
[77] Kokkou 1970, pp. 157–161; T. L. Shear 1981, p. 373; Boatwright 2000, pp. 170–171.
[78] Geagan 1979a, p. 397; T. L. Shear 1981, pp. 376–377.
[79] Kokkou 1970, pp. 165–167; T. L. Shear 1981, p. 373; Willers 1990, pp. 13–14; Willers 1996, pp. 6–7; Boatwright 2000, pp. 168–169.
[80] Graindor 1934, pp. 35–36; Kokkou 1970, pp. 171–173; Follet 1976, pp. 113–114; Willers 1990, p. 13; Boatwright 2000, p. 168.

From buildings to water supply. In the 540s, Pisistratus the tyrant had built an aqueduct to improve the city's water supply and, by extension, endear himself to the people. Hadrian began construction of a new aqueduct, one of several for which he was responsible in Achaea (including a long one to Corinth).[81] The Athenian aqueduct was discovered by chance: in 1847 workers digging to increase the water supply from what they thought was a natural spring in Ambelokipi, northwest of Athens, discovered that the water came from an underground Roman aqueduct. In 1870 more remains were found on the lower southwestern slope of Lycabettus, as well as pieces from an ornamental Ionic façade and a dedicatory inscription (dated to AD 140) stating that Antoninus Pius completed the aqueduct begun by his father, the Divine Hadrian.[82]

The water came via an underground tunnel 20 kilometers long from a source on Mount Parnes to Mount Lycabettus. On top of that hill, high above the city, Hadrian built a reservoir, fronted by an elegant Ionic portico, though the term "reservoir" is perhaps misleading. S. Leigh has convincingly argued that because its smallish capacity (estimated at 445 m^3) was far less than the daily discharge of the aqueduct (estimated at 37,152 m^3), and that because lead pipes in the front wall show that water was diverted to it from the aqueduct, it was more likely to have been a nymphaeum (monumental fountain).[83] With its elaborate portico it was clearly meant to be seen, and so would be in keeping with Hadrian's grandiose building program; especially attractive to visitors to the Panhellenion, it (like all nymphaea) was another testament to Athenian prosperity.[84]

One final monument to be mentioned here is one that Hadrian did not commission: his famous Arch, effectively creating Greek and Roman divisions of the city (Figure 15.2). We will discuss this arch in the context of his program of reform for Athens in the next chapter. But given how the city physically changed, starting in the time of Caesar in the 50s and especially under Augustus and Hadrian, as the discussion here has shown, we

---

[81] Aqueducts: Alcock 1993, pp. 124–126; see too Thompson and Wycherley 1972, pp. 197–203, on Athenian aqueducts and water supply.

[82] Smallwood 1966 no. 396, p. 133, for the inscription; see too Graindor 1934, p. 252; Kokkou 1970, pp. 169–171; Thompson and Wycherley 1972, pp. 202–203; Spawforth and Walker 1985, pp. 98–99; Willers 1990, p. 13; Boatwright 2000, pp. 167–168; and especially Leigh 1997 and Leigh 1998, discussing the discoveries as well as excellent analysis and photos of the aqueduct and remains.

[83] Leigh 1997, pp. 286–290; cf. Dickenson 2017, pp. 364–370, on nymphaea.

[84] Spawforth and Walker 1985, p. 90; cf. Boatwright 2000, p. 145.

can recognize just how apposite the inscription on that arch was: "This is the city of Hadrian, and not of Theseus."[85]

Becoming a Provincial City?

It should not be thought that Augustus had singled out Athens for the buildings he funded. Comparisons between Roman building projects at Athens with those at Ephesus and Cyrene (not to mention in the city of Rome itself) show similarities anchored less in the dominance of Rome over a place or people and more in the transformation of Rome from Republic to Empire under a monarch.[86] These similarities include, most importantly, new buildings erected in agoras, especially in the open spaces; the strengthening of the religious aspects of agoras with the addition of images of the emperor and members of the imperial family, sometimes with Roma; the preservation or relocation of monuments to do with the early history of the city; and the construction of large porticoes set some distance from the agoras and decorated with statues of the emperor and the imperial family.

The coincidences in cities throughout the east and in Athens are not accidental. For example, in addition to the many altars dotted throughout Athens, the Stoa of Zeus Eleutherius was extended with the addition of a double-chambered shrine, one time thought to have housed the imperial cult, but perhaps one to Tiberius and Livia.[87] The most obvious porticoed enclosure was the Roman Agora, which, like its counterparts at Cyrene and Ephesus, had a commercial focus.[88] All the agoras seemed to favor becoming a center for emphasizing Roman rule and a place to showcase artworks. Yet life in them continued, and people hardly avoided going to them. The Odeum soared over other buildings in the Athenian Agora and imposed a Roman presence in it, but there was still an enormous amount of space around it for people to gather, go about their business, and appreciate all the Greek monuments there.[89]

---

[85] *IG* ii² 5185 (= Smallwood 1966, no. 485, p. 179).
[86] Walker 1997.
[87] H. A. Thompson 1966; cf. Thompson and Wycherley 1972, pp. 102–103; Torelli 1995, pp. 21–22 (two cults). Walker 1997, pp. 69–72, compares religious building in agoras at Athens, Ephesus, and Cyrene (with a figure of the Athenian stoa on p. 69).
[88] Day 1942, p. 153; Thompson and Wycherley 1972, pp. 170–173; Walker 1997, pp. 73–74.
[89] Dickenson 2017, p. 262.

We should therefore heed the warning against transposing "the lofty vision of the agora as an idealized public space" onto Greek cities under the empire, and labeling them as areas that suffered popular decline.[90] Agoras changed some functions, and were hardly the democratic heart of a polis any more, but they still remained lively places where business and trade were conducted, and where people still met and talked, even if many aspects of their conversation were understandably different from Classical times.

---

[90] Dickenson 2015, for example pp. 728–732 and 739–749 (function and meaning of an agora and especially Pausanias' view of agoras, which has affected our view of them); the quote is on p. 764, and see Dickenson 2017 on the continuing vitality of agoras (not just in Athens) throughout the Hellenistic and Roman periods; but see the judicious comments of Stefanidou-Tiveriou 2008, pp. 20, 27–28, for example.

15

Hadrian's Arch

HADRIAN RULED A VAST EMPIRE from AD 117 to 138, involving himself often in the economic, social, religious, and political lives of his culturally diverse subjects.[1] He was both a military commander and a polymath: a poet, philosopher, architect, and all-round intellectual. A philhellene who in his youth had been nicknamed *Graeculus* (Grecian or Greekling, but seemingly not in a complimentary sense), he had a keen interest in Greek poetry, and embraced the old classicism of the pre-Hellenistic era.[2] This was evident even in architecture, for at his Villa at Tivoli near Rome he built a round temple to Venus, which was a replica of the Doric Temple of Aphrodite on Cnidus of the mid-fourth century BC, complete with a copy of the original nude Aphrodite of Praxiteles in the temple at Cnidus.[3]

After he assumed the throne, Hadrian went back to Athens three times (AD 124/5, 128/9, and 131/2).[4] Those visits were part of two lengthy provincial tours, the first in AD 121–125 (during which his famous Wall in northern

---

[1] On Hadrian, see Graindor 1934; Birley 2000a, pp. 132–149; Levick 2000, pp. 620–627; Boatwright 2000; biographies: Birley 2000b; Everitt 2009.
[2] Cf. Birley 1997, p. 212 with n. 24. Taste in poetry: Bowie 2002.
[3] Kleiner 1986, pp. 10–11.
[4] Dates: Follet 1976, pp. 107–116; first visit: Graindor 1934, pp. 2–17; Geagan 1979a, pp. 392; second: Graindor 1934, pp. 37–39; Geagan 1979a, pp. 394–395; third: Graindor 1934, pp. 39–41; Geagan 1979a, pp. 397–398.

England was built), and the second in AD 128–132.⁵ He had an ambitious Panhellenic program, anchored in a league of cities in the east called the Panhellenion: this gave Athens a resurgence of influence to make it the second city of the Roman Empire and benefit from the most extensive building program of any emperor.⁶

The Athenians and Hadrian

Hadrian delighted in visiting Greece, where he had a particular affinity for Athens with Eleusis a close second.⁷ He had already gone to Athens before he became emperor, in AD 112/13, when he was granted Athenian citizenship (and enrolled in the same deme, Besa, as that previous great benefactor Philopappus) and was made eponymous archon.⁸ At that time he may even have been initiated into the Mysteries, given his obvious interest in Eleusis when emperor and that he took part in the festival on each of his visits to Athens.⁹ He likely did some traveling while in Greece, almost certainly to Sparta and Corinth, and probably also to Nicopolis to listen to the lectures of Epictetus.¹⁰ He also met several distinguished men, including Plutarch, and it may have been Hadrian who put forward the names of Tiberius Claudius Atticus Herodes of Marathon and Gaius Julius Eurycles Herculanus of Sparta as the first Roman senators from mainland Greece, a milestone placed in the time of Trajan.¹¹

When Hadrian first visited Athens as emperor in AD 124/5 there were no altars to him, nor it seems anywhere else in Greece.¹² That had changed

---

⁵ Full details and chronology at Halfmann 1986, pp. 188–210; see too Graindor 1934, pp. 1–58; Day 1942, pp. 183–196; Geagan 1979a, pp. 389–399; D. Kienast 1993, pp. 206–222; cf. Levick 2000, pp. 622–625.
⁶ J. H. Oliver 1981b. Hendrick 2006 disputes the notion of a decline followed by a "Hadrianic Renaissance" based on reassessment of the literary sources of the period and their "self-serving rhetoric" (p. xiv and passim); on Hadrian, cf. his chapter 3, pp. 75–83.
⁷ Cf. the comments of Spawforth 2012, pp. 246–252. Eleusis: Clinton 1989a, pp. 1516–1523.
⁸ Archon: *IG* ii² 2024, 2025, 3286; cf. Follet 1976, p. 29.
⁹ Graindor 1934, pp. 6–8, 38–39, and 119; Clinton 1974, p. 84; Follet 1976, pp. 108–115; Geagan 1979a, p. 394; Clinton 1989a, pp. 1517–1518; Clinton 1989b, pp. 56–57; D. Kienast 1993, p. 207. See Follet 1976, pp. 113–114, for his initiation during his second visit in 124/5.
¹⁰ Birley 1997, p. 214; before emperor: pp. 212–217; cf. Sherk 1988, no. 125, pp. 165–166; Graindor 1934, pp. 1–36; Day 1942, p. 184.
¹¹ Birley 1997, for example pp. 215–217, on whom Hadrian encountered, and pp. 209–212, 218–219, and 229–244, on Herodes and Eurycles.
¹² Geagan 1979a, p. 389; Geagan 1984, p. 75; Højte 2000, p. 230.

FIGURE 15.1 Marble bust of the Emperor Hadrian, from the Pantanello at Hadrian's Villa, AD 117–118. British Museum.

by the time of his second visit in AD 128/9 when he had been given the title "Olympius" throughout the Greek-speaking east, for his name is found on no fewer than 94 altars, many calling him Hadrian the Olympian and *Hadrianos Zeus Olympios*.[13] In addition, the Athenians erected statues for

---

[13] Geagan 1984, p. 73. Salutation in Athens: Follet 1976, pp. 58–59. Altars: Benjamin 1963 (pp. 59–60 for *Hadrianos Zeus Olympios*); Geagan 2011, H285–H313, pp. 160–169;

his wife Sabina and her sister Matidia, perhaps in AD 119.[14] Hadrian also has the most number of statues of any emperor (102), perhaps because of the range of his travels and longevity of his reign; however, some bases (with or without a statue) were set up simply to express gratitude to him, as he did not visit all the places where there are dedications to him.[15]

The statues also proclaimed his association with Dionysus and Zeus. The Athenians in AD 124/5 set up a group of thirteen statues in the theater of Dionysus (one for each wedge of seats), of which four bases survive.[16] An inscription on a seat in the front row of the theater further identifies him with that god, as does his depiction with Dionysus in the relief of the *scaenae frons* (architectural background to the stage) that he had built in the theater.[17] There were also dozens of statues of him from cities all over the Greek east in the precinct of the temple of Olympian Zeus, many with his title Olympian on them, to do with his Panhellenion (to be discussed later in the chapter).[18]

One statue of Hadrian dedicated by the Athenians stands out in particular, a marble cuirassed one that stood in the Agora alongside Zeus Eleutherius in front of the Stoa of Zeus—probably the one seen by Pausanias.[19] The cuirass shows Nike crowning the goddess Athena, who is standing on the back of the wolf of Rome. The scene has been interpreted variously—symbolically showing Athens as superior to Rome, or a deliberate parallel with Theseus, also favored by the emperor, and who is named on the Arch alongside Hadrian (see further below).[20]

---

cf. T. L. Shear 1981, p. 374; Karivieri 2002, p. 42. For a Latin inscription of AD 132, see Smallwood 1966, no. 490, p. 180.

[14] Geagan 1984, p. 72.

[15] Benjamin 1963, pp. 58–59; Geagan 1979a, pp. 398–399; T. L. Shear 1981, p. 374; Højte 2000, especially pp. 228–231, also noting that a statue base need not be contemporaneous with its statue or even have one on it at all. Imperial statues generally: Hendrick 2006, chapter 9, pp. 172–207. Tribes and private individuals also honored him: see Geagan 2011, C119, pp. 57–58, for a possible statue base to him from the Aiantid tribe.

[16] *IG* ii² 3287A–D, with Graindor 1934, pp. 18–20; Benjamin 1963, nos. 2–5, p. 83; Geagan 1979a, p. 392; Geagan 1984, p. 71 with n. 6; Willers 1990, p. 50; Karivieri 2002, p. 43. Earlier statue before he became emperor: Benjamin 1963, no. 1, p. 83.

[17] Karivieri 2002, pp. 44–48.

[18] *IG* ii² 3289–3310, with Geagan 1984, p. 77; see too Geagan 2011, H261 and H262, pp. 150–151; cf. Camia, Corcella, and Monaco 2018.

[19] Pausanias 1.3.2: Hadrian a "benefactor to all of his subjects and in particular to the city of Athens."

[20] Thompson and Wycherley 1972, p. 101; H. A. Thompson 1987, pp. 10–11; Theseus: Karivieri 2002, p. 51.

It is no surprise that Hadrian was popular with the Athenians, given the amount of money he spent on the city and the measures he took to promote it in the Greek world. In his honor, they created a thirteenth tribe (the first new one in almost 300 years) named Hadrianis (which would come with the obligatory portrait on the Monument of the Eponymous Heroes in the Agora), for which a range of dates has been proposed, but most plausible is AD 126/7.[21] As emperor, he wanted to beautify Athens following the lull in building activity after the Augustan era, and here he may have followed Philopappus' example, given that both were foreigners who became citizens and were enrolled in the same deme.[22] Hadrian was undoubtedly a philhellene, but we should not forget that his attitude to Greek culture and his various benefactions were only a part, albeit a significant one, of an imperial policy to maintain his rule over the disparate peoples of his empire.[23] A lover of culture, he was also a pragmatist who did not hesitate to exploit that culture to his advantage. That is evident in the introduction of the Panhellenion, an organization of Greek cities, centered in Athens, which promoted that city in the Greek east and indeed across the Roman Empire.[24]

Constitution and Economy

Hadrian's standing in the city doubtless spurred the Athenians to do something extraordinary: they asked him to reform their constitution, including the laws of Dracon and Solon, which dated back to the end of the seventh and early sixth centuries BC.[25] Possibly the people had already started this reform and then asked for his involvement. The reorganization was completed by AD 124/5, the year of his first trip to Athens as emperor, when he may also

---

[21] Pausanias 1.5.5 (tribe), with Graindor 1934, pp. 19–21 (earlier). Dating: Notopoulos 1946; Follet 1976, pp. 117–121; Geagan 1979a, p. 393. Statue on the altar: Thompson and Wycherley 1972, p. 40.
[22] Geagan 1979a, p. 389; Perrin-Saminadayar 2007c, p. 144.
[23] Spawforth 2012, pp. 242–270.
[24] Benjamin 1963; Willers 1990; D. Kienast 1993, pp. 206–222; Willers 1996; Birley 1997, pp. 220–223; Giudice 2013; and further below. Building program connected to the Panhellenion: Spawforth and Walker 1985, pp. 92–98.
[25] Geagan 1979a, pp. 392–394. See too J. H. Oliver 1965b; Follet 1976, pp. 116–125, and especially Kapetanopoulos 1992–1998 (reform underway earlier: pp. 219 and 228–229).

have been (exceptionally) archon for a second time to commemorate the visit and his reform.[26]

We are again in the dark because of a lack of evidence as to all that Hadrian did. We know that the various democratic organs of the constitution had limped along over the years, even if officials had needed to exploit their connections to Rome and involvement in the imperial cult to get elected.[27] It seems Hadrian intended to overhaul only those aspects of the constitution he considered inefficient or obsolete. Thus he made no changes to offices such as the archonship, but reduced the Boule from 600 to 520 (to take into account the new tribe in his name), which began to meet in AD 127/8.[28] He also made changes to the *ephebeia* and built a gymnasium, giving it and the gymnasiarch their own endowments.[29] In addition he banned dual citizenship, although there were exceptions. The first Roman we know of was Quintus Trebellius Rufus of Toulouse, a knight (*eques*) who in the reign of Domitian became an Athenian citizen and archon (p. 284). Another exception was Hadrian himself, while a senator in the reign of Trajan, but these were rare occurrences.

More sweeping were his financial reforms. He decreased rates of taxation, imposed a ban on tax farming by members of the Boule (an indication perhaps that some of them may have been extorting the people), imposed greater penalties on debtors who did not pay what they owed on time, and gave the entire island of Cephallenia to the city for its revenue stream.[30] Athens' chaotic financial administration perhaps motivated him to introduce two new offices that Commodus would later reform: the *opisthodomos* (a civic treasury) and the sacred *diataxis* (treasury).[31] These oversaw payments, probably gifts, from real estate, and since they were in denarii the intended recipient was the *fiscus* (the emperor's personal treasury). Hadrian therefore may have reorganized sacred finances into an office called the *opisthodomos*

---

[26] Kapetanopoulos 1992–1998, pp. 215–218.
[27] Cf. Graindor 1934, pp. 73–98.
[28] Graindor 1934, pp. 83–85; Geagan 1979a, pp. 392–393. Magistracies: Graindor 1934, pp. 92–97.
[29] Graindor 1934, pp. 98–102 (ephebes); gymnasium: Geagan 1967, pp. 130–131; Geagan 1979a, p. 394; Kapetanopoulos 1992–1998, pp. 222–224.
[30] Tax-farming: Dio 69.16.2, with Day 1942, pp. 193–194. Cephallenia: Dio 69.16.2, but doubted by Graindor 1934, p. 55; Day 1942, p. 188; Geagan 1979a, p. 394; Boatwright 2000, p. 84, noting that the island was free (Pliny, *NH* 4.54), and so not part of the *fiscus*; most likely he made over a substantial part of its revenues to the city.
[31] J. H. Oliver 1965b, pp. 126–131; Geagan 1979a, p. 393.

with a board of treasurers; while it remained an Athenian public treasury, it had Roman methods of accounting.

Still, Athens (like the rest of Greece) was facing economic hardship, especially after Trajan's costly eastern campaigns, and revenue from foreign visitors and students was not enough.[32] Moreover, over the past decades Attica had been falling back to a position that had plagued it in the Archaic period when wealthy landowners accrued vast tracts of land at the expense of small farmers. A fragmentary inscription reveals that Hadrian ordered a list of all property and money held by individuals from all socio-economic backgrounds throughout Attica, including the names of land owners (male and female); the type of property (land with or without houses); its location (or locations); and its value (in denarii and drachmas).[33] This census provides interesting information on Attic agriculture and the countryside, including that women could own land, either in their own name or jointly with brothers or husbands—a sign of their growing status from the Hellenistic era (where previously only Spartan women could own land). Most importantly, it shows that there had been a change in land ownership, whereby wealthier landowners increased their land holdings, surely causing suffering and loss of lands on the part of the small farmers.

There was therefore a need to rein in and improve finances, as well as to monitor the well-being of smaller farmers, especially when it came to dependency on grain. To this end Hadrian introduced an annual, imperial-funded grain dole—unique to Greece, as only one other city had such a thing: Rome.[34] In addition to helping the citizens, it may have been a move to ensure the expected visitors to the Panhellenion had sufficient food supply.[35]

Arguably Hadrian's most comprehensive measure was a decree regulating the sale of olive oil, which we know of from a badly weathered inscription by the main entrance to the Roman Agora.[36] The date is controversial, but

---

[32] Visitors: Graindor 1934, pp. 59–71.
[33] Graindor 1934, pp. 79–82; Day 1942, pp. 221–237.
[34] Dio 69.16.2, with Boatwright 2000, p. 92.
[35] Spawforth and Walker 1985, p. 90; cf. Boatwright 2000, p. 145.
[36] *IG* ii² 1100 (= Smallwood 1966, no. 443, pp. 158–159), with Graindor 1934, pp. 74–79; Geagan 1967, pp. 131–132; Folet 1976, p. 117; Geagan 1979a, p. 394; Boatwright 2000, pp. 91–92. Whether Hadrian at the same time undertook work on the market is unknown: Boatwright 2000, p. 170.

the law had come into being by AD 126/7.³⁷ For some time olive oil had been sold abroad in large quantities at high prices to the detriment of the home market; Hadrian's law now regulated oil sales.³⁸ By limiting the profits of the middlemen he wanted to ensure the state had access to oil for various services, such as street lighting, at reasonable rates.³⁹ Thus his measure was directly related to the social and economic life of the citizens. The gymnasiarch, whose duty it was to ensure an adequate supply of olive oil for the baths of the gymnasia, remained the chief official, but he was assisted by subordinates called *elaiones*, who were the ones actually buying the oil.⁴⁰

The law stipulated that oil cultivators were only allowed to sell one-third of their total olive oil crop on the international market at the current rate. They had to deliver this amount at the start of the harvest to specially appointed state officials who bought it.⁴¹ An exemption was put in place for the farmers of the former estates of Hipparchus, whose lands had been callously seized by Domitian (p. 283), who had to deliver only one-eighth. Growers had to make a formal declaration as to the amount of their crop under oath.⁴² Further, the people selling the oil had to declare the amount sold, where, and even the location of the boat that was to transport the oil.⁴³ If they did not, the oil was confiscated by the state. If someone gave a false statement, he would be tried: cases involving amounts of less than 50 amphorae would be heard by the Boule; above that, by the Assembly.⁴⁴ Informers were encouraged by the award of half the value of disputed oil upon a conviction.⁴⁵ In two places the law refers to Hadrian himself: he is to be informed if an oil merchant is denounced after sailing off without making a formal declaration, and he and the proconsul are to hear appeals.⁴⁶

---

[37] Graindor 1934, p. 78, argues for AD 124/5 (but believes the law is part of Hadrian's constitution); cf. Day 1942, p. 189 n. 83; but see J. H. Oliver 1965b, p. 130 n. 11, for later dating.

[38] Graindor 1934, pp. 74–79; Day 1942, pp. 189–192; on previous export amounts: Day 1942, pp. 202 and 212–215.

[39] Some oil may also have been used in street lighting, as in other eastern cities: Graindor 1934, p. 75; cf. Day 1942, p. 192 n. 88.

[40] Geagan 1967, pp. 128–132.

[41] *IG* ii² 1100, lines 6–11.

[42] *IG* ii² 1100, lines 11–15.

[43] *IG* ii² 1100, lines 20–23.

[44] *IG* ii² 1100, lines 46–49.

[45] *IG* ii² 1100, lines 49–54.

[46] *IG* ii² 1100, lines 46–47 and 55–56.

Hadrian also introduced a law that exempted the fishermen of Eleusis from Athens' two-obol port fee while selling at Eleusis, and laid down that any profiteering by vendors would be heard by the Areopagus.[47] P. Graindor logically believed that this measure indicated that there were food shortages at Eleusis when the sanctuary was crammed with visitors during the Mysteries, and his view has largely been followed.[48] However, it has recently been argued that the law was part of a more comprehensive measure involving not just Eleusis (at the time of the Mysteries or not) but the overall issue of the exorbitantly high cost of fish in Athens.[49] Hadrian wanted to lower prices and encourage more fishermen to deliver their catches directly to the Piraeus by cutting out the middlemen who normally delivered the fish to the markets for sale.

That Hadrian would be involved at this level is likely, given his constitutional and economic reforms, but we should not see him as a micro-manager over something as trifling as the price of fish when he had an empire to run. The Greeks were as obsessed with fish as they were with sex, and the different types of fish were a status symbol, from lowly anchovies and sprats to expensive eel, tuna, and sea bass, which only the rich could afford. The brief biography of the fourth-century Athenian orator Hyperides has what seems like an excursus on his love of fish to show how he enjoyed picking out the finest fish at the market.[50] That was the fourth century but there is no reason to suppose the Athenians felt any differently so many years later. The issue of the price of fish for people was an important one then, which explains Hadrian's regulations.

Religion and Intellectual Life

Hadrian, like Augustus, was in favor of the old religious cults; he allowed the Athenians to continue celebrating their festivals, albeit with the sorts of Roman overtones that we saw with the Panathenaea under previous emperors. The choregic dedications to victorious choruses at the Great Dionysia show that this festival continued to be in favor, as it was with the Antonines after him.[51] He also initiated a program for a cultural revival

---

[47] *IG* ii² 1103 (= Smallwood 1966, no. 444, pp. 159–160), with Geagan 1979a, p. 394.
[48] Graindor 1934, pp. 127–129; Day 1942, pp. 192–193 (noting that it could be to commodities in general, not just fish); J. H. Oliver 1965b, p. 132; Boatwright 2000, pp. 90–91.
[49] Lytle 2007, and see pp. 107–110 on waiving the two-obol port or harbor fee.
[50] [Plutarch], *Moralia* 849e, with Roisman, Worthington, and Waterfield 2015, p. 257.
[51] Follet and Peppas Delmousou 2001.

of Athens, which included founding three new festivals: the Panhellenia (clearly connected to the Panhellenion), the Olympieia (associated with the cult of Olympian Zeus), and the Hadrianeia (named after himself).[52] In addition, he made changes to the Panathenaea, which had seen a decline in the number of foreign athletes.[53] These four festivals now formed their own four-yearly cycle: the Hadrianeia in the first year, the Olympieia in the second, the Panathenaea in the third, and the Panhellenia in the fourth, showing a striking promotion in the status of Athens, center of the Panhellenion, over other cities.[54] Moreover, in establishing the order of these four festivals Hadrian changed the timing of the regular Olympic festivals to prevent overlap with the Athenian ones. That they did not fare as well as those in Athens was not his concern.

Hadrian's affinity with Athenian religion and of course the Mysteries is clear, but he was also tolerant of foreign cults, including Isis, but less so Christianity, with Christians being persecuted.[55] Still, Egyptian cults could not be allowed to impact Greek ones, and especially the imperial cult, which was spreading throughout the Empire, and in Athens was centered now in the temple of Olympian Zeus.[56] Hadrian though distanced himself from how Augustus and Claudius had associated with Apollo, preferring Zeus, Dionysus, and Theseus, as his building activity demonstrates.[57]

As we noted earlier, the lifelong position of high priest of the *Sebastoi* was a plum job—even the Eleusinian priesthoods were considered as less important. Further, the post was one to which only the political elite could aspire, for eligibility was based among other things on previously holding one of the three highest public offices (eponymous archon, hoplite general, or herald of the Areopagus). Given that the numbers of the political bodies

---

[52] Follet 1976, pp. 322, 331–333, and 343–349; Geagan 1979a, pp. 397–398; Spawforth and Walker 1985, pp. 90–91; C. P. Jones 1996, pp. 37–38.

[53] Graindor 1934, pp. 47–49, 73–114; cf. J. H. Oliver 1965b, p. 126; Follet 1976, pp. 331–333; Spawforth and Walker 1985, pp. 90–91.

[54] Spawforth and Walker 1985, pp. 90–91; Boatwright 2000, pp. 94–104. The Great Panthenaea continued to be held at the beginning of the third year of the Olympiad, despite the common belief it was moved to the following year: J. L. Shear 2012.

[55] Egypt: Graindor 1934, pp. 158–165; Christianity: Graindor 1934, pp. 172–173.

[56] Graindor 1934, pp. 165–171; Benjamin 1963; Geagan 1979a, pp. 398–399; T. L. Shear 1981, p. 373 (and pp. 373–377 on the building program); cf. Willers 1990, pp. 55–60; Boatwright 2000, pp. 136–140. Altars and temples as part of emperor worship: Hendrick 2006, chapters 5–6.

[57] Karivieri 2002; see too Raubitschek 1945.

had declined, especially the Areopagus, with perhaps only 25 members, the same few influential families dominated civic life and the imperial cult.[58]

Probably after his first imperial visit to Athens, Hadrian patronized and wrote letters about Dionysus to the city's guild of artists and performers (*technitai*), which after a hiatus of two centuries became prominent.[59] The guild as a private association also worshipped other members of the imperial family and even had a seat reserved in the theater of Dionysus for an imperial priest, perhaps of Hadrian.[60] In his measures, and especially the statues to him and relief decoration in the theater of Dionysus, we see his close association with that god (probably starting in Asia Minor, where he was called the "New Dionysus").[61] He also served as *agonothetes* of the Dionysia in AD 124/5, dressing not as a Roman in a toga but in an Athenian one and wearing white shoes—a sign of pride in his citizenship and a means to endear himself to the people.[62]

Athens had been the leading center for philosophy and the arts for centuries.[63] Under Vespasian the philosophical schools had been effectively muzzled because of their proclivity to interfere in political affairs (pp. 282–283). A series of letters dated to AD 121 between Hadrian and Pompeia Plotina, the widow of Trajan, shows her resolve to change that.[64] A highly educated lady and ferocious champion of what she held dear, she had been a close friend and supporter of Hadrian since his childhood—so much so that when she died the following year (122), he deified her. She was especially interested in Epicureanism, so when it came time to appoint a new head of the Epicurean school in Athens she decided that the position should go to the current acting head, Popilius Theotimus. He was not a Roman citizen, but nevertheless she successfully petitioned Hadrian to change Vespasian's law that only Roman citizens could be heads of the schools. Her success may have been due to their relationship (and even more so her forcefulness) rather than any belief on his part that the law needed changing (especially as their

---

[58] Grijalvo 2005; Camia 2014.
[59] *IG* ii² 1105, 1106, with Graindor 1934, p. 210; Geagan 1972, especially pp. 147–151 and 155–156; Geagan 1979a, pp. 394–395.
[60] *IG* ii² 5062; note Hendrick 2006, chapter 7, p. 160.
[61] Karivieri 2002, pp. 42–48.
[62] Geagan 1979a, p. 392; Clinton 1989a, p. 1517. Pride: Geagan 1979a, p. 389.
[63] Graindor 1934, pp. 197–213.
[64] Smallwood 1966, no. 442, pp. 157–158; see too Day 1942, p. 195; Follet 1976, pp. 22–24; Follet 1994.

exchange preceded his first visit to Athens). Clearly the schools were concerned that he would change his mind after her death: four years later he had to reassure them he would not.[65]

But what propelled Athens' ascendancy in the Roman Empire was the Panhellenion, to which we finally turn.

The Panhellenion

Hadrian wanted to bring about some stability to the east by fostering a sense of unity in the cities there—and of course to rule without too many disturbances. To this end he introduced an organization of Greek cities, headed by the Athenians, to make Athens the second city of the Roman Empire.[66] The league, called the Panhellenion, took seven years to put together, and was officially launched during his third visit to Athens in the winter of AD 131/2.[67] That the initiative for this Panhellenic League came from him rather than the cities of the east seems certain.[68] Hadrian knew his Greek history, and may well have been swayed by Classical precedents: in the fifth century Athens ruled its Delian League tightly, while bringing economic benefits to its members. The Athenian League had an allied synedrion, which supposedly debated league policy and reported to the Athenian Assembly, but it was soon disregarded. In the fourth century, after defeating the Greeks at Chaeronea, Philip II had imposed a "Common Peace," the nature of which discouraged any Greek city from revolting from it and ensured Greece remained largely passive. Hence the emperor may have looked back to both of these organizations and adopted and adapted their principles to achieve peace and economic prosperity while ensuring Rome held the real power.

Since the Panhellenion was a Greek union, Rome's headship would only lead to discontent, and perhaps the same difficulty would arise in the case

---

[65] Follett 1976, pp. 23–24; J. H. Oliver 1982, especially pp. 69–75.
[66] Benjamin 1963; J. H. Oliver 1981b, p. 419; Willers 1990; D. Kienast 1993, pp. 209–210; Willers 1996; Birley 1997, pp. 220–223; Giudice 2013. A view that the impact of the Panhellenion was not so great: Spawforth 1999, pp. 350–352, but note Spawforth and Walker 1985, pp. 90–92.
[67] Graindor 1934, pp. 52–53 and 102–111; Day 1942, pp. 194–195; J. H. Oliver 1965b; Follet 1976, pp. 108 and 125–135; Geagan 1979a, p. 398; Spawforth and Walker 1985; Willers 1990, pp. 54–67 (cf. pp. 93–103); D. Kienast 1993, pp. 217–222; C. P. Jones 1996; Willers 1996; Spawforth 1999; Boatwright 2000, pp. 147–150; cf. Follet and Peppas Delmousou 1997.
[68] Spawforth and Walker 1985; Spawforth 1999, pp. 339–344; from the cities: C. P. Jones 1996.

of one of the powerful cities of Asia Minor—Ephesus, for example. There was really only one choice as leader, especially as the league was anchored as much in cultural as in practical considerations: Athens, oldest of the Greek cities, and a cultural powerhouse for centuries. Thus, Athens married together culture and politics to support Rome's policy in the east throughout the second century. In that respect, Athens was more important for Hadrian than it had been for Augustus.

Our evidence for the Panhellenion is almost entirely epigraphic.[69] Most of its members were in the Aegean region, but we find others as far afield as Asia Minor and Italy; in all, nearly thirty are known, though finds of more inscriptions could increase that figure (Map 5).[70] The Panhellenion was under the control of an archon holding office for four years, perhaps appointed by Hadrian himself, assisted by a deputy archon; since the imperial cult and games were features of the organization, there were also a priest of Hadrian Panhellenius and an *agonothetes*.[71] Each city had an annual membership, which was based on Greek ancestry and proper relations with Rome.[72] Each sent representatives (Panhellenes) who were ex-magistrates above a certain age to the council meetings, but the representatives also had to have good moral character rather than simple political experience, and be men drawn from all walks of life. That was probably why Roman citizens held the highest offices, and less than half of the Panhellenes at council meetings were not citizens, because of the emphasis on culture (*paideia*) and personal character (*aretē*).[73]

What did the Panhellenion do? It had no military role or the ability to make policy independent of Rome. It did foster communication and encourage trade between cities in the east that otherwise might not have had any interaction with one another. Also, it may have functioned as a court, and it had money, presumably from Hadrian, to make grants to athletes, maintain the shrine of the Panhellenion, and put up dedications for the first fruits to Demeter at Eleusis, to the emperor, and to others.[74] It also supervised the cult of Hadrian Panhellenios along with the Panhellenia

---

[69] C. P. Jones 1996, pp. 30–44.
[70] Spawforth and Walker 1985, pp. 79–81; Spawforth 1999, pp. 347–350; Spawforth 2012, pp. 252–255 and 261–262.
[71] Spawforth and Walker 1985, pp. 84–90; Spawforth 1999, pp. 344–347.
[72] Spawforth and Walker 1985, pp. 81–82.
[73] Spawforth and Walker, pp. 79 and 85–89; cf. Levick 2000, p. 624.
[74] Spawforth and Walker 1985, pp. 82–84; *contra* C. P. Jones 1996, pp. 36–37.

games.⁷⁵ Its religious role thus benefited not only Athens but also Eleusis, since we have two dedications that we know of from the proceeds of first fruits, going back to a fifth-century Athenian practice.⁷⁶ The origin lay in the myth that Demeter was supposed to have given grain and the Mysteries to Athens, both deemed essential to civilization, so Athens had shared both with everyone, and in return the other Greeks contributed first fruits to Eleusis in thanksgiving for Athenian generosity.⁷⁷ The Panhellenion thus revived this Classical custom, and it is likely that Hadrian, who would have known the story, was responsible for it.⁷⁸

The representatives from the member cities collected together at Athens as a council, chaired by the archon, and could make reports to Hadrian; in doing so they felt part of something bigger than just their role in local politics, and of course ambitious individuals had the opportunity to play a leading role in league affairs and even communicate league opinion to the emperor. That did not mean he was bound to follow it, just as Athens had disregarded its allied council in the fifth century and Philip II and Alexander the Great the League of Corinth in the fourth. Nevertheless, the Panhellenion was a clever move on Hadrian's part; although disaffection continued in the provinces, the connections between the member cities were important.

Athens also benefitted in prestige and income from the council representatives who travelled to the city for meetings, and especially from new, magnificent buildings (see chapter 14). All were constructed to showcase Athens as the center of the league, and for the Athenians, they echoed the power of monuments in their own imperial eras under Pericles and Lycurgus. They thus responded by setting up over ninety altars in Athens alone to their Savior and Founder, *Autokrator Hadrianos Olympios*.⁷⁹

---

⁷⁵ Benjamin 1963, p. 59; Spawforth and Walker 1985, pp. 82 and 84–86; Willers 1990, p. 60.
⁷⁶ Graindor 1934, pp. 118–135; Clinton 1989a, pp. 1520–1522; Spawforth and Walker 1985, pp. 100–102 (including under Antonines); Spawforth 2012, pp. 246–252.
⁷⁷ Story at Isocrates, *Panegyricus* 28–31.
⁷⁸ Spawforth and Walker 1985, pp. 100–101; Clinton 1989a, pp. 1520–1521; Clinton 1989b, p. 57; see too Clinton 1997, pp. 174–176.
⁷⁹ Benjamin 1963, p. 125; see the catalogue at Geagan 2011, H285–H313, pp. 160–169.

Hadrian's Arch

Hadrian's energetic building program in the city has been discussed in the previous chapter to show the physical impact it had on Athens. Here we must turn to a different monument, one foreshadowed in that chapter, which more than anything exemplifies the transformation of the city into a hybrid of Greek and Roman. This was his famous Arch, located very close to the temple of Olympian Zeus and (like today) within easy sight of the Acropolis (cf. Figure 14.5B). It was most likely dedicated by the Athenians in AD 131/2 on his third visit to Athens.[80] Made of pentelic marble of poor quality (a sign of Athens' financial straits in contrast to the quality of marble used in the imperial constructions), the arch had two stories; the lower one had two Corinthian columns on either side, and the second, narrower story had three rectangular openings, with the central one flanked by columns and a triangular pediment. Statues of Hadrian and Theseus stood next to a central opening (Figure 15.2).

On each side of the Arch was an inscription; on the east side (facing the temple of Olympian Zeus): "This is the city of Hadrian, and not of Theseus," and on the west (facing the Acropolis): "This is Athens, the ancient city of Theseus,"[81] It appears, then, that the Arch straddled two different areas, and in doing so, it has affinities with an inscribed marker supposedly set up at the isthmus of Corinth by Theseus (with whom Hadrian identified) after he had annexed Megara into Attica to show the boundary between the Peloponnese and Ionia.[82]

The purpose of the Arch has been much debated. It was once thought to have been a gate in part of the circuit wall that was in disrepair and rebuilt by Hadrian. However, repairs to the wall have been shown to be later, perhaps even in AD 267 because of the Herulian attack on the city (discussed below). Since Hadrian ruled in a time of peace, he undertook the rebuilding of very few walls and city gates throughout the whole empire, so there would have been no need to add to a defensive wall in Athens.[83]

---

[80] Graindor 1934, pp. 228–229; Day 1942, p. 187; J. H. Oliver 1965b, pp. 124–125; Kokkou 1970, pp. 167–169; Kleiner 1986, p. 11; A. Adams 1989; Willers 1990, pp. 68–85; Post 1998–1999; Karivieri 2002, pp. 49–50; Hendrick 2006, chapter 7, pp. 151–156.
[81] *IG* ii² 5185 (= Smallwood 1966, no. 485, p. 179).
[82] Plutarch, *Theseus* 25.3.
[83] Theocharaki 2011, pp. 130–131; cf. Geagan 1979a, p. 395; A. Adams 1989, p. 11. The next stage in that wall's construction was in the mid-third century AD in the reigns of Galerian and Gallienus: Theocharaki 2011, pp. 131–133. Hadrian and walls generally: Boatwright 2000, pp. 121–123.

FIGURE 15.2 Hadrian's Arch. Photo: Ian Worthington.

Since the Arch was free-standing, the idea that it served as a gate perhaps arose from its confusing integration into a Turkish wall of 1878.[84] Since the arch's style is similar to many found in the east, especially Asia Minor, it was most probably an honorary one that the Athenians set up to Hadrian for his many benefactions, not least the launching in the same year of the Panhellenion with them at its center.[85]

---

[84] A. Adams 1989, pp. 11–12; Willers 1990, pp. 70–72.
[85] A. Adams, 1989; cf. Post 1998–1999, pp. 179–181.

The two inscriptions are also controversial. The common interpretation of the eastward-facing one (following the translations) is that it refers to two distinct areas of Athens, one a new quarter of the city, established by the emperor with his building program, away from the old city, hence "city of Hadrian, and not of Theseus." There is archaeological evidence of new buildings and especially a large Roman bathhouse to the east of the arch and adjacent to the temple that possibly date to this era, which would point to the existence of a new quarter (named Hadrianopolis).[86] On the other hand, these buildings might postdate Hadrian and belong in, for example, the reign of Antoninus Pius, who completed his father's aqueduct, on which is a reference to "New Athens." If so, the east inscription cannot relate to two geographically distinct areas of the city.

A different translation has been proposed for the westward-facing inscription (toward the old city): "This is the city that used to be that of Theseus."[87] In other words, the Arch is not connected to any new quarter or indeed any particular part of Athens. Instead, the Athenians were acknowledging Hadrian as replacing the legendary Theseus as the city's founder—presumably (we imagine) for his Panhellenion that inaugurated a new era in Athenian history. In support of this view is the deliberate location of the Arch near the *temenos* of the temple of Olympian Zeus, the intended focal point of the Panhellenion. If so, then the east-facing inscription ("This is the city of Hadrian, and not of Theseus") was meant to proclaim the league was bringing a new city into being, one that had nothing to do with Theseus.

But there is a big difference between identification and replacement. Hadrian's revamping of the Panathenaea, for example, certainly indicated an affinity with Theseus, who supposedly created the festival, but we do not hear of the emperor replacing the hero as its founder. Given the Athenians' preoccupation with their past, especially evident in their religion, it is hard to imagine they would have cast aside their mythical founder so abruptly, though some altars on which he is referred to as "founder" (*ktistes*) can refer to the areas in which Hadrianic construction took place. We may imagine the Athenians going to the extreme length of abandoning their mythical past

---

[86] A. Adams 1989, p. 11 n. 9, citing sources, and p. 12 n. 14, for dating of remains; see too Zahrnt 1979; cf. Graindor 1934, pp. 226–228; Day 1942, p. 186; Willers 1990, pp. 68–72. The name is found used throughout the Empire: Boatwright 2000, pp. 104–105 and 172–173.

[87] J. H. Oliver 1965b, pp. 124–125; cf. A. Adams 1989, p. 11; Willers 1990, pp. 68–72.

and hero to try to escape some dire punishment at the hands of a tyrannical ruler, but Hadrian was clearly focused on ennobling the city.

If the Athenians were swapping Theseus for Hadrian, so to speak, then the wording of the inscription is even more puzzling—why not simply call him a "new" Theseus, as they had called previous emperors a "New Apollo," or even Julius Nicanor a "New Themistocles" and "New Homer"? Hadrian must have been well aware of the comparison of Theseus and Romulus as founders of Athens and Rome that Plutarch had made in his paired lives of these two mythical founders, so it makes more sense for the Athenians to have thanked and flattered him with an appellation like a "new" or even "second" Theseus if they were truly replacing their hero with him.

In truth, the wording of the west-facing inscription can only support the translation of "This is Athens, the ancient city of Theseus," and the eastern one, less controversially, "This is the city of Hadrian, and not of Theseus."[88] The Arch therefore had two functions. First, it was honorary as only to be expected for someone who had done so much—and since Athens was to head the cornerstone of Hadrian's policy in the east, it was also fitting to have a monument reflecting an Eastern architectural form than a Western.[89] Second, there was no new Roman quarter of Athens; instead, the east inscription symbolically draws attention to the monumental temple that was the epicenter of the Panhellenion and indeed of a new Athens, one "of Hadrian, and not of Theseus."[90] And pointing the other way was the age-old city of Theseus, all the way up to the Acropolis, so admired by Hadrian.

It is no surprise that the Athenians deliberately associated Hadrian and Theseus, while distinguishing them as two separate founders. Theseus was credited with creating a common center around the Acropolis and the sanctuary of Athena Polias for Athens while establishing the city's political, social, and religious traditions. Hadrian was taking that public life and giving it a new lease with his new Panhellenion, constructions, and even his input in the political, financial, and religious features of the city. In this regard he added to a Romanization of the city that had started to make an appearance in the first century BC.

---

[88] Cf. Zahrnt 1979, p. 393.
[89] The examples from the east given by A. Adams 1989, pp. 12–14, are compelling.
[90] Willers 1990, p. 72.

What average Athenians thought about how their city had changed we shall never know.⁹¹ But we must be careful not to assume that the lot of the ordinary people matched Athens' economic elevation, especially the Attic farmers whose lands were being swallowed up, while the upper stratum grew even richer. We hear of no dissent under Hadrian as had faced Augustus toward the end of his reign, but because Athens headed the Panhelleniondoes not mean everyone was content or grateful. Athens as a city remained beautified, culturally superior, with its prestige assured. It lacked, however, the one thing that it had always desired in its long history: freedom.⁹²

A Cultural Hegemon

Athens' decline was indeed a "a singularly fascinating story," as C. Mossé claims, dependent on many factors, as we have been tracing, until after 146 came the new normal of Roman rule for all Greece and the east.⁹³ But is "decline" really the right way to describe the city, or is that view derived from unfairly comparing the Classical city to the later one? True, there had been times when the city looked like its old defiant self, as in the Chremonidean War against Antigonus II Gonatas or in backing Mithridates against Rome, or even poised for a return to Classical independence as in 229. These times, however, were simply mirages, and not reflective of the realpolitik of Antigonid and Roman rule.

None of that meant the Athenians were down and out, yet if it were not for the city's intellectual standing its history would have been quite different under Roman rule. As has been rightly said, Athens (or Greece for that matter) did not fall into a history-free limbo when Rome annexed it in 146; instead Hellenism, and alongside it Athens' forefront position, made it exceptional.⁹⁴ Thanks to Hadrian the city enjoyed a renaissance of prestige and reputation, something other cities could not match, even as all else declined. Hellenistic and Roman Athens did not shine in the way their Classical predecessor did, but as I said at the outset of this book, they still shone, just differently.

---

⁹¹ Graindor 1934, pp. 175–196, on the city and people.
⁹² Graindor 1934, pp. 111–114.
⁹³ Mossé 1973, pp. 152–153; see too the summary of Habicht 1997a, pp. 366–369.
⁹⁴ Spawforth 2012, p. 271.

The Romans may not have had a high opinion of the Greeks because of the differences in their "national characters."[95] But in one area Roman opinion of the Greeks was paramount: culture. The Romans of course had their own culture from an early time, the result of their contacts with the Greek cities in the south of Italy (so many that the area was nicknamed *Magna Graecia*) and Sicily, and then with the peoples of Italy, such as the Etruscans, as they conquered them. But the Romans were profoundly affected by the Athenian philosophers' embassy of 155, and accelerating throughout the first century and after, they embraced the mainland Greek civilization, and when needed appropriated aspects of it for their own needs.[96] The Athenians had struggled to maintain their identity, especially when it came to their art, seeing their city move from uniquely Athenian to provincial.[97] Hence on top of Roman mastery of Greece, having their conquerors appropriate aspects of their Hellenism and plunder relentlessly must have rankled all the more.

Romans, as we have noted, came to study philosophy and rhetoric in Athens, and away from philosophy, the poets Horace and Ovid went to the city and praised their time there.[98] But mere study was not enough. The Romans borrowed extensively from the Greeks in every genre, from epic poetry to tragedy to comedy to historiography to rhetoric, and of course philosophy; the list goes on.[99] Virgil, for example, was so influenced by the Homeric poems that his *Aeneid* (recounting Aeneas' wanderings after the fall of Troy to Italy and the eventual foundation of Rome) was a fusion of Homer's *Iliad* and *Odyssey*. Of the *Aeneid*'s twelve books, the first six (Aeneas' travels to Italy) mirror the *Odyssey* (Odysseus' wanderings), and the second six (the struggles of the Trojans) mirror the *Iliad* (Trojan War). Cicero, to give another example, so admired Demosthenes' *Philippics* that he called his own harangues against Mark Antony *Philippics*, and the Romans copiously

---

[95] See Ferguson 1911, pp. 281–282, for one way of describing the differences: "The Greek was a born salesman. He loved to bargain. . . . To the blunt, practical Roman he appeared a talkative fellow."
[96] See Wardman 1976; Rawson 1989; Griffin 1994; appropriation of Hellenism: Connolly 2007; Spawforth 2012; see too the essays in Walker and Cameron 1989; Ostenfeld 2002; Follett 2004a; Perrin-Saminadayar 2007b.
[97] Alcock 1997 (Romanization); Borg 2011 (identity); T. L. Shear 1981 (the apparent transformation to a provincial city).
[98] Horace, *Epistle* 2.2.41–52; Ovid, *Tristia* 1.2.77–78.
[99] Excellent discussion of Roman plagiarisms from Greeks in Wardman 1976 (through to later Empire); Greek influences in Roman literature of first century: Townend 1996. On the influence of Plato on Plutarch, for example, and by extension Rome, see Swain 1997.

copied Greek art, which was just as well, as the Greek originals (the statue of Demosthenes, for example) are lost (see Figure 5.1).

Yet in adapting, copying, and extending the already-existing intellectual and artistic world of the Greeks, the Romans put themselves in Greece's debt. Rome did indeed roll into Greece subjugating everywhere until, in 30, it ruled the entire Mediterranean. But it was the Greeks, especially the Athenians, who arguably emerged triumphant. As Horace succinctly put it: "Captive Greece captured her rude conqueror and introduced her arts to the crude Latin lands."[100]

Aftermath: To the Herulian Sack

Hadrian's successor, his adopted son Antoninus Pius, came to the throne in AD 138.[101] He did not visit Athens, but he did complete the aqueduct begun by his father, and his interest in philosophy and rhetoric in Athens led him to create a chair of rhetoric in the city.[102] Antoninus died in AD 161, and was succeeded by his adopted sons Lucius Verus and Marcus Aurelius, with the latter ruling solely after his brother's death in AD 168. Increasing conflicts in the east (especially in Parthia and Armenia) occupied their attention, but both these emperors visited Athens.[103] Marcus Aurelius was a Stoic philosopher and trained as an orator; he studied under the foremost Greek and Roman tutors of the day, including Herodes Atticus, and he had a deep appreciation for Athens. He and his son Commodus (the future emperor) went there in AD 176, where they were initiated into the Eleusinian Mysteries. It was Commodus who succeeded his father, and his death brought the long Nerva-Antonine dynasty to a close in AD 192.[104]

The era following Hadrian saw Athens' intellectual prestige at even greater heights as the movement known as the Second Sophistic was in full swing.[105] Its scholars included Dio of Prusa, Herodes Atticus, and Plutarch, who were all responsible for a rebirth in Greek literature. In the reigns of Antoninus Pius (r. AD 138–161) and Marcus Aurelius (r. 161–180) the great orator Aelius Aristides visited Athens and lectured there; Commodus awarded

---

[100] Horace, *Epistle* 2.1.156: *Graecia capta ferum victorem cepit et artis intulit agresti Latio*.
[101] Geagan 1979a, pp. 399–410, from Hadrian to the third century.
[102] Graindor 1927b.
[103] Geagan 1984.
[104] On the Antonine emperors: Birley 2000a, pp. 149–194.
[105] On which see most recently the essays in Johnson and Richter 2017.

the rhetorician Julius Pollux a chair in rhetoric at the Academy in Athens, and Pausanias was on his famous travels, spending considerable time in Athens and Attica. It is interesting to note that the scholars and poets at Alexandria and at Pergamun might well see themselves as heirs of Athenian literary masters, yet they did not appeal to the Romans—another testament to the artistic and cultural legacy of Greece, and especially Athens.[106] As has been rightly said, "In considering the Greek renaissance in the Roman Empire, it is hard to over-estimate the role played by Athens."[107]

Athens' position as center of the Panhellenion was unchecked, festivals continued to be held, and philosophers and rhetoricians still attracted students from the provinces as well as Rome itself. In this period we must mention the benefactions of one enormously wealthy prominent individual from a family we have already met: Herodes Atticus (AD 101–177), one of the period's leading sophists, patrons of the arts, and benefactors.[108] Born in Marathon, his family was one of the most distinguished in Athens; his father was the Roman senator Tiberius Claudius Atticus Herodes, and his son was archon in AD 140 as well as being a Roman senator and a consul at Rome in AD 143.[109]

Herodes Atticus funded major construction projects all over Greece, including a theater at Corinth, stadium at Delphi, and nymphaeum at Olympia. But it was Athens that reaped the most from his philanthropy. He rebuilt the Panathenaic Stadium in marble with a seating capacity of 50,000 between AD 139/40 and 143/4 and, in AD 161, he built his famous Odeum or theater, seating five thousand people, which was set into the southwest slope of the Acropolis (Figure 15.3). The latter was a memorial to his wife, Aspasia Annia Regilla (a relation of Antoninus Pius' wife), who had recently died in suspicious circumstances. Since it was roofed, it was meant to be a more functional and modern theater than the older one of Dionysus. Most of the *cavea* (seating area) was restored for modern performances in 1950.

After Hadrian, Greece was generally free from the terrible wars that had plagued it in previous centuries, although in AD 170 a tribe known as the Costoboces invaded and burned Eleusis. Then in AD 253 a Scythian invasion penetrated as far south as Thessalonica. But the rudest break to the peace

---

[106] Woolf 1994; Connolly 2007; Spawforth 2012, pp. 264–270; cf. Graindor 1931, pp. 155–157.
[107] Camp 1989, p. 50.
[108] On whom see Graindor 1939; Ameling 1983.
[109] Day 1942, pp. 241–248; H. A. Thompson 1987, pp. 14–15; Follet 2007.

FIGURE 15.3 Theater of Herodes Atticus. Photo: Ian Worthington.

and relative prosperity that Athens and Greece were enjoying came in AD 267 when the Herulians, a Gothic tribe originally located north of the Black Sea, attacked Greece and the Balkans, capturing Byzantium and sacking Athens. They were defeated two years later. Archaeology has shown that the attack on Athens was a major one, but there is disagreement as to its extent, from every building being burned to the ground to several areas being saved, including the theaters of Herodes Atticus and of Dionysus and the temple to Asclepius on the southern slope of the Acropolis.[110] Nevertheless, the two invasions prompted the people to restore the circuit wall, which had been left unattended for centuries—under the emperor Valerian (AD 253–260) repairs were made to it after the Scythian invasion, and again under Gallienus (AD 260–268) following the Herulian attack.[111]

---

[110] Everywhere burned: Zosimus 1.39; Synkellos 1.717; see too Dexippus, *BNJ* 100 F 28, with Day 1942, pp. 258–261; H. A. Thompson 1959, pp. 61–63; Thompson and Wycherley 1972, pp. 208–210. But Castrén 1989, pp. 45–47, argues that the damage is confused with that incurred during the attack by Alaric and Visigoths in AD 396; cf. Graindor 1922b, p. 270 n. 187.

[111] Theocharaki 2011, pp. 131–133; see too H. A. Thompson 1959, p. 65.

Still, the Athenians showed their resilience had not abated over the years. Opinion is divided on exactly when they began to rebuild and return to a normal life after the Herulian sack, but it appears that this was sooner rather than later. For one thing, there was little to no interruption to the philosophical and rhetorical schools, and for another, pottery increased in manufacture (as did Athenian lamps that were far superior to the Corinthian type that had long dominated) and festivals began to be held again.[112]

Thus we move to another post-invasion era for Athens, from Macedonians to Romans, and now Gothic tribes. It was an era, however, in which the city was in a "twilight," and remained so until the light arguably fell even more in AD 529 when Justinian closed the Academy.[113] But when set against this even later period, Athens in the so-called Hellenistic and Roman periods (at least to the end of the second century AD) had shown itself to be a worthy successor of its Classical self and still highly regarded in the Mediterranean world.

---

[112] Day 1942, pp. 252–261 (a century before rebuilding); Thompson and Wycherley 1972, pp. 210–215; sooner: Castrén 1989, pp. 45–47; see too H. A. Thompson 1959, pp. 63–71.
[113] H. A. Thompson 1959; see too Thompson and Wycherley 1972, pp. 208–219; Castrén 1989.

TIMELINE

BC

359–336
Reign of Philip II of Macedonia, father of Alexander the Great.

338
Battle of Chaeronea; Philip becomes master of Greece.

337
League of Corinth assures Macedonian hegemony of Greece; Philip announces invasion of Asia.

336–323
Assassination of Philip (July 336); reign of Alexander III (the Great).

334–323
Alexander's invasion of Asia; Antipater remains behind as regent of Greece.

330–324
Lycurgan Athens period.

323
Alexander dies in Babylon (June 11); the Babylon Settlement: Philip III and Alexander IV proclaimed kings (Perdiccas as regent); Alexander's empire divided among the Successors.

323–322
Lamian War—Greece vs. Macedonia (ends summer 322 with Antipater triumphant at the battle of Crannon); suicide of Demosthenes; Antipater installs an oligarchy in Athens and establishes wealth requirement for citizenship, curtailing the democracy.

321
Ptolemy hijacks Alexander's corpse; Perdiccas declares war on Ptolemy; start of the First War of the Successors (321–320).

320
Perdiccas unsuccessfully invades Egypt and is killed; end of the First War of the Successors; Triparadeisus settlement.

319
Death of Antipater; Polyperchon his successor but Antipater's son Cassander forms alliance against him; start of the Second War of the Successors (319–316); execution of Athenian general Phocion.

317
Cassander seizes Greece and Macedonia; installs Demetrius of Phalerum in Athens as his nominal ruler; Philip III murdered.

317–307
Regime of Demetrius of Phalerum in Athens.

316
Cassander becomes guardian of Alexander IV; end of the Second War of the Successors.

315
Start of the Third War of the Successors (315–311).

311
End of the Third War of the Successors.

310 (or 309)
Cassander has Alexander IV and his mother, Roxane, murdered; end of the Argead dynasty of Macedonia.

307
Demetrius Poliorcetes seizes Athens on behalf of his father Antigonus Monophthalmus; expels Demetrius of Phalerum, who goes to Thebes and then Alexandria; start of the Fourth War of the Successors (307–301); Stratocles of Athens introduces exorbitant honors on the Antigonids,

including hailing them as savior gods and founding new tribes named after them.

306
Monophthalmus and Poliorcetes assume the kingship; other Successors follow suit; Poliorcetes defeats Ptolemy off Cyprus to establish Antigonid supremacy at sea; Cassander's unsuccessful attempt to retake Athens.

305–304
Poliorcetes' epic (but unsuccessful) siege of Rhodes; Cassander again attempts to seize Greece and Macedonia; Poliorcetes winters in Athens (304–303); forces Athenians to raise 250 talents, which he gives to his mistress Lamia for soap.

303
Poliorcetes campaigns in the Peloponnese; pressures Athenians into inducting him into the Eleusinian Mysteries.

302
Poliorcetes leaves Athens (spring); plans to resurrect the League of Corinth with both Antigonids its hegemons; coalition of Cassander, Ptolemy, Lysimachus, and Seleucus forces Monophthalmus to summon Poliorcetes to Asia.

301
Battle of Ipsus; defeat of the Antigonids and death of Monophthalmus; Poliorcetes and troops escape to Ephesus; end of the Fourth War of the Successors; Athenians expel Poliorcetes' wife Deidameia and refuse to take him back; rise to prominence of Phaedrus of Sphettus in Athens; grain shortages there cause economic distress.

297
Lachares seizes power in Athens (possibly persuaded by Cassander); death of Cassander (May).

296–295
Athenian faction captures Piraeus to defy tyranny of Lachares (winter); Poliorcetes arrives in Greece, and moderate Athenians seek his support against Lachares.

294
End of tyranny of Lachares (spring); Poliorcetes takes control of Athens and Greece; installs garrison on Museum Hill in Athens; Poliorcetes becomes king of Macedonia (fall).

293–291
Poliorcetes campaigns in Thessaly and Boeotia.

c. 292
Athenian honorary decree for Philippides.

290
Poliorcetes returns to Athens; the Athenians greet him sycophantically, especially with their ithyphallic hymn; increasing threats to his position from Ptolemy, Pyrrhus, Lysimachus, and Seleucus, as well as dissatisfaction from the Macedonians over his lifestyle and future plans.

288–287
The Fifth War of the Successors; Pyrrhus and Lysimachus invade Macedonia; Ptolemy sends military support to Athens; the Athenians revolt and attack the Macedonian garrisons (spring 287); Poliorcetes flees Greece, eventually to the court of Seleucus.

285–284
Demochares recaptures Eleusis.

283
Death of Ptolemy I, aged about eighty-two (January–February); Ptolemy II becomes king of Egypt; death of Poliorcetes (summer).

281
Unsuccessful Athenian attempt to wrest control of the Piraeus; death of Lysimachus in battle against Seleucus at Corupedium; murder of Seleucus by Ptolemy Caraunus; lengthy Wars of the Successors finally end.

280–279
Honorary statue for Demosthenes successfully proposed by nephew Demochares; Galatian invasions begin (279); death of Ptolemy Caraunus of Macedonia leaves kingdom chaotic.

277
Antigonus Gonatas defeats Galatians in Thrace in battle at Lysimacheia; seizes Macedonia and declares himself king (Antigonus II).

270–269
Honorary decree for Callias of Sphettus (for fighting against Poliorcetes in 287).

268–261

Chremonidean War; Antigonus punishes Athens; death of Zeno, founder of Stoicism (261).

256

Antigonus withdraws the garrison from the Museum Hill.

255–254

Honorary decree for Phaedrus of Sphettus (for fighting against Poliorcetes in 287); Athens remains firmly under control of Antigonus II.

242

Aratus of the Achaean League marches into Attica, but cannot win over Athens.

239

Death of Antigonus II; accession of Demetrius II.

229

Death of Demetrius II; accession of Antigonus III Doson; Athens regains independence, begins to prosper economically; Eurycleides and Micion politically dominant; start of the First Illyrian War (Rome vs. Illyrians).

228

End of the First Illyrian War.

224 or 223

Athens founds a cult to Ptolemy III and his wife Berenice, and awards other honors, including a tribe named after him (Ptolemais).

221

Death of Antigonus III; accession of Philip V.

220–217

Social War in Greece; Athens stresses its friendship to Philip V and Aetolian League.

219

Outbreak of the Second Illyrian War, which ends same year.

218–201

Second Punic Rome (Rome vs. Carthage).

215

Philip V allies with Hannibal of Carthage; Athens honors Eurycleides (a sign that he—and possibly Micion—have retired from public life or died).

214–205

The First Macedonian War (Rome vs. Philip V), during which Athens unsuccessfully tries to broker peace (209); the war ends with the Peace of Phoenice (205).

201

Athens executes two men from Acarnania for violating the Mysteries, a major trigger in warfare between Athens and Philip V; Athens turns to Attalus I of Pergamum for support.

200–196

The Second Macedonian War (Rome vs. Philip V).

200

Athens declares war on Philip V; Macedonian invasions of Attica, including burning the Academy and desecrating sacred buildings; the Athenians formally curse Philip and all Antigonid rulers; the Athenians drum up more support against Philip.

197

Titus Quinctius Flamininus defeats Philip in battle at Cynoscephalae (Thessaly); Philip survives the battle; end of Second Macedonian War.

196

Rome imposes penalties on Philip V; Roman proclamation of Greek freedom.

195

Diplomatic war between Athens and the Aetolian League; in Athens, increasing pressure by some politicians over the following years to align with Antiochus and break with Rome.

192

Apollodorus of Athens prevents Flamininus speaking in Athens; Antiochus III lands in Greece; in Athens, Leon of Aixone has Apollodorus exiled; relations between Athens and Rome stay friendly.

186–184

Rome tasks Athens and Thessaly with reorganizing the Amphictyonic Council.

179
Death of Philip V; accession of Perseus; increasing antagonism of Eumenes II of Pergamum.

171–168
The Third Macedonian War (Rome vs. Perseus).

168
Lucius Aemilius Paullus defeats Perseus at the battle of Pydna to end the Third Macedonian War; Perseus captured and taken to Rome.

167
Rome ends the Antigonid dynasty; Macedonia partitioned into four independent republics; Paullus invades and sacks Epirus; he and his son (Scipio Aemilianus) visit Athens; Athenian embassy to the Senate successfully petitions for the return of Delos and other places.

164
Athens invades territory of Oropus; Oropians appeal to Rome, which orders Sicyon to arbitrate; Athens fined but refuses to pay and maintains control of Oropus.

155
Philosophers embassy to Rome to protest the fine, which Senate reduces, but Athens still refuses to pay and relinquish Oropus; increasing number of Romans start to visit and study in Athens.

150
Andriscus, claiming to be son of Perseus, reunites Macedonia and defies Rome.

149–148
The Fourth Macedonian War (Rome vs. Andriscus); Quintus Caecilius Metellus defeats him at the second battle of Pydna; Rome now turns Macedonia and Illyria into a Roman province.

146
The Achaean War, the culmination of increasing friction between the Achaean League and Rome for many years; Lucius Mummius besieges Corinth (center of resistance to Rome), captures and razes it, killing all men, taking women and children as slaves, and plundering artworks; Rome turns Greece into a province.

134

Revolt of slaves in the Laurium mines.

123/2

First recorded foreign ephebes in Athens.

100

Second revolt of slaves in the Laurium mines.

91–88

Athens under the control of Medeius, a would-be tyrant.

88

Athenion sent to Mithridates VI of Pontus to discuss anti-Roman moves and his support of Greek freedom; Athens supports Mithridates against Rome; Aristion tyrant of Athens; around now Delos revolts in favor of Rome.

87

Lucius Cornelius Sulla and five legions sent to Greece; besieges Aristion in Athens and Archelaus (Mithridates' general) in the Piraeus, but unsuccessful; terrible conditions in Athens, including a food shortage.

86

Sulla returns to besiege Athens; sacks Athens (March 1), slaughtering many and destroying buildings; Aristion captured on Acropolis and executed (date unknown); Sulla expels Archelaus from the Piraeus and defeats him in battle at Chaeronea (Boeotia); Areopagus foremost body in Athens; Titus Pomponius (more famously known as Cicero's correspondent and confidant, Atticus) moves to Athens (or in 85) as part of an increasing number of Romans visiting the city.

68

Publius Cornelius Dolabella (governor of Smyrna) refers a homicide case to the Areopagus, possibly a sign of thawing in Athenian–Roman relations.

67

Visit of Pompey (the Great) to Athens.

62

Pompey revisits Athens and donates 50 talents to building projects.

58

Publius Clodius Pulcher introduces his *lex Clodia de provinciis consularibus*, which may have made Athens subject to Rome.

51
Visit of Julia Caesar; donates 50 talents, used to start the Roman Agora (market of Caesar and Augustus).

49/8
First Assembly decree of the post-Sullan period; outbreak of Roman Civil War (Senate vs. Caesar); Athens supports Pompey.

48
Athens besieged by Caesar's legate Quintus Fufius Calenus; Caesar defeats Pompey at the battle of Pharsalus; Pompey flees to Egypt and is murdered; Athens surrenders to Caesar.

45
End of Roman Civil War; Caesar dictator.

44
Caesar assassinated in Rome (Ides of March); Brutus and Cassius go to Greece, and at least Brutus stays in Athens, which city honors them with a statue.

42–41
Brutus and Cassius defeated at the battles of Philippi; Antony becomes ruler of the east and moves to live in Athens; goes to winter with Cleopatra VII in Alexandria (41).

40–31
Antony returns to Athens, lives there with wife Octavia; Athens honors both of them, including divine honors for Octavia; over the following years, declining relations with Octavian, Antony's disastrous invasion of the Parthian (Arsacid) Empire, and Antony's further stays in Athens.

31
Agrippa defeats Antony and Cleopatra in battle at Actium; they flee back to Egypt; Octavian takes over Athens and Greece.

30
Death of Antony and Cleopatra; Octavian annexes Egypt; Rome now controls all of eastern Mediterranean; possibly now that Athens institutes cult of the emperor.

27
Octavian becomes Augustus; Athens honors him and Agrippa.

21

Augustus' second visit to Athens; tension between him and the Athenians leads to his punitive measures against the city; eventually both sides reconcile.

19

Augustus visits Athens again; donates money to complete the Roman Agora; dedication of the temple of Roma and Augustus on the Acropolis.

15

Agrippa builds huge Odeum in the Athenian Agora.

c. 12

Introduction of the cult of Vesta in Athens.

AD

2

Gaius Caesar (Augustus' grandson) visits Athens while en route to Parthia.

13

Athenian revolt against Rome, but quickly put down.

14

Death of Augustus; Tiberius emperor; Athens bestows honors on him.

18

Germanicus Caesar (adopted son and heir of Tiberius), visits Athens while en route to Asia.

37

Death of Tiberius; Caligula emperor; Athens bestows limited number of honors on him.

41

Death of Caligula; Claudius emperor; Athens bestows various honors on him; responsible for some building projects in the city; the cult of Roma and Augustus converted to collective one of the *Sebastoi* (after 45/6).

51

Paul the Apostle arrives in Athens and preaches to the people, and also speaks before the Areopagus.

54

Death of Claudius; Nero emperor; Athens bestows some honors on him, but not as many as on Claudius.

66/7
Nero visits Greece; does not go to Athens; announces freedom of Achaea and a remission of taxes (67).

68
Death of Nero; end of Julio-Claudian dynasty; Year of the Four Emperors.

69–70
Vespasian becomes emperor, establishes the Flavian dynasty; Athenian honors run only to rededications of existing monuments; Vespasian restores the province of Achaea (in 70); introduces measures to curb the political activities of the philosophical schools in Athens.

79
Death of Vespasian; Titus emperor; Athenian honors run only to rededications of existing ones.

81
Death of Titus; Domitian emperor; few Athenian honors on him; he is the first emperor to be eponymous archon (between AD 84/5 and 92/3); arranges execution on trumped-up charges of Tiberius Claudius Hipparchus of Marathon so as to seize his lands and fortune.

96
Death of Domitian; end of Flavian dynasty; Nerva emperor and founds Nerva-Antonine dynasty; allows Atticus (the son of the Hipparchus killed by Domitian) to keep treasure he found, perhaps to show his contempt of Domitian's act.

98
Death of Nerva; Trajan emperor; Athenians set up only four statues to him.

100–102
Building of the library of Pantaenus in Athens.

112–113
Hadrian visits Athens (before becoming emperor); granted Athenian citizenship; made eponymous archon.

113
Trajan visits Athens.

114–116
Building of the elaborate funerary memorial of Philopappus atop the Museum Hill in Athens.

117

Death of Trajan; Hadrian emperor (117–138); inaugurates great building program in Athens.

121

Hadrian undoes Vespasian's measures against the philosophical schools in Athens.

124/5

Hadrian's first imperial visit to Athens; reforms Athenian constitution; introduces financial and economic reforms; introduces decree regulating the sale of olive oil (by 126/7); serves as the *agonothetes* of the Dionysia.

128/9

Hadrian's second visit to Athens; numerous Athenian honors bestowed on him, including the most numbers of statues to any emperor.

131/2

Hadrian's third visit to Athens (winter); his Panhellenion launched; temple of Olympian Zeus finished and dedicated; the Athenians commission and dedicate the famous Arch to him; Athens as center of the Panhellenion again influential in the Greek world.

BIBLIOGRAPHY

I have used the original publications and paginations for articles reprinted in collections of scholars' works (for example, Habicht 1994a; Oliver 1983; Walbank 2002).

Abramson, H., "The Olympieion in Athens and Its Connections with Rome," *CSCA* 7 (1975), pp. 1–25
Accame, S., *Il Dominio Romano in Grecia* (Rome: 1946)
Adams, A., "The Arch of Hadrian at Athens," in S. Walker and A. Cameron (eds.), *Greek Renaissance in the Roman Empire* (London: 1989), pp. 10–16
Adams, W. L., "Perseus and the Third Macedonian War," in W. L. Adams and E. N. Borza (eds.), *Philip II, Alexander the Great, and the Macedonian Heritage* (Washington: 1982), pp. 237–256
Adams, W. L., "The Successors of Alexander," in L. A. Tritle (ed.), *The Greek World in the Fourth Century* (London: 1997), pp. 228–248
Adams, W. L., "The Hellenistic Kingdoms," in G. R. Bugh (ed.), *The Cambridge Companion to the Hellenistic World* (Cambridge: 2007), pp. 28–51
Adams, W. L., "Alexander's Successors to 221 BC," in J. Roisman and I. Worthington (eds.), *A Companion to Ancient Macedonia* (Malden: 2010), pp. 208–224
Ager, S. L., *Interstate Arbitrations in the Greek World, 337–90 B.C.* (Berkeley: 1996)
Ager, S. L., "An Uneasy Balance: From the Death of Seleukos to the Battle of Raphia," in A. Erskine (ed.), *A Companion to the Hellenistic World* (Malden: 2003), pp. 35–50
Ajootian, A., "A Roman Athena from the Pnyx and the Agora in Athens," *Hesperia* 78 (2009), pp. 481–499

Alcock, S. E., *Graecia Capta: The Landscapes of Roman Greece* (Cambridge: 1993)
Alcock, S. E., "Nero at Play? The Emperor's Grecian Odyssey," in J. Elsner and J. Masters (eds.), *Reflections of Nero: Culture, History and Representation* (London: 1994), pp. 98–111
Alcock, S. E., "The Problem of Romanization, The Power of Athens," in M. C. Hoff and S. I. Rotroff (eds.), *The Romanization of Athens* (Oxford: 1997), pp. 1–7
Aleshire, S., "The Demos and the Priests: The Selection of Sacred Officials at Athens from Cleisthenes to Augustus," in R. Osborne and S. Hornblower (eds.), *Ritual, Finance, Politics*: *Athenian Democratic Accounts Presented to David Lewis* (Oxford: 1994), pp. 325–338
Allen, R. E., "Attalus I and Aegina," *BSA* 66 (1971), pp. 1–12
Allen, R. E., *The Attalid Kingdom: A Constitutional History* (Oxford: 1983)
Amela Valverde, L., "La campaña de Q. Fufio Caleno en Grecia en el año 48 A.C. y la ciudad de *Megara* La consecuencias de la guerra," *Athenaeum* 96 (2008), pp. 271–291
Ameling, W., *Herodes Atticus* (Hildesheim: 1983)
Andronikos, M., "Art during the Archaic and Classical Periods," in M. B. Sakellariou (ed.), *Macedonia, 4000 Years of Greek History and Civilization* (Athens: 1983), pp. 92–110
Anson, E. M., "Diodorus and the Date of Triparadeisus," *AJP* 107 (1986), pp. 208–217
Anson, E. M., *Alexander's Heirs: The Age of the Successors* (Malden: 2014)
Antela-Bernárdez, B., "Entre Delos, Atenas, Roma y el Ponto: Medeios del Pireo," *Faventia* 31 (2009a), pp. 49–60
Antela-Bernárdez, B., "Between Medeios and Mithridates: The Peripatetic Constitution of Athens (Agora I 2351)," *ZPE* 171 (2009b), pp. 105–108
Antela-Bernárdez, B., "A Crown for Onaso and the Archon Athenion," *ZPE* 177 (2011), pp. 91–96
Antela-Bernárdez, B., "Athenion of Athens Revisited," *Klio* 97 (2015), pp. 59–80
Antela-Bernárdez, B., "The Last Tyrants of Athens," *Karanos* 2 (2019), pp. 43–53
Ashton, N. G., "The Lamian War—stat magni nominis umbra," *JHS* 94 (1984), pp. 152–157
Atkinson, J. E., "Macedon and Athenian Politics in the Period 338 to 323 BC," *Acta Classica* 24 (1981), 37–48
Atkinson, K. M. T., "Demosthenes, Alexander and Asebeia," *Athenaeum* 51 (1973), pp. 310–335
Austin, C., "Catalogus Comicorum Graecorum," *ZPE* 14 (1974), pp. 201–225
Austin, M. M., *The Hellenistic World from Alexander to the Roman Conquest: A Selection of Ancient Sources in Translation*² (Cambridge: 2006)
Azoulay, V., and P. Ismard (eds.), *Clisthène et Lycurgue d'Athènes: autour du politique dans la cité classique* (Paris: 2011)
Badian, E., *Publicans and Sinners: Private Enterprise in the Service of the Roman Republic* (Oxford: 1972)
Badian, E., "Rome, Athens and Mithridates," *AJAH* 1 (1976), pp. 105–128

Badian, E., "Agis III Revisited," in I. Worthington (ed.), *Ventures into Greek History: Essays in Honour of N. G. L. Hammond* (Oxford: 1994), pp. 258–292

Baldassari, P., *Sebastoi Soteri* (Munich: 1995a)

Baldassari, P., "Augusto *Soter*: ipotesi sul *Monopteros* dell' Acropoli ateniese," *Ostraka* 4 (1995b), pp. 69–84

Ballesteros Pastor, L., *Mitrídates Eupátor, rey del Ponto* (Granada: 1996)

Ballesteros Pastor, L., "Atenión, tirano de Atenas," *St. Hist* 23 (2005), pp. 385–400

Bardani, V. N., and S. V. Tracy, "A New List of Athenian Ephebes and a New Archon of Athens," *ZPE* 163 (2007), pp. 75–80

Bardani, V. N., and S. V. Tracy (eds.), *Inscriptiones Graecae II/III³ 1, 5 Inscriptiones Atticae Euclidis Anno Posteriores,* Pars 1, Fascicle 5, *leges et decreta annorum 229/8–168/7* (Berlin: 2012)

Barnes, T. D., "An Apostle on Trial," *Journal of Theological Studies* 20 (1969), pp. 407–419

Baronowski, D. W., "The Provincial Status of Mainland Greece after 146 B.C.: A Criticism of Erich Gruen's Views," *Klio* 70 (1988), pp. 448–460

Baronowski, D. W., *Polybius and Roman Imperialism* (London: 2011)

Barrett, A. A., *Caligula: The Abuse of Power*² (London: 2015)

Barringer, J. M., "Panathenaic Games and Panathenaic Amphorae under Macedonian Rule," in O. Palagia and S. V. Tracy (eds.), *The Macedonians in Athens, 322–229 BC* (Oxford: 2003), pp. 243–256

Baslez, M.-F., "Citoyens et non-citoyens dans l'Athènes imperiale au Ier et au IIe siècles de notre ère," in S. Walker and A. Cameron (eds.), *The Greek Renaissance in the Roman Empire* (London: 1989), pp. 17–36

Baslez, M.-F., "La famille de Philopappos de Commagène, un prince entre deux mondes," *Dialogues d'histoire Ancienne* 18 (1992), pp. 89–101

Baslez, M.-F., "Les Notables Entre Eux. Recherches sur les Associations d'Athènes à l'Époque Romaine," in S. Follet (ed.), *L'Hellénisme d'Époque Romaine: Nouveaux Documents, Nouvelles Approches* (Paris: 2004), pp. 105–117

Bayliss, A. J., *After Demosthenes: The Politics of Early Hellenistic Athens* (London: 2011)

Baynham, E., "Antipater: Manager of Kings," in I. Worthington (ed.), *Ventures into Greek History: Essays in Honour of N. G. L. Hammond* (Oxford: 1994), pp. 331–356

Baynham, E., "Antipater and Athens," in O. Palagia and S. V. Tracy (eds.), *The Macedonians in Athens, 322–229 BC* (Oxford: 2003), pp. 23–29

Benjamin, A., "The Altars of Hadrian and Hadrian's Panhellenic Program," *Hesperia* 32 (1963), pp. 57–86

Benjamin, A., and A. E. Raubitschek, "Arae Augusti," *Hesperia* 28 (1959), pp. 65–85

Bennett, B., and M. Roberts, *The Wars of Alexander's Successors, 323–281 BC* 1 and 2 (Barnsley: 2008–2009)

Bennett, J., *Trajan: Optimus Princeps* (London: 2000)

Béquignon, Y., "Études Thessaliennes: VII. Inscriptions de Thessalie," *BCH* 59 (1935), pp. 36–77

Bernhardt, R., *Imperium and Eleutheria* (Hamburg: 1971)
Bernhardt, R., "Athen, Augustus und die eleusinischen Mysterien," *Ath.Mitt.* 90 (1975), pp. 233–237
Berthold, R. M., *Rhodes in the Hellenistic Age* (London: 1984)
Bevan, E. R., *The House of Seleucus* (London: 1902)
Bevan, E. R., *The House of Ptolemy: A History of Egypt under the Ptolemaic Dynasty* (London: 1927)
Bikerman, E., *Institutions des Séleucides* (Paris: 1938)
Billows, R., *Antigonus the One-Eyed and the Creation of the Hellenistic State* (Berkeley: 1990)
Billows, R. *Kings and Colonists* (Leiden: 1995)
Binder, W., *Der Roma-Augustus Monopteros auf der Akropolis in Athen und sein typologisher Ort* (Suttgart: 1969)
Bingen, J., *Hellenistic Egypt: Monarchy Society, Economy, Culture* (Edinburgh: 2007)
Birley, A. R., "Hadrian and the Greek Senators," *ZPE* 116 (1997), pp. 209–245
Birley, A. R., "Hadrian to the Antonines," in A. K. Bowman, P. Garnsey, and D. Rathbone (eds.), *Cambridge Ancient History*^{2} 11 (Cambridge: 2000a), pp. 132–194
Birley, A. R., *Hadrian: The Restless Emperor* (London: 2000b)
Blackwell, C. W., *In the Absence of Alexander: Harpalus and the Failure of Macedonian Authority* (New York: 1998)
Boatwright, M. T., *Hadrian and the Cities of the Roman Empire* (Princeton: 2000)
Boegehold, A. L., *The Lawcourts at Athens: The Athenian Agora* 28 (Princeton: 1995)
Borg, B. E., "Who Cared about Greek Identity? Athens in the First Century BCE," in T. A. Schmitz and N. Wiater (eds.), *The Struggle for Identity: Greeks and their Past in the First Century BCE* (Stuttgart: 2011), pp. 213–234
Bosworth, A. B., "Alexander the Great and the Decline of Macedon," *JHS* 106 (1986a), pp. 1–12
Bosworth, A. B., "Macedonian Manpower under Alexander the Great," in *Ancient Macedonia* 4 (Institute for Balkan Studies, Thessaloniki: 1986b), pp. 115–122
Bosworth, A. B., *Conquest and Empire: The Reign of Alexander the Great* (Cambridge: 1988)
Bosworth, A. B., "Philip III Arrhidaeus and the Chronology of the Successors," *Chiron* 22 (1992), pp. 55–81
Bosworth, A. B., *The Legacy of Alexander: Politics, Warfare, and Propaganda under the Successors* (Oxford: 2002)
Bosworth, A. B., "Why Did Athens Lose the Lamian War?," in O. Palagia and S. V. Tracy (eds.), *The Macedonians in Athens, 322–229 BC* (Oxford: 2003), pp. 14–22
Bosworth, A. B., "Alexander the Great and the Creation of the Hellenistic Age," in G. R. Bugh (ed.), *The Cambridge Companion to the Hellenistic World* (Cambridge: 2007), pp. 9–27
Bouché-Leclercq, A., *Histoire des Lagides*, 4 vols. (Paris: 1903–1907)
Bouché-Leclercq, A., *Histoire des Séleucides (323–64 avant J.-C.)*, 2 vols. (Paris: 1914)

Bousquet, J., "Le roi Persée et les Romains," *BCH* 105 (1981), pp. 407–416
Bowersock, G. W., "Augustus on Aegina," *CQ²* 14 (1964), pp. 120–122
Bowersock, G. W., *Augustus and the Greek World* (Oxford: 1965)
Bowersock, G. W., "The New Hellenism of Augustan Athens," *Annali della Scuola Normale Superiore di Pisa* 4 (2002), pp. 1–16
Bowie, E., "Literature and Sophistic," in A. K. Bowman, P. Garnsey, and D. Rathbone (eds.), *Cambridge Ancient History²* 11 (Cambridge: 2000), pp. 898–921
Bowie, E., "Hadrian and Greek Poetry," in E. N. Ostenfeld, *Greek Romans and Roman Greeks: Studies in Cultural Interaction* (Aarhus: 2002), pp. 172–197
Bowman, A. K., *Egypt after the Pharaohs: 332 BC to AD 642: From Alexander to the Arab Conquest* (London: 1986)
Bradley, K. R., "The Chronology of Nero's Visit to Greece, A.D. 66/67," *Latomus* 37 (1978), pp. 61–72
Braund, D., "The Emergence of the Hellenistic World, 323–281," in A. Erskine (ed.), *A Companion to the Hellenistic World* (Malden: 2003), pp. 19–34
Bremer, J. M., "Plutarch and the 'Liberation of Greece,'" in L. de Blois, J. Boens, T. Kessels, and D. M. Schenkeveld (eds.), *The Statesman in Plutarch's Works* 2 (Leiden: 2005), pp. 257–267
Bringmann, K., "Poseidonios and Athenion: A Study in Hellenistic Historiography," in P. Cartledge, P. Garnsey, and E. Gruen (eds.), *Hellenistic Constructs. Essays in Culture, History, and Historiography* (Berkeley: 1997), pp. 145–158
Briscoe, J., "The Second Punic War," in A. E. Astin, F. W. Walbank, M. W. Fredericksen, and R. M. Ogilvie (eds.), *Cambridge Ancient History²* 8 (Cambridge: 1989), pp. 44–80
Brogan, T. M., "Liberation Honors: Athenian Monuments from Antigonid Victories in Their Immediate and Broader Contexts," in O. Palagia and S. V. Tracy (eds.), *The Macedonians in Athens, 322–229 BC* (Oxford: 2003), pp. 194–205
Brown, E. L., "Antigonus Surnamed Gonatas," in G. W. Bowersock, W. Burkert, M. C. J. Putnam (eds.), *Arktouros: Hellenic Studies Presented to Bernard Knox* (New York: 1979), pp. 299–307
Bugh, G. R., *The Horsemen of Athens* (Princeton: 1988)
Bugh, G. R., "The Theseia in Late Hellenistic Athens," *ZPE* 83 (1990), pp. 20–37
Bugh, G. R., "Athenion and Aristion of Athens," *Phoenix* 46 (1992), pp. 108–123
Bugh, G. R., "Cavalry Inscriptions from the Athenian Agora," *Hesperia* 67 (1998) pp. 81–90
Bugh, G. R. (ed.), *The Cambridge Companion to the Hellenistic World* (Cambridge: 2007)
Burckhardt, L. A., "Die attische Ephebie in hellenistischer Zeit," in D. Kah and P. Scholz (eds.), *Das hellenistische Gymnasion* (Berlin: 2004), pp. 193–206
Burden, J. C., "Athens Remade in the Age of Augustus: A Study of the Architects and Craftsmen at Work," Ph.D. Diss. (Berkeley: 1999)

Burke, E. M., "*Contra Leocratem* and *De Corona*: Political Collaboration?," *Phoenix* 31 (1977), pp. 330–340
Burke, E. M., "Lycurgan Finances," *GRBS* 26 (1985), pp. 251–264
Burstein, S. M., "IG II2 1485A and Athenian Relations with Lysimachus," *ZPE* 31 (1978a), pp. 181–185
Burstein, S. M., "*IG* II² 653, Demosthenes and Athenian Relations with Bosporus in the Fourth Century B.C.," *Historia* 27 (1978b), pp. 428–436
Burstein, S. M., "Bithys, Son of Cleon from Lysimacheia: A Reconsideration of the Date and Significance of IG II², 808," *CSCA* 12 (1979), pp. 39–50
Burstein, S. M., "Arsinoë II Philadelphos: A Revisionist Review," in W. L. Adams and E. N. Borza (eds.), *Philip II, Alexander the Great, and the Macedonian Heritage* (Lanham: 1982), pp. 197–212
Burstein, S. M., *The Hellenistic Age from the Battle of Ipsos to the Death of Kleopatra VII* (Cambridge: 1985)
Burstein, S. M., *The Reign of Cleopatra* (Westport: 2004)
Burton, P.J., *Friendship and Empire. Roman Diplomacy and Imperialism in the Middle Republic (353–146 BC)* (Cambridge: 2011)
Burton, P.J., "The International *Amicitia* between Athens and Rome," *Antichthon* 47 (2013), pp. 207–218
Byrne, S. G., "The Athenian *Damnnatio Memoriae* of the Antigonids in 200 B.C.," in A. Tamis, C. J. Mackie, and S. G. Byrne (eds.), *Philathenaios: Studies in Honour of Michael J. Osborne* (Athens: 2010), pp. 157–177
Byrne, S. G., *Roman Citizens of Athens* (Leuven: 2003)
Calendra, E., "Spunti di discussion (su Atene romana e post-romana)," *Athenaeum* 86 (1998), pp. 261–272
Cameron, A., "The Garland of Philip," *GRBS* 21 (1980), pp. 43–62
Camia, F., "Political Elite and Priestly Posts in Athens during the Roman Imperial Period: Some Considerations," *ZPE* 188 (2014), pp. 139–148
Camia, F., A. Corcella, and M. C. Monaco, "Hadrian, the *Olympeieion*, and the Foreign Cities," in V. Di Napoli, F. Camia, V. Evangelidis, D. Grigoropoulos, D. Rogers, and S. Vlizos (eds.), *What's New in Roman Greece? Recent Work on the Greek Mainland and the Islands in the Roman Period* (Athens: 2018), pp. 477–485
Camp, J. M., "The Philosophical Schools of Roman Athens," in S. Walker and A. Cameron (eds.), *Greek Renaissance in the Roman Empire* (London: 1989), pp. 50–55
Campanile, D., "Cornelio Dolabella, la donna di Smirne et l'areopago," *RAL* 15 (2004), pp. 155–175
Canevaro, M., "Demosthenic Influences in Early Rhetorical Education," in M. Canevaro and B. Gray (eds.), *The Hellenistic Reception of Classical Athenian Democracy and Political Thought* (Oxford: 2018), pp. 73–92
Canevaro, M., and B. Gray (eds.), *The Hellenistic Reception of Classical Athenian Democracy and Political Thought* (Oxford: 2018)
Cargill, J., *The Second Athenian League* (Berkeley: 1981)
Carney, E. D., *Arsinoe of Egypt and Macedon: A Royal Life* (New York: 2013)
Carter, J. M., *The Battle of Actium* (London: 1970)

Castrén, P., "The Post-Herulian Revival at Athens," in S. Walker and A. Cameron (eds.), *Greek Renaissance in the Roman Empire* (London: 1989), pp. 45–49

Cawkwell, G. L., "Eubulus," *JHS* 83 (1963), pp. 47–67

Cawkwell, G. L., *Philip of Macedon* (London: 1978)

Cawkwell, G. L., "The End of Greek Liberty," in R. W. Wallace and E. M. Harris (eds.), *Transitions to Empire: Essays in Honor of E. Badian* (Norman: 1996), pp. 98–121

Champion, J., *Pyrrhus of Epirus* (Barnsley: 2012)

Champion, J., *Antigonus the One-Eyed: Greatest of the Successors* (Barnsley: 2014)

Chaniotis, A., "The Divinity of Hellenistic Rulers," in A. Erskine (ed.), *A Companion to the Hellenistic World* (Malden: 2003), pp. 431–445

Chaniotis, A., *War in the Hellenistic World: A Social and Cultural History* (Malden: 2005)

Chaniotis, A., *Age of Conquests: The Greek World from Alexander to Hadrian* (Cambridge: 2018)

Chankowski, A. S., *L'Éphébie Hellénistique. Étude d'une institution civique dans les cites grecques des îles de la Mer Égée et de l'Asie Mineure* (Paris: 2010)

Choremi-Spetsieri, A., "Vivliothiki to Adrianou," *Arch. Deltion* 51 (1996), pp. 25–32

Choremi-Spetsieri, A., and I. Tinginagka, "H Bibliotheke tou Adrianou sten Athena. T qanaskaphika dedomena," in S. Vlizos (ed.), *Athens during the Roman Period: Recent Discoveries, New Evidence* (Athens: 2008), pp. 115–131

Clarke, G. W., "The Origins and Spread of Christianity," in A. K. Bowman, E. Champlin, and A. Lintott (eds.), *Cambridge Ancient History*[2] 10 (Cambridge: 1996), pp. 848–872

Clauss, J. J., and M. Cuypers (eds.), *A Companion to Hellenistic Literature* (Malden: 2010)

Clinton, K., *The Sacred Officials of the Eleusinian Mysteries* (Philadelphia: 1974)

Clinton, K., "The Eleusinian Mysteries: Roman Initiates and Benefactors, Second Century B.C. to A.D. 267," in W. Haase (ed.), *Aufstieg und Niedergang der Römischen Welt* 2.18.2 (Berlin: 1989a), pp. 1499–1539

Clinton, K., "Hadrian's Contribution to the Renaissance at Eleusis," in S. Walker and A. Cameron (eds.), *Greek Renaissance in the Roman Empire* (London: 1989b), pp. 56–68

Clinton, K., "The Eleusinian Mysteries and Panhellenism in Democratic Athens," in W. Coulson et al., *The Archaeology of Athens and Attica under the Democracy* (Oxford: 1994), pp. 161–172

Clinton, K., "Eleusis and the Romans: Late Republic to Marcus Aurelius," in M. C. Hoff and S. I. Rotroff (eds.), *The Romanization of Athens* (Oxford: 1997), pp. 161–181

Connolly, J., "Being Greek—Being Roman: Hellenism and Assimilation in the Roman Empire," *Millenium* 4 (2007), pp. 21–42

Connor, W. R., *The New Politicians of Fifth-Century Athens* (Princeton: 1971)

Cooper, C., "Philosophers, Politics, Academics: Demosthenes' Rhetorical Reputation in Antiquity," in I. Worthington (ed.), *Demosthenes: Statesman and Orator* (London: 2000), pp. 224–245

Couvenhes, J.-C., "Le stratège Derkylos, fils d'Autoklès d'Hagnous et l'éducation des paides à Éleusis," *Cahiers du Centre Gustave Glotz* 9 (1998), pp. 49–69

Crook, J. A., "Political History, 30 B.C. to A.D. 14" and "Augustus: Power, Authority, Achievement," in A. K. Bowman, E. Champlin, and A. Lintott (eds.), *Cambridge Ancient History*² 10 (Cambridge: 1996), pp. 70–146

Culley, G. R., "The Restoration of Sanctuaries in Attica: *I.G.*, II², 1035," *Hesperia* 44 (1975), pp. 207–223

Culley, G. R., "The Restoration of Sanctuaries in Attica, II," *Hesperia* 46 (1977), pp. 282–298

Dally, O., "Athen in der frühen Kaiserzeit—ein Werk des Kaisers Augustus?," in S. Vlizos (ed.), *Athens during the Roman Period: Recent Discoveries, New Evidence* (Athens: 2008), pp. 43–53

Daly, L. W., "Roman Study Abroad," *AJP* 71 (1950), pp. 40–58

David, J.-M., *La République romaine de la deuxième guerre punique à la bataille d'Actium, 218–31* (Paris: 2000)

Davies, J. K, "Demosthenes on Liturgies: A Note," *JHS* 87 (1967), pp. 33–40

Davies, J. K., *Athenian Propertied Families* (Oxford: 1971)

Davies, J. K., "Athenian Citizenship: The Descent Group and the Alternatives," *CJ* 73 (1977), pp. 105–121

Day, J., *An Economic History of Athens under Roman Domination* (New York: 1942)

Dell, H. J., "The Quarrel between Demetrius and Perseus: A Note on Macedonian National Policy," *Ancient Macedonia* 3 (Institute for Balkan Studies, Thessaloniki: 1983), pp. 66–76

Depuydt, L., "The Time of Death of Alexander the Great," *Welt des Orients* 28 (1997), pp. 117–135

den Heijer, A., "Faithful Messenger of God: Portraits of Paul's Performance in the Book of Acts," Ph.D. Diss. (Kampen: forthcoming)

Derow, P. S., "Polybius, Rome, and the East," *JRS* 69 (1979), pp. 1–15

Derow, P. S., "Rome, the Fall of Macedon, and the Sack of Corinth," in A. E. Astin, F. W. Walbank, M. W. Fredericksen, and R. M. Ogilvie (eds.), *Cambridge Ancient History*² 8 (Cambridge: 1989), pp. 290–323

Derow, P. S., "Pharos and Rome," *ZPE* 88 (1991), pp. 261–270

Derow, P. S., "The Arrival of Rome: From the Illyrian Wars to the Fall of Macedon," in A. Erskine (ed.), *A Companion to the Hellenistic World* (Malden: 2003), pp. 51–70

Desideri, P., "Posidonio e la guerra mitridatica," *Athenaeum* 51 (1973), pp. 3–29 and 237–269

Dickenson, C. P., "Pausanias and the 'Archaic Agora' at Athens," *Hesperia* 84 (2015), pp. 723–770

Dickenson, C. P., *On the Agora: The Evolution of a Public Space in Hellenistic and Roman Greece (c. 323 BC–267 AD)* (Leiden: 2017)

Dihle, A., "Greek Classicism," in T. A. Schmitz and N. Wiater (eds.), *The Struggle for Identity: Greeks and Their Past in the First Century BCE* (Stuttgart: 2011), pp. 47–60

Di Napoli, V., F. Camia, V. Evangelidis, D. Grigoropoulos, D. Rogers, and S. Vlizos (eds.), *What's New in Roman Greece? Recent Work on the Greek Mainland and the Islands in the Roman Period* (Athens: 2018)

Dinsmoor, W. B., "The Monument of Agrippa at Athens," *AJA* 24 (1920), p. 83

Dinsmoor, W. B., *The Archons of Athens in the Hellenistic Age* (Cambridge: 1931)

Dinsmoor, W. B., "The Temple of Ares at Athens," *Hesperia* 9 (1940), pp. 1–52

Dinsmoor, W. B., Jr., "The Temple of Poseidon: A Missing Sima and Other Matters," *AJA* 78 (1974), pp. 211–238

Dmitriev, S., *The Greek Slogan of Freedom and Early Roman Politics in Greece* (Oxford: 2011)

Dmitriev, S., Demochares, *BNJ* 75 (Leiden)

Dorandi, T., "Gli Arconti nei Papiri Ercolanesei," *ZPE* 84 (1990), pp. 121–138

Dow, S., "The Egyptian Cults in Athens," *HThR* 30 (1937), pp. 183–232

Dow, S., "A Leader of the Anti-Roman Party in Athens in 88 B.C.," *CP* 37 (1942), pp. 311–314

Dreyer, B., "Der Beginn der Freiheitsphase Athens 287 v. Chr. und das Datum der Panathenäenund Ptolemaia im Kalliasdekret," *ZPE* 111 (1996), pp. 45–67

Dreyer, B., *Untersuchungen zur Geschichte des spätklassischen Athen (322–ca. 230 v. Chr.)* (Stuttgart: 1999)

Dreyer, B., "Athen und Demetrios Poliorketes nach der Schlact von Ipsos (301 v. Chr.)," *Historia* 49 (2000), pp. 54–66

Dreyer, B., "Wann endet die klassischen Demokratie Athens," *Anc. Society* 31 (2001), pp. 27–66

Dreyer, B., *Polybios—Leben und Werk im Banne Roms* (Hildsheim: 2011)

Dreyer, B., "Frank Walbank's *Philippos Tragoidoumenos*: Polybius' Account of Philip's Last Years," in B. Gibson and T. Harrison (eds.), *Polybius and His World: Essays in Memory of F. W. Walbank* (Oxford: 2013), pp. 201–211

Dubreuil, R., "The Orator in the Theatre: The End of Athenian Democracy in Plutarch's *Phocion*," in M. Canevaro and B. Gray (eds.), *The Hellenistic Reception of Classical Athenian Democracy and Political Thought* (Oxford: 2018), pp. 261–276

Duff, T., *Plutarch's Lives: Exploring Vice and Virtue* (Oxford: 1999)

Easterling, P., "The End of an Era? Tragedy in the Early Fourth Century," in A. H. Sommersten (ed.), *Tragedy, Comedy, and the Polis* (Bari: 1993), pp. 559–569

Eck, W., *The Age of Augustus* (Malden: 2007)

Eckstein, A. M., "T. Quinctus Flamininus and the Campaign against Philip in 198 B.C.," *Phoenix* 30 (1976), pp. 119–142

Eckstein, A. M., "Polybius, Demetrius of Pharus, and the Origins of the Second Illyrian War," *CP* 89 (1999), pp. 46–59

Eckstein, A.M., "Greek Mediation in the First Macedonian War," *Historia* 51 (2002), pp. 268–297

Eckstein, A. M., "The Pact between the Kings, Polybius 15.20.6, and Polybius' View of the Outbreak of the Second Macedonian War," *CP* 100 (2005), pp. 228–242

Eckstein, A. M., *Mediterranean Anarchy, Interstate War, and the Rise of Rome* (Berkeley: 2006)
Eckstein, A. M., *Rome Enters the Greek East: From Anarchy to Hierarchy in the Hellenistic Mediterranean, 230–170 BC* (Malden: 2008)
Eckstein, A. M., "Macedonia and Rome, 221–146 BC," in J. Roisman and I. Worthington (eds.), *A Companion to Ancient Macedonia* (Malden: 2010), pp. 225–250
Ehrenberg, V., and A. H. M. Jones, *Documents Illustrating the Reigns of Augustus and Tiberius*[2] (Oxford: 1976)
Ehrhardt, C., "Demetrios Ho Aitolikos and Antigonid Nicknames," *Hermes* 106 (1978), pp. 215–253
Eilers, C. F., "Athens under the *lex Clodia*," *Phoenix* 60 (2006), pp. 122–132
Ellis, J. R., *Philip II and Macedonian Imperialism* (London: 1976)
Engels, J., "Anmerkungen zum 'Ökonomischen Denken' im 4. Jahrh. v. Chr. und zur wirtschaftlichen Entwicklung des Lykurgischen Athen," *MBAH* 7 (1988), pp. 90–132
Engels, J., "Zur Stellung Lykurgs und zur Aussagekraft seines Militär- und Bauprogramms fürdie Demokratie vor 322 v. Chr," *Anc. Society* 23 (1992), pp. 5–29
Engels, J., "Macedonians and Greeks," in J. Roisman and I. Worthington (eds.), *A Companion to Ancient Macedonia* (Malden: 2010), pp. 81–98
Errington, R. M., "Philip V, Aratus, and the 'Conspiracy of Apelles,'" *Historia* 16 (1967), pp. 19–36
Errington, R. M., *Philopoemen* (Oxford: 1969)
Errington, R. M., "From Babylon to Triparadeisos," *JHS* 90 (1970), pp. 49–77
Errington, R. M., *The Dawn of Empire: Rome's Rise to World Power* (London: 1971a)
Errington, R. M., "The Alleged Syro-Macedonian Pact and the Origins of the Second Macedonian War," *Athenaeum* 49 (1971b), pp. 336–354
Errington, R. M., "Samos and the Lamian War," *Chiron* 5 (1975), pp. 51–57
Errington, R. M., "Aspects of Roman Acculturation in the East under the Republic," in P. Kneissl and V. Losemann (eds.), *Alte Geschichte und Wissenschaftsgeschichte. Festschrift Karl Christ* (Darmstadt: 1988), pp. 140–157
Errington, R. M., "Rome and Greece to 205 B.C.," in A. E. Astin, F. W. Walbank, M. W. Fredericksen, and R. M. Ogilvie (eds.), *Cambridge Ancient History*[2] 8 (Cambridge: 1989a), pp. 81–106
Errington, R. M., "Rome against Philip and Antiochus," in A. E. Astin, F. W. Walbank, M. W. Fredericksen, and R. M. Ogilvie (eds.), *Cambridge Ancient History*[2] 8 (Cambridge: 1989b), pp. 244–289
Erskine, A., "The Romans as Common Benefactors," *Historia* 43 (1994), pp. 70–87
Erskine, A., "Life after Death: Alexandria and the Body of Alexander," *G&R* 49 (2002), pp. 167–179
Erskine, A. (ed.), *A Companion to the Hellenistic World* (Malden: 2003)
Everitt, A., *Hadrian and the Triumph of Rome* (New York: 2009)
Everitt, A., *Augustus: The Life of Rome's First Emperor* (New York: 2007)

Faraguna, M., *Atene nell' eta di Alessandro: problemi politici, economici, finanziari* (Rome: 1992)
Faraguna, M., "Alexander and the Greeks," in J. Roisman (ed.), *Brill's Companion to Alexander the Great* (Leiden: 2003), pp. 99–130
Fecchi, L., "Il monópteros di Roma e Augusto sull'Acropoli di Atene," *Thalassa* 1 (2004), pp. 139–170
Ferguson, W. S., *The Athenian Secretaries* (Ithaca: 1898)
Ferguson, W. S., *Hellenistic Athens: An Historical Essay* (New York: 1911)
Fernández Uriel, P., "Nerón en Acaya: Entre el monarca helenístico y el principo julio-cludio," in Y. Perrin (ed.), *Neronia 7, Rome, l'Italie et la Grèce: hellénisme et philhellénisme au premier siècle ap. J.-C.* (Brussels: 2007), pp. 196–212
Fittschen, K., "Über den Beitrag der Bildhauer in Athen zur Kunstproduktion im Römischen Reich," in S. Vlizos (ed.), *Athens during the Roman Period: Recent Discoveries, New Evidence* (Athens: 2008), pp. 325–336
Flower, H. I., *Roman Republics* (Princeton: 2010)
Follet, S., *Athènes au IIe at au IIIe siècle: études chronologiques et prosopographiques* (Paris: 1976)
Follet, S., "Lettres d'Hadrien aux Épicuriens d'Athènes (14.2–14.3.125) SEG III 226 + IG II(2) 1097," *REG* 107 (1994), pp. 158–171
Follet, S. (ed.), *L'Hellénisme d'Époque Romaine: Nouveaux Documents, Nouvelles Approches* (Paris: 2004a)
Follet, S., "Julius Nicanor et le Statut de Salamine (*Agora* XVI, 337)," in S. Follet (ed.), *L'Hellénisme d'Époque Romaine: Nouveaux Documents, Nouvelles Approches* (Paris: 2004b), pp. 139–170
Follet, S., "Un nouvel archonte d'Athènes et les ancêtres d'Hérode Atticus au premier siècle de notre ère," in Y. Perrin (ed.), *Neronia 7, Rome, l'Italie et la Grèce: hellénisme et philhellénisme au premier siècle ap. J.-C.* (Brussels: 2007), pp. 117–125
Follet, S., and D. Peppas Delmousou, "Le décret de Thyatire sur les bienfaits d'Hadrien et le 'Panthéon' d'Hadrien à Athènes (*IG* II2 1088 + 1090 + *IG* III 3985, complétés = *TAM* V, 2, 1180 complété)," *BCH* 121 (1997), pp. 291–309
Follet, S., and D. Peppas Delmousou, "Les dedicaces chorégiques d'époque flavienne et antonine à Athènes," in O. Salomies (ed.), *The Greek East in the Roman Context* (Helsinki: 2001), pp. 95–117
Forbes, C. A., "Ancient Athletic Guilds," *CPh* 50 (1955), pp. 238–252
Fouquet, F., "Der Roma-Augustus-Monopteros auf der Athener Akropolis. Herrscherkult und Memoria 'ad Palladis templi vestibulum'?," *Thetis* 19 (2012), pp. 47–95
Fraser, P., *Ptolemaic Alexandria*, 3 vols. (Oxford: 1972)
Friend, J., *The Athenian Ephebeia in the Fourth Century BCE* (Leiden: 2019)
Frösén, J. (ed.), *Early Hellenistic Athens: Symptoms of a Change* (Helsinki: 1997)
Fuks, A., "The Bellum Achaicum and Its Social Aspect," *JHS* 90 (1970), pp. 78–89
Gabbert, J., "The Anarchic Dating of the Chremonidean War," *CJ* 82 (1987), pp. 230–235

Gabbert, J., "The Career of Olympiodorus of Athens (ca. 340–270 BC)," *Anc. World* 27 (1996), pp. 59–66

Gabbert, J., *Antigonus II Gonatas: A Political Biography* (London: 1997)

Gabriel, R. A., *Philip II of Macedon: Greater than Alexander* (Washington: 2010)

Galinsky, K., *Augustus* (Cambridge: 2012)

Garland, R., *The Piraeus* (London: 1987)

Garoufalias, P. E., *Pyrrhus, King of Epirus* (London: 1979)

Gauthier, P., "Notes sur Trois Décrets Honorant des Citoyens Bienfaiteurs," *RPh* 56 (1982), pp. 215–231

Geagan, D. J., *The Athenian Constitution after Sulla, Hesperia Suppl.* 12 (Princeton: 1967)

Geagan, D. J., "Greek Inscriptions," *Hesperia* 40 (1971), pp. 96–108

Geagan, D. J., "Hadrian and the Athenian Dionysiac Technitai," *TAPA* 103 (1972), pp. 133–160

Geagan, D. J., "Roman Athens: Some Aspects of Life and Culture. I. 86 B.C.–A.D. 267," in H. Temporini (ed.), *Aufstieg und Niedergang der Römischen Welt* 2.7.1 (Berlin: 1979a), pp. 371–437

Geagan. D. J., "The Third Hoplite Generalship of Antipatros of Phlya," *AJP* 100 (1979b), pp. 59–68

Geagan, D. J., "Tiberius Claudius Novius, the Hoplite Generalship, and the *Epimeleteia* of the Free City of Athens," *AJP* 100 (1979c), pp. 279–287

Geagan, D. J., "Imperial Visits to Athens: The Epigraphical Evidence," *Praktika, 8th Congress for Greek and Latin Epigraphy, Athens 1983* (Athens: 1984), pp. 69–78

Geagan, D. J., "The Sarapion Monument and the Quest for Status in Roman Athens," *ZPE* 85 (1991), pp. 145–165

Geagan, D. J., "A Family of Marathon and Social Mobility in Athens of the First Century B.C.," *Phoenix* 46 (1992), pp. 29–44

Geagan, D. J., "The Athenian Elite: Romanization, Resistance, and the Exercise of Power," in M. C. Hoff and S. I. Rotroff (eds.), *The Romanization of Athens* (Oxford: 1997), pp. 19–32

Geagan, D. J., *Inscriptions: The Dedicatory Monuments. The Athenian Agora* 18 (Princeton: 2011)

Gehrke, H.-J., "Das Verhältnis von Politik und Philosophie im Wirken des Demetrios von Phaleron," *Chiron* 8 (1978), pp. 142–193

Gibson, B., and T. Harrison (eds.), *Polybius and His World: Essays in Memory of F. W. Walbank* (Oxford: 2013)

Gigante, M., *Philodemus in Italy: The Books from Herculaneum*, trans. D. Obbink (Ann Arbor: 2002)

Gilley, D., and I. Worthington, "Alexander the Great, Macedonia and Asia," in J. Roisman and I. Worthington (eds.), *A Companion to Ancient Macedonia* (Malden: 2010), pp. 186–207

Giudice, A., "Atene in età adrianea: la funzione ecumenica della polis nell'ideologia del principato," *GFA* 16 (2013), pp. 347–369

Glew, D., "Mithridates Eupator and Rome: A Study of the Background of the First Mithridatic War," *Athenaeum* 55 (1977a), pp. 380–405

Glew, D., "The Selling of the King: A Note on Mithridates Eupator's Propaganda in 88 B.C.," *Hermes* 105 (1977b), pp. 253–256
Gomme, A. W., "The End of the City-State," in A. W. Gomme (ed.), *Essays in Greek History and Literature* (Oxford: 1937), pp. 204–248
Goodman, M. "Judaea," in A. K. Bowman, E. Champlin, and A. Lintott (eds.), *Cambridge Ancient History*² 10 (Cambridge: 1996), pp. 737–781
Graindor, P., "Auguste et Athènes," *RBPhil* 1 (1922a), pp. 429–443
Graindor, P., *Chronologie des archontes athéniens sous l'empire* (Brussels: 1922b)
Graindor, P., "Études sur l'éphébie attique sous l'Empire," *Le Musée Belge* 26 (1922c), pp. 165–228
Graindor, P., *Athènes sous Auguste* (Cairo: 1927a)
Graindor, P., "Antonin le Pieux et Athènes," *Revue Belge de Philologie et d'Histoire* 6 (1927b), pp. 753–756
Graindor, P., *Athènes de Tibère à Trajan* (Cairo: 1931)
Graindor, P., *Athènes sous Hadrien* (Cairo: 1934)
Graindor, P., *Hérode Atticus et sa famille* (Cairo: 1939)
Grainger, J. D., *Seleukos Nikator: Constructing a Hellenistic Kingdom* (London: 1999)
Grainger, J. D., *The League of the Aitolians* (Leiden: 1999)
Grainger, J. D., *The Roman War of Antiochus the Great* (Leiden: 2002)
Grainger, J. D., *Nerva and the Roman Succession Crisis of CE 96–99* (London: 2003)
Grainger, J. D., *The Rise of the Seleukid Empire (323–223 BC): Seleukos I to Seleukos III* (Barnsley: 2014)
Grainger, J. D., *Kings and Kingship in the Hellenistic World, 350–30 BC* (Barnsley: 2017)
Gray, B., "A Later Hellenistic Debate about the Value of Classical Athenian Civic Ideals?," in M. Canevaro and B. Gray (eds.), *The Hellenistic Reception of Classical Athenian Democracy and Political Thought* (Oxford: 2018), pp. 139–176
Green, P., *Alexander to Actium: The Historical Evolution of the Hellenistic Age* (Berkeley: 1990)
Green, P., *The Greco-Persian Wars* (Berkeley: 1996)
Green, P., "Occupation and Co-existence: The Impact of Macedon on Athens, 323–307," in O. Palagia and S. V. Tracy (eds.), *The Macedonians in Athens, 322–229 BC* (Oxford: 2003), pp. 1–7
Greenhalgh, P., *Pompey, the Roman Alexander* (London: 1980)
Grieb, V., *Hellenistische Demokratie. Politische Organisation und Struktur in freien griechischen Poleis nach Alexander dem Großen* (Stuttgart: 2008)
Griffin, M., "The Intellectual Developments of the Ciceronian Age," in J. A. Crook, A. Lintott, and E. Rawson (eds.), *Cambridge Ancient History*² 9 (Cambridge: 1994), pp. 689–728
Griffin, M., "The Flavians," in A. K. Bowman, P. Garnsey, and D. Rathbone (eds.), *Cambridge Ancient History*² 11 (Cambridge: 2000a), pp. 1–83
Griffin, M., "Nerva to Hadrian," in A. K. Bowman, P. Garnsey, and D. Rathbone (eds.), *Cambridge Ancient History*² 11 (Cambridge: 2000b), pp. 84–131

Griffin, M., "Nero and the Concept of Imperial Glory," in Y. Perrin (ed.), *Neronia 7, Rome, l'Italie et la Grèce: hellénisme et philhellénisme au premier siècle ap. J.-C.* (Brussels: 2007), pp. 97–116
Griffith, G. T., "Athens in the Fourth Century," in P. D. A. Garnsey and C. R. Whittaker (eds.), *Imperialism in the Ancient World* (Cambridge: 1978), pp. 127–144
Grigoropoulos, D., "The Population of the Piraeus in the Roman Period: A Re-Assessment of the Evidence of Funerary Inscriptions," *G&R*² 56 (2009), pp. 164–182
Grijalvo, E. M., "Elites and Religious Change in Roman Athens," *Numen* 52 (2005), pp. 255–282
Gronewald, M., "Bemerkungen zu Menander," *ZPE* 93 (1992), pp. 17–29
Gruen, E., "The Last Years of Philip V," *GRBS* 15 (1974), pp. 221–246
Gruen, E., "Philip V and the Greek Demos," in H. J. Dell (ed.), *Ancient Macedonian Studies in Honour of C. F. Edson* (Thessaloniki: 1981), pp. 169–182
Gruen, E., "Macedonia and the Settlement of 167 B.C.," in W. L. Adams and E. N. Borza (eds.), *Philip II, Alexander the Great, and the Macedonian Heritage* (Washington: 1982), pp. 257–267
Gruen, E., *The Hellenistic World and the Coming of Rome* (Berkeley: 1984)
Gruen, E., "Hellenism and Persecution: Antiochus IV and the Jews," in P. Green (ed.), *Hellenistic History and Culture* (Berkeley: 1993), pp. 238–264
Gruen, E., "The Expansion of the Empire under Augustus," in A. K. Bowman, E. Champlin, and A. Lintott (eds.), *Cambridge Ancient History*² 10 (Cambridge: 1996), pp. 147–197
Gutzwiller, K., *A Guide to Hellenistic Literature* (Malden: 2007)
Haake, M., *Der Philosoph in der Stadt. Untersuchungen zur öffentlichen Rede über Philosophen und Philosophie in den hellenistischen Poleis* (Munich: 2007)
Habicht, C., *Gottmenschentum und der griechische Städte*² (Munich: 1970)
Habicht, C., "Zur Geschichte Athens in der Zeit Mithridates' VI: Der eponyme Archon im Jahr der 'Anarchie' (88/7)," *Chiron* 6 (1976), pp. 127–142
Habicht, C., *Untersuchungen zur politischen Geschichte Athens im 3. Jahrhundert v. Chr.* (Munich: 1979)
Habicht, C., *Studien zur Geschichte Athens in hellenistischer Zeit* (Göttingen: 1982)
Habicht, C., "The Role of Athens in the Reorganization of the Delphic Amphictiony after 189 B.C.," *Hesperia* 56 (1987), pp. 59–71
Habicht, C., "Athen und die Seleukiden," *Chiron* 19 (1989), pp. 7–26
Habicht, C., "Athens and the Attalids in the Second Century B.C.," *Hesperia* 59 (1990), pp. 561–577
Habicht, C., "Zu den Epimeleten von Delos, 167–88," *Hermes* 119 (1991a), pp. 194–216
Habicht, C., "Milesische Theoren in Athen," *Chiron* 21 (1991b), pp. 325–327
Habicht, C., "Zu den Münzmagistraten der Silberprägung des Neuen Stils," *Chiron* 21 (1991c), pp. 1–23
Habicht, C., "Was Augustus a Visitor at the Panathenaea?," *CPh* 86 (1991d), pp. 226–228

Habicht, C., "Athens and the Ptolemies," *Class. Antiq.* 11 (1992), pp. 68–90
Habicht, C., "The Comic Poet Archedikos," *Hesperia* 62 (1993), pp. 253–256
Habicht, C., *Athen in hellenistischer Zeit* (Munich: 1994a)
Habicht, C., "Hellenistic Athens and Her Philosophers," in C. Habicht, *Athen in hellenistischer Zeit* (Munich: 1994b), pp. 231–247
Habicht, C., *Athen. Die Geschichte der Stadt in hellenistischer Zeit* (Munich: 1995)
Habicht, C., "Divine Honors for King Antigonus Gonatas in Athens," *Scripta Classica Israelica* 15 (1996a), pp. 131–134
Habicht, C., "Salamis in der Zeit nach Sulla," *ZPE* 111 (1996b), pp. 79–87
Habicht, C., *Athens from Alexander to Antony*, trans. D. L. Schneider (Cambridge: 1997a)
Habicht, C., "Ein neues Zeugnis der athenischen Kavallerie," *ZPE* 115 (1997b), pp. 121–124
Habicht, C., "Roman Citizens in Athens (228–31 B.C.)," in M. C. Hoff and S. I. Rotroff (eds.), *The Romanization of Athens* (Oxford: 1997c), pp. 9–17
Habicht, C., "Athens after the Chremonidean War: Some Second Thoughts," in O. Palagia and S. V. Tracy (eds.), *The Macedonians in Athens, 322–229 BC* (Oxford: 2003), pp. 52–55
Habicht, C., and S. V. Tracy, "New and Old Panathenaic Victor Lists," *Hesperia* 60 (1991), pp. 187–236
Hakkarainen, M., "Private Wealth in the Athenian Public Sphere during the Late Classical and the Early Hellenistic Period," in J. Frösén (ed.), *Early Hellenistic Athens: Symptoms of a Change* (Helsinki: 1997), pp. 1–32
Halfmann, H., *Itinera Principum: Geschichte und Typologie der Kaiserreisen im Römischen Reich* (Stuttgart: 1986)
Hammond, N. G. L., "The Campaign and Battle of Cynoscephalae (197 BC)," *JHS* 108 (1988), pp. 60–82
Hammond, N. G. L., "The Macedonian Imprint on the Hellenistic World," in P. Green (ed.), *Hellenistic History and Culture* (Berkeley: 1993), pp. 12–23
Hammond, N. G. L., *Philip of Macedon* (London: 1994)
Hammond, N. G. L., "The Continuity of Macedonian Institutions and the Macedonian Kingdoms of the Hellenistic Era," *Historia* 49 (2000), pp. 141–160
Hammond, N. G. L., and G. T. Griffith, *A History of Macedonia* 2 (Oxford: 1979)
Hammond, N. G. L., and F. W. Walbank, *A History of Macedonia* 3 (Oxford: 1988)
Hanink, J., *Lycurgan Athens and the Making of Classical Tragedy* (Cambridge: 2014)
Hannah, R., *Greek and Roman Calendars: Constructions of Time in the Ancient World* (London: 2005)
Hansen, E. V., *The Attalids of Pergamon* (Ithaca: 1971)
Hansen, M. H., *The Athenian Assembly in the Age of Demosthenes* (Oxford: 1987)
Hansen, M. H., *The Athenian Democracy in the Age of Demosthenes*² (Norman: 1999)
Hanson, V. D., *A War Like No Other: How the Athenians and the Spartans Fought the Peloponnesian War* (New York: 2006)
Hardiman, C. L., "Classical Art to 221 BC," in J. Roisman and I. Worthington (eds.), *A Companion to Ancient Macedonia* (Malden: 2010), pp. 505–521

Harding, P. E., *From the End of the Peloponnesian War to the Battle of Ipsus* (Cambridge: 1985)
Harding, P. E., *Athens Transformed, 404–262 BC: From Popular Sovereignty to the Dominion of the Elite* (London: 2015)
Harris, W. V., *War and Imperialism in Republican Rome, 327–70 B.C.* (Oxford: 1979)
Hashiba, Y., Stesicleides (Ctesicles?), *BNJ* 245 (Leiden)
Hatzopoulos, M. B., "Macedonia and Macedonians," in R. Lane Fox (ed.), *Brill's Companion to Ancient Macedon* (Leiden: 2011a), pp. 43–50
Hatzopoulos, M. B., "Macedonians and Other Greeks," in R. Lane Fox (ed.), *Brill's Companion to Ancient Macedon* (Leiden: 2011b), pp. 51–78
Hauben, H., "IG II² 492 and the Siege of Athens in 304 B.C.," *ZPE* 14 (1974), 10
Hauben, H., "The First War of the Successors (321 B.C.): Chronological and Historical Problems," *Anc. Society* 8 (1977), pp. 85–120
Hauben, H., "Arsinoé II et la politique extérieure de l'Égypte," in E. Van't Dack, P. van Dessel, and W. van Gucht (eds.), *Egypt and the Hellenistic World: Proceedings of the International Colloquium, Leuven, 24–26 May 1982* (Louvain: 1983), pp. 99–127
Hauben, H., and A. Meeus (eds.), *The Age of the Successors and the Creation of the Hellenistic Kingdoms (323–276 B.C.)* (Leuven: 2014)
Heap, A. M., *Behind the Mask: Character and Society in Menander* (London: 2019)
Heckel, W., "IG II2 561 and the Status of Alexander IV," *ZPE* 40 (1980), 249–250
Heinen, H., "The Syrian-Egyptian Wars and the New Kingdoms of Asia Minor," in F. W. Walbank, A. E. Astin, M. W. Frederiksen, and R. M. Ogilvie (eds.), *Cambridge Ancient History²* 7.1 (Cambridge: 1984), pp. 412–445
Helliesen, J., "Andriscus and the Revolt of the Macedonians, 149-148 B.C.," *Ancient Macedonia* 4 (Institute for Balkan Studies, Thessaloniki: 1986), pp. 307–314
Hendrick, K. A., "Roman Emperors and Athenian Life, from Augustus to Hadrian," Ph.D. Diss. (Berkeley: 2006)
Henry, A. S., "Athenian Financial Officials after 303 B.C.," *Chiron* 14 (1984), pp. 49–92
Henry, A. S., "Lysandros of Anaphlystos and the Decree for Phaidros of Sphettos," *Chiron* 22 (1992), pp. 25–33
Hidber, T., "Impacts of Writing in Rome: Greek Authors and Their Roman Environment in the First Century BCE," in T. A. Schmitz and N. Wiater (eds.), *The Struggle for Identity: Greeks and Their Past in the First Century BCE* (Stuttgart: 2011), pp. 115–123
Hinds, J. G. F., "Mithridates," in J. A. Crook, A. Lintott, and E. Rawson (eds.), *Cambridge Ancient History²* 9 (Cambridge: 1994), pp. 129–164
Hoët-van Cauwenberghe, C., "Condemnation de la mémoire de Néron en Grèce: Réalité ou mythe?," in Y. Perrin (ed.), *Neronia 7, Rome, l'Italie et la Grèce: Hellénisme et philhellénisme au premier siècle ap. J.-C.* (Brussels: 2007), pp. 225–249
Hoff, M. C., "The Roman Agora at Athens," Ph.D. Diss. (Boston: 1988)

Hoff, M. C., "Civil Disobedience and Unrest in Augustan Athens," *Hesperia* 58 (1989a), pp. 267–276

Hoff, M. C., "The Early History of the Roman Agora at Athens," in S. Walker and A. Cameron (eds.), *The Greek Renaissance in the Roman Empire* (London: 1989b), pp. 1–8

Hoff, M. C., "Augustus, Apollo, and Athens," *MH* 49 (1992), pp. 223–232

Hoff, M. C., "The So-Called Agoranomion and the Imperial Cult in Julio-Claudian Athens," *AA* 109 (1994), pp. 93–117

Hoff, M. C., "The Politics and Architecture of the Roman Imperial Cult at Athens," in A. Small (ed.), *Subject and Ruler: The Cult of the Ruling Power in Classical Antiquity* (Ann Arbor: 1996), pp. 185–200

Hoff, M. C., "*Laceratae Athenae*: Sulla's Siege of Athens in 87/6 B.C. and Its Aftermath," in M. C. Hoff and S. I. Rotroff (eds.), *The Romanization of Athens* (Oxford: 1997), pp. 33–51

Hoff, M. C., "Athens Honors Pompey the Great," in L. de Blois, J. Boens, T. Kessels, and D. M. Schenkeveld (eds.), *The Statesman in Plutarch's Works* 2 (Leiden: 2005), pp. 327–336

Hoff, M. C., "Greece and the Roman Republic," in J. D. Evans (ed.), *A Companion to the Archaeology of the Roman Republic* (Malden: 2013), pp. 559–577

Hoff, M. C., and S. I. Rotroff (eds.), *The Romanization of Athens* (Oxford: 1997)

Højte, J. M., "Imperial Visits as Occasion for the Erection of Portrait Statues?," *ZPE* 133 (2000), pp. 221–235

Højte, J. M., "Cultural Interchange? The Case of Honorary Statues in Greece," in E. N. Ostenfeld, *Greek Romans and Roman Greeks: Studies in Cultural Interaction* (Aarhus: 2002), pp. 55–63

Højte, J. M. (ed.), *Mithridates VI and the Pontic Kingdom* (Aarhus: 2009a)

Højte, J. M., "Portraits and Statues of Mithridates VI," in J. M. Højte (ed.), *Mithridates VI and the Pontic Kingdom* (Aarhus: 2009b), pp. 145–162

Hölbl, G., *A History of the Ptolemaic Empire*, trans. T. Saavedra (London: 2001)

Holland, L., "Plutarch's *Aemilius Paullus* and the Model of the Philosopher Statesman," in L. de Blois, J. Boens, T. Kessels, and D. M. Schenkeveld (eds.), *The Statesman in Plutarch's Works* 2 (Leiden: 2005), pp. 269–279

Hopper, R. J., "The Attic Silver Mines in the Fourth Century B.C.," *BSA* 48 (1953), pp. 200–254

Hopper, R. J., "The Laureion Mines: A Reconsideration," *BSA* 63 (1968), pp. 293–326

Horster, M., and A. Klöckner (eds.), *Civic Priests: Cult Personnel in Athens from the Hellenistic Period to Late Antiquity* (Berlin: 2012)

Hoyos, D., *Hannibal's Dynasty: Power and Politics in the Western Mediterranean, 247–183 BC* (London: 2005)

Hunt, P., *War, Peace, and Alliance in Demosthenes' Athens* (New York: 2010)

Hunter, R. L., "Literature and Its Contexts," in A. Erskine (ed.), *A Companion to the Hellenistic World* (Malden: 2003), pp. 477–493

Hunter, R. L., and C. de Jonge (eds.), *Dionysius of Halicarnassus and Augustan Rome: Rhetoric, Criticism, and Historiography* (Cambridge: 2019)
Hupfloher, A., "Der Achaierbund im 1. Jahrhundert n. Chr.: zwischen Tradition und Neuorganisation," in Y. Perrin (ed.), *Neronia 7, Rome, l'Italie et la Grèce: Hellénisme et philhellénisme au premier siècle ap. J.-C.* (Brussels: 2007), pp. 97–116
Huss, W., *Ägypten in hellenistischer Zeit, 323–30 v. Chr.* (Munich: 2001)
Johnson, A. C., "The Creation of the Tribe Ptolemais at Athens," *AJP* 34 (1913), pp. 381–417
Johnson, W. A., and D. S. Richter (eds.) *The Oxford Handbook of the Second Sophistic* (Oxford: 2017)
Jones, B. W., *The Emperor Titus* (London: 1984)
Jones, B. W., *The Emperor Domitian* (London: 1992)
Jones, C. P., *Plutarch and Rome* (Oxford: 1971)
Jones, C. P., "Three Foreigners in Attica I: Julius Nicanor," *Phoenix* 32 (1978), pp. 222–234
Jones, C. P., "The Panhellenion," *Chiron* 26 (1996), pp. 29–56
Jones, C. P., "Memories of the Roman Republic in the Greek East," in O. Salomies (ed.), *The Greek East in the Roman Context* (Helsinki: 2001), pp. 11–18
Jones, C. P., "An Athenian Document Mentioning Julius Nicanor," *ZPE* 154 (2005), pp. 161–172
Jones, C. P., "Julius Nicanor Again," *ZPE* 178 (2011), pp. 79–83
Jones, N., Philochorus, *BNJ* 328 (Leiden)
Kagan, D., *The Peloponnesian War* (London: 2003)
Kah, D., and P. Scholz (eds.), *Das hellenistische Gymnasion* (Berlin: 2004)
Kajava, M., "Vesta and Athens," in O. Salomies (ed.), *The Greek East in the Roman Context* (Helsinki: 2001), pp. 71–94
Kallet-Marx, R. M., *Hegemony to Empire: The Development of the Roman Imperium in the East from 148 to 62 B.C.* (Berkeley: 1995)
Kallet-Marx, R. M., and R. S. Stroud, "Two Athenian Decrees Concerning Lemnos of the Late First Century B.C.," *Chiron* 27 (1997), pp. 155–194
Kantiréa, M., "Remarques sur le culte de la domus Augusta en Achaie de la mort d'Auguste à Néron," in O. Salomies (ed.), *The Greek East in the Roman Context* (Helsinki: 2001), pp. 51–60
Kantiréa, M., *Les dieux et les dieux Augustes. Le culte impérial en Grèce sous les Julio-claudiens et les Flaviens. Etudes épigraphiques et archéologiques* (Athens: 2007)
Kantiréa, M., "Étude comparative de l'introduction du culte imperial à Athènes et à Éphèse," in P. P. Iossif, A. S. Chankowski, and C. C. Lorber (eds.), *More Than Men, Less Than Gods: Studies on Royal Cult and Imperial Worship* (Leuven: 2011), pp. 521–551
Kapetanopoulos, E. A., "Apolexis ex Oiou," *Athenaeum* 52 (1974), pp. 343–347
Kapetanopoulos, E. A., "Gaius Julius Nikanor, Neos Homeros kai Neos Themistokles," *Riv. Fil.* 104 (1976), pp. 375–377
Kapetanopoulos, E. A., "Salamis and Julius Nicanor," *Hellenika* 33 (1981), pp. 217–237

Kapetanopoulos, E., "The Reform of the Athenian Constitution under Hadrian," *Horos* 10–12 (1992–1998), pp. 215–237

Kapetanopoulos, E. A., "The Sarapion Monument at Athens," *Prometheus* 20 (1994), pp. 234–242

Karila-Cohen, K., "Apollon, Athènes et la Pythaïde: mise en scène 'mythique' de la cité au IIe siècle av. J.-C.," *Kernos* 18 (2005), pp. 219–239

Karivieri, A., "Just One of the Boys: Hadrian in the Company of Zeus, Dionysus, and Theseus," in E. N. Ostenfeld (ed.), *Greek Romans and Roman Greeks: Studies in Cultural Interaction* (Aarhus: 2002), pp. 40–54

Keaveney, A., *Sulla: The Last Republican*² (London: 2005)

Keaveney, A., "Notes on Plutarch, *Comparison Lysander-Sulla* 2.5–7 and 5.5," *Arctos* 52 (2018), pp. 103–118

Keaveney, A., and J. Madden, Memnon, *BNJ* 434 (Leiden)

Keesling, C. M., "Early Hellenistic Portrait Statues on the Athenian Acropolis: Survival, Reuse, Transformation," in P. Schultz and R. von den Hoff (eds.), *Early Hellenistic Portraiture: Image, Style, Context* (Cambridge: 2007), pp. 141–160

Keesling, C. M., "The Hellenistic and Roman Afterlives of Dedications on the Athenian Akropolis," in R. Krumeich and C. Witschel (eds.), *Die Akropolis von Athen im Hellenismus und in der römischen Kaiserzeit* (Wiesbaden: 2010), pp. 303–327

Kellogg, D., "*Ouk elatto paradoso ten patrida*: The Ephebic Oath and the Oath of Plataia in Fourth-Century Athens," *Mouseion* 8 (2008), pp. 355–376

Kennell, N. M., "Neron Periodonikes," *AJP* 109 (1988), pp. 239–251

Kennell, N. M., "The *Ephebeia* in the Hellenistic Period," in W. M. Bloomer (ed.), *A Companion to Ancient Education* (Malden: 2015), pp. 172–183

Kidd, I. G., "Posidonius as Philosopher Historian," in M. Griffin and J. Barnes (eds.), *Philosophia Togata: Essays on Philosophy and Roman Society* (Oxford: 1989), pp. 39–46

Kienast, D., "Antonius, Augustus, die Kaiser und Athen," in D. von Kartheinz, D. Hennig, and H. Kaleisch (eds.), *Klasiches Altertum, Spätantike und frühes Christentum* (Würzburg: 1993), pp. 191–222

Kienast, H. J., "Antike Zeitmessung auf der Agora. Neue Forschungen am Turm der Winde in Athen," *Ant. Welt.* 28 (1997a), pp. 113–115

Kienast, H. J., "The Tower of the Winds in Athens: Hellenistic or Roman?," in M. C. Hoff and S. I. Rotroff (eds.), *The Romanization of Athens* (Oxford: 1997b), pp. 53–65

King, C. J., "Kingship and Other Political Institutions," in J. Roisman and I. Worthington (eds.), *A Companion to Ancient Macedonia* (Malden: 2010), pp. 374–391

Kleiner, D. E. E., *The Monument of Philoppapos in Athens* (Rome: 1983)

Kleiner, D. E. E., "Athens under the Romans: The Patronage of Emperors and Kings," in C. B. McClendon (ed.), *Rome and the Provinces: Studies in the Transformation of Art and Architecture in the Mediterranean World* (New Haven: 1986), pp. 8–20

Kokkou, A., "Adriáneia erga eis tàs Athénas," *Arch. Deltion* 25 (1970), pp. 150–173

Konstan, D., "Comedy and the Athenian Ideal," in M. Canevaro and B. Gray (eds.), *The Hellenistic Reception of Classical Athenian Democracy and Political Thought* (Oxford: 2018), pp. 109–121

Korhonen, T., "Self-Concept and Public Image of Philosophers and Philosophical Schools at the Beginning of the Hellenistic Period," in J. Frösén (ed.), *Early Hellenistic Athens: Symptoms of a Change* (Helsinki: 1997), pp. 33–101

Korres, M., "Apó ton Stauró sten archaía Agorá," *Horos* 10–12 (1992–1998), pp. 83–104

Kosmetatou, E., "The Attalids of Pergamon," in A. Erskine (ed.), *A Companion to the Hellenistic World* (Malden: 2003), pp. 159–174

Kousser, R., "Hellenistic and Roman Art, 221 BC–AD 337," in J. Roisman and I. Worthington (eds.), *A Companion to Ancient Macedonia* (Malden: 2010), pp. 522–542

Kralli, I., "Athens and Her Leading Citizens in the Early Hellenistic Period (338–261 B.C.): The Evidence of the Decrees Awarding the Highest Honors," *Archaiognosia* 10 (1999–2000), pp. 133–162

Kralli, I., "The Date and Context of Divine Honours for Antigonos Gonatas—A Suggestion," in O. Palagia and S. V. Tracy (eds.), *The Macedonians in Athens, 322–229 BC* (Oxford: 2003), pp. 61–66

Kreuz, P.-A. "Monuments for the King: Royal Presence in the Late Hellenistic World of Mithridates VI," in J. M. Højte (ed.), *Mithridates VI and the Pontic Kingdom* (Aarhus: 2009), pp. 131–144

Kroll, J. H., "The Eleusis Hoard of Athenian Imperial Coins," *Hesperia* 42 (1973), pp. 312–333

Kroll, J. H., *The Greek Coins: The Athenian Agora* 26 (Princeton: 1993)

Kroll, J. H., "Coinage as an Index of Romanization," in M. C. Hoff and S. I. Rotroff (eds.), *The Romanization of Athens* (Oxford: 1997), pp. 135–150

Kroll, J. H., "The Evidence of Athenian Coins," in O. Palagia and S. V. Tracy (eds.), *The Macedonians in Athens, 322–229 BC* (Oxford: 2003), pp. 206–212

Krumeich, R., "Formen der statuarischen Repräsentation römischer Honoranden auf der Akropolis von Athen im späten Hellenismus und in der frühen Kaiserzeit," in S. Vlizos (ed.), *Athens during the Roman Period: Recent Discoveries, New Evidence* (Athens: 2008), pp. 353–370

Krumeich, R., "Vor klassischen Hintergrund. Zum Phänomen der Wiederverwendung älterer Statuen auf der Athener Akropolis als Ehrenstatuen für Römer," in R. Krumeich and C. Witschel (eds.), *Die Akropolis von Athen im Hellenismus und in der römischen Kaiserzeit* (Wiesbaden: 2010), pp. 329–398

Krumeich, R., and C. Witschel (eds.), *Die Akropolis von Athen im Hellenismus und in derrömischen Kaiserzeit* (Weisbaden: 2010a)

Krumeich, R., and C. Witschel, "Die Akropolis als zentrales Heiligtum und Ort athenischer Identitätsbildung," in R. Krumeich and C. Witschel (eds.), *Die Akropolis von Athen im Hellenismus und in der römischen Kaiserzeit* (Weisbaden: 2010b), pp. 1–53

Lacey, W. K., *The Family in Classical Greece* (London: 1968)
Lambert, S. D., "Connecting with the Past in Lykourgan Athens," in L. Foxhall and H.-J. Gehrke (eds.), *Intentional History: Spinning Time in Ancient Greece* (Stuttgart: 2010), pp. 225–238
Lambert, S. D., "Some Political Shifts in Lykourgan Athens," in V. Azoulay and P. Ismard (eds.), *Clisthène et Lycurgue d'Athènes: autour du politique dans la cité classique* (Paris: 2011), pp. 175–190
Lambert, S. D. (ed.), *Inscriptiones Graecae II/III3 1, 2 Inscriptiones Atticae Euclidis Anno Posteriores,* Pars 1, Fascicle 2, *leges et decreta annorum 352/1–322/1* (Berlin: 2012a)
Lambert, S. D., "The Social Construction of Priests and Priestesses in Athenian Honorific Decrees from the Fourth Century BC to the Augustan Period," in M. Horster and A. Klöckner (eds.), *Civic Priests: Cult Personnel in Athens from the Hellenistic Period to Late Antiquity* (Berlin: 2012b), pp. 67–133
Lambert, S. D., and J. H. Blok, "The Appointment of Priests in Attic Gene," *ZPE* 169 (2009), pp. 95–121
Lamberton, R., "Plutarch's Phocion: Melodrama of Mob and Elite in Occupied Athens," in O. Palagia and S. V. Tracy (eds.), *The Macedonians in Athens, 322–229 BC* (Oxford: 2003), pp. 8–13
Landucci, F., Phylarchos, *BNJ* 081 (Leiden)
Landucci, F., "Cassander and the Argeads," in S. Müller, T. Howe, H. Bowden, and R. Rollinger (eds.), *The History of the Aregeads* (Wiesbaden: 2017), pp. 269–279
Landucci Gattinoni, F., "Diodorus XVIII 39.1–7 and Antipatros' Settlement at Triparadeisos," in H. Hauben and A. Meeus (eds.), *The Age of the Successors and the Creation of the Hellenistic Kingdoms (323–276 B.C.)* (Leuven: 2014), pp. 33–48
Lane Fox, R. (ed.), *Brill's Companion to Ancient Macedon* (Leiden: 2011a)
Lane Fox, R., "'Glorious Servitude . . .': The Reigns of Antigonos Gonatas and Demetrios II," in R. Lane Fox (ed.), *Brill's Companion to Ancient Macedon* (Leiden: 2011b), pp. 495–519
Lape, S., *Reproducing Athens: Menander's Comedy, Democratic Culture, and the Hellenistic City* (Princeton: 2004)
Lape, S., "Menander's Comedy," in J. J. Clauss and M. Cuypers (eds.), *A Companion to Hellenistic Literature* (Malden: 2018), pp. 282–296
Larsen, J. A. O., "The Policy of Augustus in Greece," *Acta Classica* 1 (1958), pp. 123–130
Lawton, C. L., "Athenian Anti-Macedonian Sentiment and Democratic Ideology in Attic Document Reliefs in the Second Half of the Fourth Century B.C.," in O. Palagia and S. V. Tracy (eds.), *The Macedonians in Athens, 322–229 BC* (Oxford: 2003), pp. 117–127
Lazenby, J. F., *Hannibal's War* (Warminster: 1978)
LeBohec, S., "Phthia, mère de Philippe V: Examen critique des sources," *REG* 94 (1981), pp. 34–46
LeBohec, S., *Antigone Dôsôn roi de Macédoine* (Nancy: 1993)

Lehmann, G. A., "Der 'Lamische Krieg' und die 'Freiheit der Hellenen': Überlegungen zurhieronymianischen Tradition," *ZPE* 73 (1988), pp. 121–149

Leigh, S., "The Aqueduct of Hadrian and the Water Supply of Roman Athens," Ph.D. Diss. (Pennsylvania: 1998)

Leigh, S., "The 'Reservoir' of Hadrian in Athens," *JRA* 10 (1997), pp. 279–290

Leiwo, M., "Religion, or Other Reasons? Private Associations in Athens," in J. Frösén (ed.), *Early Hellenistic Athens: Symptoms of a Change* (Helsinki: 1997), pp. 103–117

Leon, C. F., "Antigonus Gonatas Rediscovered," *Anc. World* 20 (1989), pp. 21–25

Lévêque, P., *Pyrrhos* (Paris: 1957)

Levick, B. M., "Greece (including Crete and Cyprus) and Asia Minor from 43 B.C. to A.D. 69," in A. K. Bowman, E. Champlin, and A. Lintott (eds.), *Cambridge Ancient History*^{2} 10 (Cambridge: 1996), pp. 641–675

Levick, B. M., *Tiberius the Politician* (London: 1999)

Levick, B. M., "Greece and Asia Minor," in A. K. Bowman, P. Garnsey, and D. Rathbone (eds.), *Cambridge Ancient History*^{2} 11 (Cambridge: 2000), pp. 604–634

Levick, B. M., *Augustus: Image and Substance* (London: 2010)

Levick, B. M., *Claudius* (London: 2015)

Levick, B. M., *Vespasian*^{2} (London: 2016)

Lewis, D. M., "The Chronology of the Athenian New Style Coinage," *NC* 2 (1962), pp. 275–300

Liapis, V., and T. Stephanopoulos, "Greek Tragedy in the Fourth Century: The Fragments," in V. Liapis and A. K. Petrides (eds.), *Greek Tragedy after the Fifth Century: A Survey from ca. 400 BC to ca. AD 400* (Cambridge: 2019), pp. 25–65

Liapis, V., and A. K. Petrides (eds.), *Greek Tragedy after the Fifth Century: A Survey from ca. 400 BC to ca. AD 400* (Cambridge: 2019)

Lönnqvist, M., "Studies on the Hellenistic Coinage of Athens: The Impact of Macedonia on the Athenian Money Market in the 3rd Century BC," in J. Frösén (ed.), *Early Hellenistic Athens: Symptoms of a Change* (Helsinki: 1997), pp. 119–145

Loomis, J. W., "Cicero and Thessaloniki: Politics and Provinces," *Ancient Macedonia* 2 (Institute for Balkan Studies, Thessaloniki: 1977), pp. 169–187

Lozano, F., *La religiòn del Poder. El culto imperial en Atenas en época de Augusto y los emperadores Julio-Claudios* (Oxford: 2002)

Lozano, F., "Thea Livia in Athens: Redating IG II2 3242," *ZPE* 148 (2004), pp. 177–180

Lund, H. S., *Lysimachus: A Study in Early Hellenistic Kingship* (London: 1994)

Luppe, W., "Nochmals zur 'Imbrioi'-Didaskalia," *ZPE* 96 (1993), pp. 9–10

Luraghi, N., "Stratokles of Diomeia and Party Politics in Early Hellenistic Athens," *Class. & Med.* 65 (2014), pp. 191–226

Luraghi, N., "Stairway to Heaven: The Politics of Memory in Early Hellenistic Athens," in M. Canevaro and B. Gray (eds.), *The Hellenistic Reception of Classical Athenian Democracy and Political Thought* (Oxford: 2018), pp. 21–44

Lytle, E., "Fishless Mysteries or High Prices at Athens? Reexamining IG II (2) 1103," *MH* 64 (2007), pp. 100–111

Ma, J., "Kings," in A. Erskine (ed.), *A Companion to the Hellenistic World* (Malden: 2003), pp. 177–195

Ma, J., "Court, King, and Power in Antigonid Macedonia," in R. Lane Fox (ed.), *Brill's Companion to Ancient Macedon* (Leiden: 2011), pp. 521–543

MacDowell, D. M., *Demosthenes the Orator* (Oxford: 2009)

MacKendrick, P., *The Athenian Aristocracy, 399–31 B.C.* (Cambridge: 1969)

MacMullen, R., "Hellenizing the Romans (2nd Century B.C.)," *Historia* 40 (1991), pp. 419–438

Madsen, J. M., "The Ambitions of Mithridates VI: Hellenistic Kingship and Modern Interpretations," in J. M. Højte (ed.), *Mithridates VI and the Pontic Kingdom* (Aarhus: 2009), pp. 191–201

Malissard, A., "Tacite et les Grecs (Germanicus, Pison, Néron)," in Y. Perrin (ed.), *Neronia 7, Rome, l'Italie et la Grèce: hellénisme et philhellénisme au premier siècle ap. J.-C.* (Brussels: 2007), pp. 323–330

Malitz, J., *Nero* (Malden: 2005)

Mango, E., "Tanta vis admonitionis inest in locis. Zur Veränderung von Erinnerungsräumen im Athen des 1. Jahrhunderts v. Chr.," in R. Krumeich and C. Witschel (eds.), *Die Akropolis von Athen im Hellenismus und in der römischen Kaiserzeit* (Wiesbaden: 2010), pp. 117–155

Manni, E., *Demetrio Poliorcete* (Rome: 1951)

Marasco, G., "Sui problemi dell'approvvigionamento di cereali in Atene nell'età dei Diadochoi," *Athenaeum* 62 (1984a), pp. 286–294

Marasco, G., *Democare di Leuconoe. Politica e cultura a Atene fra IV e III sec. a. C.* (Florence: 1984b)

Mari, M., "Macedonians and Pro-Macedonians in Early Hellenistic Athens: Reflections on *asebeia*," in O. Palagia and S. V. Tracy (eds.), *The Macedonians in Athens, 322–229 BC* (Oxford: 2003), pp. 82–92

Marquaille, C., "The Foreign Policy of Ptolemy II," in P. McKechnie and P. Guillaume (eds.), *Ptolemy II Philadelphus and His World* (Leiden: 2008), pp. 39–64

Mattingly, H. B., "Some Third Magistrates in the Athenian New Silver Coinage," *JHS* 91 (1971), pp. 85–93

Mattingly, H. B., "The Beginning of Athenian New Style Silver Coinage," *NC* 150 (1990), pp. 67–78

Mattingly, H. B., "Athens between Rome and the Kings, 229/8 to 129 B.C.," in P. Cartledge, P. Garnsey, and E. Gruen (eds.), *Hellenistic Constructs: Essays in Culture, History, and Historiography* (Berkeley: 1997), pp. 120–144

Matyszak, P., *Mithridates the Great: Rome's Indomitable Enemy* (Barnsley: 2008)

Matyszak, P., *Roman Conquests: Macedonia and Greece* (Barnsley: 2009)

Mayor, A., *The Poison King: The Life and Legend of Mithridates, Rome's Deadliest Enemy* (Princeton: 2011)
McAllister, M. H., "The Temple of Ares at Athens: A Review of the Evidence," *Hesperia* 28 (1959), pp. 1–64
McGing, B. C., *The Foreign Policy of Mithridates VI Eupator, King of Pontus* (Leiden: 1986)
McGing, B. C., "Subjection and Resistance: To the Death of Mithridates," in A. Erskine (ed.), *A Companion to the Hellenistic World* (Malden: 2003), pp. 79–88
McGing, B. C., "Mithridates VI Eupator: Victim or Aggressor?," in J. M. Højte (ed.), *Mithridates VI and the Pontic Kingdom* (Aarhus: 2009), pp. 203–216
McGing, B. C., *Polybius' Histories* (New York: 2010)
McGing, B. C., "Youthfulness in Polybius: The Case of Philip V of Macedon," in B. Gibson and T. Harrison (eds.), *Polybius and His World: Essays in Memory of F. W. Walbank* (Oxford: 2013), pp. 183–199
Meeus, A., "The Power Struggle of the Diadochoi in Babylonia, 323 BC," *Anc. Society* 38 (2008), pp. 39–82
Meeus, A., "The Career of Sostratos of Knidos: Politics, Diplomacy, and the Alexandria Building Programme in the Early Hellenistic Period," in T. Howe, E. E. Garvan, and G. Wrightson (eds.), *Greece, Macedon, and Persia: Studies in Social, Political, and Military History in Honour of W. Heckel* (Haverton: 2015), pp. 143–171
Mehl, A., *Seleukos Nikator und sein Reich* (Louvain: 1986)
Mendels, D., "Polybius, Philip V, and the Socio-Economic Question in Greece," *Anc. Society* 8 (1977), pp. 155–174
Meritt, B. D., *The Athenian Year* (Berkeley: 1961)
Meritt, B. D., A. G. Woodhead, and G. A. Stamires, "Greek Inscriptions," *Hesperia* 26 (1957), pp. 198–270
Merker, I. L., "The Ptolemaic Officials and the League of the Islanders," *Historia* 19 (1970), pp. 141–160
Migeotte, L., "L'aide béotienne à la libération d'Athènes en 229 a.C.," in H. Beister and J. Buckler (eds.), *Boiotika* (Munich: 1989), pp. 193–201
Mikalson, J. D., *The Sacred and Civil Calendar of the Athenian Year* (Princeton: 1975)
Mikalson, J. D., *Religion in Hellenistic Athens* (Berkeley: 1998)
Mikalson, J. D., "Greek Religion: Continuity and Change in the Hellenistic Period," in G. R. Bugh (ed.), *The Cambridge Companion to the Hellenistic World* (Cambridge: 2007), pp. 208–222
Mitchel, F. W., "Derkylos of Hagnous and the Date of I.G. II^2, 1187," *Hesperia* 33 (1964), pp. 337–351
Mitchel, F. W., "Athens in the Age of Alexander," *G&R^2* 12 (1965), pp. 189–204
Mitchel, F. W., "Lykourgan Athens: 338–322," *Semple Lectures* 2 (Norman: 1973)
Mitchell, S., "The Galatians: Representation and Reality," in A. Erskine (ed.), *A Companion to the Hellenistic World* (Malden: 2003), pp. 280–293
Mitsis, P., "The Institutions of Hellenistic Philosophy," in A. Erskine (ed.), *A Companion to the Hellenistic World* (Malden: 2003), pp. 464–476

Morgan, M. G., "Metellus Macedonicus and the Province Macedonia," *Historia* 18 (1969), pp. 422–446
Morgan, M. G., *69 A.D.: The Year of Four Emperors* (Oxford: 2006)
Mooren, L., "The Nature of the Hellenistic Monarchy," in E. Van't Dack, P. van Dessel, and W. van Gucht (eds.), *Egypt and the Hellenistic World* (Louvain: 1983), pp. 205–240
Morris, I., "Periodization and the Heroes: Inventing a Dark Age," in P. G. Toohey and M. Golden (eds.), *Inventing Ancient Culture: Historicism, Periodization, and the Ancient World* (London: 1997), pp. 96–131
Mossé, C., *Athens in Decline, 404–86 B.C.*, trans. J. Stewart (London: 1973)
Muccioli, F., "Stratocle di Diomeia e la redazione trezenia del 'Decreto di Temistocle,'" in B. Virgilio (ed.), *Studi Ellenistici* 20 (Pisa: 2008), pp. 109–136
Müller, S., "Philip II," in J. Roisman and I. Worthington (eds.), *A Companion to Ancient Macedonia* (Malden: 2010), pp. 166–185
Müller, S., Demetrios of Phaleron, *BNJ* 228 (Leiden)
Nachtergael, G., *Les Galates en Grèce et les Sôtéria de Delphes* (Brussels: 1977)
Naco del Hoyo, T., B. Antela-Bernárdez, I. Arrayás-Morales, and S. Busquets-Artigas, "The Impact of the Roman Intervention in Greece and Asia Minor upon Civilians (88–63 B.C.)," in B. Antela-Bernárdez and T. Naco del Hoyo (eds.), *Transforming Historical Landscapes in the Ancient Empires* (Oxford: 2009), pp. 33–51
Nevett, L. C., "Continuity and Change in Greek Households under Roman Rule: The Role of Women in the Domestic Context," in E. N. Ostenfeld, *Greek Romans and Roman Greeks: Studies in Cultural Interaction* (Aarhus: 2002), pp. 81–97
Nicholson E., "Philip V of Macedon, '*Eromenos* of the Greeks': A Note and Reassessment," *Hermes* 146 (2018), pp. 241–255
Niese, B., "Die letzten Tyrannen Athens," *RhM* 42 (1887), pp. 547–581
Nilsson, M. P., *Geschichte der griechischen Religion*^{2} (Munich: 1974)
Noble, J. V., and D. J. de Solla Price, "The Water Clock in the Tower of the Winds," *AJA* 72 (1968), pp. 345–355
Notopoulos, J. A., "The Date of the Creation of Hadrianis," *TAPA* 77 (1946), pp. 53–56
Nulton, P. E., *The Sanctuary of Apollo Hypoakraios and Imperial Athens* (Providence: 2003)
Ogden, D., *Polygamy, Prostitutes, and Death: The Hellenistic Dynasties* (London: 1999)
Oikonomides, A. N., "Defeated Athens, the Land of Oropos, Caesar and Augustus. Notes on the History of the Years 49–27 B.C.," *Anc. World* 2 (1979), pp. 97–103
Oikonomides, A.N., "Philip IV of Macedonia: A King for Four Months (296 B.C.)," *Anc. World* 19 (1989), pp. 109–112
Oliver, G. J., "The Politics of Coinage: Athens and Antigonos Gonatas," in A. Meadows and K. Shipton (eds.), *Money and Its Uses in the Ancient Greek World* (Oxford: 2001), pp. 35–52

Oliver, G. J., "Oligarchy at Athens after the Lamian War: Epigraphic Evidence for the Boule and the Ecclesia," in O. Palagia and S. V. Tracy (eds.), *The Macedonians in Athens, 322–229 BC* (Oxford: 2003), pp. 40–51

Oliver, G. J., *War, Food, and Politics in Early Hellenistic Athens* (Oxford: 2007a)

Oliver, G. J., "History and Rhetoric," in G. R. Bugh (ed.), *The Cambridge Companion to the Hellenistic World* (Cambridge: 2007b), pp. 113–135

Oliver, J. H., "Greek and Latin Inscriptions," *Hesperia* 10 (1941), pp. 237–261

Oliver, J. H., "New Evidence on the Attic Panhellenion," *Hesperia* 20 (1951), pp. 31–33

Oliver, J. H., "Domitian's Freedman Antiochus," *Hesperia* 32 (1963), p. 87

Oliver, J. H., "Livia as Artemis Boulaia at Athens," *CP* 60 (1965a), p. 179

Oliver, J. H., "The Athens of Hadrian," in *Les Empereurs romains de l'Espagne. Actes du Colloque international: Madrid-Italica, 31 Mars–6 Avril, 1964* (Paris: 1965b), pp. 123–133

Oliver, J. H., "On the Hellenic Policy of Augustus and Agrippa in 27 B.C.," *AJP* 93 (1972), pp. 190–197

Oliver, J. H., "Flavius Pantaenus, Priest of the Philosophical Muses," *HThR* 72 (1979), pp. 157–160

Oliver, J. H., "A Peripatetic Constitution," *JHS* 100 (1980), pp. 199–201

Oliver, J. H., "Civic Status in Roman Athens: Cicero, *Pro Balbo* 12.30," *GRBS* 22 (1981a), pp. 83–88

Oliver, J. H., "Roman Emperors and Athens," *Historia* 30 (1981b), pp. 412–423

Oliver, J. H, "Arrian in Two Roles," *Hesperia Suppl.* 19 (Princeton: 1982), pp. 122–129

Oliver, J. H., "Roman Senators from Greece and Macedonia," in J. H. Oliver (ed.), *The Civic Tradition and Roman Athens* (Baltimore: 1983), pp. 115–136

Oliver, J. H., *The Civic Tradition and Roman Athens* (Baltimore: 1983)

O'Neil, J. L., "A Re-Examination of the Chremonidean War," in P. McKechnie and P. Guillaume (eds.), *Ptolemy II Philadelphus and His World* (Leiden: 2008), pp. 65–89

Osborne, M. J., "Athenian Grants of Citizenship after 229 B.C.," *Anc. Society* 7 (1976), pp. 107–125

Osborne, M. J., "Kallias, Phaidros, and the Revolt of Athens in 287 BC," *ZPE* 35 (1979), pp. 181–194

Osborne, M. J., "The Chronology of Athens in the Mid-Third Century BC," *ZPE* 78 (1989), pp. 209–242

Osborne, M. J., "Shadowland: Athens under Antigonos Gonatas and His Successor," in O. Palagia and S. V. Tracy (eds.), *The Macedonians in Athens, 322–229 BC* (Oxford: 2003), pp. 67–75

Osborne, M. J., "The Archons of Athens, 300/299–228/7," *ZPE* 171 (2009), pp. 83–99

Osborne, M. J., *Athens in the Third Century B.C.* (Athens: 2012)

Osborne, M. J., and S. G. Byrne, *Inscriptiones Graecae II/III3 1, 4 Inscriptiones Atticae Euclidis Anno Posteriores*, Pars 1, Fascicle 4, *leges et decreta annorum 300/299–230/29* (Berlin: 2012)

Osgood, J., *Claudius Caesar: Image and Power in the Early Roman Empire* (Cambridge: 2011)
Ostenfeld, E. N. (ed.), *Greek Romans and Roman Greeks: Studies in Cultural Interaction* (Aarhus: 2002)
O'Sullivan, L., *The Regime of Demetrius of Phalerum in Athens, 317–307 BCE* (Leiden: 2009)
Pailler, J.-M., "Domitien et la 'Cité de Pallas.' Un Tournant dans l'histoire de Toulouse Antique," *Pallas* 34 (1988), pp. 99–109
Palagia, O., "Classical Encounters: Attic Sculpture after Sulla," in M. C. Hoff and S. I. Rotroff (eds.), *The Romanization of Athens* (Oxford: 1997), pp. 81–95
Palagia, O., "Hellenistic Art," in R. Lane Fox (ed.), *Brill's Companion to Ancient Macedon* (Leiden: 2011), pp. 477–493
Palagia, O., "The Impact of *Ares Macedon* on Athenian Sculpture," in O. Palagia and S. V. Tracy (eds.), *The Macedonians in Athens, 322–229 BC* (Oxford, 2003), pp. 140–151
Palagia, O., and S. V. Tracy (eds.), *The Macedonians in Athens, 322–229 BC* (Oxford: 2003)
Papazoglou, F., "Quelques aspects de l'historie de la province de Macédoine," in H. Temporini (ed.), *Aufstieg und Niedergang der Römischen Welt* 2.7.1 (Berlin: 1979), pp. 302–369
Parker, R., *Athenian Religion: A History* (Oxford: 1996)
Paschidis, P., *Between City and King: Prosopographical Studies on the Intermediaries between the Cities of the Greek Mainland and the Aegean and the Royal Courts in the Hellenistic Period (323–190 BC)* (Athens: 2008)
Paspalas, S. A., "Classical Art," in R. Lane Fox (ed.), *Brill's Companion to Ancient Macedon* (Leiden: 2011), pp. 179–207
Pavan, M., "Nerone e la libertà dei Greci," *Atti* 12 (1982–1983) = *Neronia 3* (Rome: 1987), pp. 149–165
Pélékidis, C., *Histoire de l'éphébie attique des origines à 31 av. J.-C.* (Paris: 1962)
Pelling, C. B. R., *Plutarch, Life of Antony* (Cambridge: 1988)
Pelling, C. B. R., "The Triumviral Period," in A. K. Bowman, E. Champlin, and A. Lintott (eds.), *Cambridge Ancient History*^{2} 10 (Cambridge: 1996), pp. 1–69
Pelling, C., *Plutarch and History* (London: 2002)
Peppas-Delmousou, D., "A Statue Base for Augustus *IG* II^2 3262 + *IG* II^2 4725," *AJP* 100 (1979), pp. 125–132
Peppas-Delmousou, D., "Dédicace d'une mesure à grains par deux astynomes (IG II^2 3939 + 2878) et la politique de l'annone à Athènes sous Augustus," in S. Follet (ed.), *L'Hellénisme d'Époque Romaine: Nouveaux Documents, Nouvelles Approches* (Paris: 2004), pp. 121–138
Perlman, S., "Greek Diplomatic Tradition and the Corinthian League of Philip of Macedon," *Historia* 34 (1985), pp. 153–174
Perlman, S., "Fourth-Century Treaties and the League of Corinth of Philip of Macedon," in *Ancient Macedonia* 4 (Institute for Balkan Studies, Thessaloniki: 1986), pp. 437–442
Perlwitz, O., *Titus Pomponius Atticus* (Stuttgart: 1992)

Perrin, É., "Remarques sur la 'liberation' d'Athènes et la situation financière de la cité de 229 à 168 av. J.-C.," *AHB* 10 (1996), pp. 39–46

Perrin, Y., (ed.), *Neronia 7, Rome, l'Italie et la Grèce: Hellénisme et Philhellénisme au premier siècle ap. J.-C.* (Brussels: 2007b)

Perrin-Saminadayar, É., "L'éphébie attique de la crise mithridatique à Hadrien: Miroir de la Société Athénienne?.," in S. Follet (ed.), *L'Hellénisme d'Époque Romaine: Nouveaux Documents, Nouvelles Approches* (Paris: 2004), pp. 87–103

Perrin-Saminadayar, É., "L'accueil officiel des rois et des princes à Athènes à l'époque hellénistique," *BCH* 128–129 (2004–2005), pp. 351–375

Perrin-Saminadayar, É., *Éducation, culture et société à Athènes. Les acteurs de la vie culturelle athénienne (229–88). Un tout petit monde. De l'archéologie à l'histoire* (Paris: 2007a)

Perrin-Saminadayar, É., "Visites imperials et visites royales à Athènes au Ier siècle de notre ère," in Y. Perrin (ed.), *Neronia 7, Rome, l'Italie et la Grèce: Hellénisme et philhellénisme au premier siècle ap. J.-C.* (Brussels: 2007c), pp. 126–144

Perrin-Saminadayar, É., "Romains à Athènes (IIe et Ier siècles av. J.-C.): Entre Acculturation et Malentendu Culturel," in A. Gangloff (ed.), *Médiateurs Culturels et Politiques dans l'Empire Romain* (Paris: 2011), pp. 123–139

Perrin-Saminadayar, É., "Prêtres et Prêtresses d'Athènes et de Délos à travers les Décrets Honorifiques Athéniens (167–88 a. C.)," in M. Horster and A. Klöckner (eds.), *Civic Priests: Cult Personnel in Athens from the Hellenistic Period to Late Antiquity* (Berlin: 2012), pp. 135–159

Philipp, G., "Philippides, ein politischer Komiker in hellenistischer Zeit," *Gymnasium* 80 (1973), pp. 493–509

Poccini, J., "Man or God: Divine Assimilation and Imitation in the Late Republic and Early Principate," in K. A. Raaflaub and M. Toher (eds.), *Between Republic and Empire* (Berkeley: 1993), pp. 344–365

Poddighe, E., *Nel segno di Antipatro. L'eclissi della democrazia ateniese dal 323/2 al 319/8 a.C.* (Rome: 2002)

Pollitt, J. J., *Art in the Hellenistic Age* (Cambridge: 1986)

Pomeroy, S. B., *Families in Classical and Hellenistic Greece: Representations and Realities* (New York: 1997)

Post, A., "Zum Hadrianstor in Athen," *Boreas* 21–22 (1998–1999), pp. 171–183

Pouilloux, J., "Antigonos Gonatas et Athènes après la guerre de Chrémonidès," *BCH* 70 (1946), 488–496

Powell, J. G. F., "The Embassy of the Three Philosophers to Rome in 155 BC," in C. Kremmydas and K. Tempest (eds.), *Hellenistic Oratory: Continuity and Change* (Oxford: 2013), pp. 219–247

Pritchett, W. K., and B. D. Meritt, *The Chronology of Hellenistic Athens* (Cambridge: 1940)

Prost, F., "Les villes de la Grèce égéenne: mutations économiques et sociales entre le IVe et le IIe siècle av. J.-C.," *Pallas* 74 (2007), pp. 237–261

Pugliese, A., "The Literary Tradition on King Perseus and the End of the Macedonian Kingdom: Between History and Propaganda," *Anc. World* 45 (2014), pp. 146–173

Rathmann, M., "Athen in hellenistischer Zeit—Fremdbestimmung und kulturelle Anziehungskraft," in R. Krumeich and C. Witschel (eds.), *Die Akropolis von Athen im Hellenismus und in der römischen Kaiserzeit* (Wiesbaden: 2010), pp. 55–93

Raubitschek, A. E., "Hadrian as the Son of Zeus Eleutherios," *AJA* 49 (1945), pp. 128–133

Raubitschek, A. E., "Octavia's Deification at Athens," *TAPhA* 77 (1946), pp. 146–150

Raubitschek, A. E., "Phaidros and His Roman Pupils," *Hesperia* 18 (1949), pp. 96–103

Raubitschek, A. E., "Epigraphical Notes on Julius Caesar," *JRS* 44 (1954), pp. 65–75

Raubitschek, A. E., "Brutus in Athens," *Phoenix* 11 (1957), pp. 1–11

Raubitschek, A. E., "Greek Inscriptions," *Hesperia* 35 (1966), pp. 241–251

Rawson, E., "The Eastern Clientelae of Clodius and the Clodii," *Historia* 22 (1973), pp. 219–239

Rawson, E., "Cicero and the Areopagus," *Athenaeum* 73 (1985), pp. 44–67

Rawson, E., "Roman Tradition and the Greek World," in A. E. Astin, F. W. Walbank, M. W. Fredericksen, and R. M. Ogilvie (eds.), *Cambridge Ancient History*^{2} 8 (Cambridge: 1989), pp. 422–476

Rawson, E., "Caesar: Civil War and Dictatorship," in J. A. Crook, A. Lintott, and E. Rawson (eds.), *Cambridge Ancient History*^{2} 9 (Cambridge: 1994a), pp. 424–467

Rawson, E., "The Aftermath of the Ides," in J. A. Crook, A. Lintott, and E. Rawson (eds.), *Cambridge Ancient History*^{2} 9 (Cambridge: 1994b), pp. 468–490

Reger, G., "The Date of the Battle of Kos," *AJAH* 10 (1985) [1993], pp. 155–177

Reinach, T., *Mithridate Eupator, roi de Pont* (Paris: 1980)

Reinmuth, O. W., "The Attic Archons Named Apolexis," *BCH* 90 (1966), pp. 93–100

Reinmuth, O. W., *The Ephebic Inscriptions of the Fourth Century BC* (Leiden: 1971)

Rhodes, P. J., *The Athenian Boule* (Oxford: 1972)

Rhodes, P. J., "'Lycurgan' Athens," in A. Tamis, C. J. Mackie, and S. G. Byrne (eds.), *Philathenaios: Studies in Honour of M. J. Osborne* (Athens: 2010), pp. 81–90

Rhodes, P. J., and R. Osborne (eds.), *Greek Historical Inscriptions, 404–323 BC* (Oxford: 2003)

Rizakis, A. D., "La constitution des élites municipales dans les colonies romaines de la province d'Achaie," in O. Salomies (ed.), *The Greek East in the Roman Conte* (Helsinki: 2001), pp. 37–49

Robert, J., and L. Robert, "Bulletin Épigraphique," *REG* 61 (1948), pp. 137–212

Rödel, C., "Von Lucius Aemilius Paullus zu Augustus. Stiftungen von Römern in Athen," in R. Krumeich and C. Witschel (eds.), *Die Akropolis von Athen im Hellenismus und in derrömischen Kaiserzeit* (Wiesbaden: 2010), pp. 95–115

Roisman, J., *Alexander's Veterans and the Early Wars of the Successors* (Austin: 2012)

Roisman, J., "Perdikkas's Invasion of Egypt," in H. Hauben and A. Meeus (eds.), *The Age of the Successors and the Creation of the Hellenistic Kingdoms (323–276 B.C.)* (Leuven: 2014), pp. 455–474

Roisman, J., and M. Edwards, *Lycurgus, Against Leocrates* (Oxford: 2019)
Roisman, J., and I. Worthington (eds.), *A Companion to Ancient Macedonia* (Malden: 2010)
Roisman, J., I. Worthington, and R. Waterfield, *Lives of the Attic Orators: Pseudo-Plutarch, Photius, and the Suda* (Oxford: 2015)
Roller, D., *Cleopatra: A Biography* (Oxford: 2010)
Romm, J., *Ghost on the Throne: The Death of Alexander the Great and the War for Crown and Empire* (New York: 2011)
Roselli, D. K., "Theorika in Fifth-Century Athens," *GRBS* 49 (2009), pp. 5–30
Rosenmeyer, P. A., *Julia Balbilla* (London: 2010)
Rotroff, S. I., "From Greek to Roman in Athenian Ceramics," in M. C. Hoff and S. I. Rotroff (eds.), *The Romanization of Athens* (Oxford: 1997), pp. 97–116
Rotroff, S. I., "Minima Macedonica," in O. Palagia and S. V. Tracy (eds.), *The Macedonians in Athens, 322–229 BC* (Oxford: 2003), pp. 213–225
Rowland, R. J., "Cicero and the Greek World," *TAPhA* 103 (1972), pp. 451–461
Russo, F., "Atene e Roma, Grecia e Italia nall'excursus letterario di Velleio Patercolo, I, 17–18," *RSAnt.* 36 (2006), pp. 211–228
Ryder, T. T. B., *Koine Eirene* (Oxford: 1965)
Rzepka, J., "Anonymous," *BNJ* 257a (Leiden)
Salmenkivi, E., "Family Life in the Comedies of Menander," in J. Frösén (ed.), *Early Hellenistic Athens: Symptoms of a Change* (Helsinki: 1997), pp. 183–194
Salomies, O. (ed.), *The Greek East in the Roman Context* (Helsinki: 2001)
Sarikakis, T. C., *The Hoplite General in Athens* (Chicago: 1976)
Sarikakis, T. C., "L. Calpurnius Piso Pontifex: A Disputed Governor of Macedonia," in H. J. Dell (ed.), *Ancient Macedonian Studies in Honour of C.F. Edson* (Thessaloniki: 1981), pp. 307–314
Sawada, N., "Athenian Politics in the Age of Alexander the Great: A Reconsideration of the Trial of Ctesiphon," *Chiron* 26 (1996), pp. 57–82
Sawada, N., "Macedonian Social Customs," in J. Roisman and I. Worthington (eds.), *A Companion to Ancient Macedonia* (Malden: 2010), pp. 392–408
Schiller, K., "Gentile Affiliations and the Athenian Response to Roman Domination," *Historia* 55 (2006), pp. 264–284
Schmalz, G. C. R., "Public Building and Civic Identity in Augustan and Julio-Claudian Athens," Ph.D. Diss. (Michigan: 1994)
Schmalz, G. C. R., "Athens, Augustus, and the Settlement of 21 B.C.," *GRBS* 37 (1996), pp. 381–398
Schmalz, G. C. R., *Augustan and Julio-Claudian Athens: A New Epigraphy and Prosopography* (Leiden: 2009)
Schmitt, O., *Der Lamische Krieg* (Bonn: 1992)
Schmitz, T. A., and N. Wiater (eds.), *The Struggle for Identity: Greeks and Their Past in the First Century BCE* (Stuttgart: 2011)
Scholten, J. B., *The Politics of Plunder: The Aetolians and Their Koinon in the Early Hellenistic Era, 279–219 B.C.* (Berkeley: 2000)
Scholten, J. B., "Macedon and the Mainland, 280–221," in A. Erskine (ed.), *A Companion to the Hellenistic World* (Malden: 2003), pp. 134–158

Scodel, R., "Lycurgus and the State of Tragedy," in C. Cooper (ed.), *Politics of Orality* (Leiden: 2007), pp. 129–154

Scolnic, B., "When Did the Future Antiochus IV Arrive in Athens?," *Hesperia* 83 (2014), pp. 123–142

Scullard, H. H., "Carthage and Rome," in F. W. Walbank, A. E. Astin, M. W. Frederiksen, and R. M. Ogilvie (eds.), *Cambridge Ancient History*² 7.2 (Cambridge: 1989), pp. 537–569

Seager, R., "Sulla," in J. A. Crook, A. Lintott, and E. Rawson (eds.), *Cambridge Ancient History*² 9 (Cambridge: 1994), pp. 165–207

Seager, R., *Pompey the Great: A Political Biography*² (Malden: 2002)

Seager, R., *Tiberius*² (Malden: 2005)

Sealey, R., *Demosthenes and His Time: A Study in Defeat* (Oxford: 1993)

Seibert, J., *Untersuchungen zur Geschichte Ptolemaios I.* (Munich: 1969)

Sekunda, N. V., "IG II2 1250: A Decree Concerning the *Lampadephoroi* of the Tribe Aiantis," *ZPE* 83 (1990), pp. 149–182

Sekunda, N. V., "Athenian Demography and Military Strength 338–322 B.C.," *BSA* 87 (1992), pp. 311–355

Sève, M., "Dédicaces du Iᵉʳ siècle à Philippes," in S. Follet (ed.), *L'Hellénisme d'Époque Romaine: Nouveaux Documents, Nouvelles Approches* (Paris: 2004), pp. 37–44

Shear, J. L., "Reusing Statues, Rewriting Inscriptions, and Bestowing Honors in Roman Athens," in Z. Newby and R. E. Leader-Newby (eds.), *Art and Inscriptions in the Ancient World* (Cambridge: 2007a), pp. 221–246

Shear, J. L. "Royal Athenians: The Ptolemies and Attalids at the Panathenaia," in O. Palagia and A. Choremi-Spetsieri (eds.), *The Panathenaic Games* (Oxford: 2007b), pp. 135–145

Shear, J. L., "Demetrios Poliorketes, Kallias of Sphettos, and the Panathenaia," in G. Reger, F. Ryan, and T. Winters (eds.), *Studies in Greek Epigraphy and History in Honor of Stephen V. Tracy* (Ausonius: 2010), pp. 135–152

Shear, J. L., "Hadrian, the Panathenaia, and the Athenian Calendar," *ZPE* 180 (2012), pp. 159–172

Shear, J.L., "An Inconvenient Past in Hellenistic Athens: The Case of Phaidros of Sphettos," *Histos* 11 (2020), pp. 269–301

Shear, T. L. Jr., "The Monument of the Eponymous Heroes in the Athenian Agora," *Hesperia* 39 (1970), pp. 145–222

Shear, T. L. Jr., "The Athenian Agora: Excavations of 1971," *Hesperia* 42 (1973), pp. 121–179

Shear, T. L. Jr., "Kallias of Sphettos and the Revolt of Athens in 286 B.C.," *Hesperia Supplement* 17 (Princeton: 1978)

Shear, T. L. Jr., "Athens: From City-State to Provincial Town," *Hesperia* 50 (1981), pp. 356–377

Shear, T. L., *Trophies of Victory* (Princeton: 2016)

Sherk, R. K., *Rome and the Greek East to the Death of Augustus* (Cambridge: 1984)

Sherk, R. K., *The Roman Empire: Augustus to Hadrian* (Cambridge: 1988)

Sherwin-White, A. N., "Lucullus, Pompey and the East," in J. A. Crook, A. Lintott, and E. Rawson (eds.), *Cambridge Ancient History*² 9 (Cambridge: 1994), pp. 229–273

Shipley, G., "Between Macedonia and Rome: Political Landscapes and Social Changes in Southern Greece in the Early Hellenistic Period," *BSA* 100 (2005), pp. 315–330

Shotter, D., *Nero Caesar Augustus, Emperor of Rome* (London: 2008)

Sickinger J. P., *Public Records and Archives in Classical Athens* (Chapel Hill: 1999)

Sifakis, G. M., "Organization of Festivals and the Dioysiac Guilds," *CQ*² 15 (1965), pp. 206–214

Simpson, R. H., "The Historical Circumstances of the Peace of 311," *JHS* 74 (1954), pp. 25–31

Simpson, R. H., "Antigonus the One-Eyed and the Greeks," *Historia* 8 (1959), pp. 385–409

Sinclair, R. K., *Democracy and Participation in Athens* (Cambridge: 1988)

Smallwood, E. M., *Documents Illustrating the Principates of Nerva, Trajan and Hadrian* (Cambridge: 1966)

Smith, L. C., "Demochares of Leuconoe and the Dates of His Exile," *Historia* 11 (1962), pp. 114–118

Sordi, M., "Claudio e il mondo greco," in Y. Perrin (ed.), *Neronia 7, Rome, l'Italie et la Grèce: Hellénisme et philhellénisme au premier siècle ap. J.-C.* (Brussels: 2007), pp. 41–49

Sourlas, D. S., "L'agora romaine d'Athènes," in V. Chankowski and P. Karvonis (eds.), *Tout vendre, tout acheter* (Bordeaux: 2012), pp. 119–138

Southern, P., *Domitian, Tragic Tyrant* (London: 1997)

Spawforth, A. J. S., "Corinth, Argos, and the Imperial Cult: Pseudo-Julian, *Letters* 198," *Hesperia* 63 (1994), pp. 211–232

Spawforth, A. J. S., "The Early Reception of the Imperial Cult in Athens: Problems and Ambiguities," in M. C. Hoff and S. I. Rotroff (eds.), *The Romanization of Athens* (Oxford: 1997), pp. 183–201

Spawforth, A. J. S., "The Panhellenion Again," *Chiron* 29 (1999), pp. 339–352

Spawforth, A. J. S., *Greece and the Augustan Cultural Revolution* (Cambridge: 2012)

Spawforth, A. J. S., and S. Walker, "The World of the Panhellenion I: Athens and Eleusis," *JRS* 75 (1985), pp. 78–104

Squillace, G., "The Comparison between Alexander and Philip: Use and Metamorphosis of an Ideological Theme," in T. Howe, E. E. Garvan, and G. Wrightson (eds.), *Greece, Macedon and Persia: Studies in Social, Political and Military History in Honour of W. Heckel* (Haverton: 2015), pp. 107–113

Stefanidou-Tiveriou, T., "Tradition and Romanization in the Monumental Landscape of Athens," in S. Vlizos (ed.), *Athens during the Roman Period: Recent Discoveries, New Evidence* (Athens: 2008), pp. 11–40

Steinbock, B., "A Lesson in Patriotism: Lycurgus' Against Leocrates, the Ideology of the Ephebeia, and Athenian Social Memory," *Class Antiq.* 30 (2011), pp. 279–317

Steinhart, M., "Pausanias und das Philopappos-Monument: ein Fall von damnatio memoriae?," *Klio* 85 (2003), pp. 171–188

Stephens, S., "Ptolemic Alexandria," in J. J. Clauss and M. Cuypers (eds.), *A Companion to Hellenistic Literature* (Malden: 2018), pp. 46–61

Stewart, A., "Hellenistic Art: Two Dozen Innovations," in G. R. Bugh (ed.), *The Cambridge Companion to the Hellenistic World* (Cambridge: 2007), pp. 158–185

Stewart, A., *Art in the Hellenistic World: An Introduction* (Cambridge: 2014)

Swain, S., "Plutarch, Plato, Athens, and Rome," in J. Barnes and M. Griffin (eds.), *Philosophia Togata II: Plato and Aristotle at Rome* (Oxford: 1997), pp. 165–187

Tarn, W. W., *Antigonos Gonatas* (Oxford: 1913)

Tarn, W. W., and G. T. Griffith, *Hellenistic Civilisation*³ (London: 1952)

Taylor, L. R., *The Divinity of the Roman Emperor* (Middletown: 1931)

Taylor, M. J., "The Battle Scene on Amelius Paullus's Pydna Monument: A Reevaluation," *Hesperia* 85 (2016), pp. 559–576

Themelis, P., "Macedonian Dedications on the Akropolis," in O. Palagia and S. V. Tracy (eds.), *The Macedonians in Athens, 322–229 BC* (Oxford: 2003), pp. 162–172

Theocharaki, A. M., "The Ancient Circuit Wall of Athens: Its Changing Course and Phases of Construction," *Hesperia* 80 (2011), pp. 71–156

Thomas, O., "Ephebes Reunited: A New Edition of *IG* II(2) 1967," *ZPE* 157 (2006), pp. 71–76

Thompson, D. J., "Egypt, 146–31 B.C.," in J. A. Crook, A. Lintott, and E. Rawson (eds.), *Cambridge Ancient History*² 9 (Cambridge: 1994), pp. 310–326

Thompson, D. J., "The Ptolemies and Egypt," in A. Erskine (ed.), *A Companion to the Hellenistic World* (Malden: 2003), pp. 105–120

Thompson, H. A., "The Odeion in the Athenian Agora," *Hesperia* 19 (1950), pp. 31–141

Thompson, H. A., "Athenian Twilight: A.D. 267–600," *JRS* 49 (1959), pp. 61–72

Thompson, H. A., "The Annex to the Stoa of Zeus in the Athenian Agora," *Hesperia* 35 (1966), pp. 171–187

Thompson, H. A., "Athens Faces Adversity," *Hesperia* 50 (1981), pp. 343–355

Thompson, H. A., "The Impact of Roman Architects and Architecture on Athens, 170 B.C.–A.D. 170," in S. Macready and F. H. Thompson (eds.), *Roman Architecture in the Greek World* (London: 1987), pp. 1–17

Thompson, H. A., and R. Wycherley, *The Agora of Athens: The Athenian Agora* 14 (Princeton: 1972)

Thompson, M., *The New Style Silver Coinage of Athens*, 2 vols. (New York: 1961)

Thonemann, P., "The Tragic King: Demetrios Poliorketes and the City of Athens," in O. Hekster and R. Fowler (eds.), *Imaginary Kings: Royal Images in the Ancient Near East, Greece and Rome* (Stuttgart: 2005), pp. 63–86

Tinginagka, I., "I megali anatoliki èthousa tis vivliothikis tou Adrianou (vivliostasio)- arhitektoniki meleti-protasi sintirisis kè apokatastasis," *Arch. Deltion* 54 (1999), pp. 285–326

Tinginagka, I., "H aphanes architektonike tes Bibliothekes tou Adrianou," in S. Vlizos (ed.), *Athens during the Roman Period: Recent Discoveries, New Evidence* (Athens: 2008), pp. 133–152

Titchener, F. B., "Plutarch and Roman(ized) Athens," in E. N. Ostenfeld, *Greek Romans and Roman Greeks: Studies in Cultural Interaction* (Aarhus: 2002), pp. 136–141

Toher, M., "Herod, Athens and Augustus," *ZPE* 190 (2014), pp. 127–134

Toohey, P. G., and M. Golden (eds.), *Inventing Ancient Culture: Historicism, Periodization, and the Ancient World* (London: 1997)

Torelli, M., "L'immagine dell'ideologia augustea nell'Agora di Atene," *Ostraka* 4 (1995), pp. 9–32

Torelli, M., "Roman Art, 43 B.C. to A.D. 69," in A. K. Bowman, E. Champlin, and A. Lintott (eds.), *Cambridge Ancient History*² 10 (Cambridge: 1996), pp. 930–958

Touratsoglou, J., "Art in the Hellenistic Period," in M. B. Sakellariou (ed.), *Macedonia, 4000 Years of Greek History and Civilization* (Athens: 1983), pp. 170–191

Townend, G., "Literature and Society," in A. K. Bowman, E. Champlin, and A. Lintott (eds.), *Cambridge Ancient History*² 10 (Cambridge: 1996), pp. 905–929

Tracy, S. V., "Athens in 100 B.C.," *HSCP* 83 (1979), pp. 213–235

Tracy, S. V., "Greek Inscriptions from the Athenian Agora Third to First Centuries B.C.," *Hesperia* 51 (1982), pp. 57–64

Tracy, S. V., *Athenian Democracy in Transition: Attic Letter-Cutters of 340 to 290 B.C.* (Berkeley: 1995)

Tracy, S. V., "Athenian Politicians and Inscriptions of the Years 307 to 302," *Hesperia* 69 (2000), pp. 227–233

Tracy, S. V., "Antigonos Gonatas, King of Athens," in O. Palagia and S. V. Tracy (eds.), *The Macedonians in Athens, 322–229 BC* (Oxford: 2003), pp. 56–60

Tracy, S. V, "Reflections on the Athenian Ephebeia in the Hellenistic Age," in D. Kah and P. Scholz (eds.), *Das hellenistische Gymnasion* (Berlin: 2004), pp. 207–210

Tritle, L., *Phocion the Good* (London: 1988)

Tsouklidou, D., "Panathenaikós amphoréas próimon romaikón chrónon," in S. Vlizos (ed.), *Athens during the Roman Period: Recent Discoveries, New Evidence* (Athens: 2008), pp. 449–457

Turner, E., "Ptolemaic Egypt," in F. W. Walbank, A. E. Astin, M. W. Frederiksen, and R. M. Ogilvie (eds.), *Cambridge Ancient History*² 7.1 (Cambridge: 1984), pp. 118–174

Usher, S., "Symbouleutic Oratory," in I. Worthington (ed.), *A Companion to Greek Rhetoric* (Malden: 2007), pp. 220–235

Vanderpool, E., "Athens Honors the Emperor Tiberius," *Hesperia* 28 (1959), pp. 86–90

Vanderpool, E., "Koroni: The Date of the Camp and the Pottery," *Hesperia* 33 (1964), pp. 69–75

Vanderpool, E., J. R. McCredie, and A. Steinberg, "Koroni, a Ptolemaic Camp on the East Coast of Attica," *Hesperia* 31 (1962), pp. 26–61

Vanderspoel, J., "Provincia Macedonia," in J. Roisman and I. Worthington (eds.), *A Companion to Ancient Macedonia* (Malden: 2010), pp. 251–275

Van't Dack, E., P. van Dessel, and W. van Gucht (eds.), *Egypt and the Hellenistic World* (Louvain: 1983)

Veisse, A.-E., *Les "révoltes égyptiennes": Recherches sur les troubles intérierurs en Egypt durègne de Ptolémée III à la conquête Romaine* (Paris: 2004)

Vlizos, S. (ed.), *Athens during the Roman Period: Recent Discoveries, New Evidence* (Athens: 2008)

von den Hoff, R., "Tradition and Innovation: Portraits and Dedications on the Early Hellenistic Akropolis," in O. Palagia and S. V. Tracy (eds.), *The Macedonians in Athens, 322–229 BC* (Oxford: 2003), pp. 173–185

Walbank, F. W., *Aratos of Sicyon* (Cambridge: 1933)

Walbank, F. W., "*Philippos Tragoidoumenos*: A Polybian Experiment," *JHS* 58 (1938), pp. 55–68

Walbank, F. W., *Philip V of Macedon* (Cambridge: 1940)

Walbank, F. W., "Polybius and Macedonia," *Ancient Macedonia* 1 (Institute for Balkan Studies, Thessaloniki: 1970), pp. 91–106

Walbank, F. W., *Polybius* (Berkeley: 1972)

Walbank, F. W., "The Causes of the Third Macedonian War: Recent Views," *Ancient Macedonia* 2 (Institute for Balkan Studies, Thessaloniki: 1977), pp. 81–94

Walbank, F. W., "Sea-Power and the Antigonids," in W. L. Adams and E. N. Borza (eds.), *Philip II, Alexander the Great, and the Macedonian Heritage* (Washington: 1982), pp. 213–236

Walbank, F. W., "Monarchies and Monarchic Ideas," in F. W. Walbank, A. E. Astin, M. W. Frederiksen, and R. M. Ogilvie (eds.), *Cambridge Ancient History*^{2} 7.1 (Cambridge: 1984a), pp. 62–100

Walbank, F. W., "Macedonia and Greece," in F. W. Walbank, A. E. Astin, M. W. Frederiksen, and R. M. Ogilvie (eds.), *Cambridge Ancient History*^{2} 7.1 (Cambridge: 1984b), pp. 221–256

Walbank, F. W., "Macedonia and the Greek Leagues," in F. W. Walbank, A. E. Astin, M. W. Frederiksen, and R. M. Ogilvie (eds.), *Cambridge Ancient History*^{2} 7.1 (Cambridge: 1984c), pp. 446–481

Walbank, F. W., "Supernatural Paraphernalia in Polybius' *Histories*," in I. Worthington (ed.), *Ventures into Greek History: Essays in Honour of N. G. L. Hammond* (Oxford: 1994), pp. 28–42

Walbank, F. W., *Polybius, Rome and the Hellenistic World: Essays and Reflections* (Cambridge: 2002)

Walker, S., "A Sanctuary of Isis in the South Slope of the Athenian Acropolis," *BSA* 74 (1979), pp. 243–257

Walker, S., "Women and Housing in Classical Greece," in A. Cameron and A. Kuhrt (eds.), *Images of Women in Classical Antiquity* (London: 1983), pp. 81–91

Walker, S., "Athens under Augustus," in M. C. Hoff and S. I. Rotroff (eds.), *The Romanization of Athens* (Oxford: 1997), pp. 67–80

Walker, S., and A. Cameron (eds.), *The Greek Renaissance in the Roman Empire* (London: 1989)

Walker, S., and P. Higgs, *Cleopatra of Egypt: From History to Myth* (Princeton: 2001)

Wallace, R. W., *The Areopagos Council, to 307 B.C.* (Baltimore: 1989)

Wardman, A., *Rome's Debt to Greece* (London: 1976)

Waterfield, R., *Dividing the Spoils: The War for Alexander the Great's Empire* (Oxford: 2011)

Waterfield, R., *Taken at the Flood: The Roman Conquest of Greece* (New York: 2014)

Waterfield, R., *A Time of Transition: Antigonus Gonatas and the Greeks* (Chicago: 2020)

Webb, P. A., *The Tower of the Winds in Athens. Greeks, Romans, Christians, and Muslims: Two Millennia of Continual Use* (Philadelphia: 2017)

Wehrli, C., "Les gynéconomes," *MH* 19 (1962), pp. 33–38

Welch, K., "Titus Pomponius Atticus: A Banker in Politics," *Historia* 45 (1996), pp. 450–471

Wellesley, K., *Year of the Four Emperors* (London: 2000)

Wheatley, P., "Lamia and the Besieger: An Athenian Hetaera and a Macedonian King," in O. Palagia and S. V. Tracy (eds.), *The Macedonians in Athens, 322–229 BC* (Oxford: 2003), pp. 30–36

Whitehorne, J., *Cleopatras* (London: 1994)

Whittaker, H., "Some Reflections on the Temple to the Goddess Roma and Augustus on the Acropolis at Athens," in E. N. Ostenfeld (ed.), *Greek Romans and Roman Greeks: Studies in Cultural Interaction* (Aarhus: 2002), pp. 25–39

Wiedemann, T. E. J., "Tiberius to Nero," in A. K. Bowman, E. Champlin, and A. Lintott (eds.), *Cambridge Ancient History*^{2} 10 (Cambridge: 1996a), pp. 198–255

Wiedemann, T. E. J., "From Nero to Vespasian," in A. K. Bowman, E. Champlin, and A. Lintott (eds.), *Cambridge Ancient History*^{2} 10 (Cambridge: 1996b), pp. 256–282

Wiemer, H.-U., "Von der Bürgerschule zum aristokratischen Klub? Die athenische Ephebie in der römischen Kaiserzeit," *Chiron* 41 (2011), pp. 487–537

Will, E., "The Succession to Alexander," in F. W. Walbank, A. E. Astin, M. W. Frederiksen, and R. M. Ogilvie (eds.), *Cambridge Ancient History*^{2} 7.1 (Cambridge: 1984a), pp. 23–61

Will, E., "The Formation of the Hellenistic Kingdoms," in F. W. Walbank, A. E. Astin, M. W. Frederiksen, and R. M. Ogilvie (eds.), *Cambridge Ancient History*^{2} 7.1 (Cambridge: 1984b), pp. 101–117

Will, E. L., "Shipping Amphoras as Indicators of Economic Romanization in Athens," in M. C. Hoff and S. I. Rotroff (eds.), *The Romanization of Athens* (Oxford: 1997), pp. 117–133

Willers, D., *Hadrians panhellenisches Programm: archäologische Beiträge zur Neugestaltung Athens durch Hadrian* (Basel: 1990)

Willers, D., "Die Neugestaltung Athens durch Hadrian: Hadrians panhellenisches Programm," *Antike Welt* 27 (1996), pp. 3–17

Williams, J. M., "The Peripatetic School and Demetrius of Phalerum's Reforms in Athens," *Anc. World* 15 (1987), 87–98

Williams, J. M., "Demades' Last Years, 323/2–319/8 B.C.: A 'Revisionist' Interpretation," *Anc. World* 19 (1989), pp. 19–30

Williams, J. M., "Ideology and the Constitution of Demetrius of Phalerum," in C. D. Hamilton and P. M. Krentz (eds.), *Polis and Polemos: Essays on Politics, War and History in Ancient Greece in Honor of Donald Kagan* (Claremont: 1997), pp. 327–346

Williams, M., Apollodorus, *BNJ* 244 (Leiden)

Williams, C. K. II, "The Refounding of Corinth: Some Roman Religious Attitudes," in S. Macready and F. H. Thompson (eds.), *Roman Architecture in the Greek World* (London: 1987), pp. 26–37

Wilson, P., *The Athenian Institution of the Khoregia: The Chorus, the City, and the Stage* (Cambridge: 2000)

Wilson, R. J. A., "Sicily, Sardinia and Corsica," in A. K. Bowman, E. Champlin, and A. Lintott (eds.), *Cambridge Ancient History*^{2} 10 (Cambridge: 1996), pp. 434–448

Winterling, A., *Caligula: A Biography*, trans. D. L. Schneider, G. W. Most, and P. Psoinos (Berkeley: 2011)

Wiseman, T. P., "Caesar, Pompey, and Rome, 59–50 B.C.," in J. A. Crook, A. Lintott, and E. Rawson (eds.), *Cambridge Ancient History*^{2} 9 (Cambridge: 1994), pp. 368–423

Wiseman, T. P., "Caesar, Pompey, and Rome, 59–50 B.C.," in J. A. Crook, A. Lintott, and E. Rawson (eds.), *Cambridge Ancient History*^{2} 9 (Cambridge: 1994), pp. 368–423

Woodhead, A. G., "The Calendar of the Year 304/3 B.C. in Athens," *Hesperia* 58 (1989), pp. 297–301

Woolf, G., "Becoming Roman, Staying Greek: Culture, Identity, and the Civilizing Process in the Roman East," *PCPS* 40 (1994), pp. 116–143

Wooten, C., "Le développement du style asiatique pendant l'époque hellénistique," *REG* 88 (1976), pp. 36–64

Worthington, I., *A Historical Commentary on Dinarchus* (Ann Arbor: 1992)

Worthington, I., "The Harpalus Affair and the Greek Response to the Macedonian Hegemony," in I. Worthington (ed.), *Ventures into Greek History: Essays in Honour of N. G. L. Hammond* (Oxford: 1994a), pp. 307–330

Worthington, I., "The Canon of the Ten Attic Orators," in I. Worthington (ed.), *Persuasion: Greek Rhetoric in Action* (London: 1994b), pp. 244–263

Worthington, I., "Rhetoric and Politics in Classical Greece: Rise of the *Rhêtores*," in I. Worthington (ed.), *A Companion to Greek Rhetoric* (Malden: 2007), pp. 255–271

Worthington, I., *Philip II of Macedonia* (New Haven: 2008a)

Worthington, I., "*IG* ii² 236 and Philip's Common Peace of 337," in L. G. Mitchell and L. Rubenstein (eds.), *Greek History and Epigraphy: Essays in Honour of P. J. Rhodes* (Swansea: 2008b), pp. 213–223

Worthington, I., *Demosthenes of Athens and the Fall of Classical Greece* (New York: 2013)

Worthington, I., *By the Spear: Philip II, Alexander the Great, and the Rise and Fall of the Macedonian Empire* (New York: 2014)

Worthington, I., *Ptolemy I: King and Pharaoh of Egypt* (New York: 2016)

Worthington, I., "Why Did the Successors Meet at Triparadeisus?," *Karanos* 2 (2019a), pp. 29–32

Worthington, I., "Callias of Sphettus' Exile (*IG* ii/iii³ 1, 4 no. 911)," *ZPE* 209 (2019b), pp. 137–139

Worthington, I., "The 'Divine' Octavia and Athens, 39/8 BC," *ZPE* 210 (2019c), pp. 147–150

Worthington, I., "Augustus' Annoyance with Athens," *Arctos* 53 (2019d), pp. 247–254

Wycherley, R. E., "The Olympieion at Athens," *GRBS* 5 (1964), pp. 161–179

Xanthakis-Karamanos, G., *Studies in Fourth-Century Tragedy* (Athens: 1980)

Zahrnt, M., "Die 'Hadriansstadt' von Athen. Zu FGrHist 257 F 19," *Chiron* 9 (1979), pp. 393–398

Zambelli, M., "L'ascesa al trono di Antioco IV Epifane di Siria," *Riv. Fil.* 38 (1960), pp. 363–389

Zanker, P., *The Power of Images in the Age of Augustus*, trans. A. Shapiro (Ann Arbor: 1988)

INDEX

Foot notes are not indexed

Abydus, 150
Academy, 12, 26, 45, 99, 116, 121,
   126, 131, 151, 152, 172, 208, 219,
   229, 234, 334, 336. *See also*
   Philosophy; Plato
Acarnania/Acarnanians, 138, 149, 150,
   176–177
Achaea (province), 243, 245, 259, 260,
   268, 269, 270, 271, 272, 281,
   282, 310
Achaeans/Achaean League, 116, 120,
   127, 128, 130, 131, 133, 137, 138, 143,
   153, 154, 165, 169, 171, 173, 174–175,
   190, 243–244, 245. *See also* Leagues
Acropolis, 1, 3, 4, 36, 87, 91–92, 110,
   168, 191, 192, 196, 210, 211, 245,
   250, 256, 258, 266, 278, 279, 284,
   288, 291, 293, 297, 298, 301, 304,
   327, 330, 335. *See also* Athena;
   Religion
Acte, 64
Actium, Battle of, 2, 4, 5, 6, 68, 70,
   201, 239, 240, 246, 247, 248, 249,
   250, 251, 257, 262

Aegae, 11, 12, 48, 50, 114
Aegina, 33, 90, 148, 151, 236, 247, 248
Aelius Aristides, 285, 333
Aeschines, 22
Aeschylus, 10, 20, 42, 189
Aetolians/Aetolian League, 78, 94–95,
   95–96, 106, 112, 116, 128, 130, 131,
   132, 136, 137, 138, 139, 143, 144,
   145–146, 147, 150, 153, 155, 157,
   159–160, 161, 162, 163, 190. *See also*
   Leagues
Agis III, 21, 22
Agonothetes/agonothesia, 45, 67, 179,
   187, 199, 261, 273, 281, 300, 323,
   325. *See also* Festivals
Agora, Athenian, 1, 7, 9, 19, 20, 34, 36,
   47, 58, 60, 67, 73, 77, 82, 93, 98,
   104, 110, 134, 139, 153, 182, 188,
   195, 196, 204, 211, 227, 229, 245,
   252, 253, 257, 258, 275, 276, 278,
   279, 284, 288, 293–295, 296, 298,
   299, 309, 311–312, 316, 317. *See
   also* Agrippa, Athens; Economy/
   Finances, Athenian

INDEX

Agora, Roman, 227, 228–229, 250, 255, 259, 288, 289–290, 291, 298, 299, 306, 308, 309, 311–312, 319. *See also* Augustus; Athena Archegetis; Athens; Julius Caesar
Agoranomion, 298. *See also* Buildings
Agriculture, 85, 164, 188, 268. *See also* Farmers/Farming
Agrippa, 2, 182, 196, 224, 239, 245, 252, 258, 269, 288, 295; Odeum of, 293–294. *See also* Agora, Athenian; Buildings
Alexander III, the Great, 2, 12, 15, 16–18, 22, 23, 24, 26, 28, 29, 30, 31, 47, 74, 78, 107, 109, 139, 165, 174, 201, 204, 240
Alexander IV, 30, 47, 48, 49–50
Alexander V, 84, 93, 94
Alexander, nephew of Antigonus II Gonatas, 127, 129
Alexandria, 2, 30, 42, 51, 99, 105, 149, 177, 193, 198, 229, 231, 232, 236, 240, 260, 306, 334
Albinus, Lucius Postumius, 142, 143
Altars, 82, 191, 245, 253, 268, 279, 291, 295, 311, 314–315; to the Antigonids, 73, 82; to Caligula, 278; to Hadrian 314–315, 326, 329; to Nero, 281; to Octavian/Augustus, 245, 247; to Vespasian and Titus, 282. *See also* Athens; Imperial Cult
Ambracia/Ambracians, 176–177, 244
Ameinias, 38, 65
Amphiareus, 193
Amphictyonic Council, 68, 69, 106, 112, 162, 176, 200, 255, 268, 274. *See also* Delphi
Antigonis tribe, 73, 153
Antigonus I Monophthalmus, 29–30, 31, 36, 41, 42, 48, 49, 50, 72, 73, 75, 78, 83, 84, 108, 125, 129, 153, 189, 193, 233, 237, 259. *See also* Demetrius Poliorcetes; Successors, Wars of; Athens

Antigonus II Gonatas, 4, 46, 93, 94, 97, 100, 101, 107, 111, 113, 114–117, 118, 119–123, 125–130, 189; worshipped at Athens, 128–130
Antigonus III Doson, 132–137, 143
Antioch, 139, 198, 229, 299, 303
Antiochus I of Syria, 112, 113, 117
Antiochus III of Syria, 147, 149, 157, 160–162, 163, 169, 178
Antiochus IV of Syria, 110, 177, 178, 196–197, 219, 224, 300, 301, 303
Antipater I, Macedonian king, 84, 93, 97, 113
Antipater of Phlya, 62, 250, 253, 281
Antipater, Successor, 18, 21, 22, 25, 26, 27, 28, 29, 30, 31, 37, 38, 39, 40, 59, 60, 64, 65, 75, 110, 182, 184. *See also* Successors
Antiphilus 25
Antiochus I, 112, 113, 117. *See also* Syria
Antiochus III, 111, 147, 149, 157, 160, 161, 162, 163, 169, 178. *See also* Syria
Antiochus IV, 110, 177, 178, 196, 197, 219, 224, 300, 301, 303. *See also* Syria
Antony, Mark, 2, 4, 6, 69–70, 218, 232, 234–240, 249, 260; and Athens, 234–239. *See also* Egypt; Octavian; Rome
Apamea, Peace of, 161–162
Apellicon of Teos, 205, 206, 211
Apolexis (archon), 247, 253
Apollo, 64, 68, 69, 95, 96, 162, 166, 168, 175, 176, 187, 193, 205, 239, 249, 255, 273, 278, 279, 281, 283, 290, 291, 302, 322, 330. *See also* Delphi, Gods; *Pythais*; Religion; Temples
Apollo Hypoakraios, 255. *See also* Apollo.
Apollodorus, historian, 122, 123
Apollodorus of Otryne, 123
Apollodorus, politician, 160, 161, 163, 176,
Apollonia, 143, 151

Appian, 208, 209, 212, 213–214
Aratus of Sicyon, 127–138
Arcadia, 136, 138, 154
Arcesilaus, philosopher, 125–126
Arch of Hadrian, 3, 7, 310–311, 327–330. See also Athens; Hadrian
Archaeus (archon), 179
Archander, 129
Archedicus, 44
Archelaus of Cappadocia, 253
Archelaus, Macedonian king, 12, 115
Archelaus, Mithridates VI's general, 205, 207, 208, 210
Archons/Archonship, 35, 53, 56, 61–62, 85, 86, 88, 91, 121, 122, 133, 175, 176, 187, 198, 203, 213, 214, 253, 272, 280, 318, 322. See also Democracy
Areopagus, 35, 37, 39, 53, 54, 55, 56, 60–61, 62, 122, 123, 170, 173, 193, 201, 203, 214, 216, 218, 219, 230, 253, 254, 276–277, 281, 298, 321, 323. See also Democracy
Areus, archon, 291
Areus I of Sparta, 114, 119, 120
Ariarathes V of Cappadocia, 179
Ariobarzanes II of Cappadocia, 224
Aristion, 206, 207, 208, 209–210, 213, 214, 215, 224
Aristophanes (playwright), 10, 43, 44, 58, 77
Aristophanes of Leuconoe, 130, 131
Aristotle, 1, 10, 12, 20, 34, 45, 46, 198, 208, 211, 215, 282. See also Culture/Hellenism; Lyceum; Philosophy
Aristotle, commander, 41
Army, Athenian, 4, 112, 166
Arrheneides (archon), 115
Asander, 37
Arsinoe II, 119–120, 185
Assembly/Assemblies, 1, 19, 21, 23, 26, 32, 37, 53, 54–55, 56, 57, 58, 59, 60, 61, 63, 71, 73, 75, 76, 84, 85, 87, 88, 99, 104, 106, 112, 122, 125, 129, 131, 146, 150, 154, 160, 187, 202, 203, 214, 218, 253, 320, 324. See also Athens; Democracy
Assembly decrees: see Assembly
Athena, 3, 4, 10, 18, 26, 45, 73, 74, 75, 79, 82, 87, 88, 89, 101, 110, 116, 119, 123, 136, 168, 169, 188, 191, 196, 200, 237, 238, 245, 275, 293, 295, 297, 298, 299, 306, 316, 330; statue of spitting blood, 4, 248, 250. See also Acropolis; Athena Archegetis; Festivals; Gods; Panathenaea; Parthenon; Religion
Athena Archegetis, 250, 259, 290, 298. See also Agora, Roman; Athena
Athenion, 203–204, 205–206, 282
Athens/Athenians, *passim*; under Antipater, 18–28; and Antony, 234–239; and Augustus, 243–260, 255–260, 289–293; and Brutus and Cassius, 233–234; and Caesar, 228–229, 231–232; citizenship restrictions, 27, 37; Chremonidean War, 117–124; under Demetrus of Phalerum, 34–47, 50–51; census of Demetrus of Phalerum, 40, 182; under Demetrius Poliorcetes, 71–78, 79–83, 91–101, 190, 301; and Flavians, 282–284; and Hadrian, 303–311, 313–331, independence in 229, 132–133; and Julio-Claudians, 277–282, 298; life in, 43–45, 181–187, 201, 272–277, 311–317; 330–331, 333–336; and Nerva, 284; cursing of Philip V, 152–153; population of, 3, 40, 117, 182–183; Romans in, 157, 173, 195, 218–221, 252–253; and Sulla, 207–215, 226; possibly subject to *lex Clodia*, 216–218, 220; and Trajan, 284–285, 299; treaty with Rome, 163, 245, 278. See also Acropolis; Agora, Antigonus II Gonatas; Antigonus III Doson; Athenian; "Romanization" of Athens ;

Athens/Athenians, *passim*; under Antipater (*Cont.*) Augustus; Buildings; Culture/Hellenism; Delos; Demetrius of Phalerum; Democracy; Economy/Finances, Athenian; Egypt; *Ephebeia*; Family; Festivals; Fortifications; Fortresses; Garrisons; Gods; Grain; Greece; Guilds; Hadrian; Leagues; Macedonia; Mithridates VI; Panhellenion; Pergamum; Philip V; Philosophy; Piraeus; Religion; "Romanization;" Rome; Slaves; Statues; Syria; Temples; Walls

Attalus I, 147, 149, 150, 151, 152, 153, 154, 157, 178. *See also* Pergamum

Attalus II, 7, 178, 196, 234, 245, 277, 281, 293, 296. *See also* Pergamum

Attic/Attica, 20, 31, 32, 33, 36, 41, 43, 44, 50, 54, 55, 56, 64, 65, 71, 78, 79, 82, 90, 92, 99, 105, 120, 122, 126, 127, 128, 129, 130, 131, 133, 148, 151, 171, 173, 176, 183, 200, 220, 243, 247, 254, 256, 261, 274, 280, 296, 319, 327, 331, 334

Atticus, Titus Pomponius, 183, 219, 220–221, 229, 230

Atticus, son of Tiberius Claudius Hipparchus, 284. *See also* Hipparchus, Tiberius Claudius

Augustus, 2, 4, 108, 110, 182, 190, 191, 198, 201, 221, 224, 229, 230, 233, 239, 240, 243–244, 255–257, 258, 259, 262, 263, 264, 265, 266, 267, 268, 269, 271, 272, 273, 278, 280, 296, 303, 310, 311, 321, 322, 325, 331; and Athens, 245–252, 255–257, 260, 287–288. *See also* Agora, Roman; Athens; Buildings; Culture/Hellenism; Imperial Cult; Greece; temple of Roma and Augustus; Octavian; "Romanization;" Rome

Austin, M.M., 29

Balbilla, Julia, 186, 301
Bazaar of Pompey: see *Deigma*
Berenice, Ptolemy III's wife, 139, 190
Bithys of Lysimacheia, 131
Boeotia/Boeotians, 31, 78, 79, 94, 106–107, 111, 130, 132, 151, 154, 155, 169, 171–172, 210, 231, 243, 247. *See also* Boeotian League
Boeotian League, 106, 155, 171. *See also* Leagues
Bolgius, 111. *See also* Galatians
Boule, 37, 53, 54, 55–56, 58–59, 60, 73, 75, 88, 121, 129, 171, 188, 253, 273, 281, 298, 318, 320. *See also* Democracy
Brachylles, 155
Brennus, 111–112. *See also* Galatians
Brutus, Marcus Junius, 2, 4, 6, 218, 232, 233, 234
Buildings, by Lycurgus in Athens, 19, 20, 21, 36, 77; by Hellenistic rulers in Athens, 7, 177, 196, 223, 224, 225; by Romans in Athens, 2, 7, 182, 187, 197, 211, 212, 225, 228, 229, 230, 243, 245, 254, 274, 279, 281, 283, 287–311, 314, 317, 322, 326, 327, 329, 335. *See also* Augustus; Athens; Hadrian

Caesar, Gaius, 258, 278
Caesar, Drusus, 258, 266
Caesar, Germanicus, 266, 278
Caesar, Julius, 2, 4, 6, 175, 216, 218, 219, 226, 228, 229, 230–232, 233, 236, 237–238, 239, 247, 270, 289, 290, 310; Agora of, 228–229. *See also* Buildings; "Romanization;" Rome
Calendar: see Chronology
Calenus, Quintus Fulvius, 231
Caligula, 266, 268, 270, 278–279. *See also* Athens; Rome
Callias of Sphettus, 97, 98, 99, 100, 104, 105, 108, 117, 153. *See also* Athens; Phaedrus

Callimedes, 126
Calliphon, 209
Callippus, 111, 112, 113
Cannae, battle of, 144, 166
Carneades, 172
Cassander, 31, 33, 34, 36, 37, 40, 41, 42, 47, 48, 49, 50, 60, 71, 72, 74, 76, 78, 79, 81, 83, 84, 87, 88, 89. *See also* Athens; Greece; Macedonia; Successors
Castor of Alexandria, 140
Cato, Marcus Porcius, 161
Cavalry, Athens, 88, 106, 111, 112, 121, 123, 166, 175, 188
Centho, Gaius Claudius, 151
Centumalus, Gnaeus Fulvius, 142
Cephisodorus, 150, 159
Cerameicus, 98, 101, 115, 116, 208, 209, 211, 288
Chaeronea, battle of in 338, 1, 2, 3, 9, 14–15, 19, 21, 22, 23, 31, 91, 109, 224, 324. *See also* Demosthenes; Philip II
Chairippus, 101, 118
Chalcis, 99, 119, 129, 151, 156. *See also* "Fetters"
Chaniotis A., 6
Charias, 87, 89
Charites, shrine of, 134, 190, 193. *See also* Religion
Chios. 24, 146
Christianity, 193, 276–277, 322
Chremonides, 117, 118, 119, 124, 135. *See also* Chremonidean War
Chremonidean War, 65, 93, 106, 117–124, 125, 126, 159, 185, 331. *See also* Antigonus II; Athens; Chremonides; Ptolemy II; Sparta
Chronology, 85–86
Cicero, 183, 217, 218, 219, 220, 223, 228, 229, 230, 232, 233, 263, 332
Civil War, Roman, 230–232
Claudius, 266, 268, 275, 276, 279–281, 298, 322. *See also* Athens; Rome
Cleaenetus, 81

Cleisthenes, 55–56, 58
Cleomedon, 154
Cleomenes III, 136, 137
Cleon, 43, 58, 77
Cleopatra VII, 2, 4, 6, 185, 192, 231, 232, 236, 237–238, 239, 240. *See also* Antony; Egypt; Rome
Comedy, 1, 10, 43, 44, 46, 58, 75, 77, 88, 124, 184–185, 186, 332. *See also* Culture/Hellenism; Menander; Philippides
Corcyra, 96, 143
Corinth/Corinthians, 15, 16, 72, 83, 84, 98, 99, 119, 120, 123, 127, 128, 131, 137, 143, 151, 156, 159, 175, 176, 193, 195, 223, 232, 243, 259, 269, 270, 272, 274, 279, 288, 293, 303, 304, 310, 314, 327, 334, 336. *See also* "Fetters"
Corupedium, battle of, 107
Cos, 51, 126
Costoboces, 334
Cossutius, Decimus, 196, 197, 219, 224, 304
Courtesans, 40, 79, 125, 186. *See also* Lamia; Women
Crannon, battle of, 25, 26, 75
Craterus, 25, 26, 29, 30, 31
Crates, philosopher, 99
Critolaus, 172
Culture/Hellenism, 2, 5–6, 7, 42, 124, 141, 157, 168, 172–173, 184–185, 192, 197–198, 215, 218–221, 241, 252, 263–264, 266, 268, 287, 297–298, 313, 331–333, 333–334. *See also* Athens; Rome
Curio, Gaius Scribonius, 210
Cybernis, 112
Cynoscephalae, battle of, 154–155, 157, 159
Cyprus, 46, 74, 78, 80, 84, 96, 104

Dardanians, 131–132, 137
Deidameia, Poliorcetes' wife, 84
Deigma of Pompey, 226

Delian League, 10, 11, 59, 324. *See also* Athens

Delos/Delian, 41, 61, 66–67, 120, 159, 165, 169–171, 176, 179, 184, 188, 191, 193, 196, 198–199, 205–206, 207, 212–213, 215, 216, 217, 218, 225, 228, 259, 273, 291. *See also* Athens, Economy/Finances, Athenian

Delphi, 64, 68, 69, 95, 96, 106, 111, 112, 156, 162, 166, 168, 175, 176, 193, 198, 200, 231, 255, 259, 268, 269, 274, 283, 334. See *also* Amphictyonic Council; Apollo; *Pythais*

Demades, 24, 26, 27, 28, 31, 74

Demaenetus, 138

Demetrias, Thessaly, 94, 100, 107, 109, 152, 161

Demetrias tribe, 73, 153

Demetrius I Poliorcetes, 40, 41, 48–49, 50, 51, 61, 65, 71, 84, 89, 90, 94, 100, 103, 107, 108, 110, 117, 134, 165, 186, 301; and Athens, 71–84, 91–93, 95–99, 106, 124, 129, 153, 189, 190, 233, 237, 259; king of Macedonia, 93–94, 96–97. *See also* Antigonus Monophthalmus; Athens; Macedonia; Successors

Demetrius II, 130–132

Demetrius of Phalerum, 26, 33, 50, 59, 60, 61, 64, 72, 75, 76, 77, 80, 89, 122, 182, 184, 187, 189, 201; census of, 40; controls Athens, 34–47, 50–51; cultural life under, 42–47; statues of, 36, 40, 72. *See also* Athens; Cassander

Demetrius of Pharos, 143, 144

Demetrius, Philip V's son, 155, 164

Demetrius of Sphettus, 298–299.

Demochares, 26, 44, 74, 75, 77, 81, 86, 103–104, 106, 108, 116, 117, 118, 124

Democracy, 1, 3, 6, 10, 11, 14, 15, 18, 22, 28, 31, 32, 33, 34, 35, 37, 53–62, 70, 71, 73, 76, 77, 78, 86, 93, 101, 103, 107, 108, 116, 133, 182, 189, 190, 191, 203, 214, 229, 232, 294, 312, 318; under Antipater, 27–28, 60; under Demetrius of Phalerum, 60–61, 76; under Demetrius Poliorcetes, 71, 73, 75–76, 91–93; under Hadrian, 317–318; and Rome, 173, 183–184, 185, 191, 253; Sullan constitution, 62, 213–215;. *See also* Archonship; Areopagus; Assembly; Boule; *Epimeletes*; Herald of the Areopagus; Hoplite General; Lawcourts; Oligarchy; *Strategoi*; Tyrannicides

Demosthenes, 1, 14, 18, 19, 21, 22, 23–24, 26, 27, 28, 38, 57, 58, 72, 75, 76, 77, 107, 118, 264, 332, 333; statue of, 33, 108–110

Dinarchus, 24, 72, 86, 94, 264

Dio, Cassius, 239, 246, 248, 250, 269, 308

Diogeneia, 133. *See also* Festivals

Dio of Prusa, 262, 273, 333

Diocles (archon), 99–100, 103

Diocles, son of Themistocles, 273

Diodorus, 198, 255

Diodorus Siculus, historian, 25, 27, 32, 41, 73, 76, 86, 182, 202

Diogenes, Athenian architect, 224

Diogenes, Piraeus garrison commander, 131, 132, 133

Diogenes Laertius, 46, 75

Diogenes, philosopher, 172

Diomedon (archon), 129

Dionysia, 42, 45, 64, 68, 82, 88, 135, 188, 204, 237, 275, 276, 300, 321, 323. *See also* Dionysus; Festivals; Religion; Theater of Dionysus

Dionysius of Halicarnassus, 86, 264

Dionysius the Areopagite, 277. *See also* Paul the Apostle

Dionysus, 64, 68, 129, 187, 188, 189, 234, 237, 238, 240, 249, 298, 316, 322, 323, 334, 335. *See also* Dionysia; Gods; Guilds; Religion; Theater of Dionysus

INDEX 393

Dionysus Eleutherius, 298. *See also* Dionysus
Diotimus (archon), 99
Diphilus 43
Dodekais, 255, 274, 283. See also Apollo; Delphi; *Pythais*
Dolabella, Publius Cornelius, 216
Domitian, 67, 267, 272, 274, 283–284, 297, 318, 320. *See also* Athens; Rome
Dromocleides, 92, 94
Droysen, G., 5

Economy/finances, Athenian, 36, 66, 92–93, 104–105, 106, 123–124, 133, 135, 157, 170–171, 179, 182, 182–183, 184, 195–196, 198, 199–201, 203, 212–213, 220–221, 225, 226, 228, 229, 247, 254–255, 260, 265–266, 271, 273–274, 289, 297, 298, 303, 318–332. *See also* Athens; Delos; Economy/finances, Greece; Piraeus
Economy/finances, Greece, 175, 195, 212, 239, 244, 260, 265, 268–269, 271, 273–274, 319 *See also* Athens, Economy/finances, Athenian
Egypt/Egyptians, 1, 2, 4, 5, 6, 30, 41, 50, 78, 79, 99, 104, 120, 126, 127, 128, 133, 134, 135, 139, 140, 147, 149, 162, 171, 173, 177, 185, 189, 190, 192, 193, 224, 231, 236, 238, 239–240, 249, 276, 301, 322. See also Athens; Ptolemy I; Ptolemy II; Ptolemy III; Ptolemy IV; Rome
Eleusinion, 20
Eleusis, 20, 36, 64, 69, 81, 90, 99, 104, 105, 106, 120, 130, 139, 148, 151, 152, 187–188, 208, 228, 249, 261, 280, 302–303, 309, 314, 321, 325, 326, 334. *See also* Athens; Fortresses; Mysteries; Religion
Elis, 120, 138, 146
Emperor worship: *see* Imperial Cult
Ephebeia/Ephebes, 3, 20–21, 27, 37, 38, 63–67, 70, 72, 73, 106, 120–121, 125, 133, 134, 140, 188, 196, 198, 200, 213, 215, 218, 220, 224, 238, 254, 272, 274, 277, 278, 281, 283, 309, 318. *See also* Athens
Ephebic decrees: see *Ephebeia*/Ephebes
Ephesus, 24, 83, 84, 139, 237, 303, 311, 325
Ephialtes, 10, 56
Epicureanism, 46, 206, 220, 230, 282, 323. *See also* Philosophy; Epicurus
Epicurus, 46, 90, 218, 230. *See also* Epicureanism
Epidamnus, 142, 143, 174
Epidosis/epidoseis, 39, 132
Epimeletes, 61, 170, 199, 253, 254. *See also* Democracy
Epirus, 47, 84, 93, 95, 96, 104, 121, 130, 131, 138, 147, 151, 154, 176, 220; sack of, 167. *See also* Greece, Pyrrhus
Eponymous Heroes, monument of, 73, 153, 211, 317. *See also* Democracy
Erechtheum, 1, 110, 224, 288, 293. *See also* Acropolis
Ergochares (archon), 140
Erina of Telos, 186
Euboea, 10, 41, 90, 127, 129, 151, 157
Eubulus, 11, 19
Eucles, 290
Euctemon (archon), 87
Eumenes II, 157, 161, 165, 169, 178, 179, 196, 234, 245, 293, 296
Euripides, 10, 12, 20, 42, 189
Eurycleides, 126–127, 131, 132–133, 134, 135, 136, 139, 146, 154, 190, 192, 198. *See also* Micion
Eurycles, 245
Euthius (archon), 101
Euthydice, Poliorcetes' wife, 80
Exiles, returned by Polyperchon. 31; returned by Poliorcetes 94; returned by Perseus, 165
Exiles Decree, of Alexander the Great, 23, 24, 28

Family/families, 44, 54, 62, 80, 129, 134, 171, 173, 176, 182, 183–184, 185–186, 191, 192, 198–199, 214, 219, 228, 262, 272, 273, 323, 334. See also House; Household; Women
Farmers/Farming, 43, 54, 55, 85, 183, 189, 274, 318, 319, 320, 331
Ferguson, W.S., 6, 122, 199
Festivals, in Athens, 3, 10, 19, 37, 39, 42, 45, 64, 68, 85, 88, 95, 96, 105, 127, 177, 181, 182, 185, 187, 189, 192, 196, 238, 261, 265, 275, 321, 329, 334, 336; Roman involvement in, 191–192, 238 275, 277, 280–281, 321. See also *Agonothetes*; Gods; Diogeneia; Dionysia; Panathenaea; Priesthoods; Ptolemaea; Religion; Theseia
"Fetters" of Greece, 119, 126, 155, 157, 160. See also Chalcis, Corinth, Demetrias
Finances: see Economy/finances
Fish/Fishermen, 321
Flamininus, Titus Quinctius, 154–155, 156, 157, 159, 160, 161, 164, 180, 269, 270
Fleet, Athenian, 3, 4, 9, 15, 20, 25, 36, 40, 50, 78, 134, 231, 255
Fortifications, Athens, 63, 74, 91, 101, 120, 131, 134, 152, 208, 210, 211, 226, 231, 288, 327, 335. See also Walls
Fortresses, 20, 64, 78, 99, 105, 106, 120, 129, 131, 200. See also Eleusis; Phyle; Panactum; Rhamnus; Sunium
Fulvia, Antony's wife, 236, 237

Gabinius, Aulus, 216
Galatians (Gauls), 68, 111–113, 114, 116, 166, 176
Galba, Publius Sulpicius, 147, 151, 153
Garrisons: see Museum Hill, Munychia, Piraeus
Gauls: see Galatians
Glabrio, Manius Acilius, 161, 162
Glaucon, Chremonides' brother, 117, 124. See also Chremonides
Gods: see Apollo; Athena; Dionysius; Temples; Religion; Zeus; Zeus Eleutherius
Grain, 6, 23, 71, 74, 82, 87, 88, 90, 91, 98, 99, 103, 104, 119, 120, 121, 129–130, 133, 150, 151, 166, 179, 183, 205, 208, 210, 220, 239, 248, 249, 254–255, 274, 279, 319, 326. See also Economy/Finances, Athenian
Graindor, P., 265, 321
Greece/Greeks, 1, 2, 4, 6, 15–17, 22, 31, 33, 49, 50, 54, 79, 84, 107, 118–119, 127–128, 135, 137–138, 141–142, 145, 150, 156–157, 160, 162, 164, 165, 166, 167, 168, 173, 176, 195, 202, 212, 218–219, 223, 231–232, 233–234, 239, 241, 243–245, 248, 254, 265–266, 268–272, 310, 314, 317, 319, 321, 324–325, 331, 334, 335; proclamation of freedom in 196, 156–157; taken over by Rome in 146, 175. See also Achaea, province; Athens; Economy/finances, Greece; Macedonia; Rome
Grijalvo, E.M., 191
Guilds, 68–70, 112, 176, 204, 234–235, 249, 323. See also Guilds
Gymnasiarch, 67, 238, 254, 272, 273, 281, 318, 320. See also Gymnasium; Ephebeia
Gymnasium/Gymnasia, 20, 67, 133, 136, 140, 204, 254, 303, 309, 318, 320. See also Gymnasiarch; Ephebeia
Gynaikonomoi, 38–39. See also Demetrius of Phalerum

Habicht, C., 6, 214, 216
Hadrian, 2, 3, 4, 5, 6, 7, 67, 70, 182, 183, 186, 187–188, 197, 212, 230,

235, 267, 271, 272, 273, 274, 279, 283, 284, 288, 300, 301, 304–306, 313–331; buildings in Athens, 287, 288, 302–310, statues he set up, 304, 306. *See also* Arch of Hadrian; Athens; Buildings; Economy, Greece; Panhellenion; Rome
Hadrianis tribe, 317
Hagnonides, 32, 34
Haliartus, 169–170
Hannibal, 138, 144, 145, 147, 160, 161, 165, 166. *See also* Philip V, Rome
Harmodius and Aristogeiton: *see* Tyrannicides
Hegelochus, 297–298
Hegemachus (archon), 88
Hegesander, historian, 122
Hellenism: *see* Culture/Hellenism
Hellenistic, Hellenistic Age, 1, 3, 4, 17–18, 107–108, 240, 336; periodization, 5–7
Herculanus, Gaius Julius Eurycles, 272, 314
Heracleides Creticus, 135–136
Herald of the Areopagus, 61, 203, 214, 218, 253, 272, 280, 322. *See also* Democracy
Hermogenes, 298
Herod the Great, 251–252, 289, 299
Herodes Atticus, 283, 284, 333, 334, 335. *See also* Athens
Herodes, Tiberius Claudius Atticus, of Marathon, 272, 314, 334
Herodes of Marathon, 62, 228
Herodorus, 92
Herulian sack, 195, 317, 335, 336
Hierocles, 101
Hippachia, 186
Hipparchus, Tiberius Claudius, 283, 284, 320
Hoplite General/Generalship, 61, 62, 122, 214, 218, 253, 254–255, 272, 274, 280, 322. *See also* Democracy
Horace, 221, 332, 336

House/Houses, 38, 40, 47, 125, 135, 181–182, 185, 186, 211, 218, 230, 284, 319. *See also* Family; Household
Household, 185–186. *See also* Family; Houses; Women
Hyperides, 24, 26, 28, 31, 264, 321
Hyrcanus, John, 179

Illyria/Illyrians, 12, 17, 116, 131, 137, 142–143, 144, 145, 149, 174, 231
Illyrian War, First, 142–143
Illyrian War, Second, 143
Imbros, 72, 122, 126, 159, 188, 212
Imperial Cult, 3, 191, 193, 232, 245, 250, 257–259, 260, 261, 268, 269, 272, 273, 275, 276, 278, 279, 280, 282, 291, 298, 311, 318, 322, 323, 325. *See also* Athens; Roma; Vesta
Ipsus, battle of, 83, 84, 88
Isis, 189, 192, 193, 322

Kennell, N., 270
Kosmetes, 64, 65, 120, 215, 254. *See also* Gymnasium

Lachares, 87–90, 92, 183
Laches, 81, 103–104, 117
Lamia, Poliorcetes' mistress, 40, 80, 186. *See also* Courtesans; Women
Lamian War, 24–26, 31, 37, 64, 110
Lanassa, Poliorcetes' wife, 95, 96
Laurium, 19, 36, 40, 123, 196, 199, 247. *See also* Economy/Finances, Athenian
Lawcourts, 53, 54, 59, 60, 254, 325. *See also* Democracy
Leagues, of Philip II, 16–17, 18; of Antigonids, 83, 84; of Antigonus III, 137, 138, 139. *See also* Achaean League; Aetolian League; Boeotian League; Panhellenion
Lebadeia, 107
Leigh, S., 310
Lemnos, 41, 107, 122, 126, 159, 169, 171, 188, 212, 254

Leocrates, 21–22
Leocritus, 98
Leon, 161, 162, 163, 179, 198
Leonnatus, 25
Leosthenes, 24, 25
Lepidus, Marcus Aemilius, 150, 151, 233, 234
Lex Clodia de provinciis consularibus, 216, 217, 230
Library of Hadrian, 306–308. See also Buildings; Hadrian
Lissus, 142
Liturgy/Liturgies, 39, 45, 67, 187. See also *Agonothesia*
Livia, 246, 249, 256, 257, 258, 278, 279–280, 311
Livy, 148, 150, 153, 154, 304
Longinus, Gaius Cassius, 4, 232, 233, 234
Lyceum, 3, 4, 46, 75, 116, 172, 208, 254. See also Aristotle; Philosophy
Lycophron, Lycurgus' son, 77
Lycurgus/Lycurgan Athens, 11, 18–24, 36, 38, 42, 56, 63, 77–78, 110, 192, 210, 247, 303, 326
Lysimacheia, battle of, 113
Lysimachus, 30, 31, 49, 81, 83, 84, 87, 88, 90, 93, 96, 97, 99, 104, 105, 107, 119. See also Athens; Successors; Thrace

Macedonia/Macedonians, 1, 2, 4, 7, 9, 11–12, 15–16, 17, 18, 21, 24, 27, 29, 30, 31, 33, 43, 44, 45, 46, 47;48, 50, 51, 59, 60, 65, 69, 71, 74, 79, 80, 81, 83, 84, 85, 86, 89, 93–94, 96, 97, 98, 101, 104, 106, 107, 110, 111, 113, 114, 116, 117, 119, 120, 123, 126, 127, 128, 129, 130, 131, 132, 133, 135, 136, 137, 138, 140, 141, 142, 143, 144, 145, 147, 148, 149, 150, 151, 152, 153, 154, 155, 159, 164–167, 169, 173, 174, 175, 216, 217, 233, 234, 243–244, 260, 268, 271, 276, 287, 336; end of Argead line, 47–48; kingship of, 14; partition of, 167; annexation by Rome, 174. See also Alexander the Great; Andriscus; Antigonus II; Antigonus III; Athens; Chremonidean War; Demetrius II; Lamian War; Greece; Rome; Perseus, Philip II, Philip V, Successors
Macedonian War, First, 145–147, 157. See also Rome
Macedonian War, Second, 148–155. See also Athens, Rome
Macedonian War, Third, 166–167. See also Athens, Rome
Macedonian War, Fourth, 174. See also Rome
Medeius, 62, 198, 199, 202–203, 209, 210
Megaleas, 139
Megalopolis, 21, 173
Meidias, 76
Memmius, Gaius, 229–230
Menalippus, 224
Menander, playwright, 43–45, 72, 88, 89, 124, 184–185, 186
Menander, Titus Flavius, philosopher, 282
Messene, 90, 146, 287
Metellus, Quintus Caecilius, 174
Metrodorus, 168
Micion, 127, 132–133, 134, 135, 136, 139, 146, 154, 190, 198. See also Eurycleides
Mint Magistrates, 61, 179, 196, 213
Mithridates VI, 4, 53, 199, 201–202, 203, 204, 205–206, 207, 209, 210, 216, 224, 260, 282, 331. See also Rome; Pontus
Moschion, cook, 40
Mossé, C., 6, 331
Mummius, Lucius, 175, 232, 269
Munychia, 27, 28, 31, 49, 101. See also Garrisons; Museum Hill; Piraeus
Museum Hill, 65, 91, 97, 120, 121, 122, 126, 276, 301. See also Garrisons; Munychia; Piraeus

Mysteries, 20, 28, 81, 82, 117, 127, 143, 148, 150, 187, 193, 213, 224, 228, 229, 249, 250, 255–256, 268, 270, 274, 275, 279, 303, 314, 321, 322, 326, 333. *See also* Eleusis; Religion

Naupactus, 138, 153
Naval arsenal, 20, 210
Nero, 265, 266–267, 269–270, 271, 275, 280, 281–282, 298. *See also* Athens, Rome
Nerva, 267, 284. *See also* Athens, Rome
Nicandrus (archon), 218
Nicanor, commander Piraeus garrison, 32, 33, 34
Nicanor, Julius, 257, 260–263, 330
Nicanor, Philip V's commander, 151
Nicias (archon 296/5), 88
Nicias (archon 266/8), 120
Nicias (archon 10/9), 290
Nicocles (archon), 88
Nicopolis, 243, 244, 249, 269, 314
Nicostratus (archon), 92
Novius, Tiberius Claudius, 261, 273, 280–281, 281

Octavia, Antony's wife, 237, 238, 239
Octavian, 2, 4, 6, 66, 70, 201, 215, 218, 233, 234, 236–237, 238, 239, 240, 248, 249, 250, 257. *See also* Antony; Augustus; Rome
Odeum (Theater) of Agrippa: *see* Agrippa
Oligarchy, 11, 15, 27, 31, 32, 33, 34, 38, 54, 59, 60, 62, 81, 94, 122, 199, 214, 218, 234, 253. *See also* Democracy
Olympias, 16, 47, 185
Olympic Games, 39, 83, 95, 106, 117, 143, 144, 156, 162, 244, 269, 270, 322. *See also* Panhellenic
Olympiodorus, 81, 94, 97
Orbius, 205
Orchomenus, 120, 231
Oropus, 31, 41, 106, 171–172, 193, 232, 247
Osborne, M.J., 86

Paeonians, 12, 111
Paidotribai, 64. *See also* Gymnasium
Pammenes, 198, 291
Panactum, 64, 78, 79, 99, 105, 130. *See also* Fortresses
Panathenaea, 45, 73, 82, 87, 104, 116, 123, 177, 178, 179, 188, 191, 192, 198, 211, 238, 273, 275, 280, 321, 329; Roman changes to, 275, 280, 322, 329. *See also* Athena; Festivals; Religion
Panathenaic Stadium, 20, 274, 334. *See also* Buildings
Panhellenic, 269, 270, 314, 324. *See also* Olympic Games; Panhellenion
Panhellenion, 6, 303, 304, 306, 308, 314, 319, 324–326, 328, 329, 330, 331. *See also* Athens; Hadrian; Leagues
Pantaenus, Titus Flavius, 99
Parthenon, 1, 51, 74–75, 79–80, 82, 110, 191, 223, 281, 288, 291, 293. *See also* Acropolis; Athena
Patroclus, Ptolemy II's commander, 106, 120, 126
Patron, philosopher, 230
Paul the Apostle, 193, 276–277
Paullus, Lucius Aemilius, 166–167, 168, 169
Pausanias, 32, 81, 82, 89, 97, 101, 104, 111, 112, 113, 209, 212, 273, 302, 303, 304, 306, 316
Peithidemus (archon), 118
Pella, 12, 84, 93
Peloponnese/Peloponnesians, 21, 33, 41, 47, 79, 81, 89–90, 93, 97, 113, 114, 116, 119, 120, 127, 128, 131, 136, 137, 138, 152, 173, 175, 231, 243, 327
Peloponnesian War, 3, 9, 11, 18, 43, 58, 59, 82, 117, 214
Perdiccas, 28, 29, 30, 31
Pergamum/Pergamene, 2, 146, 147, 148, 149, 157, 160, 161, 165, 169, 173, 174, 178, 196, 198, 219, 245, 281, 332. *See also* Athens; Attalus I; Attalus II; Eumenes II; Rome

Pericles, 1, 2, 9–10, 19, 303, 326
Perseus, 164, 165–167, 168, 169, 174, 178, 220
Persian Wars, 1, 5, 10, 11, 16, 22, 95, 112, 113, 152, 208, 211, 255, 262, 271, 293, 297
Petraeus, Cassius, 245
Phaedrus of Sphettus, 76, 86–87, 98, 99, 100, 105, 108, 117, 124. *See also* Athens; Callias
Pheidostrate, Chremonides' sister, 117. *See also* Chremonides
Phila, Poliorcetes' wife, 80, 93, 97, 114, 117
Philip II, 1, 2, 9, 11, 12, 13–16, 17, 18, 19, 21, 22, 23, 28, 31, 48, 53, 58, 64, 83, 91, 93, 109, 115, 116, 118–119, 224, 270, 324. *See also* Athens; Greece; Leagues; Macedonia
Philip III Arrhidaeus, 29, 32, 47, 48
Philip IV, 84, 89
Philip V, 4, 130, 131, 132, 136–139, 143–156, 157, 159, 160, 163, 164–165, 178, 189, 190; and Athens, 150–154. *See also* Greece; Hannibal; Macedonia; First and Second Macedonian Wars; Rome
Philippides, 44, 76–77, 82, 84, 87, 88, 108, 153
Philemon, 43, 44, 124
Philippus (archon), 94
Philochorus, 124
Philocles, 151
Philodemus of Gadara, 173
Philon, architect, 20, 110
Philon, Sophocles of Sunium's prosecutor, 75
Philopappus, 186, 275–276, 299–301, 314, 317; monument of, 299, 300–302. *See also* Buildings
Philopoemen, 173–174
Philosophers' Embassy, 172, 219, 334
Philosophy/Schools of Philosophy, Athens, 1, 5, 20, 26, 42, 45–47, 67, 75, 157, 168, 172, 179, 186, 195, 198, 203, 206, 219, 230, 235, 237, 253, 263, 269, 272, 274, 282–283, 299, 323–324, 332, 334, 336. *See also* Academy; Culture/Hellenism; Epicureanism; Lyceum; Philosophers embassy; Stoicism
Phocion, 26, 28, 32–33, 34
Phoenice, Peace of, 147, 150
Phylacion, 80
Phyle, 43, 64, 78, 79, 99, 105, 130. *See also* Fortresses
Piraeus, 2, 19, 20, 26, 27, 31, 33, 34, 36, 50, 51, 63, 64, 74, 82, 89, 91, 92, 98, 99, 100, 101, 103, 111, 116, 117, 118, 119, 120, 122, 126, 128, 130, 131, 132, 133, 134, 135, 148, 150, 151, 157, 161, 168, 182–183, 192, 196, 207, 208, 210, 211, 215, 226, 231, 239, 254, 257, 273, 288, 301, 321; garrison at, 33, 50, 92, 98, 111, 116, 117, 118, 119, 120, 122, 126, 130, 131, 132. *See also* Athens; Economy/Finances, Athenian; Garrisons
Pisistratid tyranny, 37, 55, 188, 189, 196, 303, 304, 310. See also Athens; Tyrannicides
Piso, Lucius Calpurnius, 216, 217
Pius, Antoninus, 310, 329, 333, 334
Plato, 1, 10, 12, 20, 34, 45, 46, 198, 208, 219, 275, 282. *See also* Academy; Culture/Hellenism; Philosophy
Pliny, 224, 268
Plotina, Pompeia, 186, 323
Plutarch, 27, 28, 32, 51, 74, 77, 80, 86, 90, 93, 100, 132, 137, 156, 168, 182, 183, 208, 209, 214, 225, 236, 239, 247, 248, 275–276, 314, 330, 333
Pollux, Julius, 334
Polybius, 86, 132, 133, 135, 136, 139, 144, 145, 149, 150, 153, 154, 165, 169, 170
Polyperchon, 31, 32, 33, 34, 41, 47, 49, 79. *See also* Greece; Macedonia; Successors

Pompey the Great, 4, 6, 202, 210, 224, 225, 226, 227–228, 230–231. *See also* Rome
Pontus, 4, 179, 201, 210. *See also* Mithridates VI
Posidonius, 203, 204, 206, 282
Priesthoods, 62, 134, 152, 173, 189, 190, 191, 193, 253, 280, 322–323. *See also* Gods; Imperial Cult; Religion
Prytanis of Carystus, 134–135
Prytany/Prytanies, 56, 58, 85, 273
Ptolemaea, 139, 140, 190. *See also* Festivals, Ptolemy III
Ptolemais tribe, 139, 140, 177, 190. *See also* Egypt; Ptolemy III
Ptolemy I, 30, 31, 41–42, 49, 50, 51, 78, 79, 80, 83, 84, 90, 96, 97, 98, 99, 104, 105, 171, 186, 192, 240. *See also* Athens; Egypt; Greece
Ptolemy II, 51, 99, 104, 105, 117, 118, 119, 120–121, 124, 126, 128, 185. *See also* Athens; Egypt; Greece
Ptolemy III, 67, 128, 132, 135, 136, 139, 140, 150, 153, 189, 190. *See also* Athens; Egypt
Ptolemy IV, 146, 147, 149. *See also* Egypt
Ptolemy V, 147, 177. *See also* Egypt
Ptolemy VI, 177, 178. *See also* Egypt
Ptolemy Ceraunus, 51, 107, 111. *See also* Egypt; Galatians
Pulcher, Appius Claudius, 228
Pulcher, Publius Clodius, 216. *See also* lex Clodia
Punic War, Second, 138, 144, 145, 147, 149, 161
Punic War, Third, 175
Pydna, battle of in 168, 166–167; battle of in 148, 174
Pyrrhus, king of Epirus, 84, 93, 94, 96, 97, 98, 99, 104, 113, 114, 116, 121. *See also* Epirus; Macedonia
Pyrrhus of Lamptrae, 199
Pythais, 64, 65, 69, 175–176, 198, 200, 255. See also Apollo; Delphi; *Dodekais*; Religion

Religion, 3, 10, 20, 38, 45, 54, 59, 62, 64, 66, 68, 70, 73, 74–75, 79, 82, 105, 117, 127, 134, 151, 152, 181, 184, 185, 187–194, 250, 253, 254, 255–257, 258, 265, 272, 273, 276, 280, 291, 311, 321–323, 326, 329, 330. *See also* Acropolis; Gods; Festivals; Guilds; Mysteries; Priesthoods; Temples
Rhamnus, 64, 90, 106, 120, 128, 129, 130, 133, 134, 280. *See also* Fortresses
Rhetoric, at Athens, 5, 10, 34, 45, 57–58, 59, 157, 219, 241, 263, 332, 333, 334, 336. *See also* Culture/Hellenism
Rhizon, 142
Rhodes/Rhodian, 24, 48, 78, 79, 146, 148, 150, 151, 154, 162, 169, 170, 173, 176, 177, 236, 268, 277
Roma, goddess, 3, 190, 198, 200–201, 250, 257, 280, 291; cult of, 190, 200, 201, 250, 280. *See also* Athens; Temple of Roma and Augustus
Rome/Romans, 1, 2, 3, 4, 5–6, 7, 9, 16, 22, 42, 45, 53, 62, 66, 69, 70, 111, 131, 135, 137, 138, 141–143, 144, 145, 146–148, 149, 150, 151, 152, 153, 154, 155, 156, 157, 159, 160, 161, 162, 163, 164, 166–167, 168, 169–170, 171, 172, 173, 174, 175, 176, 177, 178, 180, 183, 187, 190–191, 195, 199, 200, 201–202, 203, 204, 205, 209, 210, 211, 212, 213, 214, 215, 216–217, 218, 219, 220, 221, 224, 225, 226, 229, 230–232, 233, 234, 237, 238, 240, 241, 243, 245, 248, 249, 250, 252, 253, 255, 256, 258, 259, 260, 261, 262, 263, 264, 265, 266, 267, 268, 271, 272, 273, 274, 275, 278, 279, 282, 284, 287, 288, 296, 297, 299–301, 304, 306, 308, 311, 313, 316, 318, 321, 324, 325, 330, 331–333, 334, 336; annexation of Greece, 175; proclamation

Rome/Romans (*Cont.*)
  of Greek freedom, 156–157; partition of Macedonia, 167; annexation of Macedonia, 174. *See also* Athens; Buildings; Imperial Cult; Culture/Hellenism; Greece; Illyrian Wars; Macedonia; Macedonian Wars; Mithridates VI; Panathenaea; Religion; Roma; "Romanization;" Senate; Statues
"Romanization" of Athens, 3, 173, 182, 195, 230, 252–253, 263, 266, 287–312, 330, 331
Roxane, 24, 29, 30, 48, 50, 110
Rufus, Quintus Trebellius, 284, 318
Ruler Cult, 189, 190, 193. *See also* Successors

Salamis, 10, 33, 78, 79, 99, 126, 128, 215, 257, 260–262
Sarapion of Melite, 198, 276
Sarapis/Sarapeion, 171, 189, 192–193, 276
Sculpture/Sculptors, 10, 108, 109, 198, 215, 274, 296, 297, 303. *See also* Statues
Scyrus, 159, 188, 212
Second Athenian Confederacy, 11, 59
Second Sophistic, 264, 333–334. *See also* Culture/Hellenism
Secundus, Gaius Carrinas, 281, 298
Sekoma, 255. *See also* Grain
Seleucus I, 31, 49, 83, 84, 96, 97, 99, 100, 107, 112, 301. *See also* Syria, Successors
Seleucus IV, 178. *See also* Syria
Senate, of Rome, 47, 69, 143, 147, 150, 151, 155, 156, 157, 159, 162, 163, 165, 166, 167, 169, 170, 171, 172, 174, 175, 176, 195, 202, 204, 207, 208, 212, 214, 217, 218, 219, 230, 232, 233, 239, 266, 270, 281
Slaves/Slavery, 28, 32, 40, 43, 54, 55, 58, 65, 101, 118, 146, 167, 169, 170, 175, 182, 185, 199–200, 201, 225, 239

Socrates, 1, 10, 12, 45, 198
Solon, 54–55, 56, 58, 317
Sophocles of Sunium, 47, 75
Sophocles, tragedian, 10, 20, 42, 189
Sophronistai, 64, 66. *See also* Gymnasium
Sosthenes, 111, 113
Sostratus of Cnidus, 99
Soteria, 112, 162
Sparta/Spartans, 4, 10, 11, 12, 21, 22, 33, 58, 59, 63, 82, 113, 114, 118, 119, 120, 136, 137, 138, 139, 146, 154, 160, 173, 214, 245, 246–247, 265, 269, 270, 272, 287, 314, 319. *See also* Greece
Spawforth, A., 262
Strategos/Strategoi, 35, 56, 91, 105–106. *See also* Democracy
Stallius, Gaius and Marius, 224
Statues, by Athens, 21, 67, 89, 105, 107–108, 110, 169, 215, 233–234, 253, 261, 268–269, 273, 274, 281–282, 285, 296–298, 311, of Aeschlyus, 20; of Antigonus Monophthalmus, 72–73, 108, 153; of Agrippa, 245, 293; of Antipater of Phlya, 253; of Antony, 234, 239; of Ariobarzanes II, 224; of Asander, 37; of Attalus II, 196, 234, 245, 293; of Augustus, 245, 259, 291, cf. 257; of Brutus, 233; 232; of Drusus Caesar, 278; of Gaius Caesar, 258; of Julius Caesar, 229, of Lucius Caesar, 259, 290; of Caligula and Drusilla, 278–279, of Cassius, 233; of Claudius, 279, 280–281; of Demetrius of Phalerum, 36, 40, 72; of Demetrius Poliorcetes, 72–73, 82, 108, 153; of Domitian, 283; of Eumenes II, 196, 234, 245, 293; of Euripides 20; of Eurycles, 235; of Herod, 251, 252; of Hadrian, 316, 327; of Herodorus, 93;

of John Hyrcanus, 179; of Livia, 258, 278; of Lycurgus, 77, 110; of Lysimachus, 104; of Matidia, 316; on the Monument of the Eponymous Heroes, 73; of Julius Nicanor, 260; of Novius, 273, 280; of Pharnaces and Nysa, 179; Philip V's destroyed, 152, 153; of Phocion, 33–34; of Pompey, 226; of Ptolemy III, 139, 153; of Pulcher, 228; of Rufus and family, 284; of Sabina, 316; of Sophocles, 20; of Sulla, 213; of Theseus, 327; of Tiberius, 277; of Trajan, 284, 285; of an unknown legate, 259; of the Vestal Virgins, 256. See also Acropolis; Agora; Athena; Demosthenes; Sculpture/Sculptors; Tyrannicides, "Wandering" Temples

Stoa of Attalus II, 7, 196, 277, 294. See also Attalus II, Pergamum

Stoa of Eumenes II, 196, 294. See also Eumenes II, Pergamum

Stoicism, 12, 46, 114, 115, 126, 206, 263, 282. See also Philosophy; Zeno

Stratocles, 44, 58, 72, 76–77, 80, 81, 82–83, 84, 86, 94

Strombichus, 98

Successors, wars of, 12, 18, 28, 30, 31–33, 40–42, 47–51, 78–79, 83–85, 97, 107. See also Ruler Cult

Sulla, Lucius Cornelius, 2, 4, 62, 66, 202, 207–215, 219, 220; sacks Athens, 209, 210–213, 226

Sunium, 19, 50, 64, 99, 106, 120, 126, 198, 200, 295. See also Fortresses

Syria, 2, 30, 42, 133, 147, 149, 173, 178, 189, 193, 216, 224, 233, 260, 299, 302. See also Antiochus I; Antiochus III; Antiochus IV; Athens; Rome; Seleucus I; Seleucus IV

Tacitus, 163, 271, 278, 282

Technitai of Dionysus: see Guilds

Telesphorus, 72, 89

Temples: *see* Erechtheum; Gods; Parthenon; temple of Olympian Zeus; temple of Roma and Augustus; "Wandering" temples

Temple of Olympian Zeus, 196–197, 211, 219, 224, 288, 303–306, 316, 322, 327, 329, See also Buildings; Hadrian; Panhellenion

Temple of Roma and Augustus, 110, 191, 198, 224, 256, 258, 259, 280, 288, 291–293, 294. See also Acropolis; Augustus; Buildings; Roma; "Romanization"

Teuta, 131, 142

Thalna, Publius Iuventius, 174

Theater of Dionysus, 20, 64, 70, 91, 133, 134, 196, 209, 211, 256, 258, 259, 298, 316, 323, 334, 335. See also Dionysia; Dionysus

Thebes/Thebans, 9, 14, 15, 17, 18, 21, 23, 51, 90, 95, 109, 139, 154, 231, 301

Themistocles, in Augustan-era, 255, 262–263

Theodorus of Sunium, 179, 198

Theodotus, 179, 198

Theophemus, 126

Theophrastus, commander at Eleusis, 139

Theophrastus, philosopher, 34, 46, 75, 198, 211, 215, 282. See also Culture/Hellenism; Lyceum; Philosophy

Theotimus, Popilius, philosopher, 323

Thermopylae, 10, 25, 78, 112, 161

Theseia, 173, 188, 198, 213. See also Festivals; Religion; Theseus

Theseus, 3, 173, 188, 208, 287, 302, 304, 311, 316, 322, 327, 329, 330. See also Arch of Hadrian, Theseia

Thessalonica (Thessaloniki), 48, 113, 174, 220, 243, 268, 276, 334

Thessalonice, 48, 84, 93

Thessaly, 25, 94, 107, 111, 113, 131, 132, 137, 138, 146, 154, 157, 162, 164, 166, 207, 217, 220, 245
Thirty Tyrants, 11, 33, 59, 214
Thrace/Thracians, 13, 17, 27, 30, 81, 84, 93, 107, 182, 253. *See also* Lysimachus
Thraseas, 140
Thrason, 115
Thrasyllus (archon), 281
Thymochares, 40, 41, 126
Tiberius, 257, 260, 266, 268, 271, 274, 277–278. *See also* Athens, Rome
Titus, 267, 282. *See also* Athens, Rome
Toher, M., 251
Tower of the Winds, 226, 227, 298. *See also* Agora, Roman; Buildings
Tragedy, 1, 10, 12, 20, 21, 42, 91, 189, 269, 332. *See also* Culture/Hellenism
Trajan, 186, 224, 265, 267, 268, 271, 272, 274, 284–285, 299, 300, 314, 318, 319, 323. *See also* Athens; Rome
Trasimene, battle of, 138, 144
Triparadeisus settlement, 30, 31, 80
Tyrannicides, 37, 73, 213, 233, 297

Varro, Gaius Terentius, 144
Verres, Gaius, 223
Vespasian, 47, 267, 270–271, 282–283, 300, 308, 323. *See also* Athens; Rome

Vesta/Vestal Virgins, 224, 256, 258. *See also* Imperial Cult
Vibia Sabina, 301, 306

Walls, City, 63, 74, 91, 131, 152, 208, 211, 226, 231, 288, 327, 335. *See also* Fortifications
Walls, Long, 134, 168, 207. *See also* Fortifications
"Wandering" temples, 258, 295–296, 298
Water supply, 135, 310
Women, 32, 34, 38, 43, 44, 54, 80, 117, 175, 185–186, 209, 301, 319. *See also* Courtesans; Family

Xenocles, 254
Xenocrates, 26, 28, 135

Zama, battle of, 147
Zeno, philosopher, 12, 46, 47, 114, 115, 116, 117, 122, 124, 198. *See also* Stoicism
Zenon of Marathon, 198
Zenon, Ptolemy II's admiral, 99
Zeus, 79, 110, 134, 187, 192, 193, 196, 211, 219, 224, 257, 288, 303, 304, 306, 309, 315, 316, 322, 326. *See also* Gods; Religion; Temple of Olympian Zeus, Zeus Agoraios, Zeus Eleutherius
Zeus Agoraios, 253
Zeus Eleutherius, 98, 100, 257, 278, 283, 304, 306, 311, 316. *See also* Gods; Religion; Zeus